IDEAS, relative to the manner of forwarding to the American Soldiers, the Presents of the American Women.

ALL plans are eligible, when doing good is the object; there is however one more preferable; and when the operation is extensive, we cannot give it too much uniformity. On the other side, the wants of our army do not permit the slowness of an ordinary path. It is not in one month, nor in eight days, that we would relieve our soldiery. It is immediatel[illegible] and our impatience does not permit us to proceed by the long circuity of collectors, [illegible] and treasurers. As my idea with regard to this, have been approved by some [illegible] friends, I will explain them here; every other person will not be less at li[illegible] to adopt a different plan.

1st. All Women and Girls will be received without exception, to presen[illegible] fering; and, as it is absolutely voluntary, every one will regulate it accor[illegible] ty, and her disposition. The shilling offered by the Widow or the young [illegible] ceived as well as the most considerable sums presented by the Women who hav[illegible] to join to their patriotism, greater means to be useful.

2d. A Lady chosen by the others in each county, shall be the Treasuress; an[d] to render her task more simple, and more easy, she will not receive but determinate sums, in a round number, from twenty hard dollars to any greater sum. The exchange forty dollars in paper for one dollar in specie.

It is hoped that there will not be one Woman who will not with pleasure charge herself with the embarrassment which will attend so honorable an operation.

3d. The Women who shall not be in a condition to send twenty dollars in specie, or above, will join in as great a number as will be necessary to make this or any greater sum, and one amongst them will carry it, or cause it to be sent to the Treasuress.

4th. The Treasuress of the county will receive the money, and will keep a register, writing the sums in her book, and causing it to be signed at the side of the whole by the person who has presented it.

5th. When several Women shall join together to make a total sum of twenty dollars or more, she amongst them who shall have the charge to carry it to the Treasuress, will make mention of all their names on the register, if her associates shall have so directed her; those whose choice it shall be, will have the liberty to remain unknown.

6th. As soon as the Treasuress of the county shall judge, that the sums which she shall have received, deserve to be sent to their destination, she will cause them to be presented with the lists, to the wife of the Governor or President of the State, who will be the Treasuress-General of the State; and she will cause it to be set down in her register, and have it sent to Mistress Washington. If the Governor or President are unmarried, all will address themselves to the wife of the Vice-President, if there is one, or of the Chief-Justice, &c.

7th. Women settled in the distant parts of the country, and not chusing for any particular reason as for the sake of greater expedition, to remit their Capital to the Treasuress, may send it directly to the wife of the Governor, or President, &c. or to Mistress Washington, who, if she shall judge necessary, will in a short answer to the sender, acquaint her with the reception of it.

8th. As Mrs. Washington may be absent from the camp when the greater part of the banks shall be sent there, the American Women considering, that General Washington is the Father and Friend of the Soldiery; that he is himself, the first Soldier of the Republic, and that their offering will be received at its destination, as soon as it shall have come to his hands, they will pray him, to take the charge of receiving it, in the absence of Mrs. Washington.

9th. General Washington will dispose of this fund in the manner that he shall judge most advantageous to the Soldiery. The American Women desire only that it may not be considered as to be employed, to procure to the army, the objects of subsistence, arms or cloathing, which are due to them by the Continent. It is an extraordinary bounty intended to render the condition of the Soldier more pleasant, and not to hold place of the things which they ought to receive from the Congress, or from the States.

10th. If the General judges necessary, he will publish at the end of a certain time, an amount of that which shall have been received from each particular State.

11th. The Women who shall send their offerings, will have in their choice to conceal or to give their names; and if it shall be thought proper, on a fit occasion, to publish one day the lists, they only, who shall consent, shall be named; when with regard to the sums sent, there will be no mention made, if they so desire it.

PRINTED BY JOHN DUNLAP.

Overleaf, on the Endpapers:

The Sentiments of an American Woman. *Verso:* Ideas, relative to the manner of forwarding to the American Soldiers, the Presents of the American Women. *[Philadelphia:] Printed by John Dunlap, [June 10, 1780]. Printed Ephemera Collection, Portfolio 146:3. Rare Book and Special Collections Division. Photograph by Yusef El-Amin.*

In late May 1780, General George Washington reported to Congress that serious and prolonged shortages of rations, clothing, and pay had nearly exhausted his troops. Immediate relief was needed. Aspiring "to render themselves more really useful," the women of Philadelphia, who had observed that government measures were usually slow and inadequate, took on this challenge.

Led by Esther De Berdt Reed (1747–1780), first lady of Pennsylvania, the ladies quickly organized a systematic plan for canvassing the city and suburbs. In mid-June, at least three dozen women went from house to house soliciting funds. The efforts of this "resistless force" were so successful that in her July 4, 1780, letter to Washington, Esther Reed could report that the women had raised more than $300,000 in paper currency.

Subscription papers for this pioneering charity drive, later published by Reed's grandson, list 1,645 contributors by name and amount. Although most contributions were in depreciated paper currency, more than a third of the funds were in specie. One pair of leather breeches was donated. Both the countess de La Luzerne, wife of the French minister, and the marquise de Lafayette, through the marquis, contributed generously. The ladies' campaign received repeated praise in the *Pennsylvania Packet,* where the amount the women raised was shown to rival the sum pledged by men to establish a bank—and these subscriptions from the men were expected to be returned to them with interest.

Sentiments of an American Woman—probably written by Esther Reed—sets out historical examples of aggressive female patriotism as inspiration and justification for a call to political action. Professing women's "love for the public good" to be at least equal to that of men, the writer encourages women actively to make personal sacrifices to give soldiers "extraordinary and unexpected" presents of gratitude and remembrance.

Esther Reed's patriotism is particularly noteworthy. She had come to America only a decade earlier as the bride of Joseph Reed. The conditions of war had effectively separated her from her family and friends in England. Furthermore, Esther undertook leadership of the women's relief efforts in the weeks immediately following the birth in May of her sixth child, George Washington Reed, at a time when most women would have restricted their physical and social activities severely.

On the verso of this broadsheet is a detailed plan for collecting and forwarding funds. Virginia Congressman John Walker, in his June 13, 1780, letter to Governor Thomas Jefferson, suggests that it was drawn up by François, marquis de Barbé-Marbois, secretary of the French legation, who was known to have encouraged the women's relief activities. This broadsheet, which, according to the June 13 *Pennsylvania Packet,* was published on June 10, 1780, was undoubtedly the plan enclosed by several congressional delegates with their June correspondence home.

With encouragement from Esther Reed and Martha Washington, similar fund drives were organized in Maryland, New Jersey, and Virginia. As in Philadelphia, women in these three states adapted their fundraising efforts to meet local conditions. Before year's end, the results of their collective efforts also were forwarded to General Washington.

Although the Philadelphia ladies had hoped that their contributions could be used to provide "an extraordinary bounty" beyond the food and clothing due to soldiers by the government, Washington insisted that it was shirts that would provide the greatest comfort to his men. So in late August, Esther Reed began purchasing linen. Its transformation into shirts unfortunately fell to other hands, however, for Esther Reed died suddenly on September 18, 1780, of a fever.

After an autumn of "general sickness" in the city, the Philadelphia women, wanting to stretch their funds as far as possible, began making the shirts themselves. On December 26, 1780, Sarah Franklin Bache forwarded more than two thousand shirts to Washington, with the wish that they "be worn with as much pleasure as they were made."

—Rosemary Fry Plakas

This early episode of American women's collective patriotism can be traced by consulting the following sources: *Letters of Delegates to Congress, 1774–1789,* 26 vols. (Washington: Library of Congress, 1976–2000), 15:284, 287, 315–16, 329, 355; William B. Reed, *Life and Correspondence of Joseph Reed,* 2 vols. (Philadelphia: Lindsay and Blakiston, 1847), 2: 260–71, 429–49; and *Pennsylvania Packet* (Philadelphia, John Dunlap), June 13, 17, 27; July 8; and November 4, 1780.

American Women

NOTICE.

I HEREBY forewarn all persons against crediting my wife, DELILAH McCONNELL, on my account, as she has absconded without my consent. I am therefore determined to pay none of her contracts.

WILLIAM McCONNELL.

May 15, 1828. 13—2

ᎢᏳᏛᎬᎦ.

ᎠᏂ ᏃᏉ ᏥᏁᎩ, ᏂᎦᏛ ᏴᏫ ᎢᏳᏛᏁᏗ. Ꮭ-ᏍᏗ ᎩᏳ ᏲᎾᏍᏁᏍᏗ ᎠᏴ ᎠᏆᎫᏴᏗ ᎨᏒᎢ, ᎠᏆᏟ-ᎵᎢ ᏗᎳᎵ ᏧᏁᎢᏛ. ᎠᏉᎯᏳᏅᏠᏃ ᏂᎨᏒᎾ ᎠᏆ-ᎵᏗᏒᏤ. ᏝᏍᎩᏂ ᎠᏆᎫᏴᏗ ᏲᎩ, ᏃᏉ ᏥᏁᎩ; ᎠᏴ ᎠᏆᎫᏴᏗ ᎤᏠᏤᏒ ᏓᏥᏍᏂᏁᎸᎢ.

ᎾᎵ ᎤᎩᏏᎤᏗ.

ᏍᎩᎦᏕᏏᏁ ᎢᎦ ᎠᏅᏍᎬᏗ, 1828.

"Notice: I hereby forewarn all persons against crediting my wife, Delilah McConnell." Cherokee Phoenix *(New Echota, Georgia), May 28, 1828 (Newspaper vault). Serial and Government Publications Division.*

Notices such as this bilingual one in English and Cherokee from the *Cherokee Phoenix* (New Echota, Georgia), refusing to honor an estranged wife's debts, appear in newspapers from the early nineteenth century to the present day. Since husbands were responsible for the debts and contracts of their wives, without this notice William McConnell would have been forced to pay the debts incurred after his wife's departure. In some locales, newspapers publish the only official statement of record for debt notices, bankruptcies, and estate announcements.

A Library of Congress Guide for the Study of

Contributors

Sheridan Harvey
Humanities and Social Sciences Division

Georgia Metos Higley
Serial and Government Publications Division

Pamela Barnes Craig
Law Library of Congress

Rosemary Fry Plakas
Rare Book and Special Collections Division

Jacqueline Coleburn
Special Materials Cataloging Division

Janice E. Ruth
Manuscript Division

Barbara Orbach Natanson
Prints and Photographs Division

Patricia Molen van Ee
Geography and Map Division

Robin Rausch
Music Division

Nancy J. Seeger
Recorded Sound Section—Motion Picture,
Broadcasting, and Recorded Sound Division

Rosemary Hanes with Brian Taves
Moving Image Section—Motion Picture,
Broadcasting, and Recorded Sound Division

James Hardin
American Folklife Center

Peggy K. Pearlstein and Barbara A. Tenenbaum
Area Studies Collections

Leslie W. Gladstone
Congressional Research Service

Sara Day
Publishing Office

Women's History and Culture in the United States

American Women

edited by

Sheridan Harvey
Humanities and Social Sciences Division

Janice E. Ruth
Manuscript Division

Barbara Orbach Natanson
Prints and Photographs Division

Sara Day and Evelyn Sinclair
Publishing Office

Introduction by Susan Ware
Radcliffe Institute for Advanced Studies
Harvard University

Library of Congress
Washington
2001

Title Page: ***Suffrage tent tour at Suffolk County Fair, Long Island, New York, 1914. Photograph. Harriot Stanton Blatch Papers (container 10). Manuscript Division. LC-MSS-12997-10.***

In New York State, groups like Harriot Stanton Blatch's Women's Political Union and Carrie Chapman Catt's Empire State Campaign Committee mounted an all-out effort in the summer of 1914 to sway male voters who would decide the fate of a state suffrage amendment passed by the legislature in 1913 and placed on the November 1915 ballot. As part of their southern "tent tour," WPU members set up a booth at the Suffolk County Fair on Long Island. Eager to attract working mothers to their cause and perhaps to dispel the perception of suffragists as marriage-hating spinsters, the group offered free baby-sitting to fairgoers.

Design: Adrianne Onderdonk Dudden

Library of Congress Cataloging-in-Publication Data
American women : a Library of Congress guide for the study of women's history and culture in the United States / edited by Sheridan Harvey . . . [et al.] ; introduction by Susan Ware.
p. cm.
Includes bibliographical references and index.
ISBN 0–8444–1048–9 (alk. paper)
1. Women—United States—History—Library resources. 2. Library resources—Washington (D.C.) 3. Library of Congress I. Title: Library of Congress guide for the study of women's history and culture in the United States. II. Harvey, Sheridan, 1945– III. Library of Congress.
Z7164.U5 A47 2001
[HQ1410]
026'.3054'0973—dc21 2001029547

The paper in this publication meets the requirements for permanence established by the American National Standard ANSI/NISO Z39.48.1992, Permanence of Paper for Publications and Documents in Libraries and Archives.

For sale by the Superintendent of Documents,
U.S. Government Printing Office.
Internet: bookstore.gpo.gov
phone 202.512.1800 fax 202.512.2250

Content Overview

Baker & Cornwall. Modern Manual Training School. *Photograph, 1905. Prints and Photographs Division. LC-USZ62-13380.*

Even in the new coeducational public and manual training schools around the turn of the twentieth century, courses of study were often dictated by gender. Girls in this 1905 classroom practice home economics on one side of the room while boys learn about tools for shop on the other.

Contents

8 Music Division *Robin Rausch* 253

9 Recorded Sound Section—Motion Picture, Broadcasting, and Recorded Sound Division *Nancy J. Seeger* 279

10 Moving Image Section—Motion Picture, Broadcasting, and Recorded Sound Division *Rosemary Hanes with Brian Taves* 301

Note about the essays in this guide: Interspersed among the twelve chapters describing the collections and reading rooms of the Library of Congress are five short essays written by Library staff members to demonstrate ways in which the variety of formats and the breadth of coverage of the collections can enrich the study of almost any subject you might choose to examine. We invite you to seek new avenues for your own research as you explore the Library's holdings.

National Photo Company. Women's Rowing Team, Potomac Boat Club. *Photograph, September 21, 1919. National Photo Company Collection. Prints and Photographs Division. LOT 12344-3. LC-USZ62-92402.*

Attitudes toward women's athletics, at least those of the middle class, have often been linked to educational theories prescribing appropriate activities for women. A progressive school run by the Grimké sisters before the Civil War challenged girls with calisthenic exercises and competitions in rowing, swimming, and diving. Ironically, as women forged new paths in other spheres in the wake of World War I and the aftermath of the suffrage fight, the notion of female athletic prowess suffered a setback. Many schools and colleges cut back competitive sports for women during the 1920s, and exercise became primarily a route for improving a young woman's health and looks. These members of an active Georgetown recreational club, however, seem undaunted by any threat to their femininity or by autumn temperatures.

Preface

For two hundred years, the Library of Congress, the oldest national cultural institution in the United States, has been gathering materials necessary to tell the stories of women in America. The last third of the twentieth century witnessed a great surge of popular and scholarly interest in women's studies and women's history that has led to an outpouring of works in many formats. This publication is designed to provide a guide to both old and new materials for the benefit of interested researchers whether or not they are able to visit the Library.

From its beginnings in 1800 as a legislative library, the Library of Congress has grown into a national library that houses both a universal collection of knowledge and the mint record of American creativity. Congress's decision to purchase Thomas Jefferson's personal library to replace the books and maps burned during the British occupation in 1814 set the Congressional Library on the path of collecting with the breadth of Jefferson's interests. Not just American imprints were to be acquired, but foreign-language materials as well, and Jefferson's library already included works by American and European women.

Since 1870, the single most important factor in building up the unparalleled Americana collections of the Library of Congress has been deposits under U.S. copyright laws. The constant flow of a wide variety of copyrighted materials has always included works related to women, well known and unknown, from all sorts of backgrounds and regions. Other important sources for the continual augmentation of the Library's ranging collections include purchase, gift, and exchange.

The Library of Congress has some 121 million items, largely housed in closed stacks in three buildings on Capitol Hill that contain twenty public reading rooms. The incredible, wide-ranging collections include books, maps, prints, newspapers, broadsides, diaries, letters, posters, musical scores, photographs, audio and video recordings, and documents available only in digital formats. The Library serves first-time users and the most experienced researchers alike.

To aid researchers at every level, both those who visit the Library and those who use the Library's digitized materials in their own localities, the Library has published a series of resource guides. The first—*Keys to the Encounter: A Library of Congress Resource Guide for the Study of the Age of Discovery*—was issued in 1992 to commemorate Columbus's first encounter with the American continent. *The African-American Mosaic: A Library of Congress Resource Guide for the Study of Black History and Culture* was published in 1993, and *Many Nations: A Library of Congress Resource Guide for the Study of Indian and Alaska Native Peoples of the United States* appeared in 1996.

Today, the Library is taking the lead in delivering high-quality electronic materials free of charge to the nation. One-of-a-kind primary documents from our collections are now available for examination on computer screens in schools, libraries, and homes across the country and around the world. Women's history and culture are featured prominently in these selections.

We hope that you, the user of this volume, will seek and find, either in a library near you, in person at the Library of Congress, or in a digital document that reaches you through the World Wide Web, resources that will take you further in your understanding of women's history and culture. We wish you profitable use of *American Women* and of the Library of Congress.

James H. Billington
The Librarian of Congress

Acknowledgments

A resource guide focusing on women was an idea percolating among specialists throughout the Library of Congress and among editors in the Publishing Office for many years. Convinced that the Library's resource guides provide a valuable service to both the Library's staff and its users, Director of Publishing W. Ralph Eubanks was from the start an enthusiastic supporter of the effort to identify and describe the Library's collections related to women. We owe him a great debt of gratitude for allowing us the time, resources, and independence to devote much energy and effort to pulling together the many pieces that make up this wide and detailed look at the Library's collections. The guide would never have come about without the constancy of his support or the unfailing steadiness and good counsel he was so ready to offer that held us always on course.

Staff members throughout the Library of Congress lent their support to the idea of a guide to lead researchers through the maze of resources that might shed light on women's studies. We soon assembled a team of contributors that would reflect almost all corners of the institution and its holdings. This group has proved unusually cohesive and its members have learned much from one another. During the nearly four years it has taken to complete the guide, divisional walls have become windows. Greater insight and communication have allowed relinking of different parts of the collections long since broken up by format and have promoted connections between disparate materials related to each other by subject matter. Five topical essays, written by staff members, demonstrate the potential of such cross-divisional, multidisciplinary research.

Three Library of Congress specialists in particular lent their expertise and time to the current guide, reading and evaluating the content of the manuscript as a whole through several revisions and lending assistance to all their fellow contributors. This editorial team was composed of Sheridan Harvey, women's studies specialist in the Main Reading Room of the Library; Janice E. Ruth, specialist in women's history in the Manuscript Division; and Barbara Orbach Natanson, reference specialist in the Prints and Photographs Division. Without their extraordinary knowledge of their own collections and the researchers who use them and their involvement in the Library-wide initiative to electronically integrate all of the Library's catalogs undertaken during the course of this project, this guide would not have had the close connection it does to current Library of Congress cataloging methods and policy.

To prepare to undertake a survey of this magnitude—with a large number of Library curators, librarians, and specialists interested in women's history pledged to contribute descriptions of the collections with which they were familiar—and to ensure the reliability of the information in the guide, the Publishing Office early on sought the help of a committee of scholars in the field of women's studies. The committee was headed by Susan Ware, a noted expert on twentieth-century American women and a former professor of his-

Arnold Genthe. Dressed for a Formal Visit, Chinatown, San Francisco. *Film transparency, ca. 1896-1906. Arnold Genthe Collection. Prints and Photographs Division. LC-G403-BN-0387.*

Exclusion laws in effect in the United States from 1875 kept the Chinese population small—not much greater than one hundred thousand in 1900—and predominantly male. Only members of the merchant class were permitted to bring over wives and children. A respectable young Chinese woman would have walked outside unescorted only on certain holidays and special occasions. Not surprisingly, given their small numbers and sheltered status, Chinese women appear infrequently in the photographs Arnold Genthe took of San Francisco's Chinatown. This photograph, probably taken before the1906 earthquake and fire destroyed Genthe's studio, is among more than four hundred Genthe images held by the Prints and Photographs Division. (For exclusion laws, see page 91; for the Genthe Collection, see page 206.)

tory at New York University who is currently editing the next volume of *Notable American Women* at Radcliffe. From an initial meeting in the Publishing Office in August 1997 and an all-day brainstorming session between the staff contributors and scholar advisers in May 1998 through the review of many texts, she has supported both large conceptual discussion and the perfecting of small details with unfailing energy and enthusiasm, contributing enormously to the guide's successful completion. Her introductory survey of the evolution and current state of the field of women's history provides valuable guidance and context for the chapters on specific materials.

Each of Ware's fellow scholars contributed in unique ways to shaping and polishing this guide: Eileen Boris, University of California, Santa Barbara; Joanne M. Braxton, College of William and Mary; Carol F. Karlsen, University of Michigan; Alice Kessler-Harris, Columbia University; and

"The Stock Yards. Preparation of Sausage Meat." *Jules Huret, L'Amérique Moderne, April 15, 1911 (E168.H948 fol), plate 95. General Collections.*

A French journal from 1911 offered Europeans a tour of America, including an article on the stockyards of Chicago, with which this illustration appeared. At the time, women made up 11 percent of the employees in the slaughtering and meat-packing industry in Illinois, but most supervisors, as seen here, were male. These women may be working in the fresh pork department as "trimmers of trimmings," which means they separated the lean from the fat. Those performing this job were predominantly female and worked about fifty hours a week, for which they received on the average a weekly wage of ten dollars. The same Parisian journal depicted women in classes at Tuskegee Institute and Salt Lake City Business College, included portraits of American Indian women, and presented a story on wealthy American brides who married European nobility. The Library's enormous foreigh-language collections can shed light on the lives of U.S. women and provide a vantage point that may give researchers new perspectives. (For periodicals, see p. 12.)

Vicki L. Ruiz, Arizona State University. They debated with us the proposed structure, particularly ideas for linking divisional collections and approaches to integrating ethnic and foreign-language materials, and kept us aware of literary and less strictly historical sources. The topics that they proposed helped guide the research and writing of chapters, essays, and illustration captions. Each scholar read drafts of the manuscript and offered many helpful suggestions to chapter authors and to the editors. The advisers, however, bear no responsibility for authorial or editorial errors, but all the contributors owe them a great debt of gratitude for urging them on to their best efforts.

We hope that this guide also demonstrates how women in America have been portrayed visually since Europeans first encountered Indian tribes on our soil. Jim Higgins and Yusef El-Amin of the Library's Photo Lab photographed well over a hundred original artifacts from the Library's collections, while Sandra Lawson, Eva Shade, Deborah Evans, Margaret Kieckhefer, Georgia Zola, Yvonne Brooks, Ed Russian, Charlotte Houtz, Judith Brisker, and Bonnie Coles, staff members or liaisons to the Photoduplication Service, managed the retrieval and processing of one of the largest photographic orders for a single Publishing Office project.

The design of the volume is the art and work of Adrianne Onderdonk Dudden, who has fashioned a series of resource guides for the Library of Congress. Production of the volume was directed by manager of production Gloria Baskerville-Holmes and assistant manager Clarke Allen. The index, to which all the contributors added ideas, is the work of Susan Fels.

The Library of Congress staff, from the position of Librarian of Congress to the deck attendant who brings the book or audiotape from its resting place in the stacks to the desk or listening booth where it can be read or heard, is in place to acquire, preserve, and make available the resources that scholars of women's history, their students and colleagues, and you, the reader of this guide, will one day use. To each member of the staff, we owe our thanks for making these resources available.

Sara Day, *Editor*
Evelyn Sinclair, *Editor*

Introduction

In the classic feminist text *A Room of One's Own* (1929), Virginia Woolf tells the story of going to the British Museum to do research for an upcoming lecture on women and fiction. "If truth is not to be found on the shelves of the British Museum," she asked herself, "where . . . is truth?"[1] Her search was not an especially satisfying one. She found many books written by men on the subject of women, all of them totally useless to her task at hand. She left discouraged, feeling an outsider in the men's world of knowledge and scholarship.

If Virginia Woolf were to walk into the Library of Congress or any major library or research facility today, she would have a far different experience. Instead of finding the subject of women neglected, excluded, or marginalized, she would confront a wealth of information on topics concerning women and gender that would have been inconceivable in the 1920s, or even as late as the 1960s. Now the problem is not too little material on women: it is how to master and find one's way through the explosion of feminist scholarship of the past three decades. Just as important, a whole range of previously overlooked documents and sources unearthed by feminist scholars sheds new light on women's experiences in the past and present.

This guide is designed to introduce researchers to the enormous opportunities for discovering American women's history and culture at the Library of Congress. In addition to textual sources, it covers materials such as films and sound recordings, prints and photographs, and other audio or visual material. Its intended audience includes academics, advanced graduate students, genealogists, documentary filmmakers, set and costume designers, artists, actors, novelists, photo researchers, general readers, and, of course, the modern-day equivalents of Virginia Woolf.

Few fields of American history have grown as dramatically as that of women's history over the past several decades. Courses in women's history are now standard in most colleges and universities, taught by specialists who have trained in the field; many schools also have interdisciplinary women's studies programs. Professors and graduate students continue to produce a wide range of scholarship on issues of women and gender. Textbooks that once relegated their coverage of women to luminaries such as Abigail Adams, Harriet Beecher Stowe, Sojourner Truth, or Eleanor Roosevelt now include full discussions of major topics and viewpoints in women's history as an integrated part of their general narrative. Although there is still controversy about how American history should be taught, it seems unlikely that we will ever return to the days when women were totally absent from history books or broader historical narratives.

The challenge of women's history is not a simple question of "add women and stir." It means rethinking and rewriting the story. Linda Gordon, whose pioneering work in the 1970s on the history of the birth control movement helped spur the development of the field, explained: women's history "does not simply add women to the picture we already have of the past, like painting additional figures into the spaces of an already completed canvas. It requires repainting the ear-

"Streetcars—getting on Broadway car, July 11, 1913." Photograph, 1913. George Grantham Bain Collection. Prints and Photographs Division. LC-USZ62-91532.

New York City streetcar safety and women's fashions in the summer of 1913 are subjects of this photograph taken by a Bain News Service photographer. George Grantham Bain dispensed with the services of commercial studio photographers and instead trained his office boys to photograph breaking news, interesting personalities, and aspects of daily life in the city. This particular series of photographs highlighted the difficulties women encountered in mounting steep streetcar steps with their narrow skirts and, as in this case, with children in tow. (For more about the Bain Collection, see page 193.)

lier pictures, because some of what was previously on the canvas was inaccurate and more of it was misleading."[2]

That ability to force us to look at history in new ways, with new questions and a much wider array of historical actors, is one of the most important contributions that women's history has made, and continues to make, to the writing and teaching of American history. Gerda Lerner, another pioneer in women's history and a leading feminist theorist, remarked in 1981: "What we have to offer, for consciousness, is a correct analysis of what the world is like. Up to now we have had a partial analysis. Everything that explains the world has in fact explained a world that does not exist, a world in which men are at the center of the human enterprise and women are at the margin 'helping' them. Such a world does not exist—never has. Men and women have built society and have built the world. Women have been central to it. This revolutionary insight is itself a force, a force that liberates and transforms." Knowledge is power, says Lerner: "Women's history is the primary tool for women's emancipation."[3]

Although the revival of feminism encouraged a giant leap forward in the 1970s, women's history did not start from scratch. Women's history itself has a history, which, in turn, has influenced how the field developed, what kinds of questions were asked at various points in time, and how the field interacted with larger contours of American history in general. This process is ongoing. One of the most vibrant things about the field of women's history is its determination to avoid complacency. According to Linda Gordon, women's historians have been "continuously self-critical of our generalizations."[4] To revisit some of those earlier generalizations and to examine how the questions have been recast and deepened over time provides a good introduction to the field as a whole.[5]

Some of the earliest work in American women's history dates to the nineteenth century. Usually produced by amateur historians, these works are often referred to as "compensatory" or "contributory" history because they focused on previously unknown or neglected contributions that women had made to various aspects of the American experience. Many of these early historical works were biographies of famous women, often authors, first ladies, or women otherwise defined by their relationship to prominent men, a focus that became less dominant as the field matured. Not terribly sophisticated methodologically but often written in a lively and accessible style, these early attempts to put women in history were nevertheless important for showing that the materials and resources existed to write about women's lives and their contributions to American life.

As certain American women, primarily those of the white middle class, gained access to higher education and professional training in the late nineteenth and early to mid-twentieth centuries, the range of scholarship expanded, although it remained on the margins of how American history was taught and conceptualized. Women were just not seen as subjects worthy of historical inquiry. That did not stop scholars from publishing in this field. Mary Beard's *Woman as Force in History* (1946), for example, challenged the view of women as victims by emphasizing women's agency, and Eleanor Flexner offered a meticulously researched narrative of the women's rights movement from Seneca Falls through the winning of suffrage in 1920 in *Century of Struggle* (1959). When women's history as an academic discipline began to grow dramatically in the 1970s, these pioneering books, along with feminist classics such as Simone de Beauvoir's *The Second Sex* (published in France in 1949, and available in translation in the United States in 1953), became highly influential texts for second-wave feminism.[6]

Various factors came together in the late 1960s and 1970s to fuel the growth of women's history: the waves of social protest set in motion by the civil rights movement in the 1950s, in which women as well as men participated; the climate of protest prompted by the war in Vietnam; the revival of feminism as a national issue, sparked in part by Betty Friedan's *The Feminine Mystique* (1963) and also by the emergence of women's liberation separate from the New Left; and demographic changes in women's lives, including higher workforce participation and widening access to higher education. An especially critical intellectual factor was the emergence of social history, which looked at the lives of ordinary Americans, and thus challenged the traditional focus on wars, presidents, and great men. Emboldened by the revival of feminism, many female scholars (and a few male colleagues) began actively asking new and different questions from history, often linked to the sweeping changes going on in their own lives. As historian Linda Kerber noted aptly, "activists are hungry for their history."[7] Professors who had been trained in traditional fields such as diplomatic history or Russian history switched their research interests to women's history, almost training themselves as they went. So new—and to some departments and university administrators, so threatening—

were the first courses in women's history that it practically felt like a revolutionary act to teach or take one.

In this exciting and creative time for women's history in the 1970s, much of the early research focused on the concept of separate spheres in mid-nineteenth-century America, that is, the way in which women's lives were directed toward the familial and private whereas men inhabited the wider world of politics, work, and public life. Although much of this early work targeted separate spheres as an example of the oppression of women, there was also a competing, and at times simultaneous, emphasis on the empowerment and autonomy women could enjoy in a world where, in Carroll Smith-Rosenberg's phrase, "men made but a shadowy appearance."[8] This balancing act between victimization or oppression on the one hand and women's agency or activism on the other continues to shape the field today.

Exciting as this outpouring of new research was, the limits of the separate spheres paradigm soon became apparent, one of many instances where women's history has shown its ability to criticize itself and move beyond working generalizations, or to discard them entirely. African American scholars pointed out that the separate spheres concept had little relevance to the lives of black women, for whom restriction to a domestic sphere was virtually negated by institutions like slavery or the need to seek paid employment outside the home. Scholars who studied working-class or immigrant women made the same point. The separate spheres model was also very dependent on sources from New England, with less bearing for the South or, especially, the West. Furthermore, it began to dawn on scholars that white middle-class women might have as much or more in common with men of their own social and economic class than with other women. Later scholars chipped away even more at the notion of a universal female experience by demonstrating that the line between public and private was much more fluid than prescriptive literature reflected.

This dethroning of the concept of sisterhood, and its replacement with a recognition of difference (the diversity of women's experiences, not their commonality), was well under way by the early 1980s. Difference has continued to be one of the most important organizing concepts of women's history. No longer was it enough to say "women"—scholars had to make it clear which women they were talking about. Women were divided by a range of factors that included race,

The Black Patti, Mme. M. Sissieretta Jones: The Greatest Singer of Her Race. *Color poster. New York: Metropolitan Printing Co., 1899. Performing Arts Posters. Prints and Photographs Division. LC-USZC4-5164.*

A remarkable soprano voice and a commanding presence won personal success for Matilda Sissieretta Joyner Jones. The decorations she wears in this 1899 poster testify to her professional triumphs. In 1888 she became the first black singer to appear on stage at Wallack's Theater, and in 1892 she performed at the White House for President William Henry Harrison and in London before the Prince of Wales. Jones was a performer in vaudeville and opera houses throughout her career. She was known as "the Black Patti," a reference to the celebrated Italian soprano Adelina Patti. Her success helped African Americans gain acceptance as serious artists. The presence of this poster among Performing Arts Posters in the Prints and Photographs Division offers another kind of testimony to Jones's stardom. This collection, consisting mostly of works that poster producers registered for copyright protection, contains many nineteenth-century minstrel posters, but no other portrait poster of a black performer. (For Performing Arts Posters, see page 201.)

class, ethnicity, religion, geography, age, sexual orientation, and so forth. This scholarly trend interacted with the emergence of identity politics, that is, the tendency to situate oneself politically and socially in relation to a range of self-defined identities. There was also increasing recognition of conflicts among women and the unequal power dynamics shaping relations between women: mistresses on Southern plantations and their female slaves; white professional women whose careers were made possible by cheap domestic help, usually black or minority women; or white native-born social workers and their working-class and immigrant clients. Suddenly it became much harder to make generalizations about the category of *woman*. Jacquelyn Dowd Hall challenged historians, "Think simultaneously about the construct 'woman' and about concrete, class- and race-specific historical women."[9]

Another new trend in the 1980s was the growing acceptance of the concept of *gender,* a term that was virtually nonexistent in 1970s scholarship. Gender refers to the historical and cultural constructions of roles assigned to the biological differences and attributes of men and women. If one could do a key word search of women's history scholarship of the past twenty years, "gender" would probably rival "women" as the most frequently cited word. Although there is no single women's history methodology or approach, the emphasis on gender provides a unifying theme to much of the scholarship on women being produced today. Joan Scott's enormously influential 1986 article "Gender: A Useful Tool of Historical Analysis" played a key role here.[10] Another way to date this shift is to examine the number of book titles that began to use the word in their titles, such as Ruth Milkman's *Gender at Work: The Dynamics of Job Segregation by Sex during World War II* (1987).

In addition to its fruitfulness for women's history, gender analysis has also spurred new scholarship on the construction of masculinity and the way men's roles have changed over time, although some scholars fear that this new trend is just an excuse to deflect attention away from women. In any case, the concept of gender has been stretched far beyond the realization that individuals are influenced by gender roles and expectations. Because all historical actors have a gender, practically any historical question or topic from diplomacy to leisure to state policy can theoretically be subjected to a gender analysis. As Kathleen Brown shows in her study of colonial Virginia, *Good Wives, Nasty Wenches, and Anxious Patriarchs* (1996), gender never functions in isolation, but in relationship to other factors such as race or class. Karen Anderson argues that gender should be seen "as a constituent element in all social relations, particularly race and class, and in all institutions, including families and political and economic systems and associations. Gender identities are understood as politicized identities that women and men seek to enact or reform in specific historical contexts."[11]

In the 1990s, in addition to widening attention to the intersections of race, class, and gender, practitioners of women's history and gender studies took what has been called a "linguistic turn." Spurred in part by writings from French scholars such as Jacques Derrida and especially Michel Foucault, American historians began to analyze more deeply questions of language and discourse, that is, the ways in which underlying power structures and inequalities were forged and maintained in words, speech, and other representations (see

Home Washing Machine & Wringer. *Color lithograph. New York, ca. 1869. Popular and Applied Graphic Arts. Prints and Photographs Division. LC-USZC4-4590.*

Emancipation through technology is the message of this 1869 advertisement in which low-tech drudgery is contrasted with state-of-the-art housekeeping. In fact, the image could be read as the same woman emerging from drudgery to full liberation as the mistress of the household. While previously she or her servants might have expected to labor for the better part of a day with tub and washboard, now a woman's serene engagement with the home washer and wringer requires only a small apron to protect her dress as she contemplates the promise of leisure time implicit in the figure of her elegant supervisor and studious daughter. In actuality this early mechanical washer was only a small step toward a promise reached in the twentieth century when electric power became widely available. Nevertheless, show cards such as this one used the art of color lithography to appeal to the public in window displays or on counters to attract buyers to merchandise available from retailers during this era of commercial expansion. (See historical prints, page 209.)

"Modèles de Madame Carlier." Millinery Trade Review, *February 1897 (TT650.H3), plate 4. General Collections.*

Colorful feathers, flowers, and fruit adorn the stylish hats designed in Madame Carlier's Paris establishment and worn by actresses at the Gymnase Theater. The pages of the *Millinery Trade Review* instructed American milliners on ways to create such Parisian concoctions in their own shops. This and similar trade journals provide glimpses of women's lives through employment advertisements (looking for "a lady of experience as buyer and manager of a millinery business"), obituaries, and discussions of legislation, including "anti-theater hat" bills, which sparked debate from Pittsburgh to Kansas City on whether to limit the size of hats worn by women theatergoers. (For trade journals, see page 16.)

"With Peace and Freedom Blest! Woman as Symbol" in this volume). Literary criticism and cultural analysis challenged the authenticity of the text itself, questioning its voice by showing that experience and identity were never simple or unmediated. For example, categories such as "heterosexual" and "homosexual" were shown to be historically constructed, not innate or immutable, with the emergence of a heterosexual identity (as well as other sexual orientations) a fairly recent development. Women's historians incorporated insights from much of this theoretical work into their own scholarship, deploying the use of language and the analysis of words to scrutinize topics like the body and further illuminate the arenas of race, class, and difference.

One way to think about women's history today is to realize how many of its major concerns are focused and oriented toward relationships: in addition to the reigning trilogy of race, class, and gender, the field addresses relationships between groups of women, between structures of power and their subjects, between regions and nationalities, and so forth. Many of these relationships are power relations, as Mary Beth Norton cogently documents in *Founding Mothers and Fathers: Gendered Power and the Forming of American Society* (1997), and they are all fluid formations, constantly shifting and mutating. What women's history seeks is a multifaceted approach that will be sufficient, in the words of Joanne Meyerowitz, "to illuminate the interconnections among the various systems of power that shape women's lives."[12]

One of the most far-reaching items on the women's history agenda is the continued interrogation of the concept of whiteness. Too often in the literature white women have appeared as raceless, their experiences shaped entirely by gender. In contrast, African American women and other women of color were viewed primarily in terms of their race, to the exclusion of factors such as class and gender. Yet historians now realize that everyone has ethnicity and race, that whiteness is as much a racial identity as being black or Latina. As a result, historians have been able to unmask the embedded racism of much of past white middle-class women's experiences, where such women, claiming to speak for all women, were in fact speaking from their dominant race and class positions. Such insights have significantly shaped new research in areas such as women's suffrage and the history of imperialism.

A multicultural approach, that is, one that recognizes difference and diversity in women's experiences, is also at the center of contemporary scholarship on women and gender. One of the important contributions of this approach is that it moves the field of history beyond the old framework of seeing race matters solely in terms of black and white. Here the contributions of Western historians have been especially important, because the geographical region they are describing fails to fit neatly into anything resembling a biracial dichotomy. Where would that leave Native American women, Latinas, and Asian women, who often existed side by side with black and Anglo women in Western communities? This widened field of vision once again forces historians to put issues of diversity in race, class, and gender relationships at the heart of all questions under inquiry. There is an important caveat, how-

Edward S. Curtis. Hupa female shaman. Photograph, copyright © 1923. Prints and Photographs Division. LC-USZ62-101261.

Among the Athapaskan Hupa of northwestern California, most of the shamans, or healers, were older women. Because illness was said to result from the misalignment of a person's spiritual and natural worlds, the shaman used potions, poultices, incantations, fasting, chanting, and secret rituals to drive out evil spirits and restore a person's inner balance. This photograph—a reminder of women's important cultural, spiritual, and leadership roles in many American Indian tribes—is one of approximately twenty-four hundred first-generation photographic prints deposited for copyright by Edward Curtis during his thirty-year career photographing Native Americans west of the Mississippi and collecting their legends, languages, traditions, and music for his twenty-volume work *The North American Indian*. (See the Edward Curtis Collection, page 200.)

ever: multiculturalism and diversity cannot become a question of merely recognizing and adding previously excluded groups because then diversity runs the risk of normalizing white middle-class practice and marginalizing everyone else as "other." Such an outcome, in turn, is simply a cover for existing race, class, gender, and heterosexual domination. Like most other things in life, conceptualizing women's history is always a balancing act.

One of the greatest accomplishments of women's history over the past three decades has been the extensive documentation of the contours of African American women's history. This rich outpouring of research, on everything from education to suffrage to work to slavery to music, has brought the enormous contributions made by African American women to their communities and to the country at large into the historical record. As monographs were being written and oral history interviews conducted, new documents and sources were uncovered which are now available to scholars and researchers.

Research on Asian American women, Latinas, Puerto Rican women, and immigrants from the Caribbean and South American countries has also begun in earnest, but because the fields are much newer and the number of practitioners smaller, they have not yet had the impact on broader scholarship that African American historiography has. These areas are likely to experience major growth over the next decade. From these subfields and the fruitful scholarship being done on the multicultural West, women's history has already learned the utility of concepts like borderlands, intercultural borders, frontiers, and contact zones. Once again women's history will be pushing the boundaries as it ventures into new areas of exploration and research.

Contemporary women's history scholarship also rewrites topics that had once seemed settled or fully explored by asking different questions and using new approaches. An excellent example is the women's suffrage movement (see "Marching for the Vote" in this volume). Documentation of the history of women's suffrage began in 1881 during the movement itself, with the compilation of the multivolume *History of Woman Suffrage* by Elizabeth Cady Stanton, Susan B. Anthony, and Matilda Joslyn Gage, an important if flawed source (it focused on only one wing of the movement, ignoring the contributions of the other). Eleanor Flexner's *Century of Struggle* (1959) brought the story to a new generation of readers, and the early women's rights movement became the focus of some of the most influential early works in women's history, such as Gerda Lerner's *The Grimké Sisters from South Carolina: Rebels against Slavery* (1967) and Ellen Carol Dubois's *Feminism and Suffrage: The Emergence of an Independent Women's Movement in America, 1848–1869* (1978).

Interest in suffrage has ebbed and flowed, but it has risen recently as historians probe more deeply into the embedded racism of much of the suffragists' ideology and leadership strategies. Spurred in part by scholarship on the often troubled relationship between white and African American suffragists, as well as by the new emphasis on analyzing whiteness as a category, historians have demonstrated how white suffrage leaders basically privileged the white middle-class female as the norm, the standard to be aspired to, in the United States and throughout the world. A topic that once seemed to be mainly about winning the vote now presents a window on issues such as racism, imperialism, and power.

The growing interest in suffrage is also part of a resurgence of interest in political history. In the early days of women's history, inspired largely by the dramatic growth of social history, most attention focused on the lives of ordinary women, with political elites or prominent women given a lower priority. Partly as a byproduct of moving beyond the separate spheres paradigm, historians began to realize that women had been much more involved in the public sphere than previously suspected. They may not have been voters or held political office, but they influenced public policy nonetheless: through voluntary associations, churches and charities, family connections, or even participation in mob actions or other public demonstrations not usually associated with "the weaker sex." Any former notions of women as nonpolitical have gone by the wayside. Or to put it another way, women's history has helped broaden the definition of what is political in ways that have been productive not only for research on women and gender but also for the field of American political history.

As part of a new attention to the making of public policy and how public authority is forged, historians have also turned a more critical eye to areas like the growth of the state and state policy, especially on issues affecting women and children such as welfare laws. As another example of how topics in women's history continue to grow and deepen, early work on the New Deal in the 1930s focused on the contributions that an elite band of women—primarily white but also including Mary McLeod Bethune—made to the formulation of New Deal policies. Building on that basis, later studies asked harder questions. It was no longer enough to know that women administrators were active in the New Deal; historians wanted to determine how the attitudes of those women affected the policies that they were developing and administering. In the case of social security, first passed in 1935, the law was written from a very conservative premise: that men were breadwinners, that women were primarily wives, and that any system of old-age insurance should be built on that dichotomy. Women administrators bought into this deeply gendered conceptualization and perpetuated it, despite the fact that their own lives diverged from such a model. Similar investigations into Progressive-era labor legislation and public policy from the 1960s and 1970s have uncovered previously undetected gender assumptions that now shape how historians view these periods of legislative activism.

Another field to which women's history has increasingly turned in recent years is biography. Of course, biographies of famous women have been standard fare since the nineteenth century, but in the excitement of the rediscovery of women's history in the 1960s and 1970s and the ascendancy of social history, biographies of well-known or influential women were fairly uncommon. (Gerda Lerner's book on the Grimké sisters and Kathryn Kish Sklar's 1973 biography of Catharine Beecher are notable exceptions.) And yet historians were intrigued by biography because it allowed them a window into many aspects of women's lives, be she ordinary (like Martha Ballard in Laurel Thacher Ulrich's *A Midwife's Tale*) or extraordinary (Eleanor Roosevelt as portrayed in Blanche Wiesen Cook's volumes). Especially important to the field of biography as a whole has been the insistence of feminist scholars that attention must always be paid to the interplay between the personal and the professional in forging an interpretation of a subject's overall significance.

One of the strongest continuities of women's history scholarship, stretching back to Progressive-era investigations of conditions of women's industrial work, such as Margaret Byington's *Homestead: The Household of a Mill Town* (1910) and Katherine Anthony's *Mothers Who Must Earn* (1914), is its focus on women's work, and this emphasis is alive and well. "Women have always worked" is a generalization that truly does stand up to scrutiny, and historians have documented the range of women's contributions, from industrial work to labor organizing to the significant theoretical recognition that women's unpaid domestic labor is critical to (and usually undercounted in) the wider economy. Also of interest have been the sectors of the economy where women traditionally have clustered: domestic service, waitressing, teaching, nursing, clerical work, librarianship, social work, and the like. How these occupations became typed as female, and why they have stayed that way despite monumental changes in the meaning of work and in the realities of women's lives, is a question that still tantalizes historians.

Another question that has been a constant on the women's history agenda concerns women and social change. From the beginning, historians have documented the wide variety of women's contributions to their communities and to public life. Through voluntary associations, religious groups, professional organizations, activist groups, and other forums, women have often been in the forefront of movements of social change, not always as the leaders, but certainly behind the scenes. Until recently these vital contributions have often been hidden from history, or at least overlooked. Women's activism, on the left and on the right, confirms the importance of expanding historians' notions of what constitutes the political.

An area that has always fascinated women's historians is that of sexuality. Because sexual practices are both a private activity and a public concern (expressed in such ways as laws regulating prostitution or homosexuality), it has often been easier to document the latter than the former. As part of the general challenge to a notion of a universal female experience, and influenced by the emergence of an activist gay liberation movement, innovative research has uncovered a far wider range of sexual identities and communities than previously recognized. Nor is this phenomenon limited to sophisticated urban areas like New York, Chicago, or San Francisco. Same-sex friendships, a topic that received a great deal of attention in the 1970s because of the separate spheres ideology, also continue to intrigue historians, who try to understand what these relationships meant to the women involved and then try to place the friendships into their broader historical context.

Now that America has entered the twenty-first century, it is appropriate that a fast-growing area of historical inquiry concerns women's transnationalism and globalization. The increasing number of comparative studies that cross both political and cultural boundaries also reflects this trend. Paralleling the theoretical effort to challenge and displace a white middle-class experience as the norm for all human experience is a parallel effort to dislodge the United States, and Western civilization, from a privileged position as the universal (and only) model of progress. Historians who have studied the interactions between American women's organizations and their foreign equivalents have often been struck by how deeply, and unconsciously, women who consider themselves feminists will hold up the Western model as the only one for the advancement of women. As historians document the extensive contact that American women's groups had with similar organizations beyond national borders, they show one direction that women's history will likely take in the future.

Waiting to Exhale. *Director: Forest Whitaker. Camera: Toyomichi Kurita. Screenplay: Terry McMillan and Ronald Bass. Cast: Whitney Houston, Angela Bassett, Loretta Devine, Lela Rochon. Publicity brochure. Twentieth Century Fox, 1995. Ephemera collection (box A-72). Moving Image Section, Motion Picture, Broadcasting, and Recorded Sound Division. Used with permission of Twentieth Century Fox.*

The contemporary women's film, or "chick flick," is aimed at a modern female audience. *Waiting to Exhale* combines elements from classic Hollywood movies with a new sensitivity to female and ethnic empowerment. The four beautiful, stylish, African American protagonists are successful businesswomen who learn to reject unworthy men but who continue to seek the perfect mate. (See motion pictures, page 316.)

As this necessarily abbreviated survey of the state of women's history has documented, the field is constantly generating new questions, new topics, and more sophisticated ways of interpreting and contextualizing material. But no matter what the questions are, research and documentation are needed to answer them. Sometimes it is a case of finding totally new sources and documents to tell a story that needs to be told, but far more often it is a matter of revisiting more traditional sources and asking different questions of them. That is where the rich resources of the Library of Congress come in. For practically any question in women's history, the Library of Congress is an excellent place to pursue in-depth research.

When the Library of Congress was established in 1800, it did not necessarily plan to become a major repository for material documenting the contributions of women to American life, but that, indeed, has happened over the two centuries of its existence. This material has arrived by a variety of routes, some direct and others quite circuitous. As part of the copyright registration process, books, sound recordings, motion pictures, prints and photographs, and other unique historical sources were placed on deposit in Washington. Even though the Library of Congress does not have every book ever published, its massive collections make it the library of record for the rest of the country. Its holdings include many different types of materials specifically devoted to the topic of women, but also a vast array of sources that contain unexpected nuggets of data or information for unlocking women's history.

A similar process is at work in the extensive manuscript and rare book collections: some collections, like those relating to woman suffrage, specifically relate to women, but many others, which on their face seem to have little to do with women, in fact hold major treasures. One example discussed in the chapter on manuscripts is the papers from members of Congress. Separated from their families and living a bachelor life in the nation's capital, what did congressmen do at night? They wrote home to their families about what was happening in Washington. And what did the congressional wives do? They wrote back detailed descriptions of their family and domestic concerns, and business concerns as well, thus supplying a rich source for documenting the lives of women of a certain class position. The collections were first acquired because of the importance of the male politicians, but the wives' letters are there nonetheless, ready for the kind of rediscovery and reinterpretation that is the bread and butter of women's history.

This resource guide is organized the same way that the Library of Congress is: by its major reading rooms. In each chapter you will find descriptions of important holdings and collections that relate to women's history. Perusing these chapters and seeing the wealth of material pertaining to women will suggest the kinds of topics and questions that could be researched. To demonstrate how researchers may actually use such material from the resources of the Library of Congress, five essays have been included that touch on some of the significant issues with which historians of women have grappled. These essays figuratively are the end products of a process that might begin when a researcher walks into any of the Library's reading rooms. A more detailed guide on how to use this book appears in "Using the Library of Congress," which follows. Researchers might also want to consult two previously published guides: *The African-American Mosaic: A Library of Congress Resource Guide for the Study of Black History and Culture* (1993) and *Many Nations: A Library of Congress Resource Guide for the Study of Indian and Alaska Native Peoples of the United States* (1996).

Two tips for doing research run through the entire book and have influenced its organization and presentation. The first piece of advice is not to limit research to one type of source or document, but to sample the Library's many divisions in an interdisciplinary manner. The second is that there is no single way to approach the Library's collections. Researchers should explore the finding tools, indexes, and other resources described in this volume and consult the reference staff in each reading room. Often the answers to the questions being researched can be found in a variety of places, and it is vital to cast the net widely.

One of the great attractions of doing research at the Library of Congress is the opportunity to consult many types of sources in one location, as I have found while researching a biography of radio talk show pioneer Mary Margaret McBride (1899–1976). From the 1930s through the 1950s, McBride built a loyal audience of millions of women (and not a few men) who tuned in to her program every day at one o'clock. A superb interviewer, Mary Margaret (her fans and guests were all on a first-name basis with her) welcomed the famous and the not-so-famous to her show, always eliciting interesting stories and ideas that connected her home-bound audience to the wider world. She even did her own commercials, earning a reputation as one of the most effective saleswomen on radio. If Mary Margaret said to buy a certain brand of carrots or gingerbread at the local store, her fans would pick the shelves clean.

To research this biography, I need to make use of no fewer than six collections or reading rooms at the Library of Congress, and this resource guide offers me a useful and complete introduction to each one of them. The bulk of my research is being conducted in the Recorded Sound Section, which has approximately 1,200 hours of transcribed tapes of her radio broadcasts. There I sit in a listening booth and pretend that I am one of Mary Margaret's listeners. When I want to take a break from that, I can watch her unsuccessful attempt to turn herself into a television personality in the 1950s with kinescopes and videotapes available through the Motion Picture and Television Reading Room. Historians like paper sources too, and luckily both the Recorded Sound Reference Center of the Motion Picture, Broadcasting, and Recorded Sound Division and the Manuscript Reading Room have major collections of her papers, including correspondence, letters from fans, radio logs, photographs, and memorabilia. Before McBride entered radio, she was a journalist, and I can track down articles she published through the extensive periodicals collection housed in the General Collections, which also contain the publications of many of her guests. To find newspaper coverage of her show, I can consult newspapers

"For the Benefit of the Girl Who Is about to Graduate." Lithograph. From Life, *May 22, 1890, 298-99. General Collections. LC-USZ62-58805.*

This cartoon from a May 1890 issue of the illustrated weekly humor magazine *Life* typifies a traditionalist view of education as threatening the ideal of womanhood by leading women away from their domestic duties. As the young scholar, or bluestocking, sleeps, a nightmarish army of domestic paraphernalia threatens to overwhelm her. Addressing those who questioned the value of higher education for women, most of the pioneer women's colleges advertised similar educational philosophies and goals. Their aim was to produce enlightened mothers, wives, and social exemplars. The tension between self-realization and family needs continues to be a hotly debated issue today.

from major cities across the country in the Newspaper and Current Periodical Room. If I want to find out more about the part of Missouri that she originally came from, I can go to the Geography and Map Reading Room.

I have been doing research at the Library of Congress for almost twenty-five years, and I am still learning about its rich resources. All the scholars who served as advisers to this project—Eileen Boris, Joanne Braxton, Carol Karlsen, Alice Kessler-Harris, and Vicki Ruiz—had a similar reaction as they participated in the preparation of this volume: each of us learned an enormous amount of useful, practical information about doing research at the Library of Congress, and, in fact, about doing research in general. We were collectively stimulated and excited by the possibilities of new research topics and ideas suggested by the material described. And we have all been enormously impressed by the knowledge and dedication of the members of the Library of Congress staff to making this material widely and easily accessible to researchers who wish to use it. This women's history resource guide is just the first step on what should be a fascinating and productive journey for any researcher, new or old, who enters the Library's doors. Unlike Virginia Woolf, you will not leave empty handed.

SELECTED BIBLIOGRAPHY

Anderson, Karen. *Changing Women: A History of Racial Ethnic Women in Modern America.* New York: Oxford University Press, 1996.

Armitage, Susan, and Elizabeth Jameson, eds. *The Women's West.* Norman: University of Oklahoma Press, 1987.

———. *Writing the Range: Race, Class, and Culture in the Women's West.* Norman: University of Oklahoma Press, 1997.

Bataille, Gretchen M. *Native American Women: A Biographical Dictionary.* New York: Garland Publishing, 1991.

Baron, Ava, ed. *Work Engendered: Toward a New History of American Labor.* Ithaca, N.Y.: Cornell University Press, 1991.

Baxandall, Rosalyn, and Linda Gordon, eds. *America's Working Women: A Documentary History.* 2nd ed. New York: W. W. Norton, 1995.

Boris, Eileen. *Home to Work: Motherhood and the Politics of Industrial Homework in the United States.* New York: Cambridge University Press, 1994.

Cahn, Susan. *Coming on Strong: Gender and Sexuality in Twentieth-Century Women's Sport.* New York: Free Press, 1994.

Chafe, William H. *The American Woman: Her Changing Social, Economic, and Political Roles, 1920–1970.* New York: Oxford University Press, 1974.

Clinton, Catherine, and Michele Gillespie, eds. *The Devil's Lane: Sex and Race in the Early South.* New York: Oxford University Press, 1997.

Cott, Nancy F., ed. *Root of Bitterness: Documents of the Social History of American Women.* 2nd ed. Boston: Northeastern Press, 1996.

Cott, Nancy F., and Elizabeth H. Pleck, eds. *A Heritage of Her Own: Towards a New Social History of American Women.* New York: Simon & Schuster, 1979.

Del Castillo, Adelaida R., ed. *Between Borders: Essays on Mexicana/Chicana History.* Encino, Calif.: Floricanto Press, 1990.

D'Emilio, John, and Estelle Freedman. *Intimate Matters: A History of Sexuality in America.* 2nd ed. New York: Harper & Row, 1988.

Evans, Sara M. *Born for Liberty: A History of Women in America.* New York: Free Press, 1989.

Faderman, Lillian S. *Odd Girls and Twilight Lovers: A History of Lesbian Life in Twentieth-Century America.* New York: Columbia University Press, 1991.

Giddings, Paula. *When and Where I Enter: The Impact of Black Women on Race and Sex in America.* 1st Quill ed. New York: W. Morrow, 1996.

Hewitt, Nancy, and Suzanne Lebsock, eds. *Visible Women: New Essays on American Activism.* Urbana: University of Illinois Press, 1993.

Hine, Darlene Clark, Elsa Barkley Brown, and Rosyln Terborg-Penn, eds. *Black Women in America: An Historical Encyclopedia.* 2 vols. Brooklyn: Carlson Publishing, 1993. Bloomington: Indiana University Press, 1994.

Hine, Darlene Clark, Wilma King, and Linda Reed, eds. *"We Specialize in the Wholly Impossible": A Reader in Black Women's History.* Brooklyn, N.Y.: Carlson Publishing, 1995.

Hine, Darlene Clark, and Kathleen Thompson. *A Shining Thread of Hope: The History of Black Women in America.* New York: Broadway Books, 1998.

Hodes, Martha, ed. *Sex, Love, Race: Crossing Boundaries in North American History.* New York: New York University Press, 1999.

Flexner, Eleanor. *Century of Struggle: The Woman's Rights Movement in the United States.* 1959. Revised and enlarged by Ellen Fitzpatrick. Cambridge, Mass.: Belknap Press of Harvard University Press, 1996.

James, Edward T., Janet Wilson James, and Paul S. Boyer. *Notable American Women, 1607–1950: A Biographical Dictionary.* Cambridge, Mass.: Belknap Press of Harvard University Press, 1971.

Jones, Jacqueline. *American Work: Black and White Labor since 1600.* New York: W. W. Norton, 1998.

Kerber, Linda, Alice Kessler-Harris, and Kathryn Kish Sklar, eds. *U.S. History as Women's History: New Feminist Essays.* Chapel Hill: University of North Carolina Press, 1995.

Kerber, Linda, and Jane Sherron De Hart, eds. *Women's America: Refocusing the Past.* 5th ed. New York: Oxford University Press, 2000.

Kessler-Harris, Alice. *Out to Work: A History of Wage-Earning Women in the United States.* New York: Oxford University Press, 1982.

Lerner, Gerda. *The Majority Finds Its Past: Placing Women in History.* New York: Oxford University Press, 1979.

Ling, Huping. *Surviving on the Gold Mountain: A History of Chinese American Women and Their Lives.* Albany: State University of New York Press, 1998.

Matthews, Glenna. *The Rise of Public Woman: Woman's Power and Woman's Place in the United States, 1630–1970.* New York: Oxford University Press, 1992.

Mora, Magdelena, and Adelaida R. Del Castillo, eds. *Mexican Women in the United States: Struggles Past and Present.* Los Angeles: Chicano Studies Research Center Publications, University of California, 1980.

Norton, Mary Beth, and Ruth M. Alexander, eds. *Major Problems in American Women's History: Documents and Essays.* 2nd ed. Lexington, Mass.: D.C. Heath, 1996.

Rotundo, E. Anthony. *American Manhood: Transformations in Masculinity from the Revolution to the Modern Era.* New York: Basic Books, 1993.

Ruiz, Vicki. *From Out of the Shadows: Mexican Women in Twentieth-Century America.* New York: Oxford University Press, 1998.

Ruiz, Vicki, and Ellen Carol DuBois, eds. *Unequal Sisters: A Multicultural Reader in U.S. Women's History.* 3rd ed. New York: Routledge, 2000.

Schlissel, Lillian, Vicki L. Ruiz, and Janice Monk, eds. *Western Women: Their Land, Their Lives.* Albuquerque: University of New Mexico Press, 1988.

Scott, Anne Firor. *Natural Allies: Women's Associations in American History.* Urbana: University of Illinois Press, 1991.

Shoemaker, Nancy, ed. *Negotiators of Change: Historical Perspectives on Native American Women.* New York: Routledge, 1995.

Sicherman, Barbara, and Carol Hurd Green. *Notable American Women: The Modern Period.* Cambridge, Mass.: Belknap Press of Harvard University Press, 1980.

Smith, Merril D., ed. *Sex and Sexuality in Early America.* New York: New York University Press, 1998.

Solomon, Barbara Miller. *In the Company of Educated Women: A History of Women and Higher Education in America.* New Haven, Conn.: Yale University Press, 1985.

Strasser, Susan. *Never Done: A History of American Housework.* New York: Pantheon Books, 1982; New York: Henry Holt, 2000.

Ware, Susan, ed. *Modern American Women: A Documentary History.* 2nd ed. New York: McGraw-Hill, 1997.

Woloch, Nancy. *Women and the American Experience.* 3rd ed. New York: McGraw-Hill, 2000.

Yung, Judy. *Unbound Feet: A Social History of Chinese Women in San Francisco.* Berkeley: University of California Press, 1995.

Using the Library of Congress

The Library of Congress is the largest library in the world. Its size, closed stacks, many reading rooms, and extensive multiformat collections can confuse even the most experienced reader. To make the best use of your time and its marvelous collections, you should take several steps before arriving at the Library. Begin to chart your research strategy by searching the Library of Congress Web site, <http://www.loc.gov>, which leads you to the Library of Congress Online Catalog, the American Memory Web site, and the Web pages and catalogs of individual reading rooms. The Library's main online catalog contains records for most books and periodicals as well as for many other formats such as manuscripts, sound recordings, microform materials, and maps. The American Memory Web site contains dozens of multimedia collections—with new ones being added regularly—containing digitized documents, photographs, sound recordings, motion pictures, and text from the Library's Americana collections. From the home pages of individual reading rooms, you can find information about hours and services, full-text finding aids for some special collections, and links to specialized databases and catalogs, such as the Prints and Photographs Online Catalog.

Resources at your local public or university libraries can also help you plan your visit to the Library of Congress. When looking for books and periodicals be sure to consult readily available sources—such as bibliographies and periodical indexes (see chapter 1)—in order to compile an initial list of works you want to examine. Other ways to prepare include examining notes in secondary sources and collecting names of significant individuals, organizations, places, and dates. This preliminary gathering of background information is especially important for formats, such as photographs, motion pictures, sound recordings, or maps, that may have limited subject access. For some collections, it is recommended that you call or write before arriving to discuss your projects and to schedule the retrieval of off-site collections. See specific chapters of this guide for further details. All these advance preparations will help you make the most efficient use of your time at the Library.

Similar to this research guide on U.S. women's history, two earlier guides describe Library of Congress holdings for African Americans and Native Americans: *The African-American Mosaic: A Library of Congress Resource Guide for the Study of Black History and Culture* (Washington: Library of Congress, 1993; Z1361.N39 L47 1993) and *Many Nations: A Library of Congress Resource Guide for the Study of Indian and Alaska Native Peoples of the United States* (Washington: Library of Congress, 1996; Z1209.2.U5 L53 1996). Both publications are available at libraries around the country and should be used in conjunction with this volume.

It is important to remember, too, that the Library of Congress is not always the best place for certain kinds of inquiry. Some searches are faster and easier at a public or university library. For example, to read a 1993 issue of *Working Woman* at

Mathew Brady Studio. **Camp of 31st Pennsylvania Infantry near Washington, D.C.** *Photograph, 1862, printed later. Civil War Photographs Collection. Prints and Photographs Division. LC-B8171-2405 (film negative).*

Princess Agnes Salm-Salm, wife of Prince Felix of Prussia, who served with the Union Army, observed in January 1862 that the winter camp of the Army of the Potomac was "teeming with women." Some wives insisted on staying with their husbands, which may have been the case with this woman, judging by her housewifely pose alongside a soldier, three young children, and a puppy. In addition to taking care of her own family, she may have worked as a camp laundress or nurse. Some women who lacked the marital voucher of respectability were presumed to be prostitutes and were periodically ordered out of camp. Only gradually during the four years of the war, and in the face of unspeakable suffering, were women grudgingly accepted by military officials and the general public in the new public role of nurse. (For the Civil War Photographs Collection, see page 198.)

a public library, you usually walk straight to the shelf and locate the magazine in a few minutes. At the Library of Congress, you must determine the call number, submit a call slip, and wait forty-five to ninety minutes for the issue to be brought from the stacks to a reading room in either the Thomas Jefferson or the John Adams Building. If you also want to see the most recent issue of the same magazine, you must go to another building.

Nevertheless, for many research questions the Library of Congress and its phenomenal collections are invaluable. As this volume clearly demonstrates, the Library is a complicated institution, and to make the fullest use of the multiformat collections—such as newspapers, manuscripts, maps, photographs, and sound recordings—you may need to visit several reading rooms, often in different buildings. Even collections that arrive at the Library as a unit may be split among several reading rooms. For example, from the Clare Boothe Luce collection, her personal papers are in the Manuscript Division; her photographs went to the Prints and Photographs Division; and her motion picture films and sound recordings are held by the Motion Picture, Broadcasting, and Recorded Sound Division. It is good to ask if other reading rooms hold materials from the collection you are using.

READER REGISTRATION: To use the public reading rooms in the Library of Congress, you must first get a reader identification card. The cards are issued by the Library free of charge and can be obtained by anyone over high-school age with appropriate photo-identification—a valid driver's license, state-issued identification card, or passport. Application must be made in person at the Reader Registration Station in the James Madison Memorial Building (use the main entrance at 101 Independence Avenue, SE), room LM140. Reader identification cards are valid for two years and may be renewed when they expire. Some reading rooms require additional registration. Special procedures and access policies are described at the beginning of each chapter.

For further information on services for researchers, see: <http://www.loc.gov/rr/>.

All first-time users must obtain a reader identification card. If you have the card and wish to research a topic related to American women's history, the Jefferson Building is the best place to begin your search unless you know in advance that the specific items you need are housed in the Library's specialized reading rooms. In the Jefferson Building you will find the staffed Computer Catalog Center, the Main Card Catalog, the large Main Reading Room reference collection, and most importantly, reference librarians to help you access the General Collections—which include most books and bound periodicals published after 1800—and to guide you to other reading rooms for further assistance. The Main Reading Room staff includes specialists in women's studies, American history, African American studies, literature, religion, fine arts, and more. Appointments can be made for in-depth advice. Other reading rooms have specialists appropriate to the subject or format covered there—for example, the Law Library has law specialists, the Prints and Photographs Division has specialists for formats such as posters and cartoons, and also for certain subjects, such as Native Americans and the West. It is often good to discuss your research project with the appropriate expert in a specific reading room.

One of the aims of this research guide is to show the variety of materials available in the Library for exploring the history of American women. Researchers are generally most familiar with print sources, but this volume hopes to demonstrate that other formats also are of great value. Because of the diversity of formats held by the Library, there is no one catalog that lists all items, no single system of call numbers, and no one set of authorized subject headings in use throughout the Library. Different formats require different search strategies. The following brief sections on subject headings and call numbers apply mostly to print sources—especially books and periodicals—but researchers will usually need to use published finding aids to locate items in the special collections. It is important that you consult the chapters on the various formats for a complete picture of what the Library holds and how to find it. Each chapter will explain the subject access and numbering systems used in a particular reading room.

Library of Congress Subject Headings (LCSH)

The key to searching many of the Library's online and card catalogs, especially for books, periodicals, and manuscripts, is to identify the correct Library of Congress subject headings. The Library creates highly structured, very specific headings that enable researchers to pinpoint the exact works desired. The headings have become increasingly effective for women's topics over the past thirty years. For older materials, a combination of valid subject headings and other research methods (described later in this volume) is necessary. Library of Congress subject headings are the most commonly used controlled vocabulary at the Library and also at many other libraries around the country.

Otto Henry Bacher. Women in a restaurant in a tall building. Wash drawing, ca. 1903. Cabinet of American Illustration. CAI-Bacher, no. 6 (D size). Prints and Photographs Division. LC-USZC4-1204.

Otto Henry Bacher's portrayal of women in a restaurant—both diners and waitresses—is one of several studies of women of various circumstances that Bacher made for the *Century Magazine* and other magazines. The uncaptioned image is one of those by Bacher held in the Prints and Photographs Division's Cabinet of American Illustration. A search reveals that this wash drawing may have been intended to illustrate an article by Cleveland Moffett entitled "Mid-Air Dining Clubs" published in the *Century Magazine* in September 1901, although this particular image did not appear in the issue. Moffett describes the growth of the dining clubs in New York City, the way women used their husbands' memberships to hold parties in separate ladies' dining rooms, and the pioneering Business Woman's Club, whose members, nearly three hundred working women, enjoyed its inexpensive meals and its lounges, where they could take "half an hour's nap against nerves and headache." (See the Cabinet of American Illustration, page 191.)

The multivolume *Library of Congress Subject Headings (LCSH)* (Washington: Library of Congress, annual; Z695.Z8 L524a; found in most reading rooms) lists current subject terms. Careful examination of these volumes, often referred to as the "Red Books," as well as consultation with the reference staff are crucial. Online help screens assist in identifying some of the valid subject headings but do not lead to all useful ones. No online help is as effective for determining the best subject headings as simply browsing the Red Books. The twenty-third edition of *LCSH* (2000) lists on twenty-four pages hundreds of terms under "Women," and there are many other headings, such as "Girls," "Goddesses," "Lesbians," "Mistresses," "Nuns," "Queens," and "Sisters" that apply. Individual personal and corporate names are not included in the volumes of subject headings, but they too can be searched as subjects. See chapter 1 for a more detailed description of Library of Congress subject headings. Indexing for some formats, like prints and photographs, however, uses additional headings drawn from specialized subject heading lists or thesauri.

In addition to searching the *LCSH*, other ways to select the best subject headings include talking with reference librarians, examining the subject headings assigned to a known book on the desired topic, taking a research orientation class given by staff from the Main Reading Room (call 202 707-3370 to register), or consulting a guide to research. One particularly useful volume, although out-of-date, is *Women in LC's Terms: A Thesaurus of Library of Congress Subject Headings Relating to Women* by Ruth Dickstein, Victoria A. Mills, and Ellen J. Waite (Phoenix: Oryx Press, 1988;

Ester Hernández. Libertad. *Etching, copyright © 1976. Fine Prints Collection (unprocessed). Prints and Photographs Division. LC-USZ62-127167. Courtesy of the artist.*

Chicana artist Ester Hernández, a member of the women's artist collective Las Mujeres Muralistas (Women Muralists), uses icons in almost all her work. Inspired by the nation's American Revolution Bicentennial celebrations in 1976, Hernández laid claim to the Statue of Liberty—emblem of European immigration, citizenship, plurality, freedom and also a conventional symbol of American identity—and here reworks it into a powerful symbol of resistance to assimilation. The inscription "Aztlán" (White Land) refers to the Aztec land of origin, located in the area of Arizona, Colorado, New Mexico, and California. (For fine prints, see page 209.)

Z695.1.W65 D53 1988 MRR Ref Desk, CCC, BusRR). A more general work, but extremely helpful for research on any topic, is the excellent *Oxford Guide to Library Research* by Library of Congress reference librarian Thomas Mann (New York: Oxford University Press, 1998; Z710.M23 1998 MRR Ref Desk).

Library of Congress Call Numbers

There are many numbering systems by which the Library arranges materials in its stacks. Most books and bound periodicals are placed on the shelves in Library of Congress call number order. Many other libraries, including most university libraries, use this same classification system for categorizing books by type or subject. Catalogers assign unique identifiers—call numbers—based on the content of the work (see chapter 1). Some of the special-format collections in the Library, such as manuscripts, prints and photographs, and maps, use other call number or shelving systems that may bear little relationship to the content of the collection and thus may or may not have value for subject searching. These other systems are discussed in subsequent chapters.

Catalogs

There are many ways to learn what materials are held by the Library of Congress and to find the specific numbers that are required to request items from the stacks. No single source identifies all items held by the Library. For many materials the primary catalog is the Library of Congress Online Catalog (which contains records for all formats, but does not have records for all items held by the Library). Other reading rooms have additional catalogs, bibliographies, discographies, and finding aids that you must consult to determine the full range of materials available within the Library. To access some of these special research aids, search the home pages of individual reading rooms at <http://www.loc.gov/rr/>. These specialized catalogs will be discussed in the appropriate chapters in this guide.

The Library of Congress Online Catalog is available at terminals throughout the Library and remotely from any terminal with Internet access at <http://catalog.loc.gov/>. It contains approximately twelve million records representing many, but not all, of the Library's books, serials, computer files, manuscript collections, cartographic materials, music, sound recordings, and visual materials in one integrated system. The catalog also displays searching aids for users, such as cross-references and scope notes.

The online catalog can be searched in many ways: by simple name, title, subject (LCSH), or call number or by keyword. Complicated searches are possible using commands, Boolean operators, truncation, and special cataloging codes. It is possible to limit by language, year and place of publication, types of material (e.g., limiting your search to manuscript material, computer files, or non-music sound recordings). No full explanation of this powerful system can be given here, but basic searching in the online catalog is relatively straightforward. For remote users, "Help" screens and "Search examples" are available at every step. At the Library, in the Computer Catalog Center, Jefferson Building (room LJ 139), in-person assistance is available. Online records give important location and circulation information.

The online system contains records for many older items, but about 3.2 million records, primarily for books and serials cataloged between 1898 and 1975, contain the legend "[from old catalog]," which indicates that the subject headings assigned to the item may deviate from current Library of Congress terms. For example, a researcher scanning the online catalog under the current subject heading "Women" will miss the thousands of records still listed in the same catalog under the old term "Woman." The online catalog has other pitfalls that are still being addressed; in addition to superseded subject headings, there are inputting errors and limita-

Clara Ellen Tarte Davenport and her students in Unalaska, ca. 1910–12, from "Unalaska Days: A Diary." Photographer unknown, possibly Noah C. Davenport. Noah Cleveland Davenport Papers (container 1). Manuscript Division. LC-MS-60418-1.

In August 1910, twenty-five-year-old Clara Ellen Tarte (1885–1974) married her Bellingham Normal School classmate Noah Clevelend Davenport (1885–1976) and returned with him to Alaska, where he had spent the previous year as a teacher in a federal government school on the Aleutian Peninsula. The Davenports' joint diary describes their home in the village of Unalaska and their experiences teaching school there. On September 6, 1910, Noah wrote that Clara "was pleasantly surprised at the brightness, good manners and cleanliness of the children. They were studious and not inclined to mischief."

tions on the amount of data transferred into the online records. On-site users can avoid these problems by consulting the Main Reading Room's Main Card Catalog, which includes records for books and periodicals only (see chapter 1 for a more detailed description).

Just as women have been omitted from much of history as written by male historians, so women of color have often been excluded from the works of white historians of both sexes. Some of the sources, subject headings, and search strategies outlined in this guide yield, most easily, materials describing educated, Christian, white, heterosexual, middle-class women and girls. Uncovering the history of other women—women of color, lesbians, or poor, rural, immigrant, or non-Christian women—often requires extra searching. For example, scanning the large class of American and English children's magazines using the call number beginning AP201 will miss African American children's magazines, such as *Brownies' Book* or *Ebony Jr!*, which are in AP230, and magazines in English for Jewish children, such as *Young Judean* in AP222. As a result of the major civil rights and women's movements of the last third of the twentieth century, reference sources and subject terms are much more inclusive now, but many earlier bibliographies and other reference aids omit most minority groups.

If you wish your research to cover the widest possible variety of women, it is necessary to look for materials on women in bibliographies, secondary sources, discographies, and other finding aids that focus on specific groups. For example, bibliographies on an individual group such as African Americans, Native Americans, or Muslims often lead to materials on women in these groups that will not be found in general bibliographies on "women." Russell C. Brignano's *Black Americans in Autobiography: An Annotated Bibliography of Autobiographies and Autobiographical Books Written since the Civil War* (revised and expanded edition, Durham, N.C.: Duke University Press, 1984; Z1361.N39 B67 1984 MRR Biog) lists first-person accounts of African Americans Annie L. Burton and Emma Ray that are not included in some of the bibliographies of "women's" autobiographies. The Library of Congress has both accounts, but no subject heading identifies them as African Americans or as women. The two-volume *Comprehensive Bibliography for the Study of American Minorities* by Wayne Charles Miller, 2 vols. (New York: New York University Press, 1976; Z1361.E4 M529 MRR Alc) leads to many books and articles on women in minority groups that might be difficult to find using more general bibliographies. Many similar volumes exist. (To locate them see the section on bibliographies in chapter 1.)

This point cannot be made too strongly: Researchers must remember that the infinite variety of women's experiences and the remarkable array of multiformat materials in the Library necessitate various search strategies; no one method or source works for all women. This volume suggests some of the ways to explore women's lives, but it cannot cover all methodologies. Chapter 12 illustrates through two models—American Jewish women and Latina women—the kinds of materials in the Library's many reading rooms that can be found for two specific groups. You can adapt these models to your own research needs.

Sheridan Harvey
Humanities and Social Sciences Division

American Women

FRANK LESLIE'S

Boy's & Girl's Weekly

An Illustrated Journal of Amusement, Adventure, and Instruction.

Vol. 1.—No. 18. NEW YORK, MARCH 2, 1867. Five Cents a Copy. $2.50 Yearly.

DEADLY ATTACK OF A WOLF ON A MAN.

There is a common belief that only wild beasts of the largest and savagest kind will voluntarily attack man, except when they are in large droves. There was, however, in 1859, an instance in which a wolf attacked a farmer who was chopping wood near Lexington, Sanilac County, Michigan, and with such ferocity that, despite his utmost exertions, he was overmastered by the furious animal. It appears that early one morning the unfortunate settler was engaged in lopping some branches at a short distance from his cottage, when a wolf started from a thicket, and before the farmer could defend himself, grasped his throat with such deadly power that he dropped his ax.

His cries brought his wife to the door of the cottage; seeing the danger of her husband, the noble woman, with all that scorn of danger which distinguishes her sex when those she loves are in danger, ran to the spot, and seizing the ax, struck the wolf so well-aimed a blow, that it compelled him to release the man.

Nothing daunted, the brave woman faced the furious beast with such coolness and courage that, after a short struggle, the wolf lay dead at her feet.

The woman then turned to her husband, and vainly endeavored to stop the blood which gushed from his throat. It was all in vain, for the unhappy man breathed his last in her arms.

On examination it was found that the fangs of the monster had as completely severed his windpipe as though the throat had been cut with a razor.

RECOLLECTIONS OF MY SCHOOL-DAYS AT MAPLETON HALL.

CHAPTER V.—HOME FOR THE HOLIDAYS.

The half-year term at Mapleton Hall ended with Christmas-tide. The last Friday before Christmas was always examination-day. The clergy and other professional men of the town and country attended in great ceremony. Many of the pupils' parents came into the town the day before and filled the Mapleton Tavern to overflowing.

The next afternoon they went away, taking their sons with them. During their stay the town was all bustle and excitement. The boys at the school had full liberty to visit their friends, and many were the happy greetings of father and son, mother and child, sister and brother.

The evening before examination-day Mrs. Milner gave a reception to the pupils and their friends. This entertainment commenced quite early in the evening, and before midnight her halls were deserted.

Frank and I expected no friends, and for that reason perhaps tried to look upon the affair with indifference. But when we heard that there was to be music and quadrilles, we relented a little. Then came the magic word "supper!"

"I ain't much of a ladies' man," said Frank, with all the indifference of a man of the world; "so it won't be worse than tooth-pulling to me to be without a partner; but when a young fellow with a healthy appetite like mine thinks of snubbing sponge-cake and sweetmeats, to say nothing of lemonade, that's what I call carrying the war into Africa. Don't you think, Wesley, we had better drop in about supper-time?"

DEADLY ATTACK OF A WOLF UPON A MAN, AND HEROIC CONDUCT OF THE MAN'S WIFE.

"Deadly Attack of a Wolf upon a Man, and Heroic Conduct of the Man's Wife." Engraving. From Frank Leslie's Boy's and Girl's Weekly, *March 2, 1867, p. 1 (AP200.F65). General Collections.*

A noble wife rushes to the aid of her husband, swinging an ax at the wolf clutching her husband's throat. Despite her brave efforts, the man dies in his wife's arms. Such sensational accounts, fictional and true, appeared frequently in this weekly children's magazine issued from 1866 to 1884. A publisher of illustrated magazines, Frank Leslie used the distribution networks already established for his *Lady's Magazine* and *Illustrated Newspaper* and the growing rail system to help this new children's magazine become extremely popular.

ONE GOD, ONE LAW.
ONE ELEMENT, AND ONE FAR-OFF
DIVINE EVENT TO WHICH
THE WHOLE CREATION MOVES.
HISTORY

The General Collections

Sheridan Harvey

Researchers sitting in the Main Reading Room of the Library of Congress are surrounded by images of women. From the top of the ornate dome, the female form of Human Understanding lifts the veil of ignorance to encourage scholars below in their pursuit of truth. Around the reading room, set high on great pillars, stand statues of eight larger-than-life women who symbolize aspects of civilized life and thought. The statue of History holds a book in one hand and a mirror in the other to reflect the past accurately. While the builders of the Library were reflecting a European tradition of classical symbolism, American suffragists were declaring, "Woman cannot be ignored, or civilization will suffer!"(1909).[1] The collections of the Library of Congress, like its decoration, show us our past and tell us women's stories.

Among the Library's earliest acquisitions were Mercy Otis Warren's history of the American Revolution and Phillis Wheatley's poems. As the Library began, so it has continued. Throughout its two-hundred-year history, the Library of Congress has acquired, cataloged, and preserved valuable sources for uncovering the past of women of the United States. Under the pedestrian name "General Collections," the Library gathers most of the books and bound periodicals published since 1800 that are useful to searchers of American women's history. Researchers wishing to view materials in the General Collections request them in the Main, Local History and Genealogy, Microform, and Area Studies reading rooms and at the Book Service desk in the Adams Building. (Specialized reading rooms hold books and periodicals printed before 1801, music and law materials of all dates; items written in Near Eastern and Asian languages must be requested in appropriate Area Studies reading rooms.) Within the General Collections lie nineteenth-century ladies' almanacs with hand-painted illustrations, Sears, Roebuck catalogs, slave narratives, congressional reports on women's suffrage, published collections of women's letters, diaries, and lectures presented by women astronomers.

When the modern women's movement emerged in the 1960s, many scholars began to explore the lives of women who had come before. As a result of this great upsurge of interest, the Library of Congress collections on women's history have grown enormously in the past three decades. Even before, however, many primary and secondary sources for research on this "newly discovered" topic were already housed at the Library.

When searching for primary sources—fundamental, authoritative, contemporary documents used to prepare later works—historians often overlook the abundance of *published* primary source material. Women's diaries, correspondence, and autobiographies that have been printed either by the women themselves or someone else, either at the time of composition or centuries later, are primary sources and are found in abundance in the General Collections.

In addition to primary sources, researchers also look for books and articles describing and analyzing occurrences outside the writer's personal experience. The General Collections hold thou-

Daniel Chester French. History. *Sculpture, Main Reading Room, Thomas Jefferson Building, Library of Congress. Photograph by Anne Day. With the permission of Anne Day.*

History is depicted as a female figure with bronze statues of actual male historians—Herodotus and Gibbon—on either side. Similar images of women are found throughout the Thomas Jefferson Building, where they personify Temperance, Courage, Physics, Tragedy, and many more. Representations of the female form have been used throughout time to symbolize abstract concepts. From the Statue of Liberty to blindfolded Justice, from Nike on a Rolls Royce to Aunt Jemima, women's bodies have been appropriated to convey meaning and attract attention. Although this volume focuses on historical women, allegorical women also tell us of our past. (See, for instance, the essay "With Peace and Freedom Blest!")

For a brief overview on beginning research at the Library of Congress, see **"Using the Library of Congress"** above. For a detailed explanation of each reading room and Library procedures, consult the Library's Web site at <http://www.loc.gov/rr>.

The Library's **Reference Referral Service** acts as a clearinghouse for inquiries from outside the Library about the General Collections and about the Library of Congress in general.

REFERENCE REFERRAL SERVICE
101 Independence Avenue, SE, Washington, DC 20540-4665
Telephone: 202 707-5522
Fax: 202 707-1389
E-mail: lcweb@loc.gov

Items in the General Collections may be accessed from the following reading rooms in the Thomas Jefferson Building and the John Adams Building. The researchers' entrances to both buildings are on Second Street, SE. General Collections materials may also be requested through the European, Hispanic, African and Middle Eastern, and Asian Reading Rooms, hours and access information for which are given in chapter 12.

Regulations vary from reading room to reading room, but researchers in the Jefferson Building must check almost all personal possessions, including large handbags, at the free cloakrooms in the building. Reference staff members are on duty during all hours the Library is open and should be consulted regularly for assistance.

MAIN READING ROOM
Thomas Jefferson Building, 1st floor, room LJ 100
LOCAL HISTORY AND GENEALOGY READING ROOM
Thomas Jefferson Building, ground floor, room LJ G42
MICROFORM READING ROOM
Thomas Jefferson Building, 1st floor, room LJ 139B
SCIENCE AND BUSINESS READING ROOM
John Adams Building, 5th floor, room LA 508
Hours: For the above reading rooms: Monday, Wednesday, and Thursday, 8:30 a.m. to 9:30 p.m.; Tuesday, Friday, and Saturday, 8:30 a.m. to 5:00 p.m. Closed Sunday and federal holidays.
Access and use: Appointments are not required. Reading rooms are open to those over high school age, but you must show a Library-issued reader identification card (see "Using the Library of Congress") to request materials. The Library's bookstacks are closed to the public. Books and bound periodicals are delivered to patrons in the reading rooms (delivery time is approximately forty-five to ninety minutes).

Most juvenile literature is housed in the General Collections, but there is a separate center with a specialist and a reference collection for those doing research on children's literature.

CHILDREN'S LITERATURE CENTER
Thomas Jefferson Building, lst floor, room LJ 100
Hours: Monday through Friday, 8:30 a.m. to 4:30 p.m. Closed weekends and federal holidays.
Telephone: 202 707-5535
E-mail: childref@loc.gov
Web site: <http://www.loc.gov/rr/child/>
Access and use: Appointments are recommended. Children's books can be requested from the General Collections through the other reading rooms listed above.

sands of volumes of these secondary sources, which are discussed in more detail below. An item can be both a primary and a secondary source. When Mary Ritter Beard published her *Woman as Force in History* (New York: Macmillan Company, 1946; HQ1121.B36), she had created a secondary source, a history of women. The volume becomes a primary source when later historians examine it as a pioneering contribution to the writing of women's history.

Instead of attempting to describe the innumerable women's history topics that can be researched with items from the General Collections, this chapter focuses on "types" of materials. Each type could supply evidence for multiple subjects in women's history. Some, like doctoral dissertations, are unusually plentiful at the Library of Congress; others, such as trade journals, have not been fully exploited by historians of women. Only a few titles from among many possible are given for each type. These examples are meant to suggest how these types of works could be used for future study, to emphasize the need for readers to combine the wide range of uncommon printed sources with traditional and familiar ones, and to entice readers to the Library.

Library of Congress holdings in U.S. women's history have a breadth and depth that cannot be matched elsewhere, and researchers of topics great and small will find incredible sources among the millions of items in the General Collections. Many other libraries, however, have superb American women's history collections and hold items comparable to those at the Library of Congress. The arrangement of this chapter may prove helpful to researchers using other libraries because it is not the individual items mentioned that are critical, but the types of materials. The sample subject headings and call numbers should lead to similar works in other libraries. Also, the advice on subject searching, especially on finding the most specific subject headings, is applicable to other library catalogs.

USING THE GENERAL COLLECTIONS

Whether you are looking for a biography of an Alaskan woman or a journal on women's health, a description of women's roles in the American Revolution or a book on dating rituals of the 1920s, you need three things to find such items in the General Collections—valid subject headings, appropriate catalogs, and call numbers. The section "Using the Library of Congress" provides a brief overview of these three topics and should be read in conjunction with this chapter.

Library of Congress Subject Headings

If you search the Library's online catalog for the keywords "battered women," you find more than one hundred entries and may be perfectly satisfied. But by not identifying the Library's correct subject headings, "Abused women," "Abused wives," and "Wife abuse," you may miss the best materials for your topic. A search combining these three terms yields more than one thousand records.

The current headings can be found in the multivolume *Library of Congress Subject Headings (LCSH)* (Washington: Library of Congress, annual; Z695.Z8 L524a), known familiarly as the "Red Books." The Red Books also provide call number ranges that can be searched. The "Sample LCSH" given throughout this chapter and the examples listed on the next few pages are the tiniest fraction of authoritative headings for women and women's issues. It cannot be reiterated strongly enough: Explore the Library of Congress subject headings.

The construction of Library of Congress subject headings is precise and complicated, with many rules on order and punctuation that need not be explained here. The next few paragraphs provide only the most basic guidelines on how subject headings for women's history are formed.

1 The heading "Women" can be followed by subdivisions, which can be geographical, topical, chronological, or form. For the full list of the more than three thousand authorized subdivisions, see *Free-floating Subdivisions: An Alphabetical Index* (Washington: Library of Congress, annual; Z663.72.F74 in most reading rooms).

Examples of subdivisions are: **United States, Nebraska, Folklore, History, 19th century, Bibliography, Biography,** or **Periodicals.**

These can be strung together in a fixed order: **Women—United States—Bibliography** or **Women—Massachusetts—History—Indexes.**

Several subdivisions that are particularly useful for locating primary sources are: **Sources, Diaries, Narratives, Correspondence, Interviews, Quotations,** or **Collections.**

2 The heading "Women" can be followed by an occupation, as in **Women poets; Women social reformers;** or **Women surgeons.**

3 The phrase "Women in" can be followed by terms such as **Women in literature; Women in missionary work; Women in television broadcasting;** or **Women in the professions.**

4 In keeping with the Library's cataloging policy of applying the most specific terms appropriate to an item, many words can be added to the word "Women" to narrow a search, for instance: **African American women; Hispanic American women; Korean American women; Aged women; Divorced women; Homeless women; Poor women; Rural women; Single women; Baptist women; Jewish women;** or **Women immigrants.**

Each of these terms may have subdivisions: **Homeless women—United States—Biography; Single women—Conduct of life;** or **Women immigrants—Employment—Texas.**

5 To give one longer example: the subject heading "Women artists" is related to many narrower terms and cross references, among them:

Norman Rockwell. "Rosie." Color lithograph after a painting. Saturday Evening Post, *May 29, 1943, cover (AP2.S2). General Collections. LC-USZC4-5602. Printed by permission of the Norman Rockwell Family Trust, copyright © 1943.*

Norman Rockwell's Rosie is a brawny, smudged, red-headed worker, unlike the tidier, more familiar images of Rosie the Riveter. She is a strong woman capable of doing a "man's job," and she appeared on the cover of a magazine that actively encouraged women to join the workforce during World War II. Nearly three million women answered their country's call to serve in defense plants. Rosie's patriotism is emphasized by the flag background and the placement of her feet firmly on Adolf Hitler's *Mein Kampf.*

Women artists in literature; Lesbian artists; Indian women artists; Minority women artists; Women painters; and **Women engravers.**

Each of these narrower terms may in turn have subdivisions: **Women artists—United States—Exhibitions—Periodicals;** or **African American women artists—Biography—History and criticism.**

The permutations are many and are governed by firm rules.

New subject headings are created when catalogers feel there is a sufficient mass of material to need increased specificity, and not before there is a physical item in hand to catalog. Some women's terms are of surprisingly recent creation; for example, "Lesbianism" and "Motherhood" (and "Fatherhood") are rarely found before the middle of the twentieth century. When searching for older materials, especially before 1975, be aware that current subject terms may not have been used. When a new term is created, it is not always added to the records of all previously cataloged titles. To use the online catalog effectively, you must also search those terms marked "Former heading" in the *Library of Congress Subject Headings* as well as by call numbers and keywords. Some noncurrent Library subject headings are given in this chapter's "Sample LCSH" because they appear in the online catalog. See the discussion of the Main Card Catalog below for another way to overcome the difficulty of superseded subject headings.

"Woman's Emancipation." Engraving. From Harper's New Monthly Magazine, *August 1851, p. 424 (AP2.H3). General Collections.*

"It is generally calculated that the dress of the Emancipated American female is quite pretty." So wrote Theodosia Bang to the British magazine *Punch* in 1851. She added that "With man's functions, we have asserted our right to his garb, and especially to that part of it which invests the lower extremities." Preferring to be called a woman, not the outworn feudal term "lady," she also claimed her right to male hats and cigars. Bang was writing shortly after the first women's rights conventions and the introduction of Amelia Bloomer's dress reform—the skirt worn over loose trousers. Her recommended fashions and behavior proved unacceptable to most women and men for many decades.

Library of Congress Call Numbers

To request a book or periodical to be brought to you from the General Collections stacks, you need the call number assigned to the item. These unique numbers are composed of one, two, or three letters followed by a combination of numbers and letters. For example, call numbers for many books on medicine begin with R; the range for gynecology and obstetrics is RG1–991, and for nursing, it is RT1–120. Call numbers for bibliographies begin with Z; many bibliographies on women have numbers between Z7961 and Z7965, and those specifically on the employment of women are Z7963.E7. But some bibliographies on African American women are in Z1361.N39. This last instance shows that you must be very cautious when searching for a subject by call numbers, for they are as specific as subject headings. Bibliographies solely on women usually have a different call number from those on both men and women. Bibliographies on women belonging to a specific racial, religious, or ethnic group may have a number different from the general one for "women." Nonetheless, when used carefully, this grouping by subject makes browsing the online catalog by call number another worthwhile way to search for items on a specific topic.

With the first part of a call number, you can scan the online records for books and bound periodicals in the order in which the volumes sit on the shelves, in this way coming close to "browsing the stacks" in the Library of Congress. Call number searching is especially helpful for older works that received only very broad subject headings, such as "Girls" or "Conduct of life," and for works that have no subject terms at all in the online catalog. The multivolume *Library of Congress Classification* (Washington: Library of Congress, Cataloging Distribution Service, [irregular]; Z696.U5 MRR Ref Desk) shows the full range of Library call numbers. In this chapter, call numbers for titles cited are provided in the text or in endnotes. Some sections conclude with a few examples of Library of Congress call numbers to aid in searching. Subject searching by call number works best for books and periodicals since some of the special-format collections in the Library use other call number or shelving systems that may bear little relationship to the content of the collection.

Catalogs

The Library of Congress Online Catalog, the primary catalog for the books and periodicals in the General Collections (see "Using the Library of Congress"), is the only catalog for such materials cataloged after 1980. It is available to remote users through the Library's Web site <http://catalog.loc.gov>. The online catalog also contains records for many materials cataloged before 1980, but to avoid the problem of trying to determine former subject headings and other difficulties in the online catalog (described above), researchers on site may also want to use the 22,000-drawer Main Card Catalog (MCAT) housed just off the Main Reading Room.

The MCAT remains the most accurate and complete place to identify most of the Library's book and periodical holdings published before 1980. The MCAT has consistent subject headings derived from the ninth edition of the *Library of Congress Subject Headings* (1980). Copies of this edition are available near the card catalog. This means, for example, that although you must search in the online catalog under both the current term "Women" and the former heading "Woman" to find all relevant records, in the Main Card Catalog all records with the old term "Woman" were recataloged so that they are filed together under the newer term "Women." The MCAT also often contains notes, serial holdings, and other information that is not available online. For many items in the General Collections, the only record is that which is in the card catalog. Cards were filed into the MCAT until 1980.

Reference Collections

Each of the reading rooms from which you can request materials from the General Collections has its own reference collection. These contain works such as bibliographies, encyclopedias, biographical sources, dictionaries, and handbooks that may lead to other materials in the stacks, give background information, or answer quick reference questions. The seventy-thousand-volume Main Reading Room reference collection contains numerous works to assist researchers of American women's history, and other reading rooms also hold volumes related to this subject. For women scientists, visit the Science Reference Section; for women-owned businesses consult titles in the Business Reference Section; or for ship passenger lists go to the Local History and Genealogy Reading Room. Often duplicate copies of reference works held by specialized reading rooms—for example, some books on women composers, photographers, or lawyers—are also shelved in the Main Reading Room. An advantage to a reference collection is that you can go to the shelf in the reading room and retrieve works from it yourself. To know if a title is in a reference collection, examine the complete record in the online catalog. Abbreviations such as MRR Alc (Main Reading Room alcove), MicRR (Microform Reading Room), or SciRR (Science Reading Room), which indicate reference assignments, are explained in the list of abbreviations at the back of this guide.

SELECTED HOLDINGS

It is a common myth that the Library of Congress holds two copies of every book ever printed. No library could be that large. Nonetheless, books and periodicals have been pouring into the General Collections for more than two centuries. They arrive by copyright deposit, purchase, gift, and exchange at the rate of one thousand a day, and they cover every subject dreamt of by humans. No single chapter, or even single volume, could suggest all the ways in which items in the General Collections could support research on U.S. women's history. The selected holdings described in this chapter are grouped into five broad topics—"Starting Places: General Sources for U.S. Women's History," "Magazines and Other Serial Publications," "Biographical Sources," "Women's Writings," and "Unexpected Sources"—in keeping with the focus on types of materials rather than on subjects. What follows is a rapid tour with occasional whimsical stops through the 250 miles of shelves holding the General Collections.

Starting Places: General Sources for U.S. Women's History

Sources of use to the curious can be found in numerous places. Many historians of women would not think to examine science periodical indexes such as the *General Science Index* (1978–; Z7401.G46 SciRR, MRR Alc; online, 1984–) and *Biological and Agricultural Index* (with title change, 1916–; Z5073.A46 SciRR, MRR Alc, online 1983–), yet these reference works lead to articles on sexism, patriarchy, diets of pregnant Korean Americans, and women's clubs in the environmental movement. Published congressional committee hearings debate oral contraceptives, child care, and immigrants, and trade journals sometimes include obituaries of women. The next seven sections give an overview of a few of the best places—some obvious, some not—for identifying research sources on American women's history.

Bibliographies

Would a researcher ignore a readily available list of books on her topic? Would she or he insist on repeating work that someone else had already done? This is what people do when they neglect published bibliographies. In an age of increasing reliance on computers, people forget valuable printed reference sources. Those works, often painstakingly prepared over extended periods of time, can be a boon to historians. Someone writing on women's education, for example, can search book catalogs, periodical indexes, *Dissertation Abstracts,* and indexes to congressional and government documents, or she can first turn to Kay S. Wilkins's *Women's Education in the United States: A Guide to Information Sources* (Detroit: Gale Research, 1979; Z7963.E2 W53 MRR Alc) where she will find 1,134 annotated citations to materials on her subject. Despite the drawbacks—

"The Sky Is Now Her Limit." Illustration by Bushnell, reprinted in New York Times Current History, *October 1920, p. 142 (D410.C8). General Collections.*

Only two months after passage of the constitutional amendment guaranteeing women the right to vote, a woman gazes up from under a yoke toward the heights to which "Equal Suffrage" will lead her. The rungs include ever increasingly responsible jobs, leading to political office. At the pinnacle is the presidency. Eighty years later, American women have only the final step to take.

Laura E. Foster. "Looking Backward." Cartoon. From Life, *August 22, 1912, p. 1638 (AP101.L6). General Collections.*

As fame is within her grasp, a sorrowful woman looks back at the joy she has surrendered in her quest for the vote, a career, and success. The blooming flowers of domesticity, here, give way to withered branches as woman climbs beyond her proper sphere. Even in 1912, many people, both women and men, opposed women's suffrage, arguing that women were happiest with lives centered around home, marriage, and children.

bibliographies are always selective, cover fixed time periods, and do not exist for all subjects—published bibliographies still provide an excellent starting place for most research projects and can save much time and effort.

The important microfilm set *The Bibliography of American Women* (New Haven, Conn.: Research Publications, [1975?]; 47 reels; microfilm 84/320 MicRR) gives citations to fifty thousand books and articles, not all of which are in the Library of Congress, written by and about women from 1600 to the 1920s. The format is filmed catalog cards with minimal citations; the cards are arranged three ways: alphabetically, chronologically, and by broad topics such as "Children's Books," "Cookbooks," "Domestic," "Education," "Fiction." This set is extremely valuable for identifying what has been written by a particular woman author, in a specific time period, or about American women.

The *Bibliography of American Imprints to 1901* (92 vols.) (New York: K.G. Saur, 1993; Z1215.B47 1993 MRR Alc) contains a fifteen-volume subject index that leads a searcher to early works on topics ranging from women pirates and widows to religious education for children to sex in marriage. Although not all titles listed are held by the Library of Congress, most are. This set is particularly useful because it often applies modern subject headings to works cataloged by the Library before detailed specific subject headings for women's issues were developed. You can examine this bibliography with its modern subject headings and then search the Library's catalogs to locate the item. Most books and periodicals published before 1820 are part of the *Early American Imprints*[2] microform collection (see "Microforms" below); other titles can be found in the General Collections and the Rare Book or Microform Reading Rooms.

All women, and especially women who varied from the dominant white, heterosexual, Christian, middle-class "standard," were poorly represented in reference works before the last quarter of the twentieth century. You should consult specialized bibliographies such as Gretchen M. Bataille's *American Indian Women: A Guide to Research,*[3] Aviva Cantor's *The Jewish Woman, 1900–1985: A Bibliography,*[4] Francesco Cordasco's *The Immigrant Woman in North America: An Annotated Bibliography of Selected References,*[5] and Dolores J. Maggiore's *Lesbianism: An Annotated Bibliography and Guide to the Literature, 1976–1991.*[6] Monroe Nathan Work's *A Bibliography of the Negro in Africa and America*[7] provides references to African American women, children, and families. Many other bibliographies exist and can be identified by using the subject headings given below.

BIBLIOGRAPHIES: To locate bibliographies on a given subject, refer to the many standard printed bibliographies of bibliographies, especially Patricia K. Ballou's *Women: A Bibliography of Bibliographies,* 2nd ed. (Boston: G.K. Hall, 1986; Z7961.B32 1986 MRR Alc) and *Women, Race, and Ethnicity: A Bibliography,* edited by Susan Searing and Linda Shult (Madison: University of Wisconsin System Women's Studies Librarian, 1991; Z7961.W63 1991 MRR Alc). Bibliographies of women's studies usually include sections useful to historians, and general U.S. history bibliographies contain references to materials on women.

SAMPLE LCSH: Usually the word "Bibliography" can be combined with any LC subject heading when searching the Library's catalogs. A few examples include: **Women—United States—History—Bibliography; Women's studies—United States—Bibliography; Women and religion—United States—Bibliography; African American women—Psychology—Bibliography; Women architects—California—Bibliography; Lesbian artists—Bibliography; Indian women—North America—Bibliography; Asian American women—Social conditions—Bibliography; White women—United States—History—Bibliography;** and **Working class women—United States—Bibliography.**

Secondary Sources

In this chapter's focus on *types* of materials, especially primary sources, you must not forget that the General Collections contain numerous secondary sources. Women's history surveys such as *Born for Liberty: A History of Women in America*[8] and *Century of Struggle: The Woman's Rights Movement in the United States*[9] mingle on the shelves with much more narrowly focused titles such as *Women and Urban Change in San Juan, Puerto Rico, 1820–1868*[10] and *Southern Ute Women: Autonomy and Assimilation on the Reservation, 1887–1934.*[11] Works like these and the thousands of others that exist in the General Collections are the fruit of historians' hard toil to uncover, analyze, and synthesize evidence in an effort to understand and explain how women have lived. Such texts are valuable for their depictions of women's lives in other times and places, for reminding readers of the variety of women's experiences, for models to reconstruct women's roles, for showing the significance of gender as a category for historical analysis, and for presenting different research methodologies. Secondary sources may quote primary sources that are not easily available and often provide notes and bibliographies that lead to other works. Secondary sources are indispensable to historical research and make up a major portion of the General Collections.

SEARCH TIPS: Recent secondary sources are rarely mentioned in this chapter because they are often available at other libraries around the country, and they are usually easy to find through specific LC subject headings and published bibliographies. See "Library of Congress Subject Headings" and "Library of Congress Call Numbers" above. See also the previous section on bibliographies.

Series

Many publishers group new works under a series title, and therefore identifying a useful series may lead to other volumes on related topics. The subject index in *Books in Series* (see box) directs researchers both to recent scholarly monographs on women and to published primary sources. Examples of series include Women & Children First, which has thirty-seven titles, mostly reprints of association and government reports and statistics; Women in America: From Colonial Times to the 20th Century, with more than fifty reprinted titles, often pamphlets; and Women in American History, thirty-four monographs and growing, with biographies and works on social and labor movements. Relevant series that do not specifically focus on women include the Black Heritage Library Collection (more than four hundred reprints, many literary) and American Trails (two series with accounts of overland journeys).

BIBLIOGRAPHY:
Books in Series. New York: R.R. Bowker, 1977–89. MRR Alc volumes shelved in Z1033.S5 B66 1982 and .B67. Also, look for a "series" name when examining the full record of a book on your topic. The Library's online catalog can be searched easily by series title in the "Guided Keyword" search method.

Microform Materials

When researching any topic at the Library of Congress, ask a reference librarian for help in identifying microform collections on your subject. Examples of almost every type of material mentioned in this chapter also exist in microform. Microforms are found in most reading rooms, but the largest gathering is in the Microform Reading Room. Treasures abound, and the two keys to this richness are reference librarians and *A Guide to the Microform Collections in the Humanities and Social Sciences Division of the Library of Congress* (available online and in print). This guide is an alphabetical list with brief annotations of most collections held in the Microform Reading Room. Its index provides subject access to collections that often lack subject headings in the online catalog.

It is impossible to mention all titles that might assist a women's history researcher, but there are large collections on nursing, witchcraft, slavery, religion, labor unions, missionaries, statistics, and social welfare journals. There are pamphlets in American history and in women's history, dime novels, Massachusetts vital records, congressional documents (see "Congressional Documents" below), dissertations (see the section following this), and oral histories, to name only a very few. Some are large collections acquired by the Library; others are individual book and serial titles, often filmed for preservation purposes.

Two major sets for historians are the *History of Women*,[12] a collection of more than ten thousand books and periodicals published before 1920 by and about women, and *The Gerritsen Collection of Women's History*,[13] which consists of more than forty-five hundred European and American books, periodicals, and pamphlets published between 1543 and 1945. Both collections reproduce complete runs of the *Woman's Journal* (Boston, 1870–1931) among other U.S. and foreign women's serial titles. Records for individual journal titles from these two sets appear in the online catalog. *History of Women* also has eight hundred reproductions of photographs and some manuscripts.

Because books and serials published before 1801 are kept in the Rare Book and Special Collections Division, colonial American women are rarely mentioned in this chapter. The Microform Reading Room, however, holds *Early American Imprints*,[14] two microform sets of most books, pamphlets, and broadsides printed in the United States between 1639 and 1819. These include many works by and about women from those early years, and they can be easily photocopied. More than 40 percent of the titles can be viewed in print copies in the Rare Book Reading Room (see chapter 4).

It cannot be emphasized strongly enough that there are marvelous unanticipated treats for historians of women (or any other subject) among the millions of frames in the Microform Reading Room. One collection reproduces several dozen photographs depicting Anglo and Hispanic American women in New Mexico between 1890 and 1924.[15] Another has more than sixty filmed works about the Salem witchcraft trials with descriptions of women's multiple roles in those events and accounts of individual trials.[16]

BIBLIOGRAPHY: The online version of *A Guide to the Microform Collections in the Humanities and Social Sciences Division of the Library of Congress* (Washington: Library of Congress) is updated regularly at <http://www.loc.gov/rr/microform/guide/>. For collections cataloged before 1996, you can consult the print version in most reading rooms: Z1033.M5 L53 1996.

BIBLIOGRAPHY continued:
There is limited subject access for microform collections in the online catalog, and no online record exists for most individual items within such collections.

Most guides to individual Microform Reading Room collections are shelved in the Main Reading Room reference desk area.

Doctoral Dissertations

Subjects of dissertations are extremely varied—including Basque women in the American West, roles of Iroquois women, women art collectors, Latina political activism, and a history of infant feeding in Chicago, to give just five examples. The Library of Congress is the only institution in the country to purchase microform or electronic versions of all doctoral dissertations filmed by University Microfilms, which means most U.S. dissertations. Complete dissertations since the 1940s are available on film or fiche in the Microform Reading Room and, since 1997, in full text on computer terminals at the Library. Doctoral theses contain in-depth research on an enormous variety of subjects; all have bibliographies and notes to lead to other sources. Serious researchers should look for dissertations on their topics.

A general search in the online dissertation indexes combining the keywords "women," "United States," and "history" yields more than two thousand dissertations; more specific searches would identify many others. Some additional dissertations, from universities that did not submit their dissertations to University Microfilms, were acquired in print form and appear in the card and online catalogs. Dissertations covering music and law, subjects usually accessed through other reading rooms, are found in the Microform Reading Room with most other dissertations. The Library only rarely collects master's theses or foreign dissertations.

BIBLIOGRAPHY: There are three indexes to dissertations: the print index, *Dissertation Abstracts* (with title changes, supplements, and cumulations) (Ann Arbor, Mich.: University Microfilms, 1938–; Z5053.D57 MRR Alc, and other call numbers), and the two subscription databases, *ProQuest Digital Dissertations* and *Dissertation Abstracts*. Subject access is by very broad descriptors or by keyword searches of the title and, since 1980, of the abstract. A researcher must diligently try all synonyms, plurals, and broader and narrower terms that might yield results. Both databases cover the same materials, but only *Digital Dissertations* indicates which dissertations are available in full text online.

Congressional Documents

Throughout its history, Congress has held hearings and debated matters of import to women—from obvious "women's issues" like suffrage, prostitution, and abortion to those that aroused women's concern, such as education, war pensions, immigration, pornography, and pure food and milk. Witnesses have argued for and against these subjects, and the full text of this testimony, both of individual women (and men) and of representatives of women's (and men's) organizations can be found through multiple Congressional Information Service indexes. These index U.S. congressional documents (hearings, reports, documents, and committee prints; published and unpublished) from 1789 to the present.

The *Congressional Record*, with floor debates and statements read into the record, reveals the plans, words, and opinions of congressional representatives. For example, in proposing the creation of a United States Women's Armed Services Academy in 1955, Senator Dennis Chavez praised the "spontaneous patriotism of our womanhood," adding that "women yield nothing to men in that direction. Always and always and always, American women have stood with their men in all things contributing to the welfare and security of our country."[17] Congressional documents, especially hearings, may contribute details on many topics outside the legal or political realm, such as rhetoric used by women, descriptions of family life and concerns, and ways women are treated in public. Hearings may contain reproductions of photographs, statistics, charts, or maps. See the essay "Marching for the Vote" for examples of types of information found in one hearing.

BIBLIOGRAPHY: To look specifically for congressional documents, search the Congressional Information Service indexes in print form (MRR Ref Desk, MRR Alc, LAW) and on CD-ROM, *CIS Congressional Masterfile I* and *II* (1789–, CCC). With the numbers found in the indexes, items may be requested in the Microform Reading Room or the Law Library.
SAMPLE LCSH: Print editions of many congressional documents are fully cataloged and can be found in the online and card catalogs using LC subject headings.

Indexes to Anthologies and Collections of Essays

How would a researcher studying eighteenth-century widows know that an article on this subject appeared in a collection of essays entitled *Women's Experience in America?*[18] Would someone looking for details on women shipyard workers think to look in *Hidden Aspects of Women's Work?*[19] Articles or essays published within edited volumes are rarely cataloged individually and only occasionally listed in periodical indexes, so bibliographies and indexes that capture such research are extremely valuable. The two titles used to identify the above essays are Susan Cardinale's *Anthologies by and about Women: An Analytical*

Index,[20] and the two-volume *Index to Women's Studies Anthologies: Research across the Disciplines*,[21] covering the years 1980 to 1989.

The broader *Essay and General Literature Index* (1900–, AI3.E752 MRR Alc) uses Library subject headings (such as "Woman," "Marriage," "Divorce") and covers anthologies back to 1900. *Religion Index Two: Multi-Author Works* (1970–, Z7751.R35 MRR Alc) can be searched with terms such as "Gender," "Lesbianism," or "Feminist theology," among many others.

SEARCH TIPS: The only way to know whether an index includes articles published within books is to read the introduction to the index. Occasionally, the Library of Congress catalog record for a collection of articles includes a note section with the titles and authors of each individual article. These are searchable online by keyword or as a note.

Will Grefé. "The Winter Supplies." Woman's World, *September 1915, cover (AP2.W74). General Collections.*

Woman's World was one of the most famous of the mail-order journals published in the late nineteenth and early twentieth centuries. Publishers kept subscription rates low ($0.35 a year) since the aim was to send magazines full of advertisements and coupons to as many readers as possible. From this one issue, a woman could mail in orders for a piano ($475), a kitchen range ($24.75 or $1.75 a month), women's military lace shoes ($1.39), a boy's eight-piece suit ($7.95), or women's clothes, patterns, and fashion catalogs. In a world without malls, credit cards, or the Internet, mail-order businesses put the consumer goods of American factories within reach of households throughout the country, especially after the introduction of Rural Free Delivery in 1896.

Magazines and Other Serial Publications

Items that are published periodically, like magazines and journals, are a marvelous source for history of any kind, and the Library of Congress holds thousands of serial titles of value to historians of women. Long runs of journals show changes in attitudes, in what was considered significant or marketable, and in styles of every kind—from hemlines to discourse—over an extended period. Studying many different serial titles for a given year or span of years can reveal much about the time period under examination. The span dates given for serial titles in this chapter indicate the holdings of the Library of Congress, not the full range of years in which the title was published.

Periodicals (Serials, Journals, Magazines, Annuals, Proceedings)

Published bibliographies are one of the best ways to identify magazines and journals on a given subject or published at a certain time. Two useful titles are *Women's Periodicals and Newspapers from the 18th Century to 1981: A Union List of the Holdings of Madison, Wisconsin, Libraries* compiled by Maureen E. Hady et al. (Boston: G.K. Hall, 1982; Z7965.H3 1982 MRR Alc, N&CPR) and *American Women's Magazines: An Annotated Historical Guide* by Nancy K. Humphreys (New York: Garland, 1989; Z6944.W6 H85 1989 MRR Alc, N&CPR).

The series Historical Guides to the World's Periodicals and Newspapers includes two descriptive volumes on women, both edited by Kathleen L. Endres and Therese L. Lueck: *Women's Periodicals in the United States: Consumer Magazines* (Westport, Conn.: Greenwood Press, 1995; PN4879.W6 1995 MRR Alc, N&CPR) and *Women's Periodicals in the United States: Social and Political Issues* (Westport, Conn.: Greenwood Press, 1996; PN4879.W614 1996 MRR Alc, N&CPR), as well as other volumes on African American, Native American, and children's journals, all of which lead to information on women and girls.

Titles such as Penelope L. Bullock's *The Afro-American Periodical Press, 1838–1909* (Baton Rouge: Louisiana State University Press, 1981;

PN4882.5.B8 1981 MRR Alc, N&CPR) give full publication histories and include geographical and chronological listings of journals. *The Ethnic Press in the United States: A Historical Analysis and Handbook* edited by Sally M. Miller (New York: Greenwood Press, 1987; PN4882.E84 1987 MRR Alc, EurRR, N&CPR) leads to the rich periodical literature of the varied cultures that have contributed to American life.

Because many periodicals, especially older ones, lack good indexes, researchers must scan tables of contents or flip through pages of issues from an appropriate time period. This is time-consuming but sometimes it is the only way to find substantive evidence for many research topics. It is now possible to scan tables of contents of hundreds of American journals online through the Library's subscription to the database *Periodicals Contents Index* (see "Periodical Indexes" below).

Advertisements in women's journals are a visual and verbal source of much information—from the latest household appliances to fabrics, from patent medicines to Margaret Sanger's books on birth control.[22] These advertisements show how women are portrayed at a given time, with intriguing variations by class, race, and region. Social debates about women and smoking and women and drinking can be explored. When did liquor and cigarette ads appear, and how were these items promoted to women? What arguments and words are used to sell household appliances or cleansers? How are women's bodies used to sell products to men? To women? Rarely indexed, advertisements must be located by scanning runs of periodicals.

SEARCH TIPS: Primary custody of periodicals is shared between the General Collections and the Newspaper and Current Periodical Reading Room, although some periodicals can be found in most reading rooms. The general rule is that periodicals published in the past eighteen to twenty-four months are housed in the stacks of the Newspaper and Current Periodical Reading Room; older issues are bound and kept in the General Collections. There are three major exceptions to this rule: serials published before 1801 are accessible through the Rare Book and Microform Reading Rooms, law journals of all dates are held in the Law Library, and music journals of all dates are in the Performing Arts Reading Room. Many older titles in all subjects are held only in microform and can be found through special guides in the Main Reading Room. Consult the online catalog and reference librarians to determine the locations of periodicals. See chapter 2 for further advice on how to identify which periodicals exist and for assistance on the history of magazines. See the next section for suggestions on how to locate articles within periodicals.

Some of the sections below also discuss periodicals. For missionary journals see "Travel Accounts," and for household magazines see "Cookbooks, Domestic Manuals, Journals."

"Do Remember Camels Are First in the Service." Advertisement. From the Saturday Evening Post, *April 24, 1943, back cover* (AP2.S2). *General Collections. Courtesy of RJR Tobacco Company.*

"Show your support for the boys overseas, smoke the cigarette they prefer," is the implicit message in this patriotic advertisement that gives public service announcements and links smoking with class and romance. Printed primarily in red, white, and blue, echoing the small buy-war-bonds shield, it plays to the patriotism of wartime. In the largest picture the sailor is an officer, and the woman is serious, sophisticated, and smoking. The text and illustrations at the top give real advice, but the tone is patronizing and the non-smoking women seem silly, uninformed gossips. This advertisement addresses women directly and suggests the multiple layers through which advertising can be interpreted for women's history.

Periodical Indexes

Unless otherwise indicated, all index titles in this section are available in print form in the Main Reading Room reference collection or online on terminals throughout the Library. The Newspaper and Current Periodical Reading Room holds many of the same periodical indexes in its reference collection, although not always the same run of years.

Periodical indexes (works that list articles from a selected group of journals usually alphabetically by author, title, and subject) are of enormous help to the historian, but many researchers are aware of only the most obvious, such as the commonly available *America: History and Life* (1964–, Z1236.A48, online 1964–). The *Readers' Guide to Periodical Literature* (1900–, AI3.R48, online 1983–) with its century of coverage is also familiar to most people, but many overlook its two-volume companion *Nineteenth Century Readers' Guide to Periodical Literature* (covering fifty-one periodical titles published in the 1890s, AI3.R496) and *Poole's Index to Periodical Literature* (1802–1906, AI3.P7, with supplements).

Some general twentieth-century indexes are the *International Index* (with title change, 1907–74, AI3.R49), then separated into *Social Sciences Index* (1974–, AI3.S62, online 1983–) and *Humanities Index* (1974–, AI3.H85, online 1984–); *Education Index* (1929–, Z5813.E23, online 1983–); and *Art Index* (1929–, Z5937.A78, online 1984–). These titles all provide access to articles on women, but none focuses specifically on women or on history.

With the advent of the modern women's movement in the late 1960s, the *Alternative Press Index* (1969–, AI3.A27) began early and continues still to provide good coverage from journals omitted by more mainstream indexes for topics such as women's liberation, black women, violence against women, lesbians, and a multitude of other subjects of special interest to women. Indexes focusing on women also exist; these include *Women Studies Abstracts* (1972–, Z7962.W65); *Women's Studies Index* (1988–, Z7962.W675); and *New Literature on Women* (in Swedish, *Ny Litteratur om Kvinnor,* about 60 percent in English; 1980–, HQ1686.K9). *Access: The Supplemental Index to Periodicals* (1975–, AI3.A23) covers popular titles such as *Cosmopolitan, American Girl,* and *Modern Bride.*

Computers are revolutionizing access to periodicals. An ever-increasing number of current serials receive excellent indexing, and major projects are under way to include older titles. The subscription-only database *Periodical Contents Index* (*PCI*) permits keyword searching of words in the title of an article (no subject terms are added) and by an author's name and viewing of tables of contents from more than three thousand American and European journals in the arts, humanities, and social sciences, beginning with the first issue of each title into the 1990s. Sample titles include the *Journal of the American-Irish Historical Society* (1898–1941, E184.I6 A5), *American Suffragette* (1909–11, JK1880.A6), and the journal of the American Association of University Women (various titles, 1884–1990, LC1756.A2 A5).

The Library of Congress also subscribes to two full-text databases. *JSTOR* (Journal Storage) allows keyword searching of the full text of about one hundred journals, including fifteen history titles, such as the *American Historical Review* (1895–1995), *Journal of Southern History* (1935–95), and *Journal of Negro History* (1916–97). *Project MUSE* is a database of recent issues of more than one hundred journals published by Johns Hopkins University Press and other scholarly publishers, with titles such as *American Jewish History* (1996–), the journal of the National Women's Studies Association (1999–), and the *Journal of Asian American Studies* (1998–). These two full-text databases plus *PCI* are available on terminals throughout the Library. It is likely that the Library of Congress will subscribe to other such databases as they are created; ask the reference staff about newer indexes.

Researchers know to find a good source and then scour its bibliography and notes for other helpful references, but few know to look in citation indexes to find where a specific book or journal article was later cited. This kind of search assumes that if a piece of research is subsequently cited, the citing article may be of interest to the scholar. For example, in your research on Cherokee women, you find an excellent book on your specific subject. Citation indexes identify which later articles cited the book that you have already found. Often these subsequent works, which list that known title in their notes or bibliography, may discuss the same topic. There are three citation indexes that may aid those researching women's history: *Arts & Humanities Citation Index* (print 1975–, AI3.A63; CD-ROM, 1975–); *Science Citation Index* (print 1945–, Z7401.S365 SciRR; CD-ROM, 1981–, SciRR); and *Social Sciences Citation Index* (print, 1956–, Z7161.S65; CD-ROM, 1981–).

SEARCH TIPS: Periodical indexes vary. Read the introduction to determine how to use a title efficiently and to learn what journal titles are covered, whether all articles in a journal are indexed, and whether other kinds of materials such as articles in books are included. When casting a wide net, search periodical indexes that focus on subjects that seem unrelated to your topic. For example, *Applied Science and Technology Index* (formerly *Industrial Arts Index,* 1914–, Z7913.I7 SciRR, MRR Alc; online 1983–) leads to articles on "Advertising—Women, Appeal to," and "Glass ceiling."

BIBLIOGRAPHY: For a subject guide to periodical indexes in the Main Reading Room, see *Abstracts, Indexes, and Bibliographies: For Finding Citations to Periodical Articles* (Humanities and Social Sciences Division, Research Guides, no. 5, 1993). Available online (<http://www.loc.gov/rr/main/ab_index.html>) and at MRR Ref Desk.

"Editor Polly Pigtails at Work." Polly Pigtails' Magazine for Girls, *Spring 1953, cover (AP201.C18). General Collections.*

Perky Polly and her faithful dachshund Finnegan star in this typical 1950s magazine for white middle-class girls. Polly serves as editor, explaining in the first issue (1953) that she always wanted a magazine just for girls her age with articles on subjects that girls like, such as cooking and sewing. Each issue contained a comic strip history of a famous woman—for example, Elizabeth Blackwell and Amelia Earhart—handicrafts, jokes, and short stories. After several name changes, the magazine is still published today, without the cooking and sewing, in a glossier more sophisticated format as *YM*.

Periodicals for Girls (and Boys)

The Library's long runs of children's magazines provide a valuable resource for the study of girlhood, especially of the white middle class. An impressionistic survey of many titles held by the Library reveals that when the stated audience is "boys and girls," most of the text appears to focus on boys. Perhaps further study will reveal otherwise. Nonetheless, changing views of girls can be found in the volumes of children's magazines such as *Youth's Companion* (1827–1929, incomplete, AP201.Y8 fol) and *St. Nicholas* (1873–1943, AP201.S3; microfilm 05422, reels 591–99). Careful perusal of these titles shows the kinds of stories considered appropriate for children, moral lessons advanced, behavioral strictures on young girls, and how these all varied over the years. Girls are often described as sweet, grave, earnest, busy, pretty, little, and obedient. Titles such as *Young Israel* (1871–77, AP222.Y6) and *Young Judean* (1937–78, AP222.Y73) belie the Christian bent of so many of these magazines, but usually depict girls in the same terms.

Magazines whose primary audience was girls seem to supply far more female role models than magazines addressed to all children. In girls' magazines, for example, famous women were the subjects of many of the biographical articles, and serial tales centered on female heroines. Although plots were not as adventurous as those with male heroes in general children's magazines, they depict girls as active, resourceful, intelligent beings.

Shifts in just one title show how images of girls changed (and stayed the same) over the years. The premier issue of *Polly Pigtails' Magazine for Girls* (1953, AP201.C18) contains fiction and articles on cooking, sewing, avoiding clutter, and staying thin ("Why So Fatso?"). Forty years later in the October 1993 issue of *YM* (AP201.C18), a jazzier title for the same magazine, fictional accounts are out, and the articles are "Is He Boyfriend Material?" "Super Models," and "Surviving 3 Socially Scarring Situations."[23] Cooking, sewing, and making handicrafts have given way to lip gloss, interracial dating, and advertisements for books on how to kiss. Historians of girlhood could have a field day with long runs of magazines like this one. Although the focus is primarily on the lives of white middle-class girls, the slow emergence of girls of color in print sources in the last quarter of the twentieth century is a story worth exploring.

The creators of girls' magazines intended to inform and shape girls into the model of womanhood considered appropriate for the day. These childhood magazines enable us to study girlhood and also serve as a fascinating source to trace the development of the ideal woman—to see how she has evolved and how she has remained the same over the past two centuries.

BIBLIOGRAPHY:

Kelly, R. Gordon, ed. *Children's Periodicals of the United States.* Westport, Conn.: Greenwood Press, 1984. PN4878.C48 1984 MRR Alc.

LC CALL NUMBERS: AP200 (pre-1880), AP201 (main call number for general children's magazines), AP222 (Jewish), AP230 (African American).

SAMPLE LCSH: There are no subject headings for most general children's periodicals.

Industry and Labor Union Journals

The business world was historically a man's arena, but trade and industry journals, especially in the fashion and clothing industries, yield frequent glimpses of women within this male-dominated realm. *Millinery Trade Review* (with its title change to *Hats,* 1896–1971, TT650.H3), for example, was published for those involved in making and selling women's hats, and it offers fascinating details about women in the hat business and about the workings of the fashion industry at the beginning of the twentieth century. From skimming lists of hat stores that were recently opened, sold, or in financial difficulties, and from the pages on trade representatives who sailed to Europe to gather the latest European styles, it is possible to get a sense of how many women worked in this trade and ran their own businesses. The Library holds equivalent titles for many other industries, including *Knit Goods Weekly* (with title changes, 1933–80, incomplete, TT679.K65), *Corsets and Brassieres* (1940–52, TT677.C6), and many knitting journals, like *Sweater News* (with title change, 1913–39, TT679.S8).

Material on women is much harder to find in early issues of journals for industries such as meat, brewing, mining, or transportation. Nevertheless, it is interesting to note when women appear and how they are depicted. Their absence can also be telling. The earliest images may be women in advertisements or in group pictures at conventions. During World War II, *Mass Transportation: City Transit's Industry-wide Magazine* (with title changes, 1905–71, TF701.M3) published at least two articles on the psychology of women, stating that "it is impossible to change the female" and, therefore, special psychology is necessary to train "conductorettes."[24] Only in the final decades of the twentieth century did women become part of the workforce in many industries and thus part of the journals.

Women can also be found in labor union publications. For example, the International Ladies' Garment Workers' Union issued its own journal *Justice* (1919–55, HD6350.C6 J8 fol; 1919–82, incomplete, microfilm 01646 MicRR). Some of the men's unions had a separate section for women. The *Machinists Monthly Journal* included a two-page "Woman's Sphere" (with title change, 1898–1956, HD6350.M2 M3), and reports from the women's auxiliary appeared in the *National Rural Letter Carrier* (1927–, HD6350.P77 N3).

BIBLIOGRAPHY: For recent titles, consult the *National Trade and Professional Associations of the United States and Canada and Labor Unions* (with title changes, 1966–, HD2425.D53; latest ed., MRR Ref Desk, BusRR Ref Desk, N&CPR).

SAMPLE LCSH: It is crucial to consult the *Library of Congress Subject Headings* for the names of goods and industries as they have changed over time. Search for either the name of the industry or the item produced. For labor unions, combine subject keywords "Labor unions" and "Periodicals" or search by the name of a union or industry. For older journals search by subject: **[Name of industry or item]—Periodicals.** Examples: **Textile industry; Woolen goods industry; Knit goods; Knit goods industry; Boots and shoes; Corsets—Periodicals; Meat industry and trade—United States—Periodicals.**

LC CALL NUMBERS: HD6350 (labor union periodicals). Each industry has a different call number.

Fashion Magazines and Pattern Books

A costume designer preparing for a Roaring Twenties farce and a woman trying to date a photograph of her great-grandmother have something in common: for both, the Library's large collection of fashion magazines and pattern books provides supportive materials for their quests. You can observe clothing styles appropriate for different years, seasons, activities, age levels, and classes in long runs of titles such as *Harper's Bazar* (with title change to *Harper's Bazaar,* 1867–, TT500.H3, 1867–1912; microfilm 05422, reels 430–50 MicRR), *Elite Styles* (1897–1929, TT500.E4), *McCall's Magazine* (1897–, TT500.M2), and *Pictorial Review* (1899–1939, TT500.P6). Class number TT500 leads to highly illustrated women's fashion magazines, which until the late twentieth century depict primarily middle- and upper-class white women. Catalogs for ordering dressmaking patterns, such as *Butterick Fashions* (1931–57, TT500.B8) and *Vogue Pattern Book* (with title change, 1931–, incomplete, TT500.V717), show styles for middle- and working-class women to sew.

You can trace variations in hair styles, makeup, accessories, hemlines, heel heights, and colors. Women wearing hats and gloves may tell us about the formality or modesty of an era. Images of women in illustrations, advertisements, and examples of undergarments reveal revisions in desired body shape over time—tiny waists, flat chests, long exposed legs, or cleavage. Material for clothing may vary with tariffs, rationing, or new technologies. Seasonal issues show how holidays were celebrated with decorations, food, and gifts. Maternity outfits may tell about views of pregnancy; children's clothing reflects shifts in concepts of childhood. Evidence for many kinds of history can be gleaned from these works.

SAMPLE LCSH: Fashion—Periodicals; Dressmaking—Periodicals; Dressmaking—Pattern books—Periodicals.

LC CALL NUMBERS: Since many of these journals lack subject headings, they can be searched only by call number. Most fashion and clothing journals are arranged alphabetically by original title under TT500.

"Paris Gives Full Play to Chic." Illustration from the Delineator, *August 1926, p. 28 (TT500.D3). General Collections.*

What does the well-dressed woman wear on the boardwalk? For two dollars a year, the Butterick Publishing Company brought women across the country the latest Paris styles and homemaking news. Women could purchase paper patterns for thirty to fifty cents and re-create in Nebraska or California the clothes of the haute monde. The ever-recurring issue of women's weight appears in three articles in this single issue. From 1873 to1937 the *Delineator* was one of the major American fashion magazines with a circulation in 1900 of 480,000. Its French, German, and Spanish editions displayed aspects of American attitudes and way of life to the Western world through editorials, serialized fiction, articles, and advertisements.

Publications of Organizations and Associations

The Library collects annual reports, proceedings, and journals issued by many women's organizations, as well as those to which both sexes belong. These publications show women's involvement in an enormous range of issues, among them abolition, temperance, concern for the environment, church work, and consumer safety, to name just a few. Within the General Collections you can find more than fifty years of the report of the New York-based American Female Guardian Society and Home for the Friendless (1848–1907, incomplete, HV99.N6 A4), but only fourteen issues of the annual report of Boston's Needlewoman's Friend Society (1848–69, 1894–97, incomplete, HV99.B7 N3).

You can track women's expanding roles in originally male-run groups like the National Academy of Sciences and the American Historical Association (the records of the AHA are held in the Manuscript Division), as well as in the more egalitarian National Spiritualist Association. For this last group, the Library holds carbon copy typescripts of the proceedings of the annual meetings with many statements by women (1894–1983, incomplete, BX9798.S7 A15). Membership and officer lists, budgets, reproductions of photographs, association activities, subject matter of papers presented at annual meetings, and sex of the presenters are all potential data for historical research. As with so many of these sources, the absence of women, especially women of color, in many of these volumes informs us of women's place in the organization, and perhaps in the society of the day.

BIBLIOGRAPHY: The following volumes are good sources for the names of groups and individuals.

Blair, Karen J. *The History of American Women's Voluntary Organizations, 1810–1960: A Guide to Sources.* Boston: G.K. Hall, 1989. Z7964.U49 B53 1989 MRR Alc.

Davis, Elizabeth Lindsay. *Lifting as They Climb.* Washington: National Association of Colored Women, 1933. E185.5.N278 D3 MRR Alc.

Register of Women's Clubs. 1907–33, incomplete. HQ1406.R4. Lists many women's organizations by state and town.

BIBLIOGRAPHY continued:

Scott, Anne Firor. *Natural Allies: Women's Associations in American History.* Urbana: University of Illinois Press, 1991. HQ1904.S28 1991.

SAMPLE LCSH: To locate publications by women's groups, search the catalog for the name of the group as either a name or a corporate name. For books about a group, search its name as a subject. **Women—United States—Societies and clubs—History;** [Name of the organization].

State Historical Society Publications

Most state historical associations publish journals or collections of primary sources relating to their state. Within these hundreds of volumes lurk both passing references and long narratives on women. Scanning several issues of the *Washington Historical Quarterly* (with title change, 1906–, F886.W28) located articles on the dismaying increase in divorce rates in Washington State (April 1914), Mrs. Sheffield's recollections of her 1852 trip from New York to Vancouver, and Mrs. Agnew's account of settling Idaho in 1864 (both in the January 1924 issue). The journal of the Illinois State Historical Society printed a selection of letters from a Civil War soldier to his wife. Loving in tone, proud of his service, he comments, "I shall feel the more a man, and look on you as a true heroine— And when again I appear at the head of my dear dear household, you can throw off a load of care that will make you feel, fresh, boyant & young as ever." (1862)[25] These few words alone tell us about his feelings for his wife and his position in the home and more.

State historical association journals supply details not easily found elsewhere. Excerpts from diaries, letters, obituaries, biographies of state residents, and reproductions of photographs give descriptions of daily life, games, holidays, homes, and travel. Many of these items may survive only in this published form. They are especially useful for information on genealogy, frontier life, early settlers, Native Americans, and for those examining a particular geographical area.

SEARCH TIPS: Since 1964, most state historical journals are indexed in *America: History and Life* (Z1236.A48 MRR Alc, online 1964–). For earlier years, consult the annual *Writings on American History* (1902–90, Z1236 .L331 MRR Alc, LH&G), although the references to women in it are not always easy to locate. The subscription database *Periodicals Contents Index,* available at most Library of Congress terminals, gives tables of contents of many state historical society journals; so you can rapidly scan the titles of articles and authors in each issue, but not the full text. Sometimes this is the best way to locate articles by and about women.

BIBLIOGRAPHY:

Directory of Historical Organizations in the United States and Canada. Biennial. E172.D5 MRR Ref Desk and other reading rooms. State historical associations can usually be found under the state's name in the index. The full entry lists each organization's publications.

SAMPLE LCSH: There is no single subject heading for state historical society publications. The best search is "[Name of state]—History—Periodicals," but this produces many periodicals published by other groups. A keyword search for "[Name of state]" and "state historical" often yields good results.

Biographical Sources

Readers frequently come to the Library of Congress looking for biographical facts about women. Often they know little more than a name. One scholar arrived with a reference to five Stimson sisters, whom she knew were active in the United States in the first half of the twentieth century. After searching through a combination of sources—family histories and genealogies, the Library's catalogs, biographical dictionaries, periodical indexes, and college yearbooks—she had uncovered the outlines of these women's lives, with such details as that one played college basketball, another served as dean of Goucher College, all supported women's suffrage, and four published books on topics ranging from cookery and the Army Nurse Corps to bone fractures and the history of science.

Further digging would most likely have yielded additional information. This example of a search for biographical information proved relatively straightforward as the Stimsons were educated, middle-class white women of some note. Often you will be trying to trace lesser-known, less well-documented women. The approach is similar; the results may be sparser.

Research in other reading rooms at the Library may provide further particulars, especially on more prominent women; for example, maps indicating the woman's home (G&M); local newspaper accounts (N&CPR); or occasionally photographs (P&P) and unpublished letters or diaries written by or about her (MSS).

SAMPLE LCSH: The subdivision "Biography" is not used after individual personal names; it is added to classes of people, ethnic groups, and occupational headings, such as: **Women—Biography; Hispanic American women—Biography; Women composers—Biography.**

Genealogies, Local and Family Histories, City Directories

From the Library's large collection of genealogies and regional histories you can find information on women ranging from an elusive birth date to a detailed account of the lives of several generations. Family histories can be surprisingly intimate and, in this age of self-publishing, appear in great numbers. Local histories may explain workings of nearby factories and businesses, conflicts within churches or town government, or compelling issues confronting a locale—all of which may tell us about the lives of women. Background on the places a woman lived—her schools, churches, movie theaters, gardens—are needed to write biographies and also contribute to other aspects of women's history. These volumes are rarely well indexed.

The Library also holds a vast number of United States telephone and city directories, many of which are available on microform. City directories are rich in unexpected bits of information; in addition to names and addresses, they often list spouses, occupations, and boarders, and some indicate race and marital status. Classified sections with names of businesses, organizations, and public institutions in the town reveal women's options in choosing churches, schools, clubs, newspapers, or hat makers. To discover the women's organizations in Whatcom, Washington, in 1902, or the number of midwives in Honolulu in 1936, look in the appropriate city directories. Browsing the 1863 *Washington and Georgetown Directory* shows that the most frequent occupations given for women were boardinghouse keeper, dressmaker, and milliner. The directory names one accoucheur and several women who were hucksters.[26] Scanning runs of directories for one town or state might show when women began to appear in town offices or in traditionally male occupations. Careful searching can uncover details that enrich our picture of women's lives in specific areas and at specific times. The Local History and Genealogy Reading Room has a sizable reference collection and is staffed by specialists who can provide assistance in using these sources.

BIBLIOGRAPHY:

Genealogies in the Library of Congress: A Bibliography. Edited by Marion J. Kaminkow. 4 vols. With supplements. Baltimore: Magna Carta Book Co., 1972–87. Z5319.U53 LH&G, MRR Alc.

Neagles, James C. *The Library of Congress: A Guide to Genealogical and Historical Research.* Salt Lake City: Ancestry Publications, 1990. Z1250.N4 1990 LH&G, MRR Alc. This volume lists LC holdings for city directories, and a looseleaf notebook at the LH&G reference desk adds directories microfilmed since the book's publication. City directories do not exist for all places.

PATHFINDER: Biographical Sources

To locate sources that might help you find biographical information in the General Collections, follow whichever steps are appropriate for the woman you want to know better.

1 Library of Congress Online Catalog. Search for the woman as both name and subject. For published genealogies, search under "[Last name] family" as a subject.

2 *Biography and Genealogy Master Index* (Detroit: Gale Research, 1980 and supplements; Z5305.U5 B57 MRR Biog, BusRR, LH&G; online at terminals throughout the Library). An extremely useful cumulative index to hundreds of biographical reference works and a required stop in most biographical searches. This set indexes many standard biographical sources such as *Who's Who in America, Biography Index, Notable American Women,* and *Dictionary of Literary Biography,* and so you do not need to search these titles separately.

A similar work, *IBN: Index Bio-Bibliographicus Notorum Hominum* (Osnabrück: BiblioVerlag, 1973-; Z5301.L7 MRR Alc), indexes thousands of international collective biographical volumes and includes women from the United States. By 1999, only names beginning with the letters A-G had been indexed. Most of the biographical volumes covered are not in English.

3 *Personal Name Index to "The New York Times Index," 1851–1974* (Z5301.F28 1976 MRR Biog and other reading rooms) and supplement *1975–1984* (CT104.F35 1986 MRR Biog, N&CPR).

4 *American Biographical Index* (CT213.A64 1998 MicRR). Index to a microfiche set containing the full text of more than three hundred collective biographical volumes.

5 *Biographical Dictionaries and Related Works* (Z5301.S55 1986 MRR Ref Desk, SciRR, BusRR). A two-volume bibliography of more than 16,000 collective biographies.

6 *Abstracts, Indexes, and Bibliographies: For Finding Citations to Periodical Articles* (Humanities and Social Sciences Division, Research Guides, no. 5, 1993). Available online (<http://www.loc.gov/rr/main/ab_index.html>) and in print at MRR Ref Desk.

7 Online sources, such as Internet searches, FirstSearch databases, or CD-ROM networks in various reading rooms, may supply biographical data or lead to printed works in the Library's collections. Online sources are often best for current information.

8 Directories of relevant associations and occupations.

9 Book reviews if the woman sought was an author.

10 Histories of the towns, counties, schools, churches, or organizations with which the woman was connected. (See "Genealogies . . . .")

11 City directories, if the reader has an idea of the dates and cities in which the woman resided. (See "Genealogies . . . .")

12 Librarians in the Local History and Genealogy Reading Room, for specialized genealogical materials.

13 Biographical sources about other women and men in her life.

14 *Subject Guide to Women of the World* (Lanham, Md.: Scarecrow Press, 1996; Z7963.B6 P45 1996 MRR Biog, SciRR). Useful index for identifying names of women by occupation (hospital founders, crafts, mothers of prominent men), industry, area of fame, geography.

BIBLIOGRAPHY continued:

Telephone and City Directories in the Library of Congress: A Finding Guide. Compiled by Barbara B. Walsh. Humanities and Social Sciences Research Guides, no. 37. Washington: Library of Congress, 2000. Available at MRR Ref Desk and LH&G and online at <http://www.loc.gov/rr/genealogy/bib_guid/telephon.html>.

United States Local Histories in the Library of Congress: A Bibliography. Edited by Marion J. Kaminkow. 5 vols. Baltimore: Magna Carta Book Co., 1975–76. Z1250.U59 1975 LH&G, MRR Alc, N&CPR.

SAMPLE LCSH: For genealogies, search: "[Last name] family" as a subject. For local histories, search by name of the geographical location (town, county, state, region). For city directories, search: "[Geographical location]—Directories."

LC CALL NUMBERS: There are no call numbers for U.S. telephone books and city directories. Request by name of town, state, and year. Many are self-serve in the Microform Reading Room.

Memorial Volumes

The General Collections hold about one hundred purportedly true accounts of the brief but exemplary lives and pious deaths of precocious children; and about eighty of these works describe girls. This unusual collection contains titles such as *"Asleep in Christ": A Short Narrative of Mary Harbridge* by "her pastor" I. W. Baynes (Boston: Massachusetts Sabbath School Society, 1839; BR1715.H33 B35) and *Tears and Consolations: or, A Simple Recital of the Life and Death of Little Jenny* by César Malan (Boston: Massachusetts Sabbath School Society, 1849; BR1715.J4 M3). Written by parents, ministers, or friends, these stories present views on sin in children, stress the importance of early religious education, highlight

"Death of Ann Elizabeth Pierce." Frontispiece engraving and title page from Memoir of Ann Elizabeth Pierce *(Boston: Massachusetts Sabbath School Society, 1833; BR1715.P43 P5). General Collections.*

The sorrowing family gathers by the bedside; a sister weeps, and a dying child makes a final generous gesture. Sunday school societies published small volumes intended to demonstrate the value of religious education; to promote Christian values such as reverence, obedience, and resignation; to console grieving parents and siblings; and perhaps to instill fear in errant children who would read or listen to the biographies. The death scene of young Eva in *Uncle Tom's Cabin* (1852) is a fictional version similar to these formulaic stories where a child's faith sets an example for adults and children alike.

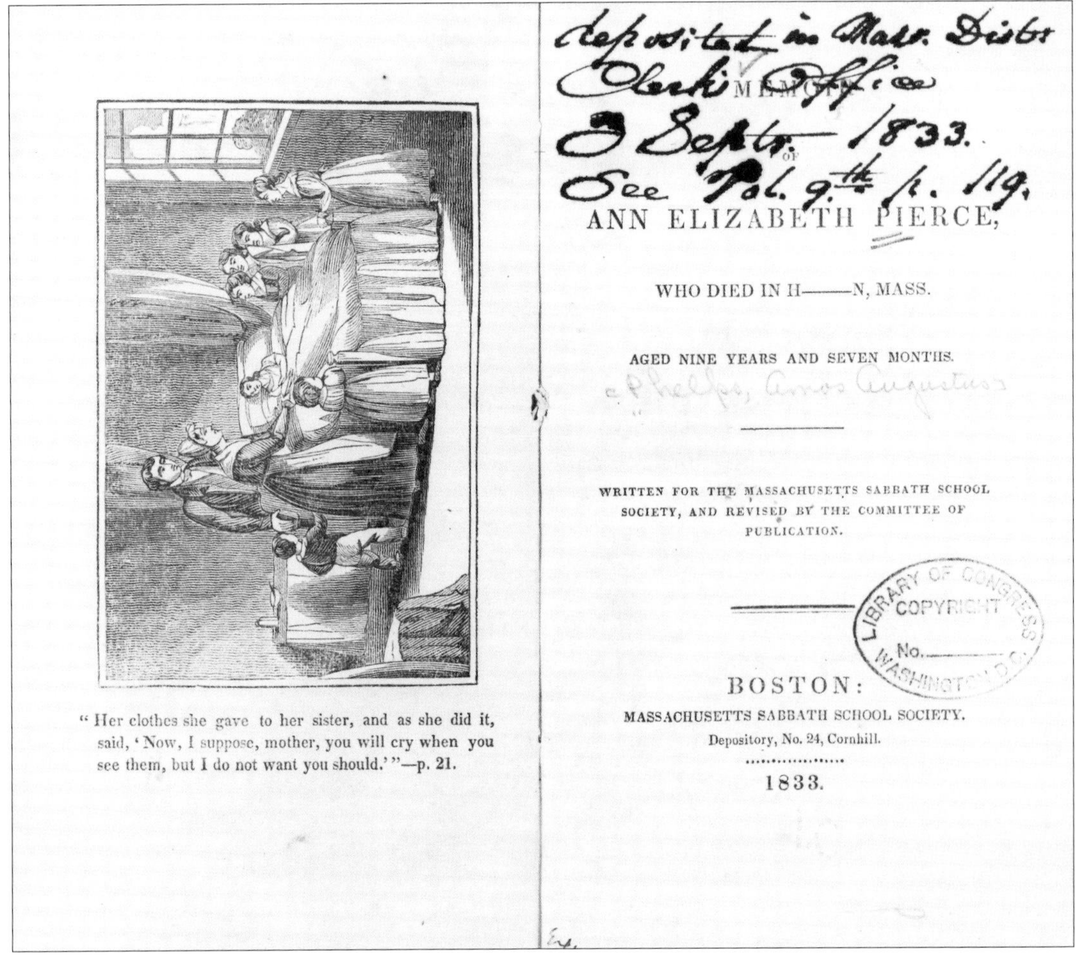

"Her clothes she gave to her sister, and as she did it, said, 'Now, I suppose, mother, you will cry when you see them, but I do not want you should.'"—p. 21.

Deposited in Mass. Distr. Clerk's Office 3 Sept. 1833. See Vol. 9th p. 119.

MEMOIR OF ANN ELIZABETH PIERCE,

WHO DIED IN H——N, MASS.

AGED NINE YEARS AND SEVEN MONTHS.

WRITTEN FOR THE MASSACHUSETTS SABBATH SCHOOL SOCIETY, AND REVISED BY THE COMMITTEE OF PUBLICATION.

BOSTON:

MASSACHUSETTS SABBATH SCHOOL SOCIETY.

Depository, No. 24, Cornhill.

1833.

the proper behavior of girls (with frequent emphasis on cleanliness and neatness), and describe how parents should approach the deaths of their children. Many were published by Sunday School societies in the first half of the nineteenth century. Other similar volumes may be found in the Rare Book and Microform Reading Rooms.

Women (and more frequently men) were memorialized in a similar fashion. Relatives or friends published biographies, often with excerpts from diaries, letters, poems, and funeral sermons. The volumes were meant to show how a life should be lived. As one author explained in writing of her grandmother, she hoped "that the example of her pure and lovely life might have its effect upon her great-grandchildren, as well as upon my own generation."[27] These biographies, usually brief, provide rare glimpses into the lives of lesser-known women. Among the topics often covered are religious practices, marital relationships, childbearing, health, travels, and how the women were perceived by friends and family.

BIBLIOGRAPHY:

Davis, Gwenn, and Beverly A. Joyce, comps. *Personal Writings by Women to 1900: A Bibliography of American and British Writers.* Norman: University of Oklahoma Press, 1989. Z1229.W8 D38 1989 MRR Alc. Search the index under "Memorial volumes."

SAMPLE LCSH: As a rule, the only subject heading for memorial volumes is the name of the child or woman, so they must be searched by call number or through bibliographies.

LC CALL NUMBERS: Mostly in BR1714-BR1715 (for children) or CT275 (for women and men). Others on women have call numbers for specific occupations, such as nurses (some in RT37) or teachers (some in LA2317).

Women's Writings

Those who would write women's history must listen to women's voices, voices that were often silenced by custom, limited education, loss of records, or lack of interested listeners. Women's words exist in the books and articles they wrote, in published diaries, journals, travel accounts, autobiographies, and collections of letters, in testimony before Congress, in legal depositions, in manuscript collections, in letters to editors, and in the vast literary output of women. Because writing could be done privately, at home, for centuries it was one of the few socially acceptable ways for women to express themselves in forms that would survive. Through their writings women tell how they felt as children, where they worked, whom they cared for, how they loved, what they served for breakfast—of birth, death, and everything in between. They talk about war, economics, science, and religion. The words of women can be found in every reading room in the Library.

Literary Works (Novels, Drama, Poetry, Short Stories)

"You will be wise to commit your novels to the flames, rather than to the hands of your daughter" (1808),[28] for "Novel reading strengthens the passions, weakens the virtues, and diminishes the power of self-control" (1843).[29] Despite these strictures, women read and wrote novels, and so did their daughters. Within the Library's general, microform, and rare book collections lies much of the literary output of American women, as well as extensive literary criticism and literary biographical works. The research possibilities from this vast array of women's voices are many, among them: what books did women and girls read; which women wrote and when, at what stages in their lives; what subjects attracted them; what words have they used; how are clothes, manners, relationships, and emotions described; and so on. (See also the sections on "Women in Popular Culture" and "Literary Works" in chapter 4, and "Literature and Journalism" in chapter 5.)

Literature has also allowed women to put their feelings and opinions before the public. Harriet Beecher Stowe's powerful antislavery novel *Uncle Tom's Cabin* (Boston: J.P. Jewett & Co., 1853; PS2954.U5 1853; many editions in RBSC) moved more readers than any abolitionist sermon. In her long poem *An Idyl of Work,* factory worker Lucy Larcom vividly recounts her mill experiences, asking poignantly, "How can I like the clatter of the looms,/The grime, the dust, the heat, the dizzy din" and later "Heads like to be employed, as well as hands;/Is there no way to give each a fair chance?" (1875).[30] In her novel *Journey to Topaz,* Japanese-American Yoshiko Uchida depicts one aspect of life in a World War II evacuation camp for her eleven-year-old heroine: "One of the worst things about being in camp was that there was no place to go to be alone. Wherever she went, people pressed close—in her own stall, at the mess hall, at school, on the track, even in the latrines and washroom."[31]

Descriptions of women and girls in literary works of any sort—westerns, mysteries, science fiction, romances, children's literature, adventure tales, novels, poems, plays, or short stories, whether by women or men—contribute evidence for women's history, but caution must be exercised when using this evidence, for it is the product of imagination as well as of experience. In the Prologue to *Journey to Topaz* quoted above, Yoshiko Uchida explains, "Although the characters are fictitious, the events are based on actual fact, and much that happened to the Sakane family also happened to my own."[32] But such forthright statements are uncommon. It is for each reader to determine to what extent fictionalized accounts of the lives of girls and women can be used as historical truths.

Cover art and illustrations within volumes give visual accompaniment to verbal depictions of women. (See chapter 2 for discussion of the pulp fiction cover collection.) Literature is one of the main avenues for women's voices, and from this vast quantity of material can be sifted information about the lives of women and girls in all time periods, regions, classes, and races.

BIBLIOGRAPHY:

Davis, Gwenn, and Beverly A. Joyce, comps. *Drama by Women to 1900: A Bibliography of American and British Writers.* London: Mansell, 1992. Z1231.D7 D38 1992 MRR Alc.

———. *Poetry by Women to 1900: A Bibliography of American and British Writers.* Toronto: University of Toronto Press, 1991. Z2013.5.W6 D38 1991b MRR Alc.

Mainiero, Lina, ed. *American Women Writers: A Critical Reference Guide from Colonial Times to the Present.* 5 vols. New York: Ungar, 1979–94. PS147.A4 MRR Biog.

Yellin, Jean Fagan, and Cynthia D. Bond, comps. *The Pen Is Ours: A Listing of Writings by and about African-American Women before 1910 with Secondary Bibliography to the Present.* New York: Oxford University Press, 1991. Z1229.N39 Y44 1991 MRR Alc.

SAMPLE LCSH: The subdivision "Fiction" can follow more recent subject headings, for example, "Man-woman relationships—Fiction." Most older literary works do not have any subject headings. The following terms help locate authors in reference and collective literary works: **Women authors, American; American literature [poetry; drama; fiction]—Women authors; American literature—[Arab American authors;** or, **Asian American, Chinese American, Catholic, etc., authors. . .]; African American women authors; Indian women in literature; Feminism and literature; Feminist literary criticism; Children's literature, American—Bibliography.**

First-Person Accounts

In autobiographies, diaries, letters, interviews, and oral histories, women describe the details of their own lives. Within the many oral history collections that are part of the series New York Times Oral History Program, we hear, for example, women of Appalachia portray lives revolving around the coal mines and California suffragists and women trade union members remember the long struggles in their respective campaigns (for an index to names, see MicRR guide; AI3.O7). From revealing abundant details on all aspects of their daily existence to how and where they expressed themselves, women's personal nonfiction writings provide the raw stuff of history. Just listen: "*July 30—Saturday*—And now Oh God comes the saddest record of my life for this day my husband accidentally shot himself and was buried by the wayside and oh, my heart is breaking" (1864).[33] Or, "By now castrating the baby goats was fairly easy for me . . . ." (1987).[34] Women do speak to us.

Women's first-person accounts are not always easily identifiable. In most cases, the sex of the author is not part of the cataloging record. The subject headings for *The Journal of Mrs. Mary Ringo: A Diary of Her Trip across the Great Plains in 1864,* quoted above, are "West (U.S.)—Description and travel" and "Overland journeys to the Pacific." The heading for most travel accounts by authors of either sex is usually the geographical location plus the subdivision "—Description and travel." Researchers must look at the records for all items under this term and try to select those by or about women. Often the name of the author is the main clue. And, of course, men's first-person accounts also contain valuable evidence about women's lives. In the past thirty years many women's diaries and letters, some that had lain unknown in attics and archives, have been printed or put on microform. More specific cataloging has improved access to recent works, but bibliographies remain the primary means of identifying most older titles.

Women have also written extensively for periodicals, but again these articles, especially those produced before 1970, are often difficult to find. Consult *Periodical Contents Index* and other periodical indexes described earlier. State historical publications and local histories also contain wonderful accounts by women.

BIBLIOGRAPHY: See "Travel Accounts" below for other bibliographies.

Arksey, Laura, Nancy Pries, and Marcia Reed. *American Diaries: An Annotated Bibliography of Published Diaries and Journals.* 2 vols. Detroit: Gale Research, 1983–87. Z5305.U5 A74 1983 MRR Alc, LH&G, BusRR.

Briscoe, Mary Louise, ed. *American Autobiography, 1945–1980: A Bibliography.* Madison: University of Wisconsin Press, 1982. Z5305.U5 A47 1982 MRR Alc, LH&G.

Cline, Cheryl. *Women's Diaries, Journals, and Letters: An Annotated Bibliography.* New York: Garland, 1989. Z7963.B6 C55 1989 MRR Alc.

Davis, Gwenn, and Beverly A. Joyce, comps. *Personal Writings by Women to 1900: A Bibliography of American and British Writers.* Norman: University of Oklahoma Press, 1989. Z1229.W8 D38 1989 MRR Alc.

Goodfriend, Joyce D. *The Published Diaries and Letters of American Women: An Annotated Bibliography.* Boston: G.K. Hall, 1987; Z5305.U5 G66 1987 MRR Alc.

Rhodes, Carolyn, H., ed. *First Person Female American: A Selected and Annotated Bibliography of the Autobiographies of American Women Living after 1950.* Troy, N.Y.: Whitston Publishing Co., 1980; Z7963.A8 F57 MRR Biog.

SAMPLE LCSH: Although there are many subject headings for first-person accounts, bibliographies often provide the best access. **American diaries—Bibliography; Diaries—Women authors—Bibliography.** You may combine

SAMPLE LCSH continued:
the following subject headings with proper names or regions or with the term "Women": **Oral history;** [Name of person]**—Interviews;** [Name of person]**—Correspondence;** [Geographic location]**—Description and travel;** [Name of war]**—Personal narratives, American** [these are mostly by men].

Travel Accounts

"I have nowhere seen woman occupying a loftier position," declared French aristocrat Alexis de Tocqueville after a visit to the United States in 1832. He went on to attribute the prosperity and strength of the young nation "to the superiority of their women."[35] Two years later, English writer Harriet Martineau reached a different conclusion, complaining that in America "woman's intellect is confined, her morals crushed, her health ruined, her weaknesses encouraged, and her strength punished."[36] These two acute observers differ in sex, class, and nationality, yet both provide historians with pointed commentary on the life and customs of American women.

Many travelers kept diaries; most wrote detailed letters to family at home, which they occasionally reworked for publication, sometimes as books, sometimes in newspapers or magazines such as the *Atlantic Monthly* or *Harper's*. These personal writings provided an acceptable way for women to present their opinions to the public.

Women's experiences far from home can also be found in reports and letters published in women's missionary journals. A single sentence from a death notice in *Spirit of Missions* shows the desired qualities of a "true woman" in 1872, and the acceptability of her "woman's work" to convert the Mormons in Utah—"Active, yet modest; helpful, without self-assertion; sensible, patient, unselfish, loving—she was a true woman, and she made her woman's work of inestimable value to us."[37]

These journals also reveal that American women who journeyed far from home to take their God to others often carried more than religion. Reporting on the Dakota Women's Society, Miss Hunter asks, "Do you think it strange that in a Christian society the women should provide the wood for their families?" She describes the household

"Miss Hartwell and Bible Women in the Foochow Mission." Photoreproduction from Life and Light, *May 1902, p. 211 (BV2612.L5). General Collections.*

"We ask your earnest prayers for these noble souls out on picket duty on the very outskirts of the army of the Lord" (November 1902, p. 496). Prayers and financial contributions were two of the frequent requests from missionaries far from home. Emily Hartwell's letters from Foochow to the Woman's Board of Missions back in Boston reveal an implicit critique of gender roles in China and an almost inevitable ethnocentrism. Working mostly with women, Hartwell points out how hard it is for those with bound feet to walk to church and bemoans the power of the mother-in-law and plural marriages. Through her educational and evangelizing efforts, she tries to subvert existing gender relationships.

duties of Dakota women and surmises that as the husband "grows in Christian character," he will assume more of the outside duties (1886).[38] Miss Hunter is trying to re-create in the lands of Native Americans her eastern, Protestant concept of the division of labor.

In journals such as *Heathen Woman's Friend* (Methodist, 1869–94, incomplete, BV2612.H4; 1869–95, microfilm 51565, reels 221–25), *Life and Light for Woman* (Congregational, with title changes, 1869–1922, BV2612.L5), and *Messenger of Our Lady of Africa* (Roman Catholic, with title change, 1931–70, BV2300.W6 A4) you find names of members of the denomination with home towns; donors and dollar amounts, and obituaries; excerpts from letters and journals of women missionaries and foreign women who have been converted; annual budgets and meeting reports; texts of original hymns sung at meetings and composed by women; and information on Native American women.

Travel accounts of all sorts—published and unpublished, by women and men, by foreigners and Americans, written for pleasure, pay, or spiritual expression—can provide a wealth of unusual detail on topics such as manners, clothing, education, childcare, health, regional differences, interpersonal relationships, and political events. Such works are rarely indexed, so only patient perusal of individual volumes will uncover the gold. In these often overlooked sources you can explore important questions of gender, class, race, and national identity and observe interactions between people of different cultures.

BIBLIOGRAPHY: See "First-Person Accounts" above for other bibliographies.

Robinson, Jane. *Wayward Women: A Guide to Women Travellers.* New York: Oxford University Press, 1990. Z6011.R65 1990 MRR Alc. Mostly British women, some of whom traveled to America.

Smith, Harold Frederick. *American Travellers Abroad: A Bibliography of Accounts Published before 1900.* 2nd ed. Lanham, Md.: Scarecrow Press, 1999. Z6011.S5 1999 MRR Alc.

Tinling, Marion. *Women into the Unknown: A Sourcebook on Women Explorers and Travelers.* New York: Greenwood Press, 1989. G200.T55 1989 MRR Biog, G&M.

SAMPLE LCSH: Women travelers—United States; Travelers—United States; Visitors, Foreign—United States; Travelers' writings, American—Bibliography; Voyages and travels—Bibliography; [Name of country or state]—Description and travel.

LC CALL NUMBERS: BV2612 and BV2350 (for some missionary journals).

Unexpected Sources

The preceding sections of this chapter describe starting places for researching American women's history, ways to identify relevant magazines and appropriate periodical indexes, biographical sources, and women's writings. There are many other types of materials that can contribute to our understanding of women's lives.

Etiquette Books and Prescriptive Literature

Authors, female and male, have always relished telling women what to do. This plentiful advice literature prescribes proper behavior for women at every stage of their lives. Nineteenth-century books on girlhood stress obedience and filial devotion as they point the way to the adult "woman's sphere" where "Woman may be well assured that the surest pathway to the highest happiness and honor lies through the peaceful domain of wifehood and motherhood. . . . To the true woman home is her throne" (1878).[39] This proper place for women was not a matter of choice: "The God who made them [the two sexes] knew the sphere in which each of them was designed to act, and he fitted them for it by their physical frames, by their intellectual susceptibilities, by their tastes and affections" (1848).[40] The Library's collections contain hundreds of titles describing a woman's duties as wife and mother in similar terms.

Combining the many subject headings for home, marriage, and wife with a broad range of call numbers, you can trace several centuries of advice to women on proper ways to behave toward a spouse. From the nineteenth-century *Marriage and the Duties of the Marriage Relations* by G. W. Quinby (Cincinnati: J.A. & U.P. James, 1852; HQ734.Q7) to the modern *Your 30-Day Journey to Being a Great Wife* by Patrick and Connie Lawrence (Nashville: Oliver Nelson, 1992; HQ759.L376 1992), writers explain the duties of each sex within marriage. In *The Young Husband's Book,* the author states that in return for supporting his wife, a husband has "a general and paramount claim to her obedience. The Scripture is so conclusive on this point that argument is unnecessary for establishing the doctrine" (1843).[41] A title such as *Woman in Girlhood, Wifehood, Motherhood: Her Responsibilities and Her Duties at All Periods of Life; a Guide in the Maintenance of Her Own Health and That of Her Children* by Myer Solis-Cohen (Philadelphia: John C. Winston Co., 1906; RG121.S67) dictates in a single volume how a woman should function in each of the three traditional phases of her life. In another grand compendium, *The College of Life, or Practical Self=Educator* [sic], *a Manual of Self-Improvement for the Colored Race,* articles on "The True Lady" and "The Model Wife" tell women to be "agreeable, modest, and dignified"

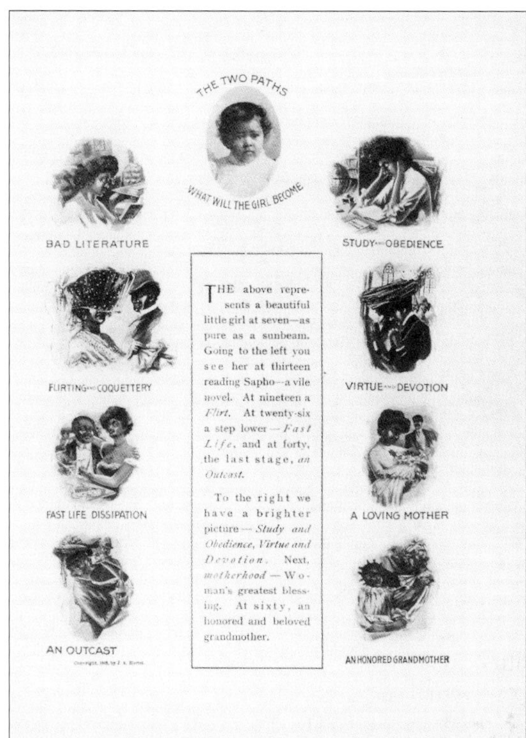
THE TWO PATHS

WHAT WILL THE GIRL BECOME

BAD LITERATURE

STUDY—OBEDIENCE

THE above represents a beautiful little girl at seven—as pure as a sunbeam. Going to the left you see her at thirteen reading Sapho—a vile novel. At nineteen a *Flirt*. At twenty-six a step lower—*Fast Life*, and at forty, the last stage, *an Outcast.*

To the right we have a brighter picture—*Study and Obedience, Virtue and Devotion.* Next, *motherhood*—Woman's greatest blessing. At sixty, an honored and beloved grandmother.

FLIRTING—COQUETTERY

VIRTUE—DEVOTION

FAST LIFE DISSIPATION

A LOVING MOTHER

AN OUTCAST

AN HONORED GRANDMOTHER

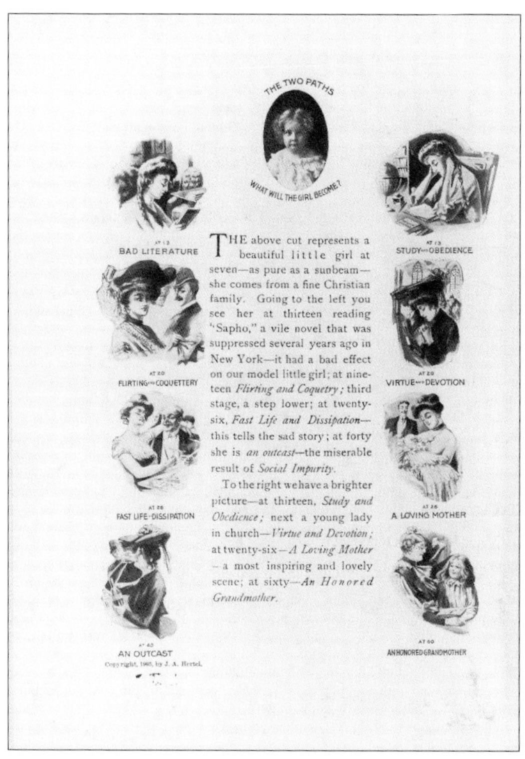
THE TWO PATHS

WHAT WILL THE GIRL BECOME?

BAD LITERATURE

STUDY—OBEDIENCE

THE above cut represents a beautiful little girl at seven—as pure as a sunbeam—she comes from a fine Christian family. Going to the left you see her at thirteen reading "Sapho," a vile novel that was suppressed several years ago in New York—it had a bad effect on our model little girl; at nineteen *Flirting and Coquetry*; third stage, a step lower; at twenty-six, *Fast Life and Dissipation*—this tells the sad story; at forty she is *an outcast*—the miserable result of *Social Impurity.*

To the right we have a brighter picture—at thirteen, *Study and Obedience*; next a young lady in church—*Virtue and Devotion*; at twenty-six—*A Loving Mother*—a most inspiring and lovely scene; at sixty—*An Honored Grandmother.*

FLIRTING—COQUETTERY

VIRTUE—DEVOTION

FAST LIFE—DISSIPATION

A LOVING MOTHER

AN OUTCAST

AN HONORED GRANDMOTHER

"The Two Paths." Illustrations from works by John W. Gibson and his wife. LEFT: Golden Thoughts on Chastity and Procreation *(Toronto, Ont., and Naperville, Ill.: J. L. Nichols & Co., 1903; HQ31.G44), between pp. 58 and 59.* RIGHT: Social Purity, or, the Life of the Home and Nation *(New York: J. L. Nichols & Co., 1903; HQ31.G46), opposite p. 59. General Collections.*

In 1903 the J.L. Nichols Publishing Company issued virtually identical books of advice for young, middle-class women and men. The two works differ only in title, introduction, and illustrations. In one volume all the illustrations depict African Americans; in the other everyone is white. This rare move by the publisher acknowledges the segregation of the day, the growth of the African American book-buying public, and the desire to promote standard values to all. Both illustrations summarize the standard messages presented to girls and women in hundreds of volumes of prescriptive literature. The rewards of education, religion, and marriage are contrasted with the downward spiral that results from novel-reading and flirtation.

and industrious (1895),[42] showing that similar behavior was expected from both white and African American middle-class women. From books like these, scholars can learn how authors felt women and girls should act and also achieve a picture of ideal daily lives, concerns, and duties.

Books on how to be a good mother are also plentiful. These works supply wonderful materials for investigating attitudes toward women, children, and family life over time. In *Advice to a Mother on the Management of Her Children,* the popular author Pye Henry Chavasse proclaimed in 1898 that a child "is the source of a mother's greatest and purest enjoyment, that he [sic] is the strongest bond of affection between her and her husband."[43] Many other works tout the joys of motherhood but then turn to practical matters such as care of a baby's teeth, constipation, and ways to keep children occupied.

Similar advice books exist for men and can be compared to those addressing women. From the differences in tone and language, topics covered, and behavior described as appropriate for each sex may come a perspective on attitudes that shape society and relations between the sexes. Frequently, men are told of their responsibilities toward the angel in the home yet warned of city haunts where "woman presides as the priestess of ruin" (1865).[44] Male opinions of women are revealed in statements such as the 1948 comment on the college woman: "She is in college for one of two basic reasons: (1) To trap an unwary male and lead him to the altar. (2) To prepare for a business or professional career."[45]

What really occurs in women's lives, of course, may bear little relationship to the conduct recommended in these works. The purity of mind advocated for nineteenth-century girls may rarely have existed in real life. Information contained in prescriptive literature must always be examined carefully and compared to experiences recounted in women's own voices, with attention to class, age, race, and regional variations. Works proclaiming the delights of motherhood can be contrasted with the cry of a Pittsburgh housewife in 1965: "I feel like a pie cut up in six pieces being served to a dinner party of ten!"[46] If a period produces many titles on the proper behavior of women, does that imply that women behaved in the prescribed manner, or were they so flouting the standards of the day that society saw a need to publicize the word on correct demeanor? Only careful research will tell.

SEARCH TIPS: Works of etiquette and advice published before 1801 will be found in the Rare Book and Microform Reading Rooms.

BIBLIOGRAPHY:

Dixon, Penelope. *Mothers and Mothering: An Annotated Feminist Bibliography.* New York: Garland, 1991. Z7963.M67 D59 1991 MRR Alc.

Hodges, Deborah Robertson. *Etiquette: An Annotated Bibliography of Literature Published in English in the United States, 1900 through 1987.* Jefferson, N.C.: McFarland, 1989. Z5877.H6 1989. Includes articles and books.

Newton, Sarah E. *Learning to Behave: A Guide to American Conduct Books before 1900.* Westport, Conn.: Greenwood Press, 1994. BJ1547.N48 1994 MRR Alc.

SAMPLE LCSH: Books on these topics have many varied subject headings and call numbers. Searches with broad subject headings such as "Woman" or "Conduct of life" are occasionally necessary. **Girls; Young women; Conduct of life; Etiquette; Woman—Health and hygiene; Beauty, personal; Love; Courtship; Marriage; Wives; Mothers; Motherhood; Home; Home economics; Domestic economy; Housewives; Cookery; Cookery, American; Food.**

LC CALL NUMBERS: For conduct of life and etiquette: BJ1651; BJ1681; BJ1853. For courtship, marriage, health, and motherhood: HQ759, HQ801; For medical works: RA778; RG121.

Sex Manuals

Forthright discussions of sexuality, especially women's, are difficult to locate in U.S. imprints before the twentieth century. As one author explained in 1896, "Works upon sexual science, physiology, anatomy, etc., are too elaborate and extensive for the average woman to study or comprehend."[47] A surprising number of books from the late nineteenth and early twentieth century, however, were published to inform girls and women about their maturing bodies, female physiology and diseases, and marital duties. Most nineteenth-century works addressing girls and women avoided male sexuality or physiology, and each sex was kept uninformed about the other.

Titles such as *What a Young Girl Ought to Know* by Mary Wood Allen (Philadelphia: Vir Publishing Co., 1897; HQ51.A4) and *The Sex Life of Girls and Young Women* by Grace Reese Adkins (Cincinnati: Standard Publishing Company, 1919; HQ51.A3 Overflow) survey health, hygiene, and sexual relations in scientific terms but with strong moral and religious messages. Discussions of sex were sometimes disguised in chapters such as "What the Flower Teaches Us" (1919),[48] but became increasingly specific and illustrated as the twentieth century progressed. Leslie J. Swabacker was unusually blunt in his *Letters to My Daughter* (1926) when he urged her to "Be the most desirable mistress in the world in your husband's eyes,"[49] and Amy Ayer exclaims that celibacy "is a crime against nature" (1890),[50] but of course she is addressing married women. In most of these works, questions of women's physiology and sexuality are inseparable from marriage and motherhood.

Some older works seem humorous today. Much medical advice is wrong. Topics such as contraception, abortion, and masturbation were ignored or discussed only with great delicacy. *Plain Facts about Sexual Life* (1877) spends twenty-two pages explaining that it would be a "breach of propriety, even in this plain-spoken work" to mention devices used to prevent conception, but the author then devotes more than one hundred pages to exposing the "Solitary Vice" of masturbation of which he also disapproves. His focus is primarily on boys, but he mentions warts, sterility, and cancer of the womb as dangers to girls.[51] By 1968, an edition of a popular marriage manual gives masturbation only a passing mention, and methods of birth control are grouped in a clear appendix (Theodoor H. van de Velde, rev. ed. *Ideal Marriage: Its Physiology and Technique* [New York: Random House, 1968; HQ21.V415 1968]; earlier editions in RBSC).

Recent transformations in public notions of female sexuality and behavior can be traced in the multiple editions and offshoots of *Our Bodies, Ourselves* by the Boston Women's Health Book Collective (New York: Simon and Schuster, 1973; HQ1426.B69, with subsequent editions and title changes).

Sex manuals for the modern woman, heterosexual or homosexual, are plentiful and easy to find. Recent titles show the variety: *Kosher Sex* by Shmuel Boteach (New York: Doubleday, 1999; HQ31.B7255 1999 Overflow), Joel D. Block's *Sex over 50* (West Nyack, N.Y.: Parker Pub., 1999; HQ31.B569 1999), *The Lesbian Sex Book* by Wendy Caster (Boston: Alyson Publications, 1993;

HQ75.5.C37 1993 Overflow), and one subtitled *Fostering Your Child's Healthy Sexual Development* by Beverly Engel (*Beyond the Birds and the Bees* [New York: Pocket Books, 1997; HQ31.E743 1997 Overflow]).

These volumes support research on many topics besides sexual reproduction. They can be used to explore issues of male-female relationships, woman-woman relationships, health and nutrition, exercise, etiquette, morality, religion, fashion, contemporary customs, and parent-child relationships.

BIBLIOGRAPHY:

Campbell, Patricia J. *Sex Education Books for Young Adults, 1892–1979.* New York: R.R. Bowker, 1979. Z7164.S42 C35.

Sahli, Nancy Ann. *Women and Sexuality in America: A Bibliography.* Boston: G.K. Hall, 1984. Z7964.U49 S26 1984 MRR Alc.

SAMPLE LCSH: Sex instruction for women [girls, youth, lesbians]; Woman—Health and hygiene; Women—Health and hygiene; Hygiene, sexual; Gynecology—Popular works; Sexual ethics; Women—Sexual behavior; Birth control; Contraception; Abortion; Beauty, personal.

LC CALL NUMBERS: HQ31, HQ46, HQ51 for many sex-advice titles.

Gift Books and Annuals

In 1832, Miss Mary Ann S. Baird received from her brother a small gilt-edged volume bound in green leather entitled *The Religious Souvenir* (Philadelphia: Key, Mielke & Biddle, 1832; AY11.R4). His inscription to her appears at the front of the Library's copy. The book contains moral and religious stories and poems with nine engravings or "embellishments," as they were often called. Miss Mary Ann was only one of thousands of American women to receive such gifts in the middle half of the nineteenth century. Each year between about 1825 and 1865, publishers issued beautifully bound, well-illustrated literary annuals to be used as gifts for friends and relatives; more than sixty titles a year appeared at midcentury.

The highly fanciful, romantic nature of the stories, delicate flower illustrations, and sentimental poetry in some gift books suggest that women and girls were the primary audience. Great care was taken in both the text and illustrations to adhere to the purest of sentiments. Nothing within the leather-bound covers would offend the most delicate sensibilities. Intended as a "family keepsake," "gift book for all seasons," or "bridal gift," these ornamental works adorned drawing room tables and provided entertainment for the whole year. Among the titles in the General Collections are *Amaranth* (14 vols.; 1831–54; AY11.A35–37), *Rose*

Rawdon, Wright, & Hatch. "The Chief's Daughter." Title page engraving after a painting by John Gadsby Chapman. From Evergreen *(Philadelphia: Carey and Hart, 1847; AY11.E7). General Collections.*

The romanticized images of Native American women that appealed to the book-buying public had little to do with the treatment meted out to indigenous peoples by the U.S. government. The shy "Chief's Daughter" seems a child of nature, yet there is sexual tension in the way she clasps her clothes to her breast. Hundreds of giftbooks published in the middle years of the nineteenth century combined stories and poems by well-known authors with engravings, often based on famous paintings. Artist John Chapman also painted the large *Baptism of Pocahontas* for the Rotunda of the U.S. Capitol.

of Sharon (1840–57; AY11.R6), *Snowflake* (1846; 1849–52; 1854–55; AY11.S58–62), and *Christian Keepsake and Missionary Annual* (1838–40, 1847–49; AY11.C53).

Gift books appeared at a time when the growing middle class had more money to spend conspicuously (a single volume could cost as much as $5.00 at a time when a textile mill worker earned about $3.50 a week) and more leisure to devote to literary pursuits. They featured the work of many American writers and illustrators and contributed to national pride by demonstrating the high level of culture in the United States.

Women regularly contributed stories and poems to the annuals and also served as editors. Lydia Maria Child, Catharine Beecher, Emma Embury, and Hannah Flagg Gould are just four of the many writers represented. Maria Weston Chapman and her sisters issued *Liberty Bell* (Boston, 1839–58; microfilm 01104, reels 491–92; and RBSC), an antislavery gift book that is unusual among such works in its realism and true tales. Researchers can explore images of women and girls in both the engravings and the stories, and examine literary pieces by women authors both well-known and unfamiliar. The Library holds more than one thousand volumes of gift books and annuals in the general, rare book, and microform collections, and has recently acquired *American Literary Annuals and Gift Books, 1825–1865* (New Haven, Conn.: Research Publications, 1966; MicRR guide no. AY10.T52 K57, Microfilm 99/21), an extensive microform set based on Ralph Thompson's bibliography and indexed by E. Bruce Kirkham (see below).

BIBLIOGRAPHY:

Faxon, Frederick W. *Literary Annuals and Gift Books: A Bibliography, 1823–1903.* 1912. Reprint. Pinner, U.K.: Private Libraries Association, 1973. Z6520.G4 F3 1973 MRR Alc.

Kirkham, E. Bruce, and John W. Fink, comps. *Indices to American Literary Annuals and Gift Books, 1825–1865.* New Haven, Conn.: Research Publications, 1975. AY10.T52 K57 MRR Alc, MicRR. Includes full tables of contents and lists of illustrations from the almost five hundred titles listed in Thompson's bibliography, with author, engraver, title, and other indexes.

Thompson, Ralph. *American Literary Annuals & Gift Books, 1825–1865.* 1936. Reprint. Hamden, Conn.: Archon Books, 1967. AY10.T5 1967 MRR Alc.

SAMPLE LCSH: Gift-books (Annuals, etc.) [former heading]; **Gift books** [current heading].

LC CALL NUMBERS: Many gift books and annuals are in class AY11.

Cookbooks, Domestic Manuals, Journals

The subject heading "Cookery, American" produces more than five thousand entries in the Library's online catalog, and many other related works can be found under terms such as "Home economics," "Domestic economy," "Home," "Housewives," "Entertaining," "Kitchens," "Desserts," and individual kinds of food. Cookbooks have always contained more than recipes, and many volumes, especially from the nineteenth century, supply advice on topics such as medicines and nursing, laundry methods, house maintenance, and etiquette.

The vast majority of such works were meant to inform women, and until the 1960s most cookbooks were written by women. Like travel accounts and literature, the volumes served as another public forum for women's words and thoughts. Popular and prolific author Catharine Beecher in her *Treatise on Domestic Economy,* for example, argued for women's superiority to men in all questions relating to morals or manners.[52]

The illustrations, descriptions of home decorations, and types of recipes seem to reflect the world of Anglo, white, middle-class housewives. These women may have been the intended audience, or, perhaps, the authors and publishers were trying to teach other groups to emulate this style of living and ideals. Occasional titles, such as *La Cuisine Creole* by Lafcadio Hearn (1885 edition, RBSC; reprint, Gretna, La.: Pelican Pub., 1990; TX715.H397 1990) or Juliet Corson's *Fifteen Cent Dinners for Workingmen's Families* (its second title page reads, "Fifteen Cent Dinners for Families of Six") (New York: The Author, 1877; TX715.C835), recognize the existence of other types of households. By the twentieth century, cookbooks increasingly reflect the growing diversity and cosmopolitan tastes of the American book-buying public. *The Historical Cookbook of the American Negro,* issued by the National Council of Negro Women, mingles recipes of Harriet Tubman's favorite cornbread with notes on African American organizations and history (Washington: Corporate Press, 1958; TX715.N326). Nilda Luz Rexach's bilingual *The Hispanic-American Cookbook* (Secaucus, N.J.: L. Stuart, 1985; TX716.A1 R49 1985) teaches Latinas and Anglos to make ripe plantain pie, and *Cookin' with Honey: What Literary Lesbians Eat,* edited by Amy Scholder (Ithaca, N.Y.: Firebrand Books, 1996; TX714.C6543 1996), focuses on another group of women.

Recipes and domestic advice appear regularly in magazines. The Library holds complete runs of many women's journals focused on the kitchen and home, such as *Household: Monthly Journal* vii.

DAILY BILLS OF FARE FOR ONE WEEK.

Day	Meal	Cents	Daily total
MONDAY	Breakfast: Boiled Rice with Scalded Milk	15	35
	Dinner: Corned Beef and Cabbage	10	
	Supper: Peas boiled in Stock	10	
TUESDAY	Breakfast: Broth and Bread	10	32
	Dinner: Baked Beans	10	
	Supper: Macaroni with Cheese	12	
WEDNESDAY	Breakfast: Toasted Bread and Scalded Milk	13	33
	Dinner: Stewed Tripe	15	
	Supper: Polenta	5	
THURSDAY	Breakfast: Rice Panada	12	32
	Dinner: Salt Pot-au-feu	10	
	Supper: Lentils stewed in Stock	10	
FRIDAY	Breakfast: Broth and Bread	10	30
	Dinner: Mutton and Turnips	10	
	Supper: Barley boiled in Broth	10	
SATURDAY	Breakfast: Mutton Broth and Bread	10	30
	Dinner: Beef and Potatoes	10	
	Supper: Beans boiled in Broth	10	
SUNDAY	Breakfast: Cocoa and Bread	7	61
	Fried Lentils	10	
	Dinner: Bean Broth	10	
	Haslet Stew	10	
	Suet Roly-poly Pudding	12	
	Supper: Cheese Pudding	12	
Total			$2 53

This leaves a balance of sixty-two (62) cents for extra bread, milk, and butter.

"Daily Bills of Fare for One Week." From Juliet Corson, Fifteen Cent Dinners *(New York, 1877; TX715.C835), p. vii. General Collections.*

For the poor, it is breakfast of bread and broth and one-dish dinners. Cookbooks and domestic journals are full of suggested menus, but most are suitable only for families with money. In 1877 Juliet Corson, superintendent of the New York Cooking School, published fifty thousand copies of this pamphlet, which was to be given to families earning one dollar and fifty cents or less a day. She included advice on shopping, recipes, and a special one-dollar Christmas dinner menu, calling for a five-pound turkey.

THE COOK. 3

Menus for the Week.

[These Menus are the copyrighted property of THE COOK, and must not be republished without due credit being given..

MONDAY.	TUESDAY.	WEDNESDAY.	THURSDAY.
Breakfast.	***Breakfast.***	***Breakfast.***	***Breakfast.***
Melons. Graham Flakes with Cream. Cold Meats. Fried Egg Plant, (260), Cucumbers.	Fruit. Shredded Oats with Cream, (292). Spanish Omelet, (330). Veal Toast.	Fruit. Graham Flakes with Cream. Fried Softshell Crabs, (154). Tomato Salad, (208).	Berries. Cracker Cream Toast. Cold Roast Lamb. Broiled Tomatoes, (4).
Dinner.	***Dinner.***	***Dinner.***	***Dinner.***
Consommé Colbert, (328). Broiled Bluefish. Cucumbers. Breast of Veal, stuffed. Sorrel, Baked Tomatoes. Queen Fritters. Water Cress Salad, (91). Blanc Mange, (320). Water Melon, (326). Cheese, Claret.	Okra Soup, (331). Boiled Sheepshead, Cream butter, (332), Boiled New Potatoes. Roast Capon. Young Carrots, Cream sauce. Stuffed Peppers, (74). Lettuce Salad, (95). Minute Pudding, (152). Canteloupes. Cheese, Coffee.	Vermicelli. Broiled Weakfish, Butter sauce. Cucumbers. Spring Lamb, Mint sauce. Green Peas, Cauliflower. Pineapple Fritters, (315). Tomato Salad. Raspberry Short Cake, (274). Camembert Cheese. Coffee.	Sorrel Soup, (333). Boiled Salmon Trout. Anchovy Sauce. Fricassee of Veal with Peas. Green Corn, String Beans. Fried Egg Plant, (260). Romaine Salad, (238). Peach Dumpling. Canned Cammebert Cheese. Coffee.
FRIDAY, (*Without Meat*).	**FRIDAY, (*With Meat*).**	**SATURDAY.**	**SUNDAY.**
Breakfast.	***Breakfast.***	***Breakfast.***	***Breakfast.***
Berries with Cream. Curry of Crayfish. (50). Tomato Omelet, (229). Breakfast Gems.	Fruit. Smoked Venison with Egg. Broiled Young Carrots. Toasted Muffins.	Cantaloupes. Rice Fritters. Broiled Spring Chicken. Hash Cream Potatoes, (226).	Peaches with Cream. Spring Lamb Chops. Broiled Potatoes, (5). Breakfast Salad.
Dinner.	***Dinner.***	***Dinner.***	***Dinner.***
Clams. Bisque of Clams, (334). Broiled Sheepshead. Cucumbers. Curry of Lobster, (335). Stuffed Tomatoes, (198). Lettuce Salad, (95). Cold Cabinet Pudding, (158). Water Melon. Rhine Wine.	Consommé Macaroni. Boiled Striped Bass. Sauce Bearnaise, (19). Leg of Mutton. Green Corn, Young Beets. Peach Fritters. Watercress Salad. Nopolitain Cream. Macaroons. Cheese, Claret.	Clams. Veal Broth with Rice. Fillets of Spanish Mackerel. Cucumbers. Fried Frogs Sauce Remoulade. Cauliflower. Roast Gosling. Tomato Mayonnaise, (263). French Rice Pudding. Cheese, Fruit, Coffee.	Clams. Cream of Cauliflower. Baked Bluefish. Sweetbreads à la Jardiniere. Stuffed Artichokes, (94). Roast Squab on toast. Escarole Salad, (267). Cold Custard, (120). Pineapple Salad, (3). Cheese, Claret.

THE NUMBERS IN THE MENUS ARE FOR REFERENCE TO THE FORMULAS IN "SEASONABLE RECIPES," ACCORDING TO WHICH DISHES SO MARKED SHOULD BE PREPARED.

"Menus for the Week." From The Cook, *July 20, 1885, p. 3 (TX1.C75). General Collections.*

For the affluent, a sample morning meal might consist of fruit, shredded oats with cream, Spanish omelet, and veal toast. This week's menu, also issued in New York, shows the variety of foods and number of dishes per meal available to the middle class. The contrast with the meagerness and the monotony of the diet of the poor is sharp. This weekly magazine of "Domestic Culinary Art for All Housekeepers" from 1885 also listed retail prices for food in Boston, New York, and Philadelphia.

Devoted to the Interests of the American Housewife, published in Brattleboro, Vermont (1869–1900; TX1.H76), and *Household Magazine,* originating in Topeka, Kansas (1900–1958; TX1.H78). Scanning such magazines presents a panorama of issues that interested small town and rural women for more than ninety years. These and other "domestic" journals supply information on almost any topic imaginable—prices, nutrition, health concerns, technological advances, women and work, women and war, women's place, male-female relationships, children, in-laws, modesty, cleanliness, religion, sports and recreation, sex, cosmetics, and fashion. "Food and Morals," "The Effort to Obtain Pure Water," "Wartime Kitchen Gadgets," articles on suffrage, and women's rights appear between recipes and fashion stories. Certain issues such as weight, body shape, and "how to please your man" recur again and again over the years. Historians in many fields will find gold in these rich and varied collections.

BIBLIOGRAPHY:

Axford, Lavonne B., comp. *English Language Cookbooks, 1600–1973.* Detroit: Gale Research, 1976. Z5776.G2 A9 MRR Alc. Provides a useful chronological index.

Dyer, Annie Isabel. *Guide to Literature of Home and Family Life: A Classified Bibliography for Home Economics.* Philadelphia: J.B. Lippincott, 1924. Z5775.D98 MRR Alc. List of magazines and trade journals, pp. 218–31.

Lowenstein, Eleanor. *Bibliography of American Cookery Books, 1742–1860.* Worcester, Mass.: American Antiquarian Society, 1972. Z5776.G2 L68 1972 MRR Alc.

Newman, Jacqueline M. *Melting Pot: An Annotated Bibliography and Guide to Food and Nutrition Information for Ethnic Groups in America.* 2nd ed. New York: Garland, 1993. Z7914.F63 N48 1993 SciRR.

SAMPLE LCSH: Cookery; Cookery, American; Domestic economy; Home economics; Food; Home; Housewives; Family.

LC CALL NUMBERS: TX1 (cookery and housekeeping periodicals).

Game and Hobby Books

Works on recreational activities prove unusual sources for many historical research topics, such as sex roles, education—both physical and moral, clothing, parental roles, and attitudes toward leisure and work, to name a few. In 1910, *Harper's Handy-Book for Girls* "points the way to all those delightful home arts and industries that the average girl loves," including decorating her own room, arts and crafts (with "simple carpentering, wood-carving, and metal work"), needle fancy work, and embroidery.[53] Because "every girl should regard the cultivation of some particular hobby as a necessity," author Elizabeth Chesser, writing in 1914, recommends learning languages (for business and travel), gardening (for closeness to nature), and collecting (to develop taste and for possible profit).[54]

Often these books show, once again, how relatively easy it is to find information about white middle- and upper-class girls. Children from other groups played some of the same games and participated in similar activities, but a researcher would find that difficult to prove from the texts and illustrations in these volumes. Life stories told by former slaves put "leisure time" in perspective. One woman remembered playing hide-and-seek and see-sawing, but remarked, "we never did have very many games, cause Maser he put us to work soon as we got big enough to work."[55]

Interest in women's sports blossomed in the last quarter of the twentieth century. More women and girls participated in sports from childhood to professional levels, and more authors wrote about them. Of the ten books in the General Collections on the All-American Girls Professional Baseball League (1943–54), all were published after 1992. Sports figures like Babe Didrikson Zaharias and Jackie Joyner-Kersee penned their autobiographies, and others wrote biographies of them for adults and for children. The Spaulding Company, makers of sports equipment, issued a series of guides to promote athletics for women. The 1930 edition of *Outdoor Baseball for Girls and Women* recommends that baseball be "an important part of the sports curriculum of every American girl" and that it is "especially important for girls in that it offers a rich opportunity for training in social adjustment."[56] Because of good subject headings and published bibliographies, books on women's sports are usually easy to find.

The Library holds many books and periodicals on other topics related to recreational and leisure activities. A few subjects include: toys, dolls, exercise, sex discrimination in sports, physical education for girls, Title IX, and lesbians in sports.

BIBLIOGRAPHY:

Remley, Mary L. *Women in Sport: An Annotated Bibliography and Resource Guide, 1900–1990.* Boston: G.K. Hall, 1991. Z7963.S6 R45 1991 MRR Alc.

Shoebridge, Michele. *Women in Sport: A Select Bibliography.* New York: Mansell, 1987. Z7963.S6 S56 1987 MRR Alc.

Wilmeth, Don B. *American and English Popular Entertainment: A Guide to Information Sources.* Detroit: Gale Research, 1980. Z7511.W53 MRR Alc.

SAMPLE LCSH: Leisure—United States [or name of state]; Hobbies; Handicraft; Games; Games for girls; Sports for women; [Name of sport] for women [or for children or girls]; Physical education for women [or children]; Sex discrimination in sports.

LC CALL NUMBERS: GV439 for physical education for girls. GV1201 and GV1203 for books and periodicals on games and hobbies. These classes also include non-U.S. materials and books for men and boys. For many topics there are no subject headings solely for works on women and girls.

School Primers and Readers

The Library holds more than two thousand elementary school primers and readers. These small volumes show the vocabulary, concepts, and literature considered appropriate for children at various age levels in different time periods. The texts and illustrations depict clothing, homes, and toys, as well as conventional views of children and adults and activities thought suitable for each sex. In a lesson from the *Franklin Second Reader* (1873) a mother advises her daughter to be good, clean, tidy, to do as she is bidden, and to attend to her sewing.[57] More than seventy years later, *School Friends* (1951) explains that mother helps us by cooking, sewing, and shopping for food, and father helps us by carpentry, lawn mowing, and fire building.[58] You can clearly see cultural norms, contemporary values, and gender stereotypes that children are taught in their school readers.

These primers, like college catalogs, education association journals, or histories of individual schools, are examples from the vast quantity of material available for studying the education of girls and women at the Library of Congress. School readers also serve historians in other fields such as sports and language.

SEARCH TIPS: Similar works, especially those published before 1801, can be found in the Rare Book and Microform Reading Rooms.

SAMPLE LCSH: Primers; Readers; Readers and speakers.

LC CALL NUMBERS: PE1117, PE1119–21, PE1123–24 (religious readers), and a few titles in PE1130.I6 (Native American readers) and PE1130.N4 (African American readers).

College Catalogs

The Library's extensive holdings of nineteenth-century and twentieth-century college catalogs are an excellent example of a primary source that can be mined by scholars from many disciplines. For education scholars, the benefits are obvious. They can easily trace curriculum variations (or compare and contrast them to men's curricula), study regulations and requirements, or observe regional, class, and racial differences. For the genealogist these volumes give names of students and faculty with home addresses. A sports historian can track alterations in physical education requirements, team sports, or styles of gym suits. Religious historians might follow shifts in compulsory church attendance and religious affiliation, or the size of church groups or choirs.

The wealth of detail on costs, classes, clothing, manners, required reading, visiting hours, buildings, and faculty is extraordinary. At Vassar, in its opening year, 1865, it was "specially desired that the dress of students shall not be expensive . . . but rather such clothing as will not be injured by active sports and vigorous exertion." Each student was to bring thick boots, a waterproof cloak, and napkin rings. Annual tuition was a hefty $350, with oil painting or riding costing an additional $60.[59] In 1903 students at the Girls Industrial College in Denton, Texas, could choose to study traditional academic subjects, domestic science (cookery or dairy work), commercial work (commercial law, stenography, bookkeeping), or domestic arts (dressmaking and millinery). In recommending the school, the catalog stresses that "Denton is a clean town morally. There are no saloons here."[60]

College yearbooks, alumni or alumnae magazines, and other educational publications can also furnish fascinating historical data. The Library does not hold all years for all colleges; for the early years especially, major institutions in the Northeast are better represented. Current collections of yearbooks are slim, but college catalogs from 1973 to the present are available on microfiche (MicRR).

SAMPLE LCSH: College catalogs rarely have subject headings. For all items published by educational institutions, search for the name of the institution as a corporate author. For alumni directories try: **[Name of institution]—Registers**

This chapter describes a few of the most noteworthy types of resources for the study of American women's history. More exist—almanacs, encyclopedias, dictionaries, interior decorating manuals, technical reports, auction catalogs, census compilations, child-care manuals, and statistical sources. The list goes on. You will find others, and you will examine those described in this chapter and put them to new uses. The study of women's lives has grown more sophisticated and innovative over the past thirty years as it has become clear that everything is subject to gender analysis. Men's studies is developing as a separate field and giving insights to women's history. These trends should continue, especially if the incredible materials in the General Collections are joined with those described in the following chapters.

POINTS TO REMEMBER

1 Consult with reference librarians regularly for advice on your search strategy.
2 Search *Library of Congress Subject Headings* ("Red Books") for the best subject headings.
3 Look for published bibliographies on your subject.
4 Ask for appropriate microform collections.
5 Don't stop your research with the General Collections. Wonderful sources exist in the special collections.

I would like to thank my colleagues in the Humanities and Social Sciences Division who cheered me on through the long months I concentrated on this guide and who also worked extra hours on the reference desk so I had time for research and writing. The following people read sections of my chapter, suggested sources, and provided valuable comments: Cheryl Adams, Paul Q. Baker, Betty M. Culpepper, David J. Kelly, David Kresh, Thomas Mann, Ardie S. Myers, Marilyn K. Parr, James P. Sweany, Barbara B. Walsh, Kathy Woodrell, and Abby Yochelson. For the sections on Library of Congress subject headings and classification, I am grateful to Thomas Mann (again), Thompson A. Yee, and Lynn M. El-Hoshy for excellent suggestions based on expert knowledge. Susan Ware gave some good advice at a crucial moment. Janice E. Ruth and Barbara Orbach Natanson commented on numerous drafts of this chapter, to its great benefit, for which I am grateful.

Official Program—Woman Suffrage Procession. *Cover illustration by Dale for the National American Woman Suffrage Association parade, Washington, D.C., March 3, 1913. Lot 5541. Prints and Photographs Division. LC-USZC4-2996.*

The dramatic flair of the program's cover shows vividly the organizers' intent to draw attention to their momentous event. The cover also displays recurring motifs of the U.S. suffrage movement–the herald sounding a horn, the motto "Votes for Women," and the colors purple, gold, and white. Such imagery was easily recognized by the general public and served as unifying symbols for those within the suffrage movement.

MOB HURTS 300 SUFFRAGISTS AT CAPITAL PARADE[1]

"There would be nothing like this happen if you would stay at home."[2]

On Monday, March 3, 1913, clad in a white cape astride a white horse, lawyer Inez Milholland led the great woman suffrage parade down Pennsylvania Avenue in the nation's capital. Behind her stretched a long line with nine bands, four mounted brigades, three heralds, over twenty floats, and more than 5,000 marchers.[3] Women from countries that had enfranchised women held the place of honor in the first section of the procession. Then came the "Pioneers" who had been struggling for so many decades to secure women's right to vote. The next sections celebrated working women, who were grouped by occupation and wearing appropriate garb–nurses in uniform, women farmers, homemakers, women doctors and pharmacists, actresses, librarians, college women in academic gowns. Harriet Hifton of the Library of Congress Copyright Division led the librarians' contingent. The state delegations followed, and finally the separate section for male supporters of women's suffrage. All had come from around the country to "march in a spirit of protest against the present political organization of society, from which women are excluded."[4]

The procession began late, but all went well for the first few blocks. Soon, however, the crowds, mostly men in town for the following day's inauguration of Woodrow Wilson, surged into the street making it almost impossible for the marchers to pass. Occasionally only a single file could move forward. Women were jeered, tripped, grabbed, shoved, and many heard "indecent epithets" and "barnyard conversation."[5] Instead of protecting the parade, the police "seemed to enjoy all the ribald jokes and laughter and part participated in them."[6] One policeman explained that they should stay at home where they belonged. The men in the procession heard shouts of "Henpecko" and "Where are your skirts?" As one witness explained, "There was a sort of spirit of levity connected with the crowd. They did not regard the affair very seriously."[7]

But to the women, the event was very serious. Helen Keller "was so exhausted and unnerved by the experience in attempting to reach a grandstand . . . that she was unable to speak later at Continental hall [*sic*]."[8] Two ambulances "came and went constantly for six hours, always impeded and at times actually opposed, so that doctor and driver literally had to fight their way to give succor to the injured."[9] One hundred marchers were taken to the local Emergency Hospital. Before the afternoon was over, Secretary of War Henry L. Stimson, responding to a request from the chief of police, authorized the use of a troop of cavalry from nearby Fort Myer to help control the crowd.[10]

Despite enormous difficulties, many of those in the parade completed the route. When the procession reached the Treasury Building, one hundred women and children presented an allegorical tableau written especially for the event to show "those ideals toward which both men and women have been struggling through the ages and toward which, in co-operation and equality, they will continue to strive." The pageant began with "The Star Spangled Banner" and the commanding figure of Columbia dressed in national colors, emerging from the great columns at the top of the Treasury Building steps. Charity entered, her path strewn with rose petals. Liberty followed to the "Triumphal March" from "Aida" and a dove of peace was released. In the final tableau, Columbia, surrounded by Justice, Charity, Liberty, Peace, and Hope, all in flowing robes and colorful scarves, with trumpets sounding, stood to watch the oncoming procession.[11] The *New York Times* described the pageant as "one of the most impressively beautiful spectacles ever staged in this country."[12]

At the railway station a few blocks away, president-elect Wilson and the presidential party arrived to little fanfare. One of the incoming president's staff asked, "'Where are all the

Suffrage Parade 3/3/13 *[Inez Milholland Boissevain]. Photograph, March 3, 1913. George Grantham Bain Collection (Lot 11052–2). Prints and Photographs Division. LC-USZ62–77359.*

Mirroring the cover of the program, lawyer Inez Milholland rode astride as the first of four mounted heralds. In her short life she shared with many of her fellow marchers a commitment to social reform. She joined organizations striving to improve the working conditions of children and the lives of African Americans. She was also a strong supporter of the shirtwaist and laundry workers. Three years after the parade, she collapsed and died at age thirty during a western suffrage lecture tour.

Florence F. Noyes as "Liberty" in Suffrage Pageant. *Photograph, March 3, 1913. George Grantham Bain Collection (Lot 11052–2). Prints and Photographs Division. LC-USZ62–70382.*

According to the Washington Post, *twenty thousand people fought madly for position near the Treasury Building to watch the allegorical pageant on the ideals toward which women and men have struggled through the ages. Florence Noyes, an interpretive dancer who participated in the Greek revival movement, arranged the dances for the allegory and played the role of Liberty. It is unlikely that the performers recognized the irony in women dressing themselves as abstract concepts and imitating the generic use of the female figure so often portrayed by male artists.*

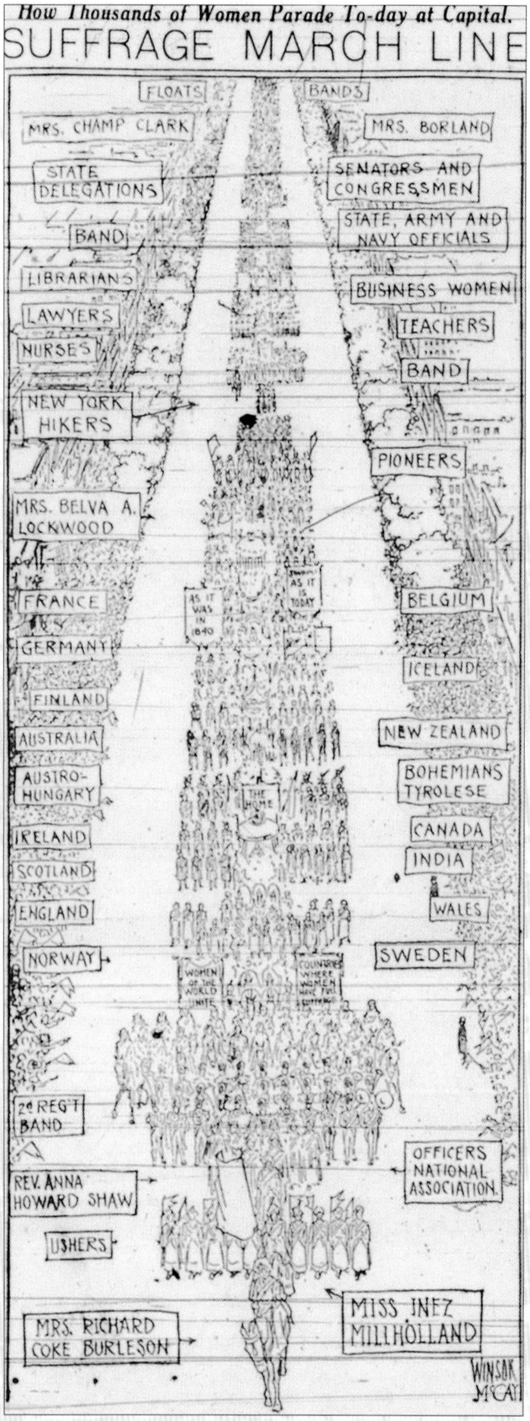

Winsor McCay. "Suffrage March Line." Drawing for the New York Evening Journal, *March 4, 1913, p. 2, col. 4. News MF 1945. Serial and Government Publications Division.*

An artist's sketch shows orderly crowds lining the avenue as the carefully organized procession marches by. Alice Paul and her committee had less than three months to plan the event and to arrange for women from countries with women's suffrage to join groups of American women representing different occupations. Despite diligent preparation, unruly crowds were to destroy the neat symmetry of the parade.

people?' —'Watching the suffrage parade,' the police told him."[13] The next day Wilson would be driven down the miraculously clear, police-lined Pennsylvania Avenue cheered on by a respectful crowd.

The Washington march came at a time when the suffrage movement badly needed an infusion of vigor, a new way to capture public and press interest. Women had been struggling for the right to vote for more than sixty years, and although progress had been made in recent years on the state level with six western states granting women suffrage, the movement had stalled on the national level. Delegates from the National American Woman Suffrage Association (NAWSA, and its predecessor associations) had arrived in the nation's capital every year since 1869 to present petitions asking that women be enfranchised. Despite this annual pilgrimage and the millions of signatures collected, debate on the issue had never even reached the floor of the House of Representatives.[14] In 1912, Teddy Roosevelt's Progressive Party became the first major political party to pledge itself "to the task of securing equal suffrage to men and women alike."[15] But the Progressives lost the election.

In November 1912, as suffrage leaders were casting about for new means to ensure their victory, Alice Paul arrived at the NAWSA annual convention in Philadelphia. A twenty-eight-year-old Quaker from New Jersey, she had recently returned to the United States fresh from helping the militant branch of the British suffrage movement. She had been arrested repeatedly, been imprisoned, gone on a hunger strike, and been forcibly fed.[16] Paul was full of ideas for the American movement. She asked to be allowed to organize a suffrage parade to be held in Washington at the time of the president's inauguration, thus ensuring maximum press attention. NAWSA accepted her offer when she promised to raise the necessary funds and gave her the title chairman of the Congressional Committee.[17] In December 1912, she moved to Washington where she discovered that the committee she chaired had no headquarters and most of the members had moved away or died.[18]

Undaunted, Alice Paul convened the first meeting of her new committee on January 2, 1913, in the newly rented basement headquarters at 1420 F Street, NW. She started raising funds; according to one friend, "it was very difficult to refuse Alice Paul."[19] She and the others she recruited worked nonstop for two months. By March 3 this fledgling committee had organized and found the money for a major suffrage parade with floats, banners, speakers, and a twenty-page official program. The total cost of the event was $14,906.08, a princely sum in 1913, when the average annual wage was $621.[20] The programs and tableau each cost more than $1,000.[21]

Suffrage groups across the nation contributed to the success of the procession. From its New York headquarters, NAWSA urged suffrage supporters to gather in Washington:

> **WHY YOU MUST MARCH**
>
> Because this is the most conspicuous and important demonstration that has ever been attempted by suffragists in this country.
>
> Because this parade will be taken to indicate the importance of the suffrage movement by the press of the country and the thousands of spectators from all over the United States gathered in Washington for the Inauguration.[22]

This call was answered. On February 12, with cameras clicking, sixteen "suffrage pilgrims" left New York City to walk to Washington for the parade. Many other people joined the original marchers at various stages, and the New York State Woman Suffrage Association's journal crowed that "no propaganda work undertaken by the State Association and the Party has ever achieved such publicity."[23] One of the New York group, Elizabeth Freeman, dressed as a gypsy and drove a yellow, horse-drawn wagon decorated with Votes for Women symbols and filled with suffrage literature, a sure way to attract publicity.[24] Two weeks after the procession, five New York suffragists, including Elizabeth Freeman, reported to the Bronx motion picture studio of the Thomas A. Edison Company to make a talking picture known as a Kinetophone, which included a cylinder recording of one-minute speeches by each of the women. This film with synchronized sound was shown in vaudeville houses where it was "hooted, jeered and hissed" by audiences.[25]

NAWSA officers prepared a strong letter to the president-elect for the "New York hikers" to carry to Washington. This letter

Rea Irvin. "Ancient History." Cover illustration from Life, *February 20, 1913; AP101.L6. General Collections.*

In suffrage cartoons women are often the aggressors, but on the day of the parade it was the men who threatened and harangued the women. The central figure resembles a classicized Susan B. Anthony in a liberty cap with anachronistic glasses and umbrella. Many of the illustrations in this "Husbandette's Number" depict large, fierce women with small, weak men.

urged that women's suffrage be achieved during his presidency and warned that the women of the United States "will watch your administration with an intense interest such as has never before been focused upon the administration of any of your predecessors."[26] Despite the tone of the letter, when the group reached Princeton, where Woodrow Wilson lived, they requested only "an audience for not more than two minutes in Washington as soon after your arrival as possible."[27] Less than two weeks after his inauguration, Wilson received a suffrage delegation led by Alice Paul, who chose to make the case for suffrage verbally and apparently did not deliver the hikers' letter. In response to the women's impassioned plea, he replied that he had never given the subject any thought, but that it "will receive my most careful consideration."[28] Hardly the whole-hearted endorsement sought by the women.

The mistreatment of the marchers by the crowd and the police roused great indignation and led to congressional hearings where more than 150 witnesses recounted their experiences; some complained about the lack of police protection, and others defended the police. Before the inquiries were over, the superintendent of police of the District of Columbia had lost his job.

The public outcry and its accompanying press coverage proved a windfall for the suffragists. The *Woman's Journal* proclaimed, "Parade Struggles to Victory Despite Disgraceful Scenes, Nation Aroused by Open Insults to Women–Cause Wins Popular Sympathy."[29] The *New York Tribune* announced, "Capital Mobs Made Converts to Suffrage."[30] At its next convention, in November 1913, NAWSA praised the "amazing and most creditable year's work" of Alice Paul's Congressional Committee, stating that "their single-mindedness and devotion has been remarkable and the whole movement in the country has been wonderfully furthered by the series of important events which have taken place in Washington, beginning with the great parade the day before the inauguration of the president."[31]

Not one to mince words, famous reporter Nellie Bly, who rode as one of the heralds in the parade, bluntly stated in the headline to her article on the march—"Suffragists Are Men's Superiors." With uncanny prescience, she added that it would take at least until 1920 for all states to grant woman suffrage.[32] Despite the pageantry of 1913, Nellie Bly was right. It was to take seven more years before the Nineteenth Amendment to the Constitution, which gave

Eliz. Freeman enrout to Wash'n. *Photograph, February 17, 1913. George Grantham Bain Collection (Lot 11052–2). Prints and Photographs Division. LC-USZ62–53218.*

Dressed as a gypsy, with her yellow cart and "Newark bargain" horse, Elizabeth Freeman was one of the most popular and colorful of the New York hikers. She used the wagon as a speaker's platform and to carry pamphlets supporting women's suffrage.

WOMAN'S JOURNAL
AND SUFFRAGE NEWS

VOL. XLIV. NO. 10 | SATURDAY, MARCH 8, 1913 | FIVE CENTS

PARADE STRUGGLES TO VICTORY DESPITE DISGRACEFUL SCENES

Nation Aroused by Open Insults to Women—Cause Wins Popular Sympathy—Congress Orders Investigation—Striking Object Lesson

Washington has been disgraced. Equal suffrage has scored a great victory. Thousands of indifferent women have been aroused. Influential men are incensed and the United States Senate demands an investigation of the treatment given the suffragists at the National Capital on Monday.

Ten thousand women from all over the country had planned a magnificent parade and pageant to take place in Washington on March 3. Artists, pageant leaders, designers, women of influence and renown were ready to give a wonderful and beautiful piece of suffrage work to the public that would throng the National Capital for the inauguration festivities. The suffragists were ready; the whole procession started down Pennsylvania avenue, when the police protection, that had been promised, failed them, and a disgraceful scene followed. The crowd surged into the space which had been marked off for the paraders, and the leaders of the suffrage movement were compelled to push their way through a mob of the worst element in Washington and vicinity. Women were spit upon, slapped in the face, tripped up, pelted with burning cigar stubs, and insulted by jeers and obscene language too vile to print or repeat.

The cause of all the trouble is apparent when the facts are known. The police authorities in Washington opposed every attempt to have a suffrage parade at all. Having been forbidden a place in the inaugural procession, the suffragists asked to have a procession of their own on March 3. They were finally told that they could have a procession but that it could not be on Pennsylvania avenue, but must be on a side street. At last they got permission to have the suffrage parade on the avenue, and asked that traffic be excluded from the street during the parade. For a long time this was denied, and only on Saturday were they successful.

Everything was at last arranged; it was a glorious day; ten thousand women were ready to do their part to make the parade beautiful to behold, to make it a credit to womanhood and to demonstrate the strength of the movement for their enfranchisement.

The police were determined, however, and they had their way. Their attempt to afford the marchers protection and keep the space of the avenue free for the suffrage procession was the flimsiest sham. Police officers stood by with folded arms and grinned while the picked women of the land were insulted and roughly abused by an ignorant and uncouth mob.

Miss Alice Paul and other suffragists were compelled to drive their automobiles down the avenue to separate the crowds so the suffragists with the banners and floats could pass. The police officials say their force was inadequate to handle the crowds, but it is noted that there was no disorder on the avenue during the inaugural procession. It is stated that federal troops were offered to the chief of police for the suffrage procession, but that he refused their aid.

At any rate, assistance was finally called from Fort Myer and mounted soldiers drove back the crowd so that a straggling line of marchers could pass through.

Not only were the suffragists bitterly disappointed in having the effect

(Continued on Page 78)

AMENDMENT WINS IN NEW JERSEY

Easy Victory in Assembly 46 to 5—Equal Suffrage Enthusiasm Runs High

The New Jersey Legislature passed the woman suffrage amendment in the Assembly last week by a vote of 46 to 5. The Senate had already voted favorably 14 to 5.

A large delegation of suffragists crowded the galleries, and when the overwhelming vote was announced there was a scene of great enthusiasm. Women stood in their seats and waved handkerchiefs and "votes for women" flags and cheered themselves hoarse.

Dr. Jekyll Becomes Mr. Hyde

Opposition was confined exclusively to the old sentimental arguments.

(Continued on Page 79)

MICHIGAN AGAIN CAMPAIGN STATE

Senate Passes Suffrage Amendment 26 to 5 and Battle Is Now On

Michigan is again a campaign State after a short lapse of four months. The amendment will go to the voters on April 7. The State-wide feeling that the women were defrauded of victory last fall will help the suffragists.

The final action of the Legislature was taken last week, when the Senate, by a vote of 26 to 5, passed the suffrage amendment, with a slight amendment to make the requirements for foreign-born women the same as those for male immigrants.

Governor Watches Debate

The debate in the Senate lasted an hour and a quarter, and was characterized by the persistent efforts of Senator Weadock and a few others to tack on crippling amendments. Several suggestions, including the disabling of women for holding office or serving on juries, were voted down in quick succession.

Gov. Ferris was among the visitors who crowded the chamber and gallery. Mrs. Clara B. Arthur, Mrs. Thomas R. Henderson and Mrs. Wilbur Brotherton, of Detroit; Mrs. Jennie Law Hardy, of Tecumseh, and other State leaders were present, supported by a large delegation of Lansing suffragists.

The final stand of the opposition was made by Senator Murtha in the hope of putting off the submission till November, 1914, and this also failed.

Of the five who opposed the measure on the final roll-call, three were from Detroit.

A complete campaign of organization and education has been mapped out by the State Association. The

(Continued on Page 74.)

General Rosalie Jones in Pilgrim Costume; Miss Inez Milholland on White Steed Leading the Parade; One of the Scores of Imposing Floats; One View of the Procession

Woman's Journal and Suffrage News, *March 8, 1913. Front page. JK1881.N357, sec. 1, no. 50 NAWSA. Rare Book and Special Collections Division.*

The organizers designed the parade to be visually effective and to attract national media attention, but it was actions of men and the inaction of police that elicited much of the press coverage with newspapers crying "Suffragists and the Mob" and "Huge Mob Blocks Suffrage Parade." Unruly crowds may have disrupted the procession, but they led to more and longer news stories and won sympathy for the cause.

women full rights to vote, finally passed both houses of Congress and was ratified by the required thirty-six states.

Behind this description of the 1913 Washington Suffrage Procession—one event in the long history of women's campaign for suffrage in the United States—lies a wealth of telling detail and the human stories that make history interesting and meaningful. A rich variety of suffrage materials in many formats lie scattered throughout the collections of the Library of Congress awaiting the curious reader in search of further details and other stories, of the sounds and sights of the fight for the vote.

The organizers of the parade intended its floats and pageant to have visual appeal for the media and thus to attract publicity for the movement. Photographers recorded the women's activities for newspaper readers and these images live on in newspapers and photo archives. Easily the single most heavily represented suffrage event in the Prints and Photographs Division's holdings, the march appears in more than forty images, including news photographs of the hike from New York to Washington, the marchers and crowds on Pennsylvania Avenue, and the pageant performed at the Treasury Building. A surviving stereograph of the parade suggests that publishers of these images, which appeared in three dimensions when seen through a special viewer, expected that the public would be willing to pay for a permanent memento of the event.[33]

The women's march also inspired cartoonists, some of whom likened the suffrage movement to colonial America's fight for independence. James Harrison Donahey, for example, substituted women for men in a cartoon based on the famous painting "Washington Crossing the Delaware." In another such cartoon, women play the fife and drums in an imitation of Archibald Willard's painting "Spirit of '76."[34] Suffrage and antisuffrage cartoons appeared frequently in magazines and newspapers of the day.[35]

Vivid details about the march also turn up in a seemingly unlikely source. The *Yidishes Tageblatt* (Jewish daily news), a Yiddish-language publication from New York City with a circulation of seventy thousand, devoted two columns to the women's parade. The article claimed that twenty-five lost children stayed in police stations overnight and eighteen men asked the police to find their wives.[36]

A 1974 magazine interview with eighty-nine-year-old Alice Paul reveals the problems for the historian of hindsight and memory. In two major respects Miss Paul's recollections of the event, sixty-one years after it occurred, differ from those of contemporary sources. She remembers a fairly peaceable parade in which the police did as well as could be expected: "Of course, we did hear a lot of shouted insults, which we always expected. You know the usual things about why aren't you home in the kitchen where you belong. But it wasn't anything violent."[37] The Senate hearings, on the other hand, show that many people felt the crowd was hostile and the police inept.

The other major point in which Paul's memory differs from contemporary accounts is on the question of the place of African American women in the procession. In her view, the "greatest hurdle" in planning the parade came when Mary Church Terrell wanted to bring a group from the National Association of Colored Women. NAWSA had stated firmly that all women were welcome, but Paul knew "members from the South said they wouldn't march." She recalls that the compromise was to have white women march first, then the men's section, and finally the Negro women's section.[38] A different picture appears in the *Crisis,* the journal of the National Association for the Advancement of Colored People. After initial difficulties and attempts to segregate the African American women, "telegrams and protests poured in and eventually the colored women marched according to their State and occupation without

James Donahey. Gen. Rosalie Jones crossing the Delaware. *Cartoon drawing for the* Cleveland Plain Dealer, *February 15, 1913. Prints and Photographs Division. LC-USZ62–55985.*

The women's campaign was a source of many cartoons—for and against suffrage—in newspapers and magazines throughout the country. In this favorable image, General Rosalie Jones, who led the New York hikers to Washington, is likened to General George Washington leading his troops through dangerous waters to his victory against enemy forces. Support for suffrage divided many families, often along generational lines—Jones's mother, Mrs. Oliver Livingston Jones, greeted her daughter on her arrival in Washington, but she was planning an anti-suffrage automobile tour for that summer.

let or hindrance."[39] Ida B. Wells-Barnett was among those who objected strongly to a segregated parade; she walked with the Illinois delegation.

Moving beyond sources related to a single event to examine other aspects of the history of women's suffrage, researchers visiting the Library of Congress will discover collections of major significance in many different reading rooms. Records of the National Woman's Party, the National American Woman Suffrage Association (NAWSA), and the National Association of Colored Women (on microfilm), as well as the family papers of the Blackwells and the La Follettes, all contain material relating to the effort to enfranchise women (MSS). The libraries of Susan B. Anthony and of NAWSA are preserved as separate collections (RBSC). The National Photo Company, George Grantham Bain, and League of Women Voters collections each contain relevant images (P&P). Innumerable journal articles, autobiographies, and extensive secondary literature address the subject (GenColl, MicRR). Congressional hearings, related laws (LAW), and contemporary press coverage of the entire movement (N&CPR) are also available. These and many other sources open vast avenues for continuing the investigation of the long and fascinating fight for women's right to vote.

One of the great rewards of research is the exhilaration of new discoveries—uncovering a new fact, locating an unknown photograph, or hearing the voice of a person you are studying. At the Library of Congress you can hold a letter written by Alice Paul, follow the path of the suffrage parade on a map of Washington, or scan old newspapers for Nellie Bly's forthright words. If you listen carefully, our foremothers will speak to you. If you tell their story, they will live again.

This essay could not have been written without contributions by Janice Ruth, MSS; Georgia Higley, N&CPR; Barbara Natanson, P&P; Rosemary Plakas, RBSC; Rosemary Hanes, MBRS; Peggy Pearlstein, AMED; and Audrey Fischer, PAO.

Background Image: "Exhibit no. 36." Halftone photograph from Suffrage Parade, Hearings *(Washington: GPO, 1913; JK1888 1913b), opposite p. 502. General Collections.*

A copy of one of the many photographs entered as evidence of the misbehavior of the crowds during the suffrage procession appeared in the report on the Senate inquiry. Parade supporters demonstrated that the police had not kept the route clear and that the women were in danger.

THE WORLD.  PAGES 21 TO 28.

NEW YORK, SUNDAY, JANUARY 26, 1890.

ROUND THE WORLD WITH NELLIE BLY.

CUT OUT THIS GAME, PLACE IT ON A TABLE OR PASTE IT ON CARDBOARD AND PLAY ACCORDING TO SIMPLE DIRECTIONS BELOW.

NELLIE BLY

THE WORLDS GLOBE GIRCLER

GOOD BY PHILEAS! — JULES VERNE

1st DAY — THE START
2nd DAY — CLEAR — GO AHEAD 3 DAYS
3rd DAY — RAIN — GO BACK 1 DAY
4th DAY — STORM — GO BACK 2 DAYS
5th DAY — ICEBERGS — GO BACK TO PORT
6th DAY — CLEARING — GO TO SOUTHAMPTON
7th DAY — FAIR SAILING
8th DAY — SOUTHAMPTON — GO TO AMIENS
9th DAY — AMIENS — ONE MORE THROW
10th DAY — GO BACK 5 DAYS
11th DAY — BRINDISI — GO BACK 2 DAYS
12th DAY
13th DAY — LOSE NEXT THROW
14th DAY — GO TO 18th DAY
15th DAY — ISMAILIA
16th DAY — RED SEA
17th DAY — GO BACK 5 DAYS
18th DAY — STRIKES A ROCK — GO BACK 18 DAYS
19th DAY — ADEN — GO AHEAD 5 DAYS
20th DAY — ARABIAN SEA — ANOTHER THROW
21st DAY — LOSE 2 THROWS
22nd DAY — INDIAN OCEAN
23rd DAY — INDIAN OCEAN
24th DAY — INDIAN OCEAN
25th DAY — INDIAN OCEAN
26th DAY — COLOMBO
27th DAY — CEYLON — LOSE NEXT THROW
28th DAY — BAY OF BENGAL — GO TO SIAM
29th DAY — BAY OF BENGAL
30th DAY — MALACCA STRAITS — PIRATE SHIP — GO BACK 5 DAYS
31st DAY — OFF SUMATRA
32nd DAY — MALACCA STRAITS — GO AHEAD 1 DAY
33rd DAY — SINGAPORE
34th DAY — SIAM — GO AHEAD 2 DAYS
35th DAY — CHINA SEA
36th DAY — SIMOON — GO BACK 10 DAYS
37th DAY — BORNEO — GO BACK 5 DAYS
38th DAY — CHINA SEA — GO BACK 2 DAYS
39th DAY — CHINA SEA — GO BACK 3 DAYS
40th DAY — HONG KONG — GO TO 18th DAY
41st DAY — 1 MORE THROW
42nd DAY — CHINA
43rd DAY — CANTON — LOSE NEXT THROW
44th DAY
45th DAY
47th DAY — GO BACK 1 DAY
48th DAY
49th DAY — YOKOHAMA — GO AHEAD 5 DAYS
50th DAY — YOKOHAMA — LOSE NEXT THROW
51st DAY — YEDDO — ONE MORE THROW
52nd DAY — YOKOHAMA
53rd DAY — YOKOHAMA — DELAY — GO BACK 5 DAYS
54th DAY — YOKOHAMA
55th DAY — ON THE PACIFIC — GO BACK 2 DAYS
56th DAY — STORMY — GO BACK 10 DAYS
57th DAY — CLEAR — GO AHEAD 1 DAY
58th DAY — BREAK IN MACHINERY — GO BACK 3 DAYS
59th DAY — CLEAR
60th DAY — FAIR — GO AHEAD 2 DAYS
61st DAY — CLEAR — GO BACK 3 DAYS
62nd DAY — STORM — GO BACK 13 DAYS
63rd DAY — COLLISION
64th DAY — ON A RAFT — LOSE 2 THROWS
65th DAY — RESCUED — GO BACK 5 DAYS
66th DAY — CLEAR — GO AHEAD 1 DAY
67th DAY — PACIFIC OCEAN — LOSE 1 THROW
68th DAY — GOLDEN GATE
69th DAY — SIERRA MOUNTAINS — SNOW BOUND — LOSE 3 THROWS
70th DAY — CHEYENNE — INDIANS — GO BACK TO GOLDEN GATE
71st DAY — OMAHA — GO IN CENTRE
72nd DAY — CHICAGO — LOSE 1 THROW
73rd DAY — FIRST PART OF

ALL RECORDS BROKEN

NELLIE BLY

SPEEDING ACROSS THE ATLANTIC

OVER A MILE A MINUTE

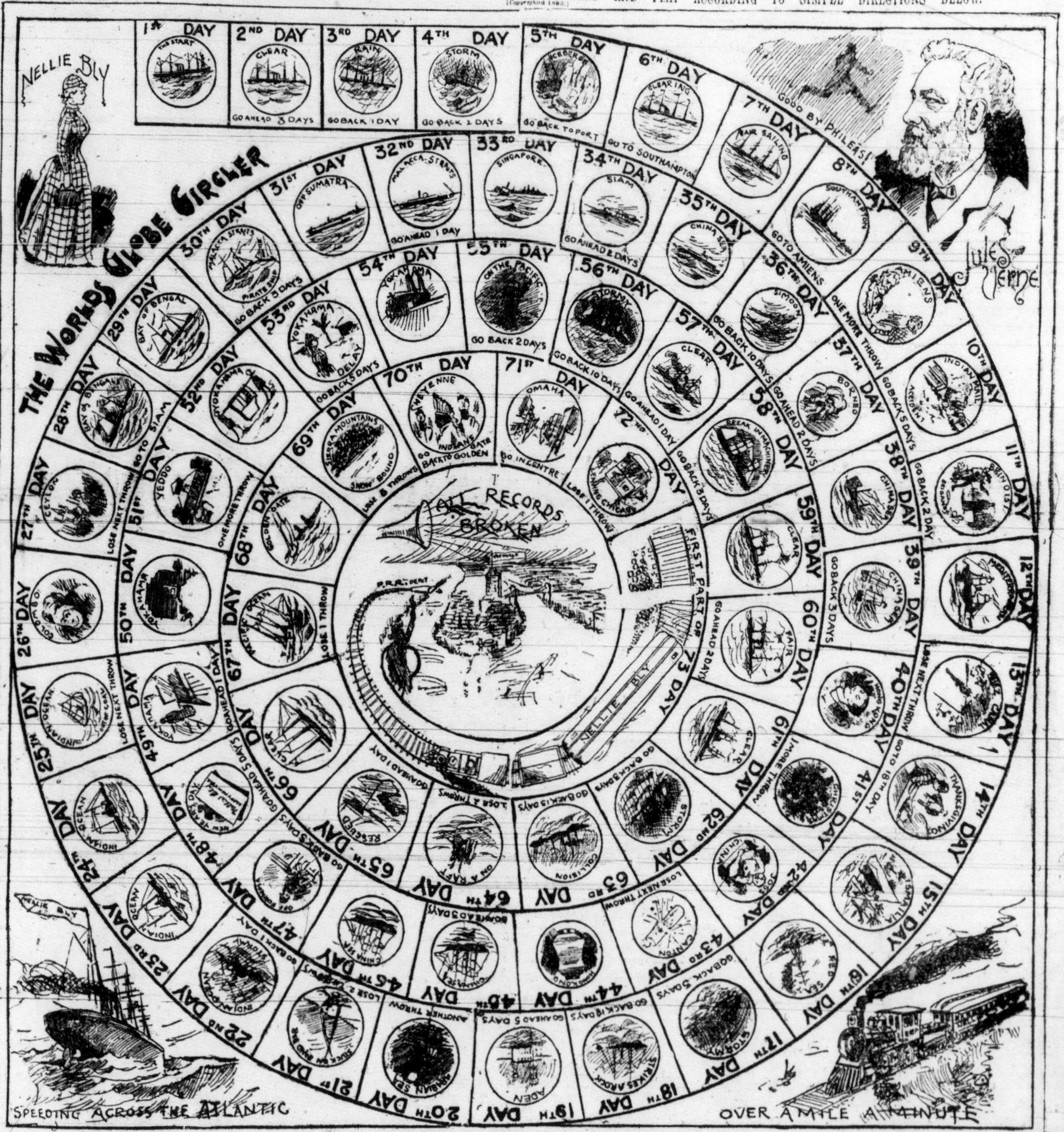

Any number of Persons can play. Use checkers, pennies or any kind of counters to represent the voyagers. Use either a "teetotum" or dice. A play of "one" puts voyagers at first day, a play of "two" at second day and so on. Follow directions on any given day or space that player may happen to reach, i. e., "go back a day;" "lose one throw," etc. If no directions are given, remain on space. The directions, however, are to be followed only when player reaches a space by the throw of dice or turn of the "teetotum." For instance, having gone back a day or more as directed, players are to disregard the directions found at second resting place. The object of the "game" is to complete the circuit of the world and reach New York first.

2 Serial and Government Publications Division

Georgia Metos Higley

Women are the best reporters in the world. In regard to feature writing—by which I mean emotional writing—women from the very start have headed for first flight. I think men have shoved them out of many a position in which, to my mind, they could prove themselves superior.
—*Eleanor "Cissy" Patterson.*[1]

The collections of the Serial and Government Publications Division trace their origins to the first acquisitions of the United States Congress. In May 1789, Congress resolved that each member of the Senate and House should be furnished one newspaper of his choice at public expense. Once the Library of Congress was established, in 1800, the Librarian was involved in the selection. By 1867 a small, separate periodicals reading room was established for members of Congress. Thirty years later, the Periodicals Division was established. A separate newspaper-periodical reading room for scholars and the public was created in 1900.

Today, the Serial and Government Publications Division has custody of one of the world's largest collections of current and retrospective newspapers, current periodicals, government publications, and several special holdings of a serial nature. Although no single collection in the division focuses on women in American history and culture, all its collections are rich sources for primary and secondary material about women.

Every aspect of American life is found in newspapers, and the Library's newspaper collection documents the activities of Americans from colonial times to the present. Perhaps no other source can provide clues as to how Americans lived in the past and how Americans viewed both momentous events and daily occurrences of their time. Newspapers serve as memory or as forums for discussion. They verify, refute, or circulate rumor. Newspapers provide a documentary history of the lives, events, and interests of famous, infamous, and ordinary people. As sources for the study of women's history, newspapers document the place of women in society and acknowledge society's recognition of women as audience and as contributors. Although underestimated by many, both the role and the influence of women as producers of the news are important aspects of American women's history. A researcher using the Library's newspaper collection in the Serial and Government Publications Division can trace the presence of women both in the newspaper industry and in the news itself.

Periodicals, too, form part of the journalistic history of America. Both the interests of contemporary American women and their current involvement in the magazine industry are well-represented in the Library's immense periodical collection.

Government publications from the days of the Continental Congress have become part of the Library's collections. Many U.S. government publications can be found in the General Collections and in the Law Library. The Serial and Government Publications Division's collection contains federal publications arranged by document classification and Federal Advisory Committee documents. International publications of the United Nations and other international organizations include information about Americans and American interests. Data about women found in government publications include a broad spectrum of statistical, analytical, descriptive, historical, and popular information.

Popular, if stereotypic, views of women can be found in the division's special collections. Wish-fulfillment, idealism, and extremism of all genres are represented in the comic book collection and pulp fiction covers. These collections offer unique

"Round the World with Nellie Bly." New York World, *January 26, 1890 (News MF 1363). Serial and Government Publications Division.*

Arguably one of the best-known journalists in America, Nellie Bly (1864–1922), born Elizabeth Jane Cochran, achieved international fame with her round-the-world journey in 1889–90 for the *New York World.* On November 14, the *World* heralded her as a "veritable Phineas Fogg," living out Jules Verne's *Around the World in Eighty Days.* Besides the *World*'s exhaustive coverage, other holdings of the Serial and Government Publications Division can be used to follow her trip in newspapers from across the United States and around the world.

opportunities to consider how women were and are portrayed in some of America's most popular media.

USING THE COLLECTIONS

Some preparation is required before you visit the Serial and Government Publications Division. Although some finding aids are unique to the division, other resources available at repositories and research libraries nationwide can be very useful. The division's Web site and the Library's online catalog can provide invaluable information to help you make the most of the time you spend in the Newspaper and Current Periodical Room (N&CPR) looking at material. Advance preparation will allow you to quickly place requests for the material you need from the division's closed stacks.

Newspapers

A newspaper is a serial publication, appearing usually at least weekly, which serves as a primary source of information on current events of general interest. While format can vary widely, newspapers are normally published without a cover, but with a masthead or banner, and are normally larger than 12 by 17 inches.

—Library of Congress collection policy statement for U.S. newspapers (November 1996)

NEWSPAPER AND CURRENT PERIODICAL ROOM
James Madison Memorial Building, 1st floor, room LM133
Hours: Monday, Wednesday, and Thursday, 8:30 a.m. to 9:30 p.m.; Tuesday, Friday, and Saturday, 8:30 a.m. to 5:00 p.m.
Closed Sunday and federal holidays.
Telephone: 202 707-5690; TTY 202 707-9952
Fax: 202 707-6128
Address: Serial and Government Publications Division, Library of Congress, 101 Independence Avenue, SE, Washington, DC 20540-4760
E-mail: serref@loc.gov
Web site: <http://www.loc.gov/rr/news/ncp.html>
Access and use: Use of material in the Serial and Government Publications Division collections follows guidelines similar to those for the General Collections. See the division's Web site for information on services and facilities. Although no appointments are necessary, researchers from outside the Washington, D.C., metropolitan area are advised to write, e-mail, or telephone before visiting to verify holdings, because some collections are stored off-site and require advance notice for retrieval. Some of the division's special collections have use restrictions, and consultation with serial reference specialists before arrival is essential. Photocopying from microfilm, periodicals, and current newspapers is permitted, but photocopies of bound newspapers, rare material, and comic books must be ordered through the Library's Photoduplication Service.

The Library's newspaper collection is the largest such collection in the United States. On a current basis, the Serial and Government Publications Division receives major titles published in all 50 states and from over 179 foreign countries. Although the division does not receive every newspaper published in the United States or the world, the collection's sheer size, breadth, and diversity of viewpoints are unmatched. Scholars researching a broad geographic area or a subject encompassing whole regions of the United States or foreign countries are able, in a visit to a single institution, to examine a wide range of newspaper titles with comprehensive, long runs. Most newspapers are housed in the Serial and Government Publications Division. Newspapers written in non-roman alphabets, however—Slavic, Asian, or Near Eastern, for instance—are housed in the appropriate Area Studies divisions (see chapter 12).

Other titles that many researchers may consider to be newspapers (such as Anne Royall's *Paul Pry*, the *New York Ledger*, *Woodhull & Claflin's Weekly*, and *Equal Rights* of the National Women's Party) are classified as periodicals in the Library of Congress because they are subject-specific and are not designed for general interest. These are available in the General Collections, the Microform Reading Room, or the Rare Book and Special Collections Division. Newspapers that the Library classifies as periodicals generally include the underground press, military camp newspapers, and trade newspapers.

Most of the division's newspaper collection is on microfilm. "In general the Library prefers archival microfilm as the permanent medium . . . . Reader demand and political, historical, economic, or cultural significance are factors which may justify retention of the original paper format, although such retention will be on an exceptional basis only" (Collections Policy Statement, Newspapers—Foreign—Current, May 1993).[2] The division does hold, however, a large collection of bound and portfolio newspapers from the late seventeenth through the early twentieth century. Seventeenth- and eighteenth-century newspapers (originals and facsimiles) are considered rare and require special handling and permission for use, as do selected titles from later time periods (for instance, originals of the early nineteenth-century *Cherokee Phoenix* or a Civil War wallpaper edition of the *Vicksburg Daily Citizen*). To use these, you must fill out and sign a special request form indicating that you agree to abide by the conditions of use for this material. Nineteenth-

and twentieth-century bound newspapers are housed in remote storage and must be requested in advance.

Newspaper titles are listed in the Library's catalog, but holdings information is only beginning to be included in catalog listings. Such information will be added to the catalog in the near future. If you are coming from outside the Washington area, you should either contact the Newspaper and Current Periodical Room to verify specific holdings or try to find such information through your local library. The United States Newspaper Program (USNP), a union database managed by OCLC (Online Computer Library Center), contains holdings information of U.S. newspapers held by the division. Division reference specialists routinely consult the USNP database for division holdings as well as holdings in other institutions for referral purposes. This database is available only for newspapers published in the United States; there is no equivalent for foreign-published newspapers held in U.S. libraries.

Possibilities for finding information about women in the division's newspaper collections are vast. This section suggests sources and search strategies for researching women's roles in the news business and women in the news. None is exhaustive but each discussion demonstrates the possibilities available to researchers.

Dick DeMarsico. "Little Denise Davidson, 5 months old, sleeps peacefully while her mother, Mrs. Donald Davidson, of 278 Clinton St., Bklyn., marches with ban-the-bomb group outside the United Nations. . . ." Photograph, 1962. New York World-Telegram and Sun Collection. Prints and Photographs Division. LC-USZ62-126854.

This resolute mother protests against President Kennedy's decision to resume atom-bomb testing in the wake of Soviet aggression. The editors of the *New York World-Telegram and Sun* chose woman as activist to appear on page 1 over a photograph of a more violent ban-the-bomb protest in Japan which they placed on page 2. Headlined as "While Mother Marches," this photo shows the very local, even personal immediacy the newspaper gave to international news so as to connect with readers (News MF 1465, April 26, 1962, pp. 1–2).The photograph, which is held in the New York World-Telegram and Sun Newspaper Photograph Collection (see page 195), demonstrates how photo morgues, such as those available in the Prints and Photographs Division, provide one useful way to locate articles in newspapers that otherwise lack subject access through newspaper indexes or detailed histories. Viewing a photograph in its publication context, in turn, often amplifies our understanding of the content of the image.

Finding Aids and Guides to the Library's Newspaper Collections

Information about newspapers held by the division is contained in several lists available only in the Newspaper and Current Periodical Room or on its Web site. Data about microfilm holdings for U.S. and foreign newspapers is recorded in card files available in the reading room. Frequently requested newspaper titles are listed in "Commonly Used U.S. Newspapers on Microfilm," available at <http://www.loc.gov/rr/news/cunom_us.html>. An inventory of bound newspapers (U.S. states and territories and foreign country holdings after 1801), completed in 1998, is on the Newspaper and Current Periodical Room Web site. See also <http://www.loc.gov/rr/news/bound/us/inventor.html> for links to the "19th and 20th Century U.S. Newspapers in Original Format: Inventory of Volumes Held in Remote Storage" and "19th and 20th Century Foreign Newspapers in Original Format: Inventory of Volumes Held in Remote Storage." Specific issue-level information is available in a bound-volume card file. U.S. newspapers published before 1801 held by the division are listed in "American Eighteenth Century Newspapers in the Library of Congress: A Checklist," compiled by Travis Westly (N&CPR). Extremely useful for researchers who need to know what is available for a single year or a specific time period in multiple geographic areas is the "Chronological Index of Newspapers for the Period 1801–1967 in the Collections of the Library of Congress" compiled by Paul E. Swigart (N&CPR). This twelve-volume set is arranged first by year and then by state and city. It lists newspapers in both microfilm and bound volumes.

As holdings information is added, the Library's online catalog will become the primary way to determine the Library's holdings of newspapers, and researchers will be able to determine what is available by accessing the catalog through the World Wide Web.

Newspapers by Place and Date: Directories and Union Lists

Directories and union lists identify titles of newspapers published in a specific city or town for specific years.

SEARCH TIP: One of the first steps in newspaper research is to identify newspaper titles for specific locations or time periods. Division specialists frequently consult the following five sources to identify U.S. newspapers:

Brigham, Clarence S. *History and Bibliography of American Newspapers, 1690–1820.* 2 vols. Worcester, Mass.: American Antiquarian Society, 1947. Z6951.B86 N&CPR.

Widely used to identify early newspapers, Brigham's work includes historical information about each newspaper as well as holdings information. The work is arranged first by state and then by newspaper title. It includes indexes to titles and printers. Edward Lathem's *Chronological Tables of American Newspapers, 1690–1820* (Z6951.L3 N&CPR) is a chronological arrangement of Brigham.

North, S. N. D. *History and Present Condition of the Newspaper and Periodical Press of the United States.* Washington: U.S. Government Printing Office for the Census Office, Department of Interior, 1884. HA201 1880.B1 vol. 8 N&CPR.

Completed for the tenth census (1880), this history of the newspaper and periodical press from 1639 to 1880 provides statistics, a catalog of periodical publications issued in 1880, and a chronology of the U.S. newspaper press. Although not every state's press history is included, the chronology, arranged by state and territory, contains valuable historical information not easily found elsewhere.

N.W. Ayer & Son's American Newspaper Annual. Philadelphia: N.W. Ayer and Son, 1880–1986. Z6951.A97 N&CPR full set

Published annually, the "Ayer's Directory," as it is commonly known, is a list of newspapers (and many periodicals) published in the United States and Canada, arranged geographically. Ayer's includes a classed listing of newspapers and periodicals, as well as subject listings, such as culinary and housekeeping, fashion, matrimonial, millinery, woman's handiwork, and women's clubs (these categories became increasingly detailed over time). It was continued by *Gale Directory of Publications and Broadcast Media* (New York: Gale, 1987–), with expanded coverage of radio and television stations.

Rowell's American Newspaper Directory. New York: George P. Rowell & Company, 1869, 1871–85, 1886–1909. Z6951.R88 N&CPR.

A predecessor and later a competitor of *Ayers, Rowell's* lists newspapers and periodicals of the United States and the territories geographically. It has a large section on advertising rates and circulation data and includes listings related to women, such as "Woman's Rights." It was absorbed by *Ayer's American Newspaper Directory* in 1910.

Working Press of the Nation. Volume 1, *Newspaper Directory.* Chicago: R.R. Bowker, 1945–. Z6951.W6 N&CPR.

Volume 1 of the three-volume *Working Press* is categorized first according to type of newspaper (daily, weekly), then by subject groupings (feature syndicates, news and photo services), which are not limited to a specific newspaper. One of its strengths is its index to editorial personnel.

SAMPLE LCSH: Useful subject headings for locating these and other newspaper directories in the Library's catalog include: **American newspapers—Bibliography; American newspapers—Directories; Newspapers—Directories; Newspaper publishing—Directories; Press—United States—Directories.**

Union lists assist in locating newspaper holdings beyond the Library of Congress, and they verify the existence of newspapers. Widely available, these lists provide valuable information that will help you prepare for a visit to the Library of Congress or to newspaper repositories around the country. In addition to the USNP mentioned earlier, two print union lists are particularly useful: *American Newspapers, 1821–1936,* edited by Winifred Gregory (New York: Bibliographical Society of America, 1937; Z6951.A498 N&CPR), and the three-volume *Newspapers in Microform, 1948–1983,* 6th edition (Washington: Library of Congress, 1983; Z6945.U5 N43 N&CPR). Union lists may include useful editorial information and listings of variant titles as well.

SAMPLE LCSH: To find union lists for specific ethnic groups, states, or regions, search under: **African American newspapers—Bibliography—Union lists; American newspapers—Bibliography; Catalogs, Union—Southern States** [or —specific state]; **Newspapers—Bibliography—Union lists.**

Newspaper Indexes

For newspapers, unlike periodicals, there are no comprehensive retrospective indexes (such as the *Readers' Guide to Periodical Literature*) covering multiple titles over long time periods. Indeed, many newspapers lack any kind of indexing at all, so creative strategies are necessary in order to find pertinent articles about women or by women reporters. The *New York Times,* well-known for its reporting quality, is equally noteworthy for its index, which covers its entire lifespan from 1851 to the present (AI21.N45 N&CPR). The *New York Times* has issued specialized indexes too, such as *Women, 1965–1975* (Glen Rock, N.J.: Microfilming Corp. of America, 1978; Z7961.W62 N&CPR). But this is unusual, and few newspapers have such extensive indexing.

Of the major newspapers published today, the majority have indexes going back only to the 1970s and 1980s. For example, the index to the *Los Angeles Times* begins in 1971 (AI21.L65 B44a and AI21.L65 L67 N&CPR), and the *Philadelphia Inquirer* has no printed index at all. Numerous electronic indexes (CD-ROM or online) may be available through information brokers such as Dialog Information Service and Lexis/Nexis. Many newspapers are providing Web access to their archives, usually on a fee or subscription basis. Today, *Newspaper Abstracts* and *Proquest Newstand,* published electronically by University Microfilms International, are among the few indexes that are widely available in libraries and that cover multiple newspapers on a current basis. The division's Web site points to online newspaper indexes <http://www.loc.gov/rr/news/oltitles.html>, and includes lists such as the Special Library Association's comprehensive "U.S. News Archives on the Web" at <http://www.ibiblio.org/slanews/internet/archives.html>.

Likewise, ethnic and minority newspapers lack comprehensive retrospective indexes. *Ethnic Newswatch,* published electronically by SoftLine Information, Inc., covers the ethnic, minority, and native press in America from 1995 to present. All major ethnic and minority groups (in broad categories) are represented in this very useful index, and full text of articles are available for many hard-to-locate newspapers (often difficult to find outside the local community). The database includes many titles not held by the Library.

An important retrospective print index for the minority press found in the Library is the *Black Newspapers Index* (formerly *Index to Black Newspapers*) published since 1977 (Ann Arbor, Mich.: University Microfilms International; AI3.I46 N&CPR). It indexes eight of the highest circulating black newspapers, among them the *Chicago Defender, New York Amsterdam News,* and *Los Angeles Sentinel.*

Although dated, two reference sources provide information regarding the existence and location of specific newspaper indexes: *Lathrop Report on Newspaper Indexes: An Illustrated Guide to Published and Unpublished Newspaper Indexes in the United States and Canada,* compiled and edited by Norman M. Lathrop and Mary Lou Lathrop (Wooster, Ohio: Norman Lathrop Enterprises, 1979–80; Z6293.L37 1979 N&CPR), and the three-volume *Newspaper Indexes: A Location and Subject Guide for Researchers* by Anita Cheek Milner (Metuchen, N.J.: Scarecrow Press, 1977–82; Z6951.M635 N&CPR). The division makes every effort to collect indexes for newspaper titles it holds. Nevertheless, many indexes exist only as card files or limited-copy bound sets available solely where the newspaper is published, making preparation before using the Library's newspaper collection advisable.

When all other strategies have been exhausted, you may need to search a newspaper date by date and page by page to locate articles of interest. To avoid this time-consuming effort, you should use secondary sources to narrow your search to a limited time period whenever possible. Using periodical indexes and existing newspaper indexes may help you narrow your field of inquiry even when the newspapers you need have no index. Information you discover through these indexes may be transferable to the research at hand—it may help you identify the date of an event, determine approximate date ranges to focus on, or discover biographical information. Secondary sources such as books, journal articles, and dissertations are also extremely useful. Newspaper histories may refer to specific stories or columnists for which the newspaper is known. Biographies of publishers, editors, and reporters may also yield unexpected leads.

Bibliographies

Numerous bibliographies treat newspapers and newspaper history. Most general bibliographies refer to women in journalism, more often noting them in the index than devoting entire chapters to women. Warren Price's massive *Literature of Journalism: An Annotated Bibliography* (Minneapolis: University of Minnesota Press, 1959; Z6940.P7) considers the press in Britain, Canada, and the United States; this work, and its supplements, is one of the standard bibliographies of the field. Another noteworthy bibliography, limited to the American press, is *Newspapers: A Reference Guide* by Richard A. Schwarzlose (New York: Greenwood Press, 1987; Z6951.S35 1987 N&CPR). Schwarzlose includes all aspects of the study of newspapers: history, production, society, technology, and reference sources. William David Sloan's *American Journalism History: An Annotated Bibliography* (New York: Greenwood Press, 1989; Z6951.S54 1989 N&CPR) cites articles that discuss the history of newspapers from 1690 to the present, categorized by chronological period. Mentioned in the index are scholarly articles on individual women journalists, newspaper coverage of women, and the suffrage movement.

SAMPLE LCSH: For finding newspaper bibliographies, the following headings are useful: **American newspapers—History—Bibliography; Journalism—Bibliography; Newspaper publishing—United States—Bibliography.**

Newspaper Histories

Several authors have attempted comprehensive histories of U.S. newspapers, but few have succeeded in documenting the diversity and progress of newspaper publishing as well as Frank Luther Mott. His classic *American Journalism: A History, 1690–1960* (New York: Macmillan, 1962; PN4855.M63 1962 N&CPR) is one of the best sources to begin a study of newspaper history. Mott provides both broad scope and insights about individual newspapers. His exhaustive footnotes and detailed accounts include minutiae absent from other newspaper histories. For instance, Mott (p. 599) links the development of the women's pages of the late nineteenth century not to the increasing presence of women in the workplace but to department store advertising. Concentrating on an earlier period, Isaiah Thomas's *History of Printing in America* (New York: Burt Franklin, 1873; E172.A3 v.5–6 N&CPR) describes printing in the colonies through 1775. Thomas discusses not only the printing process itself and the newspaper press in each colony but also individual newspapers and biographies of printers. He was one of the first to point out the involvement of women in early American printing.

A slightly different approach is taken in *The Press and America: An Interpretive History of the Mass Media* (Boston: Allyn and Bacon, 1996; PN4855.E6 1996 N&CPR), edited by Edwin Emery until his death in 1993. Revised irregularly, this book covers the modern era of American journalism in detail, with less emphasis on the early American and colonial press but better coverage of the increased role of women as editors, journalists, and columnists of the twentieth century. Emery also discusses the relationship of print journalism to television and radio media.

Most major newspapers have a published history of the newspaper compiled by the newspaper itself or by independent historians. These histories may be useful starting points for finding information about women journalists—as long as the researcher knows the newspaper for which these particular journalists worked. For example, Lloyd Wendt's discussion of Sigrid Schultz (1893–1980) in his history of the *Chicago Tribune* provides valuable information about the risks Schultz took to report on Nazi oppression. It highlights her 1938–39 articles, written under the pseudonym "John Dickson" to avoid discovery by the Nazis (pp. 574–75, 665–66), which exposed the concentration camps and helped determine the editorial stance of the paper against Nazism and Fascism.[3]

Association histories and publications are also helpful in documenting the involvement of women journalists in their field. The Women's National Press Association was launched in the 1880s, and some of the most famous women journalists of the day were founders and members. The National Federation of Press Women and its state chapters have been active since 1937. Associations and clubs for journalists and for women journalists in particular may have biographical information not easily obtained elsewhere.

SAMPLE LCSH: Useful, though general, subject headings for these and other newspaper histories include: **American newspapers—History; Journalism—United States; Press—United States; Printing—America—History;** name of newspaper searched as a subject (e.g., *Chicago Tribune*).

De Yongh. The New York Times: The Model of Decent and Dignified Journalism. Easter. *Poster, color lithograph by Lieber and Maass Lith., New York, 1896. Artist Posters. Prints and Photographs Division. LC-USZC4-1429.*

This stunning poster was undoubtedly an effort by the owners of the *New York Times* to resuscitate the ailing newspaper in the 1890s. In contrast to populist newspapers, such as the *New York World* and *New York Journal,* whose colorful posters and newsprint blazoned their sensationalist brand of journalism, the *New York Times* was known as a "sober, conservative, dignified paper." Holding the Easter lily of purity and rebirth, the idealized image of pure young womanhood symbolized how the owners of the *Times* intended to triumph over competitors: "The truth is great and will prevail." Contrary to what the colors in this promotional poster might suggest, the newspaper itself lacked the feature stories, comic strips, household hints, and advice columns that appealed to women readers of competitor newspapers and which would have provided a way for women reporters to enter its newsroom. Perhaps not surprisingly, women journalists flourished in the popular press but made little headway on the pages of traditionalist newspapers such as the *New York Times* until the early twentieth century.

Margaret Fuller. Engraving with signature. Biographical file. Prints and Photographs Division. LC-USZ62-47039.

Already a noted feminist and intellectual, Margaret Fuller (1810–1850) became the literary editor of Horace Greeley's *New York Daily Tribune* in 1844. Her work was bylined with a star (*), and inspired the pun that she was the "star" of the *Tribune*. In 1846 she became the newspaper's foreign correspondent and covered the 1848 revolution in Italy, but she died tragically in a shipwreck in 1850.

Researching Women in the Newspaper Industry

Several works investigating the presence of women in the newspaper field have appeared recently. Until the 1980s, most discussions of individuals involved in newspaper production focused on men—as editors, publishers, columnists, and reporters. Few women, unless they were so renowned that the history of the news would be incomplete without them—as was the case with Ida B. Wells-Barnett and Nellie Bly—were highlighted in the histories, and even fewer treatments of women's roles were published.

One of the few early works on women and the press was written by *New York Herald Tribune* reporter Ishbel Ross. *Ladies of the Press* (New York: Arno Press, 1936, 1974; PN4872.R7 1974 N&CPR) is a colorful history of women in the newspaper business from colonial times to the twentieth century. Roughly chronological in arrangement, its index is helpful in locating specific women. *Great Women of the Press* by Madelon Schilpp and Sharon Murphy (Carbondale: Southern Illinois University Press, c1983; PN4872.S34 1983 N&CPR) is a biographical introduction to women in the press, from Elizabeth Timothy, as the first woman publisher, to war correspondent Marguerite Higgins (1920–1966). Although not as comprehensive as Ross's work, *Great Women* establishes the importance and credibility of women in the newspaper industry.

BIBLIOGRAPHY: Other reference works that cover specific aspects of women as reporters include:

Edwards, Julia. *Women of the World: The Great Foreign Correspondents.* Boston: Houghton Mifflin Company, 1988. PN4872.E39 1988 N&CPR.
A history that tells how women joined the ranks of the elite reporters—foreign correspondents—beginning in the nineteenth century.

Mills, Kay. *A Place in the News: From the Women's Pages to the Front Page.* New York: Columbia University Press, 1990. PN4784.W7 M55 1990 N&CPR.
Mills, then with the *Los Angeles Times,* provides an insider's view of women's presence in the newsroom.

Streitmatter, Rodger. *Raising Her Voice: African-American Women Journalists Who Changed History.* Lexington: University Press of Kentucky, 1994. PN4872.S66 1994 N&CPR.

SAMPLE LCSH: Useful biographical headings include: **Women journalists—United States—Biography; Foreign correspondents—United States—Biography; Women journalists—**[state]**—Biography; African American journalists—Biography.**

Several periodicals discuss women in their various roles as reporter, subject, and audience. While some are indexed in abstracting and indexing sources such as the general *Readers' Guide to Periodical Literature* and the more journalism-specific *Communications Abstracts,* many periodicals are not indexed.

BIBLIOGRAPHY: Periodicals that cover the newspaper industry include:

The Journalist (The Journalist Publishing Company, New York; PN4700.J8) 1:1 (March 22, 1884) through 39:13 (January 1907).
Although primarily intended for the newspaper and journalism *man,* it contains biographies of women journalists (with portraits), reports of women appointed to positions of editor or bureau chief, and the rise of women's magazines. *The Journalist* also published irregularly a special "Woman's Number," first published in 1889 with over fifty biographies of women reporters.

Editor & Publisher (Editor and Publisher Company, New York; PN4700.E4 N&CPR), 1901 to the present.
Covering all aspects of journal and newspaper publishing, it absorbed: *The Journalist, Newspaperdom,* and *Fourth Estate;* and it publishes several annual publications, including *Editor & Publisher International Yearbook.*

Publishers' Auxiliary (National Newspaper Association, Washington, D.C., etc.; PN4700.P8), 1865 to present.
It is self-proclaimed as the "newspaper industry's oldest newspaper." (LC holdings begin in 1891.)
Other journals that discuss and analyze all aspects of newspapers include:[4] *American Editor: The Bulletin of the American Society of Newspaper Editors; Columbia Journalism Review; Journalism History; Journalism Quarterly* (continued by *Journalism and Mass Communication Quarterly); Nieman Reports;* and *Quill.*

SAMPLE LCSH: Journalism—Periodicals; Journalism—United States—History—Periodicals; Mass media—Periodicals; Press—Periodicals; Press—United States—Periodicals.

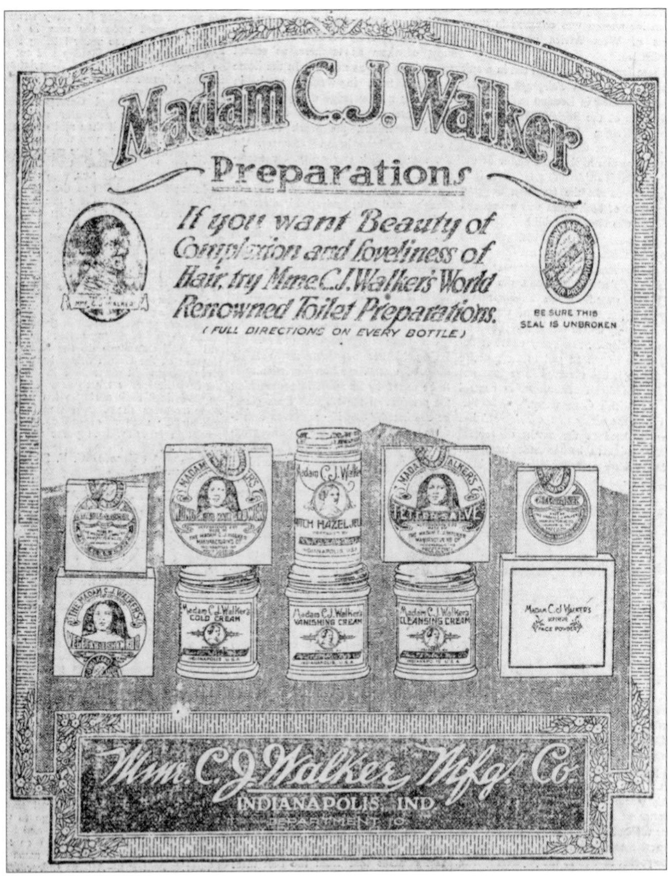

"Madam C.J. Walker Preparations," Madam C.J. Walker Manufacturing Company, Indianapolis, Indiana, advertisement. From New York Age, *January 17, 1920 (bound newspaper, no. 10330). Serial and Government Publications Division.*

Madam C. J. Walker (1867–1919) was one of the first American women to become wealthy solely through her own efforts. In addition to personal appearances by Madam Walker and traveling saleswomen called "Walker's Agents," advertisements in African American newspapers and periodicals promoted her hair and complexion products. By 1917, this daughter of former slaves had built the largest black-owned company in the United States. Advertisements for hair-straightening products were (and continue to be) very common in the African American press.

Women in the Newspapers

Researching women as the subject of news articles can be done using standard search strategies—searching available and pertinent newspaper indexes, reviewing newspaper histories for discussions of women in newspapers, and scanning secondary sources (books, dissertations, journal articles) for useful citations. To study an individual woman, researchers may need to search the broader topics she is associated with (instead of her name), since names are not always listed consistently in indexes. General and subject-specialized periodical indexes may provide approximate dates for researching women and women's issues in local (unindexed) newspapers. More recently, scholarly attention has turned to what is not usually indexed—advertisements, want ads, and obituaries—to discover how women were viewed during their lifetime and what newspapers considered to be of importance to a female audience.

Current Periodicals

Custody of serials is shared between the General Collections and the Serial and Government Publications Division. Serials can also be found in most reading rooms. As a general rule, periodicals published in the past eighteen to twenty-four months should be requested in the Newspaper and Current Periodical Room; older issues are bound and available from the General Collections. Four major exceptions are (1) law journals, which are kept in the Law Library; (2) music journals, which are found in the Performing Arts Reading Room; (3) non-roman alphabet materials (the Slavic-, Asian-, and Near Eastern-language publications located in the Area Studies reading rooms, described in chapter 12), and (4) periodicals published before 1801, which are accessible through the Rare Book or Microform Reading Rooms. Many older titles are held only in microform and can be found through special guides in the Main Reading Room. Consult the online catalog and reference librarians to determine the locations of periodicals.

Although the Serial and Government Publications Division retains only the unbound, current issues of periodicals received by the Library, division staff members are specialists in serial publications in general. Therefore, this discussion includes information about retrospective periodicals that are outside the custodial responsibilities of the division but well within the intellectual scope of the reference specialists. Although some periodical indexes are best suited for researching older periodicals and others cover only current titles, the strategy for researching periodical literature is largely the same for whatever time period interests you. This section will focus on how to identify which periodicals exist and provide assistance on the history of magazines.

Only a small percentage of periodicals can be found in abstracting and indexing services. Many academic journals covering women's studies are indexed in such services as *Women Studies Abstracts, America: History and Life, Contemporary Women's Issues,* and several of the H.W. Wilson indexes (for instance, *Social Sciences Index* and *Humanities Index*), but others must be discovered through periodical directories and new journal title announcements. Popular and special interest periodicals are even less accessible through traditional scholarly and general indexes. Readers often discover titles through advertisements, word of mouth, Web sites, and newsstands. Responsive to the varied interests of the Library's researchers and the size of the American publishing industry, the Library's current periodicals collection has an extensiveness unmatched by any other library. (See "Magazines and Other Serial Publications" in chapter 1 for information on how to locate specific articles within periodicals.)

Like the book collection of the Library of Congress, the periodical collection is international in scope but is particularly strong for titles published in the United States. The majority of the Library's U.S. titles are received through copyright deposit. Because publishers have the option of making group deposits of a run of issues, some periodicals are not received on a current basis but instead are mailed in bunches. Therefore, the Library can receive a title but lack current issues, a practice in keeping with the Library's mission of collecting and preserving for the future.

Periodical literature is collected according to guidelines established in collection policy statements. The Library does not receive or keep every periodical published or distributed in the United States. Generally, the Library retains significant holdings of U.S. periodicals, selects representative titles from trade industries and high circulation newsletters, and collects only a few regional newsletters.

Currently, the Library's online catalog provides access only to the titles of periodicals it holds; information about specific issues held is incomplete. Therefore, as with newspapers, you should contact the Library in advance to determine which specific periodical issues it holds. Magazines are cataloged by Library of Congress subject headings, with some exceptions. Erotic magazines (such as *Playboy*) and supermarket tabloids (*National Enquirer*) generally are assigned no subject headings. Some periodicals are assigned no subject or classification access. Once bound, these few titles are identified with the prefix "WMLC" ("with minimum-level cataloging"). *Sister 2 Sister* (WMLC 96/519), *Family Circle Easy Gardening* (WMLC 93/3584), and *Knockouts: For the Woman with the Will to Win* (WMLC 95/68) fall in this category.

Directories and Union Lists

A key to locating needed periodicals in the Library of Congress collections is to have accurate titles and places of publication for them. Directories identify title changes, provide publishing information that can distinguish otherwise similar titles, and, more important for researchers, can provide subject access to journal titles that may not be indexed in bibliographies and indexes.

SEARCH TIP: Directories commonly used by division specialists include the following, which are available in most libraries:

Ulrich's International Periodicals Directory. New York: R.R. Bowker, 1932–present. Z6941.U5 N&CPR; also on CD-ROM and the Web.

Ulrich's is published annually and provides subject access to periodical information. A worldwide, comprehensive directory, *Ulrich's* is also useful for periodicals published in the United States, one of the largest publishing countries in the world. It includes descriptive information other directories lack, for instance, refereed titles and indexing sources. "Women's Health," "Women's Interests," and "Women's Studies" are terms useful for locating current women's history and policy titles.

The Serials Directory. Birmingham, Ala.: EBSCO Publishing, 1986–present. Z6941.S464 N&CPR, CD-ROM only 2000–.

A competitor of *Ulrich's,* this international directory is published by a subscription agent for libraries. Useful features for journal titles include a content description, indexing and abstracting sources, and whether or not the journal produces its own index.

Standard Periodical Directory. New York: Oxbridge Communications, Inc., 1964/65–present. Z6951.S78 N&CPR.

Although initially intended as a directory of U.S. and Canadian journals, *Standard* includes some international titles as well. Like *Ulrich's,* it has a section covering "Women's" periodicals.

Directories specific to electronic journals are available through the World Wide Web. The N&CPR Web page includes listings of electronic journals under "Other Internet Resources—Periodicals" at <http://www.loc.gov/rr/news/extper.html>.

Besides locating other libraries and assisting in verifying holdings information, many union lists provide publication history and editorial information to help you verify citations and trace title changes. The most comprehensive and indispensable title is *Union List of Serials in Libraries of the United States and Canada,* 3rd ed. (New York: H.W. Wilson Company, 1965; Z6945.U45 1965 N&CPR). First coordinated by the American Library Association in 1913, this five-volume set lists more than 150,000 serials from 1,000 libraries (including the Library of Congress); among them are annual publications, monographic series, children's magazines, and some pulp magazines. It excludes most newspapers, government publications, almanacs, law reports, house organs, and college student publications. Its value to researchers lies in its comprehensive gathering of serial titles and comparative information about collections held across various libraries. It is not intended to provide subject access to serials and lacks any kind of thematic organization of material.

SEARCH TIP: Published union lists are also available for subjects or special interest areas and, to a lesser extent, for geographic regions of the United States: **Feminism—Periodicals—Bibliography—Union lists** [by subject]; **African American—Periodicals—Bibliography—Union lists** [by ethnic group]; **Serial publications—Bibliography—Union lists.**

Bibliographies

Greenwood Press has published a series called Bibliographies and Indexes in Women's Studies. Several academic journals include women's studies as a research category in their year-in-review or recent scholarship sections, as, for example, any issue of the *Journal of American History* will demonstrate for recent work. Typical historical bibliographies of women's magazines include *Sources on the History of Women's Magazines, 1792–1960: An Annotated Bibliography,* compiled by Mary Ellen Zuckerman (New York: Greenwood Press, 1991; Z6944.W6Z83 1991 N&CPR) and *American Women's Magazines: An Annotated Historical Guide* by Nancy K. Humphreys (New York: Garland, 1989; Z6944.W6H85 1989 N&CPR). See chapter 1 for tips on researching articles about women and women's interests in periodicals.

SAMPLE LCSH: Women—United States—History—Sources—Bibliography; Women—United States—Periodicals; Feminism—United States—Periodicals.

Histories of Periodicals

Histories of periodicals provide valuable clues about the reading habits of women, the place of women's magazines in the history of American media, and the involvement of women in the magazine industry.

Frank Mott holds the same position of authority for periodicals that he does for newspapers. His five-volume *History of American Magazines* (Cambridge, Mass.: Harvard University Press, 1968; PN4877.M63 1938 N&CPR) is a history of the American magazine press in general, from 1741 to 1930, and a collection of in-depth, lengthy descriptions of specific magazines, arranged chronologically. This work is particularly useful for researching women's publications and women's issues. Each volume has whole chapters and sections on women in magazines:

Volume 1, 1741–1851, has sections on "The Place of Woman," "Women and Periodicals," "Women's Magazines," and "The Woman Question."

Volume 2, 1850–65, includes sections on "Magazines and the 'Woman Question'" and "Magazines for Women and the Home," as well as "sketches" of magazines such as *Ladies' Repository* and *Frank Leslie's Magazine for Women.*

Volume 3, 1865–85, has an entire chapter devoted to "Women and Their Magazines" as well as profiles of *Harper's Bazaar* and the *Delineator.*

Volume 4, 1885–1905, has a chapter entitled "Women's Activities," discussing fashion, the right to work, education, and women's clubs, and descriptions of *Ladies' Home Journal, Cosmopolitan,* and *Woman's Home Companion.*

Volume 5, 1905–30, includes an extensive index to the set, with two pages devoted to variations of the term "Woman," and descriptions of *Better Homes and Gardens, Good Housekeeping,* and *House Beautiful.*

BIBLIOGRAPHY: Other useful histories, which describe women in periodicals, include the following:

Richardson, Lyon N. *History of Early American Magazines, 1741–1789.* New York: Thomas Nelson, 1931. PN4877.R5 1931 N&CPR.

This one-volume history focuses on the development of the magazine press in colonial America. It is representative of the kind of survey that typically refers to articles of interest to women readers of the time or highlights published stories written by women.

Tebbel, John, and Mary Ellen Zuckerman. *The Magazine in America, 1741–1990.* New York: Oxford University Press, 1991. PN4832.T43 1991 N&CPR.

Organized chronologically, this is a one-volume treatment of magazine history.

Another type of periodical history is one that considers specific subject areas and individual periodicals. Several popular, long-lived women's magazines contain histories that describe the development of women's presence in the mainstream press as well as the history of a periodical.

BIBLIOGRAPHY: Examples of compiled magazine histories include the following:

American Mass-Market Magazines. Edited by Alan Nourie and Barbara Nourie. New York: Greenwood Press, 1990. PN4877.A48 1990 N&CPR

Nourie and Nourie include historical articles about magazines as diverse as the *Columbian Lady's and Gentleman's Magazine, Playgirl, Vanity Fair,* and *Mother Jones.*

Damon-Moore, Helen. *Magazines for the Millions: Gender and Commerce in the Ladies' Home Journal and the Saturday Evening Post, 1880–1910.* Albany: State University of New York, 1994. PN4879.D36 1994 N&CPR

A critical analysis of the development of the two magazines.

Women's Periodicals in the United States: Consumer Magazines. Edited by Kathleen L. Endres and Therese L. Lueck. Westport, Conn.: Greenwood Press, 1995. PN4879.W6 1995 N&CPR

This compilation profiles some of the most profitable and influential women's magazines.

SEARCH TIPS: Subject headings for general histories of periodicals are very general, lumped under the term "American periodicals—History." Subject headings for women's magazines, gender studies, and individual periodical titles are much more specific.

SAMPLE LCSH: Women's periodicals, American—History; Women's periodicals, American—History—[time period]; Name of periodical searched as a subject [e.g., *Ladies' Home Journal*]; **Sex role in mass media.**

Statistics: Market Research

Circulation information for many periodicals is available through directories (see above) and industry organizations such as the Magazine Publishers of America. One useful way to judge the impact and importance of a periodical is to discover who reads it. Who reads *Ladies' Home Journal* or *Walking Magazine?* How many women read *Time* and *Newsweek?* At what age do young girls begin reading *Cosmopolitan?* The answers to these kinds of questions identify women as the intended audience of a publication and determine how companies choose to spend their advertising dollars to reach their target audience. Market research addresses the question: How important are women as consumers?

BIBLIOGRAPHY: Two services that provide statistics on market research that cover a wide range of media and specialized markets are Standard Rate and Data Service (SRDS) and Simmons Market Research Bureau, whose publications include the following:

SRDS Consumer Magazine Advertising Source. Des Plaines, Ill.: SRDS, 1995–present. HF5905.S725; current issues, N&CPR.

Published monthly. Titles are organized by categories such as "Women's," by which magazine title information is listed. Includes circulation, editorial profiles (intended audience), and geographic distribution of copies. For example, the August 2000 SRDS reported that the greatest number of copies of *Latina* magazine were sold in the Middle Atlantic States (New Jersey, New York, and Pennsylvania).

Study of Media and Markets: Magazine Audiences and Readers per Copy. New York: Simmons Market Research Bureau, Inc. 1974–present. HC101.S527 BusRR latest edition.

Updated annually. Information is organized by broad subject categories and by very detailed statistical elements. For example, in 1994 *Study of Media and Markets* reported that twice as many mothers read the *National Enquirer* and the *Star* as read *Cosmopolitan* (7,416,000 vs. 3,565,000 in 1994), and women college graduates making over $40,000 were more likely to read *Newsweek* than high school graduates making the same amount (3,701,000 vs. 459,000 in 1994).

Government Publications

The majority of any government's publications are serial in nature. The division's collection includes periodicals published by the federal government, state and local governments, foreign governments, and international organizations. Official serial publications of U.S. states and foreign governments are housed in the division until bound. In addition to government-produced periodicals, the division has depository collections for U.S. publications issued by the U.S. Government Printing Office, for the United Nations (UN), and for the European Union (EU). Besides these depository arrangements, the Library has established exchange and special agreements with a number of international organizations and foreign governments in order to receive needed publications and documents. Organizations such as the Organization of American States, the International Labour Organization, and many UN-affiliated organizations share their publications with the Library. Researchers investigating what the role of American women is in the international arena and how American women fare on a worldwide basis will find the statistics collected by governments and reports generated through government- and organization-sponsored studies and research among the most important sources to review.

Federal Depository Collection

As the largest publisher in the world, the U.S. Government Printing Office issues monographs, serials, maps, posters, and online databases on behalf of federal government agencies. These publications document the workings of the federal government.

In 1979, the Library became a selective federal government depository, receiving specified categories of material issued by federal agencies and published by the GPO. Like the General Collections, the depository collection excludes most publications in agriculture and technical medicine. The closed stacks collection is arranged by the Superintendent of Documents (SuDoc) classification number. By receiving publications directly from the GPO and arranging them by SuDoc number, the division provides quicker access to U.S. government materials, because they, unlike those destined for the General Collections, are not cataloged and assigned Library of Congress classification before they are made available to the public. The SuDoc collection contains many documents available elsewhere in the Library, but its value lies in the immediacy of its public access and in its organizing principles, which group together materials from each government agency for comparative research.

Access to the depository material is available through numerous sources. Like the other 1,400 depository libraries in the United States, the Library of Congress has access to government databases such as StatUSA, an economic and commercial database issued by the Commerce Department (<http://www.stat-usa.gov>), and GPO Access (<http://www.access.gpo.gov/>), a Web site containing databases and textual documents of congressional and executive agencies. The *Catalog of U.S. Government Publications* is available in several formats (in print or on CD-ROM) from several sources (among them OCLC FirstSearch, Dialog, and Marcive) and can be searched on the Web from January 1994 to the present at <http://www.access.gpo.gov/su_docs/locators/cgp/index.html>. Printed resources are best for older government publications (housed in the General Collections) that have not yet been added to computer databases. Electronic resources offer the easiest and most effective access to current government publications housed in the division.

SEARCH TIPS: In addition to the Library's online catalog, many resources are available for subject, title, and author access to older government publications. The *Monthly Catalog of United States Government Publications* (Washington: U.S. Government Printing Office, 1896–present; Z1223.A18 N&CPR) has annual indexes. A number of cumulative subject, title, and author indexes have been published both by the GPO and by private publishers. Congressional hearings are available in many divisions of the Library (see chapters 1 and 3), and have specialized indexes of their own.

SAMPLE LCSH: To locate indexes to U.S. government publications, search under: **Government publications—United States—Indexes; Government publications—United States—Bibliography—Union lists.**

Federal Advisory Committee Collection

When Congress passed the *Federal Advisory Commission Act of 1972*, the Library of Congress was designated by statute as the archival repository for Federal Advisory Commission (FAC) documents. Federal Advisory Commissions are the committees, boards, commissions, "blue ribbon" panels, councils, and similar groups that have been established to advise officers and agencies in the executive branch "as a useful and beneficial means of furnishing expert advice, ideas, and diverse opinions to the federal government" (*Federal Advisory Commission Act of 1972*, Pub. L. 92–463, Sec. 1, Oct. 6, 1972, 86 Stat. 770). These blue ribbon panels include advisory experts, political stakeholders, and consultants on whom Congress and the executive branch depend for advice and recommendations about a narrowly defined field. Most executive branch FACs are established by statute, executive order of the president, or presidential proclamation. Each is coordinated and supported by a parent federal agency.

The Library's collection of FAC material is primarily maintained in the Serial and Government Publications Division. Unless findings of a commission are deemed important enough to be published as government publications—an example is the Glass Ceiling Commission reports—the FAC material is not available elsewhere in the Library. Therefore, the Library's online catalog does not hold comprehensive records of FAC material. A card file index of FAC material received by the division is available in the Newspaper and Current Periodical Room. The FAC collection always includes the charter for each commission documenting its scope, membership, activities, and lifespan and may also include reports, records of public hearings, and issue briefs.

An important directory for using FAC material is the *Encyclopedia of Governmental Advisory Organizations* (Detroit, Mich.: Gale Research; JK468.C7 E5 N&CPR), issued annually. Indexed by keyword, each entry provides the address, authorizing authority, program description, members, and publication information. Both current and terminated commissions are included, so the *Encyclopedia* should be considered a first resource for this collection. Useful keywords include: gender, women (and variations), maternal, sex, family (and variations), and affirmative action.

Since 1972 the Office of Management and Budget and the General Services Administration have issued the *Annual Report of the President on Federal Advisory Committees* (JK468.C7 U55a N&CPR full set). This report lists existing FACs for the year by parent agency; each entry indicates the number of meetings held during the year, the actual and proposed costs, and the type of authorizing basis for each. Another useful reference source is Steven D. Zink's *Guide to the Presidential Advisory Commissions, 1973–84* (Alexandria, Va.: Chadwyck Healey, Inc., 1987; JK468.C7 Z56 1987 N&CPR). Although limited in scope to the time period indicated, the guide provides a detailed account of significant FACs, summarizing each FAC's activities and recommendations and giving meeting dates and bibliographic information for all reports issued.

International Organizations: Collections

Because the United States is a world power and key player in international affairs, sources that provide information about American women, their place in the world, and their involvement in international politics are significant. The division receives publications from the United Nations, World Health Organization (WHO), International Labour Organization (ILO), and Food and Agriculture Organization (FAO), as well as many other international organizations. By far the most heavily used is the depository collection of United Nations material.

Like U.S. government publications, the UN material in the Library's online catalog does not reflect all the official materials received by the Library. Available in paper or microfiche, UN material includes documents arranged by UN document number, official records produced by the major UN bodies (General Assembly, Security Council, Economic and Social Council, Trusteeship Council), and serial publications. Reference material in the Newspaper and Current Periodical Room provides a gateway to the division's (and the Library's) UN collection. The *Yearbook of the United Nations* (1946 to present; JX1977.A37 Y4 N&CPR full set) provides an overview of each year's activities, with full text of many UN resolutions and references to document numbers for background research. Women figure prominently in its extensive index. The United Nations produces print and online indexes to its publications and documents. Together with reference sources produced by private publishers, these indexes offer the best ways to access the wealth of UN material available to researchers.

SEARCH TIPS: For help in finding UN documents and publications, general indexes with a variety of formats and coverage exist. The *Index to United Nations Documents and Publications on CD-ROM* (networked through N&CPR) by Readex is the most comprehensive and the easiest to use, indexing documents and publications currently and retrospectively. It includes full text of many resolutions.

AccessUN (<http://infoweb.newsbank.com>) covers UN material from 1998. General indexes in paper format (all available in N&CPR) include: *UN Documents Index, 1950–73* (Z6482.U45); *UNDEX: United Nations Documents Index, 1974–78* (Z6481.U4); and *UNDOC: Current United Nations Documents Index, 1979–96* (Z6481.U19); *United Nations Documents Checklist,* 1996–97; and *United Nations Documents Index,* 1998– (Z6481.U19).

Official Web sites of the United Nations are also access points. Besides the main Web site of the United Nations (<http://www.un.org/>), which serves as a gateway to each UN assembly, agency, and program, specialized Web sites gather information about women's programs and serve as host sites for women's conferences. "WomenWatch: The UN Working for Women" (<http://www.un.org/womenwatch/un/index.html>) gathers sources about women from UN organizations, treaties, conferences, statistics, and country profiles.

Together with U.S. government publications, publications of international organizations contain an official view of women in America and the world and document what is important to the national and international community. Women are ubiquitous in these publications, and American women figure prominently in all. International reports and statistics also provide a basis for comparing the condition of the American woman to that of her counterparts around the world.

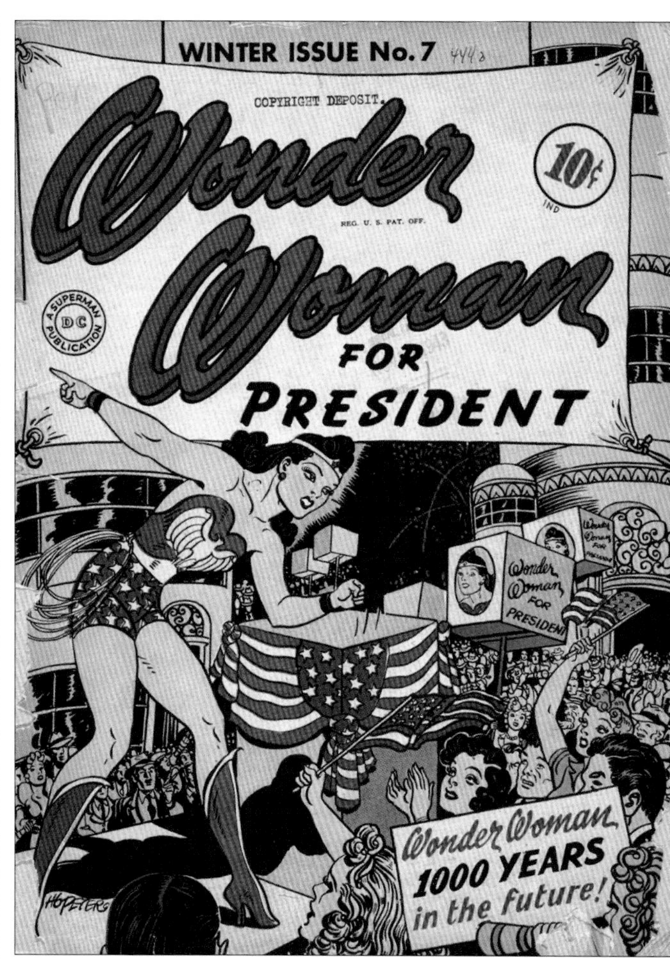

"Wonder Woman for President." Wonder Woman, *no. 7, Winter 1943. DC Comics, Inc. Copyright deposit. Serial and Government Publications Division. Wonder Woman is a trademark of DC Comics © 2001. All rights reserved. Used with permission.*

Wonder Woman was created by Dr. William Moulton Marston, a psychologist who took the pen name of Charles Moulton. In her, he created a role model for American girls in the 1940s who might have aspired to be president of the United States. His campaign scene, however, posted a deflating sign in the foreground: "Wonder Woman 1000 Years in the Future!"

Popular Culture Collections

When originally published, comic books and pulp magazines were considered disposable publications. Today they are collectors' items and sources for the scholarly analysis of American popular culture. Despite use restrictions owing to their fragility and rarity, these collections can be used by researchers to study twentieth-century American attitudes and popular interests.

Comic Books

The largest collection of comics books in the United States is housed in the Serial and Government Publications Division. The collection includes U.S. and foreign comic books—over 5,000 titles in all, totaling more than 100,000 issues. Primarily composed of the original print books, the collection includes color microfiche of a handful of the early comic books (such as *Wonder Woman, Superman,* and *Action Comics*) and special reprints. Although the collection is most comprehensive from 1950, scattered issues from numerous titles date back to the 1930s. A small number of comic books make up the Underground Comic Book collection of titles "recommended for mature readers." The Library acquires comic books published and distributed in the United States almost exclusively through copyright deposit. Titles are added to the collection on the basis of quality of text and graphic depiction; significance of the artist, writer, or publisher; originality of story or main character; the title's popularity as reflected in circulation statistics or media attention; representation of new ideas or social trends; or availability through copyright.

Comic books are circulated for use in the Newspaper and Current Periodical Room for those doing research of a specific nature, leading toward a publicly available work such as a publication, thesis, or dissertation; a radio, film, or television production; or a public performance. Self-service photocopying of comic books is prohibited. In some cases photocopies may be obtained through the Photoduplication Service of the Library of Congress. When researching comic books, collectors are usually interested in price and condition, whereas women's studies scholars may look on them as an art form, a popular culture medium, or a historical artifact. Unfortunately, many periodicals that focus on comic books are not indexed in abstracting and indexing services.

SEARCH TIPS: Two useful, but unindexed, journals are *Comics Journal* and *Comic Book Checklist & Price Guide* (PN6714.C655). Current awareness publications, each includes articles reviewing past and present comic books, character development, artists, and history.

Finding women characters in comics is relatively easy using encyclopedias and histories of comic books such as *Crawford's Encyclopedia of Comic Books* (Middle Village, N.Y.: Jonathan David Publishers, 1978; PN6725.C7 N&CPR) and Mike Benton's *The Comic Book in America: An Illustrated History* (Dallas, Tex.: Taylor Publishing, 1989; PN6725.B38 1989 N&CPR). Comic book scholarship is accessible through indexes such as *Women Studies Abstracts* (Z962.W65 MRR Alc), *MLA International Bibliography* (Z7006.M64 MRR Alc; OCLC FirstSearch), and *America, History and Life* (Z1236.A488 N&CPR, ABC-CLIO database). Much more difficult to research are women illustrators and writers who worked on women's comic books or on the male superhero issues. These women are often unidentified even in the fine print of the comic book.

Subject headings for comic book research tend to be very general (comic books and comic strips are considered together in Library of Congress subject headings) but lead to some surprisingly specific sources. For example, the subject heading "Women—Comic books, strips, etc." includes the title *The Poison Maiden and the Great Bitch: Female Stereotypes in Marvel Superhero Comics* by Susan Wood (San Bernardino, Calif.: R. Reginald/Borgo Press, 1989; PN6725.W66 1989) and Trina Robbins's *The Great Women Superheroes* (Northampton, Mass.: Kitchen Sink Press, c1996; PN6725.R59 1996).

SEARCH TIPS: The comic book collection can be searched by individual title in the Library's online catalog. Subject headings are used sparingly to describe individual titles, and many are given the general heading of "Comic books, strips, etc." In cases where a single character is the focus of a comic book, the name of the character is the subject heading, e.g., "Wonder Woman (Fictitious character)."

EXAMPLES: *I Love Lucy Comics* (Comics box 161) has the subject "Women comedians—Comic books, strips, etc.—Periodicals." The sole subject heading for *Romance Trail* (Comics box 312) is "Western comic books, strips, etc."

SAMPLE LCSH: Comic books, strips, etc.**—United States—History and criticism; Cartoons and comics; Heroes; Popular culture—United States.**

Pulp Fiction

The pulp fiction collection at the Library of Congress consists of issues received for copyright deposit at the time of their publication, dating from the 1920s to the 1950s. The collection consists of approximately 310 titles and 14,000 issues. The majority were held by the Serial and Government Publications Division until preserved on film. Three extremely rare and valuable titles are available in the Rare Book and Special Collections Division: *Amazing Stories, Black Mask,* and *Weird Tales.* Microfilmed titles, available in the Microform Reading Room, can be found by searching the Library's online catalog. For these, the division retains all original color covers in preservation sleeves.

An inventory of the collection is available in the Newspaper and Current Periodical Room in a card file arranged by title. Each issue (and any duplicates) received was checked in on a card and assigned a box location. "Pulp Fiction in the Library of Congress: A Finding Aid" compiled by Janelle M. Zauha in August 1992 (N&CPR Reference Desk) provides holdings information and notes on the collection that supplements the card file index. A list of titles that have been microfilmed is available at <http://www.loc.gov/rr/news/pulp.html>.

Secondary sources provide overviews, histories, and bibliographies for the pulps. Lee Server's *Danger Is My Business: An Illustrated History of the*

Fabulous Pulp Magazines (San Francisco: Chronicle Books, 1993; PN4878.5.S47 1995 N&CPR) is a profusely illustrated, highly readable overview of these "fabulous" titles. Server highlights the most prolific and most accomplished writers and categorizes pulps by genre—such as adventure, private eye, romance, horror, or science fiction titles. In contrast, *Cheap Thrills: An Informal History of the Pulp Magazines* by Ron Goulart (New Rochelle, N.Y.: Arlington House, 1972; PS379.G6 N&CPR) relies less on illustration and concentrates on one particular period, detailing the "heyday of the pulp magazine" from 1920 to 1940. Cover art is also a subject of interest, as Jaye Zimet's *Strange Sisters: The Art of Lesbian Pulp Fiction, 1949–1969* (New York: Viking Studio, 1999; NC973.5.U6 Z56 1999) documents.

One of the most exhaustive indexes and checklists to the pulp magazines is *The Pulp Magazine Index* compiled by Leonard A. Robbins (Mercer Island, Wash.: Starmont House, 1988; Z1231.F4 R54 N&CPR), a multivolume set with indexes by author, artist, character, and magazine. Other indexes to pulp fiction focus on specific genres, as does *Mystery, Detective, and Espionage Fiction: A Checklist of Fiction in U.S. Pulp Magazines, 1915–1974* by Michael L. Cook and Stephen T. Miller, in two volumes (New York: Garland Publishing, 1988; Z1231.D47C66 1988 N&CPR).

SEARCH TIP: Pulp fiction tends to be classed by genre, and there is no subject heading for "pulp fiction" per se. To find information about the pulps, the following, very general Library of Congress subject headings are useful, but they obviously apply to other literary topics as well.
SAMPLE LCSH: Popular literature; Literature and society—United States—History—20th century; Magazine covers—United States. Genre headings for pulp fiction include: **Detective and mystery stories, American; Spy stories, American; Crime in literature; Western stories; Science fiction—American.**

FINDING THE WOMEN

The collections of the Serial and Government Publications Division can be characterized as treasure troves of material on women waiting to be unearthed. Often requiring imaginative search strategies and patient, time-consuming scanning of material, the collections are nonetheless rich sources for making discoveries about both the emergence of women in the media and society's perception of American women.

Newspapers and Women

Open any newspaper today and women can be found on every page—in articles, in advertisements, as reporters, and as publishers. Finding the women in the newspapers of yesteryear is more of a challenge—women involved in the production of newspapers were often unnamed, women reporters had to prove their competence, and newspaper publishers and advertisers only slowly recognized the importance of women as audience and as consumers.

Women and the News Business

The collection of the Serial and Government Publications Division reflects the presence of women in the newspaper business from its colonial beginnings. In the early eighteenth century, women often worked alongside their husbands and brothers to publish a newspaper as a family business. In some cases, a wife became a publisher upon her husband's death, usually until a son could take over the paper. The influence of women as active participants in the family newspaper business is an enduring feature of newspaper history to the present day, as Katharine Graham's leadership at the *Washington Post* exemplifies.

As the *South Carolina Gazette* (News MF 1468) documents, the first woman publisher was Elizabeth Timothy (ca. 1700–1757), who ran the Charleston newspaper in 1739 upon the death of her husband, Lewis Timothy. According to Kay Mills in *A Place in the News* (New York: Dodd, Mead, 1988; PN4784.W7M55 1988 N&CPR), Lewis Timothy went into business with Benjamin Franklin, who later found the widow a far better business partner than her husband. "Her accounts were clearer, she collected on more bills, and she cut off advertisements if payments were not current" (p. 16). Elizabeth Timothy identifies herself as the successor to her husband as editor, but her son Peter is listed as the printer (even though he did not actually take over the newspaper until years later). Mary Katherine Goddard (1738–1816), printer and publisher of the *Maryland Journal* (News box 8, folio 8–15, and News BD 235–36) of Baltimore, during her brother's absence from 1774 to 1783, supported the patriots during the American Revolution, printed and distributed the first official copy of the Declaration of Independence, and published "extraordinaries" that chronicled American successes during the Revolution, among them her July 12, 1775, account of the battle of Bunker Hill.

Talented American women found opportunities in the newspaper business as publishers and as editors. Cornelia Walter (1813–1898) became the first woman to edit a daily newspaper in America while working at the *Boston Transcript* from 1842 to 1847. Her departure was noted by newspapers around the country, and the newspaper's owners

The New Northwest.

DUNIWAY PUBLISHING COMPANY, Proprietors.

OFFICE—Cor. Front & Washington Streets

TERMS, IN ADVANCE:

One year ... $3 00
Six months ... 1 50
Three months ... 1 00

ADVERTISEMENTS inserted on Reasonable Terms.

The New Northwest.

FREE SPEECH, FREE PRESS, FREE PEOPLE.

VOLUME IX. PORTLAND, OREGON, THURSDAY, NOVEMBER 27, 1879. NUMBER 11.

The New Northwest

A Journal for the People.
Devoted to the Interests of Humanity.
Independent in Politics and Religion.
Alive to all Live Issues, and Thoroughly Radical in Opposing and Exposing the Wrongs of the Masses.

Correspondents writing over assumed signatures must make known their names to the Editor, or no attention will be given to their communications.

New Northwest *(Portland, Oregon), Thursday, November 27, 1879 (Oregon portfolio 9354-X). Serial and Government Publications Division.*

Abigail Scott Duniway, Engraving, 1870–90. Biographical file. Prints and Photographs Division. LC-USZ61-787.

Abigail Scott Duniway (1834–1915) edited and published the *New Northwest* from May 1871 to 1887 as part of her fight for women's suffrage in Oregon. Advertisements for the *New Northwest* describe it as "not a Woman's Rights, but a Human Rights organ, devoted to whatever policy may be necessary to secure the greatest good to the greatest number. It knows no sex, no politics, no religion, no party, no color, no creed. Its foundation is fastened upon the rock of Eternal Liberty, Universal Emancipation, and Untrammeled Progression." Many of the agents authorized to distribute copies of the newspaper throughout the Pacific Northwest were women.

commended her work (*Boston Transcript;* News MF 1868, September 1, 1847, 1):

> The experiment of placing a lady as the responsible editor of a Daily Paper was a new and doubtful one. It was a bold step on her part to undertake so much labor and responsibility. She made the trial with fear and trembling, and her success has been triumphant. The task had never been undertaken in this or any other country, to the knowledge of the publishers, by one of her sex; it was consequently the more trying, and her victory the more brilliant.

Ida B. Wells-Barnett (1862–1931) became part owner and editor of the *Memphis Free Speech and Headlight* in 1889. American expatriate Mary Ann Shadd Cary (1823–1893), abolitionist and free woman of color, published newspapers in Canada.

The newspaper collection also represents the gradual emergence of women as reporters and columnists. Not until the nineteenth century do women begin to establish reporting careers in their own right. Horace Greeley appointed the already notable Margaret Fuller (1810–1850) as the first woman literary critic of the *New York Tribune* (News MF 1358), for which she also wrote investigative articles on women prisoners, prostitution, and insane asylums. She became one of America's first women foreign correspondents and covered the Italian republican uprisings of 1848–49. By midcentury, Jane Cunningham Croly (1829–1901), who wrote under the pen name Jennie June, was one of the first women syndicated columnists. Through her fashion columns in the *New York World* (News MF 1363, 1862–72), *New York Times* (News Self-Service, 1864–72), and *New York Daily Graphic* (News MF 2980, 1873–78; originals in P&P, 1872–78), Jennie June is credited with starting the woman's page in newspapers. By the end of the nineteenth century, her column regularly appeared in newspapers in every state in the country, and she was considered the best known woman journalist in America.[5] Presidential wives also found self-expression as columnists: Eleanor Roosevelt (1884–1962) penned the column "My Day," which was syndicated nationwide, and, more recently, Hillary Rodham Clinton (b. 1946) wrote a weekly newspaper column.

Women who were associated with some of the great newspaper dynasties became journalistic leaders in their own right. Helen Rogers (1882–1970) married into the Reid family of the *New York*

Tribune (News MF 1358) and served as the paper's vice president. In that position of influence she actively campaigned for women's suffrage and hired women for the newspaper staff, employing more women than any other U.S. daily. (See chapter 5 for the Reid Family papers.) In 1930, Eleanor "Cissy" Patterson (1881–1948), granddaughter of *Chicago Tribune* (News Self-Service) editor Joseph Medill, became editor and publisher of the *Washington Herald* (News MF 1011), soon to become the largest morning circulation newspaper in Washington.[6] Patterson's niece, Alicia Patterson (1906–1963), became editor of the Long Island daily *Newsday* (News MF 2463) in 1940 and held that position until her death.

Women Reporters

Their experiences in the field as reporters often caused women to become reform-minded. While working for the *Chicago Herald* (News MF 2133), Teresa Howard Dean (d. 1935) was assigned to cover the Sioux Ghost Dance phenomenon. Initially neutral on government Indian policy, she arrived in Pine Ridge, South Dakota, only weeks after the Wounded Knee massacre of December 1890, and there she gradually developed sympathy and respect for the Sioux. Dean criticized fellow reporters who used the massacre as an opportunity for self-promotion.[7] Likewise, many women reformers were inspired by their stints as reporters early in their careers to support reforms. The "sob sisters," reporters Winifred Black (1863–1936), Dorothy Dix (aka Elizabeth Meriweather, 1861–1951), Ada Patterson (1867–1939), and Nixola Greeley-Smith (1880–1919) were known for their investigative, undercover exposés that often led to reform of public institutions.[8] In 1921 reporter Genevieve Forbes Herrick (1894–1962) disguised herself as an immigrant to expose conditions at Ellis Island for an article in the *Chicago Tribune* that led to national scrutiny.

Minority women journalists found opportunities in the ethnic press. African American women journalists rose to prominence after the Civil War. Ida B. Wells-Barnett, a well-known activist and a former slave, wrote for the *New York Age* (News MF 1316) in the 1890s and championed women's rights and human rights in her stories, speaking out against lynchings that targeted blacks. Victoria Earle Matthews (1861–1907) worked for several New York dailies, including the *New York Times* and the *New York Herald* (News MF 1330), as well as prominent black newspapers such as the *Chicago Defender* (News MF 1057), *Washington Bee* (News MF 1008), and *Detroit Plain Dealer* (News MF 1217). During World War II the five women who made up the "Mosquito Patrol" (so called for their slender frames, rapidity of movement, and accuracy of reporting)—Ruth A. Jenkins (1921?–1997), Louise Hines, Mae Medders (1923?–1996), Audrey Weaver (1913–1996), and Frances Murphy—reported on segregation and discrimination at home for the *Baltimore Afro-American* (News MF 1182) while their male colleagues covered the war.

Foreign newspapers are also revealing as sources for studying American women. Not only do they illustrate what women and men outside the United States have considered important in America, but they have provided employment for American women reporters. One of many women journalists following World War I who saw Europe as a place of opportunity, Dorothy Thompson (1893–1961) achieved initial fame as foreign correspondent for the *Manchester Guardian* (News MF 328) and the *Philadelphia Public Ledger* (News MF 1449). She interviewed politicians such as Czechoslovakian president Tomás Masaryk and German Nazi leader Adolf Hitler. Thompson interviewed Hitler in 1931, and dismissed him as "inconsequent and voluble, ill-poised, and insecure," an opinion she was to regret later. Eventually her anti-Nazi reports led to her expulsion from

New Editor-In-Chief

—From a Drawing by Neysa McMein

MRS. ELEANOR MEDILL PATTERSON, who will become Editor-in-Chief of The Washington Herald, August 1. Her appointment was announced yesterday.

ANNOUNCEMENT

The Washington Herald makes the following announcement:

Mrs. Eleanor Medill Patterson, beginning August 1, will assume the direction of The Washington Herald, as editor-in-chief.

Mrs. Patterson and her family have long been known in Washington in official and other circles.

The new editor of The Washington Herald comes naturally by journalistic ability. Her grandfather was Joseph Medill, founder of the Chicago Tribune, and she has been very successful as a writer of novels and signed articles.

Mrs. Patterson is a first cousin of the late Senator Medill McCormick, and of R. R. McCormick, publisher of the Chicago Tribune. She is the sister of Joseph Medill Patterson, publisher of the New York Daily News and Liberty Magazine.

Mrs. Patterson has long been anxious to engage in active newspaper work which has occupied members of her family for three generations.

For a long time she endeavored to purchase The Washington Herald, of which she now becomes the active editor. But, Hearst newspapers are not for sale.

Mrs. Patterson will work as editor of The Herald under the regular Hearst newspaper contract.

Mrs. Patterson, who was formerly the Countess Gizycka, and who subsequently married the well known lawyer, Elmer Schlesinger, at her mother's request has resumed her maiden name which is the same as her mother's, Eleanor Medill Patterson.

Mrs. Patterson's mother is one of the two daughters of Joseph Medill.

The Washington Herald feels sure that Mrs. Patterson, who, in accordance with Galton's law, inherits the genius of her grandfather, will be very successful and INTERESTING as editor of a Washington daily newspaper.

"New Editor-in-Chief." Washington Herald, *July 23, 1930 (News MF 1011). **Serial and Government Publications Division.***

Eleanor Medill Patterson (1881–1948) was the granddaughter of *Chicago Tribune* editor Joseph Medill and sister of *New York Daily News* publisher Joseph Medill Patterson. Despite her family heritage, she had little journalistic work experience until she was appointed editor of the *Washington Herald* in 1930, taking over one of the failing newspapers of the William Randolph Hearst empire. By 1936 she had doubled its daily circulation to over 100,000. She is among the few women to be named editor of a daily newspaper and certainly unusual in being so prominently welcomed to her position, as this front page article in the *Washington Herald* did in its announcement.

SUNDAY, JANUARY 10, 1892—THIRTY-TWO PAGES.

SITUATIONS WANTED—FEMALE.

Miscellaneous.

WANTED—MALE HELP.

Bookkeepers and Clerks.

Stenographers.

Salesmen.

WANTED—MALE HELP.

Salesmen.

Solicitors and Canvassers.

Boys.

Trades.

WANTED—MALE HELP.

Miscellaneous.

WANTED—FEMALE HELP.

Bookkeepers and Clerks.

Stenographers.

Dressmakers.

"Wanted—Male Help; Wanted—Female Help." From Chicago Tribune, *January 10, 1892 (bound newspaper, no. 7635). Serial and Government Publications Division.*

This page from an 1892 *Chicago Tribune* typifies the employment advertising practices of a century, with the headings "Wanted—Male Help" and "Wanted—Female Help." Until the late 1960s and early 1970s most newspapers had separate listings by gender for help-wanted ads. The impetus for change was the Civil Rights Act of 1964. In 1968 the Equal Employment Opportunity Commission issued guidelines for employment ads: "The placement of an advertisement in columns classified by publishers on the basis of sex, such as columns headed 'male' or 'female,' will be considered an expression of preference, limitation, specification, or discrimination based on sex" (29 CFR 1604.5). The American Newspaper Publishers Association challenged the guidelines and voiced many of the arguments held by advertisers and publishers, including anticipated advertising revenue losses and inconvenience to job seekers. By the mid-1970s, challenges by women's groups, public opinion, and failed court cases led to the eradication of separate want ads. Judge Kramer's opinion in the 1972 case *Pittsburgh Press Company v. Pittsburgh Commission on Human Relations* captures the new attitude: "It is no longer possible to state that all women desire, or have an 'interest' in, any one type or classification of work. Some women have the desire, ability and stamina to do any work that men can do. Once we accept such a premise it then becomes logically impossible to permit continued segregation of employment want ads by column headings for any job" (*Pittsburgh Press v. Pittsburgh Commission on Human Relations,* 287 A.2d 161 1972).

Germany. She became a columnist for the *New York Herald-Tribune* (News MF 1330) in 1936, and her controversial column "On the Record" gave her the reputation for being the most famous woman in America after Eleanor Roosevelt.[9] Less well known is war correspondent Frances Davis, who, as the London *Daily Mail*'s (News MF 2211) only woman reporter in the 1930s, was seriously wounded covering the Spanish Civil War.[10]

Women in the News

As one of the most readily accessible media for the general population of America, newspapers present a rich and full picture of the daily life of women over time. Not only is the content of the articles revealing, but their placement in an issue or on a page, next to an advertisement or a photograph, speaks volumes about the newspaper editors' assumptions about audience views of women.

Announcements of births, weddings, and deaths traditionally document women's place in society. The presence or absence of obituaries for women, as well as their content, is indicative of women's status in society. Likewise, employment ads in newspapers indicate wider societal viewpoints, and not just by job titles and salaries: until the late 1960s, want ads segregated by gender were commonplace in all major newspapers.

Of course, women were also the subject of newspaper articles. As early as colonial times, articles reporting crimes against women or by women were numerous, the more sensational the better. One of the first news reports about a colonial American woman described a purported kidnapping of a servant girl by four Indians. However, according to a handwritten notation on the page containing this report in the Library's copy of the *Boston Newsletter* of May 8, 1704 (News MF 1930 ESR Mass Na reel 1), this was a false report: "This story was a fiction contrived by the girl to excuse her too long stay at the spring with a young man who met her there." In the early American press, women were depicted in two basic, and opposite, ways—as either the virtuous woman or the vicious woman.

"To Married Women—Madame Restell, Female Physician," from New York Herald, *April 13, 1840 (News MF 1330).*

"Mrs. Bird, Female Physician," and "To the Ladies—Madame Costello, Female Physician," from New York Sun, *February 24, 1842 (News MF 1357).*

"French Periodical Pills," from Boston Daily Times, *January 6, 1845 (bound volume, no. 8256).*

Serial and Government Publications Division.

Besides the ubiquitous advertisements for hair products, complexion lotions, clothing, and dry goods that appeared in every newspaper, some newspapers accepted advertisements for thinly disguised treatment for unwanted pregnancies. Advertisers cloaked their remedies in phrases such as "Preventive Powders for married ladies, whose health forbids a too rapid increase of family," "treatment of obstinate case of female irregularity, stoppage of suppression," and relief "from severe pains which they occasionally suffer periodically." One advertisement by a Dr. L. Monroe in the *Boston Daily Times* (January 6, 1845, p. 4, c. 6) carefully advises that "ladies married should not take them if they have reason to believe they are enciente [*sic*], as they are sure to produce a miscarriage."

In New York, the *Sun* and the *Herald* accepted advertisements from abortionists such as Madame Restell, Madame Costello, and Mrs. Bird. Their ads were not, however, universally accepted. The *New York Tribune* refused them all, and Horace Greeley even campaigned through editorials to bring attention to the "infamous and unfortunately common crime—so common that it affords a lucrative support to a regular guild of professional murderers, so safe that its perpetrators advertise their calling in the newspapers" (*New York Herald,* August 20, 1871, p. 4, c. 3). The presence of such advertisements in major newspapers, the success of abortion practitioners (Madame Restell became a millionaire), and the relative lack of prosecution despite its illegality and public censure suggest nineteenth-century society's ambivalence toward abortion.

Elizabeth Blackwell (1821–1910), the first American woman to receive a medical degree, labored against the misconception, fostered by newspaper advertisements of the day, that a female physician was by definition an abortionist. In *Pioneer Work in Opening the Medical Profession to Women* (London: Longmans, Green, and Co.,1895; R133.B63 GenColl), Blackwell states the dilemma when recounting her decision to pursue a medical degree: "There was at that time a certain Madame Restell flourishing in New York. This person was a noted abortionist, and known all over the country. She was a woman of great ability, and defended her course in the public papers. She made a large fortune, drove a fine carriage, had a pew in a fashionable church, and though often arrested, was always bailed out by her patrons. She was known distinctively as a 'female physician,' a term exclusively applied at that time to those women who carried on her vile occupation" (pp. 29–30). Not until the passage of the Comstock Act of 1873 did the "public papers" cease to carry such advertisements.

Later, the undercover investigations by Nellie Bly (1864–1922), Winifred Black, and others focused on women in jeopardy, and society's horrified reaction to their discoveries often led to reform. Nellie Bly's portrayal of a deranged, Spanish-speaking woman committed to Blackwell's Island asylum published in the *New York World* (News MF 1363) was one of the first exposés concerning the taboo subject of mental illness.[11] When Winifred Black, writing as Annie Laurie,

TO MARRIED WOMEN—MADAME RESTELL, *Female Physician*, is happy to have it in her power to say that since the introduction into this country, about a year ago of her celebrated Preventive Powders for married ladies, whose health forbids a too rapid increase of family; hundreds have availed themselves of their use, with a success and satisfaction that has at once dispelled the fears and doubts of the most timid and skeptical; for, notwithstanding that for twenty years they have been used in Europe with invariable success, (first introduced by the celebrated Midwife and Female Physician. Madame Restell, the grandmother of the advertiser, who made this subject her particular and especial study,) still some were inclined to entertain some degree of distrust, until become convinced by their successful adoption in this country. The results of their adoption to the happiness, the health, nay, often the life of many an affectionate wife and a fond mother, are too vast to touch upon within the limits of an advertisement—results which affect not only the present well-being of parents, but the future happiness of their offspring. Is it not but too well known that the families of the married often increase beyond the happiness of those who give them birth would dictate? In how many instances does the hardworking father, and more especially the mother, of a poor family, remain slaves throughout their lives, tugging at the oar of incessant labor, toiling to live, and living but to toil; when they might have enjoyed comfort and comparative affluence; and if care and toil have weighed down the spirit, and at last broken the health of the father, how often is the widow left, unable, with the most virtuous intentions, to save her fatherless offspring from becoming degraded objects of charity or profligate votaries of vice? And even though competence and plenty smile upon us, how often, alas! are the days of the kind husband and father embittered in beholding the emaciated form and declining health of the companion of his bosom, ere she had scarce reached the age of thirty—fast sinking into a premature grave—with the certain prospect of himself being early bereft of the partner of his joys and sorrows, and his young and helpless children of the endearing attentions and watchful solicitude which a mother alone can bestow, not unfrequently at a time when least able to support the heart-rending affliction! Is it desirable then—is it moral for parents to increase their families, regardless of consequences to themselves or the well being of their offspring when a simple, easy healthy and CERTAIN remedy is within our control? The advertiser feeling the importance of this subject and estimating the vast benefits resulting to thousands by the adoption of means prescribed by her, would respectfully arouse the attention of the married, by all that they hold near and dear to its consideration. Is it not wise and virtuous to prevent evils to which we are subject by simple and healthy means within our control? Every dispassionate, virtuous, and enlightened mind will unhesitatingly answer in the affirmative. This is all that Madame Restell recommends or ever recommended. Price Five Dollars a package, accompanied with full and particular directions. For the convenience of those unable to call personally, "Circulars" more fully explanatory, will be sent free of expense (postage excepted) to any part of the United States. All letters must be post-paid, and addressed to MADAME RESTELL, Female Physician. Principal office. 148 Greenwich street, New-York. Office hours from 9 A. M to 7 P. M. Philadelphia office, 39½ South Eighth street.

ap10 1m*

MRS. BIRD, Female Physician, where can be obtained Dr. Vandenburgh's Female Renovating Pills, from Germany, an effectual remedy for suppression, irregularity, and all cases where nature has stopped from any cause whatever. Sold only at Mrs. Bird's, 83 Duane st, near Broadway.

n24 3m*

TO THE LADIES—Madame Costello, Female Physician, still continues to treat, with astonishing success, all diseases peculiar to females. Suppression, irregularity, obstruction, &c., by whatever cause produced, can be removed by Madame C. in a very short time. Madame C's medical establishment having undergone thorough repairs and alterations for the better accommodation of her numerous patients, she is now prepared to receive ladies on the point of confinement, or those who wish to be treated for obstruction of their monthly periods. Madame C. can be consulted at her residence, 34 Lispenard st, at all times.—All communications and letters must be post paid.

f2f 1m*

FRENCH PERIODICAL PILLS.

Warranted to have the desired effect in all cases.

THESE Pills contain a portion of the only article in the whole meteria medica, which can regulate the system and produce the monthly turns of females that can be taken, without hazarding life, and this article is not to be found in any of the pills or nostrums which are pictured forth so largely in the papers of the day. It has frequently occurred that the unhappy patient has by the use of these pills and nostrums given nature such a shock that they have never since enjoyed health, and they never can. It seems that they are got up and advertised merely for the object of making money, regardless of the consequences, and the venders are usually considered beneath responsibility, by all who know them.

The French Periodical Pills are the result of thn combined knowledge and experience of some of the oldest and most distinguished physicians of Europe, and have been used by females embracing the gentility and most of the nobility of France, for the last twenty-three years. To eulogize their virtues would not add to their merits. We will only say TRY THEM, and if they do not prove to be what they are here represented to be, your money shall be refunded.

They contain no medicine detrimental to the constitution, but restore all debilitated constitutions to their wonted energy and healthfulness by removing from the system every impurity.

The only precaution necessary to be observed is ladies married should not take them if they have reason to believe they are en ciente, as they are sure to produce a miscarriage, almost without the knowledge of the patient, so gentle yet active are they,

All letters to be directed to DR. L. MONROE, U. S. Agent and Importer. No 58 Union street, Boston.

N. B. The above Pills can only be obtained at 58 Union street, all sold elsewhere in Boston, are counterfeit, and only calculated to deceive.

N. B Full directions accompanying the Pills.

3 w* d 11

THE BLACK LIST OF STATES.

Below we give the black list of States, showing the limit at which fathers, brothers and husbands have placed the age at which a little girl may consent to her ruin:

SEVEN YEARS.
Delaware.

TEN YEARS.
Alabama, North Carolina, South Carolina.

TWELVE YEARS.
Kentucky, Louisiana, Texas, Wisconsin, Virginia.

THIRTEEN YEARS.
Iowa, New Hampshire, Utah.

FOURTEEN YEARS.
Arizona, California, Connecticut, Georgia, Idaho, Illinois, Indiana, Maine, Maryland, Michigan, Minnesota, Missouri, Nevada, New Mexico, North Dakota, Ohio, Oregon, Vermont, West Virginia.

FIFTEEN YEARS.
Montana.

SIXTEEN YEARS.
Arkansas, District of Columbia, Massachusetts, Mississippi, New Jersey, New York, Pennsylvania, Rhode Island, South Dakota, Tennessee, Washington.

SEVENTEEN YEARS.
Florida.

Kansas and Wyoming have raised the age of consent to eighteen years.

Colorado has made it twenty-one. The bill was introduced by a woman, and the Legislature so records in its archives.

"In Possession." Milwaukee Journal, *February 22, 1895 (News MF 1533). Serial and Government Publications Division.*

The *Milwaukee Journal* was one of many newspapers that sponsored a women's edition for charitable purposes. This lighthearted cartoon captures the sense and sensibility of the special edition: for a single day the *Journal* was completely staffed by women and run according to women's rules (note the "No Smoking" sign), with the men waiting nearby to congratulate them—and return to the status quo.

Alice Russell Glenny. Women's Edition (Buffalo) Courier. *Color lithograph, poster. Artist Posters. Prints and Photographs Division. LC-USZC2-1727.*

The *Buffalo Courier's* Women's Edition of forty pages (versus the usual ten) was published May 8, 1895. Women's editions were promoted with colorful posters and flyers to attract readers and advertisers alike; this one was designed by Alice Russell Glenny (1858–1924).

"The Black List of States." Courier-Journal *(Louisville, Kentucky) March 27, 1895 (News MF 1158). Serial and Government Publications Division.*

Women writers and editors used the women's editions to comment about issues of importance to them. The Louisville women who produced this issue of the *Courier-Journal* took the opportunity to highlight what they considered a social injustice: the age (which varied by state) at which young girls could dispose of property or contract legal marriage. The thick black edging was typically used for death announcements, and readers would undoubtedly have understood the message it was intended to suggest.

went undercover as a vagrant in 1890 for the *San Francisco Examiner* (News Self-Service), her writings increased the newspaper's circulation and led to a complete review of hospital services for the poor as well as the creation of San Francisco's first ambulance service.

Women as Audience

Newspaper publishers and advertisers were quick to realize the purchasing power of women. In the nineteenth century, sections of the newspaper were directed to women in their roles as homemakers and mothers. Eliza Jane Poitevent Holbrook Nicholson (1849–1896) increased readership when she added women's and children's features to the *New Orleans Daily Picayune* (News MF 1167) after becoming publisher in 1876. The women's pages that originated in the late nineteenth century targeted the women's market and quickly became ubiquitous, appearing in ethnic and small town newspapers as well as those of large metropolitan areas. To attract women readers, publishers hired women reporters to report on society news, community projects, homemaking tips, fashion, and recipes.

Many prominent women reporters got their start on the women's page and then moved on to investigative journalism, but others found their niche in covering women's issues. Inez Callaway Robb (1901–1979) was a society editor for the *New*

York Daily News (News MF 1343) in the 1920s, but earned a 1957 Newspaper Women's Club award with her syndicated news column "Assignment America." In the 1920s, Helen Rowland (1875–1950) attained great popularity with her column, variously titled "Widow Wordalogues," "Meditations of a Married Woman," and "Marry-Go-Round." Helen Worden also found great success in the women's pages of the *New York World* (News MF 1363) and *World-Telegram* (News MF 1365) with her "Sally Lunn" cooking column and "What Society Is Wearing." Although often dismissed as fluff, the women's pages provide a picture of what family and household life was like over time. Beginning in the mid-twentieth century, women's pages began to disappear, replaced by lifestyle and entertainment sections of more general interest. More recently, women's pages are being reinvented again to target an important audience. In 1990, the American Society of Newspaper Editors produced "Womenews," a prototype section, and the *Chicago Tribune* followed with a weekly Sunday section called "Womanews."

In addition, advertisers deliberately appealed to women. Although little quantitative research has been done on this subject, it is clear that nineteenth- and twentieth-century newspaper ads targeted women as customers. In contrast, seventeenth- and eighteenth-century newspapers lacked illustrated advertisements or were limited to announcements. Even though advertisements are not indexed, they, like the women's pages themselves, illustrate the varied interests of women over time and assist researchers who are reconstructing the daily life of women in the past. Nineteenth-century advertisements for corsets, sewing machines, and medicinal cures can be found next to those for plows and wagons.

Contemporary Women's Magazines

Perhaps even more than the daily newspaper, current periodicals represent the diversity of interests of the American reading public. Through home subscriptions, newsstand purchases, library reader requests, and electronic subscriptions, Americans choose what interests them, and their "votes" determine what continues to be published in the United States. More than 75,000 periodicals are published each year in the United States and Canada alone, and that number swells to over 125,000 worldwide.[12] Consumer magazines alone account for more than 20,000 North American titles, and women's magazines have consistently

PATHFINDER: Women's Editions of Daily Newspapers

In the mid-1890s, philanthropic projects of women's clubs in large and small urban areas led to the appearance of women's editions of daily newspapers. Distinctly different from the women's pages common in many papers, women's editions involved the takeover of the newspaper by women for that day's edition. In many cases, women wrote, edited, typeset, and published the day's paper, filling it with lavish illustrations and numerous advertisements. Generally, the editions were much longer than the regular issues, and often they contained multiple sections.

Women's editions were published on religious or civic holidays, usually for fund-raising purposes. For example, the December 21, 1895, special edition of the *San Francisco Examiner* sold 130,000 copies and raised $10,000 for a local hospital. While thematically the editions often reflected the observed holiday, the content of these newspapers included local, national, and international news common to all newspapers. They covered women's issues and concerns to a greater extent than the regular edition. The front page of the 1895 "Charity Edition" of the *Milwaukee Journal* included the headline "Women Own It All," referring to the Washington, D.C., gathering of the Daughters of the American Revolution and the National Council of Women. That same issue also illustrated the sporting page with women playing golf and riding a bicycle. The editors of the Christmas 1895 *Rocky Mountain News* (News MF 991) created a "Man's Page" to highlight the "facts, fancies, faults, foibles, fads and fashions" of the nineteenth-century man. In a more serious vein, the *San Francisco Examiner*'s edition included an excerpt from the autobiography of Elizabeth Cady Stanton, and the *Louisville Courier-Journal* printed a "Black List of States" giving the legal age "at which a little girl may consent to her ruin."[13]

Although few women involved in producing the edition considered themselves career reporters or publishers, they were quite serious and proud of their work. Mrs. John Watkins Mariner, editor of the *Milwaukee Journal* (News MF 1533) "Charity Edition" of February 22, 1895, had two reasons for her involvement as editor: "The first and paramount one was, of course, to raise money for the poor; the second one was to succeed. I wanted to show what women could do."[14] That the men also took the women seriously is evident in the editorials about the edition and the advertisements that celebrated it. One of these, entitled "Well Done!" comes from the *Louisville Courier-Journal* (News MF 1158) of March 28, 1895; the January 24, 1895, issue of the *Cleveland Plain Dealer* (News MF 1411) carries such an advertisement; and another is "Empress of the Dailies: Something about the Paper the Ladies Will Publish" from the December 23, 1894, *San Francisco Examiner*, p. 17 (News MF 984). Researcher Ann Colbert has identified well over one hundred of these special issues from both major cities and small towns.[15] Of these, the division has a representative sample, primarily on microfilm.

The women's editions of these newspapers, opportunities for local women to express their social and political interests, also represent a brief time in the late nineteenth century when men supported, if only for a day, women's ventures into a male-dominated occupation.

ranked in the top ten magazine categories. Women represent 51 percent of Americans, and their purchasing power has long been recognized by advertisers, marketers, and publishers. In 1998 women's interest magazines were among the top twenty-five best-selling new magazine titles published.[16] Women's magazines account for half of the top ten magazines by circulation: *Better Homes and Gardens, Family Circle, Good Housekeeping, Ladies' Home Journal,* and *McCall's.*[17]

Women's consumer magazines may be the most popular magazines read by American women but they cover only some of the subjects of interest to women. The current periodical collection of the Serial and Government Publications Division is one of the few places where researchers in women's studies can find many of the most popular magazines side by side with the most esoteric. The diversity and size of the collection are its strengths. In addition to U.S. material, the division has a substantial collection of foreign periodicals in all western European languages; the United States is a fascinating object of study and imitation for many around the world. Periodicals can be used in a variety of ways to study women's issues: articles, columns, photographs, layout, and advertisements can all contribute to an understanding of popular and scholarly interests concerning women.

The current periodicals are arranged in closed stacks by title of journal—the title as listed in the Library of Congress Online Catalog (which may vary from its popular title owing to cataloging practices). On these shelves can be found *Cosmopolitan, More, Mode, Jane,* and *W,* but also *Out, Curve,* and *Bust.* General women's magazines (*McCall's, Good Housekeeping,* and *Ladies' Home Journal*) share shelf space with magazines targeting a narrower consumer audience (*Working Mother* and *New Woman*). Also available are supermarket tabloids; the *National Enquirer* (with older issues available on microfilm for use in the Microform Reading Room) and other tabloids include gossip, fashion, and rumor, making them among the most popular weeklies in America. Ethnic women have also become the focus of publishers: *Latina* and *Estylo* are directed toward Hispanic American women, and *Essence, Heart & Soul,* and *Sisters in Style* are among those targeting African American women.

Popular consumer magazines represent only one aspect of women's interests. Less common are literary and art journals created by feminists or intended for them: *Calyx, Kalliope, Hurricane Alice, Iris: A Journal about Women,* and *Writing for Our Lives.* Gender issues, politics, and public affairs have a woman's aspect, as represented in *Chrysalis, Issues Quarterly, Woman of Power, Peace and Freedom,* and *Z Magazine.* Publications investigating women in business, as professionals, and as activists include *Romance Writers Report, Soroptimist, Choices, For Entrepreneurial Women, Working Woman,* and *Social Anarchism.* Hobbies and home crafts are well represented in current periodicals (*McCall's Quilting, Boating for Women, Sportswoman, Taste of Home*) and reflect the diverse interests of women outside the workplace. Care-giving, single-parenting, and relationships are also important to women, as is religion (*Today's Christian Woman, Friendly Woman,* and *Church Woman*).

Eroticism and exploitation are represented in the collection as well. Copies of Hugh Hefner's *Playboy,* Larry Flynt's *Hustler,* and *Oui* are held in the division until bound to be permanently housed in the Rare Book and Special Collections Division. Similarly, *Playgirl* issues are available until bound. These titles share shelf space with *Easyriders* (entertainment for adult bikers) and *Biker* (intended "for dissenting adults only").

The current periodical collection contains thousands of titles that include articles by and about women. Although indexing is the preferred and invaluable way to discover women as subjects of articles and as authors, it is not uncommon for researchers in the Newspaper and Current Periodical Room to request all issues of a title in order to page through the publication and discover the women for themselves.

An emerging trend in periodicals is the "born digital" journal. The Internet is an increasingly important publishing medium, and more individuals, organizations, and publishers are taking advantage of its immediacy and accessibility to publish journals directly on the Web. Many journals (and newspapers) are publishing editions in paper and on the Web simultaneously but with different content. The Library's initial digital collecting efforts in serials have been concentrated on acquiring access to collections of periodicals, such as *Project Muse* (<http://muse.jhu.edu/journals>) and *JSTOR* (<http://www.jstor.org/jstor/>) (discussed in chapter 1). Recently an initiative to begin collecting digital serials in an organized way by extending already established Library of Congress collection policies to them has begun. Eventually born-digital periodicals like *Postmodern Culture* and *Salon* will be as accessible through the Library's online catalog as any print journal is today.

Women and Government Publications

Issues important to women are also policies of interest to governments and international organizations. Employment, health, education, and economic parity can be researched at state, national, and international levels through government publications housed in the Serial and Government Publications Division. Foreign government publications contain varied levels of detail concerning women in any particular country, and U.S. state publications reflect the importance of women in the American home, workplace, and society too. Their importance is mirrored on the national level as well. International organizations have also made conscious efforts to include women in their policy deliberations.

U.S. Government Publications

The Government Printing Office publishes technical reports, treatises, and histories, as well as popular, consumer-oriented information to educate and notify the American public about questions affecting large segments of the population, such as the importance of the census, child safety, or nutrition issues. The federal government is one of the largest research and analysis organizations in the world. Agencies conduct their own investigations and sponsor research through advisory commissions and contracts. The amount of information about women in government publications is vast and includes a broad range of data and a great variety of information. You can find here the number of Navajo women who are heads of household (that is, no spouse is present in the home) (U.S. Bureau of the Census, *1990 Census of Population, Characteristics of American Indians by Tribe and Language,* C 3.286:CD 90 SSTF 13) or how many women suffer from migraine headaches each year (U.S. National Center for Health Statistics, *Vital and Health Statistics,* Series 10, HE 20.6209:10/). Special programs available for women are made known in publications like the annual *Catalog of Federal Domestic Assistance* (PREX 2.20)—where women can find out how to benefit from such programs as the Women's Special Employment Assistance or Women's Business Ownership Assistance.

The SuDoc classification system groups print, electronic, and microfiche publications by issuing agency. Therefore, all publications issued by the Women's Bureau (such as the *Women's Newsletter*) are grouped together under the SuDoc **L 36.102-L 36.116** range. The annual Census Bureau publication *Fertility of American Women: Current Population Reports* (C 3.186/10) is housed with other Census publications such as *Households, Families, Marital Status, and Living Arrangements* (C 3.186/9) and *Household and Family Characteristics* (C 3.186/17). The series Women-Owned Businesses (C 3.250) is found with the Census series for the Construction Industry and Retail Trade. The annual *Data on Female Veterans* (VA 1.2/12) is one of many publications issued by the Department of Veterans Affairs' Statistical Policy and Research Service. This grouping may help researchers determine how an agency considers women in the context of its larger mission and gives researchers access to some of the primary data on which publications concerning women are based.

Corra la voz acerca de los Mamogramas y la prueba de papanicolaou o prueba pap: un recurso educativo para los profesionales de la salud [Spread the word about mammograms and the Pap test: an educational resource for health care professionals] (Washington: National Institutes of Health, National Cancer Institute, 1999; SuDoc no. HE 20.3152:P 19/7/DISPLAY). Serial and Government Publications Division.

An important purpose of government publications is to educate the public and publicize government-sponsored outreach services. This publication about mammograms was published in both English and Spanish. Colorful pictures introduce the importance of mammograms and Pap tests for women.

Federal Advisory Committees

Because Federal Advisory Committees reflect public policy issues of interest to the federal government and the public, they often take up social, scientific, health, and workplace issues. Women are the specific subject of a number of the FACs, including the Glass Ceiling Commission mentioned earlier. A twenty-one-member panel created in November 1991, it was formed to "focus greater attention to the importance of eliminating artificial barriers to the advancement of women and minorities to management and decisionmaking positions in business, and promote work force diversity" and to "facilitate, establish procedures, and make recommendations for the Frances Perkins-Elizabeth Hanford Dole National Award for Diversity and Excellence in American Executive Management" (Advisory Committee Charter, March 26, 1992). The resulting reports, *Good for Business* (Y 3.2:G46/B96) and *A Solid Investment* (Y 3.2:G 46/IN 8), were published as government publications. In 1997 the Defense Department established an eleven-member Advisory Commission on Gender-Integrated Training and Related Issues in the Military Services. The 1976–78 National Institute of Child Health and Human Development's Contraceptive Development Contract Review Commission (Health and Human Services), composed of clinical and research experts, determined methodologies for testing and monitoring the use of synthetic contraceptive drugs in male and female clinical trials. More recently, in March 1999, the President's Commission on the Celebration of Women in American History issued recommendations on how best to acknowledge the accomplishments of American women.

Federal Advisory Committees also document women's expanding role as experts and advisers. Women appointed to serve on such committees are either acknowledged experts in their fields or political stakeholders. For example, the annual report for the 1993 Women's Health Initiative Program Advisory Committee lists author Gail Sheehy and activist Linda Chavez among the twenty-three members of its panel. Editor Janet W. James and director Jeannette B. Cheek of the Schlesinger Library on the History of Women in America were members of the 1972 Advisory Committee on Women's Papers, recommending that the National Historical Publications Commission publish the papers of more than ninety women and women's organizations (Report of the Special Committee of the National Historical Publications Commission on Women's Papers, 1973).

Women and International Organizations

The United Nations has a variety of programs that highlight women's issues, promote human rights and gender equality, and monitor women's involvement in economic and social issues around the world. Official UN records, reports, studies, and statistical compendia include a wealth of information about American women, placing them and U.S. policies toward women's issues within a larger context. Because the collection dates to the founding of the United Nations and includes all of its member countries, it is quite feasible to do longitudinal, comparative studies on women's health, education, employment, and human rights.

American women have been involved in the United Nations since its founding. Eleanor Roosevelt was the first chairperson of the UN Commission on Human Rights. Jeane Kirkpatrick was named ambassador to the United Nations from 1981 to 1985. Madeleine Albright served from 1993 to 1997. Public statements by these and other American women who have spoken before the UN General Assembly and UN agencies attest to their power and influence in world affairs—and all are documented in the proceedings, press releases, and voting records of the institution.

The United Nations' policy toward women is represented in its many and varied agencies and programs that monitor women worldwide: UNICEF, the Women's Development Fund, the Commission on the Status of Women, and the International Research and Training Institute for the Advancement of Women. To date, the United Nations has sponsored four international conferences on women, the latest taking place in Beijing, as well as the United Nations Decade of Women (1976–85). The UN General Assembly has convened special sessions regarding women, most recently in June 2000, "Women 2000: Gender Equality, Development, and Peace for the Twenty-first Century." Beginning in 1970 within its own bureaucracy, the United Nations promoted balance and equality for women in the workforce. Enduring UN conventions, such as the Convention on the Elimination of All Forms of Discrimination against Women (CEDAW), are supported and promoted by Americans.

Other organizations, such as the World Health Organization and the Food and Agriculture Organization, related to the United Nations through treaty, also sponsor programs supporting women and children. The International Labour Organization promotes standards for women in the workforce. All produce statistics, reports, and studies which provide the basis for comparing American women with their counterparts around the world.

Carrie Chapman Catt, "Wonder Women of History," Wonder Woman, *no. 26, December 1947. Ellen Swallow Richards, "Wonder Women of History,"* Wonder Woman, *no. 50, November/December 1951. DC Comics, Inc. (Copyright deposit). Serial and Government Publications Division. Wonder Woman is a trademark of DC Comics © 2001. All rights reserved. Used with permission.*

"Wonder Women of History" appeared as a regular feature in the *Wonder Woman* comic book, with Florence Nightingale as the first, in issue no.1 of 1942, and ending with Gail Laughlin in issue no. 66 of May 1954. Since Wonder Woman's strength, speed, and agility are the result of her Amazon training rather than super powers, this feature also reinforced a major theme of the series: *any* young girl could become a wonder woman through personal initiative. Women from a variety of ethnic backgrounds, occupations, and historical time periods were included. Each biography was one to four pages in length.

Women in Popular Culture Collections

The special collections of the Serial and Government Publications Division contain two collections that represent the popular culture of America: comic books and pulp fiction.

Comic books began as a popular, relatively inexpensive American art form in the 1930s and have continued to flourish today. In addition to their value as collectibles, comic books are potentially rich sources for research in the arts, advertising, sociology, popular culture, and history. Perhaps no other medium provides such a popular representation of stereotypes, archetypes, national interests, and fads as do comic books. Comic books have evoked fervent reactions by detractors and enthusiasts who have interpreted their illustrations and story lines for their own ends. Women characters in comic books run the gamut from superhero, child, sidekick, romantic interest, model, outlaw, and ultimate erotic fantasy to serious career woman.

The first woman superhero, Wonder Woman, appeared in *All Star Comics,* no. 8, in December 1941 (Comics box 13a, and Comics microfiche) in a nine-page story of the Amazon princess Diana who nursed American Captain Steve Trevor back to health following an airplane crash. She debuted as the lead character in the inaugural issue of *Sensation Comics* (Comics box 329a–29b), arriving in the United States with Captain Trevor. Her creator, Dr. William Moulton Marston, a psychologist, who took the pen name of Charles Moulton, wanted Wonder Woman to be a role model for young girls of the 1940s and created a strong, self-reliant, and confident female superhero. In contrast, *Marge's Little Lulu* (Comics box 206a–6c), a comic book based on the *Saturday Evening Post* cartoon character, captured children's ingenuity and adult absurdity.

Since Wonder Woman's appearance, women in comic books have been represented in various ways, reflecting women's actual, imaginary, and stereotypical roles over time. Strong villains and heroines, such as those in *Planet Comics* (Comics box 282), appeared during World War II and represented women's contributions to the war effort. Such comic books existed side by side with *Canteen Kate* (Comics box 56b) and *Wartime Romances* (Comics box 426a).

Comic books can be found on all subjects. They

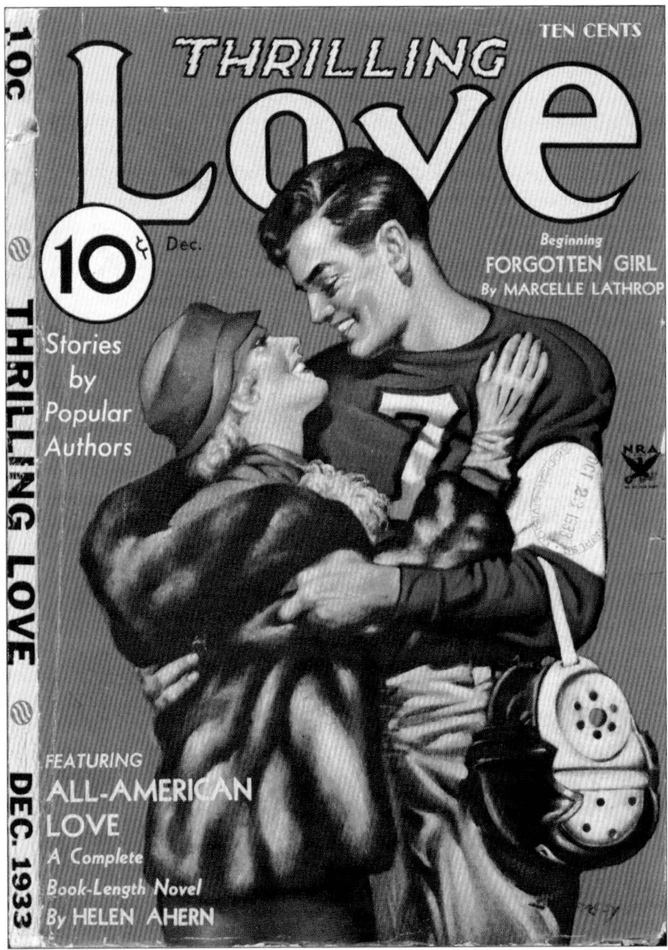

Thrilling Love, *December 1933 (Cover KM). Serial and Government Publications Division.*

The 1930s saw the expansion of the pulp magazine industry. Hundreds of titles appeared, covering all genres and special interests, from horror to true crime to racy magazines. Covers reflected the content of each issue, and a number of stereotypic views of women prevailed—woman as exotic temptress, woman in jeopardy (often in painful contortions) needing rescue, and woman as romantic interest. This *Thrilling Love* cover typifies the popular true-to-life romances—the sports hero being congratulated by an adoring All-American girl. The romance pulps were one of the few genres where women authors could receive credit for their work, as Marcelle Lathrop and Helen Ahern did here.

present beauty pageants, as does *Miss America* (Comics box 239b), or real and imagined movie stars, such as *Dale Evans* (Comics box 82a) and *Katy Keene* (Comics box 181a). Some, like *Nyoka, the Jungle Girl* (Comics box 264), show exotic locales. More recent acquisitions reflect the comic book industry's affiliation with horror, fantasy, and computer games—from *Elvira, Mistress of the Dark* (aka Cassandra Peterson) (Comics box 606), and *Elfquest,* created by husband and wife team Wendy and Richard Pini (Comics box 95c and 501a), to Anne Rice's *Vampire Lestat* (Comics box 17b). Underground comic books such as *Love and Rockets* (Comics box 559) and *Wimmen's Comics* (Comics box 521) represent the extreme in the industry. There are even comic books that satirize other comic books—just as *Not Brand Echh* (Comics box 263a), illustrated by Marie Severin, plays off other Marvel comics.

Another important collection that represents popular culture from the 1920s through the 1950s is the Library's collection of pulp fiction. "The Pulps," so called because they were printed on cheap, highly acidic paper, grew out of the dime novel industry of the nineteenth century (see chapter 4). Cheap, portable, disposable, and usually sensational in presentation and content, pulps can be considered predecessors to today's paperback books. At five to twenty-five cents an issue, pulp fiction was a literature accessible to Americans at every income level—often sold at newsstands and drugstores. Until the mid-1950s, pulp fiction was the literature of choice for the reading public, before it was supplanted by comic books and paperbacks.

Pulps presented stereotypic views of society, often within a fantastic, unusual setting. Every genre of literature is represented; indeed, the pulps popularized several genres and writing styles. They introduced writers such as Edgar Rice Burroughs, Ray Bradbury, and Max Brand to the reading public. Pulp fiction writers were often prolific, usually followed a formulaic style and plot, and were paid by the word. As Lee Server points out, publishing houses of pulp fiction were considered writing factories, and deceased authors could have their name appropriated by anonymous hacks in order to attract buyers and to increase revenue.[18]

Discussion of women in pulps often focuses on characters, which tended to be stereotypic and one-dimensional, and on cover artwork, which was deliberately enticing, exotic, and shocking. Women characters abounded in the pulps, sometimes as main characters but more often as companions, sidekicks, or inamoratas of male protagonists. Sue McEwen, the daughter of policeman Gilbert McEwen, had a supporting role in several Moon Man stories from *10 Detective Aces* (Microfilm 95/1697 MicRR). *Love Romances* and *Popular Love* glamorized women and fostered ideal love while appealing to women readers. *Oriental Stories* and *Dime Mystery Magazine,* intended for male audiences, studied the darker side of eroticism and romantic obsession.

Covers frequently depicted women as femmes fatales, damsels in distress, or the objects of either desire or torture. Few women artists are identified in histories or checklists. Margaret Brundage, an artist for *Weird Tales,* is one of the few women artists that we know of in the field. According to Tony Goodstone, author of *The Pulps: Fifty Years of American Pop Culture* (New York: Chelsea House, 1970; PZ1.G6524 Pu N&CPR), Brundage's highly erotic covers were controversial even for *Weird Tales* readers. Researching women writers of pulp fiction is equally difficult. As with comic books, writers wrote under several names, used initials, and in some cases made every attempt to conceal their gender. Some women, however, did achieve recognition in the field. Mary Elizabeth Counselman (1911–1995) wrote supernatural stories in *Weird Tales.* Dorothy McIlwraith was editor of *Short Stories* until 1938. In 1940, she joined the editorial staff of *Weird Tales,* where she served as editor until 1954.

As one kind of American popular culture, the pulps are a rich source for researchers to discover the place of women in American society and imagination. The stories and cover art in the division's collection capture a period of American history in which readers looked for escapism, titillation, and armchair adventure.

This chapter makes no claim to be an exhaustive study of women in the Serial and Government Publications collections. Instead, it offers research methodologies and possibilities, and it points out ways the collections can support various kinds of research concerning women. Newspapers, periodicals, government publications, and the popular comic books and pulp magazines can all contribute to the stories of American women. As this chapter suggests, there are many stories yet to be told.

For encouraging my participation in this project, I would like to thank the chief of the Serial Division, Karen Renninger, who not only offered her support but also read various drafts of the manuscript. Colleagues who generously shared their expertise and who critiqued multiple drafts include Mark Sweeney, head of the Newspaper Section; Lyle Minter, head of the Reference Section; and reference specialists Travis Westly and Sara Striner. I am indebted to my reference colleagues in the division who worked extra hours in the Newspaper and Current Periodical Room so that I could complete this chapter.

3 Law Library of Congress

Pamela Barnes Craig

The Law Library of Congress contains the largest body of United States federal and state law, foreign law, international law, and comparative law and legislation in the world. The breadth and depth of the Law Library's collections are extraordinary. Federal and state laws and court decisions from the colonial period to the present shed light on U.S. history. Laws of Massachusetts that date from the late seventeenth century and Virginia Court Reports dating from the early eighteenth century are available both in printed editions, housed with the Law Library's Rare Book Collection, and in microform.

Besides these primary source materials, legal treatises—for instance, *Blackstone's Commentaries* (see bibliography after section on Property Law)—form a strong component of the Law Library collections. Many early editions of common law treatises—from which numerous modern laws are derived—are among the holdings, as are legislative histories. For example, a collection of bound federal bills dating back to the 16th Congress is available for consultation. Through all these varieties of resources, the Law Library of Congress presents a wealth of legal information to support the study of women's issues.

Charles Dana Gibson. Studies in Expression: When Women Are Jurors. *Drawing, [1902?] Published in* Life, *October 23, 1902. Cabinet of American Illustration (CAI—Gibson, no. 23 [C size]). Prints and Photographs Division. LC-USZ62-46321.*

Women were virtually nonexistent on juries in 1902 when Charles Dana Gibson, creator of the famous "Gibson Girls," drew this caricature for *Life.* On rare occasions, however, women were called to serve in cases that involved female defendants. Despite the fact that juries are selected from voter rolls and the passage of the Nineteenth Amendment qualified women as "electors," the states did not immediately pass legislation to include them for jury selection. As late as 1942 only twenty-eight state laws allowed women to serve as jurors, but these also gave them the right to claim exemption based on their sex. The Civil Rights Act of 1957 gave women the right to serve on federal juries, but not until 1973 could women serve on juries in all fifty states.

Historically, the legal rights of women have been determined by men. Some legal historians even argue that women in the United States had no "legal rights" until 1920 when the Nineteenth Amendment was ratified. Although the lives of women had been affected by laws, women themselves had played no direct role in legislating or enforcing these laws. They could not vote to elect legislators and thus had no direct leverage in the electoral process. It seems ironic that Justice, the symbol of the United States court system, is female, yet for years women were not able to participate in the judicial system except as defendants or third parties. For the most part, women did not enter the courtroom as lawyers until the late nineteenth century, and they could not serve as jurors until the twentieth century.

Nevertheless, there were a number of laws from as early as the seventeenth century that specifically addressed women. Protective legislation limiting the number of hours women and children could work and court decisions addressing a woman's guilt or innocence in criminal proceedings or whether or not she could keep or devise her inherited property are examples.

Despite this wealth of legal information to support the study of women in diverse academic areas, court decisions and statutory language have been underused by scholars in disciplines other than legal history. The reasons for this vary, but most law librarians will agree that the challenges of legal research and a lack of knowledge about law may discourage historians and others from doing research in this area. The vast array of materials in the Law Library can be overwhelming to the researcher, especially if the methodology of legal research is unfamiliar. Because there are few guides, indexing sources, or treatises specifically addressing women's issues, using legal resources can be challenging—but can also result in rewarding discoveries.

USING THE COLLECTIONS

Using the legal collections of the Law Library requires an understanding of legal resources and basic legal methodology, as well as some knowledge of specific tools for research. Below is a discussion of methodology that will give a brief overview of legal research. Following that are sections on federal and state law that will give examples of laws that directly related to women and to the issues that affected them. Property, suffrage, and employment are areas that have distinct laws with a long history. Other issues are interesting for their exclusivity, such as laws relating to slavery and indentured servants. Civil rights and discrimination in employment—legislation that is fairly recent and whose basic issues are familiar to most women—will illustrate the major differences between federal and state law and their interdependence.

Catalogs and Subject Headings

As in other parts of the Library of Congress, the Library's online catalog can be used to find books and periodicals in the Law Library collections. It is important to gain some familiarity with classification of legal materials, specific subject headings, and catalogs that may be helpful.

The Law Library collections have various classification numbers (or call numbers). Most law materials are in class K, which is often subdivided according to country: K is international law, KF is United States law, KD is British law, and KZ is used to classify international treaties. Since class K was one of the most recently developed classes, many of the books housed in the Law Library carry earlier classification numbers. For example, books in the American State Trials Collection may be identified by the call number: LAW <Trials "Kinney">. Other class numbers include J1–J14 (official country gazettes) and JX (presently being converted to KZ). A card catalog is also available and is helpful for finding books that were published before 1980 for which the classification number is not given in the online catalog. Books written in non-roman-script languages that do not have transliterated titles can also be located through the card catalog.

SAMPLE LCSH: Subject headings for women in Law Library catalogs follow the pattern used for the General Collections: **Women—Legal status, laws, etc.; Women—Employment—Law and legislation; Women (International law); Women teachers—Legal status, laws, etc.; Women—Suffrage—Law and legislation; Women judges.** Some headings, however, are unique to law: **Abortion—Finance—Law and legislation; Trials (Divorce); Trials (Rape); Dower; Widow's allowance;** and **Lawyers' spouses** (formerly **Lawyers' wives)** are examples.

LAW LIBRARY READING ROOM
James Madison Memorial Building, 2nd floor, room LM 201
Hours: Monday through Saturday, 8:30 a.m. to 5:00 p.m. Closed Sunday and federal holidays.
Telephone: 202 707-5079; TTY 202 707-9949
Fax: 202 707-3585
Address: Law Library of Congress, 101 Independence Avenue, SE, Washington, DC 20540-3000
E-mail: law@loc.gov
Web site: <http:/www.loc.gov/rr/law>
Access and use: In the open bookstacks of the Law Library Reading Room, federal laws, current state laws, administrative materials, and treatises are immediately accessible to the public. Most of the law collections, however, are located in closed bookstack areas that are not open to readers. These materials must be requested in the Law Library Reading Room, and you should allow approximately one hour for their retrieval. To request materials, you will need a valid Library of Congress reader identification card.

Professional legal reference specialists are available to help you. In addition, the Law Library's staff of foreign-trained lawyers is available on a limited basis to respond to public reference questions concerning foreign laws, administrative regulations, and court decisions.

To use the **Law Library Rare Book Collections,** you will need to follow security procedures. First make an appointment with the rare book law librarian to identify the material you need. Subject catalogs and other bibliographical guides will help you identify desired items as Law Library materials. If the rare book librarian determines that no alternate sources are available, you may complete a registration form and be given access to the rare book materials.

The Law Library Reading Room Card Catalog can be used to find call numbers for materials that are not available through the Library's online catalog. Many of the rare materials have not been cataloged and given a Library of Congress call number, and for these, the card catalog may be one of the only sources for finding a particular book or series. Other, published catalogs are also helpful and should be consulted to identify useful material.

Legal Research Methodology

Legal research can be time consuming and sometimes offers limited results, but there are fundamental principles that will aid the process. Consulting general sources will help you identify specific legal research resources, their arrangement, and the methods used to obtain information from them.

BIBLIOGRAPHY:

Cohen, Morris, Robert C. Berring, and Kent C. Olson. *How to Find the Law.* 9th ed. St. Paul: West Publishing Co., 1989.

Cohen, Morris L., and Kent C. Olson. *Legal Research in a Nutshell.* 7th ed. St. Paul: West Publishing Co., 2000.

Jacobstein, J. Myron, Roy M.. Mersky, and Donald J. Dunn. *Fundamentals of Legal Research.* 7th ed. Westbury, N.Y.: The Foundation Press, 1998.

Wren, Christopher, and Jill Robinson Wren. *The Legal Research Manual: A Game Plan for Legal Research and Analysis.* 2nd ed. Madison, Wis.: A-R Editions, 1996. Chapter 1.

In legal treatises, periodicals, digests, and codes, a variety of index terms are useful in researching issues concerning women. For modern sources, index terms familiar since the 1960s, such as "woman," "sexual harassment," and "marriage," can be used. The best technique for searching an index is to begin with a narrow term and broaden the search. For instance, if you are trying to determine if a state has laws on the battered wife syndrome, start with the narrow term "battered wife syndrome." If that does not yield results, broaden your search to "spousal abuse." If you do not find either of these phrases, use the broader term "domestic violence." Searching under antonyms, synonyms, and associated words of all kinds may lead to useful information.

Researching historical issues can be problematical because the legal status of women changed over time. The researcher must try to think the way an eighteenth-, nineteenth-, or early twentieth-century legal scholar might have thought. Most legislation pertaining to women has been enacted indirectly. Married women were considered "silent partners" in marriage relationships. As a result, "woman" or "women" were rarely used as indexing terms. By and large, indexing terms reflected a woman's relationship to a man. Terms such as "wives," "dower" (a dower[1] being the portion of real and personal property of a deceased husband that the law gives to his widow during her life), "widows," *"coverture," "femes covert"* (married women), *"femes sole"* (single women), or "females" were used.

Normally, unless the application of a law treats men and women differently, there will be no distinct subject terms for indicating gender in an index. For instance, contract law applies to any party to a contract regardless of gender or position as long as the requirements for contracting are met, so there are no distinct headings for women; whereas property law, a substantive area, has distinct headings for women, because widows held a unique position in estate and succession laws. It is important to remember to make the distinction between law and social conditions in dealing with women's issues. Often, it was not the wording of the law that prohibited women from doing certain things, but rather it was the social interpretation of the law influenced by mores that restricted women's behavior.

There are two types of authority in the law: mandatory and persuasive. Mandatory authority is authority the courts must heed (or to which the courts must pay attention). Persuasive authority can persuade a court to its opinion, but it is not binding. Mandatory authority is found in primary sources which include legislation, judicial decisions, and administrative regulations. Persuasive authority is found in both primary and secondary sources. Secondary sources are treatises, legal periodical articles, legal encyclopedias, and other commentary about the law. Very often it is easier to look at secondary sources to understand the primary sources, but to legislators, judges, lawyers, regulators, and those involved with the law, primary sources ultimately are the only sources that matter. For other academic specialists, particularly historians, the background information for the creation of legislation and court documents pertaining to a case can be essential for analyzing the social and political climate of the time.

Legal treatises, which are secondary sources, are good sources for general information on substantive law, though most do not focus specifically on women's issues and rights. Consulting a treatise on a specific subject will usually yield some background information and, more important, citations to statutory or case law. Many of the treatises focusing on women were not published until the 1970s, but a few were published earlier. An early one that did relate specifically to women was *Woman's Manual of Law* by Mary A. Greene (1857–1936) written in 1902 to "present in a clear, simple, and if possible, entertaining way, those principles of law governing the business world and domestic life which most men understand in some degree, or think they do, but which most women do not understand, and wish they did."[2]

Although the term *law* is often used generically, there are three major categories of primary law: (1) statutory law, (2) regulatory law, and (3) common law. Any or all of these categories might apply to any given topic relating to women. Statutory law is created by a legislative body, such as the U.S. Congress or the State of Maryland General Assembly. Regulatory law is created and enforced

IN GOD WE TRUST!
JOHN RUTLEDGE,
BORN IN S.C. 1739, APPOINTED JULY 1st 1795, DIED JULY 23d 1800.
JOHN JAY,
BORN IN N.Y. DEC. 12th 1745, APPOINTED SEPT. 26th 1789, DIED MAY 17 1829.
OLIVER ELLSWORTH,
BORN IN CONN. APRIL 29th 1745, APPOINTED 1796, DIED NOV. 26th 1807.
JUSTICE
LIBERTY
JOHN MARSHALL,
BORN IN VA. SEPT. 24th 1755, APPOINTED JANY 31st 1801, DIED JULY 6th 1835.
ROGER BROOK TANEY,
BORN IN MARYD. MARCH 17th 1777, APPOINTED 1831, DIED OCT. 12th 1864.
E PLURIBUS UNUM
CONSTITUTION OF THE UNITED STATES.
SAL'N PORTLAND CHASE,
BORN IN N.H. JANY 13th 1808, APPOINTED 1864, DIED MAY 7 1873.
MORRISON R. WAITE,
BORN IN CONN. NOV. 29th 1816, APPOINTED 1874, DIED MARCH 23d 1888.
MELVILLE W. FULLER,
BORN IN MAINE, FEBRUARY 11th 1833, SWORN IN OCT. 8th 1888.
THE CHIEF JUSTICES OF THE UNITED STATES.
COPYRIGHTED 1894 BY KURZ & ALLISON,
PUBS. 76 & 78 WABASH AVE., CHICAGO.

by an administrative body, for instance, the U.S. Department of Labor or the State of Michigan Fair Employment Practices Commission. Common law is created by a judicial body, such as the Fourth Circuit Court of Appeals or the Virginia Supreme Court. In many instances, these laws are interdependent, although they may appear to function independently (see the discussion of federal law that follows). To add to the complexity, these types of laws are created by the appropriate body in each of the different jurisdictional units: federal, state, regional, county, and city. In other words, each jurisdictional entity has governmental bodies that create statutory, regulatory, and common law.

Another consideration involving jurisdictions is the governance of various legal issues.[3] Civil rights, immigration, interstate commerce, and constitutional issues are subject to federal jurisdiction. Issues such as domestic relations, which includes domestic violence, marriage and divorce, corporations, property, contracts, and criminal laws, are generally governed by states, unless there is federal preemption.[4] State laws and terminology will vary from state to state, and there are few comparative guides available. It is better to look at a specific state's laws or court decisions or to compare several specific states' laws and court decisions rather than to attempt to generalize about the legal criteria followed by all states.

When your legal research involves case law (or common law), it is important to know something about the significance of precedents or the doctrine of *stare decisis,* which refers to "adhering to or abiding by" settled decisions. Simply put, lower courts are bound to follow decisions of higher courts in the same jurisdiction. For example, a federal district court in Maryland is required to follow the decisions of the Fourth Circuit Court of Appeals and the U.S. Supreme Court, but it is not bound by the decisions of other district courts or by the Maryland state courts. Historically, this doctrine has hindered women in the courts, because once a precedent has been set, it is difficult to receive a different ruling unless the law that the judges or justices are interpreting is itself changed. Recently, however, *stare decisis* has been one of the major reasons that women have won cases concerning employment in the courts. Many precedents based on Title VII of the Civil Rights Act of 1964 favor women.

State legal materials resemble federal legal materials in many ways, but there are differences in the types of publications in which they are readily available. The nature of legal materials and publishing practices may differ depending on jurisdiction. Resources on the federal level are easier to obtain because materials are published by both private and government publishers. U.S. Government Printing Office (GPO) publications are readily available in government depository collections in libraries across the United States. Each state, however, follows its own publishing practices.

Differences are especially significant in the publication of court decisions. Many decisions regarding women's issues have been rendered on the trial level in state courts, and few state trial court decisions are published, because they do not establish legal precedent. (This reinforces the importance of the American State Trials Collection for studying historical development of the law.) Other cases, like the breast implant class action suit, are settled out of court, and there is no official publication of the proceedings or the terms of the settlement. Further, attempting to trace a particular piece of state legislation to its origin in colonial times can be difficult because of imprecise terminology and inconsistent publishing practices.

Most primary sources are chronologically arranged. To find them, you must be able to read legal citations, which are fairly uniform in their format. In such citations, the number preceding the name of the source ordinarily refers to a volume or title number. The number following the name of the source refers to the page number on which the cited material begins or the section number if the first number is a title. For instance, Pub.L. 88–352, Title VII, 78 *Stat.* 241, indicates that Public Law 88–352, Title VII, can be found in volume 78 of the *U.S. Statutes-at-Large* on page 241. The *United States Code* citation for the same law, 42 *U.S.C.* § 2000e *et seq.,* indicates that the beginning of the codified law is found in Title 42 of the *United States Code,* section 2000e. Similarly, *Meritor Savings Bank v. Mechelle Vinson et al.,* 106 *S.Ct.* 2399 (1986), indicates that the Supreme Court decision is found in volume 106 of *West's Supreme Court Reporter* on page 2,399. Tables of

Kurz & Allison. The Chief Justices *[of the]* United States. *Lithograph, 1894. Prints and Photographs Division. LC-USZ62-17681.*

Although Justice and Liberty traditionally have been symbolized by female figures, the legislative and judicial bodies have been dominated by men throughout the history of the United States of America. Sandra Day O'Connor and Ruth Bader Ginsburg now serve as associate justices on the Supreme Court, but to date only males have held the position of chief justice of the U.S. Supreme Court.

abbreviations will help you identify an abbreviation. Legal dictionaries, dictionaries of legal abbreviations, and the *Bluebook: A Uniform System of Citation* provide commonly used abbreviations and acronyms.

Statutory law can be found in two types of publications: compilations of statutes or codified laws.[5] Both the compilations and the codes have the same wording, but their formats are different. A federal law is given the number of the U.S. Congress that passed it and a second number that represents the chronological order of its passage. "Pub. L. 88–352" indicates the 352nd law passed by the 88th Congress. After passage, a law is codified, or published according to its subject category. Public Law 88–352 can also be found in the *United States Code,* where the citation is 42 *U.S.C.* § 2000e *et seq.* Remember, though, that not all laws are codified.

If you are looking for statutory law on a general subject, the code is the best place to look. A code usually has a multivolume index that includes the codified laws, which are published there with amendments integrated into the original law, as currently in force. Public laws, however, are separate entities—the original law and each of its amendments remain separate. There is no general index to them. To find a specific public (or session) law, you need to know either the Congress that passed it or the year it was enacted, because indexes are published only at the end of each session of Congress.

To get a clearer picture of the passage of a law, the underlying legislative intent, and any political ramifications, it is often necessary to consult legislative history materials. Among these are, primarily, committee reports, hearings, and debates. Committee reports and hearings are published either as separate entities or in compilations. Debates are found in the *United States Congressional Record.* Again, federal legislative materials are easier to find, for most states do not actively publish these materials. To locate these state materials, find out if the state legislative branch has a legislative reference bureau or library available.

Administrative agencies serve two major functions: rule-making and adjudication (or enforcement). The rules and regulations of administrative agencies and executive documents are generally published in a register and compiled in a code. For example, federal materials are published in the *Federal Register* (F.R.) and the *Code of Federal Regulations* (C.F.R.). The State of Michigan publishes the *Michigan Register* and the *Administrative Code of Michigan.* Decisions rendered by an agency's adjudicatory body may be published as well. If a decision or order is not published, anyone wanting a copy must contact the agency to receive one.

As in searching for laws, the general subject of a regulation can be searched in the general index that a code provides. To find a rule or regulation in a register, the researcher should know the date of the final regulation or the year of enactment. Most registers have no general index that covers all regulations currently in force.

Court systems vary depending on whether they are federal or state. All court systems have two major levels: a trial court (district court) and a court of last resort (supreme court). Some have an immediate appeals court (court of appeals). The court system may also include various special courts that have limited jurisdiction. The federal system has three levels (district courts, courts of appeal, and a supreme court), whereas the District of Columbia, for example, has only two (the Superior Court and the Court of Appeals).

A suit is initiated in a trial court. If someone chooses not to accept the decision of the judge and jury, he or she can file an appeal in the immediate court of appeals. This court will affirm (support) the trial court's decision or reverse it. That decision can then be appealed to the court of last resort. Unlike the immediate court of appeal, to which citizens have a right to appeal, the court of last resort must be petitioned. The judges or justices determine whether or not they will hear the appeal. A state supreme court decision can be appealed to the United States Supreme Court.

Decisions rendered by judicial bodies are published in reporters (or reports), which vary in type. Again, it is important to remember that not all judicial opinions are published. There are reporters for all levels of federal courts, and virtually all of the opinions of the state courts of last resort are published. State immediate appellate court decisions are generally published. State trial court opinions, however, are rarely reported, but New York (in its *Miscellaneous Reports*) and Pennsylvania (in the *Pennsylvania District and County Reports*) do publish such decisions selectively. Most other state court decisions and any trial transcripts must be obtained through the clerk of the court in the specific jurisdiction where the trial was held.

Court records and briefs can be used to get background information on a specific court opinion. The Law Library of Congress has records and briefs for most U.S. Supreme Court opinions from 1832 to the present in both print and microfiche, as well as the privately published *Land-*

EXECUTOR'S NOTICE.

THE Subscribers having been duly appointed Executors to the last Will and Testament of

ANNA CARPENTER,

late of Newport, widow, deceased, request all persons having demands against said Estate, to present them for settlement, and those indebted, to make immediate payment to

STEPHEN GOULD, } Exc'rs.
EDWARD W. LAWTON. }

Newport, 12th mo. 6th, 1834.

ADMINISTRATOR'S NOTICE.

THE Subscriber hereby gives notice; That he has been duly appointed Administrator, with the Will annexed, on the Estate of

Mrs. *FRANCES WOODMAN*,

late of Newport, widow, dec. and requests all persons having demands against said Estate, to present them for settlement, and those indebted to make immediate payment to

JOHN STEVENS, *Adm'r.*

Newport, Nov. 15.

GUARDIAN'S NOTICE.

THE Subscriber having been appointed by the Hon. Court of Probate for the town of Newport, on the 26th day of June, 1832, Guardian of the persons and estates of *Ann C. Maxson*, aged 14 years, and *James M. Maxson*, under 14 years, minors, and children of *John S. Maxson*, dec. and having accepted said trust, and given bonds as the law directs she requests all persons having any demands against said minors to present them for settlement, and those indebted to make immediate payment to

ABBY MAXSON, *Guardian.*

Newport, Feb. 14.

EXECUTRIX'S NOTICE.

THE Subscriber, having been duly appointed Executrix to the last Will and Testament of

Rev. MICHAEL EDDY,

late of said Newport, deceased, requests all persons having demands against said Estate, to present them for settlement, and those indebted, to make immediate payment to

PHEBE EDDY, *Exe c'rx.*

Newport, August 29.

PROBATE NOTICES.

Court of Probate, Newport, April 6, 1835.

THE Administration Account on the Estate of MARY PITMAN, single woman, late of Newport, deceased, was this day presented for examination, and for allowance It is ordered, that the same be received, and consideration thereof referred to a Court of Probate, to be holden at the State-House in Newport, on the first Monday in May next, at 9 o'clock A. M. and that previous notice be given by publishing a copy of this order three several times in the *Newport Mercury*, to all persons interested to appear at said time and place, and be heard. *By Order,*

B. B. HOWLAND, *Probate Clerk.*

ADMINISTRATRIX'S NOTICE.

THE Subscriber having been appointed by the Hon. Court of Probate, Admniistratrix on the Estate of

JAMES TAYLOR,

late of Newport, Druggist & Apothecary, deceased, and having given bonds as the law requires, hereby gives notice to all persons having claims against said Estate, to present them for settlement, and those indebted to make payment without delay, to

ANN TAYLOR, *Adm'x.*

Newport, July 10, 1835.

GUARDIAN'S NOTICE.

THE Subscriber hereby gives notice, That he has been appointed by the Court of Probate for the town of Portsmouth, Guardian to *ELIZABETH ALMY*, of said Portsmouth, adjudged by said Court of Probate as incapable of managing her Estate ;—and having given bonds according to law, he requests all persons having demands against said Elizabeth, to exhibit them to him within six months from the date hereof, and those indebted, to make immediate payment.

JOHN ALMY, *Guardian.*

Portsmouth, July 25, 1835.

Executor's Notice for Will of Anna Carpenter and Administrator's Notice for Estate of Mrs. Frances Woodman, January 10, 1835; and Guardian's Notice by Abby Maxson for two children, February 24, 1835; Executrix Notice for Rev. Michael Eddy, deceased, Phebe Eddy, Exect'rx; Probate Notice for Mary Pitman, single woman, April 6, 1835; and Administratrix Notice for estate of James Taylor and Ann Taylor, Adm'x; Guardian's Notice for Elizabeth Almy ("incapable of managing her Estate"), John Almy, Guardian; July 15, 1835. All from the Newport Mercury, *Newport, Rhode Island (Bound volume, no. 9658). Serial and Government Publications Division.*

Legal notices are published frequently in newspapers. These ads serve to notify the public and specific individuals about legal transactions that are in process. In the case of guardianship, those who are opposed are given the opportunity to state reasons why the transaction should not go forth. Executrix, administratrix of estates, and probate officers give notice so that any debts can be satisfied and contracts can be fulfilled or notice given as to why they will not be completed. Much can be learned about women's roles in the management of estates and family under the law from such notices.

mark Briefs and Arguments of the Supreme Court of the United States: Constitutional Law.[6]

Because court reporters are arranged chronologically, digest systems must be used to find court decisions by subject. Each of the major legal publishing firms has its own digest system. The most widely used of these is the American Digest System created by West Publishing Company.[7] This standard system of subjects and topic areas is used in all of the company's digests, including digests for each jurisdiction and various subject digests, such as the *Merit System Protection Board Digest.* In addition, table-of-cases volumes can be used when the parties to litigation are known but the legal citation is not.

Legal encyclopedias, also secondary sources, give overviews of many aspects of law and numerous citations to relied-upon authority. They combine primary and secondary sources to give succinct statements of applicable law. Today, there are two major legal encyclopedias: *Corpus Juris Secundum* (CJS) (1936–) and *American Jurisprudence (AmJur)*, 2nd edition, (1952–). For historical research, the older editions, *Corpus Juris* (1914–37) and *American Jurisprudence* (1936–52), are useful, as well as *The American and English Encyclopaedia of Law* (1887–96; 2nd edition, 1896–1905) and *Ruling Case Law* (1914–21). It is important to remember that each of these encyclopedias is different. Different topics, different subject headings, and different case law may be provided in each. In *Corpus Juris Secundum* each section has a summary of the law, usually in boldface type, and a reference to a topic heading (a key number) used in the West Digest System, which gives further access to related case law. In *American Jurisprudence,* research references (usually to *American Law Reports,* or ALR) are given

PATHFINDER: Using Encyclopedias

If a social historian wanted to explore power relationships between husband and wife by examining terms of antenuptial agreements concerning children, she or he might begin by searching the index of *Corpus Juris Secundum,* where the researcher would find, among others, the entries "Antenuptial Contracts–Parent and child–religion, custody of children, Parent&C §28" and "religious education, Parent&C §14."

The subject "Parent & Child" is located in CJS, volume 67a, where the summary reads: "Religious education of children of tender years is a right and duty of parents; and where one parent has custody, such parent has the right to control the religious education of a child, except to the extent that an agreement providing otherwise is recognized. Library References: Parent and Child (key) 2(1), 3.1(12)," giving the West key numbers, locators of related case law.

If the researcher were to search the index of the current edition of *American Jurisprudence,* on the other hand, she would find the topic "Antenuptial Settlements, obligations, and other matters—Children and minors—religious training, Par & C § 21." The summary statement for "Parent & Child," section 21, in volume 59 reads: "An agreement between the parents, antenuptial or otherwise, as to the religious training to be given their children, has usually been held to have no binding effect in proceedings involving custody. And it has been held that such an agreement does not bind the custodian. However, some courts have enforced such agreements, except where to do so would adversely affect the child's welfare."

Tracing antenuptial agreements back through earlier encyclopedias yields slightly different results. In *Corpus Juris* the heading "Antenuptial contract" has subheadings relating only to husband and wife. A cross-reference from "Antenuptial settlements" to "Marriage settlements, this index" leads to "Marriage Settlements—Children." Under "Parent and Child," however, CJ gives the subheading "Religious education and affiliations of child, Parent & C 7" about which the encyclopedia states: ". . . The general rule is that an infant is to be brought up in the religion of the father, . . . and an antenuptial agreement that the children shall be brought up in a different religion from that of the father is not binding at law or in equity."

In *The American and English Encyclopedia of Law* (1905), the term "antenuptial contracts" is subsumed under other headings. For instance, "Husband and wife," "Separate property of married women," and "Antenuptial settlements" are all under "Marriage settlements." The summary for "Parent and Child—Right of Custody—Religious Education" states: "In the United States this question seems not to have been considered. The duty of a parent to give religious instruction to his children and his right to do so without interference are recognized. . . ." However, the initial statement under the right of custody reads: "At common law the father has the paramount right to the custody of his children, as against the world."

Footnotes cite judicial opinions concerning these various issues. For the heading under "Parent and Child" [§ 7] 4. Religious Education and Affiliations of Child," which states that "an antenuptial agreement that the children shall be brought up in a different religion from that of the father is not binding at law or in equity," CJ provides a footnote citing *Com. v. McClelland,* 70 *Pa. Super.* 273 (1918). The case is found in *Pennsylvania Superior Court Reports,* volume 70, page 273, and concerns two children whose father was Protestant and whose mother was Catholic. Their father signed an agreement stating that he was willing to have his children raised in the Catholic faith. Their mother subsequently was institutionalized for insanity. At this point, the father began taking the children to his Protestant church. After the father's death, his in-laws protested the court's placement of his daughters with a Protestant family and filed suit, but the court decided to follow the wishes of the daughters.

It is in this way that a researcher can use legal encyclopedias to help her follow the gradual and complex evolution of custom, practice, and statutory, regulatory, and common law.

under each major heading. Using encyclopedias is a good way to begin research if you are unfamiliar with law and legal concepts.

This guide can give only a brief overview of the fundamentals of legal research. The best way to become familiar with legal materials is to have a law librarian guide you the first time you undertake it. Although it may not make doing the research less complex, it will make the process more comfortable, which will allow you, the researcher, to consider the possibilities of what you are finding rather than becoming frustrated by the citation numbers, legal jargon, and variety of publishing practices.

SELECTED AREAS FOR RESEARCH

Within the Law Library, it is helpful to view its resources in the three general categories addressed above—the collections that are considered rare materials, either because of their age or scarcity; the material that has to do with federal law; and the various kinds of state materials relating to state law.

Rare Book Collection

The Rare Book Collection of the Law Library of Congress contains a large and diverse assortment of materials. These unique holdings include the laws from colonial America, historical laws of other countries, and treatises. Laws, court decisions, and treatises written and published before 1801 are considered rare, as are certain "one of a kind" items published after 1801. Most of these materials are in their original printings.

Territorial and state session laws make up the major portion of the Rare Book Collection. Included are the laws of the Hawaiian Islands before 1896, when they were ruled by Queen Liliuokalani. Another unique collection is the Native American Nations laws, including the Creek, Choctaw, and Cherokee tribal codes. Some of these codes are written in the vernacular script of the tribe. Several tribes have been recognized as strongly matrilineal, as reflected in their codes. Among reprints of colonial court records are records of the Massachusetts' executor of wills as well as other property records. The American State Trials Collection reveals that women played a significant role in some trials. Included are several domestic homicide trials in which the wife is charged with poisoning her husband or as acting as an accessory in a murder or is a victim of murder.

The Rare Book Collection includes historical laws and treatises from France, Spain, Russia,

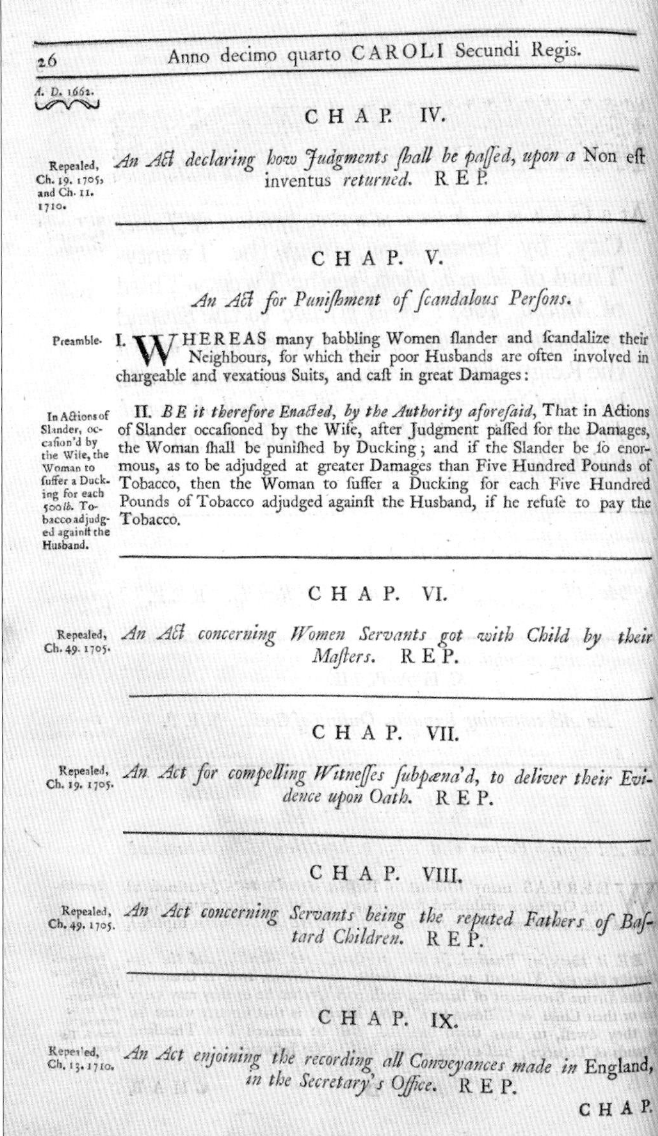

26 Anno decimo quarto CAROLI Secundi Regis.

A. D. 1662.

CHAP. IV.

Repealed, Ch. 19. 1705, and Ch. 11. 1710.

An Act declaring how Judgments ſhall be paſſed, upon a Non eſt inventus *returned.* REP.

CHAP. V.

An Act for Puniſhment of ſcandalous Perſons.

Preamble. I. WHEREAS many babbling Women ſlander and ſcandalize their Neighbours, for which their poor Husbands are often involved in chargeable and vexatious Suits, and caſt in great Damages:

In Actions of Slander, occaſion'd by the Wife, the Woman to ſuffer a Ducking for each 500*lb.* Tobacco adjudged againſt the Husband.

II. *BE it therefore Enacted, by the Authority aforeſaid,* That in Actions of Slander occaſioned by the Wife, after Judgment paſſed for the Damages, the Woman ſhall be puniſhed by Ducking; and if the Slander be ſo enormous, as to be adjudged at greater Damages than Five Hundred Pounds of Tobacco, then the Woman to ſuffer a Ducking for each Five Hundred Pounds of Tobacco adjudged againſt the Husband, if he refuſe to pay the Tobacco.

CHAP. VI.

Repealed, Ch. 49. 1705.

An Act concerning Women Servants got with Child by their Maſters. REP.

CHAP. VII.

Repealed, Ch. 19. 1705.

An Act for compelling Witneſſes ſubpæna'd, to deliver their Evidence upon Oath. REP.

CHAP. VIII.

Repealed, Ch. 49. 1705.

An Act concerning Servants being the reputed Fathers of Baſtard Children. REP.

CHAP. IX.

Repealed, Ch. 13. 1710.

An Act enjoining the recording all Conveyances made in England, *in the Secretary's Office.* REP.

CHAP.

"An Act for Punishment of Scandalous Persons." From A Complete Collection of the Laws of Virginia at a Grand Assembly held at James City 23 March, 1662 *(London, [1684?]; Law<United States Virginia 2>). Law Library of Congress.*

This 1662 Virginia law was designed to discourage married women from bringing scandal to their husbands by gossiping about their neighbors. If the assessed damages were 500 pounds of tobacco and the husband refused to pay the debt, the wife was punished by dunking.

Great Britain, and other Commonwealth countries. The laws of Great Britain are the most extensive because of their significance in America and their influence on America's laws. Often the colonies based their original laws on the British or other European systems. *The Statutes of the Realm of Great Britain,* dating back to 1235, are the oldest. Law in Louisiana, the only civil law state, was, on the other hand, influenced by French and Spanish civil codes. The *Coutumes of France,* dating back to the fifteenth century and the precursor to the contemporary French Civil Code, are in this collection. The Castillian Leone Code, *Las Siete Partidas,* the precursor to the Spanish Civil Code, as well as a collection of Imperial Russian materials including the laws in force during the reign of Catherine the Great (1762–96) can be found in the Rare Book Collection. Although the collections consist primarily of laws, there are a number of treatises. One treatise pertaining to women is *Laws Respecting Women regarding their Natural Rights, or the Connections and Conducts,* published in Great Britain in 1777.

Territorial and State Session Laws

The Territorial and State Session Laws in the Rare Book Collection include a large number of early colonial and state marriage, property, and dower laws in their original text. The laws date from late seventeenth-century Massachusetts and early eighteenth-century Virginia. An edition of *The General Laws and Liberties of the Massachusetts Colony in New-England, Revised and Reprinted* (London, 1675) is one of the earliest.[8] A section on dowries states:

> It is Ordered by this Court and the Authority thereof, that every Married Woman, (living with her Husband in this Jurisdiction, or other, where absent from him with his consent or through his meet default, or inevitable providence, or in case of Divorce, where she is the innocent party) that shall not before Marriage be estated by way of joynture, in some Houses, Lands, Tenements or other Hereditaments for term of life, shall immediately after the death of her Husband, have Right and Interest by way of Dowry, in and to one third part of all such Houses, Lands, Tenements and Hereditaments. . . .[9]

These session laws contain a wealth of information about the lives of men and women during the colonial period. Interestingly, the laws on marriage in Virginia in 1722 indicate that a marriage license could be paid for in shillings and pence or in tobacco:

> An Act concerning Marriages.
>
> Ministers shall not marry People without License, of thrice Publication of Banes, according to the Rubrick. . . . . Fees for Marriage Licenses.

	s.		l.
To the Government	20	or	200 of Tobacco
To the Clerk of the County Court	5	or	50
To the Minister if by License	20	or	100
If by Banes	5	or	50
For publishing the Banes and Certificate	1 s. 6d	or	15

> If these Fees be not paid in ready Money, they shall be paid at the Time of Year in Tobacco of the Growth of the Parish where the *Feme* shall live, and on Refusal of payment be leviable by districts as *per* Clerks Fees.[10]

Such laws, written in the script of the colonial period, reveal aspects of colonial life that were important enough to legislate and litigate.

American State Trials Collection

The American State Trials Collection is an extraordinary body of state trials published from colonial times. Even today, when publishing court decisions is much more common, state trials are rarely among those that are printed. The judicial opinions and trial transcripts found in this collection include cases on adultery, murder, libel, and rape. Many of these trials took place before there were female attorneys or women jurors. Some resulted in interesting verdicts considering the period and the views held by men about women. In the case of *The Commonwealth (Massachusetts) v. Fairchild,* a Congregational minister was convicted of seduction in 1844 and banned from the church by an ecclesiastical court. In a subsequent civil trial, he was acquitted of adultery.[11] In other trials, wives were acquitted of charges brought against them. In *Commonwealth (Massachusetts) v. Kinney,* 1840, "Hannah Kinney was acquitted of the charge of murdering her husband by arsenic poison." The jury took only three minutes of deliberation to reach its decision.[12]

Books written about such trials or newspaper articles reporting the events of a trial as they unfolded show how highly publicized some of them were. Such complementary materials will be found not in the Law Library but in other Library of Congress collections, such as the General Collections or the collections of the Rare Book and Special Collections Division and the Serial and Government Publications Division.

BIBLIOGRAPHY:

Catalogue of the Library of the Law School of Harvard University. Cambridge, Mass.: Harvard Law School, 1909. This catalog is an alphabetical listing of items available in 1909 in the Harvard Law School. It is one of the few indexes published during the early twentieth century and is a good source for finding trials and other legal items published during the

BIBLIOGRAPHY continued

nineteenth century and held in the rare book collections of the Law Library of Congress or other libraries.

Cohen, Morris L. *Bibliography of Early American Law.* Buffalo, N.Y.: William S. Hein & Co., 1998 (KF1 .C58 1998). This bibliography is excellent for determining the types of materials available for doing research and where, including the Library of Congress, to find them. Cohen's chapters on trials provide excellent access points to the American State Trials Collection.

Marvin, J. G. *Legal Bibliography or a Thesaurus of American, English, Irish, and Scotch Law Books together with Some Continental Treatises.* Philadelphia: T & J. W. Johnson, 1847. An alphabetical listing by title or author of works available during the period of its publication includes some entries that are annotated.

Soule, Charles Carroll. *The Lawyer's Reference Manual.* Boston: Soule and Bugbee, 1883. A subject index of law book and court report citations, the manual includes some entries that pertain to women, such as "Divorce," "Divorce and Matrimonial Causes," "Dower," and "Husband and Wife."

State Law

As noted earlier, state materials are diverse. Each state has different laws, follows precedents set by different court cases, uses different terminology, and publishes legal materials according to its own dictates. Property law, a substantive area that has a distinct set of laws applicable only to women, is a good example to examine on the state level. The practice of law by women, employment practices, and suffrage are three other areas with important historical ramifications for women that are governed by state law.

Property Law

Generally, property is divided into two major areas: realty and personalty. Realty is land, whereas personalty is possessions—for instance, jewelry, money, furniture, or slaves. State laws regulate who may purchase property, who may own it, and how it will be distributed upon the death of the owner or owners. This premise applies unless the land is federal property, in which case the federal government makes the determination.

Property laws have been important from the beginning of this nation, especially since many new citizens did not or could not own property in their countries of origin. Disagreement among the colonies about continuing British legal traditions resulted in differences in colonial laws—some colonies wanted to remain true to British legal tra-

382 MARCH TERM 1805.

MARTIN *vs.* COMMON-WEALTH & *al.* In Error.

to have declared that they had become aliens would not have answered the purpose—it was necessary further to provide for the disposition of their estates. The statute is grounded on the position that every *British* subject who owned lands here and had withdrawn himself from this country to put himself under the protection of the *British* government had forfeited his estate. Their case was distinguished from that of aliens in general. The title of the Commonwealth arose under the statute, provided the process pointed out should be regularly followed, not *merely* because they were aliens, but because they were aliens in a *particular way*--because they had deserted their country. The statutes were not a war upon enemies, as such, as is said by the *Attorney General;* had they been, the legislature would have extended them to *all* British subjects owning lands *here.*

The real question is whether the statute was intended to include persons who have, by law, no wills of their own. The statute extends to persons who have *freely* renounced their relation to the State. Infants, insane, *femes-covert,* all of whom the law considers as having no will, cannot act *freely.* Can they freely renounce? The statute meant such, and such only, as could. Is the State entitled to the *personal* services of a *feme-covert* to defend it in war? Can she render any? What aid and comfort can she give to an invading enemy? Has she the controul of property? Is she ever required to take the oath of allegiance?--As to the provision in the statute for dower; that has no relation to *her* property—it is merely the donation of the State, giving to her a part of that which was absolutely its own. There was the same provision also in the *conspirator-act.* It has been said that the husband abjured the realm, and that this dissolved the marriage contract--this is a strange consequence, and one till now unheard of.

"The real question is whether the statute was intended to include persons who have, by law, no wills of their own. . . . Infants, insane, femes-covert, *all of whom the law considers as having no will, cannot act* freely." Martin vs. Commonwealth et al. *in* Reports of Cases Argued and Determined in the Supreme Judicial Court, of the Commonwealth of Massachusetts *(Boston, 1816; KFM2445.A19 1804). Law Library of Congress.*

James Martin, the son of William and Anna Martin, filed a writ of error in 1801 in order to recover property owned by his parents that had been confiscated by the Commonwealth of Massachusetts in 1781. William, a British Loyalist, had renounced his citizenship with the newly united American colonies at the outbreak of the Revolutionary War in 1775 and had taken his family to live in Canada. James Martin was able to recover the family property on the basis of several legal arguments. Two of the strongest arguments presented by his attorney, a Mr. Parsons, were that his mother, Anna Martin, had no choice but to follow her husband to Canada because the law assumed that *femes-covert* had no will of their own, and that she was the owner of the property because she brought it to her marriage. A husband had rights to his wife's estate only for his natural life.

dition, whereas others chose to abandon some or all of the traditions. With its very structured property and inheritance common law tradition, Great Britain allowed women to file suit in chancery courts, known as "equity courts." The route a colony took on such an issue determined to a large extent the rights and privileges that women living in that colony possessed.

Some colonies, like Virginia, had liberal laws that gave widows the right to own or control the use of land as part of their dowry rights.[13] Connecticut, on the other hand, gave women no rights to own their property or their husbands' real property. Other colonies gave wives the right of *private examination.*[14] Their laws required husbands to get the signature of their wives before title to joint property or property brought to the marital state by the wife could be conveyanced or transferred.[15] Virginia adopted the British chancery court system, which gave women the ability to challenge male descendants' claims to land. In the western territories, because of the influence of Spanish civil law, women might enjoy community property rights.

PATHFINDER: Property Rights

While reading an article on community property in New Mexico, you see a commentary on a court decision that interests you. A footnote gives the legal citation as *McDonald v. Senn et al.*, 53 N.M. 198, 204 P.2d 990 (1949).[16] The Law Library of Congress has both reporters, *New Mexico Reports* (N.M.) and the *Pacific Reporter, Second Series* (P.2d), but you choose to use the *Pacific Reporter,* the regional reporter. As you begin reading the decision, you discover that the New Mexico community property law was adopted in common law in 1876; the statute was passed later. The statute was based on California law, which was modeled on the civil law of Spain and Mexico.

You are interested in looking at both the earliest statutes on community property in California and some judicial decisions interpreting those laws. You can either (1) find the case citations from California listed in the *McDonald* decision, or (2) find the statutory citations from California listed in the decision. The most expedient is to use the statutory citations.

The California statutory citation for community property, written in the dissent, is "Section 161a of the California Civil Code, . . . adopted in 1927." [17] Start your search for the earliest statutes with this citation to the law being interpreted here. In the *Civil Code of the State of California . . . 1927,* section 161a of the appendix is an amendment to an earlier law. Sections 159–181 in the main body of the *Civil Code* give the law antedating this amendment. Because this edition of the Civil Code is annotated, you find a short history of the legislation here. Following section 159, "Husband and wife. Property relations," you read:

> Legislation §159. 1. Enacted March 21, 1872; based on Stats. 1850, p. 254, §§ 14, 15, 22, 23; Field's Draft, N. Y. Civ. Code, § 80.
> 2. Amended by Code Amdts. 1873–74, p. 193, inserting "in writing" after "may agree." [18]

To follow the tracings, first consult the *Civil Code of the State of California, 1872.* Section 164 of the code states: "All other property acquired after marriage, by either husband or wife, or both, is community property." [19] The notes in the annotations indicate that the first mention of community property occurs in the California Constitution, 1849, Article XI. Sec. 14. The *General Laws of the State of California, from 1850 to 1864, Inclusive* quotes the section:

> *Husband and Wife*
> *An Act defining the rights of husband and wife.*
> *Passed April 17, 1850, 254.*
> §3564. Sec. 2. All property acquired after the marriage by either husband or wife, except such as may be acquired by gift, bequest, devise, or descent, shall be common property.[20]

The California Constitution of 1849, Article XI: Promiscuous Provisions. 215. section 14, states: "All Property, both real and personal, of the wife, owned or claimed by her before marriage, and that acquired afterwards by gift, devise, or descent, shall be her separate property; and laws shall be passed more clearly defining the rights of the wife, in relation as well to her separate property, as to that held in common with her husband." [21]

Also interesting is a mention of a treatise entitled *Civil Laws of Spain and Mexico,* a translation of the civil law of Spain published in 1851, in the discussion of *McDonald v. Senn.* Chapter 4 of the treatise, "Rights and duties of Husband and Wife in relation to the property acquired during marriage, Section 1, Community of Goods," states: "Art. 43. The law recognizes a partnership between the husband and wife as to the property acquired during marriage, and which exists until expressly renounced, in the manner prescribed in Section 3." [22]

Court decisions can be found in the notes provided in the annotated codes or by using the state digests. In this instance, the *Civil Code of the State of California* is annotated and provides a number of citations to secondary sources: "1) *California Jurisprudence:* See articles Husband and Wife; Divorce and Separation, vol. 9, p. 821. 2) A.L.R. Notes: Liability of husband for services rendered by wife in carrying on his business, note 23 A.L.R. 18." [23] (A.L.R. is *American Law Reports.*) *The General Laws of the State of California* is annotated also and provides a number of judicial decisions in the marginal notes: "Separate property of husband. 13 Cal. 9. 18 Cal. 654. Common property." [24] The first, 13 Cal. 9, is a case named *Barker v. Koneman* (1859), an appeal from a district court concerning property left in trust for the widow. The case 18 Cal. 654, or *Lewis v. Lewis,* is an appeal from probate court in 1861 determining the value difference between the late husband's separate estate and the common property.[25]

Interpreting and tracing the citations to statutory law and court decisions may initially seem complex, but once you begin to find the relevant footnotes and recognize legal citations, the research process is the same as it is in other subject areas.

The importance of courts is evidenced by the relative abundance of published court opinions. Some cases even reached the U. S. Supreme Court. One of the earliest, *Jones v. Porters,* was decided in 1740 in a Virginia court.[26] In it, the court nullified a conveyance made by a married couple because the wife's private examination had not been recorded. Without the private examination on record, purchases could be nullified, as illustrated by a 1691 law of New York: "An Act declaring what are the Rights & Privileges of Their Majesties Subjects inhabiting within Their Province of New-York: That no Estate of a *Feme Covert* shall be sold or conveyed, but by Deed acknowledged by her in some Court of Record, the Woman being secretly examined, if she doth it freely, without threats or compulsion of her Husband."[27]

Between the late eighteenth and the end of the nineteenth century, the U.S. Supreme Court rendered over one hundred decisions in which women and property rights or conveyancing of property were at issue. One of the first cases was *Barnes' Lessee v. Irwin* in 1793, which concerned a wife's inherited property and an antenuptial agreement.[28] The high court ruled in favor of the defendant, upholding the validity of the antenuptial agreement and the wife's right to grant ownership through her will. The importance of property ownership and the right to devise were clearly evident in the pervasive laws and court decisions rendered in colonial America and the early United States of America.

Married Women's Property Laws

During the nineteenth century, states began enacting common law principles affecting the property rights of married women. Married women's property acts differ in language, and their dates of passage span many years. One of the first was enacted by Connecticut in 1809, allowing women to write wills. The majority of states passed similar statutes in the 1850s.[29] Passed in 1848, New York's Married Women's Property Act was used by other states as a model:

AN ACT for the effectual protection of the property of married women.

Passed April 7, 1848.

The People of the State of New York, represented in Senate and Assembly do enact as follows:
Sec. 1. The real and personal property of any female who may hereafter marry, and which she shall own at the time of marriage, and the rents issues and profits thereof shall not be subject to the disposal of her husband, nor be liable for his debts, and shall continue her sole and separate property, as if she were a single female.
Sec. 2 The real and personal property, and the rents issues and profits thereof of any female now married shall not be subject to the disposal of her husband; but shall be her sole and separate property as if she were a single female except so far as the same may be liable for the debts of her husband heretofore contracted.
Sec. 3. It shall be lawful for any married female to receive, by gift, grant devise or bequest, from any person other than her husband and hold to her sole and separate use, as if she were a single female, real and personal property, and the rents, issues and profits thereof, and the same shall not be subject to the disposal of her husband, nor be liable for his debts.
Sec. 4. All contracts made between persons in contemplation of marriage shall remain in full force after such marriage takes place.[30]

Legal historians usually refer to the Civil War period to illustrate the changes in the law brought about by amendment. Amendments based on different economic, social, and political conditions can change the emphasis of the original legislation. Before the Civil War, married women's property laws were concerned with equity procedures, focusing on the appropriate pleadings a wife should use to file a suit but not altering a husband's privileges granted by prior common law principles. After the Civil War, laws were concerned with equalizing property relations between husband and wife. As Joan Hoff-Wilson concludes in *Law, Gender, and Injustice* (1991), these laws "ranged from the simple ability of wives to write wills with or without their husbands' consent, to granting *feme sole* status to abandoned women, to allowing women some control over their own wages, to establishing separate estates for women, to protecting land inherited by widows from their husbands' creditors, to allowing widows legal access to their husbands' personal estates."[31]

The Homestead Act of 1862 demonstrates that the federal government did not make gender one of the criteria for homestead ownership, and this concept was adopted by several western states as well:

Sec. 1 . . . head of a family, or who has arrived at the age of twenty-one years, and is a citizen of the United States, . . . shall, from, and after the first January, eighteen hundred and sixty-three, be entitled to enter one quarter section or a less quantity of unappropriated public lands, upon which said person may have filed a preemption claim, or which may, at the time the application is made, be subject to preemption at one dollar and twenty-five cents, or less, per acre; . . . .
Sec. 2: And be it further enacted. . . . upon application to the register of the land office in which he or she is about to make such entry, make affidavit before

the said register or receiver that he or she is the head of a family. . . .[32]

At the turn of the century, it was the effectiveness not the language of the law that diminished the rights of females. Some state legislatures began enacting laws that recognized separate and inherited estates of women as part of family income, granting creditors the right to claim women's property to pay family debts. As estates, trusts, and succession laws were passed, the rights of dower were abolished. Even after these laws had been repealed, many states kept portions of the older laws. For example, intestate succession (without a will) generally allowed a widow to take one-third of the husband's estate as earlier rights of dower had specified.

Spain and Mexico, civil law countries, influenced the way property laws developed in the western United States. Early community property legislation was enacted in this region. One of the earliest mentions of the distinction between the wife's separate property and common property is in the California Constitution of 1849: Section 14: "All property, both real and personal, of the wife, owned or claimed by her before marriage, and that acquired afterward by gift, devise, or descent, shall be her separate property; and laws shall be passed more clearly defining the rights of the wife in relation as well to her separate property, as to that held in common with her husband."[33]

Although the states passed legislation naming marital property as community property, husbands were the ones who managed and disposed of the property. Only if the husband died was the wife allowed to manage the property, as this 1879 Texas law illustrates:

> Art. 2181. The surviving wife may retain the exclusive management, control and disposition of the community property of herself and her deceased husband in the same manner, and subject to the same rights, rules and regulations as provided in the case of a surviving husband, until she may marry again.
>
> . . . .
>
> Art. 2852. All property acquired by either husband or wife during the marriage except that which is acquired by gift, devise or descent shall be deemed the common property of the husband and wife, and during the coverture may be disposed of by the husband only.[34]

BIBLIOGRAPHY:

Blackstone, William. *Commentaries on the Laws of England.* Reprint, 1967; Oxford, 1803 (KF385 .B55 1967). This multivolume treatise, a standard for the study of British and early American law, should be consulted by any researcher who is interested in colonial law. It outlines and summarizes the common law of England.

Chused, Richard. "Married Women's Property Law, 1800–1850." *Georgetown Law Journal* 71: 1359. A law journal article that gives a good

BIBLIOGRAPHY continued

overview of this group of laws, it suggests locations of collections that would interest researchers and provides passage dates and statistics on the impact of legislation.

Hoff-Wilson, Joan. *Law, Gender, and Injustice: A Legal History of U.S. Women.* New York: New York University Press, 1991 (KF4758 .H64 1990).

Laws Respecting Women. London: St. Paul's Church-Yard, 1777 [Law E Treat 'Laws'] {LLRBR}. Chronicling the laws affecting women in Great Britain, this treatise provides an eighteenth-century perspective. Interestingly, it presents some issues that society today would view as modern, for instance, the monetary payment a wife should receive if she and her husband agree to live separately.

Salmon, Marylynn. *Women and the Law of Property in Early America.* Chapel Hill: University of North Carolina Press, 1986 (KF524 .S24 1986). An excellent source for studying property laws in Massachusetts, Connecticut, New York, Pennsylvania, Maryland, Virginia, and South Carolina and their effect on women during the period 1750–1830. This overview addresses the impact these laws had on the social structure of the colonies.

Slavery and Indentured Servants

Just as a high premium has always been placed on real property, personalty has been valuable and its ownership the subject of law and contested in court as well. Before the Civil War, slaves and indentured servants were considered personal property, and they or their descendants could be sold or inherited like any other personalty. Like other property, human chattel was governed largely by laws of individual states. Generally, these laws concerning indentured servants and slaves did not differentiate between the sexes. Some, however, addressed only women. Regardless of their country of origin, many early immigrants were indentured servants, people who sold their labor in exchange for passage to the New World and housing on their arrival. Initially, most laws passed concerned indentured servants, but some time around the middle of the seventeenth century, colonial laws began to reflect differences between indentured servants and slaves. More important, the laws began to differentiate between races: the association with "servitude for natural life" with people of African descent became common. *Re Negro John Punch* (1640) was one of the early cases that made a racial distinction among indentured servants.[35]

Virginia was one of the first states to acknowledge slavery in its laws, initially enacting such a law in 1661.[36] The following year, Virginia passed two laws that pertained solely to women who were slaves or indentured servants and to their illegitimate children. Women servants who produced children by their masters could be punished by having to do two years of servitude with the

Margaret Sanger, The Fight for Birth Control *(New York: Max Maisel, 1916; HQ763.P3 pamphlet 47). Rare Book and Special Collections Division.*

Margaret Sanger's "fight for birth control" involved many confrontations with the law. As a consequence of distributing three issues of her journal *The Woman Rebel,* which contained articles on sexuality, she was indicted in 1914 for violating the Comstock Act of 1873 (*An Act for the Suppression of Trade in, and Circulation of, obscene Literature and Articles of immoral Use,* c. 258, 17 Stat. 598), which classified materials "for the prevention of conception" as obscene and made it illegal to send them through the mail. In 1916, she and her staff were arrested for operating the first birth control clinic, which was located in Brooklyn. Sanger was convicted in 1917. The appeals court affirmed the conviction (*People v. Sanger,* 166 NYS 1107 [1917]), and she served one month in the penitentiary for women in Queens, New York.

As women's suffrage passed into law, Sanger gradually won support for family planning from the public and the courts. She organized the first American (1921) and international (1925) birth control conferences and formed the National Committee on Federal Legislation for Birth Control in 1929. In 1936 the *United States v. One Package* (86 F2d 737 [1936]) decision changed the Comstock Act's classification of birth control literature as obscene, and in 1971 Congress amended the statute to remove any trace of prevention of conception. The U.S. Supreme Court decision *Griswold v. Connecticut* (381 U.S. 479 [1965]) ended the ban on the use of contraceptives by married couples, and *Eisenstadt v. Baird* (405 U.S. 438 [1972]) allowed unmarried couples to legally use birth control devices. Sanger's publications and papers are discussed in chapters 4 and 5 respectively, but a visit to the Law Library provides an examination of the laws that relate to birth control and family planning.

churchwardens after the expiration of the term with their masters. The law reads, "that each woman servant gott with child by her master shall after her time by indenture or custome is expired be by the churchwardens of the parish where she lived when she was brought to bed of such bastard, sold for two years. . . ."[37]

The second law, which concerned the birthright of children born of Negro or mulatto women, would have a profound effect on the continuance of slavery after the slave trade was abolished—and on the future descendants of these women. Great Britain had a very structured primogeniture system, under which children always claimed lineage through the father, even those born without the legitimacy of marriage. Virginia was one of the first states to legislate a change:

Act XII
Negro womens children to serve according to the condition of the mother.

WHEREAS some doubts have arrisen whether children got by any Englishman upon a Negro woman should be slave or ffree, *Be it therefore enacted and declared by this present grand assembly,* that all children borne in this country shalbe held bond or free only according to the condition of the mother, *And* that if any christian shall committ ffornication with a Negro man or woman, hee or shee soe offending shall pay double the ffines imposed by the former act.[38]

Most slave states enacted similar laws. After the slave trade officially ended, many slave owners tried to ensure sufficient numbers of slaves were available to run their plantations. Young slave women of breeding age became more valuable. There are a number of court cases where slave women either killed their masters who forced them to have sexual relations or killed the children rather than have the children enslaved.[39]

Miscegenation laws, forbidding marriage between races, were prevalent in the South and the West. Because English masters had had little regard for indentured servants of non-Anglo ethnic groups, they allowed and sometimes encouraged commingling of their servants. Being seen in public or bringing legitimacy to these relations, however, was not lawful. This is evidenced by a court decision from 1630, the first court decision in which a Negro woman and a white man figured prominently. *Re Davis* (1630) concerned sexual relations between them, the decision stating, "Hugh Davis to be soundly whipt . . . for abusing himself to the dishonor of God and shame of Christianity by defiling his body in lying with a Negro, which fault he is to actk. next sabbath day."[40]

Virginia passed its first miscegenation law in 1691 as part of "An act for suppressing outlying Slaves."

> And for prevention of that abominable mixture and spurious issue which hereafter may encrease in this dominion, as well by negroes, mulattoes, and Indians intermarrying with English, or other white women, as by their unlawfull accompanying with one another, *Be it enacted by the authoritie aforesaid, and it is hereby enacted,* that for the time to come, whatsoever English or other white man or woman being free shall intermarry with a negroe, mulatto, or Indian man or woman bond or free shall within three months after such marriage be banished and removed from this dominion forever. . . .[41]

Another section of the law closed the loophole created by the 1662 birthright law, which mandated that technically, children born of a free white mother and Negro father were free. This amendment stated that a free white woman who had a bastard child by a Negro or mulatto had to pay fifteen pounds sterling within one month of the birth. If she could not pay, she would become an indentured servant for five years. Whether or not the fine was paid, however, the child would be bound in service for thirty years.

The laws that restricted slaves or indentured servants addressed the owners and would penalize them for breaking the law. It would have been difficult to penalize someone who was a slave for life; laws governing their condition allowed them to be whipped, beaten, or killed under certain circumstances. Nor could they go to court to seek redress. It was not permitted for a colored person to testify against a white Christian, as illustrated by the 1717 Maryland law:

> II. Be it Therefore Enacted, *by the right honourable the Lord Proprietary, by and with the advice and consent of his Lordship's Governor, and the Upper and Lower Houses of Assembly, and by the authority of the same,* That from and after the end of this present session of assembly, no Negro or mulatto slave, free Negro, or mulatto born of a white woman, during his time of *servitude by law,* or any Indian slave, or free Indian natives, of this or the neighbouring provinces, be admitted and received as good and valid evidence in law, in any matter or thing whatsoever depending before any court of record, or before any magistrate within this province, wherein any christian white person is concerned.[42]

Against these overwhelming restrictions, there were a number of court cases in which slaves filed suit seeking their freedom or freed Negroes claimed property that had been inherited from their former owners. Elizabeth Freeman (1732/34–1829), a slave, presented her case for freedom in a Massachusetts court *pro se* in 1783 and won.[43] In addition there were the cases where the slave or freed Negro was the defendant; *Celia, a Slave* is a narrative account of such a trial in Missouri in 1855.[44]

White women were often involved in litigious situations involving slaves through the workings of the dower laws. In some states women could inherit personalty but could only receive a life estate in real property.[45] This situation created many problems, particularly if slaves were needed to make profits from the land. For example, if a woman chose to free her inherited personalty at death, her descendants would have no one to work the land unless they farmed it with paid workers or purchased new slaves. Frequently, wills or contracts that granted freedom or conveyed realty or personalty as dower were contested in court.

The laws and resulting court cases that involved slavery and indentured servants have had a major impact on America, its men and women alike, in both the past and the present. Through the years, the laws that the states passed became steadily more restrictive toward slaves, mulattoes, and freed Negroes. In 1850, the federal government became involved with the passage of the Fugitive Slave Act, responding to strong lobbying efforts by slaveholders wanting to counteract abolitionist forces.[46] In the face of these all-encompassing laws, women with extraordinary courage fought for a better life. For example, Harriet Tubman (ca. 1821–1913) returned to the South nineteen times to bring over three hundred fugitives to freedom, and Charlotte Forten (1837–1914), a free privileged Negro from Philadelphia, went to South Carolina during the early Civil War to teach "the contrabands of war."[47]

In 1865, the Thirteenth Amendment to the United States Constitution ended slavery and involuntary servitude. Many laws that had been passed and judicial precedents that had been established before that date would not be changed until the middle or late twentieth century.

BIBLIOGRAPHY:

Catterall, Helen Tunnicliff. *Judicial Cases concerning American Slavery and the Negro.* Reprint, New York: Octagon Books, 1968 (KF4545.S5 C3 1968).

BIBLIOGRAPHY continued

Finkelman, Paul. *Slavery in the Courtroom.* Washington: Library of Congress, 1985 (KF4545.S5 A123 1985).

Giddings, Paula. *When and Where I Enter: The Impact of Black Women on Race and Sex in America.* New York: Bantam Books, 1985 (E185.86 .G49 1985).

Ham, Debra Newman, ed. *The African American Odyssey.* Washington: Library of Congress, 1998 (E185.53.W3 L53 1998).

McLaurin, Melton A. *Celia, a Slave.* Athens, Ga.: University of Georgia Press, 1991 (KF223.C43 M34 1991).

Belva Lockwood. Photograph, n.d. Prints and Photographs Division. LC-BH834-55.

In 1879, Belva Lockwood was admitted to the U.S. Supreme Court bar, the first woman to be admitted to it. The same court, however, refused to issue a writ of mandamus ordering the Commonwealth of Virginia to admit her to its bar, thereby setting the legal precedent allowing states to limit their definition of "person" to males only.

Women Lawyers

Women have been a part of the legal system since the early years of this nation, but for a long time, they were prohibited through various means from practicing law. There have been some exceptions. Margaret Brent (ca. 1601–1671), for example, arrived in the New World in 1638, received a land grant in St. Mary's City, and became executrix for Governor Leonard Calvert of Maryland. She appeared before the provincial court to file suits against her own debtors and to plead cases for others.[48] Luce Terry (1730–1821) in 1796 was "the first voice of a black woman in the nation to influence law before a court on which a member of the U.S. Supreme Court sat when she gave an oral argument in a Vermont court before Justice Samuel Chase who was riding the circuit in New England."[49]

Initially, women were denied admission to law schools, and later they were denied admission to state bar associations. State legislative bodies or the administrative offices of a state's supreme court determine the requirements for bar admission and the codes of professional ethics. Myra Bradwell (1831–1894), for example, filed a petition with the U. S. Supreme Court to appeal the decision of the Illinois Supreme Court that denied her admission to the state bar in 1872 after she had completed her legal studies and passed the bar examination.[50] Her argument was based on the Immunities and Privileges Clause of the Fourteenth Amendment, which says: "No state shall make or enforce any law which shall abridge the privileges or immunities of citizens of the United States. . . ."[51] The U.S. Supreme Court ruled that the immunities and privileges clause did not apply to the "right to admission to practice in the courts of a State," and thereby set a precedent of noninterference by the federal government in state employment affairs that would remain in place for decades. The justices conceded that Mrs. Bradwell was a "citizen" according to the Constitution, but the fact that she was married presented the Court with problems. Justice Bradley concurred in the Court's opinion, and his view of women would prevail in future judicial opinions:

> It certainly cannot be affirmed, as an historical fact, that this has ever been established as one of the fundamental privileges and immunities of the sex. On the contrary, the civil law, as well as nature herself, has always recognized a wide difference in the respective spheres and destinies of man and woman. Man is, or should be, woman's protector and defender. The natural and proper timidity and delicacy which belongs to the female sex evidently unfits it for many of the occupations of civil life. The constitution of the family organization, which is founded in the divine ordinance, as well as in the nature of things, indicates the domestic sphere as that which properly belongs to the domain and functions of womanhood. The harmony, not to say identity, of interest and views which belong, or should belong, to the family institution is repugnant to the idea of a woman adopting a distinct and independent career from that of her husband.[52]

In 1893 Belva A. Lockwood (1830–1917), a trained attorney who was the first woman admitted to practice before the U.S. Supreme Court, filed suit for mandamus in this same court to force the Commonwealth of Virginia to admit her to the state bar. Stating its precedent, the U.S. Supreme Court "denied leave" to bring her argument:

> In *Bradwell v. the State,* 16 *Wall.* 130, it was held that the right to practise law in the state courts was privilege or immunity of a citizen of the United States; that the right to control and regulate the granting of license to practise law in the courts of a State is one of those powers that was not transferred for its protection to the Federal government, and its exercise is in no manner governed or controlled by citizenship of the United States in the party seeking such license.[53]

Belle Babb Mansfield (1846–1911), the first woman admitted to a state bar in the United States, was formally admitted to the Iowa State Bar in June 1869 after a ruling in the Iowa courts in her favor.[54] Charlotte E. Ray (1850–1899 or 1900), a Howard University graduate, was the first African American woman lawyer; she was admitted to the District of Columbia Bar in 1872 without a fight because she applied for admission under the name C. E. Ray and the admissions committee thought she was male.[55]

Today women lawyers are enjoying opportunities that would surprise and delight women of the nineteenth and early twentieth centuries. An 1890 commentary by Lelia Robinson (1850–1891), the

CHAP. 30.] LUNATICS AND DRUNKARDS. 371

person, if there be any of sufficient ability to pay the same.

SEC. 45. This act shall take effect and be in force from and after its passage.

Approved, December 9th, 1869.

FEMALE SUFFRAGE.

CHAPTER 31.

AN ACT TO GRANT TO THE WOMEN OF WYOMING TERRITORY THE RIGHT OF SUFFRAGE, AND TO HOLD OFFICE.

Be it enacted by the Council and House of Representatives of the Territory of Wyoming:

SEC. 1. That every woman of the age of twenty-one years, residing in this territory, may, at every election to be holden under the laws thereof, cast her vote. And her rights to the elective franchise and to hold office shall be the same under the election laws of the territory, as those of electors. *Women's rights.*

SEC. 2. This act shall take effect and be in force from and after its passage.

Approved, December 10th 1869.

COUNCIL AND REPRESENTATIVE DISTRICTS.

CHAPTER 32.

AN ACT APPORTIONING THE TERRITORY OF WYOMING INTO COUNCIL AND REPRESENTATIVE DISTRICTS, AND FOR OTHER PURPOSES.

Be it enacted by the Council and House of Representatives of the Territory of Wyoming:

SEC. 1. That hereafter the council of the territory of Wyoming shall consist of nine members, and the house of representatives of thirteen members. *Number in legislature.*

SEC. 2. The members of the council and house of

"An Act to Grant to the Women of Wyoming Territory the Right of Suffrage, and to Hold Office." From General Laws, Memorials and Resolutions of the Territory of Wyoming, Passed at the First Session of the Legislative Assembly, convened at Cheyenne, October 12th, 1869 *(Cheyenne, 1870; Wyo 1 1869). Law Library of Congress.*

Wyoming was the first territory to grant women full suffrage rights. Several western states and territories followed this 1869 precedent in granting women the right to vote before the passage of the Nineteenth Amendment to the U.S. Constitution in 1920.

Chic Young. "Blondie: The Night Shift." Drawing, 1933. Published September 5, 1933. Prints and Photographs Division. LC-USZ62-126672. Reprinted with special permission of King Features Syndicate, Dean Young, and Jeanne Young O'Neil.

Protective legislation, state laws limiting the number of hours a woman or child could work and guaranteeing a minimum wage, was common during the late nineteenth and early twentieth centuries. This drawing from the popular comic strip shows Blondie implementing the notion of protective legislation to ensure equality in her primary workplace, the home. Shortly after her marriage to Dagwood Bumstead in 1933, Blondie organized local housewives and lobbied for an eight-hour day. She led Dagwood to the sink full of dirty dishes with a wink to newspaper readers.

first woman admitted to the Massachusetts bar, traces the beginnings:

> [B]ut it remained for the United States to inaugurate the era of the woman lawyer of to-day. And this was so short a time ago,—for the woman lawyer in the abstract has not yet attained her majority,—that the novelty of her very existence has scarcely begun to wear off, and the newspapers publish and republish little floating items about women lawyers along with those of the latest sea-serpent, the popular idea seeming to be that the one is about as real as the other.[56]

As the woman lawyer is taken increasingly more seriously, books for women attorneys address such issues as how to become partners in large law firms, "rain-making (or generating business for a law firm)," and marketing as a sole practitioner. More important, women attorneys are receiving favorable decisions in court concerning their rights as attorneys, not just their right to be members of a state bar.[57]

BIBLIOGRAPHY:

Drachman, Virginia G. *Sisters in Law: Women Lawyers in Modern American History.* Cambridge, Mass.: Harvard University Press, 1998 (KF299.W6 D7 1998).

Morello, Karen. *The Invisible Bar: The Woman Lawyer in America 1638 to Present.* New York: Random House, 1986 (KF299.W6 M67 1986). This treatise, an often-cited source, is an excellent historical account of women practicing law in the United States.

Robinson, Lelia. "Woman Lawyers in the United States." *The Green Bag* 2 (1890):10. In this popular magazine published in Boston in the 1890s, Robinson gives the contemporary view of women lawyers.

Smith, J. Clay Jr., ed. *Rebels in Law: Voices in History of Black Women Lawyers.* Ann Arbor: University of Michigan, 1998 (KF299.A35 R43 1998). This excellent chronicle of the African American woman's experience in law is told in the words of various authors. Although it describes some of the same hardships as other accounts of women lawyers, *Rebels in Law* is unusual in showing how these women had to struggle with other social restrictions, such as racism.

State Suffrage Laws

When it was ratified in 1920, the Nineteenth Amendment to the United States Constitution granted the right to vote to women. Before that time, some states had passed legislation allowing women to vote, beginning with Wyoming in 1869:

> Be it enacted by the Council and House of Representatives of the Territory of Wyoming:
>
> Sec. 1. That every woman of the age of twenty-one years, residing in this territory, may, at every election to be holden under the laws thereof, cast her vote. And her rights to the elective franchise and to hold office shall be the same under the election laws of the territory, as those of electors.
> Sec. 2. This act shall take effect and be in force from and after its passage.
> Approved, December 10th 1869.[58]

Western territories such as Colorado, Utah, and California followed Wyoming's example in the years from 1869 to 1911. Other states and municipalities granted women limited suffrage, like Kentucky, which gave widows with children the right to vote in school elections as early as 1838.[59] During the women's suffrage movement, New Jersey became a rallying cry for the early suffragists in their demonstrations and court cases. Interestingly, New Jersey had given women who met the enumerated requirements the right to vote in its 1776 constitution:

IV. That all inhabitants of this Colony, of full age, who are worth fifty pounds proclamation money, clear estate in the same, and have resided within the county in which they claim a vote for twelve months immediately preceding the election, shall be entitled to vote for Representatives in Council and Assembly; and also for all other public officers, that shall be elected by the people of the county at large.[60]

Sixty-four years later, however, the state constitution of 1844 took away those suffrage rights, regardless of a woman's standing, stating that "One. Every white male citizen of the United States, of the age of twenty-one years, who shall have been a resident of this State one year . . . ." would be entitled to vote.[61]

To force the issue of national suffrage, women filed court cases. The case of *United States v. Susan B. Anthony* was a highly publicized one.[62] When Anthony tried to vote in New York for a member of Congress in 1872, the United States brought criminal charges against her. The court found Susan B. Anthony guilty and fined her $100 plus court costs. That same year, Mrs. Virginia Minor (1824–1894), a Missourian, attempted to register to vote, despite a Missouri statute limiting voting rights to the "male citizen of the United States." Eventually, the U.S. Supreme Court heard Minor's case and decided in favor of the state: "Being unanimously of the opinion that the Constitution of the United States does not confer the right of suffrage upon any one, and that the constitutions and laws of the several States which commit that important trust to men alone are not necessarily void, we Affirm the Judgment."[63] Because the various state laws on voting rights were arbitrary, it was necessary for the suffragists to mount a national effort for securing the franchise. The Nineteenth Amendment gave women some leverage in the electoral process.

Protective Legislation

Before the passage of the Civil Rights Act of 1964, a federal law, employment issues that affected women were governed solely by state law. After the Civil War, large numbers of women went to work outside their homes. In his speech before his colleagues in the U.S. House of Representatives to encourage the extension of equal suffrage in Alaska on Wednesday, April 24, 1912, Congressman Edward T. Taylor of Colorado stated:

But to-day one-fifth of all the women of this country are compelled to earn their own living by their daily labor. Nearly 7,000,000 women are wage earners to-day, and the number is constantly increasing. Woman suffrage is not responsible for bringing about that condition. It is the economic change that is going on in the life of this Republic. If the right to vote was taken away from the laboring men of this country to-morrow, they would within one year, and in many places within one week, be reduced to a condition of practical slavery; and it is little less than inhuman to compel the 7,000,000 women to work in this country under conditions that would be absolutely intolerable to men.[64]

These women were generally single, widowed, or had been deserted. Some of them held jobs as school teachers or worked in other professions. Most jobs held by women were low-paying and involved substandard conditions. Some suffrage organizations advocated improvement of working conditions for women. These groups were largely responsible for the changes in labor laws that are referred to as "protective legislation."

Protective legislation limited the number of hours that a woman or child could work in certain jobs and guaranteed them a minimum wage. The legal result, however, was that men and women were treated differently in the work place. The major justifications were that (1) physical differences between men and women would make it dangerous for women to work (2) the chronic fatigue of long hours would result in the deterioration of women's health and (3) future generations would be affected by this deterioration in women's health.[65] Wisconsin, the first state to pass this legislation, enacted a protective law in 1867, but a law passed in Massachusetts in 1874, and amended in 1902, provided the most common model:

No woman shall be employed in laboring in a manufacturing or mechanical establishment more than ten hours in any one day, except as hereinafter provided in this section, unless a different apportionment in hours of labor is made for the sole purpose of making a shorter day's work for one day of the week; and in no case shall the hours of labor exceed fifty-eight in a week. . . .[66]

Although the laws were designed to protect the working woman's health, welfare, and morals until she married, not all employers and employees were satisfied with the legislation. Employers filed suit to have the statutes voided for being unconstitutional. *Muller v. Oregon* was one of the most famous of these cases.[67] In it, the U.S. Supreme

Court upheld the constitutionality of such laws. Oregon's defense team was led by Louis D. Brandeis, a progressive attorney who became an associate justice of the Supreme Court before *Muller* was decided.[68]

Promulgation of minimum wage laws for women in the states followed their legislation of maximum hours. An example is the 1918 District of Columbia law that later became the subject of litigation:

Sec. 23. That this Act shall be known as the "District of Columbia minimum-wage law." The purposes of the Act are to protect the women and minors of the District from conditions detrimental to their health and morals, resulting from wages which are inadequate to maintain decent standards of living; and the Act in each of its provisions and in its entirety shall be interpreted to effectuate these purposes.[69]

Employers contested these laws too; law suits were filed declaring them unconstitutional and in violation of the liberty-of-contract doctrine.[70] In 1923, *Adkins v. Children's Hospital* was appealed to the U.S. Supreme Court, which ruled the law unconstitutional.[71] Other state courts, following the precedent set by the Supreme Court, ruled that their state statutes were likewise unconstitutional. Fourteen years later, however, the U.S. Supreme Court reversed its decision and held that a law concerning the minimum wage for women in the State of Washington was constitutional.[72]

Although these laws guaranteed a minimum wage for women and children, they created unintentional inequities. Protective legislation gave courts the grounds for rendering inequitable decisions. It was not until the Civil Rights Act of 1964 that women enjoyed legislation granting equality in the workplace and the firm legal grounds to enforce such laws in court.

In employment, as in suffrage and possession of property, the legal history of women's struggle for equality mirrored what was happening in the society at large and amplifies our understanding of it.

Federal Law

Two examples of federal law illustrate how federal and state laws complement one another and show the role of the courts and executive agencies in carrying out the laws—sometimes to the benefit and sometimes to the detriment of women.

Civil Rights

The Civil Rights Act of 1964 is generally perceived as having granted women more freedom in the workplace and a right to expect equal treatment.[73] Despite glass ceilings and other impediments, the passage of this act was a major legal victory. It was the cumulation of several struggles that began early in United States history.

The Civil Rights Act of 1964 exemplifies how various categories of law interact. As statutory law, the act forbade gender-based discrimination in the employment arena:

§ 703. (a) It shall be an unlawful employment practice for an employer—
(1) to fail or refuse to hire or to discharge any individual, or otherwise to discriminate against any individual with respect to his compensation, terms, conditions, or privileges of employment, because of such individual's race, color, religion, sex, or national origin; or
(2) to limit, segregate, or classify his employees in any way which would deprive or tend to deprive any individual of employment opportunities or otherwise adversely affect his status as an employee, because of such individual's race, color, religion, sex, or national origin.[74]

The courts broadened the scope of the law when interpreting the statutory language. For instance, the court introduced the concept of "hostile environment" as a criterion to be used to determine whether or not the law had been violated:

Since the Guidelines were issued, courts have uniformly held, and we agree, that a plaintiff may establish a violation of *Title VII* by proving that discrimination based on sex has created a hostile or abusive work environment. As the Court of Appeals for the Eleventh Circuit wrote in *Henson v. Dundee,* 682 *F.2d* 897, 902 (1982): "Sexual harassment which creates a hostile or offensive environment for members of one sex is every bit the arbitrary barrier to sexual equality at the workplace that racial harassment is to racial equality. Surely, a requirement that a man or woman run a gauntlet of sexual abuse in return for the privilege of being allowed to work and make a living can be as demeaning and disconcerting as the harshest of racial epithets."

Accord, *Katz v. Dole,* 709 F.2d 251, 254–255 (CA4 1983); *Bundy v. Jackson,* 205 U.S.App.D.C., at 444–454, 641 F.2d, at 934–944; *Zabkowicz v. West Bend Co.,* 589 F.Supp. 780 (ED Wis.1984).[75]

As the number of court cases and judicial precedents increased, the body of common law grew and expanded the concept that originated from Title VII of the Civil Rights Act of 1964.

In accordance with legislative language and judicial interpretations, various administrative agencies further delineated the statute by implementing affirmative action programs with guidelines that were applicable only to a specific agency, thus creating a body of regulatory law. An example from the Department of Justice:

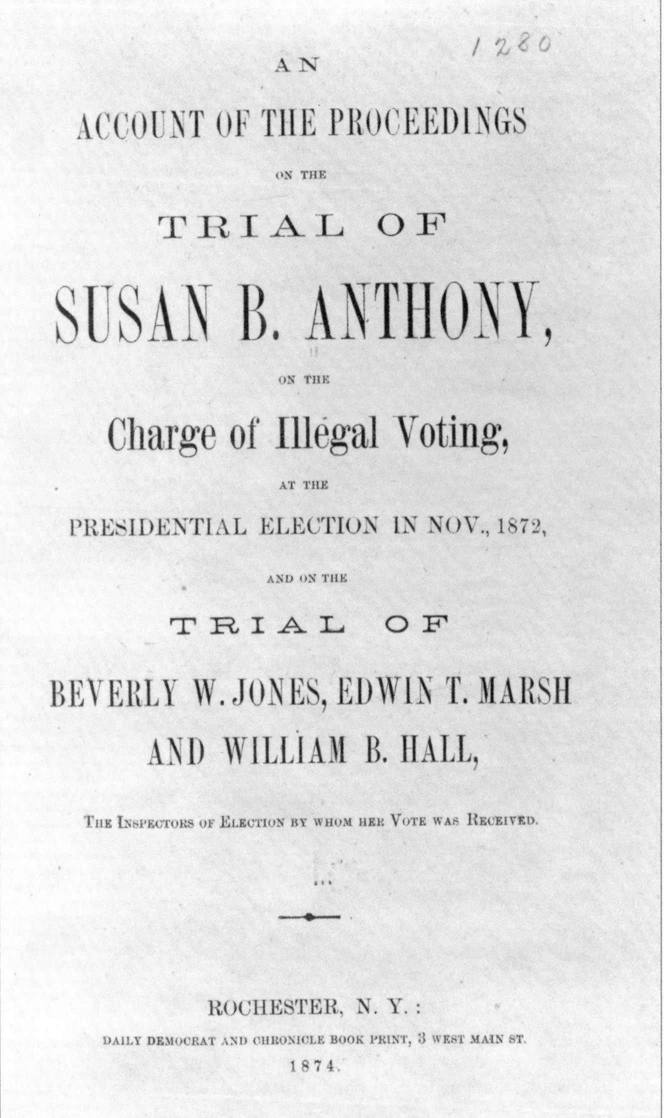
AN ACCOUNT OF THE PROCEEDINGS ON THE TRIAL OF SUSAN B. ANTHONY, ON THE Charge of Illegal Voting, AT THE PRESIDENTIAL ELECTION IN NOV., 1872, AND ON THE TRIAL OF BEVERLY W. JONES, EDWIN T. MARSH AND WILLIAM B. HALL, THE INSPECTORS OF ELECTION BY WHOM HER VOTE WAS RECEIVED.

ROCHESTER, N. Y.:
DAILY DEMOCRAT AND CHRONICLE BOOK PRINT, 3 WEST MAIN ST.
1874.

Susan B. Anthony, An Account of the Proceedings on the Trial of Susan B. Anthony, on the Charge of Illegal Voting, at the Presidential Election in Nov., 1872 *(Rochester, N.Y., 1874; JK1899.A6 A5 Anthony). Susan B. Anthony Collection, Rare Book and Special Collections Division.*

Susan B. Anthony's annotated copy of the printed transcript of her trial for attempting to vote in the 1872 presidential and congressional election documents her efforts to test the citizenship clause of the Fourteenth Amendment. Anthony was indicted and found guilty in a federal court for attempting to vote for a member of Congress. Although the U.S. Supreme Court eventually decided in *Minor v. Happersett* that suffrage was a privilege to be granted by states, the trial offered Anthony an opportunity to publicize her arguments both in pretrial lectures and subsequent presentations that brought many new converts to the cause.

Subpart A—Equal Employment Opportunity within the Department of Justice

AUTHORITY: 5 *U.S.C.* 301, 28 *U.S.C.* 509, 510; E.O. 11246, 3 *CFR* 1964–1965 Comp., p. 339; E.O. 11478, 3 *CFR* 1966–1970 Comp., p. 803.

§ 42.1 Policy
(a) It is the policy of the Department of Justice to seek to eliminate discrimination on the basis of race, color, religion, sex, sexual orientation, national origin, marital status, political affiliation, age, or physical or mental handicap in employment within the Department and to assure equal employment opportunity for all employees and applicants for employment.
(b) No person shall be subject to retaliation for opposing any practice prohibited by the above policy or for participating in any stage of administrative or judicial proceedings related to this policy.
[Order No. 2037–96, 61 *FR* 34730, July 3, 1996; 61 *FR* 43119, Aug. 20, 1996.][76]

When you try to locate law concerning a specific aspect of the Civil Rights Act, it is important to review all of these sources to fully understand the issue.

Often, in order to learn why a law was enacted or how the law is intended to apply, you must also review the legislative history documents promulgated during the consideration of the passage of the law. These include U.S. House of Representatives and Senate bills, congressional committee reports, hearings transcripts, and the *Congressional Record* of debates.[77] Using the Civil Rights Act of 1964 as an example, we can look at the fact that the *Congressional Record* reports that an amendment adding women to the protected class was offered by Congressman Howard Smith of Virginia during floor debate.[78]

Amendment offered by Mr. Smith of Virginia: On page 68, line 23, after the word "religion," insert the word "sex". . . .
Now, I am very serious about this amendment. It has been offered several times before, but it was offered at inappropriate places in the bill. Now, this is the appropriate place for this amendment to come in. I do not think it can do any harm to this legislation; maybe it can do some good. I think it will do some good for the minority sex.[79]

Although women have worked outside the home since the beginnings of this country, they did not possess the legal right to challenge inequities in the workplace. When women gained legal equality in the workplace, federal statutory law created rights and remedies based on which women could file suit against an employer or potential employer for employment discrimination.

Legal history shows that women have not always possessed this right by either federal or state law, resulting in there being few remedies available to them in court.

Nevertheless there have been many suits filed. Often these resulted in dismissal "for lack of a cause of action" because of the grounds on which they were brought. Nineteenth-century women filed suits against discrimination based on the Fourteenth Amendment's privileges and immunities clause and failed to win favorable results. Today, women file suits based on the Fourteenth Amendment's equal protection clause and on the Civil Rights Act of 1964, Title VII, and win favorable decisions. As a result, a considerable body of precedent has been set in the court, giving women the rights and remedies they need to enforce equal treatment in employment settings.

Immigration

The Immigration Act of 1875 was the first immigration law that excluded groups of people from the United States—and women were part of that exclusion. Commonly referred to as the Asian Exclusion Act, this legislation prohibited the importation of Chinese labor forces who did not voluntarily consent to come to work in America and Chinese women for the purposes of prostitution: "Sec. 3. That the importation into the United States of women for the purposes of prostitution is hereby forbidden."[80] In 1903 the immigration law was amended to include in the exclusion any woman or girl, regardless of her country of origin. The 1903 law read: "Sec. 3: That the importation into the United States of any woman or girl for the purposes of prostitution is hereby forbidden."[81] Not until 1910 were the words "woman or girl" removed from the law, and it was amended to read, "That the importation into the United States of any alien for the purpose of prostitution or for any other immoral purpose is hereby forbidden."[82] The same year, the Mann Act, or White Slave Traffic Act was passed, which punished those who imported or transported women across state lines for immoral purposes.[83]

Although the laws were enacted to limit the trafficking of women for prostitution, they were used in a negative way to prevent women who were single and unemployed from entering the United States when they did not appear to have a means of support. The immigration laws enacted from 1875 to 1910, in conjunction with the prevailing opinion that the European countries were encouraging their paupers and undesirables to emigrate, assumed that single women would become wards of the state or turn to prostitution in order to make a living.[84] Even though these laws were passed during the late nineteenth and early twentieth centuries, some of the views they supported remained entrenched well into the late twentieth century.

The Law Library of Congress has a wealth of material that provides sources for research in women's history, in both the basic and the more tangential issues that have had an impact on women's individual lives and on the society in which they have found themselves. Legal materials add a dimension to scholarly studies that has not often been exploited. Although the law may not be as immediately interesting as journals or scrapbooks of individual women, the fact that the legal community and the people who formed it took the time to legislate and later to litigate an issue indicates that such an issue was integral to the times in which they lived. To omit a consideration of how the law developed is to disregard a crucial aspect of the lives of women.

I would like to thank the editorial team and academic advisers for their challenging questions and comments, my law librarian colleagues for their time and research skills, and those colleagues who encouraged me to make "how to find the law" an integral part of this guide.

"Supporters of the proposed Federal equal rights amendment demonstrating yesterday in Lafayette Park across from the White House." Photograph by Teresa Zabala, June 30, 1982, for the New York Times, July 1, 1982, p. A12. Serial and Government Publications Division. Copyright © 1982 The New York Times. Teresa Zabala, NYT Pictures.

On the day the Equal Rights Amendment (ERA) died, Eleanor Smeal, president of the National Organization of Women (NOW), spoke to an estimated two thousand cheering supporters across from the White House in Lafayette Park, vowing to continue the fight. She said that NOW planned to spend $3 million in the November elections to defeat state legislators who voted against the ERA.

At a National Organization for Women (NOW) rally in Lafayette Park, across from the White House, on June 30, 1982, NOW president Eleanor Smeal rallied an estimated two thousand supporters, including seven hundred nurses in town for the American Nurses Association convention.[1] Although they were there that day mourning the defeat of the Equal Rights Amendment (ERA), Smeal urged them not to forget that "We are a majority. We are determined to play majority politics . . . . We are not going to be reduced again to the ladies' auxiliary."[2] In San Francisco, outside the Civic Center, about one thousand women counted down the ERA's last six hours, a rain-soaked vigil that was reported, filmed, and recorded by many women journalists and technicians.[3]

That same night, at a party in a Washington, D.C., hotel, the ERA's demise was celebrated by opponents, fourteen hundred strong, as "a great victory for women."[4] The *Washington Post* account of that evening describes the entrance into the ballroom of the leader of the ERA opposition, Phyllis Schlafly, as the band played "Somewhere over the Rainbow." During the festivities, the crowd was entertained with renditions of "Ding, Dong, the Witch Is Dead" and "I Enjoy Being a Girl." Triumphantly addressing the crowd, Schlafly called for "a mighty movement" that will "set America on the right path."[5]

What caused the rejection of the Equal Rights Amendment? Why the intense emotions that caused ERA proponents to write the names of opponents in pigs' blood on the floors of the Illinois state capitol or opponents to pronounce apocalyptically that if the amendment was ratified husbands would no longer have to support their wives, that women would be drafted, and that toilets would be made unisex? What, if any, was the legacy of the often bitter ratification campaign that divided American women for nearly a decade beginning in 1972?

The proposed Equal Rights Amendment, only fifty-one words in length, was contentious from its inception. In a form suggested by Alice Paul, a constitutional amendment was first introduced in 1923—only three years after the Nineteenth Amendment granted women the right to vote—unleashing sixty or more years of national debate. Paul was a militant leader in the suffrage movement, founded the National Woman's Party (see chapter 5), and for fifty years served as a tactician for the ERA. Her original wording, drafted in 1923, has been changed several times, but the text submitted to the states for ratification in 1972 is essentially hers:

"Sec. 1. Equality of rights under the law shall not be denied or abridged by the United States or any State on account of sex.

"Sec. 2. The Congress shall have the power to enforce, by appropriate legislation, the provisions of this article.

"Sec. 3. This amendment shall take effect two years after the date of ratification."[6]

Almost immediately in 1923, a split developed between the more militant feminists whose goal was full equality under the Constitution and the social reformers and organized labor who feared that the amendment would be used to strike down laws that they had secured to protect women in the workplace. (See "Protective Legislation" in chapter 3 and also chapter 5 under National American Woman Suffrage Association, League of Women Voters, National Consumers' League, National Women's Trade Union League of America, and Women's Joint Congressional Committee.) Opposition to the ERA began to dissipate somewhat in the 1930s. Roosevelt's New Deal enacted social welfare laws that regulated wages and hours and instituted fair labor standards for both male and female workers, rendering protective laws less necessary. Yet the split continued, because certain groups—such as agricultural workers and domestics, areas where women workers concentrated—were still exempted from these standards.[7] According to Cynthia Harrison, "between 1945 and 1960, the proponents of the ERA and the defenders of protective labor legislation would not reconcile their views, based as they were in opposite philosophies of women's needs."[8] The liberal-labor coalition's concerns about the threat to protective legislation were not finally removed until passage of Title VII of the Civil Rights Act of 1964, when a high volume of sex discrimination complaints and suits confirmed the argument that protective labor laws acted as a limitation on women's employment opportunities.[9]

In the 1960s, the period generally referred to as the second women's rights movement began with John F. Kennedy's appointment of the first President's Commission on the Status of Women (PCSW), chaired by Eleanor Roosevelt. The work of this and other early commissions successfully focused public attention on a broad range of initiatives designed to address the unequal position of American women, both under U.S. law and in customary practice.[10] According to Marguerite Rawalt, the only pro-ERA appointee, the creation of the PCSW, consisting almost entirely of women who still opposed the ERA, was intended to forestall consideration of the amendment. Labor's continued opposition to the ERA made it a politically risky issue for a Democratic president. Recollections of differences in perspectives and values between such commissioners as Rawalt, who at the time was president of the National Associa-

Demonstrators opposed to the ERA in front of the White House, February 4, 1977. Photograph by Warren K. Leffler. U.S. News & World Report Collection. Prints and Photographs Division. LC-U9–33889A, frame 31–31A.

In February 1977 demonstrators gathered at 1600 Pennsylvania Avenue to protest White House involvement in the effort to ratify the federal equal rights amendment, reminding President Carter that daughters might become subject to registering for the draft and First Lady Rosalynn Carter that women feared losing their social security benefits. The chairman of Stop ERA, Phyllis Schlafly, elucidated the principle underlying their protest in a press release: "now the Carters insist upon intruding into the amending process of our Constitution which is absolutely *a legislative matter reserved strictly to Congress and the state legislatures."*

tion of Women Lawyers, and Esther Peterson, the highest-ranking woman in the Kennedy administration as director of the Women's Bureau and an assistant secretary of labor, can be heard on National Public Radio's 1981 program "The ERA in America."[11]

It has been argued that many of this first presidential commission's accomplishments were long-range. One was to make discussion of women's roles and status respectable and to give women's issues a prominent place on the national political agenda for the first time since ratification of the Nineteenth Amendment.[12] Possibly the most divisive issue for the commission, however, was the problem of how to achieve constitutional equality for women. After receiving divergent views from national women's organizations and labor union groups, the commission declared that equality of rights for all persons is embodied in the Fifth and Fourteenth Amendments to the Constitution and recommended that prompt judicial clarification of this principle be sought from the Supreme Court, which could confer equal rights to women by interpreting the Fourteenth Amendment's equal protection clause to give sex the same "suspect" test as race and national origin.[13] It also found that an equal rights amendment "need not now be sought," but protective legislation for women should be maintained and expanded.[14]

"When would the government act?" was the activists' question, and "*Now*" became the mantra. Outraged by the refusal of the newly formed Equal Employment Opportunity Commission to prosecute job discrimination cases on the basis of sex through Title VII, Marguerite Rawalt, Betty Friedan, and others founded the National Organization for Women in 1966. Passage of the ERA was its first agenda item.[15] Four years later, on July 20, 1970, Representative Martha Griffiths, a Democrat from Michigan, collected enough signatures for a discharge petition, by-passing veteran House Judiciary Committee chair Emanuel Celler, a liberal Democrat from New York with strong labor ties who had refused to hold hearings on the ERA for two decades.[16] Opening House hearings on the amendment on August 10, Griffiths pleaded, "Give us a chance to show you that those so-called protective laws to aid women—however well-intentioned originally—have become in fact restraints, which keep wife, abandoned wife, and widow alike from supporting her family."[17]

Approved by 352–15 in the House in 1971, the amendment moved to the Senate, where Senator Sam Ervin, a Democrat from North Carolina and chair of the Senate Judiciary Committee, was its chief opponent. A strict constitutionalist, Ervin in fact attacked the amendment on the basis of traditional views of gender.[18] Much anti-ERA literature subsequently was based on Ervin's public statements.[19] Despite continued opposition of some segments of organized labor, the ERA was passed by the Senate on March 22, 1972, and it was submitted to the states for ratification.[20]

Phyllis Schlafly and Gladys O'Donnell at the Women's Press Club, Washington, D.C. Photograph, 1967. New York World-Telegram and Sun Collection. Prints and Photographs Division. LC-USZ62-119255.

Phyllis Schlafly (right) and Gladys O'Donnell were opposing candidates for the presidency of the National Federation of Republican Women. O'Donnell, a strong supporter of the ERA, was elected at the NFRW convention in Chicago in 1967. The Republican Party had endorsed the ERA in their quadrennial conventions since 1940, four years longer than the Democrats.

Bella Abzug. Signed photograph, ca. 1979. ERAmerica Records (box 177). Manuscript Division. LC-MS-60475-2.

Bella Abzug (D-N.Y.), one of the strongest voices for the ERA in the House, cofounded the National Women's Political Caucus (NWPC) with Betty Friedan, Gloria Steinem, and Shirley Chisholm in 1971 in the expectation that it would reach a broader range of women than did the National Organization for Women. During a confrontation over the amendment, Judiciary Committee Chairman Emanuel Celler (D-N.Y.) is reported to have argued that women should know their place, noting that no women were present at the Last Supper. Abzug, a committee member, allegedly responded, "Manny, women may not have been at the Last Supper, but we sure as hell will be at the next one."(Abzug obituary, Congressional Quarterly, *April 4, 1998, p. 903).*

Representative Martha Griffiths (D-Mich.). Washington, D.C., August 12, 1970. Photograph by Warren K. Leffler. U.S. News & World Report Collection. Prints and Photographs Division. LC-U9–23069.

Long a champion of equal rights, Representative Martha Wright Griffiths, a Democrat from Michigan, was instrumental in adding sex discrimination to the types of discrimination specified in the landmark 1964 Civil Rights Act and in directing the Equal Rights Amendment (ERA) through the U.S. House of Representatives. Of the ERA, Griffiths said, "This amendment, if passed, would be like a beacon which should awaken nine sleeping Rip Van Winkles to the fact that the twentieth century is passing into history." Griffiths served in the U.S. Congress for twenty years, after which she served two terms as lieutenant governor of Michigan, ending in 1991.

In the years between 1972 and 1977, the federal amendment proposing equal rights for women was considered by the legislatures of every state, in some cases more than once, and thirty-five of them ratified it.[21] In addition, between 1971 and 1978, fifteen *states* adopted equal rights amendments to their own constitutions, providing a legal basis for equal treatment to women in those jurisdictions. These served to demonstrate the protections that such an amendment could provide and as an argument for passage of a federal amendment. At the same time, other states began making changes in their laws to eliminate distinctions that unfairly precluded women from receiving equal treatment.

One problem encountered early in the ratification campaign was the portrayal of women and women's rights by the press generally, which seemed to enjoy making them subjects of heavy-handed jokes. When Gloria Steinem was invited to speak at a National Press Club luncheon in January 1972, a short time after the club had agreed to admit women journalists, she used the occasion to take up not only the serious issues of feminism and the ERA but also the crippling effect for both sexes of a male-dominated vision of the world. A tape of the session, held in the Motion Picture, Broadcasting, and Recorded Sound Division, records her comments on the way men tended to assume that they represented the norm, so that when the press presented issues important to the lives of women, reporters seldom found it necessary to seek out women as sources.[22] As an example she cited a recent story on abortion in which the interviewees consisted of a number of men, plus one nun. Conservative women, on

Edward Sorel. Sic transit Gloria. *Drawing, pen and ink, 1974. Prints and Photographs Division. LC-USZC4–4872. Courtesy of Edward Sorel.*

Edward Sorel made this caricature of Gloria Steinem as a female St. George slaying the male dragon with her staff in response to her remark in the New York Times Magazine *of August 11, 1974, that "Women's obsession with romance is a displacement of their longings for success." Sorel's drawing is both a satirical swipe and a measure of respect for the efficacy of her crusading efforts. Steinem's persona—the apparent contradiction between the radical vehemence of her feminist statements and her well-groomed good looks and evident liking for men—provided a challenge to the press's tendency to stereotype pro- and anti-ERA women.*

the other hand, particularly Schlafly, were convinced that the "liberal" press was on the side of the ERA. Other interviews illustrating the flavor of the debate over the ERA, also available in MBRS, are those with Gloria Steinem and Jill Ruckelshaus, both active in the ratification campaign, on *Meet the Press,* September 10, 1972 (RWC 7731 B2); and with Eleanor Smeal, president of the National Organization for Women, also on *Meet the Press,* November 20, 1977 (LWO 15563 1–2), and at the National Press Club, June 25, 1981 (RXA 1902 B).

Scholars have speculated about the causes of the dramatic slowing in the ratification process that followed the first three months of 1973. It has been suggested that the Supreme Court's decision on abortion in *Roe v. Wade* on January 22, 1973, coupled with nationwide admiration for Senator Sam Ervin's chairmanship of the Senate Watergate hearings that began in May, made ERA proponents' task much harder. Decriminalization of abortion angered fundamentalists and social conservatives, and Ervin, leader of the Senate opposition to the ERA since 1969 and now seen as a savior of the Constitution, became their champion in the southern states that refused to ratify the ERA.[23]

Preparations for International Women's Year (IWY) and its culminating event, the National Women's Conference in Houston in 1977, infused the ERA ratification effort with new energy. And just in time, for not only had ratification slowed markedly but five states had voted to rescind their previous ratifications.[24] The designation of 1975 as International Women's Year, a United Nations initiative, had come in response to the rising demand for women's rights, not only in the United States, but around the world.[25]

The agenda for the national conference consisted of twenty-six items nominated for action by the state groups. The preceding year was spent researching and surveying particular aspects of gender discrimination, and 115 suggestions for remedial action were submitted to the president.[26] Included were recommendations on issues such as employment, reproductive freedom, the legal status of homemakers, rape, the media, and the proposed Equal Rights Amendment. All twenty-six agenda items were approved, but the only one totally unchanged by the delegates to the National Conference was the one that stated, "The Equal Rights Amendment should be ratified."

Many more socially conservative women were politicized by the Houston conference. Shocked by the delegates' overwhelming support for the ERA, gay rights, federal funding of abortion, government-sponsored child care, and contraception for minors without parental consent, all advocated in the name of "women's rights," they were also angered that this "feminist" convention was supported by taxpayers.[27] A privately funded opposition rally in Houston was held by Schlafly and her Stop ERA and Eagle Forum organizations. The ERA campaign was denounced as an assault on the family and on the role of women as wives and mothers.[28]

An important offshoot of the IWY national conference was a new organization named ERAmerica, whose records are held by the Manuscript Division (see chapter 5).[29] Created at the request of a number of nongovernmental groups, ERAmerica was set up as a private national campaign organization. Its role was to direct the final months of the ratification drive in the fifteen remaining unratified states. Throughout this ratification effort, ERAmerica worked with more than two hundred participating organizations that lobbied for the amendment, mounted campaigns in unratified states where success was believed possible, organized a national educational program, served as a clearinghouse for information, and did fund-raising and public relations. In this way, it and allied groups became agents for the hands-on engagement of numerous activist women with the nuts and bolts of political campaigning and with the political process at the state and local level.

The records of ERAmerica are a rich source of detail on the way much of the political training of pro-ERA volunteers was accomplished. Since ERAmerica could pay only a handful of professional staff, it was necessary to recruit volunteers from organizations within the targeted states, and these people represented a broad spectrum of backgrounds and interests.[30] By the same token, the anti-ERA effort had a strong educational value for conservative women, many of whom became effective lobbyists for their points of view. As the Reverend Jerry Falwell remarked the day after the ERA died, "Phyllis has succeeded in doing something nobody has ever done . . . She's mobilized the conservative women of this country into a powerful political unit."[31]

At the national level, the case for passage of the amendment was carried to the general public by magazine articles in such publications as *Women's Day* and *Working Women*. These discussed issues like discriminatory wages, battered wives, loopholes in a homemaker's right to spousal support, publicly funded boys-only schools, and the lack of protections for women in the areas of marital and property rights, child support payments, and credit access.[32] Also

The Woman's Salon. *Poster, 1977. Photograph © copyright by Freda Leinwand. Yanker Poster Collection (POS 65–U.S. 309). Prints and Photographs Division. Courtesy of Ruth Wallach and the archives of the University of Southern California.*

On Sunday, November 20, 1977, members of the Woman's Salon gave readings and presented talks on such subjects as the history of salons as catalysts of culture at the National Women's Conference in Houston. This New York literary salon had first gathered as the Woman's Salon in the living room of Gloria Orenstein (second from right) in 1975. Although its members were not among the conference delegates who debated topics such as the ERA, abortion, lesbian rights, child care, minority women, the establishment of a cabinet-level women's department, homemakers, health, or battered women in Houston, they took their feminist concerns to the political arena where these discussions were taking place, and afterward received a letter of appreciation from the presiding officer of the conference, Bella Abzug, for their participation. The photograph used for the poster shows Erika Duncan reading from her work "The Death of Clair" at the salon on January 31, 1976.

First Lady Betty Ford with Liz Carpenter and Elly Peterson. Photograph, 1977. ERAmerica Records, box 177. Manuscript Division. No negative available.

President and Mrs. Ford were longtime supporters of the ERA: Gerald Ford supported Martha Griffiths in her discharge petition of August 1970, although he did not sign it, and Betty Ford, along with Lady Bird Johnson and Rosalynn Carter, endorsed the ERA before more than two thousand delegates and twenty thousand guests at the 1977 National Women's Conference in Houston. Liz Carpenter—journalist and former press secretary to Lady Bird Johnson—and Elly Peterson became codirectors of ERAmerica.

cited in the ERAmerica records was a speakers bureau organized for radio, television, and personal appearances by well-known figures like Maureen Reagan, Liz Carpenter, Erma Bombeck, Alan Alda, Polly Bergen, and others who could attract an audience and articulate the rationale for improving the status of women.

Although the amendment was ratified by thirty-five states, it did not gain approval of the necessary three-fourths or thirty-eight states before the 1982 deadline. There is no question, however, that public opinion regarding the need for change was substantially altered by the years of debate. Surveys taken by Louis Harris and the Roper Organization from 1970 through 1985 show steadily growing support for strengthening the status of women.[33] In answer to the question, "Do you favor most of the efforts to strengthen and change women's status in society today?," 40 percent of women and 44 percent of men who responded approved the idea at the beginning of the 1970s. Fifteen years later in 1985, 73 percent of women and 69 percent of men favored such changes.

Out of the gradual shift in public opinion, legislative gains followed, and a significant number of women's rights measures were passed in this period. Between the 92nd Congress, beginning in 1971, and the 95th Congress, ending in 1978, ten statutes were enacted prohibiting discrimination on the basis of sex with regard to education, employment, credit, and housing, more than during any other period in the history of the Congress.[34] Other legislation focused on women's interests has been enacted in the years following. Since the 1980s, with the major civil rights statutes in place, other legislative gains have included measures to provide pension rights and survivor benefits to divorced spouses under various public pension plans; to strengthen the Fair Housing Act to ban discrimination against families with children; to ban discrimination on the basis of sex in public jobs programs; to fund training programs for men and women who are entering nontraditional occupations and for individuals who are single parents or displaced homemakers; to improve child support enforcement programs; to clarify the application of Title IX of the Education Amendments of 1972, which prohibits discrimination on the basis of sex in federally assisted education programs and activities (by restoring the broad coverage originally enacted); and to provide for the protection of jobs and health insurance after childbirth or family health emergencies.

The Supreme Court of the United States also revealed an awareness of the ratification arguments and, in the 1970s and 1980s, moved toward a more rigorous standard of review in sex discrimination cases, although it fell short of applying the "suspect" category test it applied to race and national origin. The papers of Justice Ruth Bader Ginsburg, who in this period argued many landmark women's rights cases for the American Civil Liberties Union, are held in the Manuscript Division (chapter 5).[35] Copies of the final Supreme Court opinions (or decisions), records, and briefs can be found in the Law Library.

Between 1970 and 1990, the number of women winning elective offices increased markedly, and their influence was significant in promoting legislation supportive of women's interests.[36] The number of women mayors in cities with populations over 30,000 increased from 1.6 percent in 1973 to 18 percent in 1993. In the same period, women in state legislatures grew from 5.6 percent to 20.4 percent, women in the U.S. House went from 3.7 percent to 10.8 percent, and women senators from zero to 6 percent. Other women established "firsts" as candidates. Shirley Chisholm was the first African American woman to run for president in 1972 and Patricia Schroeder ran in 1988. Geraldine Ferraro was nominated by a national party for vice president in 1984.

The importance of electing women to office at all levels is best revealed in the pattern that women officeholders established early on. Many of these women from both parties have tended to promote legislation having an impact on the lives of women, children, and families, in areas such as health, welfare, and education. Many others have supported women's rights generally.[37] Moreover, the influence of elected women has changed over time as their numbers have increased, and they have proved equally effective as men at securing passage of their legislative priorities.

In the end, change over these years came from many quarters and for many reasons. The long public debate over the status of women and the call for a constitutional amendment heightened expectations that changes would be made, and changes did follow. Women at the grass-roots level joined together in examining problems believed by some to have been caused by gender discrimination and women's less-than-equal status. They reached out for new solutions. Inevitably women on both sides of the ERA question became involved in the political process and began learning how the levers of power are activated at different levels of government. The cumulative effect of all these forces stimulated a chain of elective, legislative, and judicial actions that made, and arguably continue to make, a positive contribution to substantive changes in women's status in this country.

For help with this essay, I am much indebted to the editors in the Publishing Office Sara Day and Evelyn Sinclair for their support and encouragement. I wish also to thank Nancy Seeger and Rosemary Hanes, MBRS, Barbara Natanson, P&P, Pam van Ee, G&M, Georgia Higley, SER, Sheridan Harvey, HSS, Pamela Craig Barnes, LAW, and Janice Ruth, MSS, for their help with suggesting and locating materials in their collections.

'For Better or For Worse' gives a woman's view of family life, 3-D

Miss Manners, 2-D
Splitsville, 3-D
Single-minded cooking, 3-D

Giancarlo Giannini plays eight comic roles in a hilarious Italian film, 4-D

wednesday/savvy

section D

The up-and-down life of the ERA

Present status of the Equal Rights Amendment

How working women view the ERA struggle

There's no 'mystique' about Betty Friedan, — she's tough, dedicated and to the point

savvy FARE

Frank Peters. Present Status of the Equal Rights Amendment. *Color map in "Wednesday Savvy" section,* St. Petersburg Times, *October 17, 1979. ACSM Map Design Competition Collection (G370.F8 1979 .P4 MLC ACSM 7920). Geography and Map Division. Copyright © 1976 The St. Petersburg Times. Art by Frank Peters.*

A map submitted to the American Congress on Surveying & Mapping for its annual map design competition in 1979 shows the regional nature of the states opposing ratification of the ERA. The southeastern and parts of the southwestern portions of the United States formed two distinct blocks, shown as three-dimensional entities, that never passed the ERA. Interestingly, the states that revoked ratification are all contiguous with one of the two blocks of states that never ratified the proposed amendment. Made to accompany a survey of "The up-and-down life of the ERA" in Florida's St. Petersburg Times, *the map and the article made it clear that the ERA was not to be won in Florida. In fact, the ERA died in the important non-ratifying states of Florida, Illinois, and North Carolina on the day presidential candidate Ronald Reagan won a landslide victory, November 4, 1980.*

Published by Chas. Magnus, 12 Frankfort St. N.Y.

SOLDIER'S WIFE.

They tell me he has gone to fight
  For honor of our land;
For Freedom's cause, our soldiers brave
  March onward, hand in hand.
'Tis well indeed, in such a cause
  Such gallant hearts to find! —
Forgive my tears! why should I weep,
  Tho' I am left behind?

My little ones cling round my knee,
  And lisp their father's name;
They cannot tell their Country has
  For him a greater claim:
Yes, wife and children, home and land
  Must be by him resign'd —
But honor calls — why should I weep,
  Tho' I am left behind?

Glory may wait our deeds of arms,
  And Vict'ry crown the strife:
But while your hearts with pleasure throb,
  Think of the Soldier's Wife;
Think of the agonizing fear,
  The deep suspense of mind —
For, he may fall — Then I must weep
  For I am left behind!

4 Rare Book and Special Collections Division

Rosemary Fry Plakas and Jacqueline Coleburn

I am obnoxious to each carping tongue
Who says my hand a needle better fits,
A Poets pen all scorn I should thus wrong,
For such despite they cast on Female wits:
If what I do prove well, it won't advance,
They'l say it's stoln, or else it was by chance
—*Anne Bradstreet, 1678*[1]

This gentle protest against indiscriminate condemnation of women's writings was penned by Anne Bradstreet (1613–1672), the first woman poet to be published in colonial America. Bradstreet received praise and approval from her male contemporaries, including influential clergyman Cotton Mather, and her poems on a variety of subjects, sacred and secular, were published in London in 1650 by a kinsman. They were subsequently published posthumously in an expanded compilation in Boston in 1678. Both in her breadth of subjects—her poems addressed not only home and family, but nature, history, philosophy, and religion—and in her sensitivity to prejudices against women's writings, Bradstreet is a worthy pathfinder for the women who have followed her.

The Rare Book and Special Collections Division reflects the eclectic interests of its premier patron, Thomas Jefferson, his unrelenting passion for learning, and his belief that the unrestricted pursuit of knowledge is crucial to the continuing health of the nation. After the British burned the Capitol and the congressional library in 1814, Jefferson offered to sell his book collection to Congress. Jefferson's great library of books in several languages and covering an amazing variety of subjects became the foundation for the new Library of Congress in 1815 and today is the cornerstone of the Library's rare collections. Jefferson sought out the writings of several American and English women. While president he subscribed to Mercy Otis Warren's *History of the Rise, Progress, and Termination of the American Revolution* (Boston: Manning and Loring, 1805; E208.W29 Jefferson) for himself and his cabinet. He owned a volume of Warren's poems, as well as a volume by Phillis Wheatley. Jefferson also acquired Catherine Macaulay's *History of England,* Lady Mary Chudleigh's essays on ethics, and Jane Marcet's *Conversations on Chemistry.* And he owned a 1623 compilation on English laws relating to women and a 1742 copy of Mary Eales's *Compleat Confectioner,* as well as novels by Eliza Haywood, Mary Manley, Teresia Phillips, and Anne Germaine, Baronne de Staël-Holstein.

The Library did not create a separate Rare Book and Special Collections Division until 1934 when the division moved into its present reading room and stack area, but the institution had been actively seeking out collections of rare materials since the visionary Ainsworth Rand Spofford was Librarian of Congress (1864–97). The purchase of the private library of Peter Force in 1867, as well as gifts from major donors, notably the medical library of Joseph Meredith Toner in 1882, strengthened its rare Americana holdings, including sources related to the history of women in the United States.

Today the division's collections number nearly eight hundred thousand books, broadsides, pamphlets, theater playbills, title pages, prints, posters, photographs, and medieval and Renaissance manuscripts. The division's materials have come into its custody for a variety of reasons, including their importance in the history of printing, monetary value, association interest, binding, fragility, or need for security. Most Library holdings printed in the Roman alphabet before 1800 are found here, including nearly half of all such printing in what is now the United States.

As its name suggests, the division's holdings are organized in two ways. The Rare Book Classified Collection is a microcosm of the General Collec-

Soldier's Wife *(New York: Charles Magnus, n.d.; Broadside Song Sheets). Rare Book and Special Collections Division.*

The solemn plight of the soldier's wife is depicted in this illustrated Civil War song sheet, representative of a genre that peaked in popularity during the war years. Wives, mothers, and sweethearts left behind were often the subjects of these sentimental and patriotic ballads.

tions, arranged by the same subject classifications and including books, pamphlets, and serials acquired by transfer, gift, and purchase, on all subjects and concerning all time periods. Special Collections include well over one hundred separate collections created either by the donor or by Library staff and tend to have a specific subject or format focus. Both arrangements are strong in Americana and offer rich sources for the study of the contributions and impact of women as participants in American history and culture. Major subject strengths include women's suffrage, women's contributions to various nineteenth-century social reform movements, and selected literary works by women. These strengths were developed over time through a combination of factors including generous gifts of participants like Susan B. Anthony and Carrie Chapman Catt, gifts by collectors like Katherine Bitting and Marian S. Carson, and ongoing acquisition through copyright deposit and purchase.

Readers at the Library of Congress are often surprised when their call slips are returned to them in the Main Reading Room and they are told to request the item in question in the Rare Book Reading Room. Why is a certain 1867 pamphlet advocating women's suffrage in the rare book collections while so many similar nineteenth-century publications are accessible in the General Collections? Out of all of the editions and copies of *A Vindication of the Rights of Woman* by Mary Wollstonecraft, why are some of them considered rare books while others are readily available from the Main Reading Room? Why on earth is *Sex* by Madonna in a rare book room?

RARE BOOK AND SPECIAL COLLECTIONS READING ROOM
Thomas Jefferson Building, 2nd floor, room LJ 239
Hours: Monday through Friday, 8:30 a.m. to 5:00 p.m.
Closed weekends and federal holidays.
Telephone: 202 707-3448
Fax: 202 707-4142
Address: Rare Book and Special Collections Division, Library of Congress, 101 Independence Avenue, SE, Washington, DC 20540-4740
E-mail: rbsc@loc.gov
Web site: <http://www.loc.gov/rr/rarebook>
Access and use: Before using the Rare Book Reading Room, you must obtain a reader identification card and check your personal belongings in lockers. Only pencils may be used when taking notes. No self-service photocopying is permitted. Requests for photocopying materials, including xerography, microfilming, and the preparation of color transparencies, should be directed to the Library's Photoduplication Service.

Most of the books kept in the rare book vault are truly rare and need special housing and protection because of their historical and literary significance and monetary value. Some are valued as artifacts as much, if not more than, for the information they contain. Others are part of a special collection that needs to be kept whole. Often a book's presence in the Rare Book and Special Collections Division has to do with how the Library acquired it. For instance, Carrie Chapman Catt (1859–1947), the suffragist leader in command during the last charge for women's suffrage, donated the reference library of the National American Woman Suffrage Association (NAWSA) to the Library in 1938. The collection, including copies of the suffrage pamphlet and Wollstonecraft's *Vindication* mentioned above, is kept together because of its historically important provenance and because of its relevance to American scholarship, hinging as much on its existence as NAWSA's library as it does on the individual books the library contains.

Another copy of *Vindication* (Boston: Peter Edes, 1792; HQ1596.W6 1792a Anthony) is in the Susan B. Anthony Collection, her gift to the Library in 1903. The significance of this first American edition is enhanced by its provenance and particularly its inscription from Anthony, "a great admirer of this *earliest* word for *woman's* Right to Equality of rights ever penned by a *woman*. As Ralph Waldo Emerson said, 'A *wholesome* discontent is the *first step toward progress*.' And here in 1892[*sic*], we have the first step—so thinks Susan B. Anthony." Anthony had serialized the *Vindication* in her newspaper the *Revolution*, hung Wollstonecraft's picture on the wall of her Rochester home, and invoked Wollstonecraft's memory in her last suffrage speech in 1906. These acts and the sentiments of the inscription all point to the place of honor held in Anthony's heart by this early champion of feminist ideology.

Sex by Madonna (New York: Warner Books, 1992; ML420.M1387 A3 1992) is indeed in the rare book vault. The Library collects books and other formats that document our culture, whether it be folk, popular, or elite. The Library's copies of *Sex* are the sort of material that is at high risk for theft or mutilation.

Also, the division collects and preserves in their original condition the first editions of many contemporary American women writers, including Maya Angelou, Gwendolyn Brooks, Rita Dove, Louise Erdrich, Louise Gluck, Maxine Kumin, Joyce Carol Oates, Sonia Sanchez, and Alice Walker. A reader interested in the literary content of a work should request it in the Main Reading Room and receive a General Collections copy, which will probably arrive in a sturdy library binding with the call number embossed on the cover and fitted with a bar code. If you need to see the book as it was first presented to the public for sale, you should go to the Rare Book Reading Room, which is equipped to handle fragile material, and request the Rare Book copy. In most cases, you will receive a book that is relatively untouched, in its original dust jacket, as it would have been issued from the publisher.

USING THE COLLECTIONS

Significant progress has been made in recent years to provide online cataloging records for the division's holdings. The phrase "Request in: Rare Book/Special Collections Reading Room" appears at the bottom of online records for rare books. If the book is in a special collection within the division's holdings, an abbreviation of that collection name is part of the call number. Examples include "Am Imp" for the American Imprint Collection and "Carson" for the Marian S. Carson Collection. Special card files in the reading room still provide valuable access information for collections that have not been cataloged and for cataloged collections for which there are no records online. Other special files have provenance, inscription, and binding information on books from many collections. These and other finding aids are mentioned, where appropriate, throughout the chapter. The division's own dictionary catalog contains 650,000 cards that provide access to almost the whole of the division's collections by author or other form of main entry and, in some instances, by subject and title also. The card file was closed in 1991 and no cards have been added since then. It remains available in the reading room for access to those collections whose records are not yet online. There is no single catalog that contains records for all items held in the Rare Book and Special Collections Division. Some items are found only in published bibliographies or divisional finding aids.

Most Library of Congress patrons who use the rare book collections are looking for early printed books and pamphlets. When searching for older material, whether online or in printed guides, it is critical that you use both new and old search terms. Popular vocabulary, and therefore library subject headings, have changed over time, and the Library of Congress has not had the resources to update every heading. Updating and adding to the online catalog is an ongoing process. Some older records will still be under the heading "Negroes" or "Afro-Americans" rather than the current heading "African Americans." "Woman" has been updated to "Women." This pattern extends to more specific headings such as "African American women" and "African American women authors." Refer to chapter 1 for an overview of subject searching at the Library. Throughout this chapter, we suggest effective search strategies for particular rare book collections and formats.

SELECTED COLLECTIONS

This discussion of the division's resources centers around six areas of strength both in the Library's rare collections and for many aspects of women's history: the domestic sphere, religious example and spirituality, reform efforts that made a difference, women in popular culture, collections formed by women, and literary works. Women's domestic and family responsibilities, including cooking and medicine, are documented in books, the magazines and newspapers published for women, and the extensive children's book collection. Religion and spirituality can be studied in many early imprints, including sermons and captivity narratives. As the country grew, women became active in a variety of reform movements, for which the Library's collections are particularly strong in abolition and suffrage. Resources documenting women's role in popular culture feature women as both creators and subjects of mass culture. Women have been collectors of traditional rare book collections, including Americana and cookery, as well as compilers of more humble scrapbooks. A discussion of literary works suggests both limitations and unique aspects of rare holdings. In the following pages, we will guide you through the collections, offer examples of what a reader will find there, and point out what is unique in our holdings.

The Domestic Sphere

> Your sex requires the utmost circumspection; what among men is reputed a venial fault, is an absolute crime with us.
>
> *Advice from a Lady of Quality to her Children* (Newbury-Port: John Mycall, 1789 Juv), 175.

Today we are shocked both by the double standard described above and by its general acceptance. Women's limited role in the early days of the country is often described, encouraged, and reinforced in the literature of the time. The many early imprints written for and by American women held in the rare book collections offer a

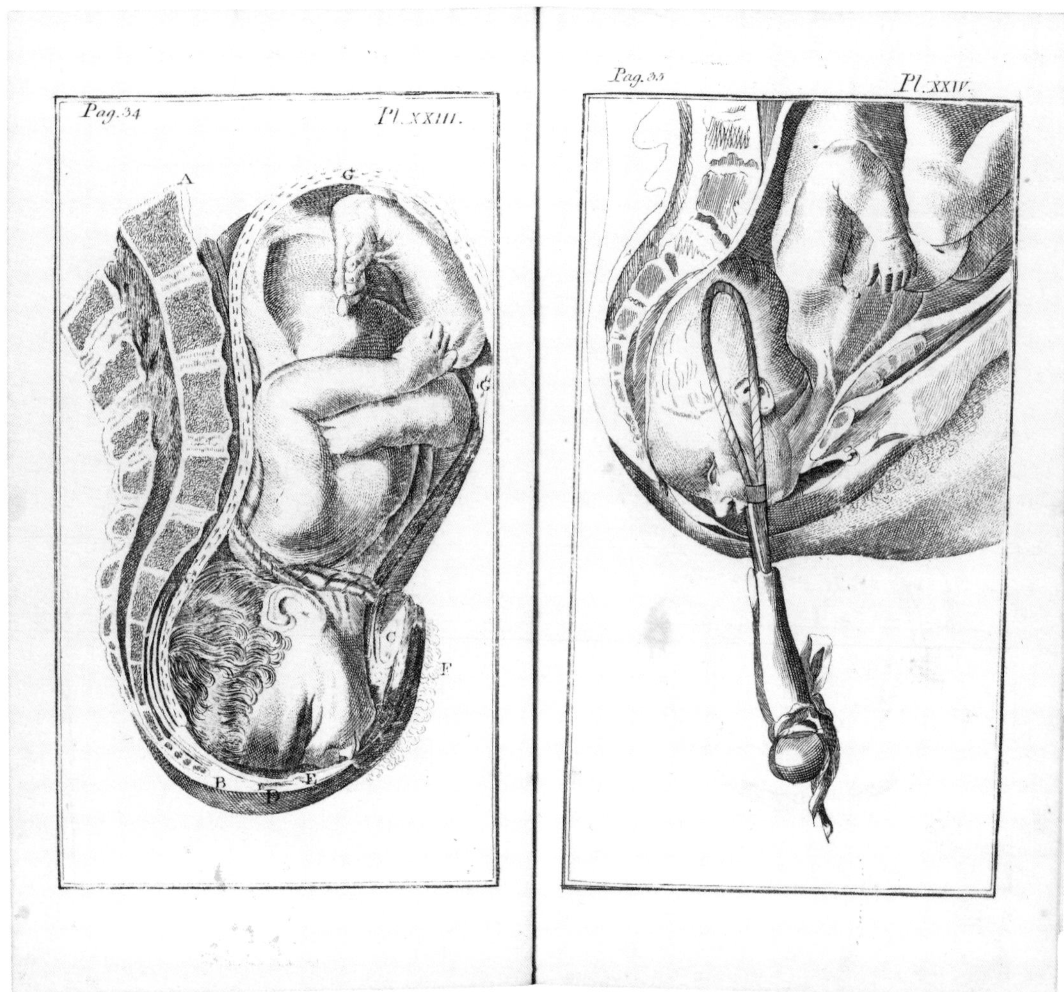

John Norman. "Child birth." Engraving. From William Smellie, An Abridgement of the Practice of Midwifery *(Boston: Printed and sold by J. Norman, 1786; RG93.S63 Toner), plates 23–24. Rare Book and Special Collections Division.*

William Smellie (1697–1763) introduced innovative obstetrical procedures into the practice of midwifery that greatly increased the chances of live birth. His 1754 London treatise outlining safe rules for the use of forceps in child delivery was widely reprinted in the United States, beginning with this 1786 Boston edition. As male doctors took over a formerly female ritual, the practice of midwifery began to decline.

contemporary view of the images of women, an American woman's image of herself, and a look at how these changed over time.

Early works on women's role in society are classified in HQ1201 throughout the special collections (see chapter 1 for an overview of call numbers). These include the first American printings of popular foreign titles like M. Antoine Léonard Thomas's *Essay on the Character, Manners, and Genius of Women in Different Ages* (Philadelphia: Robert Aitken, 1774; HQ1201.T5 Am Imp) and Thomas Gisborne's *An Enquiry into the Duties of the Female Sex* (Philadelphia: James Humphreys, 1798; HQ1201.G6 1798 Carson). Pierre Joseph Boudier de Villemert's *The Ladies Friend* (Philadelphia: John Dunlap, 1771; HQ1201 .B74 1771 Am Imp) encourages women to study the arts, literature, and history, and *The Lady's Pocket Library* (Philadelphia: Mathew Carey, 1792; HQ1201.L22 1792 Am Imp) is a compilation of advice to young ladies on friendship, love, and marriage.

Amelia Simmons's *American Cookery* (Hartford: Hudson & Goodwin, 1796; TX703.S5 1796 Am Imp) is the first cookbook written by an American and published in the United States. Numerous recipes adapting traditional dishes by substituting native American ingredients like corn meal and squash are printed here for the first time, including "Indian Slapjack," "Johny Cake," and "Pompkin Pudding." More often, American households relied on local reproduction of popular English works such as the first American printings of Susannah Carter's *The Frugal Housewife, or, Complete Woman Cook* (Boston, 1772; TX705.C32 Am Imp) and Richard Briggs's *The New Art of Cookery . . . being a Complete Guide to all Housekeepers* (Philadelphia, 1792; TX703.B7 Bitting). Early manuscript recipe books written by women include *Mary Coates's Book* (RS125.C55 1740 Carson), a book of home remedies and cookery, and several eighteenth-century cookbooks in the Elizabeth Robins Pennell Collection. Pre-1801 works on cooking are found at classifications TX703 and TX715. Recipes and household hints sometimes accompany tips on kitchen gardening in almanacs, as exemplified by Caroline Gilman's *Lady's Annual Register and Housewife's Memorandum-Book* (Boston, 1838–43; AY201.B7 L333 Am Almanac).

Early midwifery and obstetrics gather in class RG93 and include works like Charles White's *A Treatise on the Management of Pregnant and Lying in Women . . .* (Worcester, Mass.: Isaiah Thomas, 1793; RG93.W5 1793 Am Imp). The first American edition of William Smellie's *An Abridgement of the Practice of Midwifery* (Boston: J. Norman, 1786; RG93.S63 Toner) contains thirty-nine engravings of the birth process and eighteenth-century obstetrical equipment. *Outlines of Theory and Practice of Midwifery* and *A Treatise on the Management of Female Complaints* by the Scottish doctor Alexander Hamilton are also in the collections in many U.S. editions. The subject heading of "Obstetrics—Early works to 1800" will lead the researcher to these and similar studies. Most of such early medical books are in the Joseph Meredith Toner Collection. A Washington physician and a medical historian, Dr. Toner gave his extensive collection to the Library in 1882. His collection includes books on early gynecology, obstetrics, midwifery, women's hospitals, and advice to new mothers (all of which are classed in RG).

Magazines and newspapers designed for a female audience in the nineteenth century give today's reader insight into the concerns and expectations of women at that time. For the most part, the primary audience for these publications was middle-class white women. The Rare Book and Special Collections Division holds a sampling of these publications with titles ranging from the *Domestic Monthly* to the *Revolution*. (The *Revolution* and other reform publications will be discussed in a later section).

Traditional women's magazines in the collection include the first of this genre published in the United States, the *Lady's Magazine, and Repository of Entertaining Knowledge* (Philadelphia,

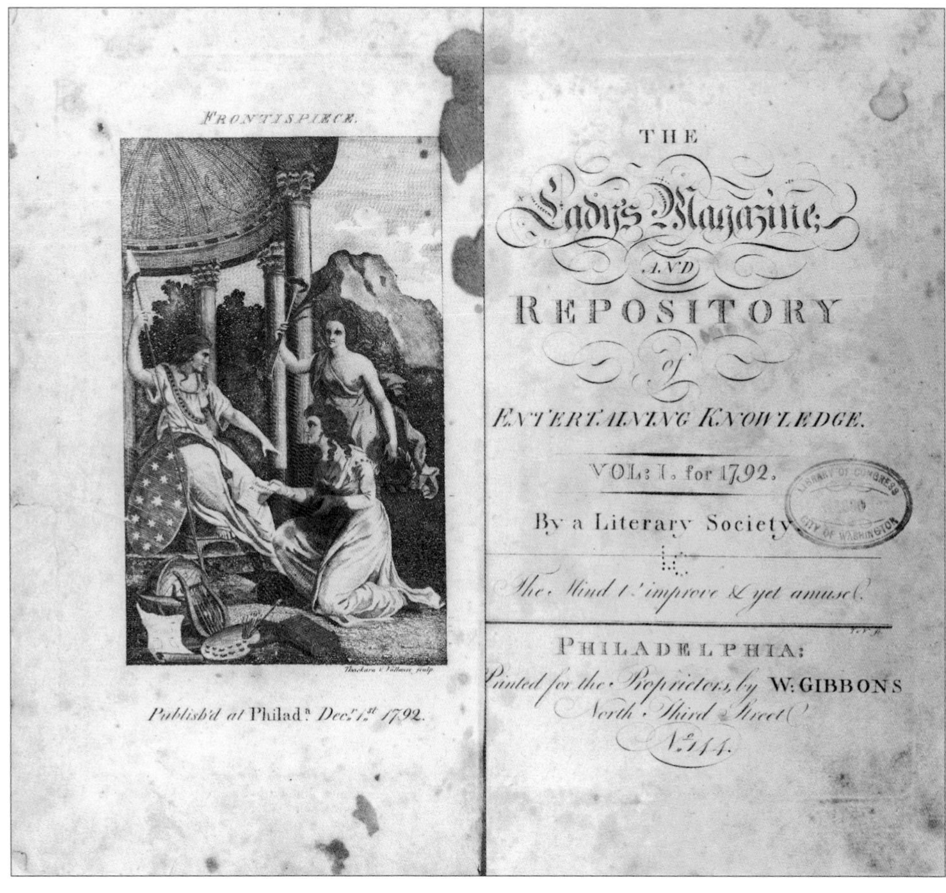

Thackara & Vallance. Frontispiece engraving, with title page. From The Lady's Magazine; and Repository of Entertaining Knowledge *(Philadelphia, 1792; AP2.A2 L2). Rare Book and Special Collections Division.*

In this frontispiece illustration, the "Genius of the Ladies Magazine" presents Liberty with a copy of Mary Wollstonecraft's *Vindication of the Rights of Woman,* thus linking the great English feminist with this first effort to provide a magazine of literary selections to inspire and amuse American women. Wollstonecraft's *Vindication,* which argues that equal educational opportunities for women will confirm their equal mental abilities, is reviewed here in the first issue.

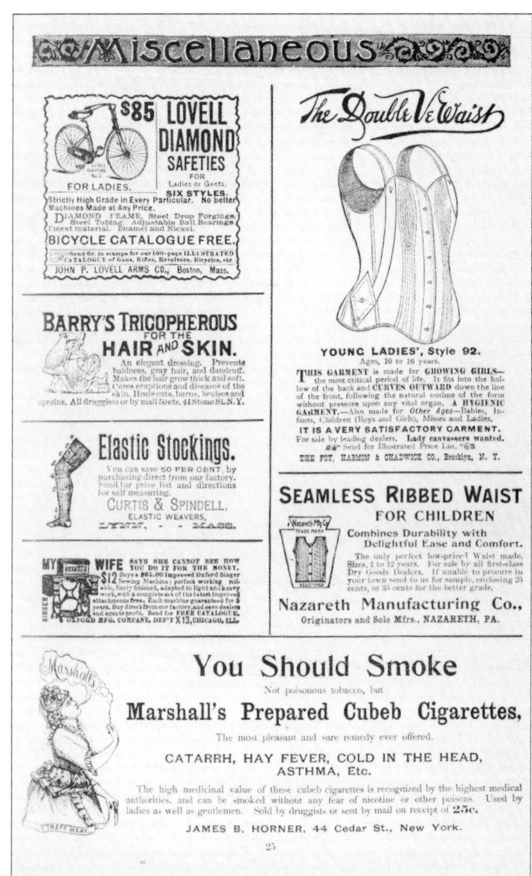
Miscellaneous

$85 LOVELL DIAMOND SAFETIES FOR Ladies or Gents. SIX STYLES. FOR LADIES.
Strictly High Grade in Every Particular. No better Machines Made at Any Price.
DIAMOND FRAME, Steel Drop Forgings, Steel Tubing. Adjustable Ball Bearings. Finest material. Enamel and Nickel.
BICYCLE CATALOGUE FREE.
Send 6c. in stamps for our 100-page ILLUSTRATED CATALOGUE of Guns, Rifles, Revolvers, Bicycles, etc.
JOHN P. LOVELL ARMS CO., Boston, Mass.

BARRY'S TRICOPHEROUS FOR THE HAIR AND SKIN.
An elegant dressing. Prevents baldness, gray hair, and dandruff. Makes the hair grow thick and soft. Cures eruptions and diseases of the skin. Heals cuts, burns, bruises and sprains. All druggists or by mail 50cts. 44 Stone St. N.Y.

Elastic Stockings.
You can save 50 PER CENT. by purchasing direct from our factory. Send for price list and directions for self measuring.
CURTIS & SPINDELL. ELASTIC WEAVERS, LYNN, - - MASS.

MY WIFE SAYS SHE CANNOT SEE HOW YOU DO IT FOR THE MONEY.
$12 Buys a $65.00 Improved Oxford Singer Sewing Machine; perfect working reliable, finely finished, adapted to light and heavy work, with a complete set of the latest improved attachments free. Each machine guaranteed for 5 years. Buy direct from our factory, and save dealers and agents profit. Send for FREE CATALOGUE.
OXFORD MFG. COMPANY, DEP'T X13, CHICAGO, ILL.

The Double Ve Waist
YOUNG LADIES', Style 92.
Ages, 10 to 16 years.
THIS GARMENT is made for GROWING GIRLS—the most critical period of life. It fits into the hollow of the back and CURVES OUTWARD down the line of the front, following the natural outline of the form without pressure upon any vital organ. A HYGIENIC GARMENT.—Also made for *Other Ages*—Babies, Infants, Children (Boys and Girls), Misses and Ladies.
IT IS A VERY SATISFACTORY GARMENT.
For sale by leading dealers. Lady canvassers wanted.
Send for Illustrated Price List.
THE FOY, HARMON & CHADWICK CO., Brooklyn, N. Y.

SEAMLESS RIBBED WAIST FOR CHILDREN
Combines Durability with Delightful Ease and Comfort.
The only perfect low-priced Waist made. Sizes, 1 to 12 years. For sale by all first-class Dry Goods Dealers. If unable to procure in your town send to us for sample, enclosing 25 cents, or 35 cents for the better grade.
Nazareth Manufacturing Co., Originators and Sole Mfrs., NAZARETH, PA.

You Should Smoke
Not poisonous tobacco, but
Marshall's Prepared Cubeb Cigarettes,
The most pleasant and sure remedy ever offered.
CATARRH, HAY FEVER, COLD IN THE HEAD, ASTHMA, Etc.
The high medicinal value of these cubeb cigarettes is recognized by the highest medical authorities, and can be smoked without any fear of nicotine or other poisons. Used by ladies as well as gentlemen. Sold by druggists or sent by mail on receipt of 25c.
JAMES B. HORNER, 44 Cedar St., New York.

25

Miscellaneous advertisements. From Godey's Lady's Book and Magazine *(February 1893; AP2.G56). Rare Book and Special Collections Division.*

This single page of advertisements offers a glimpse of the variety of products from personal care to recreation that were available for "growing girls" as well as for mature women on the eve of the twentieth century.

1792–93; AP2.A2 L2). A sampling of early nineteenth-century titles includes the *Ladies' Weekly Museum, or, Polite Repository of Amusement and Instruction* (New York: J. Oram, 1814–18; AP2.L22), the *Ladies Garland* (Harper's Ferry, Va., 1824–26; AP2.L13), the *Ladies Companion* (New York: W. W. Snowden, 1834–44; AP2.L11), and the *Bower of Taste* (Boston, 1828–30; AP2.B842), which was edited by Katharine Augusta Ware (1797–1843). Sarah Josepha Hale (1788–1879), who did not support the women's rights movement but was a strong advocate for the education of women and for women joining the teaching profession, edited the *American Ladies' Magazine* (Boston: Putnam & Hunt, 1828–36; AP2.A343) and, later, *Godey's Lady's Book* (Philadelphia, 1830–98; AP2.G56). For the most part, these publications reinforced the domestic sphere as the world for women. They offered advice, covered fashion news, instructed in child care, and promoted etiquette. They included book reviews, human interest news, and short stories and serial fiction, generally of an uplifting, edifying nature.

The advertisements in such periodicals can be as enlightening as the text. The products that were available and how they were pitched to readers offer strong indications about self-image, ongoing concerns, and the everyday lives of the readership. An advertisement in *Godey's Lady's Book* for March 1893 advises: "You should smoke not poisonous tobacco but Marshall's prepared cubeb cigarettes. The most pleasant and sure remedy ever offered [for] catarrh, hay fever, cold in the head, asthma, etc." In the same issue an advertisement for "Doctor" Warner's corsets asserts that "the Coraline we use is superior to whalebone and absolutely unbreakable."

A survey of children's literature offers a glimpse of what impressionable youngsters were reading and learning, and what their parents and teachers wished to impress upon them. When investigating children's reading matter, however, it is important to remember that, early in our history, books were expensive and generally available only to the well-to-do. The Juvenile Collection contains nearly fifteen thousand children's books, chiefly American. Most of the collection is arranged chronologically. The earliest book, *A Course of Sermons on Early Piety . . .* by Increase Mather (Boston: S. Kneeland, 1721; BX7233.A1 C6 Juv) was printed in 1721. Significant selections from each year continue through the twentieth century. A section arranged alphabetically by author and title contains the work of thirty-six American authors considered significant, of which fourteen are women. The collection includes many books and serials written for children of both sexes by women authors, fiction written specifically for girls, and instructional and advice books for girls and young women.

Lydia Maria Child (1802–1880) edited the *Juvenile Miscellany* (Boston, 1826–34; AP200.J7), the first American magazine for children, and penned many monographic works. Sarah Josepha Hale's "Mary Had a Little Lamb" first appeared in *Juvenile Miscellany*. Other early magazines for children grew out of the Sunday school movement, including the *Children's Magazine* (New York: General Protestant Episcopal Sunday School Union, 1829–40, 1871–74; AP200.C5), the *Encourager* [Methodist] (New York, vol. 1, 1846; AP200.E6), the *Catholic Youth Magazine* (Baltimore: Murphy, 1858–61; AP200.C3), and the *Ju-*

venile Instructor [Mormon] (Salt Lake City: Cannon, 1866–73, AP201.J7). Later Mary Mapes Dodge (1831–1905) edited *St. Nicholas* (New York: Scribner, 1873–1919; AP201.S3), which focused more on entertainment than instruction.

Susan Warner (1819–1885), under the pseudonym Elizabeth Wetherell, wrote many domestic stories for girls, featuring pious, earnest young women such as Ellen Montgomery, the orphan heroine of *Wide, Wide World* (New York: George Putnam, 1851; PS3155.W6 Juv), Warner's first and most popular novel. The first edition of *Little Women* (Boston: Roberts Bros., 1868; PZ7.A335 Li Juv) by Louisa May Alcott was published in 1868, introducing more believable and natural girl characters. Also in the collection are the first works published under Alcott's name, *Flower Fables* (Boston: Briggs, 1855; PS1017.F6 Juv) and her rare piece *Nelly's Hospital* (U.S. Sanitary Commission [1865]; E621.A35 Juv), which was written after she returned from volunteering at a military hospital.

Isabella M. Alden (1841–1930), who used the pseudonym Pansy, and Martha Finley (1828–1909), who wrote under the pseudonym Martha Farquharson, were prolific and popular nineteenth-century authors whose stories often featured girls and their adventures. Harriet Mulford Stone Lothrop (1844–1924) wrote the Five Little Pepper books and many others under the pseudonym Margaret Sidney. The collection also holds many first editions by Laura Ingalls Wilder (1867–1957), with illustrations by Helen Sewell. Other women authors of children's books include Rebecca Sophia Clarke, Mary A. Denison, Theodosia Maria Foster, Frances Griswold, Clara Guernsey, Augusta Larned, Johanna Matthews, Julia Mathews, and Sarah Stuart Robbins.

Advice to girls and young ladies has been a part of literature for children for many years. With the Juvenile Collection and complementary parts of the Carson Collection and the rare book classified collection, it is possible to trace development and changes in this genre. The eighteenth-century author of *Advice from a Lady of Quality to Her Children* (Newbury-Port: John Mycall, 1789; LC262.A3 Juv) advises, "The books you read should be as pure as your heart, and be reduced within a narrow compass. It is a mistake to pretend that our sex ought to STUDY" (p. 181). In *A Mirror for the Female Sex, Historical Beauties for Young Ladies* (Hartford: Hudson and Goodwin, 1799; HQ1229.P58 Juv), on the other hand, Mary Hopkins Pilkington declares, ". . . it does not appear to me that a woman will be rendered less acceptable in the world, or worse qualified to perform any part of her duty in it, by having employed her time from 6 to 16 in the cultivation of her understanding"(p. 58).

By the mid-nineteenth century Lydia Howard Sigourney (1791–1865), a retired teacher, wrote in *The Book for Girls* . . . (New York: Turner & Hayden, 1844; PZ6.S578 Bo Juv), "No female should consider herself educated, until she is mistress of some employment or accomplishment, by which she might gain a livelihood, should she be reduced to the necessity of supporting herself" (p.117). More works offering advice to young women in the classified rare book collection, as in the General Collections, can be found under HQ1229, for example, Eliza Farrar's *Young Lady's Friend* (Boston, 1837; HQ1229.F22) and an American reprint of British author John Ruskin's *Letters and Advice to Young Girls and Young Ladies* (New York: J. Wiley, 1879; HQ1229.R9). Emily Thornwell's *Lady's Guide to Perfect Gentility* (New York: Derby & Jackson, 1857; BJ1856.T5 Toner) was so popular that it was reissued ten times between 1857 and 1890.

To search for a specific title in the Juvenile Collection, a reader needs to check three separate places. Search the online catalog first. Records of all children's books cataloged after 1982 are online. A card file in the Rare Book Reading Room covers titles cataloged between 1974 and 1982. Most of the collection, however, is described in a two-volume guide published in 1975. *Children's Books in the Rare Book Division of the Library of Congress* (Totowa, N.J.: Rowman and Littlefield, 1975; Z1038.U5 U54 Rare Bk Ref) is arranged by author and date of publication.

Collector Marian S. Carson's special interest in children's literature brought to the Library of Congress a splendid gathering of nearly three hundred rare and fragile children's books and games, printed primarily in Philadelphia and New York during the first half of the nineteenth century. *Dame Partlet's Farm* (Philadelphia: Johnson and Warner, 1810; PZ6.D178 1810 Carson) celebrates the ability of a widow to use her outstanding reading skills and her industry to provide for her children and share with the poor. Through charming verse and delightful engravings, *Disastrous Events Which Attended Joe Dobson* (Philadelphia: William Charles, 1813; PZ6.D57 1813 Carson) recounts the results of a husband's bet that he can do more household work in any day than his wife can do in two. Switching roles for a day, Joe Dobson suffers calamities while milking, spinning, cooking, and washing, whereas his wife successfully completes her work at the plow and the mill and returns to cook dinner as well. *The Little Girl's Own Book* by Lydia Maria Child (Boston: Carter, Hendee, 1835; GV1204.998 C55 1835 Carson) describes games and amusements specifically for girls. *The Diligent Girl as Lady of the House* (Germany: 187-?; GV1203.C235, box 3, no.1 Carson) is a game, printed in English, Italian, French, and German, that reinforces domesticity as well as language proficiency.

The American Toilet by Hannah Lindley Murray (New York: Imbert's Lithographic, 1827; BJ1531.M86 1827 Carson), a particular treasure in the Marian S. Carson Collection, was directed at the training of modest young ladies. Each page is illustrated with an item from a lady's dressing table, part of which is actually a hinged paper flap. Each instrument of vanity lifts to reveal a virtue, such as the breast pin that opens to reveal "charity." "Virtues—Juvenile literature" and "Toy and movable books—Specimens" will help the reader find books on this subject and in this genre.

Religious Example and Spirituality

Religious topics dominate in titles published before 1801 in what is now the United States, nearly half of which are organized chronologically in the American Imprint Collection (see Microfiche 85/431 (Z) in the Microform Reading Room). There are numerous sermons and most of the works about individual women are funeral sermons. Increase Mather, Cotton Mather, and other leading ministers eulogized relatives and members of their congregations, extolling their piety and virtue. Pastor Benjamin Colman's *The Honour and Happiness of the Vertuous Woman* (Boston: B.Green, 1716; HQ1221.C73 Am Imp), memorializing Elizabeth Sewall Hirst (1681–1716), is representative.

A handful of execution sermons may be of particular interest to those studying early American women. Cotton Mather and Benjamin Colman both preached about the life and death sentence of Margaret Gaulacher, who murdered her illegitimate child in 1715. Colman's sermon is entitled *The Divine Compassions Declar'd and Magnified . . . a Sermon Preach'd . . . upon the Sorrowful Occasion of a Miserable Woman Present, under Sentence of Death for the Murder of her Spurious Infant* (Boston: T. Fleet, 1715; BV4627.M8 M38 1715 Am Imp). Mather's work, *A Sorrowful Spectacle in Two Sermons Occasioned by the Just Sentence of Death on a Miserable Woman for the Murder of a Spurious Offspring . . . with Some Remarkable Things Relating to the Criminal, Proper for all to be Informed of* (Boston: T. Fleet, 1715; BV4627.M8 M38 1715 Am Imp), goes beyond a sermon and includes some titillating facts about this fallen (and soon to be deceased) woman. Along the same lines, Henry Channing preached at a 1786 execution, publishing the sermon under the title *God Admonishing His People of their Duty . . . a Sermon . . . Occasioned by the Execution of Hannah Ocuish, a Mulatto Girl, Aged 12 Years and 9 Months, for the Murder of Eunice Bolles, Aged 6 Years and 6 Months* (New-London: T. Green, 1786; E90.O2 C54 Am Imp). Similar works can be identified using the subject heading "Sermons," often subdivided by denomination, or the more specific "Funeral sermons" or "Execution sermons." The subdivision "Early works to 1800" is currently used in the catalog to separate out those works published before 1800 and is an effective way to retrieve early religious materials.

The doctrinal writing of English Quaker Mary Brook (ca. 1726–1782), *Reason of the Necessity of Silent Waiting,* was reprinted in several editions in colonial America, as were the devotional exercises of her countrywoman Elizabeth Singer Rowe (1674–1737) and the religious tracts of Hannah More (1745–1833). Religious poems of Martha Brewster, Jane Dunlap, and Phillis Wheatley are also represented, as well as Hannah Adams's (1755–1832) dictionary of religion, *An Alphabetical Compendium of the Various Sects which have appeared in the World from the Beginning of the Christian Era to the Present Day* (Boston: B. Edes & Sons, 1784; BL31.A3 1784 Am Imp).

Women played a central role in many of the Indian captivity narratives as participants and in some cases as narrators. Mary Rowlandson's narrative was the earliest account published separately. The division has a photostat of one of the rare 1682 editions and several eighteenth-century printings of this classic narrative, including the 1720 edition entitled *The Soveraignty & Goodness of God, Together with the Faithfulness of His Promises Displayed; Being a Narrative of the Captivity and Restauration of Mrs. Mary Rowlandson* (Boston: T. Fleet, 1720; E87.R862 1720 Am Imp). Rowlandson describes her captivity as a spiritual experience and attributes her return to God's providence. Similar religious messages are found in many of the narratives that followed hers, whether written by Puritans, Catholics, or Quakers.

Some of the female captives offer a positive view of Indian culture. Notably, Mary Jemison, captured at twelve in 1755, recounts the kindness and generosity of her adopted Seneca family in *A Narrative of the Life of Mrs. Mary Jemison*

AN
AFFECTING NARRATIVE
OF THE
Captivity and Sufferings
OF MRS.
MARYSMITH
Who with her Husband and three daughters, were taken prisoners by the INDIANS, in August last (1814) and after enduring the most cruel hardships and torture of mind for sixty days (in which time she witnessed THE TRAGICAL DEATH OF HER HUSBAND and helpless Children) was fortunately rescued from the merciless hands of the Savages by a detached party from the army of the brave
GENERAL JACKSON.
Now commanding at New-Orleans.
PROVIDENCE, (R. I.) PRINTED BY L. SCOTT.

Hand-colored woodcut frontispiece and title page. From An Affecting Narrative of the Captivity and Sufferings of Mrs. Mary Smith *(Providence, R.I., [1815]; E87.S663). Rare Book and Special Collections Division.*

Typical of the captivity narratives created to arouse anti-Indian hostility, this extremely rare fictitious account describes the 1814 capture of Mary Smith in West Florida, where, after witnessing the excruciating torture of her daughters by savage "monsters of barbarity," she manages to kill her sleeping captor and is eventually rescued through "kind Providence," by Tennessee troops.

(Canandaigua, N.Y.: J.D. Bemis, 1824; E87.J46). Capitivity narratives published after the American Revolution became a popular source of anti-Indian propaganda. Many describe the brutal torture of young girls and women. Presented as fact, such narratives were frequently exaggerated and sometimes, like Mary Smith's sensational account, completely fabricated. Ann Eliza Bleecker (1752–1783), drawing on her perilous experiences on the New York frontier, first adapted the Indian captivity theme to a popular literary genre. Her sentimental novel *The History of Maria Kittle* (Hartford: E. Babcock, 1797; PZ3.B6156 1797 Am Imp), set during the French and Indian War, was published first in 1790.

In contrast to the negative image of Native Americans depicted in the majority of captivity narratives, some of the missionary literature attempts to describe native cultures and traditions, but also stresses the importance of education. Beginning in 1830, Sarah Tuttle produced a series of missionary tracts, *Letters and Conversations on the Indian Missions,* for the Massachusetts Sabbath School Union that describes mission life among the Choctaw, Cherokee, Chickasaw, Seneca, and Sioux and appeals to Sunday school youth to collect money to support mission schools. While sympathetic to the zeal and courage of most missionaries, Mary Henderson Eastman (1818–1890) also recognizes their failure to understand the native culture. In her works, *Dahcotah, or, Life and Legends of the Sioux around Fort Snelling* (New York: J. Wiley, 1849; E99.D1 E19) and *American Aboriginal Portfolio* (Philadelphia: Lippincott, Grambo, 1853; E77.E125), Eastman attempts to celebrate the moral character of the Dakota and to preserve their legends and character traits both through prose descriptions from her observations and the drawings of her husband, Capt. Seth Eastman. Julia Moss Seton's *Indian Costume Book* (Santa Fe, N.M.: Seton Village Press, 1938; E98.C8 S5) includes descriptions and photographs of women's ritual and everyday clothing, hair designs, and beadwork.

The division has an important collection of Shaker literature, significant here because of the nineteenth-century Christian sect's commitment to the equality of women. Members were dedicated to a life of perfection, seeking "the kingdom of heaven upon earth."[2] Their efforts toward perfection included hard work, pacifism, communal living, and celibacy. They believed in God as a spirit being, both a spiritual father and mother, and in the equality of the sexes. Martha Anderson wrote, in her *Social Life and Vegetarianism,* "As there is perfect equality of the sexes in our home, guaranteed by the law of absolute purity, which frees women from masculine dominance, the sisterhood are insured the right to manage their own affairs."[3]

It was the Shakers' pacifism during the Revolutionary War that first called outside attention to the group and its activities. Mother Ann, as the leader Ann Lee was called by followers, and five others were jailed for several months in 1780 because of their opposition to the war. The sect's opposition to war continued and is spelled out in *A Declaration of the Society of People . . . Shewing their Reasons for Refusing to Aid or Abet the Cause of War and Bloodshed by Bearing Arms, Paying Fines, Hiring Substitutes, or Rendering an Equivalent for Military Services* (Albany, N.Y.: E. & E. Hosford, 1815; BX9789.W2 A5 1815). Almost all the Shaker items can be found in the catalog with classification numbers between BX9751 and BX9793. Much of the literature is an explanation of Shaker beliefs, but it also includes works on the Shakers' famous woodworking, seed supply businesses, and inventions. Six scrapbooks filled with newspaper and journal clippings, programs, and poetry compiled by members document the years 1841 to 1882. Many Shaker works are by and about women, including biographies of their women leaders. Additional Shaker materials, including correspondence, diaries, hymns, and other papers may be found in the Library's Manuscript Division (see chapter 5) and Shaker maps in the Geography and Map Division (see chapter 7).

Mary Baker Eddy (1821–1910) is another pioneering religious reformer whose writings are well represented in the divisional holdings. Her first major work, *Science and Health* (Boston: Christian Scientist Publishing Company, 1875; BX6941.S4 1875), explores the relationship between spirituality and healing and has been reprinted often in various editions and translations. In addition to Eddy's other books, sermons, speeches, and magazine writings, the division has scrapbooks compiled by Stella Hadden Alexander, one volume (New York, 1935; BX6931.Z8 A6), and Alice Morgan Harrison, three volumes, 1900–1931 (New York, 1936), which document the activities of Eddy and her disciple Augusta E. Stetson (1842–1928), as well as the Christian Science movement.

The central role played by African American women in organizing sabbath schools and benevolent societies is acknowledged in the *National Baptist Magazine* (Nashville, Tenn., 1899; E449.D16 C:9 Murray Pam), where the Reverend J. Francis Robinson celebrates the "pious, consecrated, self-sacrificing women" who bring "stability and support" to such endeavors. This echoes Bishop Benjamin Arnett's praise of black women's efforts in establishing the New Asylum for Orphan and Friendless Colored Children and other benevolent societies in Cincinnati in *Proceedings of the Semi-Centenary Celebration of the African Methodist Episcopal Church* (Cincinnati, 1874; E449.D16 D:2 Murray Pam) and James Holloway's recognition of the influence of female Sabbath School teachers in *Why I Am a Methodist* ([Charleston, S.C., 1909]; E185.A254 H:134 Afr Am Pam).

Reform Efforts That Made a Difference

Men, their rights and nothing more; women, their rights and nothing less.

The Revolution

Women's participation in all the major reform movements may be traced through an abundance of material in the division, chiefly from the nineteenth century, in a variety of formats, including magazines and newspapers, books, pamphlets, scrapbooks, and broadsides, many of which complement collections of personal papers held in the Manuscript Division (see chapter 5). Playing a significant role in the antislavery movement, women developed skills and expertise that they would apply to other reform efforts. Lydia Maria Child's *Appeal in Favor of That Class of Americans Called Africans* (Boston: Allen and Ticknor, 1833; E449.C53) not only presents the first comprehensive synthesis of facts and arguments refuting myths of black intellectual inferiority but also is credited with bringing many women into the antislavery movement and broadening the male leadership. Angelina Grimké (1805–1879), who had freed her slaves and left the South, became an abolitionist lecturer and organizer. Her *Appeal to the Christian Women of the South* (New York, American Anti-Slavery Society, 1836; E185.A254 G:117 Afr Am Pam) is extremely rare because so many of the copies were destroyed by Southern postmasters.

Women's innovative organizational efforts can be followed in reports of the *Proceedings of the Anti-Slavery Convention of American Women* (Philadelphia: 1837–39: E449.A621/E449.A6234/E449.A6235), an early attempt at interracial cooperation. Maria Weston Chapman (1806–1885), who was active in the Massachusetts Anti-Slavery Society and American Anti-Slavery Society, organized antislavery fairs and edited the first successful antislavery annual gift book, *The Liberty Bell* (Boston: American Anti-Slavery Society, 1839–58; E449.L69), to raise funds for the cause.

The pages of the early women's rights newspapers offer us a window on the beginning of

Fredrikke S. Palmer. "The Anti and the Snowball—Then and Now." From Agnes E. Ryan, The Torch Bearer *(Boston: Woman's Journal and Suffrage News, 1916; JK1881.N357 sec. 7:1, no. 20 NAWSA). Rare Book and Special Collections Division.*

This clever cartoon graphically depicts the changing attitudes of the opposition toward the suffrage movement. In the early years the woman's cause was belittled as being inconsequential and inappropriate. As it gained strength and support, in part through the efforts of the *Woman's Journal,* the movement's opponents, sometimes known as "Anti's," finally realized that it was only a matter of time until they would be silenced by a suffrage victory.

that long struggle. *The Lily* (Seneca Falls, N.Y., 1849–51; HV5285.L5), "devoted to the interests of woman," was initially begun by Amelia Jenks Bloomer (1818–1894) as a temperance newspaper soon after the Seneca Falls women's rights convention. Regular contributions by Elizabeth Cady Stanton quickly transformed it into the first women's rights newspaper and a champion of the dress reform now associated with its editor. In 1853 Paulina Wright Davis (1813–1876) began publishing *The Una: A Paper Devoted to the Elevation of Woman* (Providence, R.I., 1853–55; HQ1101.U5 Anthony) in Rhode Island and then moved it to Boston. In the prospectus on the first page of the first issue, February 1, 1853, Davis explains that *The Una* signifies the truth she will seek in "discussing the rights, sphere, duty, and destiny of woman, fully and fearlessly." The *Revolution* (New York: Anthony, 1868–71; HN51.R5 Anthony; JK1881.N357 sec. 1, nos. 2–6), easily the most radical of women's rights periodicals, was founded by Susan B. Anthony and Elizabeth Cady Stanton in 1868. Demanding "Principle, not Policy; Justice, not Favors," the *Revolution* advocated not only universal suffrage, but also equal pay and an eight-hour work day. Anthony's personal copy of the fifth volume (January–May 1870) is inscribed to her mother: "Lucy Read Anthony, from her 'Strong Minded' Daughter . . . Dec. 25th 1870." When she donated this volume to the Library of Congress in 1903, Anthony further inscribed it: "This was the end—May 26, 1870 of my experiment in newspaperdom."[4] In 1870 in Boston, Lucy Stone began the more moderate, and more successful *Woman's Journal,* which became the official voice of the National American Woman Suffrage Association (NAWSA) in 1890 and continued publication under modified titles and shifting financial support until 1931 (JK1881.N357 sec. 1, nos. 7–68 NAWSA).

The **Susan B. Anthony Collection** includes printed speeches, pamphlets, convention proceedings, serials, and scrapbooks that document the formative years of the suffrage movement and complement the personal papers held in the Manuscript Division (see chapter 5). Particularly illuminating is Anthony's annotated copy of *An Account of the Proceedings on the Trial of Susan B. Anthony, on the Charge of Illegal Voting, at the Presidential Election in November 1872* (Rochester, N.Y., 1874; JK1899.A6 A5 Anthony), which documents Anthony's efforts to test the citizenship clause of the Fourteenth Amendment, as to whether it guaranteed universal suffrage (see illustration, page 90). The collection is of interest both to those investigating the history of the movement and those interested in Anthony herself. Anthony's scrapbooks are particularly significant as they chronicle the history and progress of the suffrage movement and demonstrate the gradual change in public opinion from 1848 to 1900 through newspaper clippings, programs, trial reports, letters, and memorabilia. Thirty-three volumes of Anthony's scrapbooks, as well as one volume compiled by her sister, Mary Anthony, are also available on microfilm (microfilm 42106 MicRR).

Many of Anthony's 272 books are inscribed to her by the author or donor and later by her to the Library of Congress. Her inscriptions highlight the importance of the book in her life and work. For example, Anthony's copy of Elizabeth Barrett Browning's *Aurora Leigh* (New York and Boston: C.S. Francis & Co., 1857; PR4185.A1 1857a Anthony), celebrating a woman's choice of career over marriage, was given to her by her mother. Anthony notes that she had carried it about in her satchel, read and reread it, and "always cherished it above all other books." Anthony's inscriptions include comments about her niece and "right hand" assistant Rachel Foster Avery, as well as Lydia Maria Child, Paulina Davis, Frances Ellen Harper, Sojourner Truth, and Harriet Tubman. Elizabeth Cady Stanton inscribed her autobiography, *Eighty Years and More* (New York: European Publishing Co., 1898; JK1899.S7 A3 c. 3 Anthony), to Anthony in a bold hand: "We cement our friendship of half a century with an exchange of our autobiographies . . . 1899."[5]

The reference library of the National American Woman Suffrage Association (NAWSA) was donated to the Library in 1938 by the organization's last president, Carrie Chapman Catt (the association's records and Catt's personal papers are in the Manuscript Division; see chapter 5). The nearly one thousand titles in the NAWSA library include books, pamphlets, serials, convention proceedings, and scrapbooks, some formerly owned by Susan B. Anthony, Alice Stone Blackwell, Julia Ward Howe, Mary A. Livermore, Elizabeth Smith Miller, Elizabeth Cady Stanton, Lucy Stone, and other suffrage leaders. The original arrangement of the **NAWSA Collection** has been retained, divided into sixteen sections under one classification number: JK1881.N357. Although primarily documenting the suffrage movement from the point of view of the white middle- and upper-class leadership, it has sections on working women and on prostitution. Biographies of women of various nationalities and time periods and literary works by and about women are also well represented. The suffrage movement in England, particularly the work of the Women's Social and Political Union, is also covered.

Many of the individual books in this collection are not unique to the Library of Congress or other libraries that collect in the field of women's history. As with the Anthony Collection mentioned above, the NAWSA collection is of particular interest when studied as a whole, as the reference library of one of the leading suffrage organizations in the country. Provenance is an important aspect of its value to scholars. There are many editions and copies of Stanton's *Woman's Bible* in the Library, but this collection holds Catt's personal copy, inscribed by Stanton, which has bound with it a rare Stanton pamphlet, *Bible and Church Degrade Woman* (Chicago: H. L. Green, [1898]; JK1881.N357 sec.5, no. 25 NAWSA).[6] The NAWSA library also includes Lucy Stone's personal copy of Margaret Fuller's *Woman in the Nineteenth Century* (Boston: Jewett & Co., 1855; JK1881.N357 sec. 1, no. 162 NAWSA), some very rare early suffrage pamphlets, and a typescript of Maud Wood Park's (1871–1955) "Front Door Lobby," which describes the NAWSA Congressional Committee's efforts during the last push to get the federal suffrage amendment adopted.

Catalog records for items in the NAWSA collection are accessible online. Beyond the author, title, and subject headings, each bibliographical record contains the name of the collection. This allows the reader to browse the collection as a whole, using a "name" search with "National American Woman Suffrage Association Collection." A selection of 167 items from this collection is also available over the Internet through the National Digital Library (NDL) American Memory Program, entitled "Votes for Women: Selections from the National American Woman Suffrage Association Collection, 1848–1921" (<http://memory.loc.gov/ammem/naw/nawshome.html>).

The Rare Book and Special Collections Division's significant cache of **suffrage scrapbooks** offers a unique look at a slice of social history, documenting the gradual evolution of public sentiment and the changing strategies of several generations of activists as they struggled to win the vote for women. The scrapbooks are the creations of women whose interests complement each other and represent a range of activities over time and differences in focus.

Like Susan B. Anthony, Matilda Gage (1826–1898) was active in the National Woman Suffrage Association and compiled four volumes of newspaper clippings, 1850–76, that cover women's professional accomplishments and crimes against women, as well as suffrage issues (JK1901.G16). Ida Husted Harper (1851–1931), a suffrage writer and Anthony biographer, compiled fourteen volumes of her published writings and activities between 1896 and 1920 (JK1896.H4). They include Harper's articles in the *New York Sun*, 1899–1903, extensive coverage of the California campaign of 1896, accounts of the international congresses and related social activities, 1899–1915, and detailed coverage of suffrage victories, 1916–20. These are supplemented by six boxes of suffrage pamphlets published between 1848 and 1922 (JK1896.H42), as well as additional Harper material now in the Manuscript Division.

Seven scrapbooks compiled between 1897 and 1911 by Elizabeth Smith Miller (1822–1911) and her daughter Anne Fitzhugh Miller (1856–1912) of Geneva, New York (JK1882.N357 sec. 16, no. 3–9 NAWSA), document suffrage activities at the local, state, national, and international levels. Creator of the bloomer costume, Elizabeth Miller was the daughter of the abolitionist Gerrit Smith and a cousin of Elizabeth Cady Stanton. In addition to their leadership in the suffrage cause, both women were active supporters of higher education for women. The Millers organized the Geneva Political Equality Club and represented it at New York State and national suffrage conventions and parades. They were often hosts to national and international suffrage leaders, including Emmeline and Sylvia Pankhurst. The Millers' scrapbooks contain much more than the clippings one might expect. They filled their pages with programs, photographs, pins and ribbons, and other artifacts and memorabilia from years of local organizing, lobbying, and national involvement, as well as correspondence with influential people and government officials.

May Wright Sewall (1844–1920) held executive offices in both the National and the International Council of Women. She documented these organizations' activities in four volumes of clippings, 1894–1904 (HQ1114.N3). Harriet Taylor Upton (1853–1945) of Warren, Ohio, treasurer of the National American Woman Suffrage Association, compiled "Oklahoma Indian Territory," which contains newspaper clippings about the Oklahoma bill for statehood and the campaign for women's suffrage in 1904 and 1905. It also holds an annual report of the Oklahoma NAWSA chapter outlining their successes, and signed by Kate H. Biggers (F699.S4).

Progress in the education of girls and women can be studied in a variety of the division's collections. Judith Sargent Murray (1751–1820) was one of the most powerful and prolific early advocates of improved educational opportunities for females of all ages. In her first published essay, "Desultory Thoughts upon the Utility of Encouraging a Degree of Self-Complacency, Especially in Female Bosoms," which appeared in the October 1784 issue of the *Gentleman and Lady's Town and Country Magazine* (Boston, 1784; AP2.A2 G3), Murray, writing as "Constantia," argues for better education for girls in order to encourage their achievement and self-respect. In addition to poetry, drama, and extensive correspondence, Murray wrote eloquent essays, as "Constantia" and "The Gleaner," for the *Massachusetts Magazine* advo-

"Men's League for Woman Suffrage." Miller Scrapbook (Geneva, New York, 1910–11; JK1881.N357, sec. 16:9 NAWSA), pp. 82–83. Rare Book and Special Collections Division.

In their suffrage scrapbooks from the years 1910 and 1911, Elizabeth and Anne Miller tried to capture all aspects of the movement. Here they recognize the importance of men's efforts in "Winning Freedom for Your Daughters," particularly documenting the work of their friends Max Eastman and Nathaniel Schmidt, professor at Cornell University, in organizing the Men's League for Woman Suffrage of the State of New York. George Foster Peabody, William Dean Howells, and John Dewey were among other prominent charter members.

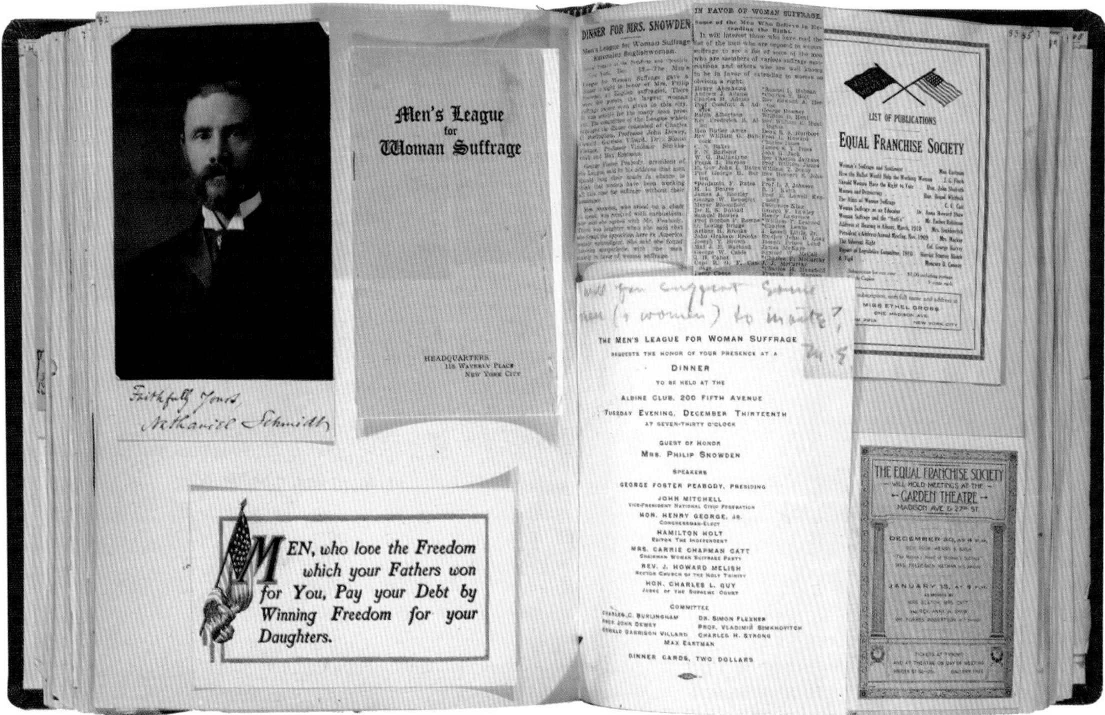

cating women's equality at home and in employment and religious independence as manifest in Universalism.

On the threshold of a lifetime of self-education, Murray at sixteen had declared *The Oeconomy of Human Life* to be the best book ever written. Murray's interest in this popular work on conduct apparently was shared by First Lady Martha Washington, whose inscribed 1790 Philadelphia edition (BJ1561.D6 1790 Carson) was collected by Marian S. Carson along with two other earlier editions. Carson further showed her interests in women and education by acquiring several textbooks written for young ladies, reports of girls schools, and advice books and guides to conduct. Of special note are Milcah Martha Moore's *Miscellanies, Moral and Instructive* (Philadelphia: Joseph Crukshank, 1793; PE1120.M55 1793 Carson), which was reprinted at least fifteen times during the author's lifetime, and an extremely rare copy of a history of the first Philadelphia charter school for girls, *The Rise and Progress of the Young Ladies' Academy of Philadelphia* (Philadelphia: Stewart & Cochran, 1794; LC1421.R57 1794 Carson). This school history complements two related essays on education. In *Thoughts on Education* (Philadelphia: Thomas Dobson, 1787; LB41 .S93 Franklin), John Swanwick, a "Visitor" of the Academy, proposes that all useful and ornamental branches of knowledge, including languages, mathematics, science, and instrumental music, be included in the curriculum. James A. Neal's *An Essay on the Education and Genius of the Female Sex* (Philadelphia: J. Johnson, 1795; LC1421 .N4 Am Imp) is published with an account of the 1794 commencement ceremonies of the academy. Other early works on the education of girls are classified in LC1421.

Emma Hart Willard (1787–1870) proposed a plan for improving female education with state funding in *An Address to the Public* (Middlebury, Vt.: J. W. Copeland, 1819; LC1756.W6). This address and other relevant lectures and proposals may be located under the subject heading "Women—Education," as well as the older heading, "Education of women." Willard was a leader in teacher education at her Troy, New York, school and in Europe. She also wrote textbooks on history and geography and scientific treatises on respiration.

Some understanding of the education of Native American women may be gleaned from reports of training at Eleazar Wheelock's Indian Charity School in Connecticut in *A Continuation of the Narrative of the Indian Charity–School* (London: J. and W. Oliver, 1769; E97.6.M5 C69). More than a century later, the mission work of various Catholic sisterhoods in schools, hospitals, and orphanages throughout the United States is described in *Mission Work among the Negroes and the Indians* (Baltimore: Foley Bros., 1893; E185 .A254 M:195 Afr Am Pam). In a government report on education of Indians at Hampton Institute (Senate Ex. Doc. no. 31; E97.6.H3 L38 1892), 205 girls and women are described and some are photographed doing various tasks or with their families. *Then and Now at Hampton Institute, 1868–1902* (Hampton, Va: Hampton Institute Press, 1902; E449.D16 16:11 Murray Pam) also includes photographs of female Indian students, as well as a listing of graduates and their careers.

Contrasts in educational opportunities available to black girls are evident by sampling other titles in the Daniel Murray Pamphlet Collection. *Catalogue of Pupils of Saint Frances' Academy for Colored Girls* (Baltimore: John Murphy & Co., 1868; E449.D16 23: 21 Murray Pam) offers courses in French, embroidery in silk, tufted work, wax flower and fruit work, music, and painting, in addition to religious training, history, arithmetic, geography, and writing. More typical is the *Annual Report of the Colored Industrial Training School* (Spartanburg, S.C., 1892; E449.D16 18:7 Murray Pam), which lists ninety-eight girls receiving training in cooking, sewing, and general housekeeping. High praise for the success of nursing programs at Hampton and Spelman is offered by *A Report Concerning the Colored Women of the South* (Baltimore, 1896; E449.D16 22:1 Murray Pam).

The pamphlet collections collectively are a rich source of information on women's history, women's movements, and issues affecting women's lives. Nineteenth-century reform movements, including contemporary writings on suffrage, abolition, education for women, prison reform, and temperance, are documented in them. These primary sources will allow the reader to follow the arguments on these and other issues, both pro and con. More than thirty thousand pamphlets are found in such groupings as the **YA Pamphlet Collection,** the **Daniel Murray Pamphlet Collection,** the **African American Pamphlet Collection,** the **Radical Pamphlet Collection,** and the bound pamphlet collections. Although most pamphlets have individual bibliographic records online, they do not have individual classification numbers. This accession-type numbering means that pamphlets on one subject or by one author will be scattered throughout the collections. Pursuing online access to them by

ANARCHISM

AND

OTHER ESSAYS

BY

EMMA GOLDMAN

WITH BIOGRAPHIC SKETCH

BY

HIPPOLYTE HAVEL

MOTHER EARTH PUBLISHING ASSOCIATION

210 EAST THIRTEENTH STREET

NEW YORK

1910

"Emma Goldman." Frontispiece illustration and title page. From Emma Goldman, Anarchism and Other Essays *(New York: Mother Earth Publishing Association, 1910; HX844.G6 1910 Avrich). Rare Book and Special Collections Division.*

Considered by some as "the most dangerous woman in America," Emma Goldman (1869–1940) was a controversial crusader for the rights of women and workers. Believing that woman suffrage would not solve all women's problems, she strongly advocated sexual independence and was jailed for distributing birth control literature. Goldman's published writings and correspondence are well represented in the division's various radical literature collections.

subject heading or author and title is most efficient.

The **YA Pamphlet Collection,** a huge, miscellaneous nineteenth-century pamphlet collection, includes speeches by Victoria Woodhull (1838–1927) and other early feminists as well as works by and about Maria Mitchell (1818–1889), the first American woman astronomer and an advocate of higher education for women.

The **Daniel Murray Pamphlet Collection** and the **African American Pamphlet Collection** include significant material by African American women authors and activists, particularly during the last quarter of the nineteenth century. The Murray Pamphlet collection includes several works by noted abolitionist and suffragist Frances E. Watkins Harper (1825–1911), including her speech *Enlightened Motherhood* (Brooklyn: The Society, 1892; E449.D16 19:6 Murray Pam) given before the Brooklyn Literary Society, and some of the antilynching writings of journalist and lecturer Ida B. Wells-Barnett (1862–1931). In *The Progress of Colored Women* (Washington: Smith Brothers; E449.D16 A:13 Murray Pam), a speech Mary Church Terrell (1863–1954) delivered before the Fiftieth Anniversary Convention of the National American Woman's Suffrage Association in 1898, she calls for the end of racial injustice and gender bias in education and employment. The Murray collection of nearly 350 pamphlets has been digitized as an American Memory collection entitled "African American Perspectives" (<http://lcweb2.loc.gov/ammem/aap/aaphome.html>). The African American Pamphlet Collection, which numbers nearly four hundred works published between 1824 and 1909 and includes works related to women's education and social conditions, is also available in American Memory as "From Slavery to Freedom: The African-American Pamphlet Collection" found at <http://memory.loc.gov/ammem/aapchtml/aapchome.html>.

The **Radical Pamphlet Collection** of approximately four thousand items is organized as a group, with the call number HX81.A53 1870. The pamphlets are arranged alphabetically by author, organization, or title, and a container list is available in the Rare Book Reading Room. Pamphlets by Emma Goldman (1869–1940) are here, including *Marriage and Love* and *Anarchism, What It Really Stands For,* both published in 1914. Works on women and communism by Elizabeth Gurley Flynn (1890–1964), member of the National Board of the Communist Party, U.S.A., and Olive Johnson's (1872–1954) pamphlets on women and the Socialist movement are also in this collection.

The division holds five more special collections of radical literature, representing the ideologies and activities of groups across the political spectrum. The **Anarchism Collection** (1850–1970) includes foreign-language titles intended for urban immigrant communities in the United States, such as works by Emma Goldman and the Yiddish-language newspaper of an anarchist group of the International Ladies' Garment Workers' Union. The **Anarchism Pamphlet Collection** consists of approximately eight hundred pamphlets, broadsides, and posters printed between 1895 and 1972 and is strong in materials relating to anarcho-syndicalism as well as anarchism. Finding aids are available in the reading room.

The **Paul Avrich Collection** of nearly twenty

thousand, twentieth-century American and European anarchist publications and manuscripts was donated to the Library by Dr. Paul Avrich, its collector. It features much material concerning Emma Goldman, including a number of rare pamphlets and extensive correspondence. Materials related to Mollie Steimer (1897–1980), a participant in the controversial Abrams case concerning American civil liberties and free speech, and extensive correspondence with Clara Larsen are notable. Contributions of women to the development of anarchist colonies and schools, especially Stelton Modern School, can be traced in the correspondence of Elizabeth Ferm (1867–1944) and Nellie Dick. Also significant is correspondence of Jo Ann Burbank, Minna Lowensohn, Dora Keyser, and Pauline Turkel. Significant serials holdings include several issues of *Association of Libertarian Feminists News* (Revere, Mass., 1979–85) and *Rebel Woman* (Portland, Ore., 1973–74). Manuscript material is arranged alphabetically by individual or organization; pamphlets are arranged alphabetically by author. A finding aid is available in the reading room and catalog records for books in the Avrich Collection are available online.

The **House UnAmerican Activities Committee Collection** includes four thousand pamphlets that were produced by those under committee review and collected by the committee. The wide range of topics they address includes labor, communism, socialism, fascism, and black power. Access to this collection is available through a finding aid in the reading room or the Chadwyck-Healey microfiche publication *Radical Pamphlets in American Collections* (MicRR).

The **M & S Collection** of ten thousand, twentieth-century radical books, pamphlets, newspapers, magazines, broadsides, and printed ephemera represents many little-known and short-lived groups that generated publications between 1950 and 1981. Publications are arranged by format and then alphabetically by group. Included are scattered issues of the newspapers *Women and Revolution* and *Women United;* the magazines *Freewoman* and *Minute Woman;* and broadsides by Female Liberation, National Organization for Women, Women's Committee against Genocide, and Women's International League for Peace and Freedom, as well as many pamphlets related to abortion and other topics relevant to women. A finding aid is available in the reading room.

The **Printed Ephemera Collection** (formerly the Broadside Collection) contains nearly thirty thousand broadsides, as well as posters, programs, and other ephemera. Items generated by the women's movement and other reforms in which women participated, as well as advertisements of products intended for women, literary and social programs, menus, and poetry written and printed by women, are found here. For instance, Esther De Berdt Reed, first lady of Pennsylvania, calls on her sisters to live simply and make personal sacrifices in order to save money to send to the soldiers in "Sentiments of an American Woman" ([Philadelphia, June 10, 1780]; Printed Ephemera, Port. 146:3). Philadelphia women raised more than $300,000 in paper currency in only a few weeks. Their patriotism inspired similar efforts in other states. (See endpapers.) The work of women in support of the abolitionist cause is well documented by notices of antislavery fairs and appeals from female anti-

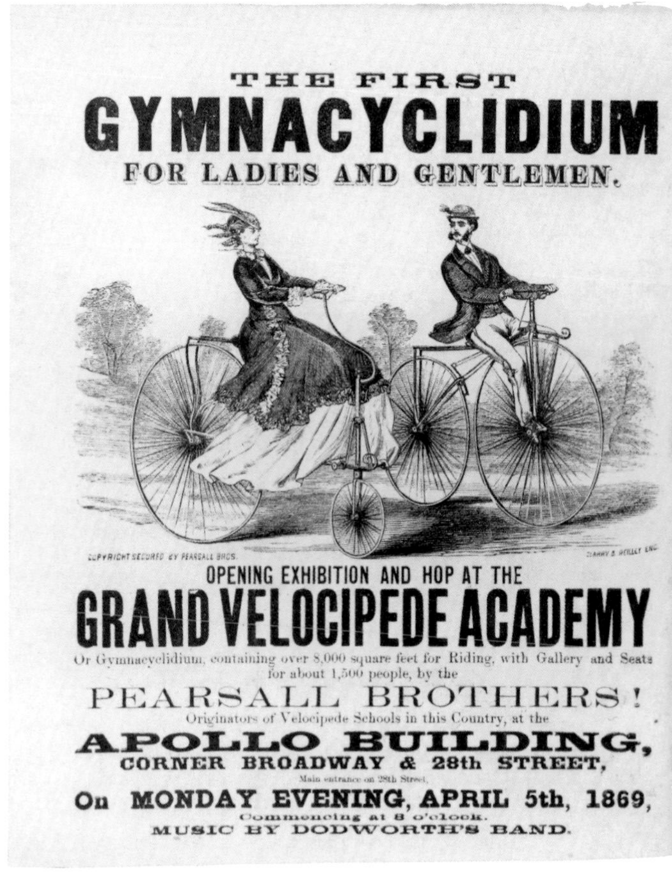

The First Gymnacyclidium for Ladies and Gentlemen. *Illustrated advertising leaflet with engraving by Clarry & Reilley Inc. (New York, 1869; Port 341:18 Pr Eph). Rare Book and Special Collections Division.*

The Pearsall Brothers introduced their "peerless" ladies' two-wheeled velocipede as "proper and practical" and "requiring no change of dress." At their fashionable New York City resort for bicycle exercise, special hours were set aside for ladies to exercise, but no ladies could take lessons unless accompanied by a member of their family.

slavery societies. The efforts of female teachers to educate the freedmen is reported in a fund-raising leaflet, "Education among the Freedmen" (Philadelphia, 1862; Printed Ephemera, Port. 157:41), which shows schoolyard activities at Sea-Island School, No. 1, St. Helena Island, South Carolina.

As the nation prepared to celebrate its one hundredth anniversary in 1876, the rights of full citizenship promised by the Declaration of Independence were still not enjoyed by women. In "Declaration and Protest of the Women of the United States" (Philadelphia, 1876; Printed Ephemera, Port. 160:3), the National Woman Suffrage Association lists wrongs and oppressions against women that violate the fundamental principles of government and are in their eyes grounds for impeachment of the nation's rulers. "Woman Suffrage Co-Equal with Man Suffrage" (New York, 1910; Printed Ephemera, Port 132:2) is representative of the suffrage posters created by the National American Woman Suffrage Association to gain the attention of a variety of constituencies in the first decade of the twentieth century.

Broadsides cataloged before 1972 are listed in the *Catalog of Broadsides in the Rare Book Division* (Boston: G. K. Hall, 1972; Z1231.B7 A5 Rare Bk Ref). Those cataloged between 1972 and 1986 are represented in a card file in the reading room. Beginning in 1986, individual online records have been created. The printed catalog is four volumes, organized geographically, by author and title, and chronologically, but it provides no subject access. The Printed Ephemera Collection is currently being digitized for American Memory as "An American Time Capsule: Three Centuries of Broadsides and Other Printed Ephemera" (<http://memory.loc.gov/ammem/rbpehtml/pehome.html>). Digitized text searching online will provide subject links not otherwise available for this collection.

The division's holdings on birth control, family planning, and the birth control movement are classified in HQ, along with books on sex and marriage. Two volumes labeled "Pamphlets on contraception" (HQ763.P3 and HQ763.P33) contain seventy-two pamphlets, many of which were given to the Library by Margaret Sanger (1879–1966), a pioneering advocate of birth control, in December 1931. The pamphlets, most of which were published in the 1920s, cover the history of the movement, include two editions of Sanger's *Family Limitation,* and present arguments both for and against birth control (see chapter 5 for Sanger's personal papers and illustration, page 83).

The division holds several treatises on abortion at HQ767 and a pamphlet describing the activities and court trials of the New York abortionist Anna Trow Lohman in *Restell's Secret Life* (Philadelphia: Old Franklin Publishing House, 1884; HV6534.N5 A6 1884). Stories based on court cases and police reports dealing with various "wrongs afflicted on young women," including deception, domestic violence, and murder, are found under HV6534.N5 A6 1869–1886.

A glimpse of the variety of work available to women is offered in *Life in New York, In Doors and Out of Doors* (New York: Bunce & Brother, 1851;

A Terrible Blot on American Civilization *(front) and* Vote against Those Who Voted to Protect the Lynching Industry *(back). Illustrated flyer (Washington: District of Columbia Anti-Lynching Committee North Eastern Federation of Colored Women's Clubs, [1922]; Port. 208:36 Pr Eph). Rare Book and Special Collections Division.*

Once women's suffrage was finally achieved, women's organizations encouraged women to use their new political tool. This North Eastern Federation of Colored Women's Clubs flyer shows women joining men to make a stand against lynching by exercising their right to petition and to vote.

HD6096.N6 B8) through forty engravings accompanied by profile stories. The tedious suffering of the needlewoman is contrasted with the pleasant surroundings of the shop woman. Most descriptions discuss actual tasks, working conditions, and wages. Teaching and nursing are praised and jobs related to printing are encouraged, whereas corset makers are chided for bringing misery to other women. Tasks performed by poor girls, including fruit vending and ash picking, are described by Emma Brown and illustrated by Katherine Peirson in *The Child Toilers of Boston Streets* (Boston: D. Lothrop & Co, 1879; HD2350.U5 B72). Lucy Stone's copy of Caroline Dall's *Woman's Right to Labor* (Boston: Walker, Wise, and Co., 1860; JK1881.N357 sec. 9:9 NAWSA) and the memorial edition of her *The College, the Market, and the Court; or Woman's Relation to Education, Labor, and Law* (Boston: Rumford Press, 1914; JK1881.N357 sec. 9:22 NAWSA) are among the labor works gathered in the NAWSA Collection. Here also are several works by Charlotte Perkins Gilman, including *Women and Economics* (Boston: Small, Maynard & Company, 1898; JK188 .N357 sec. 6:20 NAWSA), as well as Alice Henry's *Trade Union Woman* (New York: D. Appleton and Company, 1915; sec. 3:9 NAWSA) and a complete set of the *Bulletin of the Women's Bureau* of the Labor Department (Washington: U.S. Government Printing Office, 1919–37; sec. 3: 27–34 NAWSA).

R. Major. "The Press Feeder." Engraving from Life in New York, In Doors and Out of Doors *(New York: Bunce & Brother, 1851; HD6096.N6 B8). Rare Book and Special Collections Division.*

Press-feeder was one of several jobs in the printing industry here considered appropriate for young women in mid-nineteenth-century New York. In *Life in New York,* teachers and nurses were praised, but corset-makers were chided for bringing misery to other women.

Women in Popular Culture

A wealth of relatively untapped materials await the persistent researcher interested in expanding our understanding of women as both creators and subjects of popular culture. The **Dime Novel Collection** includes nearly forty thousand titles, acquired primarily by copyright deposit, and is representative of the popular pulp fiction published between 1860 and 1933, which, through wide distribution, helped to shape the nation's perception of itself (see also chapter 2). The first dime novel, *Malaeska: The Indian Wife of the White Hunter* (Beadle's Dime Novels, series 17, no. 1), was an American romance by Ann S. Stephens (1813–1886). In fact, women wrote many of the stories in this collection of dime novels, which also often feature women or depict them in their cover art. Two extremely rare pieces by Louisa May Alcott (1832–1888), *The Skeleton in the Closet* and *The Mysterious Key,* appear in 1867 issues of the Ten Cent Novelettes (series 189). One particularly intriguing title in the Police Gazette Library (series 128), *Female Sharpers of New York, Their Haunts and Habits, Their Wiles and Their Victims* (1883), describes the shadowy activities of blackmailers, streetwalkers, shoplifters, witches, and gamblers. Among other authors represented are Mary A. Denison (1826–1911), Laura Jean Libbey (1862–1924), Mrs. Alexander McVeigh Miller (n.d.), Elizabeth Oakes Smith (1806–1893), and Metta V. Victor (1831–1885), who was editor of *Home.* Beadle's Handbooks (series 20) includes manuals on dressmaking and millinery, beauty, letter writing, and household management. An extensive run of the Seaside Library includes the work of Charlotte Mary Brame (1836–1884), Margaret Wolfe Hungerford (1855–1897), Mary Elizabeth Maxwell (1837–1915), and Margaret Oliphant (1828–1897) and is accessible through a separate card file. There is no subject guide to this popular fiction, but bibliographies and series guides can help to identify genres that may be fruitful and the reference staff can offer informed guidance.

The **Manuscript Play Collection** consists of more than three thousand typescripts submitted for copyright deposit, 1876–1945, and includes works by and about women, some of which were never published or performed. A reading room card file, arranged alphabetically by author, provides access to this collection. Representative titles include Mrs. C. F. McLean's "The Flying Machine" (Cincinnati, Ohio, 1894), Guido Marburg's "Typewriter Girl" (New York, 1897), Garda Brown Wise's "Must Women Choose?" (New York, 1924), and Frank McGrath's "Carry Nation, a Chronicle Play" (1932). Other copyright deposit playscripts are held in the Manuscript Division (see chapter 5).

Also acquired through copyright deposit are nearly six thousand dramas, published between 1870 and 1920, for use by amateur performers. Representative works by and about women in this **Reserve Storage Drama Collection** include Ida M. Buxton's *Matrimonial Bliss* and *A Sewing Circle* (Clyde, Ohio: A. D. Ames, 1884 and 1885), *Woman's Rights, a Comedy by Sylvan Drey of the Baltimore Bar* (Baltimore, 1882), J. A. Fraser's *Bloomer Girls, or Courtship in the Twentieth Century* (Chicago: Dramatic Publishing Co., 1896), and Sophie Perkins's *Walk This Way, Please, a Satire on Shopping* (Chicago: T. S. Denison, 1917). A reading room card file, arranged alphabetically by author, provides access to this collection.

Performance information on some nineteenth-century actresses and playwrights may be culled from over three thousand playbills in the **Theater Playbills Collection.** Primarily announcing performances of plays in Washington, D.C., and New York City, these playbills also describe productions of *After Dark or Neither Maid, Wife, nor Widow* in Hoboken, New Jersey, in 1868, and *Bachelor's Wives* in Cedar Rapids, Iowa, in 1896. Other play titles include *Becky Sharp, Belles of the Kitchen, School of Reform, Telephone Girl, Temperance Town, Way to Win a Woman,* and *Women of Achievement.* A reading room card file, labeled "Playbills" and arranged alphabetically by play title, provides access to this collection.

Insights into the place of women in popular culture may be gleaned from browsing through more than four thousand, nineteenth-century **Broadside Songs** held in the division. Lyrics of popular songs honor mothers and celebrate women at work and at leisure. Representative titles include "My Mother Dear," "Human Equality," "The Song of the Shirt," "Red Petticoat," "The Wife's Lament," "A New Temperance Song," and "Gay and Happy," which is listed as being "composed and sung by Miss Anne Rush, the Philadelphia Vocalist." This collection has been digitized and is available as an American Memory collection entitled "America Singing: Nineteenth-Century Song Sheets" (<http://memory.loc.gov/ammem/amsshtml/amsshome.html>).

Collections Formed by Women

The **Katherine Golden Bitting Collection** on Gastronomy and the **Elizabeth Robins Pennell Collection** of cookbooks are significant for the study of women's history in two important ways. Gastronomy and cookery have traditionally and historically been part of a woman's world, and women were logically the intended audience for many of these books. The collections and the related bibliographies also shed light on the two individual women who assembled these collections.

Bitting's interest in book collecting was sparked by her career as a food chemist. She wrote extensively on food preservation and began collecting books on gastronomy in the process of her research. More than four thousand volumes that she collected were donated to the Library between 1939 and 1944, among them eighteenth- and nineteenth-century books on food preparation from England and the United States, as well as European works. Bitting included American regional cooking in her collection. Cookbooks produced by churches and community organizations throughout the United States contain recipes for very local and specific tastes. These often hard-to-find cookbooks offer insight into the development of regional cuisines.

On the other hand, Elizabeth Robins Pennell's cookbook collection is primarily European and is strongest in French and Italian works from the sixteenth through eighteenth centuries. She was a journalist, and often worked together with her husband, artist Joseph Pennell.

Both women published extensive bibliographies. Bitting's work, *Gastronomic Bibliography* (San Francisco, 1939; Z5776.G2 B6 Rare Bk Ref), is a classic in the field. Pennell's *My Cookery Books* (Boston and New York: Houghton, Mifflin, 1903; Z5777.P41 Rare Bk Ref) is a particularly beautiful book, designed by Bruce Rogers. Both bibliographies are important tools for approaching the collections and are available in the Rare Book Reading Room. For a fuller description of these collections, see Leonard Beck, *Two "Loaf-givers," or a Tour through the Gastronomic Libraries of Katherine Golden Bitting and Elizabeth Robins Pennell* (Washington: Library of Congress, 1984; Z663.4.T95 1984 Rare Bk Ref).

Another of the division's major women collectors, Marian Carson, amassed an amazing array of books, pamphlets, broadsides, and printed ephemera on a variety of subjects, including early American printing, nineteenth-century social history, culinary arts, and children's literature. In addition to the cookbooks, conduct books, books on

Claire Van Vliet. "Lady Freedom." Cover design for Rita Dove, Lady Freedom among Us *(West Burke, Vt.: Janus Press, 1993; PS3554.O884L33 1994 Janus Pr). Rare Book and Special Collections Division. With permission of the artist, Claire Van Vliet.*

Bound in the folds of this three-dimensional representation of "Lady Freedom" designed by Claire Van Vliet is the text of the poem *Lady Freedom among Us,* written by United States Poet Laureate Rita Dove on the occasion of the return of the statue of Freedom to the dome of the United States Capitol on October 23, 1993.

education, and children's books and games discussed above, she brought to the Library an impressive body of printed material that celebrates the social diversity of American life while documenting the political, cultural, and economic growth of the American Republic during its first century. *Gathering History: the Marian S. Carson Collection of Americana* (Washington: Library of Congress, 1999; Z1201.G38 1999) showcases this collection.

The **Janus Press Collection and Archive** (1955–) includes fine press and handmade books and printed ephemera created and published since 1955 by Claire Van Vliet, contemporary printer, printmaker, and publisher. In addition to Van Vliet's contributions, a significant number of works are collaborations with other women authors and illustrators, including Ruth Fine, Susan Johanknecht, Margaret Kaufman, Barbara Luck, and Helen Siegl. Subjects include quilts, recipes, abused women, and a housewife's diary.

The archive also contains material relating to the production of books and ephemera bearing the Janus Press imprint, as well as other projects carried out with the assistance of its founder. An open collection, it currently numbers nearly five thousand items and includes correspondence, proofs, paste-ups and layouts, book designers' mockups, drawings, woodblocks, etched and engraved plates, notes, and receipts. Material is arranged chronologically by publication date of the work to which it relates. A finding guide is available in the reading room and on the Internet.

Another realm of collecting is the scrapbook, and the division holds examples on a variety of subjects compiled by women, besides the suffrage scrapbooks mentioned earlier. Not only are scrapbooks significant for what they contain—excerpts from contemporary newspapers, photographs, and keepsakes—but they give us insight into what was important to the compilers. Jessica Randolph Smith compiled "Stars and Bars" (CR113.5 S5) in 1916, covering the design and history of the first Confederate flag. "Scrapbook of the Confederate Veteran, Her Dead Son," compiled by Cassie Moncure as a memorial to her son, describes the Civil War, life in the South, and Southern families. Mary M. North compiled two scrapbooks, the first about the American flag, Flag Day, and other patriotic issues, the second a Civil War army nurses' scrapbook, now available on microfilm (Microfilm 19739 E MicRR). Thomas Shuler Shaw filled two scrapbooks with correspondence and clippings about Mary E. Wilkins (1852–1930), novelist and short story writer, in preparation for a biography, which he apparently never completed.

Literary Works

American literature holdings in the Rare Book and Special Collections Division are far from comprehensive, as most late nineteenth- and twentieth-century works remain in the General Collections, but there is sufficient unique material to merit attention. The division routinely collects current copyright deposits of nearly eighty contemporary American women writers. For certain works by contemporary women writers and artists the Library's only copies are found in the Press Collection or the Artists' Books Collection. For example, Susan E. King's *Women and Cars* (Los Angeles: Paradise Press, 1983; N7433.5.K56 A4 1983 Artists' Bks) and her *Georgia* (Los Angeles: Paradise Press, 1981; PS3561.I4834 G46 1981 Press) are in the Rare Book and Special Collections Division only and five of Johanna Drucker's works are found only in the Artists' Books Collection. Three of Sylvia Plath's works, including *The Green Rock* (Ely: Embers Handpress, 1982; PS3566.L27 G7 1982 Press), are found only in the Press Collection, as is Arthur Miller's *Homely Girl* (New York:

Peter Blum, 1992; PS3525.I5156 H66 1992 Press), with etchings by Louise Bourgeois. Works found in these collections are often published in limited editions, sometimes numbering as few as ten, and with unusual artwork or bindings.

Significant holdings by a number of earlier writers include works by Laura Benet, Elizabeth Bishop, Alice Brown, Pearl S. Buck, Alice Carey, Emily Dickinson, Edna Ferber, Charlotte Perkins Gilman, Ellen Glasgow, Louise Imogen Guiney, Sarah Josepha Hale, Lorraine Hansberry, Lillian Hellman, Zora Neale Hurston, Edna St. Vincent Millay, Margaret Mitchell, Marianne Moore, Margaret Bayard Smith, Gertrude Stein, Eudora Welty, and Edith Wharton. Some of these were acquired as part of special collections like the Oliver Wendell Holmes Collection and the Finkelstein Collection. Others are particularly interesting because of inscriptions, unusual provenance, or special illustrations. For example, a unique extra-illustrated copy of Helen Hunt Jackson's *The Procession of Flowers in Colorado* (Boston: Roberts Brother, 1886; QK150.J12 1888) has six spectacular full-page watercolors of Colorado wildflowers in addition to the twelve in-text marginal watercolors and a tailpiece. Original artwork by Jackson's good friend Alice Stewart delayed actual publication of this limited edition of 100 copies for two years. A number of the novels of Sarah Orne Jewett (1849–1909) are in bindings designed by her friend Sarah Wyman Whitman (1842–1904), one of Houghton Mifflin's most respected designers. In particularly good condition are five in the Oliver Wendell Holmes Collection: *Country of the Pointed Firs* (Boston: Houghton, Mifflin, 1896; PS2132.C64 1896 c. 3 Holmes), *Deephaven* (Boston: Houghton, Mifflin, 1894; PS2132.D4 1894 Holmes), *Life of Nancy* (Boston: Houghton, Mifflin, 1895; PS2132.L55 1895 Holmes), *The Queen's Twin* (Boston: Houghton, Mifflin, 1899; PS2132 .Q4 Holmes), and *Tales of New England* (London: R. Osgood, McIlvaine & Co., 1893; PS2132.T34 1893 Holmes). Both Willa Cather's *Death Comes for the Archbishop* (New York: Alfred A. Knopf, 1927; PS3505.A87 D4 c. 2) and *Lost Lady* (New York: Knopf, 1926; PS3505.A87 L6 1923 c. 2) have signed inscriptions by the author, expressing her admiration for Marian MacDowell, who supported Cather's writing (see "The House That Marian Built" in this volume).

By looking at aspects of the Rare Book and Special Collections Division's holdings ranging from religion and reform to popular culture and literature, we have attempted to highlight the strengths of rare book holdings related to United States women's history, to demonstrate the richness and variety of these resources, and to point out some of the division's contemporary holdings and unique treasures. Because the Rare Book Classified Collection mirrors holdings in the General Collections, most of the same subjects and formats are found in both and may be accessed using the same subject headings and search strategies. Because not all of the division's special collections have online access, it is important to consult special card files and finding aids in the Rare Book Reading Room in addition to the online catalog. While we could not touch on all subjects and formats that might interest researchers, we hope this survey of holdings will suggest new ways in which the division's resources can be used to complement materials found in other Library divisions to further the understanding of American women and celebrate their complex contributions to our world.

Sarah Wyman Whitman. Signed trade binding for Sarah Orne Jewett, The Queen's Twin *(Boston: Houghton, Mifflin, 1899; PS2132.Q4 Holmes). Rare Book and Special Collections Division.*

The stylized simplicity of Boston artist Sarah Wyman Whitman's cover designs changed the direction of trade binding design during the 1890s. Whitman was a respected adviser to publisher George Mifflin and produced memorable cover designs for many Houghton Mifflin literary authors, including Margaret Deland, Celia Thaxter, and Nathaniel Hawthorne.

We wish to thank both Mark Dimunation, chief of the Rare Book and Special Collections Division, and Susan H. Vita, chief of the Special Materials Cataloging Division, for their support of this publication. For assistance with photography, thanks also to Margaret Kieckhefer.

The Womans Bible
Chapter. II.
by
Elizabeth Cady Stanton

(very small print) Genesis II 21—25,

21 And the LORD God caused a deep sleep
to fall upon Adam, and he slept; and he
took one of his ribs, and closed up the flesh
instead thereof.
22 And the rib, which the LORD God had
taken from man, made he a woman, and
brought her unto the man.
23 And Adam said, This *is* now bone of my
bones, and flesh of my flesh: she shall be
called Woman, because she was taken out
of man.
24 Therefore shall a man leave his father
and his mother, and shall cleave unto his
wife: and they shall be one flesh.
25 And they were both naked, the man and
his wife, and were not ashamed.

As the account of the creation in the first chapter, is in harmony with science, common sense, & the experience of mankind in natural laws, the enquiry naturally arises why should there be two contradictory accounts in the same book, of the same event? It is fair to infer that the second version, which is found in some form, in the different religions of all nations, is a mere allegory, symbolizing some mysterious conception of a

5 Manuscript Division

Janice E. Ruth

Spanning all time periods and embracing all occupations, the Library's manuscript sources for the study of women's history are among the finest and most comprehensive in the country. Contained in hundreds of collections are documents reflecting the full range of women's experiences, from Abigail Adams's declaration to her sister in 1799 that she would "never consent to have our sex considered in a inferior point of light,"[1] to the remarks of cabinet secretary Patricia Harris, the daughter of a dining car porter, who told a skeptical senator at her 1977 confirmation hearing, "If my life has any meaning at all, it is that those who start out as outcasts can wind up being part of the system."[2] The Manuscript Division's collections document the efforts of Harris and of countless other women not only to join "the system" but also to reform and transcend it. These women, in the words of pioneer physician Elizabeth Blackwell, "did not wish to give them[selves] a first place, still less a second one—but the most complete freedom to take their true place whatever it may be."[3] This chapter—and the larger work of which it is a part—offers researchers the tools to uncover and interpret what that "true place" has been for American women throughout our nation's history.

American historian Mary Ritter Beard, author of the pathbreaking *Woman as Force in History* (1946), was fond of quoting French historian Fustel de Coulanges's declaration, "No documents, no history." Fearful that women would be "blotted from the story and the thought about history as completely as if they had never lived," Beard tried unsuccessfully in the 1930s to create a World Center for Women's Archives to preserve women's documentary heritage and to ensure that the "women of today know about the women of yesterday to whom they are so closely linked for better or worse" and that the "women of tomorrow" will "know about the women of today."[4] The goals espoused by Beard—collecting primary documents by and about women, and providing adequate access to them—have been concerns of the Library's Manuscript Division since its establishment in 1897.

The division's earliest chiefs vigorously solicited the collections of notable women who were involved in the suffrage and abolition campaigns. They also sought the papers of first ladies, of women who achieved various "firsts" in history, and of women who were pioneers in fields formerly restricted to men. To this day, these collections sustain heavy research use. Also obtained were the records of women's voluntary associations and national reform and trade organizations founded and supported by women. Other materials, which were not always consciously sought, were letters and diaries documenting women's everyday existence and revealing women's hopes, disappointments, and accomplishments. Although unsolicited, these items were also preserved—but as part of multigenerational family papers or as unnoticed groupings buried in the papers of a more famous husband, father, or brother.

Elizabeth Cady Stanton. The Woman's Bible. *Draft manuscript, ch. 2, p. 1 (Genesis 2. 21–25). Elizabeth Cady Stanton Papers (container 3). Manuscript Division. LC-MS-41210-3.*

Although most often identified as a suffragist, Elizabeth Cady Stanton (1815–1902) participated in a variety of reform initiatives during her lifetime. She actively supported dress reform and women's health issues, greater educational and financial opportunities for women, more liberal divorce laws, and stronger women's property laws. Even more controversial were Stanton's views on religion and on the Church's role in limiting women's progress, ideas that culminated in 1895 with her publication of *The Woman's Bible,* shown here in draft form. Assisted by a committee of academic and church women, Stanton reproduced sections of biblical text followed by feminist commentary. Although *The Woman's Bible* was never accepted as a major work of biblical scholarship, it was a best-seller, much to the dismay of many suffragists. Younger members of the National American Woman Suffrage Association felt that the book jeopardized the group's ability to gain support for a suffrage amendment, and they formally denounced the publication, despite Susan B. Anthony's pleas not to embarrass their former president publicly.

The papers of these unknown female relatives reflect the daily activities, concerns, and observations of American women from the colonial period through the twentieth century. Used together with the papers of male family members, they provide important information on American family life, including courtship, marriage, child rearing, socialization of children, gender roles, social and economic relationships between men and women, and the impact of wars, politics, and other national and international events on individuals and families.

Most of the women represented in the division's holdings are white and from middle- and upper-middle-class families. Some important examples of African American women may be found, but fewer sources exist in the division written by Native Americans or by women of Asian, Hispanic, or other origin. Information about the latter groups, however, and about women in general, appears in the papers of male legislators, judges, missionaries, doctors, educators, soldiers, and scientists, whose writings often reveal white society's attitudes about ethnicity, race, and gender. These collections are examples of how sources originally acquired to support one field of research can be mined by historians pursuing other areas of inquiry. Thus, through a combination of men's and women's collections, documenting the lives of both notable and unknown women, the Manuscript Division offers unique opportunities for students of American women's history. Its holdings can help researchers of the next millennium remedy the neglect Clara Barton noted at the beginning of the twentieth century when writing to Mary S. Logan about Logan's efforts to compile a history of American women: "From the storm lashed decks of the Mayflower . . . to the present hour; woman has stood like a rock for the welfare and the glory of the history of the country, and one might well add . . . unwritten, unrewarded, and almost unrecognized."[5]

MANUSCRIPT READING ROOM
James Madison Memorial Building, 1st floor, room LM101
Hours: Monday through Saturday, 8:30 a.m. to 5:00 p.m. Closed Sunday and federal holidays.
Telephone: 202 707-5387
Fax: 202 707-6336
Address: Manuscript Division, Library of Congress, 101 Independence Avenue, SE, Washington, DC 20540-4680
E-mail: mss@loc.gov
Web site: <http://www.loc.gov/rr/mss>
Access and use: Although no appointments are necessary, researchers are advised to write or telephone prior to visiting, since many collections are stored off-site and advance notice is needed to retrieve them for research use. In addition, some collections carry access restrictions, and permission may need to be sought before use. Because the Manuscript Division's holdings are rare and irreplaceable, their use is limited primarily to patrons conducting serious research who have exhausted available secondary sources. Student access is generally limited to those engaged in graduate study. Undergraduates who are working on a senior thesis or similar project under the direction of a faculty member will be admitted after an introduction in person or writing by their advisers. First-time researchers are required to read and sign a form agreeing that they will abide by the formal rules and regulations for using the reading room. All researchers must complete a registration card every two years and must present a Library of Congress reader identification card at that time. Pencils, note cards, and notepaper are provided. Only materials essential to research are allowed in the reading room. As a rule, researchers are permitted to make copies of original manuscript material on the photocopiers in the reading room, with the exception of bound documents, fragile items, or collections that carry restrictions on photoduplication. Additional information on the division's services and facilities, including its interlibrary loan policies, may be obtained on the Manuscript Division Web site.

USING THE COLLECTIONS

The Manuscript Division's holdings of more than 53 million items, contained in approximately eleven thousand collections, account for nearly one-half of the entire Library of Congress collection of 121 million items. They differ from the holdings of the National Archives and Records Administration, which principally maintains the official records of the United States government. Instead, most of the division's collections comprise the personal papers of individuals and families, along with a smattering of organizational records. They generally are limited in focus to American history and culture. They also tend to reflect events, people, and organizations of national significance, although aspects of state and local history are invariably documented in the state files of national groups and in the letters and diaries of women and men who lived in, traveled to, or otherwise represented communities across the country. Most of the division's collections were donated as gifts, although some were acquired through purchase or government transfer. They range in size from one item to more than 2.5 million items, and they contain various types and formats of material. Supplementing the division's original manuscript sources are microfilm copies of related collections in other American and foreign repositories, including, for example, some of the Spanish reproductions cited in chapter 12 and in the essay "Women on the Move" in this volume.

Understanding what constitutes a manuscript collection and how such materials are organized and described for patron use is an important prerequisite for a successful research trip. Archives and manuscripts have several different kinds of value. Some, such as illuminated manuscripts, are valued as artifacts or objects of art. Other manuscripts are valued because of their association with a famous person—autographs might be a good example of this. Although some of the division's manuscripts have artifactual and associational value, most are collected for their informational or evidentiary value. They are primary sources, often unique ones, upon which the writing of history may be based. They provide evidence of human activity, and as such, are generated naturally during the course of an individual's or an organization's life. Scholars often use these manuscripts, however, for purposes unrelated to the reasons the documents were created. For example, an organization may create membership records because it needs to send out renewal notices or match members' skills to specific tasks the group has undertaken. Later, after the group's records are donated to an archival repository, a scholar might examine those same membership lists, not because she intends to send invoices to those individuals but because she is attempting to construct a socioeconomic or regional analysis of women who joined voluntary associations at a given time in our nation's history.

Manuscript librarianship is based on the premise that the context in which documents were created must be understood before their content can be identified, authenticated, and interpreted. This leads to the central organizing principle of archives and manuscripts, which is known as *provenance* or *respect des fonds*. This concept assumes that because manuscripts and archives are the organic byproducts of individuals and organizations, they cannot be understood apart from the life of the individual or the functions of the organization that created them. Documents are therefore kept together as discrete units of material linked to their creator or collector. They are not pulled out of their collections and subjectively reorganized according to some other scheme, such as subject matter, geographical focus, or time period. Moreover, whenever possible, the original order of documents within a collection is also preserved to help validate the documents' authenticity and to reveal as much as possible about the functions and activities that generated them. No single document can be understood in isolation; it is almost always part of a larger file, record series, or collection. These principles of provenance and original order are apparent in the Manuscript Division's arrangement and description of its collections.

As reflections of personal lives, professional careers, and organizational activities, the division's collections contain many different types of manuscripts, including diaries, personal and official correspondence (incoming and sometimes copies of outgoing letters), school papers, speeches, drafts of literary manuscripts and other writings, notebooks, account books, ships' logs, commonplace books (containing handwritten recipes, poetry, and other musings), autograph and commemorative albums, scrapbooks, press clippings, subject files, photographs, legal and financial papers, and other documents in every conceivable format—originals, letterpress copies, carbons, and photocopies that have been handwritten, typewritten, and computer-generated during the past three hundred and fifty years. Consider the kinds of material that you or members of your family have accumulated over the years. All of those types of material are likely to be represented somewhere in the division's holdings, although rarely will one collection contain every type and format. Collectively these materials constitute what is meant by the terms *papers* and *records* as used throughout this chapter.

Sometimes when an archivist processes a manuscript collection, certain types of materials that require special equipment or handling, particularly films, sound recordings, rare books, and photographs, may be transferred to another custodial division in the Library, where they are often identified by the same collection name assigned to the manuscript materials. Examples of such transfers are given in chapters 6, 9, and 10, but further inquiries would reveal other instances of collateral material spread across Library divisions.

Some types of manuscripts naturally yield more information than others—correspondence, minutes, and diaries come easily to mind—but occasionally a new generation of scholars brings a fresh appreciation to underused document types. For example, students of women's and African American history have made interesting use of previously ignored women's household account books to understand social and economic relationships between men and women, free and slave, within plantation economies, or they have used these sources to illustrate household consumption patterns and to document women's participation in local, regional, and national economic networks.

Although the Manuscript Division may acquire a collection because of an individual's prominence or contribution to one particular field or endeavor, that person's collection may likely contain papers reflecting the full range of her life's activities, including documents relating to her schooling, religious beliefs, family background, professional affiliations and activities, committees on which she served, organizations which she joined, her relationship with her employer or employees, her charitable and philanthropic acts, and her hobbies and avocational interests, all of which may be totally unrelated to the work for which she is best known. Some documents in a collection may tell us very little about the person in whose papers they came to reside. Instead they are important for the data they reveal about other people, places, or events. The best examples of this might be incoming letters from friends and associates; constituent mail received by politicians; medical and school records retained by doctors and educators; and legal case files compiled by lawyers, judges, and civil rights organizations. Although a collection may be centered on a prominent individual or family, it can nevertheless be a source of information on ordinary women and the seemingly mundane events and activities that characterize daily life.

Archivists attempt to convey to researchers the diversity of information in manuscript collections through catalog records and finding aids, but even these access tools cannot identify everything of significance. Scholars must supplement these tools with sound background research on their topics and a willingness to wade through often large and complex bodies of materials.

Manuscript Catalog Records

Every collection held in the Manuscript Division is represented by a record in the Library of Congress Online Catalog. Each catalog record includes information on the title or creator of the collection; size, dates, and type of material; data about the person or organization featured in the collection; a brief summary of the collection's scope and content; and a controlled listing of the principal subjects and people represented. The catalog is updated daily and may be accessed from terminals throughout the Library and from remote locations through the Internet.

As with any catalog, the amount of information given for each collection is limited and touches only on the major topics and correspondents. Primarily a browsing device, the catalog is useful for locating the most likely sources on a topic and for providing an overview of the division's holdings. You may search for manuscript material in conjunction with a search of the Library's books and other formats, or you may limit your search to manuscript records only. Familiarity with the *Library of Congress Subject Headings* (*LCSH*) is essential, as the search strategies and subject terms used in locating manuscript records are the same as those described in "Using the Library of Congress" and chapter 1 of this guide. In addition to searching by name, title, and subject, the catalog also permits various types of keyword searches, which are useful for locating words and phrases in the summary scope and content notes of manuscript records, including the "natural language" version of words for which the arcane subject headings may not be readily apparent. Keyword searching is also a good way of finding collections that contain certain types of manuscript material that are sometimes themselves the focus of a research project, such as diaries, ships' logs, speeches, account books, and so on.

When you search the catalog, it is important to cast a wide net. For example, when researching an individual, search not only for that person's name but also for the names of family members, friends, colleagues, organizations, and anyone else with whom he or she may have corresponded. Searches by occupation and subject are also helpful in identifying collections related to the individual you are researching. Locating individuals by their religious or ethnic identities, however, is often more difficult, unless those aspects of people's lives so permeated their papers as to be obvious subject headings to the processing archivist or cataloger. When searching for collections by race or ethnicity of the creator, you may find it helpful to supplement your catalog search with a search of available printed guides.[6] (See also the tips in chapter 12.)

Keep in mind that when doing manuscript research, you will likely need to consult collections not because of any interest per se in the creator of those materials but because the creator may have had an association with events and activities that are the real focus of your research. The catalog record, however, cannot describe the entire scope and diversity of the creator's experiences, nor can it identify all of the people, events, or subjects represented in a given collection. It distills in a few paragraphs the information contained in a multipage finding aid, which in turn is only a summary description of the documents that make up the collection. Even when a search of the catalog is unpromising, a follow-up search of collection finding aids may yield results.

Finding Aids

Finding aids, which are sometimes called inventories or registers, are created by division archivists in the course of processing a collection. These guides embody the archival view of the materials not as discrete individually described items but as groups of related documents that are arranged and analyzed collectively in an effort to preserve their context and reflect their provenance and the relationship between items. Although finding aids occasionally vary in format according to the nature of the collection, most division finding aids are divided into several parts. The first part includes information about the source or creator of the collection, the custodial history of the documents, and the conditions under which they may be consulted, reproduced, or quoted. A biographical note or organizational history lists the important dates and events in the life of the individual or organization featured in the collection. A scope and content note describes the arrangement of the collection, the major topics covered, and any notable gaps or weaknesses in the collection. The series description outlines the major groups or series of papers. The container list, which is usually in hierarchical outline form, identifies in progressive detail the contents of the papers together with the corresponding microfilm reel number or container number of each file. A few finding aids also include partial or complete name indexes to the correspondence contained in the collection.

Detailed finding guides or registers exist for virtually all of the division's larger collections. More than two thousand are available for use in the reading room, and photocopies of these may be ordered for a fee. About seven hundred of the division's finding aids were reproduced on microfiche by a commercial publisher and distributed under the title *National Inventory of Documentary Sources in the United States: Manuscript Division, Library of Congress* (Teaneck, N.J.: Chadwyck-Healy, 1983; Microfiche Ref). Copies of this microfiche are available in libraries throughout the country. In the last few years, the division has begun converting its paper finding aids to electronic form for distribution over the Internet. Only a small percentage have been converted so far, but they are freely accessible from the division's Web site, their full text searchable for now through character-string searches and later through more advanced techniques. Searching the online versions allows researchers to uncover more quickly than before the names of people, places, groups, and subjects that do not appear in the abbreviated catalog records. Yet even with such enhancements, finding guides are still only aids to research. They cannot substitute for a scholar's detailed examination of the actual papers.

Women's History Guides and Access Tools

Supplementing the Manuscript Division's catalog records and finding aids are several guides and articles relating specifically to the division's women's history holdings. The most accessible is the two-volume *Women's History Sources: A Guide to Archives and Manuscript Collections in the United States* (New York: R. R. Bowker Company, 1979; Z7964.U49 W64), edited by Andrea Hinding. Through the help of various field-workers, Hinding compiled a guide comparable in format to the more general *National Union Catalog of Manuscript Collections* (Washington: Library of Congress, 1959–93; Z6620.U5 N3; also available online[7]) in that it provides brief catalog descriptions of women's history collections located in archival repositories throughout the country. Hinding's guide is arranged geographically by state and city and then alphabetically by name of repository within each city. The entries for each repository are further arranged alphabetically by name of collection. A cumulative index permits subject and name searches across repositories. The field-worker who surveyed the Manuscript Division's catalogs, finding aids, and some actual collections in the mid-1970s identified 506 collections relating to women's history.

In 1983–84, division reference librarian Marianne L. Roos conducted her own survey of the division's catalogs and indexes and prepared a 276-page unpublished guide to women's history sources in the division. Embracing a broad view of women's history, Roos identified more than fourteen hundred collections containing papers written by or about women. Accompanying her guide are two appendixes that sort the collections by occupation of the men and women represented, and a third appendix that indicates which collections contain correspondence and which include diaries or journals. Roos's draft guide is available for use in the reading room. It lacks an index, but patient readers will be rewarded with revealing references to women in collections not usually considered prime sources for women's history.[8]

Another, more narrowly focused guide to the Manuscript Division's women's history collections is Roy R. Thomas's *The Progressive Era and World War I, 1896–1920: A Bibliography of Manuscript Sources Selected from the Library of Congress Collections* (Washington: Catholic University of America, 1972; Z1244.T47), which describes more than seven hundred division collections, including seventy collections of women's personal papers, organizational records, and family papers. The full guide is available in the General Collections. An unpublished copy of the women's history subset is in the Manuscript Division.

Although it is not possible to list them all here, numerous published articles about individual collections have appeared in both the *Quarterly Journal of the Library of Congress,*[9] 1943–83 (before 1964 titled *Quarterly Journal of Current Acquisitions*) and in the annual *Library of Congress Acquisitions: Manuscript Division* (1979–present). The latter publication also lists and summarizes all annual receipts. Other divisional guides containing references to women's papers are cited elsewhere in this chapter, and a separate guide to women's diaries is under way. Researchers interested in diaries should consult with the division's reference staff.

SELECTED COLLECTIONS

The breadth and depth of the division's holdings preclude compiling an exhaustive list of women's history sources in this chapter. Instead, the following ten sections attempt to identify the division's major collecting areas and to describe some of the significant women's papers in each category. Many collections could easily have appeared in more than one category, reflective of the many roles and interests of their creators, but such overlap was resisted in favor of highlighting the collection's main emphasis. Collections of men's papers are also included, but since virtually every collection in the division contains at least some correspondence with women, references to men's papers are generally limited to the most relevant examples within each topic. Special access tools are noted when appropriate, and researchers are encouraged to consult the Library's catalog and reference librarians for additional information. The names of cited collections appear in boldface to assist researchers in seeking additional information or requesting access to materials. The item count and span dates of the collections are also provided, as are the birth and death dates of most of the women whose papers are described.

Microfilm editions of original manuscript materials held in other repositories are not described in this chapter, but a search of the Library of Congress Online Catalog will identify titles that are available for use in the Manuscript Reading Room. The accessibility of such microfilm allows scholars to consult in one research trip various women's history sources scattered across the country. It permits, for example, the researcher interested in Jane Addams to consult both the microfilm edition of her papers held by Swarthmore College as well as original items relating to her in this division's Breckinridge Family Papers. It enables researchers studying women's roles in antilynching campaigns to access this division's original records of the National Association for the Advancement of Colored People at the same time they consult the microfilm records of the Association of Southern Women for the Prevention of Lynching held at Atlanta University's Robert W. Woodruff Library. Many of the microfilm editions held by the Manuscript Division were produced by commercial vendors and acquired through copyright deposit, including the series *Women's Studies Manuscript Collections from the Schlesinger Library, Radcliffe College* and the important multirepository compilations *Grassroots Women's Organizations* and *Southern Women and Their Families in the 19th Century: Papers and Diaries.*

Women's Suffrage

The long and difficult struggle for women's suffrage is one of the best-documented, most widely researched, and most seriously debated topics in American women's history. That historians know as much as they do about the suffrage campaign is in large part because of its participants' conscious efforts to record their movement's history. In the late 1870s, in the very midst of their campaign, leading suffragists Susan B. Anthony, Elizabeth Cady Stanton, and Matilda Joslyn Gage began chronicling the movement in *The History of Woman Suffrage,* published in three monumental volumes between 1881 and 1886. The early leaders supplemented this history by publishing various autobiographies and memoirs and by assiduously collecting clippings, books, and pamphlets about their efforts.

In 1903 Librarian of Congress Ainsworth Rand Spofford convinced his friend **Susan B. Anthony** (1820–1906) to donate her collection of books and other printed matter to the national library, where they now reside in the Rare Book and Special Collections Division (see chapter 4). Following receipt of these printed sources, the Library's curators began amassing manuscripts, photographs, and other papers relating to the struggle for women's rights, assembling in the process a compelling documentary history of the suffrage campaign from its early connections to the abolition and temperance campaigns (see "Reform" below) to its final victory in August 1920.

Among the first suffrage manuscripts acquired were the papers of Anthony's close friend and colleague **Elizabeth Cady Stanton** (1815–1902), who had launched the suffrage campaign by "sending forth that daring declaration of rights" at the country's first women's rights convention in Seneca Falls, New York, in 1848.[10] Four portfolios of Stanton documents accompanied Anthony's gift to the Library in 1903, to which the Library added other items donated by Stanton's children or purchased from dealers. Today, the Stanton Papers (1,000 items; 1814–1946; bulk 1840–1902) document her efforts on behalf of women's legal status and women's suffrage, the abolition of slavery, civil rights for African Americans, and other nineteenth-century social reform movements. The collection includes an official report and contemporary newspaper clippings relating to the historic 1848 convention, drafts of Stanton's memoirs *Eighty Years and More: Reminiscences, 1815–1897,* and a draft of her controversial *The Woman's Bible,* a critical attack on church authority, which nearly splintered the suffrage movement when published in 1895.

Anthony's personal papers (500 items; 1846–1934; bulk 1846–1906) did not join her book collection at the Library until 1940, when her niece, Lucy E. Anthony, donated a small collection relating to her aunt's interests in abolition and women's education, her campaign for women's property rights and suffrage in New York, and her work with the National Woman Suffrage Association, the organization Anthony and Stanton founded in 1869 when the suffrage movement split into two rival camps at odds about whether to press for a federal women's suffrage amendment or to seek state-by-state enfranchisement. Also included are six scrapbooks compiled by Anthony's younger sister Mary, containing a valuable compilation of newspaper clippings, convention programs, and other contemporary accounts, which would be impossible to reassemble today.

Joining Stanton and Anthony as the third member of the nineteenth-century suffrage triumvirate was **Lucy Stone** (1818–1893). Two years after Stanton and Lucretia Mott organized the 1848 convention, Stone helped coordinate the first national American women's rights convention, held in Worcester, Massachusetts. For many years, Stone earned a living as an antislavery and women's rights lecturer, and from 1872 until her death in 1893, she coedited with her husband, Henry Brown Blackwell, the premier women's suffrage newspaper, the *Woman's Journal.* Stone's papers and those of her husband are held in the division's **Blackwell Family** Papers (29,000 items; 1759–1960; bulk 1845–90). They include information about the couple's famous wedding ceremony, in which they eliminated the bridal vow "to obey" and circulated a written protest against nineteenth-century marriage laws, which denied women all legal standing. The collection is an important source on the early suffrage movement, its connections to the abolitionist cause, and its unsuccessful campaign for a universal suffrage amendment as part of the American Equal Rights Association. Also documented is the movement's split after the Civil War into the American Woman Suffrage Association led by Stone, Blackwell, and Julia Ward Howe, and the National Woman Suffrage Association led by Stanton and Anthony.

The Blackwell Family Papers document the national suffrage movement with a special emphasis on New England, whereas the papers (300 items; 1869–1905) of Michigan suffragist **Olivia Bigelow Hall** (1823–1908?) provide a picture of the local suffrage scene. In the last third of the nineteenth century, Hall organized meetings in her hometown of Ann Arbor, obtained speakers for rallies there, and corresponded with national leaders Susan B. Anthony, Anna Howard Shaw, Carrie Chapman Catt, and members of the American Equal Rights Association and National Woman Suffrage Association.

In 1890, the competing wings of the women's suffrage movement reunited as the National American Woman Suffrage Association. Ideological differences remained, but the need for two national organizations seemed less important to a new generation of women entering the movement, including Stone's daughter, **Alice Stone Blackwell** (1857–1950), and Stanton's daughter, Harriot Stanton Blatch, both of whom helped to broker the merger. Alice Stone Blackwell's papers, dating from 1848 to 1957, constitute the largest group in the **Blackwell Family** Papers, and they reflect her significant role in the women's suffrage movement, her editorship of the *Woman's Journal,* and her literary endeavors translating and promoting the work of Armenian, Russian, and Spanish poets.

Harriot Stanton Blatch (1856–1940) helped to pave the way for the 1890 merger by insisting ten years earlier that her mother and Anthony include a discussion of Stone and the American Woman Suffrage Association in their *History of Woman Suffrage.* They consented and asked Blatch to write the chapter. She later helped to revitalize the suffrage movement in the early 1900s, when she returned to the United States after living in England for many years and introduced to

American suffragists some of the militant street tactics that characterized the British campaign. As founder of the Equality League of Self-Supporting Women (later renamed the Women's Political Union), Blatch attempted, at least initially, to blend varying class interests of suffragists and was successful in pushing a suffrage amendment through the New York state legislature in 1913, which became law four years later by state referendum. Her papers (14 volumes; 1907–15) document the New York campaign, the centennial celebration of her mother's birth, and her efforts to bring Emmeline Pankhurst and other British suffragists on speaking tours of the United States. A third source of information about the 1890 merger is the papers of **William Dudley Foulke** (2,500 items; ca. 1470–1952; bulk 1868–1935), president of the American Woman Suffrage Association from 1886 to 1890 and chairman of the woman's suffrage congress at the World's Columbian Exposition in Chicago in 1893.

Through the efforts of Blackwell, Blatch, Foulke, and others, the **National American Woman Suffrage Association** (NAWSA) came into existence and exerted an immediate impact on the movement, leading to suffrage victories in Wyoming, Colorado, Idaho, and Utah in the 1890s. Although most of the material in the NAWSA records (26,700 items; 1839–1961) dates from 1890 to 1930, the collection includes some information on the movement's early pioneers, including Anthony, Stanton, Sarah M. Grimké, Julia Ward Howe, Mary A. Livermore, Lucretia Mott, and Emma Willard. More recent leaders include Ida Husted Harper, Mary Garrett Hay, Belle Case La Follette, Maud Wood Park, Mary Gray Peck, Rosika Schwimmer, and Anna Howard Shaw. Of particular note in the records are progress reports from affiliated state and local suffrage organizations, papers relating to the work of the Congressional Union (which later became the National Woman's Party), literature on antisuffrage groups, information about international suffrage leaders and alliances, and files relating to suffrage songs and plays. (See chapter 4 for information on NAWSA's working library.)

Included among the NAWSA manuscript materials are items relating to the Leslie Woman Suffrage Commission, which was established by NAWSA president Carrie Chapman Catt (1859–1947) with a one-million-dollar bequest she inherited in 1914 from newspaper publisher Miriam Florence Leslie. Catt appointed journalist Ida Husted Harper to the commission's newly created Leslie Bureau of Suffrage Education, with the job of generating press releases and reports in favor of the federal suffrage amendment and responding to editorials critical of women's suffrage and of the tactics used by the NAWSA's militant offshoot organization, the National Woman's Party. In addition to the NAWSA materials, Harper's work is documented in a separate Manuscript Division collection of **Leslie Woman Suffrage Commission** Records (1,200 items; 1911–18).

The records of the **National Woman's Party** (438,400 items; 1891–1974) trace the development of that organization from its beginnings in late 1912 when Alice Paul and Lucy Burns, young Americans who had worked with the Pankhursts in the British suffrage movement, sought appointments on the lethargic NAWSA Congressional Committee so that they could work toward passage of a federal suffrage amendment. Their first activity was to organize the massive March 3, 1913, national suffrage parade (see "Marching for the Vote" in this volume), which was followed by other efforts to increase pressure on Congress and President Woodrow Wilson. Finding themselves at odds with the NAWSA leadership, Paul and Burns left the Congressional Committee in late 1913 to form the Congressional Union, a NAWSA affiliate that became independent of the parent body in February 1914 and was later reorganized as the National Woman's Party (NWP) in June 1916.

The NWP records held by the division are divided into three major groups. Group I, dating mainly 1912–20, covers all aspects of the party's suffrage campaign, including its use of pickets, parades, demonstrations, arrests, hunger-strikes, and other "militant" tactics. Hundreds of photographs of individuals, groups, and events are found here. Groups II and III date from 1913 to 1974 and include some suffrage material but relate primarily to the organization's post-1920 initiatives, principally its efforts to gain passage of a federal Equal Rights Amendment (ERA), drafted by Paul and first introduced in Congress in December 1923. The organization also fought successfully for more favorable nationality laws and equal citizenship rights for women, including the Cable Act of 1922 and its subsequent revisions, the Dickstein-Copeland Bill of 1934 and the Equal Nationality Treaty of 1934. State laws also came under the NWP's review, and the organization's Legal Research Department prepared extensive reports on women's legal status in each state and drafted bills for state legislatures concerning parents' custody rights, jury service, property rights, reinstatement of maiden name after marriage, divorce rights, estate administration, and guardianship issues. The dissolution of the NWP in the early 1990s, following a contentious internal legal fight, may be traced in the records of the **Woman's Party Corporation** (11,480 items; 1918–98; bulk 1985–95).

Through the combined efforts of the NAWSA, the NWP, and scores of state and local suffrage organizations, a final successful push toward suffrage was mounted in the 1910s. Key to this victory was NAWSA president Carrie Chapman Catt's secret "Winning Plan," a well-executed, two-pronged attack that called for the careful coordination of state work with a new lobbying effort in Washington for a federal amendment. Details about Catt's strategy may be found in the NAWSA records as well as in the **Carrie Chapman Catt** Papers (9,500 items; 1848–1950; bulk 1890–1920), which reflect her steadfast dedication to two major goals–the right of women to vote and world peace. Catt sought to achieve the latter by building on the ties she formed while president of the International Woman Suffrage Alliance from 1904 to 1923.

Also active in the last stages of the suffrage campaign was **Maud Wood Park** (1871–1955), who became the first president of the League of Women Voters. Her collection (3,700 items; 1844–1979; bulk 1886–1951), especially her correspondence with her second husband, Robert F. Hunter, is a particularly rich source of information on the tactics, strategy, and ideology of the suffrage and early women's rights movement. Concerned with preserving the movement's history, Park corresponded with many of the women involved, collected information about them, and supported efforts to create collections of women's rights materials at both Radcliffe College in Cambridge, Massachusetts, and the Library of Congress.

Other collections relating to the twentieth-century suffrage campaign include two that concern the national movement as well as aspects of the local campaign in the District of Columbia. As a member of the NWP, **Anna Kelton Wiley** (1877–1964) was arrested and jailed for picketing the White House in 1917. She served two terms as chairman of the party in the early 1930s and 1940s and edited its periodical *Equal Rights* for five years. Wiley was the consummate Washington, D.C., club woman, holding memberships in more than forty organizations, many of which are documented in her voluminous papers (110,000 items; 1798–1964; bulk 1925–60), as are her activities on behalf of women's rights, Indian rights, consumer protection, and improved child care.

Mary Church Terrell (1863–1954) cofounded the National Association of Colored Women in 1896 and became its first president. Her papers (13,000 items; 1851–1962; bulk 1886–1954) are a valuable source of information on African American women's involvement in the campaigns for women's suffrage and the Equal Rights Amendment. They reflect the key roles she played in the National Woman's Party, NAWSA, and the Women's International League for Peace and Freedom. They document, too, her work as a member of the District of Columbia School Board (1895–1911), as an adviser to the Republican Party during the 1920s and 1930s, and as chairman in the 1940s of the Coordinating Committee for the Enforcement of the D.C. Anti-Discrimination Laws, which challenged the legality of segregated restaurants and movie theaters in the nation's capital. Among Terrell's many correspondents were important black women leaders such as Mary McLeod Bethune, Nannie Helen Burroughs, and Addie W. Hunton. Related information may be found in the papers of Terrell's husband, **Robert H. Terrell** (2,750 items; 1870–1925; bulk 1884–1925).

Dozens of other manuscript collections also contain information relating to women's suffrage, including the papers of various presidents and members of Congress, some of which are mentioned later in this chapter. Other collections may be found by skimming relevant finding aids and by searching for the term "suffrage movement" in the index to this volume and for "women suffrage" in LCOC.

Reform

Complementing the division's suffrage collections are numerous materials documenting women's involvement in the nineteenth-century abolition and temperance movements as well as their work in twentieth-century campaigns for African American civil rights, women's reproductive rights, and a host of Progressive reform initiatives. Women's reform efforts brought them into arenas and activities often thought to be outside women's proper sphere. Most of the reformers represented in the division's collections were from the middle and upper classes, but their papers and those of the organizations they founded have been successfully used by historians studying the con-

Julia Bracken Wendt. Drawing of the National Women's Trade Union League seal, ca. 1908–9. National Women's Trade Union League Records (oversize cabinet 2, drawer 1). Manuscript Division. LC-MS-34363-1.

The National Women's Trade Union League, founded in 1903 to improve women's working conditions through protective legislation and to secure their right to organize and bargain collectively, differed from other social reform organizations in that its members included both working women and their middle-class allies. Within a few short years of its modest beginnings, the league began to exert considerable political influence and acquired the visual representations of officialdom, including a newly patented seal. At an executive board meeting in March 1909 and again six months later at the league's national convention, the organization's secretary reported that the new seal, drawn by Chicago sculptor Julia Bracken Wendt (1871–1942), had "brought about most happy results." The seal was added to the national office's letterhead, became "increasingly popular with all the Local leagues on all their publications," was fashioned into a pin, and—most satisfying of all—was reproduced and framed at Samuel Gompers's request to hang in his presidential office at the headquarters of the American Federation of Labor in Washington, D.C.

fluence of class and gender and analyzing elite attitudes toward the people they hoped to assist or reform or both.

Many early suffragists, including Susan B. Anthony, Elizabeth Cady Stanton, and members of the Blackwell family, participated in the abolition campaign, and their papers illustrate the adoption of techniques and strategies from that struggle for use in the women's suffrage crusade. The papers of **Julia Ward Howe** (1819–1910) and **Anna E. Dickinson** (1842–1932) also show the overlap in the two movements. Howe's papers (200 items; 1845–1917) consist chiefly of speeches and writings, many pertaining to her wide-ranging interests in education, immigration, prison reform, and race relations. Dickinson was a teenage phenomenon on the antislavery lecture circuit, whose electrifying speeches made her one of the campaign's most sought-after speakers. Her familiarity with the stage later led to a career as an actress and playwright. As reflected in her papers (10,000 items; 1859–1951; bulk 1859–1911), Dickinson had a particularly close relationship with Susan B. Anthony and shared the latter's interest in women's rights and temperance. She also corresponded with escaped slave and abolitionist orator **Frederick Douglass,** whose own papers (7,400 items; 1841–1967; bulk 1862–95) provide an interesting perspective on women's rights. Douglass collected speeches and articles by Belva A. Lockwood, Ida B. Wells, and Frances Willard, as well as correspondence with such notables as Susan B. Anthony, Clara Barton, Elizabeth Palmer Peabody, and Frances Willard. His collection also contains correspondence of his first wife, Anna Murray Douglass (d. 1882), and his second wife, Helen Pitts Douglass (1838–1903), a lecturer and women's rights activist whom he married in 1884.

Letters from abolitionist Angelina Grimké Weld (1805–1879), discussing her philosophical disagreements with her sister Sarah Grimké, the importance of women's associations, and her reaction to the bloomer costume, are among the papers of her husband, **Theodore Dwight Weld** (32 items; 1783–1888). Similar small collections are available for antislavery stalwarts **Lydia Maria Child** (26 items; 1856–76), **Harriet Beecher Stowe** (14 items; 1866–85), **Frances Wright** (100 items; 1843–96), and **Myrtilla Miner** (see "Education" below). The papers of male abolitionists also contain letters and other documents relating to women's participation in the antislavery campaign. Notable among the division's many holdings in this area are the records of the **Western Anti-Slavery Society** (2 volumes; 1834–58) and the papers of **Henry Ward Beecher** (5,400 items; 1836–86; bulk 1840–65), **Salmon P. Chase** (12,500 items; 1755–1898; bulk 1824–72), **Theodore Parker** (180 items; 1832–1910; bulk 1850–60), **Lewis Tappan** (5,200 items; 1809–1903), **John C. Underwood** (165 items; 1856–98; bulk 1857–72), and **Elizur Wright** (5,300 items; 1793–1935; bulk 1830–85).

Some antislavery proponents—both black and white—believed that freed slaves should be resettled in Africa rather than remain in the United States. The voluminous records of the **American Colonization Society** (190,198 items; 1792–

1964; bulk 1823–1912) document one group's efforts to establish in Liberia a settlement for free blacks. Information about women is scattered throughout the society's records—on passenger lists, in correspondence about potential emigrants, and in documents relating to society members, financial contributors, and slave owners. (For related daguerreotypes, see chapter 6.)

The nineteenth- and early twentieth-century temperance campaign was another reform initiative in which women played a major role. In addition to some of the collections previously cited, three others merit mention. The records of the **Women's Organization for National Prohibition Reform** (350 items; 1896–1933) document that group's efforts to repeal the Eighteenth Amendment because it believed other methods, such as a liquor control system, would be more effective in achieving temperance. The connection between temperance and divorce reform may be traced in the papers of Congregational minister and reformer **Samuel W. Dike** (9,800 items; 1870–1913), which include correspondence and reports of the National Divorce Reform League (later the National League for the Protection of the Family), statistics and news clippings relating to divorce and polygamy, and a few letters from Julia Ward Howe and **Frances Elizabeth Willard** (1839–1898), president of the Women's Christian Temperance Union (WCTU). A separate collection of Willard Papers (18 items; 1889–97) also exists, as does a speech (1 item; 1898) on the WCTU's early years by **Eliza Jane Thompson** (1816–1905).

Besides engaging in the temperance and suffrage movements, women responded to the upheaval and opportunities of turn-of-the-century industrial America, by banding together to form numerous national and local organizations dedicated to enhancing social justice and advancing the general welfare. The Manuscript Division holds the records of a number of these national groups as well as the personal papers of some of the key participants.

Women played a leading role in the work of the **National Consumers' League** (NCL), founded in 1899 to coordinate the work of local consumers leagues, which had formed earlier that decade for the purpose of improving the lot of women and child workers through public action. The NCL monitored the conditions under which goods were manufactured and distributed, and it encouraged consumers to use their purchasing power to force employers to provide healthy working conditions and reduce the use of child labor. The league also took an interest in issues of public health, consumer product labeling, and equal pay. Although the organization's records (81,500 items; 1882–1986; bulk 1920–50) primarily concern national office activities, some material is available on state and local leagues. Extensive files relate to the landmark case of *Adkins v. Children's Hospital* (1923), in which the Supreme Court invalidated a District of Columbia minimum wage law; the Equal Rights Amendment, which the league opposed; radiation and radium poisoning among women workers in watch factories; and in the 1950s and 1960s, Mexican American farm laborers and migratory workers. For the period before 1932, the records reflect the major role played by the league's first general secretary, Florence Kelley, but numerous other women reformers and women's organizations are also represented, including Grace Abbott, Molly Dewson, Julia C. Lathrop, and Frances Perkins. Related material may be found in the papers (16 items; 1865–1941) of league investigator **Pauline Dorothea Goldmark** (1873–1962).

Several of the groups reflected in the NCL files are also represented by their own set of archives. The records (7,400 items; 1903–50) of the **National Women's Trade Union League of America** (NWTUL) document that group's struggle to improve working conditions for women in industry and to ensure their right to organize and bargain collectively. From its founding in Boston in 1903 to its dissolution in 1950, the league supported labor strikes, especially in the garment industry, and lobbied for legislation relating to the eight-hour day, minimum wages, federal aid to education, civil rights, and social security. Correspondents include Mary E. Dreier, Pauline M. Newman, Margaret Dreier Robins, and Rose Schneiderman.

The **National Council of Jewish Women** (NCJW) was organized in 1893 at the conclusion of the World's Parliament of Religions held in conjunction with the World's Columbian Exposition in Chicago. Its two primary goals were social reform and the promotion of Judaism among women. Special concerns emerged with each decade of the council's existence, and these topics are documented in the files of both the national office (48,000 items; 1893–1989; bulk 1940–81) and the Washington, D.C., office, established in 1944 for the purposes of lobbying Congress (169,200 items; 1924–81; bulk 1944–77). Issues include child care, education, foreign economic assistance, food and nutrition, immigration, international relations, Jewish culture, nuclear warfare, and women's rights. In the 1950s, the council coordinated a Freedom Campaign against McCarthyism. Civil rights and sex discrimination took precedence in the 1960s, and abortion and the Equal Rights Amendment gained prominence in the 1970s.

Documentation on the early history of the NCJW may be found in a small collection of papers (2,000 items; 1817–1986; bulk 1892–1942) relating to its first president, **Hannah G. Solomon** (1858–1942). Most of the papers relate to Solomon's position as chair of the Jewish Women's Congress at the World's Parliament of Religions and her role in founding the NCJW with social worker Sadie American. Of particular note is the correspondence between American and Solomon discussing the women's efforts to establish local sections and reflecting the tension within the council as it struggled to decide whether to focus on social welfare work or religious education. In 1904, Solomon represented the NCJW at the Berlin conference of the **International Council of Women** (ICW), which had been formed in 1888 as a part of the Peace and Disarmament Committee of the Women's International Organisations. A small body of ICW records (4,200 items; 1931–57) pertain to that committee and to several international conferences.

Once women's suffrage was secured, the National American Woman Suffrage Association (see "Women's Suffrage" above) regrouped as the **League of Women Voters** (514,400 items; 1884–1986; bulk 1920–79) and directed its focus toward many of the same social and political issues that occupied other women's groups. Its emphasis was on educating voters, particularly newly enfranchised women, about candidates and campaign issues, especially relating to child labor and welfare, citizen participation, civil rights, consumer affairs, environmental concerns, ratification of the Equal Rights Amendment, immigration, labor, national security, and women's legal status and rights. In addition to promoting its own programs, the league was also a prime mover behind the **Women's Joint Congressional Committee** (WJCC) (6,200 items; 1920–70; bulk 1920–53), an umbrella organization of various women's and social reform groups that was formed in 1920 to serve as an information clearinghouse and lobbying force for pending federal legislation. Among the charter members were the League of Women Voters, National Consumers' League, National Women's Trade Union League of America, National Council of Jewish Women, and six other groups. More organizations joined a few years later to promote legislation against lynching and for maternity and infant health protection (including support for the 1921 Sheppard-Towner Act), independent citizenship for married women (as partially realized in the 1922 Cable Act), funding for the federal women's and children's bureaus, and creation of a Department of Education.

One group that did not join the WJCC was the National Woman's Party (NWP), the leading proponent of the Equal Rights Amendment (ERA), which NWP chair Alice Paul had drafted in 1923. The WJCC resisted the ERA as a threat to the sex-based protective labor legislation that its members had fought for years to secure. Several decades passed before the influential League of Women Voters and other former WJCC members supported the ERA, which Congress did not pass until 1972 (see "The Long Road to Equality" in this volume). Aspects of the failed struggle to ratify the amendment may be traced in the records of **ERAmerica** (62,300 items; 1976–82), a nationwide alliance of about 200 civic, labor, church, and women's groups founded in 1976. The organization mounted major campaigns in Illinois, Oklahoma, and key southern states, as reflected in the files of honorary cochairs Liz Carpenter and Elly Peterson, and of various other staff members. Materials from anti-ERA organizations, such as the Eagle Forum and Moral Majority, are also found here, as are files on issues that became linked to the ERA, such as abortion, comparable worth, and pension rights of former military spouses.

Women's involvement in the twentieth-century civil rights movement is another aspect of reform particularly well documented by the division's holdings—both in the papers of individuals and in the records of numerous organizations. One of the largest and most frequently consulted collections consists of the records of the **National Association for the Advancement of Colored People** (2,575,375 items; 1842–1992; bulk 1919–78). Founded in 1908 as the National Negro Committee, a biracial protest group, the NAACP developed into the nation's premier civil rights organization, focusing much of its attention on obtaining legal equality for African Americans. Women have played a key role in the association from its earliest beginnings, and material by and about women appears throughout the collection. Of particular importance are the diaries, correspondence, and other papers of Mary White Ovington (1865–1951), one of the group's founders, who in her forty years with the organization served as an officer of the New York City branch, national secretary, and chairman of the board. Other officials include Daisy Bates, Mildred Bond, Hazel Bowman, Serena Davis, Joan Franklin, Addie W. Hunton, Ruby Hurley, Daisy Lampkin, Catharine D. Lealtad, Juanita Jackson Mitchell, Constance Baker Motley, June Shagaloff, and Althea T. L. Simmons. The collection's voluminous finding aid lists numerous women correspondents, including Mary McLeod Bethune, Myrlie B. Evers, and Pauli Murray, and files on the National Training School for Girls, the National Woman's Party, women's suffrage, the Equal Rights Amendment, the Women's Army Auxiliary Corps, and the Young Women's Christian Association.

For fund-raising and tax purposes, the NAACP established in 1939 the **NAACP Legal Defense and Educational Fund** (1,057,500 items; 1915–87; bulk 1940–87), the records of which cover many of the same topics found in the files of the parent organization. Of interest to women's historians are the papers of attorney Constance Baker Motley (b. 1921), an expert in housing issues; materials relating to Josephine Baker's discriminatory treatment; and files concerning the fund's handling of rape cases.

In 1910, just two years after the creation of the NAACP, three New York City welfare organizations merged to become the National League on Urban Conditions among Negroes, later the **National Urban League** (NUL). The division holds the records of the NUL's national headquarters (483,600 items; 1910–86; bulk 1930–79), Washington, D.C., bureau (26,100 items; 1961–85) and southern regional office (106,600 items; 1900–1988; bulk 1943–78). Among these materials are the personal papers (1931–86) of league employee Ann Taneyhill; files on Marian Anderson, Isobel Chisholm, and Malvina Hoffman; and information on aid to dependent children, black women in World War II, Camp Fire Girls, child care, Delta Sigma Theta Sorority, domestic workers, African American social workers, and the Young Women's Christian Association. The Southern Regional Office records contain files on Bethune-Cookman College, the Big Brother and Big Sister movement, and the Women in Non-Traditional Jobs Program.

Although labor issues and labor unions came under the purview of both the NAACP and NUL,

#17

The summer after my marriage I was desperately ill and my life was despaired of. My recovery was nothing short of a miracle and my case is recorded in medical history. In five years we lost three babies, one after another, shortly after birth, which was a great blow both to Mr. Terrell and myself.

The maternal instinct was always abnormally developed in me. As far back as I can remember, I have been very fond of children. I can not recall that I have ever seen a baby, no matter what its color, class or condition, no matter whether it was homely or beautiful, no matter whether it was clad in rags or more dainty divinity that I did not think it was cunning and dear. When, therefore, my third baby died two days after birth, I literally sank down to the very depths of despair.

For months I could not divert my thoughts however hard I tried. I could not read understandingly. It was impossible for me to fix my mind on what I saw in print. When I reached the bottom of a page in a book, I knew no more about its contents than did some one who had never seen it. Right after its birht the baby had been placed in an improvised incubator and I was tormented by the thought that if the genuine article had been used its little life might have been saved. I could not help feeling that the methods used in caring [illegible] my baby had caused its untimely end.

A few of my friends were unable to understand how a woman could grieve so deeply as I did over the death of a baby that had lived only a few days. But I sometimes think a woman suffers as much, when she loses her baby at birth, as does a mother who loses a baby which she has had much longer. There is the bitter disappointment of never having enjoyed the infant to whose coming the mother has looked forward so long and upon which she has built such fond hopes.

Acting upon my physician's advice I left home, where everything reminded me of my sorrow and visited my dear, sunny mother in New York. She would not allow me to talk about my baby's death and scouted the idea that its life might have been saved. Nobody could remain long in the company of my mother with her cheerful disposition and hearty, infectious laugh without being cheered and encouraged, no matter how unhappy he or she had previously been. This short visit to my mother did much for me physically, spiritually and mentally. Many a human being has lost his reason, because he has allowed himself to brood over his trouble indefinitely, when a slight change of scene and companionship might have saved it.

Mary Church Terrell. "A Colored Woman in a White World." Draft manuscript. Mary Church Terrell Papers (container 36). Manuscript Division. LC-MS-42549-3.

A graduate of Oberlin College and a Washington, D.C., educator and community activist, Mary Church Terrell (1863–1954) devoted her entire life to speaking out against racial injustice and women's inequality. As the first African American woman to serve on the District of Columbia School Board and as cofounder of the National Association of Colored Women, Terrell encountered and overcame numerous obstacles during her lifetime. In her 1919 diary (held in private hands), she wrote of her intention to pen an autobiography in which she would "be courageous and tell everything," but the resulting 1940 publication, *A Colored Woman in a White World,* reflected the tendency of most public figures to be more circumspect in published form than in private correspondence and diaries. Nevertheless, the raw emotion of losing three children within her first five years of marriage is very much evident in this draft page from Terrell's book. Difficult pregnancies, death from childbirth, and the loss of young children were facts of life for many American women, but such afflictions were even more prevalent among the poor and disadvantaged. As Terrell suggests in this manuscript, she believed that her babies might have survived had she and her infant children received better medical care than was available in Washington's segregated hospital system. (Diary quoted from Dorothy Sterling's biographical essay on Terrell in *Notable American Women: The Modern Period,* ed. Barbara Sicherman and Carol Hurd Green [Cambridge: Belknap Press of Harvard University Press, 1980], 680.)

those topics are more fully explored in the records of the **Brotherhood of Sleeping Car Porters** (BSCP) (41,000 items; 1920–68; bulk 1950–68) and in the personal papers of the brotherhood's founder **A. Philip Randolph** (13,000 items; 1909–79; bulk 1941–68). Women are not the focus of either collection, but both sources contain financial records and miscellaneous papers relating to the BSCP's Ladies Auxiliary. In addition, the BSCP records contain information on the work of railroad maids and correspondence from such prominent women as Josephine Baker, Mary McLeod Bethune, Freda Kirchwey, Eartha Kitt, and Anna M. Rosenberg.

Nearly twenty-five years after establishing the BSCP, Randolph joined Roy Wilkins and Arnold Aronson in founding the **Leadership Conference on Civil Rights** (93,350 items; 1943–91; bulk 1960–87), a coalition of more than one hundred national organizations dedicated to the enactment and enforcement of civil rights legislation on the federal level. Yvonne Braithwaite, Shirley Chisholm, Patricia Roberts Harris, Coretta Scott King, Esther Peterson, Natalie P. Shear, and Glenda Sloan are among the correspondents, while subject files of interest are titled affirmative action, displaced homemakers, Equal Rights Amendment, International Women's Year, women's rights, women's issues, and World Conference of the United Nations Decade for Women. Dozens of women's organizations are also represented in the collection, including such diverse groups as B'nai B'rith Women, National Association of Colored Women's Clubs, National Council of Catholic Women, and Women's Legal Defense Fund.

In 1970 civil rights lawyer William L. Taylor established the **Center for National Policy Review** (50,300 items; 1959–86; bulk 1971–85) to monitor the government's enforcement of and compliance with federal civil rights laws. Coming under the center's consideration were the Women in Construction Compliance Monitoring Project, Title IX, sex and pregnancy discrimination, the feminization of poverty, and the Equal Rights Amendment.

In addition to organizational records, the division holds the personal papers of numerous individuals active in civil rights and social reform. Some of these collections are described elsewhere in this chapter, including the papers of **Belle Case La Follette** and **Fola La Follette** (Congressional Collections); **Alice Stone Blackwell, Carrie Chapman Catt, Anna Kelton Wiley,** and **Mary Church Terrell** (Suffrage); **Nannie Helen Burroughs, Charl Ormond Williams, Booker T. Washington,** and members of the **Moton Family** (Education); and **Margaret Sanger** and other public health activists (Science and Medicine). Others are described immediately below.

Social worker and lawyer Sophonisba Preston Breckinridge (1866–1948), author of *Women in the Twentieth Century: A Study of Their Political, Social, and Economic Activities* (1933), became the first dean of the University of Chicago School of Civics and Philanthropy (later the School of Social Service Administration) in 1907. An adviser to both Grace Abbott and Jane Addams, Breckinridge was affiliated with the Immigrants Protective League and was an expert on issues of public welfare, delinquent children, and juvenile court legislation. Her papers and those of her sister-in-law, Madeline McDowell Breckinridge (1872–1920), a women's rights activist and reformer, are part of the **Breckinridge Family** Papers (205,000 items; 1752–1965).

Another large collection of family papers, relating to the **Grosvenor Family** (67,300 items; 1827–1981; bulk 1872–1964) of Massachusetts and Washington, D.C., documents the community work of Elsie May Grosvenor (1878–1964), including her support for the Clarke School for the Deaf, her advocacy of women's suffrage, and her campaign for pure milk. The **Hale Family** Papers (7,500 items; 1698–1916; bulk 1810–1909) contain more than three thousand love letters exchanged between Edward Everett Hale, a married Unitarian clergyman, and his much younger assistant, Harriet E. Freeman, a financially independent single woman who was active in efforts to preserve forest lands and to protect the rights of Native Americans. Social reformer **Charlotte Everett Wise Hopkins** (1851–1935) served as chairman of the District of Columbia section of the woman's department of the National Civic Federation. Her small collection (150 items; 1916–18) concerns a host of municipal reform efforts in the areas of housing, pure milk, garbage collection, playgrounds, juvenile delinquency, and war relief. Reformer and nurse **Ellen Newbold La Motte** (1873–1961) collected reports and other materials relating to international drug trafficking and her interest in curbing drug abuse, particularly opium addiction (360 items; 1919–33).

Leading postwar philosopher and political scientist **Hannah Arendt** (1906–1975) fled Nazi Germany for Paris in 1933, worked with the Jewish Agency for Palestine, and was detained in a concentration camp before succeeding in emigrating to the United States in 1941. In the United States, she continued her career as a lecturer, writer, social critic, and college educator. Topics covered in her papers (28,000 items; 1898–1977; bulk 1948–77) include the Holocaust, education, violence, justice, and women's liberation.

In 1980, **Anne B. Turpeau** (b. 1924) and **Faith Berry** (b. 1939) were part of the American delegation to the World Conference of the United Nations Decade for Women in Copenhagen, Denmark. Turpeau, a social activist affiliated with the Washington Urban League and the District of Columbia Commission for Women, collected files (20,000 items; 1915–86; bulk 1960–86) relating to the UN conference and to numerous African American women's groups, including the Organization of Black Activist Women, Black Women's Agenda, and National Council of Negro Women. Berry's papers (2,500 items; 1963–84; bulk 1971–83), on the other hand, primarily relate to her research on the life and literary career of poet Langston Hughes and her work as media coordinator for the President's Advisory Committee for Women.

The work of women reformers may also be researched through the papers of male colleagues. One such example is social reformer **John Adams Kingsbury** (57,400 items; 1841–1966; bulk 1906–39), director of the New York Association for Improving the Condition of the Poor and commissioner of Public Charities of New York City. Kingsbury corresponded with Jane Addams, Mary E. Dreier, Alice Hamilton, Helen Keller, Frances Perkins, Margaret Sanger, Lillian Wald, and others about various public health issues, unemployment, welfare, and world peace. His papers also include letters his maternal grandparents exchanged during the 1840s and 1850s and school papers and correspondence of his mother from the 1860s to 1880s.

Education

Campaigns to improve the quality of women's primary education and to ensure their access to schools of higher learning were among some of the first reform efforts undertaken by women. Great debates raged as to the amount and content of schooling women should receive. Women's physical and mental capacities came into question, and their struggle to gain admittance to predominantly male schools and programs has continued to this day.

In 1804, Washington society leader **Margaret Bayard Smith** (1778–1844) lamented how her "passionate fondness for reading" was "opposed by circumstances and the friends with whom [she] lived" who oversaw her education. She declared that "had I been a boy and conducted regularly through the paths of science—how much more useful—how much more happy might I have been!"[11] Obstacles such as those described by Smith and other aspects of women's education and their entry into the teaching ranks may be explored in a host of collections held by the Manuscript Division. The topic, in fact, is an overwhelming one, since more than 330 collections are identified when searching the catalog for the term "educators." Division collections are replete with notebooks, letters, and diaries written by girls and young women while in school. Many of the women whose papers are described elsewhere in this chapter retained documents from their school days, and these materials are usually identified in the finding aids for those collections. Family papers often include information on women's education; see especially the papers of the **Bancroft-Bliss Family** (5,800 items; 1788–1928; bulk 1815–75); **Alexander Graham Bell Family** (147,700 items; 1834–1974); **Montgomery Family** (12 items; 1872–1938); **Pratt Family** (2 volumes; 1802–08); **Singleton Family** (900 items; 1758–1860; bulk 1829–55); **Willard Family** (119,900 items; 1800–1968; bulk 1890–1954); and the various families in the **Marian S. Carson** Collection (14,250 items; ca. 1650–1995; bulk 1700–1876).[12] Also of note are early nineteenth-century student work books kept by **Bathsheba Barton** (1 item; 1819); **Ann Maria Churchill** (3 items; ca. 1830); **Sarah Hall** (1 item; 1813); and **Caroline Dana Jarvis** (1 item; 1819).

One aspect of women's education that is especially well documented is the founding of schools for African American women. Abolitionist **Myrtilla Miner** (1815–1864) overcame local opposition to establish and maintain the Miner School for Free Colored Girls in antebellum Washington, D.C., in 1851. Her papers (600 items; 1825–1950; bulk 1851–58) contain student essays and correspondence, including exchanges with prominent abolitionists and with novelists Emma Dorothy Eliza Nevitte Southworth and Harriet Beecher Stowe, relating to the school and to Miner's interests in feminism, spiritualism, hydrotherapy, and alternative medical treatments. Sharing Miner's initiative was **Lucy Salisbury Doolittle** (1832–1908), who in the 1860s obtained funds from the New York National Freedman's Relief Association and opened an industrial school for black women in the Georgetown neighborhood of the District of Columbia. All that remains of Doolittle's papers (11 items; 1864–67) are a few letters and a notebook recording class attendance and students' completion of sewing assignments.

More than fifty years after Miner's and Doolittle's pioneering efforts, African American educator and religious leader **Nannie Helen Burroughs** (1879–1961) founded a trade school for young black women in Washington, D.C. Records relating to the National Training School for Women and Girls (later the National Trade and Professional School for Women and Girls), established in 1909, may be found in the Burroughs collection (110,000 items; 1900–1963; bulk 1928–60), which also contains material concerning her activities with the National Baptist Convention, National League of Republican Colored Women, and National Association of Wage Earners.

A contemporary of Burroughs, **Charl Ormond Williams** (1885–1969), was active in the field of education and educational reform through her association with the National Education Association and her participation in the 1944 White House Conference on Rural Education. Her papers (3,200 items; 1924–59; bulk 1935–45), including correspondence with Mary Ritter Beard, Mary McLeod Bethune, Clare Boothe Luce, and Margaret Chase Smith, relate to those issues and to school segregation, the Democratic Party, and the 1944 White House Conference on How Women May Share in Post-War Policy Making.

Industrial education and occupational training for black women and girls are topics that also appear in the papers of several educators affiliated with Tuskegee Institute in Alabama. The voluminous papers of Tuskegee's founder **Booker T. Washington** (375,550 items; 1853–1946; bulk 1900–1915) contain records of the school's Women's Department and files relating to women's industries, industries for girls, and hospital and nurses' training. As one of the premier black leaders of his generation, Washington corresponded with many prominent women activists, reformers, and educators, including Jane Addams, Alice Stone Blackwell, Nannie Helen Burroughs, Alice Moore Dunbar, Helen Keller, Ida M. Tarbell, and Mary Church Terrell.

Washington's successor as president of Tuskegee was Robert Russa Moton, whose papers are included with those of his wife, educator Jennie Dee Booth Moton (1880–1942), and their daughter, government official Charlotte Moton Hubbard (1911–1994). The **Moton Family** Papers (8,700 items; 1850–1991; bulk 1930–40) document the family's efforts to promote educational and economic opportunities for African Americans and to improve race relations. Under Robert Moton's leadership, Tuskegee developed from a vocational and agricultural high school into a fully accredited college. Jennie Moton served briefly as director of the school's Department of Women's Industries and later was a field agent for the Agricultural Adjustment Administration (AAA) and president of the National Association of Colored Women (NACW). Her AAA files include correspondence, statistical reports, and narrative accounts of her activities among black Americans in the rural South, and her NACW files include correspondence with Jessie Daniel Ames, Bertha LaBranche Johnson, and Charlotte Payne. When Charlotte Moton Hubbard was appointed deputy assistant secretary of state for public affairs in 1964, she became the highest-ranking black woman in President Lyndon Johnson's administration, a testament to her many years of work in education, community relations, and government service. Other African American educators whose papers are of interest to women's historians include third Tuskegee president **Frederick D. Patterson** (15,000 items; 1861–1988; bulk 1965–88) and civil rights leader and pioneer researcher in African American history **Lorenzo Johnston Greene** (44,100 items; 1680–1988; bulk 1933–72).

African Americans are not, however, the only group whose educational activities are represented in the division's holdings. Education and social customs of the native people of Alaska are reflected in two collections. A diary and papers (10 items; 1910–12) kept by **Clara Ellen Tarte Davenport** (1885–1974) and her husband, **Noah Cleveland Davenport,** recount their voyage from Seattle, Washington, to the Aleutian island village of Unalaska and their teaching experiences after arriving there. The ecclesiastical records of the **Russian Orthodox Greek Catholic Church of America, Diocese of Alaska** (87,000 items; 1733–1938), covering the administration of numerous parishes and chapels, contain information on women missionaries who traveled to Alaska and on native women who joined the church or attended its schools. (See page xxxv.)

Correspondence of Harriet Fidelia Coan (1839–1906), a teacher in Punahou, Hawaii, may be found in the papers (5,000 items; 1818–1923; bulk 1832–82) of her parents, Presbyterian minister **Titus Coan** and his wife, Fidelia Church Coan (1810–1872). The diary (1 item; 1835–37) of Bostonian **Caroline B. Poole** (1802–1844) describes her daily life as a teacher in Monroe, Louisiana, and the **Julia G. Alexander Collection of Alexander and Graham Family Papers** (35 items; 1812–61) contains a notebook and other items relating to the New York and Tennessee teaching career of Sarah Ann Graham Alexander (1807–1839?). **Harry Augustus Garfield**'s correspondence with his sister, Mary Garfield Stanley Brown (1867–1947), concerns her education in Cleveland, Ohio, and at Miss Porter's boarding school in Farmington, Connecticut. Also in Garfield's papers (60,000 items; 1888–1934) are letters of his daughter Lucretia Garfield Comer (1894–1968) relating to her schooling, her work as a teacher with the Pine Mountain Settlement School in Kentucky, and her views on World War I, peace, and social reform. Education of Native Americans, particularly Navajo Indians, is the focus of a small collection of papers (200 items; 1951–74) relating to the career of **Hildegard Thompson** (1901–1983), who served for a time as chief of the education branch of the U.S. Bureau of Indian Affairs.

Alice Hirsch, a student of **Maria Kraus-Boelté** (1836–1918), compiled a collection (200 items; 1904–13) about her mentor, a pioneer in children's early education, who helped establish in 1873 the New York Seminary of Kindergarteners, a training school for kindergarten teachers. The papers of **Lyman Bryson** (12,000 items; 1893–1977; bulk 1917–59), on the other hand, contain his correspondence with Lucy Wilcox Adams, Mary L. Ely, and other women teachers about adult education programs.

Two other male educators, whose careers and writings bear on women's educational history and women's role as mother, are **William Torrey Harris** (13,000 items;1866–1908) and **Angelo Patri** (30,000 items; 1904–62; bulk 1924–62). Harris served as superintendent of schools in nineteenth-century St. Louis, Missouri, and wrote on the benefits of women's education, including articles titled "Ought Young Girls to Read the Daily Newspapers?" (1888) and "Why Many Women Should Study Law" (1901). Following in Harris's footsteps was Patri, an author and public school principal in New York City, who for forty years wrote a syndicated column "Our Children," which popularized John Dewey's progressive educational principles. Patri also wrote articles for numerous magazines aimed at women, including *Farmer's Wife, McCall's, Parents Magazine,* and *Young Wives.* Of particular note in his papers are letters from troubled parents seeking his child-rearing advice during the Depression.

Religious leaders also frequently expressed opinions about women's education. Methodist clergyman and educator **Matthew Simpson** (5,000 items; 1829–1929; bulk 1833–84) supported female education and wrote about female heroism. Information about the Northfield Seminary for girls may be found in the papers of nineteenth-century evangelist **Dwight Lyman Moody** (200 items; 1854–1937; bulk 1864–99).

Many women who achieved fame in their professions held university teaching positions at some point in their lives, including **Sophonisba Breckinridge** (see "Reform" above), **Margaret Mead** (see "Science and Medicine" below), **Helen Taft Manning** (1891–1987), and **Elizabeth Reynolds Hapgood** (1894–1974). Manning, the daughter of President William Howard Taft, was a history professor, dean, and president of Bryn Mawr College who corresponded with her father about her career, family matters, and Washington politics (350 items; 1908–56; bulk 1917–29). Hapgood, the wife of diplomat and author **Norman Hapgood** (6,000 items; 1823–1977), was an editor and translator who became head of the Russian Department at Columbia University in 1915 and founder of the Russian Department at Dartmouth College in 1919. The papers (4,000 items; 1895–1968; bulk 1922–68) of sociologists **Helen Merrell Lynd** (1896–1982) and her husband **Robert Staughton Lynd** relate to their academic careers at Columbia University and Sarah Lawrence College and their authorship of the famous cultural studies on *Middletown* (1929) and *Middletown in Transition* (1937).

Several women whose papers are in the division served in high-level government positions relating to education. In the mid-to-late 1960s, economist **Alice M. Rivlin** (b. 1931) was with the Department of Health, Education, and Welfare (HEW), first as assistant secretary for program coordination and later for planning and evaluation. Her papers (10,000 items; 1964–88) cover those years as well as her tenure with the Congressional Budget Office and the Brookings Institution, and her service on the boards of the Black Student Fund, Bryn Mawr College, and Harvard University. She kept files on aging, education, income maintenance programs, public welfare, social policy, and social unrest in the late 1960s, including materials on the National Advisory Commission on Civil Disorder (Kerner Commission) and the Poor People's Campaign.

Letters from Lindy Boggs, Evangeline Bruce, India Edwards, Florence Jaffray Hurst Harriman, and Margaret Chase Smith are among the papers (36,500 items; 1914–91; bulk 1942–68) of **Katie**

S. Louchheim (1903–1991), deputy assistant secretary of state for cultural and educational affairs in the 1960s and director of women's activities for the Democratic National Committee during the previous decade. Also represented is Louchheim's work with the United Nations Relief and Rehabilitation Administration and her interest in Lady Bird Johnson's landscape beautification projects, women's rights, and social life in Washington, D.C.

Following a two-year stint as secretary of housing and urban development in Jimmy Carter's cabinet, lawyer and educator **Patricia Harris** (1924–1985) became Carter's secretary of health, education, and welfare (later health and human services). Her papers (113,400 items; 1950–83; bulk 1977–80) pertain primarily to these cabinet posts and include information on abortion, civil rights, consumer protection, discrimination, energy, the environment, housing, immigration, the Iran hostage crisis, and urban policy. Also serving in Carter's cabinet, as secretary of education from 1979 to 1981, was lawyer and federal judge **Shirley M. Hufstedler** (b. 1925). Policy statements and other materials (1,360 items; 1979–81) document Hufstedler's promotion of educational programs, including the Youth Act of 1980, which was never enacted. Papers concerning Hufstedler's legal career and her tenure on the U.S. Court of Appeals for the Ninth Circuit have not yet been received but are expected in the future.

Science and Medicine

Information about women's health and women's involvement in the medical profession may be found in a variety of manuscript collections, including such familiar sources as women's diaries, family correspondence, and the papers of medical practitioners and also in some unexpected places, including, for example, the papers of a public relations executive. Some of these collections may be located by searching the manuscript records in the Library's online catalog for likely subject headings such as "Physicians," "Nurses," "Medicine," "Hygiene," and "Psychoanalysts." Other sources can be discovered only by plowing through hundreds of collections of family correspondence and diaries in which the writers unfailingly describe pregnancies, childbirth, illnesses, diseases, and medical treatments that they or members of their families experienced. Unearthing these sources requires a definite commitment of time and energy on the part of the researcher.

For example, among the correspondence between Elizabeth Randolph and her father, **William B. Randolph** (7,500 items; 1696–1884; bulk 1795–1855), a prosperous Virginia plantation owner, are numerous letters detailing Elizabeth's treatment for an undisclosed medical condition in 1829–30, which involved leeching, bleeding, and a lengthy convalescence at a relative's home. Both **Louisa Lee Schuyler** (1837–1926), a former U.S. Sanitary Commission volunteer, and novelist Constance Cary Harrison (1843–1920), wife of **Burton N. Harrison** (18,600 items; 1812–1926; bulk 1913–21), described in their diaries charity

Clara Barton. War lecture, ca. 1866. Clara Barton Papers (container 152). Manuscript Division. LC-MS-11973-12.

Twenty years before founding the American Red Cross, for which she became famous worldwide, Clara Barton (1821–1912) came to the aid of Union soldiers fighting in the American Civil War. At first, War Department regulations and nineteenth-century female stereotypes limited her involvement, but before the war's end, she "broke the shackles and went to the field," nursing hundreds of wounded and dying soldiers at Cedar Mountain, Second Bull Run, Antietam, and elsewhere. Although by no means the only woman to engage in such work, Barton became one of the most famous because of the postwar lectures she delivered to raise money for her efforts to identify dead and missing soldiers, especially those who perished at Andersonville prison. As this page from one of her lectures illustrates, in the days before laser printers and word processors with multiple font sizes, orators typically enlarged their handwriting to increase legibility of their remarks, which were often read in dimly lit settings.

I was strong — and I thought I ought to go to the rescue of the men who fell —:
But I struggled long and hard with my sense of propriety — with the appalling fact — that I was only a woman, whispering in one ear — and the groans of suffering men, dying like dogs — unfed and unsheltered, for the life of the very Institutions which had protected and educated me — thundering in the other.
I said that I struggled with my sense of propriety — and I say it with humiliation and shame —. Before God and before you I am ashamed that I thought of such a thing —
But when our armies fought at Cedar Mountain I broke the shackles and went to the field

work they did at New York's Bellevue Hospital in the 1870s. In 1881, writer Mary S. Logan (1838–1923), wife of Gen. **John Alexander Logan** (46,000 items; 1836–1925; bulk 1860–1917) received the advice, presumably unsolicited, from a relative who wrote, ". . . you are approaching a time of life when great changes take place in the female system; when it is necessary to carefully keep away tendencies to congestion of the brain, which are always imminent when natural discharges cease."[13] At the end of her 1886 diary, women's rights activist Helen Pitts Douglass (1838–1903), wife of **Frederick Douglass** (7,400 items; 1841–1967; bulk 1862–95), noted instructions for curing various illnesses—such as consumption, diabetes, and apoplexy—by applying electrodes to parts of the body. Located in the **Arthur Family** Papers (20,000 items; 1817–1972; bulk 1874–1972) are diaries of Myra Fithian Andrews Arthur (1870–1935), wife of rancher Chester Alan Arthur, in which she records her reaction to her husband's infidelities; her contemplation of suicide; her divorce; and her health, including a severe brain clot in 1904 and menopause in 1916, which she believed contributed to her husband's philandering. Myra Arthur spent several days in bed each month, perhaps while menstruating, and her diary entries for those days contain the one-word comment "unwell."

These examples intend to show that by their very nature, collections of personal manuscripts contain a wealth of information about the health and well-being of the individuals and families featured in the papers. They also reflect the important role women have traditionally held in caring for the sick and elderly in America. With the rise of the women's rights movement in the nineteenth century and greater wartime demands for their services, women's socially sanctioned role as family nurse-maids evolved into greater professional opportunities and medical training. The Library's manuscript collections document this development of women's medical careers.

Having completed her medical education at Geneva College in west central New York in 1849, **Elizabeth Blackwell** (1821–1910) is widely considered to be the first American woman to receive an academic medical degree. Her papers, part of the larger **Blackwell Family** collection (29,000 items; 1759–1960; bulk 1845–90), describe her pioneering efforts to open the medical profession to women, including her difficulties in establishing in 1854 the New York Infirmary for Women and Children with her sister Dr. **Emily Blackwell** (1826–1910) and their colleague Dr. Marie Zakrzewska and her struggle fifteen years later to found a women's medical college in the United States. Elizabeth and Emily wrote numerous pieces on women's health concerns, but they also lived up to the family's reputation for producing reformers and strong supporters of women's political rights.

When the Civil War broke out, the Blackwell sisters were involved in the establishment of the U.S. Sanitary Commission and helped to select and train nurses for war work. As the repository for more than a thousand Civil War collections, the Manuscript Division holds extensive material relating to women's medical involvement in the war.[14] For example, letters from convalescent soldiers and from Alden M. Lander, the superintendent of women nurses, are among the papers (515 items; 1856–67) of nurse-physician **Esther Hill Hawks** (1833–1906), who after the war established schools and distributed supplies for the National Freedman's Relief Association. The papers of Sara Iredell Fleetwood (1811–1908), a teacher and nurse who was superintendent of nurses at the Freedmen's Hospital in Washington, D.C., are included among those of her husband **Christian A. Fleetwood** (400 items; 1797–1945; bulk 1860–1907), a free black soldier who was awarded the Congressional Medal of Honor. Catherine Oliphant (d. 1916) sought a pension for her services as a laundress and nurse in her husband **Benjamin F. Oliphant**'s regiment (22 items; 1864–1916). **Mary Ann Bickerdyke** (1817–1901) was a nurse and agent for the U.S. Sanitary Commission whose heroic service on the field and in hospitals earned her the gratitude of countless Union soldiers. After the war, "Mother" Bickerdyke became an attorney assisting army veterans in securing military pensions. Her papers (1,800 items; 1855–1905) cover both phases of her life and include files relating to the Woman's Relief Corps of the Grand Army of the Republic, Mary A. Livermore, and Lucy Stone. Also an agent for the U.S. Sanitary Commission was nurse **Lydia J. Stull,** who reviewed court-martial cases of Union soldiers held in military prisons (23 items; 1865).

Many Civil War nurses and physicians later recorded their reminiscences. Physician **Harriette C. Keatinge** (1837–1909) wrote about the burning of South Carolina by Gen. William T. Sherman's troops, her husband's capture by Union forces, and her experiences traveling with Sherman's army to join her husband (3 items; 1903–9). The papers (4 items; 1916–30) of **Martha Elizabeth Wright Morris** (1832?–1919) contain an address she gave in 1916 describing her wartime activities, including her work with the U.S. Sanitary

Commission and her acquaintance with Confederate spy Rose O'Neal Greenhow. A biographical sketch (1 item; n.d.) of **Carrie Eliza Cutter** (1842–1862) details her activities and death from fever while serving as a nurse with a New Hampshire regiment during the war.

Perhaps the best known of all Civil War nurses was **Clara Barton** (1821–1912), who later founded the American National Red Cross. At the war's outbreak, Barton was a forty-year-old Patent Office clerk in Washington, D.C., who embraced the task of collecting much-needed provisions and medical supplies for the Union army. Frustrated by bureaucratic delays, she began to distribute the supplies herself and also started nursing the wounded in military hospitals and battlefields, earning the nickname "Angel of the Battlefield." Barton became famous for her Civil War exploits mainly because of a series of phenomenally successful postwar lectures she delivered about her war experiences and her later efforts to identify dead and missing soldiers. In preparing these lectures, Barton drew not only from memory but also from diaries and notes she had kept at the time, which are now part of her personal papers (70,000 items; 1834–1918).

During Barton's last years with the American National Red Cross, the organization was criticized for its inefficiency and came under rebuke during the Spanish-American War from Surgeon General George M. Sternberg, who believed that women nurses should not be permitted on the battlefield but instead should be confined to base hospitals. Sternberg appointed physician and anthropologist **Anita Newcomb McGee** (1864–1940) as acting assistant surgeon general and charged her with recruiting qualified graduate nurses to staff army hospitals and later to serve in overseas camps. At the end of the war, McGee helped organize a permanent Army Nurses Corps. Her papers (3,000 items; 1688–1932) document her medical and army careers as well as her role in forming the Women's Anthropological Society of America and her research on communal societies in the United States, including the Shakers and the Oneida community.

The discord within the American National Red Cross was fueled in part by a power struggle between Barton and newly appointed executive committee member **Mabel Thorp Boardman** (1860–1946), who eventually succeeded Barton as the organization's leader in 1904. Boardman's papers (4,000 items; 1853–1945; bulk 1904–29), which include extensive correspondence with William Howard Taft and other national officials, trace the Red Cross's growing ties to the federal government and its emergence as the leading voluntary organization providing disaster and war relief and promoting public health and safety.

During the First World War, more than eighteen thousand Red Cross nurses served with the Army and Navy Nurse Corps. Some of these nurses—such as **Dorothy Kitchen O'Neill** (69 items; 1918–19), who was stationed at American Red Cross headquarters in Savenay, France—worked at American base hospitals, at field units, and aboard ships, whereas others, including **Helen Culver Kerr** (200 items; 1918–19), served at home combating the 1918 influenza epidemic and providing medical services to military camps, munitions plants, and shipyards. Some American Red Cross nurses served as part of the British Expeditionary Force (B.E.F.). Edith Hulsizer Copher (1891–1935), for example, went to France as a dietitian with a B.E.F. Red Cross unit formed by Dr. Harvey Cushing of the Harvard Medical School, and her letters in the **Hulsizer Family** Papers (145 items; 1915–41; bulk 1917–19) provide not only an account of the medical conditions in army facilities but a glimpse of the social life and everyday concerns of the young hospital staff.

The long hours, stress, and exposure to disease took a toll on army medical personnel. Obituaries in the **Breckinridge Family Papers** (205,000 items; 1752–1965) suggest that fatigue and overwork contributed to the death of Mary Curry Desha Breckinridge (d. 1918), a Red Cross nurse who joined a Chicago hospital unit serving in France during the war. Several hundred letters written to and from Breckinridge describe her experiences. At the start of World War I, Red Cross official Grace Elizabeth Allen (1886–1976) was just entering nursing school in Washington, D.C. Several volumes of her meticulous diary in the **Allen Family** Papers (500 items; 1865–1976) discuss her training and wartime work at Columbia Hospital in the nation's capital.

Although World War I led to a marked increase in the number of women involved in public health nursing, many women had entered the field years earlier as part of settlement house work and other Progressive reform initiatives. Nurse, author, and public health activist **Lavinia L. Dock** (1858–1956) collected writings on various aspects of nursing as well as other papers (350 items; 1908–49; bulk 1935–38) relating to her involvement with the International Council of Nurses, the American Association of the Red Cross, and the Henry Street Settlement in New York City. The papers (3,000 items; 1891–1969; bulk 1910–69) of nurse

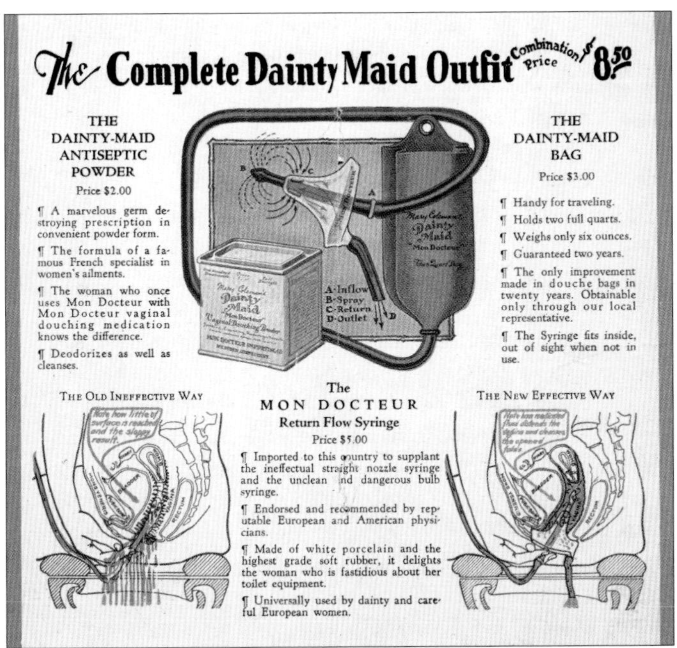

"The Complete Dainty Maid Outfit." Advertisement, n.d. Margaret Sanger Papers (container 252). Manuscript Division. LC-MS-38919-8.

Margaret Higgins Sanger (1879–1966), a public health nurse, was arrested in October 1916 after opening the first American birth control clinic in Brooklyn, New York, in violation of state law prohibiting the distribution of contraceptive information. A leader in both the national and international birth control movements, Sanger assembled a collection of personal papers and organizational records documenting her long struggle for women's reproductive rights. Like many of her contemporaries, she retained all kinds of printed matter accumulated during her career, including pamphlets like this one relating to women's gynecological health and hygiene.

Florence Deakins Becker (1878–1969) relate principally to her crusade against tuberculosis and cancer. Documents concerning the Visiting Nurses Association are among the papers of Helen Newell Garfield (1866–1930) included in the **James Rudolph Garfield** Papers (70,000 items; 1879–1950; bulk 1890–1932).

After serving as a nurse in France during World War I, Mary Breckinridge (1881–1965), a relative of Mary Curry Desha Breckinridge, went to England to study midwifery and then returned to the United States to found the Kentucky Committee for Mothers and Babies in 1925, which became known three years later as the Frontier Nursing Service (FNS), a social welfare project aimed at providing medical care to families living in inaccessible mountain communities. Documents regarding the FNS may be found in the Mary Breckinridge files in the **Breckinridge Family** Papers. As a young woman, photojournalist **Mary Marvin Breckinridge Patterson** (b. 1905) served as a guide and courier for doctors associated with her cousin's Frontier Nursing Service. She later made a film about the project (see chapter 8). Patterson's papers (1 volume; 1939–40) consist of radio transcripts documenting her years as a correspondent during World War II, but additions to this collection are expected, which will cover her FNS work and her philanthropic activities as a community activist and diplomat's wife.

Among the most famous of public health nurses was **Margaret H. Sanger** (1879–1966), who for many years led the campaign for birth control in the United States and abroad. In 1914, believing that effective birth control was essential for women's freedom and independence, Sanger published the illustrated pamphlet *Family Limitation,* in direct violation of the 1873 federal Comstock law, which prohibited the dissemination of contraceptive information (see pages 83, 117). Two years later she opened the nation's first birth control clinic, which resulted in her much-publicized arrest and imprisonment. Undeterred, Sanger proceeded to organize the first American and international birth control conferences, founded numerous organizations, and mounted important legal battles, including the landmark Supreme Court case *United States v. One Package.* Her papers (130,000 items; 1900–1966; bulk 1928–40) include the records of various birth control groups with which she was associated and document her interest in socialist politics and liberal reform groups.

In the early 1950s, Sanger introduced philanthropist Katharine Dexter McCormick to biologist **Gregory Pincus** (44,000 items; 1920–69; bulk 1950–67), who was then studying the hormonal aspects of mammalian reproduction and had recently begun testing the therapeutic properties of steroid compounds for the drug company G.D. Searle. Shortly thereafter, McCormick provided funding for Pincus to develop the "birth control pill," an oral contraceptive released on the market as Enovid in 1960. The Pincus Papers include correspondence with McCormick, Sanger, and G.D. Searle officials; reports of trial tests in Puerto Rico and Haiti recording women's experiences, side effects, and personal feelings about the pill; and files relating to the Planned Parenthood Federation and the Worcester Foundation for Experimental Biology.

Although Sanger and many of her followers campaigned for birth control as a woman's right, other advocates of contraception, including geneticist and demographer **Robert C. Cook** (19,600 items; 1882–1992; bulk 1940–70) focused

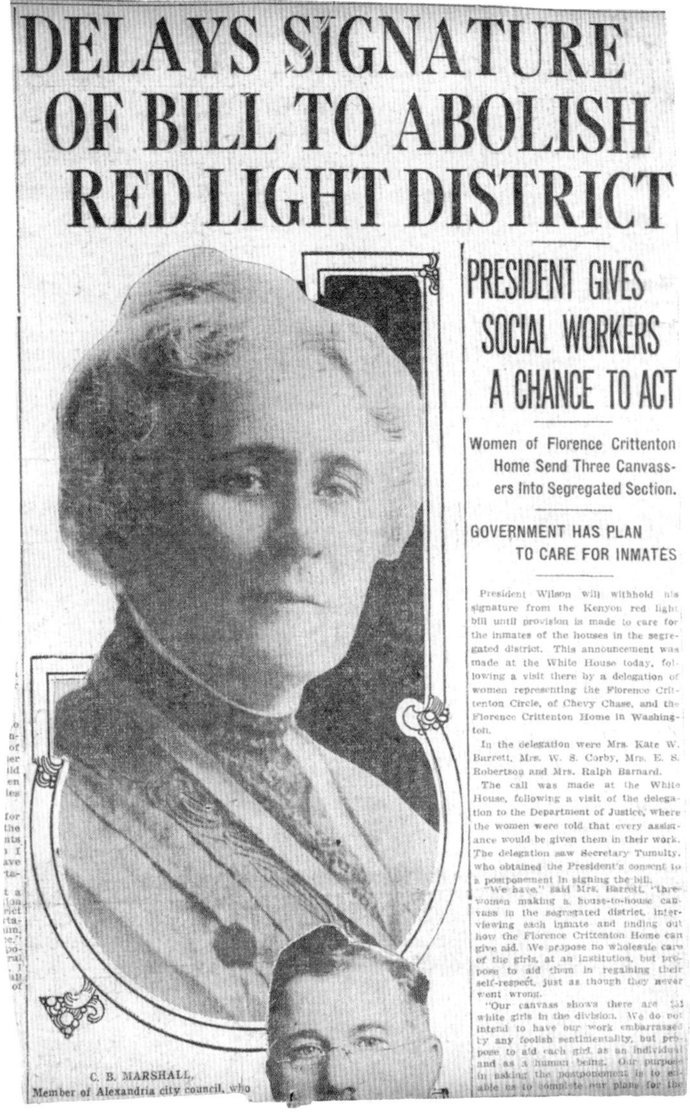

DELAYS SIGNATURE OF BILL TO ABOLISH RED LIGHT DISTRICT

PRESIDENT GIVES SOCIAL WORKERS A CHANCE TO ACT

Women of Florence Crittenton Home Send Three Canvassers Into Segregated Section.

GOVERNMENT HAS PLAN TO CARE FOR INMATES

President Wilson will withhold his signature from the Kenyon red light bill until provision is made to care for the inmates of the houses in the segregated district. This announcement was made at the White House today, following a visit there by a delegation of women representing the Florence Crittenton Circle, of Chevy Chase, and the Florence Crittenton Home in Washington.

In the delegation were Mrs. Kate W. Barrett, Mrs. W. S. Corby, Mrs. E. S. Robertson and Mrs. Ralph Barnard.

The call was made at the White House, following a visit of the delegation to the Department of Justice, where the women were told that every assistance would be given them in their work. The delegation saw Secretary Tumulty, who obtained the President's consent to a postponement in signing the bill.

"We have," said Mrs. Barrett, "three women making a house-to-house canvass in the segregated district, interviewing each inmate and finding out how the Florence Crittenton Home can give aid. We propose no wholesale care of the girls, at an institution, but propose to aid them in regaining their self-respect, just as though they never went wrong.

"Our canvass shows there are [illegible] white girls in the division. We do not intend to have our work embarrassed by any foolish sentimentality, but propose to aid each girl as an individual and as a human being. Our purpose in asking the postponement is to enable us to complete our plans for the

C. B. MARSHALL, Member of Alexandria city council, who

Newspaper clipping, ca. January 1914. Kate Waller Barrett Papers (container 4). Manuscript Division. LC-MS-11882-4.

Kate Waller Barrett (1858–1925), physician and leader in the National Florence Crittenton Mission for unwed mothers, was among the delegation of women reformers who successfully lobbied President Woodrow Wilson in January 1914 to postpone enacting a law that would dismantle the capital city's notorious red-light district until arrangements could be made to assist and rehabilitate the many prostitutes who would be displaced from the triangular area that stretched below Pennsylvania Avenue two blocks from the White House to the edge of Capitol Hill. Wilson was sympathetic to the reformers and later supplied Barrett with a letter of support for the Crittenton Mission's work to be used in the organization's fund-raising campaigns. Scrapbooks of newspaper clippings, like this one from the Barrett Papers, are often found in collections of personal papers. They provide access to articles not easily located in unindexed newspapers and provide clues about other sources to consult, in this case, the papers of Woodrow Wilson, which contain scattered letters from Barrett and a case file on the 1914 Kenyon Act to Enjoin and Abate Houses of Lewdness, Assignation, and Prostitution (S. 234).

on issues of eugenics and population control. Cook's papers include more than two hundred essays by him and others on birth control, overpopulation, medicine, and fertility.

Other aspects of women's reproductive health emerge from the papers of two women doctors, born more than fifty years apart. Before becoming a physician in midlife, **Kate Waller Barrett** (1858–1925) assisted her minister-husband in pastoral work among Georgia prostitutes. After receiving her medical degree in 1892, she became affiliated with Charles N. Crittenton and later assumed leadership of his National Florence Crittenton Mission, a series of homes designed to rescue "fallen women." Under Barrett's direction, the missions gradually gave up the goal of reclaiming prostitutes and concentrated on providing homes, guidance, medical care, and vocational training to pregnant unmarried women, encouraging these women to keep their babies rather than abort their pregnancies or give their children up for adoption. Barrett's papers (625 items; 1895–1950) touch on this work as well as on her affiliation with the National Council of Women and her efforts to secure passage of the Mann Act and other women's rights legislation.

Physician, pharmacologist, and U.S. Food and Drug Administration (FDA) official **Frances Oldham Kelsey** (b. 1914) is best known for her refusal to approve the commercial distribution of the sedative drug thalidomide in the United States, a decision for which she received the President's Award for Distinguished Federal Civilian Service in 1962. Her papers (12,000 items; 1913–97; bulk 1960–70) concern the tragedy surrounding the use of this drug, primarily in Europe, by pregnant women whose children were born with missing, stunted, or malformed limbs. Against great pressure from drug manufacturers, Kelsey and her supervisors held firm, and the publicity generated by their stance helped spark passage of the Kefauver-Harris Amendments, mandating that drug manufacturers provide the FDA with proof of a new drug's safety and effectiveness.

Although much of the focus here has been on women medical practitioners, the papers of male physicians are also good sources of information about women's medical issues and women's involvement in medical professions. Examples that illustrate this point include the papers of physician **Joseph Meredith Toner** (237,000 items; 1741–1896), which contain an eighteenth-century manuscript on midwifery and nineteenth-century medical papers on pregnancy, childbirth, venereal disease, and uterine hemorrhaging (see also the

Toner collection in chapter 4); and the papers of pathologist and physician **John W. Colbert** (400 items; 1895–1966; bulk 1903–44), documenting his training of nurses in Puerto Rico in 1904–05, his work with Red Cross nurses during World War I, and his advocacy of women's participation in war efforts as the founder of the Woman's Ambulance and Defense Corps of America in the 1940s.

Research in the papers of other male doctors would undoubtedly reveal additional source material of interest to women's historians, as would a broader search of the division's catalogs for the names of individual women doctors and nurses, medical conditions, and organizations and associations. Casting a wide net often results in some unexpected finds, such as when a search for the term "American Nurses Association" uncovers the papers of public relations executive **Edward L. Bernays** (227,000 items; 1777–1994; bulk 1920–90), whose clients included many women in the fields of arts and politics. Bernays also represented *Good Housekeeping, Cosmopolitan,* the Lucy Stone League, and various pharmaceutical companies. For one of his ad campaigns for the American Tobacco Company, Bernays sought to link women's equality with smoking in public, and he arranged for society women to light up during New York's 1929 Easter Parade and for college coeds to lobby for the right to smoke on campus. The Bernays Papers are a good source not only for women's medical issues but also for studying how advertising was directed toward women, who were thought to control household budgets. They also document the important role his wife, Doris Fleischman Bernays (1891–1980), played in his business affairs and include some of her correspondence, a draft manuscript of her book *A Wife Is Many Women* (1955), and background information for her pioneering 1928 book *An Outline of Careers for Women.* Correspondence also exists for Edward and Doris's daughter, novelist Anne Bernays.

Edward and Doris Bernays were masterful at using psychology in their public relations campaigns, at times manipulating consumers with a knowledge of human behavior that rivaled that of Edward's uncle, noted psychoanalyst **Sigmund Freud** (45,000 items; 1810–1990), whose papers are also held by the division. In fact, the division holds numerous psychoanalytical collections documenting women's roles as both patients and practitioners in this field. These collections, some of which are currently restricted, generally include personal and professional correspondence, patient case files, research findings, and drafts of scientific papers. Among the women psychoanalysts are Freud's daughter **Anna Freud** (1895–1982), an expert in the field of child analysis (60,000 items; 1880–1988; bulk 1946–82); French-born psychoanalyst **Princess Marie Bonaparte** (1882–1962), whose papers include records of her own analysis and dreams (3,300 items; 1913–61); Austrian-born **Berta Bornstein** (1900?–1971), one of the first Freudian child psychoanalysts practicing in the United States (21,000 items; 1933–71; bulk 1945–70); and German émigrés **Paula Elkisch** (725 items; 1924–78; bulk 1947–78), **Frieda Fromm-Reichmann** (2,025 items; 1922–85), **Edith Jacobson** (2,800 items; 1922–77), and **Edith Weigert** (16 items; 1935–71). Jacobson was an authority on mental depression, and drawing from her own experiences in Nazi Germany, she became an expert on the psychological effects of imprisonment on female political prisoners. **Muriel Gardner** (1901–1985) is best known as the psychoanalyst of Sergius Pankejeff, the "Wolf-Man" of Freudian analysis (3,000 items; 1890–1986; bulk 1946–84). And noted New York analyst **Elisabeth R. Geleerd** (1909–1969) researched and wrote on a variety of topics, especially in the areas of child analysis and educational standards for analysts (6,500 items; 1927–69; bulk 1945–69). Women's historians should not limit themselves to the papers of women psychoanalysts, however. Much can be gained by consulting the papers of leading male practitioners, including for example, the papers of **Karl Abraham** (500 items; 1907–26), which consist chiefly of correspondence between Abraham and Sigmund Freud relating to their respective views on sexual trauma and fantasy, hysteria, and neuroses.

Complementing the division's many psychoanalytical collections are the papers of numerous psychologists, including several women whose focus was on children's mental health. **Frances G. Wickes** (1875–1967), one of the primary representatives of the Jungian school of psychology in the United States, was a pioneer in therapeutic work with disturbed children. Her papers (4,000 items; 1897–1968; bulk 1939–68) include patient files and research papers, among them materials for her publications *Inner World of Childhood* (1927) and *Inner World of Man* (1938). Additional Wickes material may be found in the papers of her literary executor, poet **Muriel Rukeyser** (see "Literature and Journalism" below). **Louise Bates Ames** (1908–1996), child psychologist, author, and cofounder and codirector of the Gesell Institute of Child Development, devoted her entire life to analyzing and explaining child behavior. She was an early proponent of Rorschach testing, and her lectures, television appearances, and newspaper column "Child Behavior" (later "Parents Ask"), which she wrote from 1951 to 1973, established her as an authority on child development. Her papers (14,000 items; 1915–89; bulk 1950–75) also include those of her associate **Frances Lillian Ilg** (1902–1982), and additional material on both Ilg and Ames may be found in the **Arnold Gesell** Papers (90,000 items; 1870–1971; bulk 1910–50). The papers of educators and psychologists **Mamie Phipps Clark** (1917–1983) and her husband **Kenneth Bancroft Clark** (168,500 items; 1897–1994; bulk 1935–90) document their contributions to the civil rights movement and to providing equal educational opportunities for blacks. They studied the psychological effects of racial discrimination, and their findings were used in the legal fight for school desegregation.

As in the case of psychoanalysts, the papers of male psychologists are also of value to women's historians, since many of these men helped to shape society's opinions about women. **James McKeen Cattell** (49,000 items; 1835–1948; bulk 1896–1948) was an editor and psychology professor who wrote about various family and women's issues, including such articles and speeches as "The Causes of the Declining Birth Rate" (undated draft) and "The Declining Family and Its Causes" (1914). Similarly, educator and psychologist **Edward L. Thorndike** (100 items; 1900–1938) lectured about careers for college women and wrote articles titled "The Feminization of American Education" (undated draft) and "The Failure of College Women to Marry" (undated newspaper article).

Psychologists and psychoanalysts are not the only ones to have expressed concern about children's mental health. Jeannette Ridlon Piccard (1895–1981), a chemist by training who is best known for her accomplishments as a balloonist and aerospace consultant, also worked with emotionally disturbed children. Her papers, part of the **Piccard Family** collection (73,000 items; ca. 1470–1983; bulk 1926–83), touch on all aspects of her amazingly diverse life, including her aeronautical achievements, her firm commitment to women's rights, and her activities as one of the first women Episcopal priests, after her ordination in 1974.

In addition to those in the medical fields, other women scientists whose work is represented in the division include Dr. Winifred Gray Whitman, who collaborated with her husband **Merle Antony Tuve** (147,000 items; 1901–82; bulk 1941–66) in analyzing the effects on animals of high frequency resonance radiation; naturalist and ornithologist **Harriet Mann Miller** (1831–1918), who wrote under the pseudonym Olive Thorne Miller (46 items; 1891–1909); and various geographers, explorers, and anthropologists who joined the **Society of Woman Geographers** (11,700 items; 1925–87).

Anthropology may be the scientific field about which the division has the most information on women's participation. Among its largest collections are the papers of anthropologist and educator **Margaret Mead** (1901–1978). Beginning with her first book, *Coming of Age in Samoa* (1928), which compared the experiences of American and Samoan teenagers, Mead used her research on Pacific Island cultures as a framework for analyzing American society. She was particularly interested in gender and race as cultural constructs, and she served as a mentor and promoter of many young women, especially those pursuing careers in anthropology. Her correspondence, speeches, and writings, including her many articles for *Redbook* and other women's magazines, cover a variety of topics of interest to women's historians. Also included in her collection (522,450 items; 1838–1987; bulk 1911–78) are papers of her colleagues Jane Belo, Ruth Benedict, Edith M. Cobb, Lenora Schwartz Foerstel, Margaret Lowenfeld, Lola Romanucci, and Martha Wolfenstein. Another of Mead's colleagues, anthropologist **Rhoda Bubendey Metraux** (b. 1914), donated her own collection of papers (49,000 items; 1905–80; bulk 1948–70), which includes material on several of their joint projects. Born a half-century before Mead was author and explorer **Mary French Sheldon** (1847–1936). Although she was not as consciously comparative in her approach as Mead, Sheldon nevertheless revealed attitudes about gender issues in American society in her studies of women and children in the Belgian Congo in the 1890s (1,350 items; 1885–1936).

Although many scientific pursuits were considered off limits to most women, the fields of agriculture and horticulture seem to have been more accessible, perhaps because of women's traditional roles in maintaining family farms and gardens. The **Charles Cotesworth Pinckney Family** Papers (8,000 items; 1703–1947) contain letter books of Elizabeth Lucas Pinckney (1723–1793), one of America's earliest agricultural innovators, whose experiments with indigo helped to establish that crop as an important southern export in the eighteenth century. (Also of note in this collection is a plantation book that lists the names of male and female slaves along with their birth dates and a description of the work they performed.[15]) In more recent years, Pennsylvania horticulturist and city planner **Mira Lloyd Dock** (1853–1945) accumulated papers (2,500 items; 1814–1947; bulk 1896–1930) dealing with forestry, gardening, park development, and city beautification. Other work by women landscape architects may be unearthed in the records of the **American Society of Landscape Architects** (11,000 items; 1900–1960; bulk 1925–55).

The division's holdings relating to male scientists are quite extensive, but only a few examples are needed to illustrate their potential interest to women's historians. The papers of geologist, Indian agent, and explorer **Henry Rowe Schoolcraft** (25,000 items; 1788–1941; bulk 1820–56), include the papers of his wives and daughters as well as stories about Native American women in the Michigan area. Schoolcraft's first wife, Jane Johnston Schoolcraft (1800–1842), was part Ojibwe Indian, and her papers consist of poems she wrote before and after her marriage, writings about Indian girlhood and Ojibwe tales and legends, and a journal (1828) detailing her agricultural and household activities while her husband was away from home. The papers of Henry's second wife, novelist Mary Howard Schoolcraft, a member of a wealthy slave-owning family who left her home in South Carolina to live with Henry in Washington, D.C., reflect her thoughts about women's need for economic independence; southern women and slavery; and Washington politics and society. Also of interest to historians of Native American women are the papers of zoologist and ethnologist **C. Hart Merriam** (5,000 items; 1873–1938), whose wife Virginia Elizabeth Gosnell (d. 1937) accompanied him on his many trips to the American West to study Native American culture, record local flora and fauna, and compile Indian vocabularies. The family papers of inventor and educator **Alexander Graham Bell** (147,700; 1834–1974) include correspondence and other papers of his mother Eliza Grace Symonds Bell (1809–1897) and his wife Mabel Gardiner Hubbard Bell (1857–1923), both of whom were deaf, as well as his daughters Marian Hubbard Bell Fairchild (1880–1962), a suffragist and author, and Elsie May Bell Grosvenor (1878–1964), a suffragist and explorer.

Papers of Presidents and First Ladies

The Manuscript Division's presidential collections are among its most prized holdings. As the nation's oldest and most comprehensive presidential library, the division holds the papers of twenty-three presidents of the United States ranging in time from George Washington to Calvin Coolidge. (Subsequent presidents have their own libraries administered by the National Archives and Records Administration.) Included in these collections are the papers of many first ladies, documents relating to public policies and programs affecting women, correspondence with women relatives and friends, and letters from women constituents attempting to gain presidential favor for political and cultural initiatives. All twenty-three presidential collections have been microfilmed, and the microfilm editions are available in repositories throughout the country. Published indexes list many of the documents by name of writer or recipient, together with the date, series number, page count, and other information as appropriate. Unfortunately, distinguishing between men's and women's names is difficult because many of the indexes list only the first initial of the first name.

Two additional reference aids are helpful in identifying first ladies' materials. A card index in the Manuscript Reading Room identifies each first lady and lists names of collections, container numbers, and brief descriptions of the materials in those collections relating to her. Another useful source is Mary M. Wolfskill's "Meeting a New Century: The Papers of Four Twentieth-Century First Ladies," in *Modern First Ladies: Their Documentary Legacy,* compiled and edited by Nancy Kegan Smith and Mary C. Ryan (Washington: National Archives and Records Administration, 1989; CD3029.82.M63 1989). In this article, Wolfskill describes the papers of Edith Kermit Roosevelt, Helen Herron Taft, Ellen Axson Wilson, and Edith Bolling Wilson.

Although most first ladies have been the subject of at least one biography, it has only been in the past two decades that scholarship on presidential wives and on the role and function of first ladies has emerged as a separate area of inquiry within the field of women's history. Recent books have examined the "office" of first lady and have focused attention on the influence these women exerted not only on their husbands but also in the larger arenas of politics and public opinion. Information on first ladies can be found in the division's presidential collections and in the papers of numerous cabinet officials and legislators with whom they had a social or political connection. In addition, three first ladies—**Dolley Madison** (1768–1849), Lucretia Rudolph Garfield (1832–1918), and Edith Bolling Galt Wilson (1872–1961)—are represented by their own collections of papers, which are arranged and described separately from their husband's presidential collections.

Madison's papers were among the first materials acquired by the division when they were transferred to the Library from the Smithsonian Institution in 1866, seventeen years after her death. As the young widow of John Todd Jr., Dolley married James Madison in 1794, and from 1801 to 1809 she acted as White House hostess for fellow Virginian Thomas Jefferson while her husband served as the president's secretary of state. From 1809 to 1817, she was first lady during her husband's presidency. She was noted for her friendliness and charm, and her papers (1,700 items; 1794–1852; bulk 1836–49), most of which date after her husband's death, reflect her warm personal relationships and the use of her influential position to assist others. Notable are the letters she exchanged with her son John Payne Todd, nieces Anna Causten and Rebecca Todd, and nephews Richard D. Cutts and Samuel P. Todd. Additional materials relating to her may be found in the papers of **James Madison** (12,000 items; 1723–1859; bulk 1771–1836), **William C. Rives** (50,400 items; 1674–1939; bulk 1830–90), and others.

The first lady with the largest collection in the Manuscript Division is **Lucretia Rudolph Garfield** (1832–1918), wife of James A. Garfield, who was elected president in 1880 and was assassinated less than a year later by a disgruntled job seeker. Her collection (55,000 items; 1807–1958) pertains to her husband's assassination, their children, and her interests in art, literature, civic and political affairs, women's rights, genealogy, and the publication of her husband's papers and biography. Of particular significance is her correspondence with her children and their families, some of which is included in the separately maintained papers of her sons **Harry Augustus Garfield** (60,000 items; 1888–1934) and **James Rudolph Garfield** (70,000 items; 1879–1950; bulk 1890–1932). Lucretia also appears in her husband's papers, which include not only family diaries and the president's correspondence with his mother and daughter, but also his professional correspondence with Susan B. Anthony, Almeda A. Booth, Lucy Stone, and Frances Willard.

Edith Bolling Galt Wilson (1872–1961), the second wife of President Woodrow Wilson, is represented by a large collection (19,000 items; 1833–1961), most of which dates after her husband's death in 1924. Drafts of Edith's memoirs are noteworthy, as is her correspondence with political leaders, including other twentieth-century first ladies and feminist Carrie Chapman Catt. An additional ten thousand items relating to Edith may be found in her husband's papers, including documents from her White House years. The **Woodrow Wilson** Papers (278,700 items; 1786–1957) are also a rich source of information about Ellen Axson Wilson (1860–1914), the president's first wife who died after only seventeen months in the White House. Besides materials relating to his wives, Wilson's papers are rich in documents concerning the women's suffrage campaign and passage of the Nineteenth Amendment, protective labor legislation, Progressive reform, and women's involvement in World War I and the pacifist movement.

The papers of journalist and Woodrow Wilson biographer **Ray Stannard Baker** (30,000 items; 1836–1947; bulk 1907–44) contain transcripts of letters Wilson wrote to his first wife and copies and originals of the president's correspondence with Jane Addams, Mabel T. Boardman, Carrie Chapman Catt, Ida M. Tarbell, and others. Additional Wilson family materials may be found in the papers of Senator **William Gibbs McAdoo** (250,000 items; 1786–1941), who married the president's daughter Eleanor Wilson McAdoo (1889–1967), and in a small collection of **Wilson-McAdoo Family** papers (1,093 items; 1860–1966; bulk 1912–43), which consists chiefly of the papers of Margaret Woodrow Wilson (1886–1944) and Eleanor Wilson McAdoo. These papers include information on Margaret's brief singing career, her promotion of schools as community centers, and her experiences in India as a follower of Hindu mystic Sri Aurobindo Ghose.

Although only three first ladies are represented by their own collections in the Manuscript Division, the papers of other presidential wives and of women who served as White House hostesses for unmarried presidents may be found among those of their husbands, children, and other relatives and associates. Letters from Martha Washington (1731–1802) are rare, but about forty pieces of original correspondence may be found in the papers of her husband **George Washington** (77,000 items; 1592–1943; bulk 1748–99), and numerous other reproductions are contained in the **Washington Family** Papers (800 items; 1582–1965; bulk 1700–1900). The nation's first president counted among his correspondents numerous women, including Sarah Franklin Bache, Sarah Fairfax Carlyle, Elizabeth Graeme Ferguson, Judith Sargent Murray, and Mercy Otis Warren. The **Adams Family** Papers are held in the Massachusetts Historical Society (a microfilm copy is available in the division), but a significant

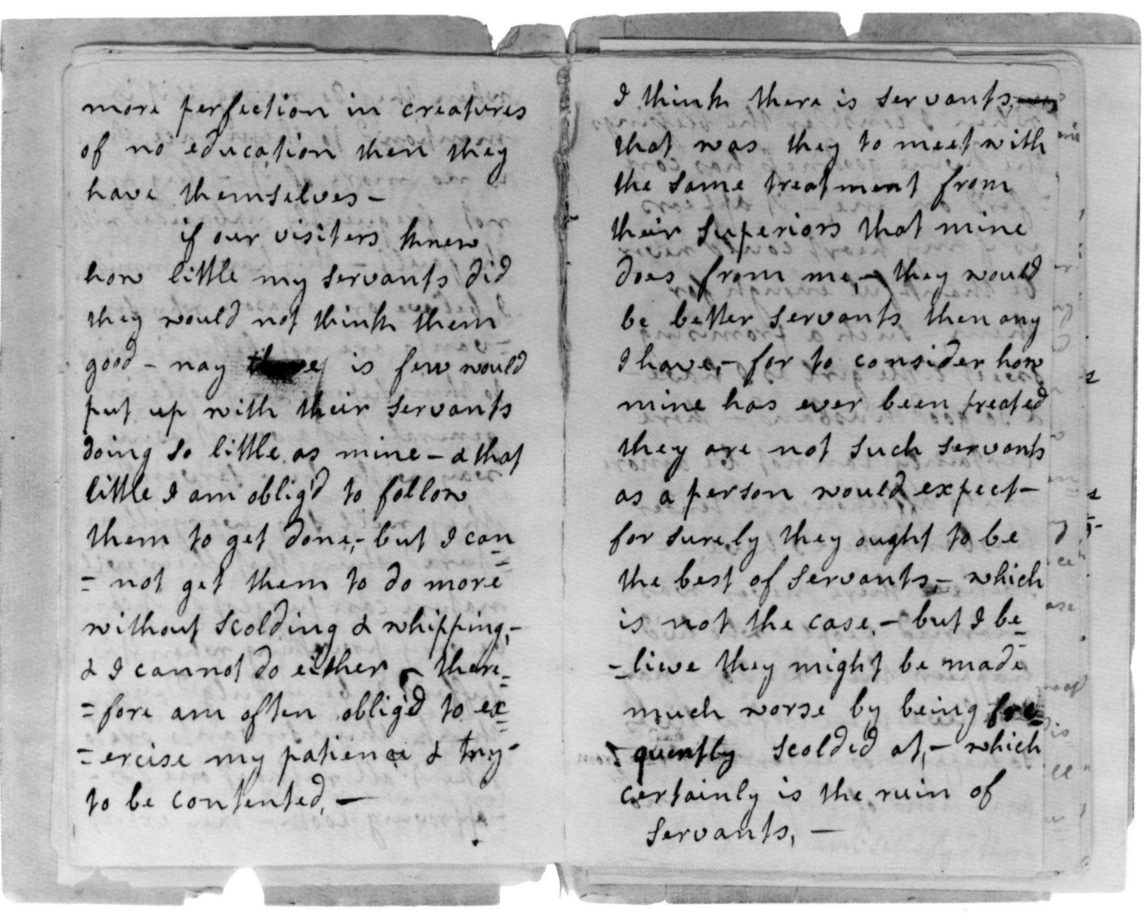

more perfection in creatures
of no education then they
have themselves—
if our visiters knew
how little my servants did
they would not think them
good—nay there is few would
put up with their servants
doing so little as mine—& that
little I am oblig'd to follow
them to get done,—but I can
=not get them to do more
without scolding & whipping,—
& I cannot do either—there=
=fore am often oblig'd to ex
=ercise my patience & try
to be contented,—

I think there is servants
that was they to meet with
the same treatment from
their superiors that mine
does from me—they would
be better servants then any
I have—for to consider how
mine has ever been treated
they are not such servants
as a person would expect—
for surely they ought to be
the best of servants—which
is not the case,—but I be
=lieve they might be made
much worse by being fre
=quently scolded at,—which
certainly is the ruin of
servants,—

Elizabeth Foote Washington. Journal, 1779–1796, spring 1789 entry. Washington Family Papers (container 2). Manuscript Division. LC-MS-56408-3.

Supplementing the Manuscript Division's twenty-three presidential collections are numerous other papers of presidential family members, many of which contain diaries and letters written by women. Included in the papers of the Washington family is this slim volume of sporadic journal entries written by Elizabeth (Betsy) Foote Washington from November 1779, just before her marriage to her cousin Lund Washington, to December 1796, a few months after the death of her husband, her "dear partner and companion." Lund Washington was George Washington's distant cousin, who lived at Mount Vernon and managed the future president's estate from 1765 to 1785, at which time Lund and Betsy moved to their own newly built home south of Alexandria. Betsy intended her journal to be a record for her daughters of how to conduct a household, and on several occasions she discussed her relationship with her servants, whom she obviously felt took advantage of her and her unwillingness to scold or whip them, as noted in this spring 1789 entry. Betsy's daughters would never read their mother's instructions, as both girls died in infancy, leaving Betsy to fret in her last entry about what would become of her journal and to worry that her "female servants will take every manuscript Book they can lay their hands on, & many of my other religious Books—tho' it is my intention, if I am in my senses when on my death bed, [that] I should have a friend with me—to warn them of my servants."

number of original letters from Abigail Adams (1744–1818) are contained in the **Shaw Family** Papers (650 items; 1636–1892; bulk 1770–1870)—mostly letters to her sister Elizabeth Shaw Peabody—and in the papers of President **Thomas Jefferson** (25,000 items; 1606–1902; bulk 1775–1826).

Journal entries and correspondence of Emily Donelson (1807–1836), who acted as White House hostess for President Andrew Jackson, are found in the papers of her husband **Andrew Jackson Donelson** (4,000 items; 1779–1943; bulk 1813–69), the president's nephew, military aide, and private secretary. A collection of **Singleton Family** Papers (900 items; 1758–1860; bulk 1829–55) contains approximately one hundred letters relating to Angelica Singleton Van Buren (1816–1877), White House hostess for her father-in-law, President Martin Van Buren. Included are letters from her mother giving advice on manners and education during her school years in Philadelphia, correspondence about the family plantation in South Carolina, and a few letters discussing life in the White House after her marriage to Abraham Van Buren.

The small collection of **John Tyler** Papers (1,400 items; 1691–1918) includes letters of his wife Julia Gardiner Tyler (1820–1889) and other family papers reflecting social life in Virginia. The papers of President **James K. Polk** (20,500 items; 1775–1891; bulk 1830–49) include three volumes of papers of his wife, Sarah Childress Polk (1803–1891), whom he married in 1824 and who acted as his secretary and political adviser. Most of her documents pertain to the management of her plantation in Mississippi after her husband's death in 1849, but also included are approximately ninety letters she and her husband exchanged from the time he left Congress in 1839 through his presidency (1845–49).

The **Franklin Pierce** Papers (2,350 items; 1820–69) contain only two letters from Jane M. Pierce (1806–1863) to her husband and only six from her to other people, leading the president's biographer to conclude that Pierce destroyed his correspondence with his wife, who predeceased him. Fortunately, the **Pierce-Aiken Family** Papers (575 items; 1797–1903; bulk 1830–70) include not only letters from Jane Pierce but also a rich correspondence of three generations of women in the Pierce-Aiken families, including Jane's mother Elizabeth Appleton (d. 1844), her sisters Mary M. Aiken (d. 1883) and Frances Packard (d. 1839), and various aunts and nieces.

Harriet Lane Johnston (1830–1903) served as White House hostess for her uncle **James Buchanan** (1,500 items; 1825–87), and her papers form part of his collection. Small collections of incoming letters to Mary Todd Lincoln (1818–1882), family correspondence and incoming letters to Julia Dent Grant (1826–1902), family and personal correspondence of Ellen Lewis Herndon Arthur (1837–1880), and incoming correspondence and genealogical materials of Frances Folsom Cleveland (1864–1947) may be found in the papers of their respective husbands, **Abraham Lincoln** (40,550 items; 1774–1948), **Ulysses S. Grant** (50,000 items; 1843–1969; bulk 1843–1908), **Chester Alan Arthur** (4,400 items; 1843–1960; bulk 1870–88), and **Grover Cleveland** (100,300 items; 1859–1945; bulk 1885–1908). The Lincoln Papers also include correspondence with Jessie B. Fremont, Eliza P. Gurney, and Sarah Josepha Hale; the Arthur Papers include correspondence of Mary S. Logan, Katherine Chase Sprague, and Frances Willard; and the Cleveland Papers contain printed matter on divorce and women's suffrage.

Edith Kermit Roosevelt (1861–1948), an intensely private woman, destroyed many of her personal files, but letters and other documents written by, to, and about her have survived in the papers of her husband President **Theodore Roosevelt** (276,000 items; 1759–1993; bulk 1889–1919), step-daughter **Alice Roosevelt Longworth** (1884–1980) (3,000 items; 1890–1946; bulk 1899–1936), and sons **Theodore Roosevelt Jr.** (25,000 items; 1780–1962; bulk 1920–44) and **Kermit Roosevelt** (56,900 items; 1885–1975). Correspondence found in her husband's papers documents her social responsibilities as first lady and her interest in Anglo-American relations, especially as evidenced by her letters to diplomats Whitelaw Reid and Cecil Spring-Rice.

Scattered among the papers of her husband **William Howard Taft** (676,000 items; 1784–1973) are numerous papers of Helen Herron Taft (1861–1943), including diaries kept before her marriage in 1886, during her honeymoon and subsequent travels abroad, and while serving as first lady. Helen's correspondence with her husband documents her tremendous influence in molding his career and shaping his opinions on political matters and foreign affairs. Additional Helen Taft materials may be found in the papers of her children **Robert A. Taft** (522,000 items; 1885–1980; bulk 1938–53), **Charles P. Taft** (185,000 items; 1816–1983; bulk 1937–79), and **Helen Taft Manning** (see "Education" above). Also of note in the William Howard Taft Papers is the president's extensive correspondence with American Red Cross administrator **Mabel Thorp Boardman** (see "Science and Medicine" above).

The lives and accomplishments of modern first ladies may also be researched in the division, even though their personal collections and those of their husbands are held elsewhere in the country. For example, the division's first ladies card index reveals more than ninety-one collections containing Eleanor Roosevelt material. Jacqueline Kennedy Onassis items may be found in collections ranging from architect **Ludwig Mies van der Rohe** (22,000 items; 1921–69; bulk 1938–69) to Senator **Daniel P. Moynihan** (164,000 items; 1786–1978; bulk 1955–75) to National Gallery of Art director **David E. Finley** (31,000 items; 1921–77). Correspondence with Lady Bird Johnson is contained in the papers of historian and presidential adviser **Eric Frederick Goldman** (27,600 items; 1886–1988; bulk 1940–70), among others, and information on her landscape beautification projects may be found in the **Katie Louchheim** Papers (see "Education" above). Nancy Reagan scholars will undoubtedly need to consult the papers of her husband's treasury secretary and chief of staff **Donald T. Regan** (78,000 items; 1919–93; bulk 1981–87), with whom she had a sometimes contentious relationship.

Complementing the division's presidential collections are the papers of White House staff members **Edith Benham Helm** (1874–1962) and **Victoria Henrietta Kugler Nesbitt** (1874–1963). Helm served as social secretary to Edith Bolling Wilson, Eleanor Roosevelt, and Bess Truman, and her papers (10,000 items; 1918–53) relate mainly to White House social functions and to President Wilson's trips to Europe for the Paris Peace Conference. Nesbitt was a housekeeper for Franklin D. Roosevelt's family, and her collection (4,500 items; 1933–49) contains correspondence (including some exchanged with Eleanor Roosevelt about domestic matters), manuscripts of her books *White House Diary* (1948) and *The Presidential Cookbook* (1951), and a nearly complete set of White House menus.

Women who wrote about the White House and its occupants include both Ruth Painter Randall (1892–1971), whose book *Mary Lincoln: Biography of a Marriage* (1953) is represented in the papers of her husband, Civil War historian **J. G. Randall** (35,000 items; 1779–1970; bulk 1916–70), and Mary S. Logan, wife of **John Alexander Logan** (see "Congressional Collections" below). Political correspondents **Ruby A. Black** (1896–1957), **May Craig** (1889?-1975), and **Bess Furman** (1894–1969) covered the White House, reporting particularly on Eleanor Roosevelt and other modern first ladies (see "Literature and Journalism" below).

Congressional Collections

Surpassed perhaps only by the division's rich presidential holdings are its more than nine hundred collections relating to members of Congress. Most of these congressional collections are identified in John J. McDonough's *Members of Congress: A Checklist of Their Papers in the Manuscript Division, Library of Congress* (Washington: Library of Congress, 1980; Z1236.U613 1980). Ranging in time from the first Continental Congress in 1774 to the 105th Congress in 1998, they cover the entire breadth of United States history. Women appear throughout these collections as members of Congress, as spouses and children of members, and as constituents, lobbyists, and members of special interest groups. They also make their presence felt as the focus of legislation aimed to restrict, protect, enhance, or define women's status in society.

Of the women who have served in Congress, the Manuscript Division holds the papers of two: Illinois representative Ruth Hanna McCormick Simms (1880–1944) and Connecticut representative Clare Boothe Luce (1903–1987). Simms's papers, part of the larger **Hanna-McCormick Family** collection (47,300 items; 1792–1985; bulk 1902–44), focus on her political activities, including her role as chair of the Women's National Executive Committee of the Republican Party, her service in the House of Representatives (1929–31), her unsuccessful Senate campaign in 1930, and her work as presidential campaign manager for Thomas E. Dewey in 1944. Her general correspondence files include a number of letters by Harriet Taylor Upton and others concerning efforts to mobilize women politically, a topic also addressed in many of Simms's speeches. Scrapbooks of newspaper clippings relate to her 1903 wedding to Medill McCormick, the women's suffrage campaign in 1914–15, her farm and personal affairs in 1925–27, and her involvement in congressional and presidential politics in the late 1920s and again in 1940. Less documentation exists on her ownership of a dairy farm designed to produce sanitary milk for invalids and children, her operation of two newspapers and a radio station, and her creation of a girls' school in New Mexico.

An author and playwright, **Clare Boothe Luce** served in Congress from 1943 to 1947 as a Republican representative from Connecticut. Six years later, she was appointed U.S. ambassador to Italy (1953–57), and in the 1970s and 1980s, she served on the President's Foreign Intelligence Advisory Board. Her voluminous papers (460,000 items; 1862–1988; bulk 1930–87) document both her political career and her literary endeavors as an editor at *Vanity Fair* (1930–34), author of such Broadway hits as *The Women* (1936) and *Kiss the Boys Good-bye* (1938), adviser to her husband Henry Robinson Luce on publishing matters at Time Inc., World War II correspondent for *Life* magazine, and syndicated newspaper columnist (1948–86). The collection also reflects her personal life, her conversion to Roman Catholicism in 1946 and subsequent religious activities, and her advocacy of working women and greater public roles for women.

As a member of the House Military Affairs Committee, Luce received letters from women in the military, and her congressional and subject files reflect her interest in wartime economic and labor issues, including universal military service for men and women and the concerns of military nurses. Other files relate to child care programs, maternity and infant health care issues, women diplomats, and women in politics. Much to her dismay, Luce found herself heading a crusade against the shortage of women's stockings in postwar America. She also became embroiled in the controversy that arose when the Daughters of the American Revolution refused to admit African Americans to Constitution Hall. Many of Luce's speeches while in Congress related to women, such as "The Role of American Women in Wartime" (1942) and "Equality of Women and Men" (1947).

Although the division does not hold the corpus of their personal papers, several other women members of Congress are represented in division collections, although none by a substantial number of documents. Material on Jeannette Rankin (1880–1973) of Montana, the first woman elected to Congress, appears in the papers of Mary Church Terrell and the records of the National American Woman Suffrage Association, National Consumers' League, Suffragists Oral History Project collection, and Bancroft Library Oral History Collection. Information about Maine representative and senator Margaret Chase Smith (1897–

James Henry Hammond. Plantation manual, 1857–58. James Henry Hammond Papers (container 43). Manuscript Division. LC-MS-24695-1.

A slave owner, Senator James Henry Hammond (1807–1864) of South Carolina compiled a detailed manual of instructions for the operation of his plantation, covering such diverse topics as crops, allowances, hogs, children, the overseer, and on the pages shown here, the old, the pregnant, and nursing mothers. Undoubtedly with an eye toward protecting and controlling his property, Hammond carefully outlined the number of months women slaves could nurse their babies, the length of time they could spend each day with their infants, the amount of work they were expected to perform, and even the body temperature they should maintain before nursing. The volume was compiled in 1857–58, around the same time that Hammond made his celebrated March 4, 1858, speech in the United States Senate arguing that "In all social systems there must be a class to do the menial duties, to perform the drudgery of life. . . . It constitutes the very mudsill of society." He went on to utter the oft-repeated words, "You dare not make war on cotton—no power on earth dares make war upon it. Cotton is king."

Sucklers. —

Sucklers are not required to leave their houses until sun-rise, when they leave their children at the children's house before going to field. The period of suckling is 12 mos. Their work lies always within 1/2 a mile of the quarter. They are required to be cool before commencing to suckle — to wait 15 minutes, at least, in summer, after reaching the children's house before nursing. It is the duty of the nurse to see that none are heated when nursing, as well as of the Overseer & his wife occasionally to do so. They are allowed 45 minutes at each nursing to be with their children. They return 3 times a day until their infants are 8 mos. old — in the middle of the forenoon, at noon, & in the middle of the afternoon: 'till the 12th mo. but twice a day, missing at noon during the 12th mo. at noon only. On weaning, the child is removed entirely from its Mother for 2 weeks, & placed in charge of some careful woman without a child, during which time the Mother is not to nurse it at all.

Remarks. — The amount of work done by a Suckler is about 3/5 of that done by a full-hand, a little increased toward the last.

Old & Infirm. —

Those, who from age & infirmities are unable to keep up with the prime hands are put in the sucklers gang.

Pregnant. —

Pregnant women, at 5 mos. are put in the Sucklers gang. No plowing or lifting must be required of them.

~~Sucklers, old, infirm & pregnant, receive the same allowances as full-work hands.~~

1995) may be found in the papers of Florence Ellinwood Allen, William Rea Furlong, Katie Louchheim, Edgar Mowrer, and Charl Ormond Williams. Letters of California representative Helen Gahagan Douglas (1900–1980) are in the collections of Reinhold Niebuhr, Kermit Roosevelt, and Paul F. and Claire Ginsburg Sifton. A file on Ohio representative Frances Payne Bingham Bolton (1885–1977) is in the Records of the Society of Woman Geographers. Ruth Bryan Owen Rohde (1885–1954) correspondence may be found in the papers of Bess Furman and Laurence A. Steinhardt, and New York congresswoman Bella Abzug (1920–1998) is represented in the Records of ERAmerica. The Former Members of Congress oral history collection contains the narratives of twelve women ranging from Utah representative Reva Zilpha Beck Bosone (1895–1983), a descendant of Mormon pioneers, to Hawaii representative Patsy Mink (b. 1927), a supporter of women's rights, bilingual education, and civil rights for minorities.

Although most of the division's congressional collections revolve around the careers of male representatives and senators, they are nevertheless rich sources of information for women's history. They include letters from female constituents as well as subject files on legislation affecting women's work, health, and legal status. Moreover, few men enjoyed successful congressional careers without the support and involvement of their wives and other female family members. In the eighteenth and much of the nineteenth centuries, women generally did not accompany their husbands to Washington. They remained behind to raise children and take care of the family home, farm, or business. Even in the twentieth century, second homes were beyond the means of most members. Fortunately for the historian, families separated physically from one another turned to correspondence and poured out in letters all the affection, concern, and news they were unable to share in person. Wives and other relatives informed the member of happenings at home, advised him on local reaction to pending legislation, and peppered him with questions about his health, the nation's business, and the latest fashions and social activities in the capital. Members responded by describing in candid detail their living arrangements and social life, their opinions of their colleagues, their views on historically important issues, their assessments of women's dress and appearance, and any other thoughts and observations they thought would be of interest to the recipient.[16]

Josiah Bartlett, a physician and delegate to the Continental Congress,[17] received weekly letters from his wife Mary Barton Bartlett (m. 1750), who was in charge of running the family's farm during his long and frequent absences. The Bartlett collection (10,000 items; 1710–1931; bulk 1800–1890) contains four notebooks (1816–21) of Hannah E. W. Thompson Bartlett documenting her years at Bradford Academy and also Hannah Bell's "Ladies Album" of poems and verses written by herself and female friends during the 1840s. Several generations of women are represented in the papers of the **Field-Osgood Family** (1,600 items; 1702–1938; bulk 1780–1930), including Maria Bowne Franklin Osgood, wife of New York legislator Samuel Osgood, and her daughter, Susan K. Osgood Field. Of particular interest is Susan's correspondence, 1814–21, with her married sisters and cousins. Their correspondence reflects the everyday life of young women of the early nineteenth-century merchant class. Also of note are manumission papers and a letter from Maria concerning her obligations to Chloe Field, an African American woman. The **Ralph Izard Family** Papers (660 items; 1778–1826; bulk 1801–14) contain weekly correspondence of the South Carolina senator's wife Alice Delancey Izard (1745–1832) with her daughter, daughter-in-law, and granddaughter concerning family matters and social affairs in Charleston, South Carolina, and Philadelphia.

For the first half of the nineteenth century, researchers have a number of fine collections to consult. The papers of **Levi Woodbury** (17,000 items; 1638–1914; bulk 1804–97) include correspondence with his wife Elizabeth Williams Clapp Woodbury (1796–1873) during their courtship and early years of marriage, letters they exchanged when he was in Washington and she was at home in New Hampshire, letters she wrote to her parents and children, and diaries (1860–76) and correspondence of their daughter Virginia Woodbury Fox. The **William C. Rives** collection (50,400 items; 1674–1939; bulk 1830–90) includes the papers of Judith Page Walker Rives (1802–1882), a writer whom William married in 1819. Her letters discuss her life in Albemarle County, Virginia, and a diary, in the form of letters to her sister, describes the couple's life in France during William's term as minister to that country.

Job Pierson (600 items; 1755–1908; bulk 1809–96) was an Albany, New York, lawyer who served four years in the House of Representatives during Andrew Jackson's administration. During that time, he wrote more than 350 letters to his wife, Clarissa Bulkeley Pierson (1794–1865), who remained at home with their young children. He provided her with candid assessments of his colleagues and his opinions on political issues; described visits to the White House; informed her of his presumably innocent infatuation with Emily Donelson, Jackson's hostess; expressed his concern for their children's education and the burdens his absence was placing on her; relayed the latest gossip about boardinghouse life, including stories of a senator seducing a chambermaid and of other boarders entertaining prostitutes in their rooms; and on one occasion chastised her for writing him a letter that had "too much of the querulous spirit in it. This should not be so—Women should always be sunshine & flowers."[18]

The Civil War is richly represented in the papers of **Philip Phillips** (7,000 items; 1832–1914), representative from South Carolina who married Eugenia Levy Phillips (1820–1902) in 1836. Of interest are letters from Eugenia's sister Phebe Levy and copies of Eugenia's reminiscences detailing her arrest and imprisonment in Washington, D.C., as a Confederate spy, her parole and return to the South, her experiences in New Orleans, and her work with sick Confederate soldiers at La Grange, Georgia. Harriet Ward Foote Hawley (1831–1886), the wife of Connecticut representative and senator **Joseph R. Hawley** (13,200 items; 1638–1906; bulk 1841–1906), wrote to her husband and others during the Civil War about her hospital work at Hilton Head, South Carolina, and after the war about her work as organizer and president of the Washington Auxiliary of the Women's National Indian Association. **Henry Dawes** (22,000 items; 1833–1933; bulk 1848–87) of Massachusetts served in Congress during and after the Civil War, and his papers include those of his wife, Electa Sanderson Dawes (1822–1901), who kept her husband informed of happenings in his district, and of his daughter Anna L. Dawes (1851–1938), a journalist, antisuffragist, and Indian reformer who worked with Mrs. Hawley. Henry Dawes himself corresponded with muckraking journalist and author Ida M. Tarbell. Anna Dawes maintained a lengthy correspondence with ethnologist Alice C. Fletcher and with New England writer Sarah Orne Jewett, with whom Dawes lived for many years.

The papers of Mary S. Logan (1838–1923), editor of the women's periodical the *Home Magazine,* arrived with the papers (46,000 items; 1836–1925; bulk 1860–1917) of her husband, **John Alexander Logan,** army officer and Illinois senator. Mary Logan served as a nurse during the Civil War, founded the Women's Relief Corps of the Grand Army of the Republic, and worked on the 1893 World's Columbian Exposition. She was also interested in women's history and wrote several books, including *The Part Taken by Women in American History* (1912) and the unpublished "Ladies of the White House." Unlike Logan, Issa Desha Breckinridge (1843–1892) spent the Civil War living in exile in Canada, while her husband, William C. P. Breckinridge, served in the Confederate army. Her papers, now part of the **Breckinridge Family** collection (205,000 items; 1752–1965), relate mainly to family affairs during and after the war.

Nathaniel Prentiss Banks's family papers (50,000 items; 1829–1911; bulk 1860–80) contain letters exchanged with his wife Mary Theodosia Palmer Banks (m. 1848), including letters she wrote after the Civil War while traveling abroad in France, Italy, and Switzerland. A scrapbook of clippings about Josephine Wilson Bruce (1853–1913) in the papers of her husband, **Blanche Kelso Bruce** (2 items; 1878–90), an African American senator from Mississippi, describes their marriage in 1878 and how she was received in Washington society during her husband's years in Congress. Diaries of Margaret Blaine Damrosch (1867–1949), daughter of Maine senator **James Gillespie Blaine** (7,000 items; 1777–1945; bulk 1870–92), concern the daily activities of a Washington, D.C., teenager, including her school lessons, domestic tasks, parties involving "kissing games," and painting lessons. Life in the late-nineteenth-century West is described in the papers (9,000 items; 1883–1917) of **Thomas Henry Carter,** senator from Montana, which include correspondence of his wife, Ellen Galen Carter (m. 1886), and the recollections of his sister Julia Ann Carter Lang (b. 1856?). The activities of a wealthy woman in the early twentieth century are documented in the diaries and correspondence of Abby Chapman Aldrich (1845–1917), wife of philanthropist and Rhode Island senator **Nelson W. Aldrich** (42,700 items; 1762–1930).

One of the most important twentieth-century congressional collections is also one of the best for studying women's history. The massive **La Follette Family** collection (423,800 items; 1844–1988; bulk 1910–53) includes the papers of Progressive senator Robert M. La Follette of Wisconsin, his wife Belle Case La Follette (1859–1931), their son, Senator Robert M. La Follette Jr., and their daughter, Fola La Follette (1882–1970).

Belle wrote and spoke on behalf of women's suffrage, civil rights, child labor legislation, education reform, and the post–World War I peace movement, addressing these and other issues in correspondence with such women as Jane Addams, Mary Ritter Beard, and Emma Wold. Fola La Follette, a teacher and actress, exchanged letters with Emily Newell Blair, Eva Le Gallienne, Mary McGrory, and Lillian Wald.

Both Robert Sr. and Robert Jr. corresponded with the leading women reformers of the day, and their papers contain numerous files relating to women's suffrage and women's rights. The younger La Follette's congressional papers also include Senate files on military nurses' training, Women's Army Auxiliary Corps, Women's Conservation Corps, and equal rights. Received with the La Follette collection were the papers of New York attorney Gilbert E. Row, concerning divorce, gender discrimination, and the legal problems of Margaret Sanger, Agnes Smedley, and Rosika Schwimmer. Additional correspondence of Fola and Belle La Follette may be found in the papers of Fola's husband, playwright and copyright specialist **George Middleton** (15,000 items; 1894–1967; bulk 1911–58), whose efforts to protect authors' literary rights brought him into contact with members of the theatrical and literary communities, including Edna Ferber, Lillian Gish, and Katharine Hepburn.

One of the division's largest congressional collections (260,000 items; 1905–40; bulk 1912–40) consists of the papers of **William Edgar Borah,** longtime senator from Idaho. His congressional files date from the early 1910s though the 1930s and include information on suffrage, the Equal Rights Amendment, the Children's Bureau, prohibition, child labor laws, birth control, and divorce legislation, as well as correspondence with Jane Addams, Carrie Chapman Catt, and other women leaders. Legislative files relating to suffrage, subject files concerning the General Federation of Women's Clubs, and correspondence with his wife, Mimosa Gates Pittman (1872–1952), including letters she wrote while staking claims in Alaska, may be found in the papers (55,000 items; 1898–1951) of Nevada senator **Key Pittman.**

Although principally known for his interests in agriculture, atomic power, and Native Americans, **Clinton Presba Anderson** (250,000 items; 1938–72; bulk 1948–72), senator and representative from New Mexico, also maintained congressional files relating to equal rights bills in the 1950s, legislation in the early 1960s to improve widows' benefits, and speeches delivered to various women's organizations. Among Anderson's predecessors in the Senate was fellow New Mexican **Bronson Cutting,** a newspaper publisher turned politician, whose papers (33,000 items; 1899–1950; bulk 1910–35) contain numerous files relating to military pension claims made by his constituents, many of whom were widows of Hispanic descent.

New York representative **Emanuel Celler** (195,000 items; 1924–73; bulk 1945–73) served for more than twenty years as chairman of the powerful House Judiciary Committee. Although he was a strong supporter of civil rights, Celler repeatedly used his position to keep the Equal Rights Amendment from reaching the House floor for a vote. (See "The Long Road to Equality" in this volume.) **Edward William Brooke** (240,000 items; 1956–88; bulk 1963–78) was the first popularly elected African American to serve in the Senate (1967–78), and he introduced legislation designed to make housing affordable for families and tenants of public housing (many of whom are women). He also proposed legislation to increase social security pensions and expand health care for the elderly. His papers include files on abortion, the Equal Rights Amendment, women's issues, and nurses' training. Before entering the Senate, Brooke was attorney general of Massachusetts in the 1960s, and his files from that period include materials relating to Albert DeSalvo, the self-confessed Boston Strangler.

Correspondence with women relatives and files relating to suffrage, the Equal Rights Amendment, birth control, and related issues may also be found in the collections of **Irvine Luther Lenroot** (10,000 items; 1890–1971; bulk 1900–1944); **Henry Justin Allen** (80,000 items; 1896–1942; bulk 1919–42); **Richmond Pearson Hobson** (27,300 items; 1889–1966; bulk 1890–1937); **John Sharp Williams** (36,000 items; 1902–24; bulk 1914–24); **James Martin Barnes** (12,000 items; 1924–58); **Victor Murdock** (38,300 items; 1824–1971; bulk 1909–40); **Robert A. Taft** (522,000 items; 1885–1980; bulk 1938–53); and **Thomas J. Walsh** (262,000 items; 1910–34).

Legal Collections

In addition to its strong presidential and congressional collections, the Manuscript Division also holds the nation's largest gathering of papers of chief justices and associate justices of the United States, as well as the papers of many judges of the lower federal courts. Complementing these judicial collections are the papers of numerous attorneys general, solicitors general, private lawyers, and public interest groups, all of which provide excellent sources of historical information on the country's legal affairs, including the laws and court cases that have shaped women's status, rights, and freedoms for more than three centuries. Although principally relating to areas of federal law, these collections touch on a host of legal matters of interest to women's historians, including such issues as nationality, citizenship, property and dower rights, voting rights, sexual discrimination, sexual harassment, working conditions, pay equity, and reproductive rights, to name just a sampling. They often contain details about legal cases and background on a judge's decision-making process that are not found in the official court reporters and similar published accounts (see chapter 3). Noted here are the papers of prominent women judges and attorneys, followed by a sampling of men's collections relevant to women's legal history. Since many of these legal collections carry access restrictions (which vary from collection to collection and are too complex to explain here), researchers are reminded to contact the Manuscript Division Reading Room before visiting.

Only two women have served on the U.S. Supreme Court during its first two hundred years of existence, and the Manuscript Division holds the papers of both—**Sandra Day O'Connor** (b. 1930) and Ruth Bader Ginsburg. O'Connor donated the first of her papers (71,475 items; 1963–88) to the division in 1991, ten years after her appointment to the Court. These relate to her first five years on the Court and to her career in Arizona as a state senator (1969–75), a Maricopa County Superior Court judge (1975–79), and a judge on the Arizona Court of Appeals (1979–81), with the Supreme Court files making up the bulk of the collection. These are divided into three subseries: administrative files, case files, and docket sheets. As the first woman justice, O'Connor received hundreds of letters in 1981 from well-wishers, including many from women and girls of all ages inspired by the justice's appointment. In 1988, following her surgery for breast cancer, she received numerous cards and letters from women who had also undergone mastectomies. O'Connor's handwritten notes of the major issues, oral arguments, and opinions of her colleagues highlight her case files, including those relating to *Mississippi University for Women v. Hogan,* a 1982 gender discrimination case; *City of Akron v. Akron Center for Reproductive Health,* a 1983 abortion rights case; and *Grove City College v. Bell* , a 1984 Title IX sexual discrimination case.

In 1993, **Ruth Bader Ginsburg** (b. 1933) joined O'Connor on the Court, and five years later donated to the Library two installments of her papers (16,450 items; 1925–99; bulk 1970–97) covering her academic career as the first tenured woman professor at Columbia University Law School (1972–80), her appointment to the U.S. Court of Appeals for the District of Columbia Circuit (1980–93), and her accomplishments as a pioneering litigator for women's rights, a role which earned her the title "the Thurgood Marshall of gender equality law." Papers relating to many of the constitutional law cases that Ginsburg argued for the American Civil Liberties Union in the 1970s are found here. Files for *Reed v. Reed* (1971), the landmark case in which the Supreme Court declared unconstitutional an Idaho law that favored the appointment of a man over a woman to act as administrator of an estate, document the first time the Court used the equal protection clause of the Fourteenth Amendment to protect a woman's right to equal treatment under the law. Also represented are several cases, such as *Frontiero v. Richardson* (1973) and *Craig v. Boren* (1975), in which Ginsburg and others attempted to convince the Court to apply an elevated standard of review, comparable to the standard applicable to race, religion, and national origin, when considering the constitutionality of laws that differentiate on the basis of sex. Other important cases represented in the collection include *Weinberger v. Wiesenfeld, Healy v. Edwards, Califano v. Goldfarb,* and *Duren v. Missouri.* Complementing her ACLU files are scores of speeches and writings reflecting her advocacy of women's issues and her support of the failed Equal Rights Amendment.

More than fifty years before O'Connor and Ginsburg began their judicial careers, **Florence Ellinwood Allen** (1884–1966) became the first woman to sit on an American court of last resort when she was appointed an associate justice of the Ohio Supreme Court in 1922. From 1934 to 1959, she served on the U.S. Court of Appeals for the Sixth Circuit and was thought by many to be worthy of a Supreme Court nomination. Her papers (2,700 items; 1907–65) relate to her judicial career, her activities on behalf of suffrage and women's rights, and her interest in peace through international law. Another pioneering judge was **Juanita Kidd Stout** (1919–1998), who in 1959

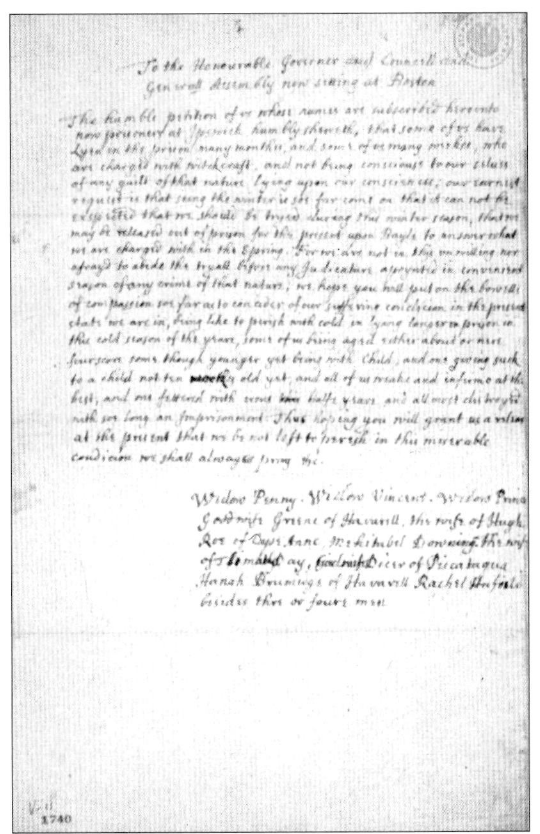
To the Honourable Governor and Council and General Assembly now sitting at Boston

Witches petition, ca. 1692. John Davis Batchelder Autograph Collection (vol. 11, item 1740). Manuscript Division. LC-MS-12021-A7 (color slide).

People were executed for witchcraft throughout the colonies during the seventeenth century, but especially in Massachusetts. Many of the accused were women, prompting some recent historians to suggest that charges of witchcraft were a way of controlling women who threatened the existing economic and social order. In 1692 the famous Salem, Massachusetts, witchcraft trials took place, and that summer hundreds of people in the colony were arrested. Shown here is an appeal from ten women "besides thre or foure men" who were confined without trial in the Ipswich jail for many months. The petitioners—some "fettered with irons," some pregnant, and all "weake and infirme"—request that they be released on "bayle" to stand trial the following spring so that they do not "perish with cold" during the winter months.

became the first African American woman to serve as a judge in Pennsylvania and the first in the country to win election to a court of record. Her obituary called her the "judicial scourge of murder, mayhem, and bad grammar,"[19] because she was known to take tough stances on convicted criminals and was adamant about the importance of education to deter crime. Her recently acquired collection (31,000 items; 1929–98) deals primarily with her judicial career.

Although a woman did not become attorney general of the United States until Janet Reno's appointment in 1993, numerous women did serve in the Justice Department before that time, including **Mabel Walker Willebrandt** (1889–1963), a former Los Angeles public defender (with special responsibility for cases involving women), who in 1921 became the second woman to receive an appointment as assistant attorney general and the first to serve an extended term. Although not known as a prohibitionist before her appointment, Willebrandt became one of the fiercest defenders of the Eighteenth Amendment, earning the nickname "Prohibition Portia." She also was responsible for establishing the first federal prison for women and played an important role in Herbert Hoover's successful presidential campaign. Her papers (2,000 items; 1881–1978; bulk 1921–29), especially her letters to her parents, concern her Supreme Court appearances, social and political life in Washington, Republican Party politics, and the role of women in politics. Additional items relating to her may be found in the papers of Justice **Harlan Fiske Stone** (26,500 items; 1889–1953; bulk 1925–46), who was attorney general during part of Willebrandt's tenure at the Justice Department.

Deputy attorney general for Pennsylvania **Regina Clark McGranery** (1907–1975) and her husband **James P. McGranery,** attorney general of the United States (74,800 items; 1909–75; bulk 1943–75) were active in the Democratic Party and the Catholic Church. Regina's papers reflect the political role of women during the New Deal and document her career as a lawyer and a leader in the Girl Scouts and Woman's National Democratic Club. The couple's law office files contain material on birth control, sterilization, and women's religious organizations.

As suggested by the O'Connor and Ginsburg collections, the papers of Supreme Court justices and appeals court judges contain a wealth of information on federal case law relating to women of all classes, races, and regions. Many of these judges and justices also had earlier careers as lawyers or state judges, and thus their papers may reflect aspects of state law as well. For a sense of the division's collections relating to the Supreme Court, consider that it holds the papers of nearly every chief justice from 1796 to 1969. Locating material relating to women and the law in the eighteenth- and nineteenth-century collections is more difficult than in those of the twentieth century, as fewer challenges to women's legal position reached the nation's highest court in earlier years. Nevertheless, many of the early collections do contain correspondence with women family members and friends, some of which touch on legal matters. For example, the papers of Chief Justice **Salmon P. Chase** (12,500 items; 1755–1898; bulk 1824–72) contain correspondence with his third wife, Sarah Bella Ludlow Chase (d. 1852), and his daughters Janette Chase Hoyt and Catherine "Kate" Chase Sprague (1840–1899), in which he discusses his career and advises Kate against seeking a divorce.

Among twentieth-century chief justices, the papers of **Earl Warren** (250,000 items; 1864–1974; bulk 1953–74) are notable for the many landmark decisions identified with his tenure in the areas of civil rights, race relations, criminal procedure, freedom of speech and press, and church-state relations. Included are case file materials for *Griswold v. Connecticut,* the 1965 privacy rights case that overturned one of the last state laws prohibiting the prescription or use of contraceptives by married couples. The *Griswold* decision is also represented in the papers of **William O. Douglas** (634,000 items; 1801–1980; bulk 1923–75), who wrote the Court's majority opinion in the case.

Besides Douglas's papers, the division holds those of other associate justices who served under Warren or his successors, several of which are particularly relevant to women's legal history, especially the papers of **Felix Frankfurter** (70,625 items; 1846–1966; bulk 1907–66), an associate justice from 1939 to 1962. Letters from the justice's wife, Marion Denman Frankfurter (d. 1975), describe her activities at Smith College (1910–12) and graduate studies in social work, her support of suffrage, her work with the American National Red Cross during World War I, and her research and editing of her husband's articles. Marion's sister, Helen Denman, wrote about her experiences as a traveling secretary in the 1920s for the Young Women's Christian Association (YWCA). While a professor at Harvard Law School, Felix Frankfurter assisted the National Consumers' League and other groups in their efforts to obtain protective legislation for women in the workplace. He was the lead attorney for the appellants in the 1923 Supreme Court case *Adkins v. Children's Hospital,* and his papers contain files relating to that case and more generally to child labor and minimum wage legislation. He counted among his correspondents notable women such as Grace Abbott, Molly Dewson, Alice Hamilton, Belle Moskowitz, and Frances Perkins. Frankfurter's fellow New Deal appointee **Hugo L. Black** (130,000 items; 1883–1976; bulk 1926–71) also maintained files from his Senate and judicial careers on wages and hours legislation, pure food and drug bills, and birth control.

Since the 1960s, the number of Supreme Court cases relating to women's legal rights has grown substantially as the judicial system has ruled on issues of job discrimination, privacy, reproductive rights, affirmative action, and sexual harassment. These topics and others are particularly well represented in the papers of **William J. Brennan** (388,000 items; 1945–98; bulk 1956–90), **Byron R. White** (183,500 items; 1961–92), **Thurgood Marshall** (173,700 items; 1949–91; bulk 1961–91), and **Harry A. Blackmun** (530,000 items; 1913–99; bulk 1959–94). Blackmun wrote the majority opinions in the landmark 1973 abortion rights cases *Roe v. Wade* and *Doe v. Bolton.* As a result, he received much correspondence (more than eight thousand items of which were retained in his papers) from supporters and detractors on both sides of this contentious issue. Most of the critical letters stemmed from the 1973 cases or were received before oral arguments in the controversial 1989 ruling *Webster v. Reproductive Health Services,* in which the Court upheld Missouri's restrictions on abortion and accepted limits on the use of federal funding for abortion-related services.

Legal case files form an important component of recent judicial collections, and such files are generally arranged by date of term and docket number, which may be a year or two earlier than the date of decision. Legal casebooks, digests, and other sources described in chapter 3 are helpful in identifying decisions relevant to women. Also useful is Elizabeth Frost-Knappman and Kathryn Cullen-DuPont's *Women's Rights on Trial: 101 Historic Trials from Anne Hutchinson to the Virginia Military Institute Cadets* (Detroit: Gale Research, 1997; KF220.F76 1997).

Supplementing the papers of Supreme Court justices are the papers of many lower-court judges, especially those who played a vanguard role in the modern civil rights movement, such as **Simon Ernest Sobeloff** (95,000 items; 1882–1973; 1950–73), **J. Skelly Wright** (81,200 items; 1933–87; bulk 1948–86), and **Frank Minis Johnson** (116,000 items; 1945–89; bulk 1955–86). Wright's papers include letters from his former law clerk Susan Estrich (b. 1952), who later became the presidential campaign manager for Michael Dukakis and a noted legal expert on rape. The papers of U.S. District Court judge **Gerhard A. Gesell** (60,000 items; 1956–93) include materials on *United States v. Vuitch* (1971), an im-

FILED MAY 19 1923

Nation Wide Conference

called by

National Consumers' League

on the

Minimum Wage Decision

of the Supreme Court of the United States

This decision affirms your constitutional right to starve

National Consumers' League. Report of Conference on Minimum Wage Decision of the Supreme Court, April 20,1923. Cover with cartoon by Rollin Kirby, which the NCL reproduced courtesy of the New York World. *League of Women Voters Records (container I:25). Manuscript Division. LC-MS-29660-2.*

At the same time that women were campaigning for the vote, they were also lobbying for social welfare legislation, including protective laws establishing minimum wages and restricting the number of hours women could be forced to work. On April 9, 1923, the Supreme Court ruled in *Adkins v. Children's Hospital* that such minimum wage laws for women were unconstitutional because they interfered with the liberty of contract guaranteed by the Fifth and Fourteenth Amendments. Two weeks after that decision, which according to cartoonist Rollin Kirby guaranteed women the constitutional right to starve, the National Consumers' League (NCL) convened a meeting of groups supporting minimum wage legislation to consider next steps. The report of that meeting may be found not in the NCL records held by the Manuscript Division but in the records of an allied organization, the League of Women Voters, which had joined the NCL and other groups three years earlier to form a lobbying organization known as the Women's Joint Congressional Committee. Locating manuscript materials for a research project often involves expanding your search beyond the most obvious sources to include the papers of individuals and organizations that may have had an association with events and activities that are the focus of your research.

portant abortion case that laid the groundwork for *Roe v. Wade*. Also of interest is Gesell's sentencing file (1968–92), which reflects the vast economic and demographic changes in the District of Columbia over a twenty-year period and contains valuable social data about families, crime, the judicial system, and race relations.

Joining the papers of federal judges are those of several state judges, most notably Charles Mason, justice of the Iowa territorial supreme court, and **Ben B. Lindsey** (95,000 items; 1886–1954), a judge and social reformer who helped to develop the juvenile court system in Colorado and California. Mason's diaries, 1836–82, located in the **Charles Mason Remey Family** Papers (1,225 items; 1778–1949; bulk 1855–1932) describe his work on behalf of women's rights, including his support of equal pay for equal work. Lindsey corresponded with many women reformers, and his subject files concern child labor laws, penal reform, women's suffrage, birth control, marriage, divorce, sex education and hygiene, and the Women's Protective League.

A catalog search for the subject term "lawyers" (limited to manuscript records) identifies more than five hundred collections, many of which contain items of interest to women's historians. For example, attorney **Winn Newman** (126,500 items; 1876–1993; bulk 1979–91) specialized in litigation involving the rights of women and minorities, including lawsuits involving the comparable worth of women employees, sex and pregnancy discrimination, union access to equal opportunity data, and pay equity. Correspondence with Eleanor Roosevelt, client files relating to Lillian Hellman, and a speech and other items concerning the National Organization for Women are among the papers of lawyer and civic activist **Joseph L. Rauh Jr.** (107,650 items; 1913–88; bulk 1950–84).

Multigenerational family papers, organizational records, and dozens of other collections also merit investigation by students of women's legal history. For example, some of the early presidential collections, including the papers of **George Washington, Thomas Jefferson,** and **James and Dolley Madison,** contain legal documents relating to women's dower rights. After the American Revolution, Loyalist women, who had remained in the colonies after their husbands had fled, asserted rights and claims to family property seized by the new government, as evidenced by documents in Elizabeth Graeme Ferguson's papers in the **Marian S. Carson Collection** (14,250 items; ca. 1656–1995; bulk 1700–1876) and in the records of the **Great Britain Commission Appointed to Enquire into the Losses of American Loyalists** (6,000 items; 1784–90).

Other collections also reflect how individual women in the course of their everyday lives came into contact with the judicial system. A letter from **Frances Alexander** in 1820 records her efforts to obtain an affidavit for her case against Edward May for assault and battery. The reminiscences (1 item; 1893) of **Harriet Ann Moore Page Potter Ames** (b. 1810) describe her efforts in Texas in the mid-1800s to win a conviction against the murderers of her husband and daughter. Letters of school girl Lillian Gobitas Klose (b. 1923) and her brother **William Gobitas** (100 items; 1935–89; bulk 1935–40) relate to the Supreme Court case *Minersville v. Gobitis* [*sic*] concerning the children's refusal on religious grounds to salute the American flag at their Pennsylvania school in 1935. The records of civil rights organizations such as the **National Association for the Advancement of Colored People** and the **NAACP Legal Defense and Educational Fund** (see "Reform" above) contain files relating to legal issues affecting African American women, and legal files in the **National Woman's Party** Records (see "Women's Suffrage" above) document that group's efforts to contest the constitutionality of laws discriminating against all women.

Military and Diplomatic Affairs

Military and diplomatic collections are another strength of the Manuscript Division. Included are the papers of hundreds of career military officers, volunteers, and enlisted personnel as well as defense secretaries, war correspondents, and private citizens caught in the path of war. Joining these military collections are the papers of more than three hundred diplomats and more than half of the individuals who have served as secretary of state. Most of these collections relate to men, which is not surprising, given women's relatively late admittance to the military and diplomatic ranks. Nevertheless these sources, like the division's presidential, congressional, and legal holdings, contain information of interest to those researching the history of women in this country. Material abounds about women's role in managing households, farms, and businesses when their husbands and fathers left to fight in wars or assume overseas diplomatic posts. Sometimes wives accompanied their husbands to frontier outposts and to overseas embassies and consulates, becoming by extension unofficial representatives of the United States government. By World War I, women were being officially recruited for war work, but before that time, they had worked as army cooks, seamstresses, and laundresses, engaged in espionage, nursed the sick and wounded, and supported the military effort in various other ways, sometimes even going so far as to disguise themselves as men to go into combat. A quick survey of the division's military and diplomatic collections suggests the wealth of information waiting to be mined by women's historians who have not always examined these sources with the same interest and enthusiasm as other collections.

Although the division's military holdings span the entire history of the United States, they are particularly rich for the eighteenth and nineteenth centuries. The Revolutionary War is the focus of innumerable collections, many of which are described in the publication *Manuscript Sources in the Library of Congress for Research on the American Revolution,* compiled by John R. Sellers et al. (Washington: Library of Congress, 1975; Z1238.U57 1975). These collections cover both Loyalists and patriots. For example, surgeon **Isaac Foster** (69 items; 1769–1899), a patriot, described for his wife, Mary Russell Foster, his military activities and travels during the American Revolution, and she wrote to him about domestic life and the impact of war on the economy, especially in the Boston area. After her Loyalist husband and their daughter fled to England during the Revolutionary War, Grace Galloway (d. 1782) remained in Philadelphia in an unsuccessful attempt to save the family property. Her correspondence in the **Joseph Galloway Family** Papers (260 items; 1743–1823) describes her daily experiences, her need to smuggle her letters through enemy lines, and the attack on the family's home during the riots following the British surrender at Yorktown. **Christian Barnes** (54 items; 1768–84), the wife of merchant Henry Barnes, similarly described the hardships faced by Loyalists in Massachusetts and related her family's experiences after the war when they and other Loyalists relocated to Bristol, England.

The period between the Revolution and the Civil War is one for which the Library holds a number of interesting naval collections, including several that document the role of wives in maintaining the family home and raising children while their husbands were away at sea for months or even years at a time. The **Browning Family** Papers (900 items; 1824–1917; bulk 1835–55) include numerous letters that Eleanor Hanlon Browning (1809–1857) wrote to her naval officer husband when he was on duty on various ships from 1834 to 1850. Minerva Denison Rodgers (1784–1877) managed her family's household affairs and kept her husband, Commodore John Rodgers, apprised of domestic matters while he was at sea. Observing their mother's life no doubt helped to prepare the Rodgerses' daughters, Ann Rodgers Macomb (1824–1916) and Louisa Rodgers Meigs (1817–1879), for similar roles in their marriages to military men, as reflected in the letters they exchanged with their spouses. Also included in the **Rodgers Family** Papers (14,850 items; 1740–1987; bulk 1804–1932) are letters of a granddaughter, Minerva Macomb Peters, recounting the difficulties she faced in adjusting to frontier life in Wyoming, where she and her husband settled after their marriage in 1881, and to the life of a diplomat's wife later that decade when her husband accepted a post in the U.S. consular service in Germany.

Some wives such as Harriet D. Welles traveled with their seafaring husbands. Harriet's diary in the **Roger Welles** collection (2,100 items; 1884–1926) describes navy life aboard the USS *New Orleans* and the people and customs in Shanghai, Hong Kong, and Manila during a tour of duty to China in ca. 1910. The division's naval collections span all time periods, and more than 370 of them can be found by searching the catalog for the subject term "naval officers." Many of these include letters or diaries of wives, including the papers of **Reginald R. Belknap** (7,100 items; 1784–1929; bulk 1900–1929), **George Dewey** (25,000 items; 1805–1949; bulk 1885–1931), **Edward Everett Hayden** (11,000 items; 1817–1965; bulk 1879–1932), **Richmond Pearson Hobson** (27,300 items; 1889–1966; bulk 1890–1937), **Charles A. Lockwood** (7,000 items; 1904–67; bulk 1940–60), and **William Sowden Sims** (43,000 items; 1856–1951; bulk 1900–1936). Besides the catalog, descriptions of many naval collections may be found in the printed guide *Naval Historical Foundation Manuscript Collection: A Catalog* (Washington: Library of Congress, 1974; Z1249.N3 U5 1974). Complementing these many naval collections are several dozen whaling collections that also provide documentation about nineteenth-century marriages and domestic situations characterized by seafaring husbands' long absences from home.[20]

No military topic is better documented in the Manuscript Division's collections than the Civil War. The division holds the records of the **Confederate States of America** (18,500 items; 1858–72) and the papers of many of the leading generals and of hundreds of noncommissioned officers and enlisted personnel on both sides of the conflict. A leading component of most of these collections is family correspondence, notably letters between wives and husbands, and parents and children. These range from the **Thomas Ewing Family** Papers (94,000 items; 1757–1941; bulk 1815–96)—which include letters Ellen Ewing Sherman (1824–1888) wrote to her mother describing the various army camps where she visited her husband, Union general William T. Sherman—to letters that Confederate army officers **Roger Weightman Hanson** (175 items; 1856–88) and **John Singleton Mosby** (40 items; 1861–1904; bulk 1860–69) exchanged with their wives. Some women, including Ellen Marcy McClellan (1838–1907), used their diaries not only to record their own personal thoughts and ac-

Antonia Ford Willard. Lace cap and collar. Willard Family Papers (container I:172). Manuscript Division. LC-MS-45757-6.

When division archivists sort, arrange, and describe a manuscript collection, they occasionally discover locks of hair, articles of clothing, jewelry, pressed flowers, pieces of wedding cake, wallets, badges, pins, or other three-dimensional artifacts tucked in among the papers. Generally these items are not retained within the Manuscript Division, although notable exceptions to this policy abound, including this delicately crafted lace cap and collar, purportedly made by Antonia Ford Willard (1838–1871) while in prison on charges of spying for the Confederate army. Willard, who later married her captor, Union Major Joseph Clapp Willard, wrote a poem about these items, which began with the verse "This collar my Mamma must wear, And she must wear alone, I've made it in my prison cell, Don't think me quite a drone."

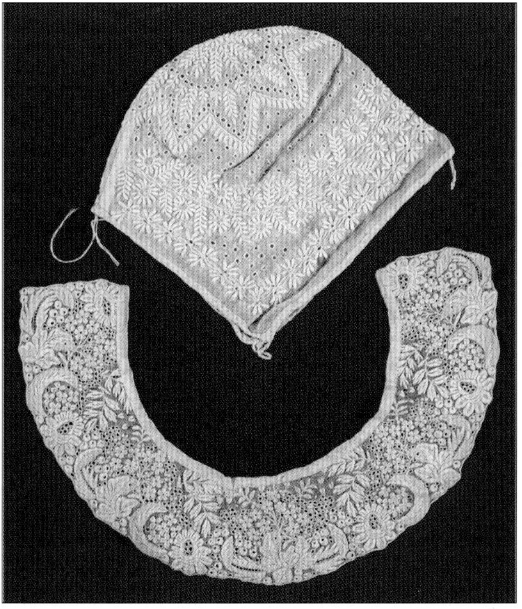

E. Carra[nce]. Watercolor drawing in souvenir autograph album. Mary Curry Desha Breckinridge file, Breckinridge Family Papers (container 845). Manuscript Division. LC-MS-13698-4.

Mary Curry Desha Breckinridge (d. 1918) was one of more than eighteen thousand Red Cross nurses who served with the Army and Navy Nurse Corps during World War I. Affiliated with a Chicago hospital unit assigned to France, Breckinridge earned the respect of her colleagues and the gratitude of the soldiers whom she nursed. Before fatigue and poor health forced Breckinridge to leave France, she assembled in this souvenir autograph album various poems, sketches, notes of appreciation, and remembrances, including some written by her patients.

tivities, but also to record for their families and posterity their husbands' accomplishments. The remaining three volumes, 1866–72, of Ellen's deliberately detailed diaries were recently added to the **George Brinton McClellan** Papers (33,000 items; 1823–98; bulk 1850–85).

Other parts of this chapter (see especially "Reform," "Science and Medicine," and "Congressional Collections" above) discuss collections reflecting women's roles as Civil War nurses, laundresses, welfare agents, and suppliers of food and clothing. Another area of continuing research interest is the role women played gathering intelligence information for both armies. Union signal officer **James M. McClintock** (84 items; 1862–87) received help from his daughter in transcribing intercepted Confederate messages. Quaker Rebecca M. Bonsal, a Union supporter living in Winchester, Virginia, in 1864, smuggled military intelligence to Union army officer **Philip Henry Sheridan** (18,000 items; 1831–91; bulk 1862–87), thus enabling him to capture the town. The papers of the socially and politically active **Willard Family** of Virginia and Washington, D.C. (119,900 items; 1800–1968; bulk 1890–1954) include the papers of Antonia Ford Willard (1838–1871), an accused Confederate spy who was a commissioned aide-de-camp to Gen. Jeb Stuart. Her letters discuss the effects of the war on noncombatants, the whereabouts of friends and family in the Confederate army, and her secret romance with and subsequent marriage to Union Maj. Joseph Clapp Willard, who had arrested her for wartime espionage. Additional correspondence, research notes, and clippings about Willard and her part in the Confederate capture of Gen. Edwin Henry Stoughton were assembled by Antonia's daughter-in-law, Belle Layton Wyatt Willard (1873–1954), whose own papers provide important insights into her life as a diplomat's wife and businesswoman involved in her family's extensive real estate and hotel operations. Information on other women spies may be found in the papers of **Philip Phillips** (see "Congressional Collections" above), **John C. Babcock** (60 items; 1855–1913), who served in the military intelligence bureau of the Army of the Potomac, and in the aforementioned records of the **Confederate States of America.** For descriptions of other Civil War collections, consult the Library's catalog and the printed guide *Civil War Manuscripts: A Guide to Collections in the Manuscript Division of the Library of Congress,* compiled by John R. Sellers (Washington: Library of Congress, 1986; Z1242.L48 1986).

Among the military collections described in *Many Nations: A Library of Congress Resource Guide for the Study of Indian and Alaska Native Peoples of the United States,* edited by Patrick Frazier et al. (Washington: Library of Congress, 1996; Z1209.2.U5 L53 1996), are several that touch upon women's experiences in the West. **Elizabeth Burt** (b. 1839), a volunteer nurse during the Civil War, married soldier Andrew Sheridan Burt and accompanied him throughout his long army career to various military outposts on the western frontier. A picture of their life together, including information on their relations with Native Americans, can be pieced together by reading Burt's letters to her daughter and the typescript copy of her autobiographical account, "An Army Wife's Forty Years in the Service, 1862–1902," contained in her papers (60 items; 1797–1917). Diaries of Sadie Pollock Carlton list her monthly expenses and describe her activities living with her husband **Caleb Henry Carlton** (2,500 items; 1831–1954; bulk 1844–1916) in army forts in Nebraska, Texas, and South Dakota between 1879 and 1894. In letters to his father and sister, army officer **John**

Porter Hatch (150 items; 1843–68) described the hardships of a frontier assignment and the pain of being separated from his wife.

As noted elsewhere in this chapter (see "Reform," "Science and Medicine," and "Congressional Collections" above), many of the division's collections concern women's relief work and their activities as nurses during the Spanish-American War and World War I. The papers (21,500 items; 1900–1975; bulk 1955–75) of pioneer aviator **Marjorie Claire Stinson** (1896–1975), on the other hand, document her work as a flight instructor and reflect women's role in aviation during the First World War. **Emma L. George**'s papers (52 items; 1915–20) relate to her association with the Woman's Land Army of America, which recruited and trained women to work farms left untended by men in the military. Included are letters from appreciative farmers, poems and songs about the "farmerettes," and recruitment and training material. Several collections reflect women's efforts to memorialize those who participated in the Great War, including the records of the **American Gold Star Mothers, Inc.** (4,000 items; 1917–41) and the papers of **Lydia S. M. Robinson** (13,500 items; 1914–42, bulk 1914–18), **Eva Roberts Cromwell Stotesbury** (122 reels; 1914–19), and **Mary Edith Powel** (32,000 items; 1747–1922; bulk 1890–99).

In many respects, World War II marked the watershed of women's participation in the United States military. The Women's Army Auxiliary Corps (WAAC)—later the Women's Army Corps (WAC)—was established in May 1942. Two months later, the Navy began recruiting women into its Women Accepted for Voluntary Emergency Service (WAVES). Women also entered the U.S. Marines and Coast Guard, and women pilots became members of the Women's Auxiliary Ferrying Service (WAFS) and the Women Airforce Service Pilots (WASP).[21] Before becoming a state legislator and first secretary of health, education, and welfare, **Oveta Culp Hobby** (1905–1995) was a United States army colonel and the director of the Women's Army Corps during World War II. Correspondence, photographs, and printed matter (2,200 items; 1941–52) document her career with the War Department and the mobilization of American women for military service. Correspondence with Hobby may also be found in the papers of high-ranking Air Force officer and aviation pioneer **Ira Eaker** (77,300 items; 1918–89; bulk 1942–82), who supported the training of women pilots; who successfully lobbied Hobby and his superiors for a WAC Company to be assigned to his command, first in England and later near the front in Italy; and, who, despite his own reservations, put before his commanders the request of Dixie Tighe, a woman war correspondent who wanted to go on a bomber mission as her male counterparts had. Of the WACs in Italy, Eaker wrote of their "superb" work habits, suggesting that "one girl is worth three men," and raved that despite "extremely unpleasant conditions . . . this little group of American girls is exhibiting the best and most cheerful type of morale of any soldiers I have ever seen."[22]

Army officer **Henry Harley Arnold** (160,000 items; 1903–89; bulk 1940–46) saved among his papers letters from mothers whose sons served in the Air Force during World War II and many subject files relating to the WAC, the WASP, the Women's Flying Corps, women nurses, and career opportunities for women after the war. Air Force officer **Noel Francis Parrish** (29,500 items; 1894–1987; bulk 1930–87) is best known for overseeing the training of African American male pilots at Tuskegee Army Air Field during World War II, but he was also interested in the work of the Women's Army Corps and corresponded with Pam A. McClellan about the training of women pilots.

Dixie Tighe was just one of many women covering the war for news media (see Janet Flanner and May Craig under "Literature and Journalism" below). Another was **Betty Wason** (b. 1912), a Columbia Broadcasting System war correspondent in Europe from 1938 to 1941, who for part of that time was stationed in Greece and made nightly broadcasts from there to the United States. Of note among Wason's papers (21 items; 1941–43) is a diary with brief entries describing the German invasion of Greece and her evacuation from Athens via Berlin and Lisbon to New York. Among the many collections that describe the home front during World War II are the papers of labor relations consultant **Maurice F. Neufeld** (12,000 items; 1919–90; bulk 1932–87), which include correspondence from his wife Hinda Cohen Neufeld, an administrator with the New York State Division of Women in Industry and Minimum Wage.

The government as well as many of the women themselves saw their military work during World War II as a temporary measure. Some, of course, remained to make a career for themselves, but women were not fully integrated into all the branches until the late 1970s, did not gain admittance to the four major military academies until 1975–76, and only in recent years have begun to reach the highest ranks. Asian affairs analyst and Indonesian expert **Jeanne S. Mintz** (1922–1994) was one of the first American women to be given operational responsibility for high-level military policy. Early in her career, she was an adviser to the Indonesian ambassador to the United Nations and worked for two Washington, D.C., think tanks doing national security work for the Department of Defense. During the Vietnam War, Mintz supervised special operations teams responsible for emplacing remote sensors along North Vietnamese supply routes. She joined the Defense Department in 1970 and held numerous positions before retiring as an assistant deputy undersecretary for Asia, Middle East, and the Southern Hemisphere. In her last position, she was involved in missile nonproliferation treaty negotiations and in Israel-Egypt peace talks. Her papers (23,400 items; 1928–93; bulk 1943–65) touch on all aspects of her career but are strongest for the period of the 1940s through 1960s.

Fifty years before Mintz took part in these peace negotiations, Congresswoman Ruth Bryan Owen Rohde (see "Congressional Collections" above) became the first American woman appointed to a major diplomatic post when she was named minister to Denmark in 1933, a period in her life that is reflected in letters she exchanged with diplomat **Laurence A. Steinhardt** (42,500 items; 1929–50). Four years later, **Florence Jaffray Hurst Harriman** (1870–1967) became the second woman to join this elite club. Her papers (9,000 items; 1912–50) relate primarily to her service as U.S. minister to Norway (1937–41) and her subsequent activities in world peace organizations. When Franklin D. Roosevelt posted her to Norway, he had not anticipated Germany's invasion of that country, but Harriman, an early suffragist, displayed great courage during this dangerous period. She negotiated the release of an American ship captured by the Germans, accompanied the Norwegian government into exile in Sweden, and arranged for the evacuation of American citizens. In 1998, Harriman's granddaughter donated additional papers covering Harriman's work in the Woodrow Wilson presidential campaign and her role as cofounder of the Women's National Democratic Club. Also of interest is Harriman's correspondence with World War I general John J. Pershing and Secretary of the Treasury William Gibbs McAdoo, with whom she had close relationships.

From 1953 through 1956, **Clare Boothe Luce** (see "Congressional Collections" above), served as U.S. ambassador to Italy under President Dwight D. Eisenhower, and in 1965, President Lyndon Johnson appointed **Patricia Harris** (1924–1985) U.S. ambassador to Luxembourg (see "Education" above). Joining Harris in breaking the State Department's racial barriers were economist and diplomat **Mabel M. Smythe** (b. 1918) and her husband, sociologist and diplomat **Hugh H. Smythe,** whose papers (34,000 items; 1921–94) document their long careers in foreign service and their efforts to promote greater appreciation throughout the world for cultural, racial, and gender differences. Included are materials on Mabel's work in the 1950s as a research director for the NAACP and the NAACP Legal Defense and Educational Fund; her memberships in the 1960s on the U.S. Advisory Commission on International Educational and Cultural Affairs, the Bureau of Educational and Cultural Affairs, and various United Nations commissions; her concurrent ambassadorships to Cameroon (1977–80) and Equatorial Guinea (1979–80), and her duties as deputy assistant secretary of state for African Affairs in the early 1980s. Throughout her life, Smythe held numerous teaching positions in economics and African Studies both in the United States and Japan, and she was a prolific writer and advocate for issues relating to Africa, multiculturalism, African American civil rights, women's issues, and the improvement of health and economic conditions in the United States.

The most recent woman diplomat whose papers have come to the Library is **Pamela Digby Churchill Hayward Harriman** (1920–1997), who was involved in national and international politics and diplomacy since the opening days of World War II. Her large collection of papers (501,650 items; 1940–97), which has not yet been processed, covers all aspects of her extraordinary life, with the bulk of the material documenting her civic and political activities during her last twenty years. During this period, she became a leading figure in the Democratic Party, served on the board of directors of the Commission on Presidential Debates (1987–93), was chair and cofounder of the major fund-raising committees "Democrats for the 80s" and "Democrats for the 90s," and was national cochair of the successful Clinton-Gore presidential campaign in 1992. The following year, President William Jefferson Clinton appointed her ambassador to France. Her papers reflect to a lesser degree her three marriages—to Prime Minister Winston Churchill's son, Randolph Churchill, Broadway agent and pro-

Women's Army Auxiliary Corps, Third Platoon, Company 1, Fort Des Moines, Iowa. Photographer unknown, ca. August–September 1942. Oveta Culp Hobby Papers (container 14). Manuscript Division. LC-MS-26146-1.

On May 14, 1942, Congress passed legislation establishing the Women's Army Auxiliary Corps (WAAC), and just two months later the first 440 recruits reported to Fort Des Moines, Iowa, for basic training, among them approximately forty African American women. The War Department and WAAC director Oveta Culp Hobby (1905–1995) had assured Congress that Negro WAAC officers and auxiliaries would constitute at least 10 percent of the corps, but aggressive recruitment at black colleges and the assistance of influential reformer and educator Mary McLeod Bethune (1875–1955) were needed to attract enough qualified applicants to meet this quota and to dispel black women's fears of discrimination within the segregated armed services. The black press and civil rights organizations such as the NAACP, critical of the appointment of Hobby, a white southerner, carefully monitored the situation at Fort Des Moines and attempted to use the training facility as a test case to challenge the army's segregation policies. Some of the first African American women to be trained at Fort Des Moines, the women of the Third Platoon, Company 1, shown here with their commanding officer Capt. Frank Stillman, were in all likelihood part of either the first or second classes to graduate, respectively, on August 29 and September 11, 1942.

ducer Leland Hayward, and businessman and statesman W. Averell Harriman—and the various love affairs and liaisons with powerful men that had brought her so much press attention during her lifetime and spurred interest in several biographies and a made-for-television movie after her death.

Vastly outnumbering the papers of women diplomats are the papers of men who held positions in the foreign service. Included in many of these collections are letters and diaries written by wives or other female relatives who accompanied male diplomats to their foreign posts. The family papers of these men and women not only reflect the life of American families living abroad but also sometimes reveal aspects of American women's status and experiences at home. Much can be gleaned about a person's beliefs and interests from what they choose to observe and write about. A careful reader of diaries and letters often discovers references to the appearance, condition, and rights of women in the country where the writer is stationed, with their consequent direct or implicit comparisons to American women at home.

Included in the **Bancroft-Bliss Family** collection (5,800 items; 1788–1928; bulk 1815–75) are the papers of Elizabeth Davis Bancroft (1803–1886) dating from her boarding school days through both of her marriages, including her second union with historian and diplomat George Bancroft, U.S. minister to England from 1845 to 1849. Elizabeth's observations of the contemporary scene in England provided the source material for *Letters from England, 1846–1849* (New York: C. Scribner's Sons, 1904; DA625.B21), manuscript drafts of which are in the collection. Elizabeth's daughter-in-law, Eleanor Albert Bliss (d. 1874), also became an unofficial ambassador when her husband, Alexander Bliss (Elizabeth's son from her first marriage), became secretary of the U.S. legation at Berlin in the late 1860s and early 1870s.

Permelia Stevens Wadsworth Buckalew accompanied her husband **Charles Rollin Buckalew** (300 items; 1839–90) to Ecuador when he was appointed U.S. minister to that country in 1859, and her diary contains short entries recording her activities and observations of the country and its people. The **Anson and Edward L. Burlingame Family** Papers (550 items; 1810–1936) contain lengthy letters from Anson's wife Jane Cornelia Burlingame (d. 1888) describing for her father and sons the couple's official and private activities in China, where Anson served as U.S. minister from 1862 to 1867, and later in London, Paris, Berlin, and St. Petersburg, where he was negotiating treaties on behalf of the Chinese government. **Frances Hawks Cameron Burnett** (1884–1957) was an author and poet who became more involved than many diplomatic wives in the activities and concerns of her host country Japan. While stationed there with her husband Col. Charles Burnett, the U.S. military attaché, Burnett became active in the Boy Scouts of Japan (Nippon Renmei Shonendan), founded the Japan Humane Society (Nippon Jindo Kai), enjoyed the social life in Tokyo and at the Imperial Court, and promoted better relations between the United States and Japan. Much of her collection (700 items; 1818–1936; bulk 1911–36) is written in Japanese.

The papers of Helen Moore Bristol (1867–1945) document her life, first as an Alabama debutante and later as the wife of naval officer and diplomat **Mark L. Bristol** (33,000 items; 1882–1939; bulk 1919–39), the U.S. High Commissioner to Turkey. The papers of another diplomatic representative to Turkey, **Charles Monroe Dickinson** (1,000 items; 1897–1923), contain numerous documents concerning the abduction of Ellen Maria Stone (1846–1927), an American missionary in Macedonia who was carried off by brigands near the Turkish-Bulgarian border in 1901 and was held for ransom for six months.

Detailed descriptions of Italian customs, travels through Europe and the Far East, and the daily routines of life in the foreign service are the topics covered in three volumes of letters (1903–49; bulk 1903–07) written by **Mary Reed Edwards** (1862–1931), wife of a military attaché, to her mother in Tacoma, Washington. The papers of jurist and diplomat **Philip C. Jessup** (120,000 items; 1574–1983; bulk 1925–83) include those of his wife, Lois Walcott Kellogg Jessup (1898–1986), relating to her work for the American Friends Service Committee, the U.S. Children's Bureau (preparing reports on children in Europe during World War II), and the United Nations. Notebooks cover her travels to Africa, Latin America, and the Middle East where she made special efforts to see conditions and observe the activities of women.

Among daughters who accompanied their fathers to diplomatic posts, one of the more controversial was **Martha Dodd** (1908–1990), daughter of **William Edward Dodd** (20,000 items; 1900–1940), American ambassador to Germany from 1933 to 1937. According to some sources, Dodd had an affair with Rudolf Diels, head of the Prussian secret police, before denouncing fascism and becoming the lover of Boris Winogradov, an official at the Soviet embassy in Berlin. After Winogradov was recalled to the Soviet Union, Dodd returned to the United States and published an edited version of her Berlin diary, *Through Embassy Eyes* (1939), and helped her brother publish their father's diaries. Her own collection (4,900 items; 1898–1990; bulk 1950–90) relates to her Berlin experiences as well as to her exile with her millionaire husband, Alfred Kaufman Stern, to Cuba and Czechoslovakia following their indictment for participation in Soviet espionage in the 1950s.

Joining the papers of American diplomats are the papers (525 items; 1925–94; bulk 1930–49) of writer Courtney Letts Borden de Espil Adams (1899–1995), the American-born wife of Felipe Espil, the Argentine ambassador to the United States. Adams kept a detailed record of the "diplomatic, residential, and official life in Washington" in a series of diaries dating from 1933 to 1953, which she intended for publication. In October 1943, Espil was recalled to Argentina, and the diaries cover the couple's time there and at subsequent posts in Europe. When living in Washington, Adams became good friends with both Mathilde Welles, wife of Undersecretary of State Sumner Welles, and Frances Hull, wife of Secretary of State Cordell Hull. Hull and Welles were often at odds over policy, and the long conflict between the two men is documented from the perspective of their wives through conversations Adams reported in her diaries and correspondence she exchanged with the women.

Although not diplomats per se, author **Lilian Thomson Mowrer** (1889–1990) and her husband **Edgar Ansel Mowrer,** a syndicated columnist and American editor of the periodical *Western World,* both wrote and lectured on politics and world affairs, particularly on the diplomatic policies of France, Germany, Italy, and the United States. Their collection (52,500 items; 1910–70; bulk 1940–60) includes Lilian's papers documenting her activities with the Women's Action Committee for Lasting Peace and Women's World Fellowship.

Literature and Journalism

All areas of American studies, including our country's rich cultural and literary legacy, are reflected in the Library's manuscript holdings. Numerous collections document women's contributions to American literature and journalism. These include collections of papers that women generated as well as the papers of their male colleagues, editors, critics, and publishers. Most of these collections include drafts of literary manuscripts, research notes, transcripts of interviews, and other artifacts of the trade that illustrate the evolution of literary styles, genres, and themes. In addition, the best collections also contain rich correspondence files that reveal aspects of the writer's personality and reflect the cultural and political world in which they lived.

One of the country's earliest historians, poets, and playwrights was **Mercy Otis Warren** (1728–1814), whose pioneering account of the *History of the Rise, Progress, and Termination of the American Revolution* (1805) may be read in the original longhand draft (7 volumes; 1801–05) held by the division. Nineteenth-century novelist Constance Cary Harrison (1843–1920), the wife of Jefferson Davis's private secretary, wrote satires about southern and New York society. Her papers, part of the **Burton N. Harrison Family** collection (18,600 items; 1812–1926; bulk 1913–21), contain diaries, manuscripts of writings—including her autobiography *Recollections Grave and Gay* (1911)—and correspondence with Varina Howell Davis, Lady Fairfax, Minnie Maddern Fiske, Louise Chandler Moulton, and others. Popular novelist **Emma Dorothy Eliza Nevitte** [E.D.E.N.] **Southworth** (1819–1899), whose books are replete with tales of abandoned and mistreated women, is represented by a small collection of papers (500 items; 1870–1918; bulk 1890–99) consisting principally of letters she wrote to her daughter, Charlotte Southworth Lawrence, during the last decade of her life.

Among the division's twentieth-century literary holdings are the papers of prolific novelist **Gertrude Franklin Horn Atherton** (1857–1948), consisting of correspondence and manuscripts (35 items; 1889–1943) of her books *The Jealous Gods* (1928), *Golden Peacock* (1936), and *The Horn of Life* (1942). The papers of **Peter Marshall,** a Presbyterian clergyman and Senate chaplain (10,000 items; 1933–61), contain the writings of his wife Catherine Marshall (1914–1983), including her most famous book, *A Man Called Peter* (1951), which was turned into a motion picture. **Shirley Jackson** (1919–1965), a writer whose short stories frequently focused on witchcraft, the occult, and abnormal psychology, is perhaps best known for a macabre story about a community's yearly ritual of selecting a person to be brutally stoned to death. Drafts of "The Lottery" are among Jackson's papers (7,400 items; 1932–70), which also contain diaries, letters, and files on the vaguely autobiographical works *Life among the Savages* (1953) and *Raising Demons* (1957), in which she presents a humorous albeit strange account of raising children, cleaning house, and cooking meals in a disordered suburban environment. Other Jackson items are in the papers of her husband, literary critic and educator **Stanley Edgar Hyman** (14,000 items; 1932–78).

Few American women novelists have generated as much controversy as Russian expatriate **Ayn Rand** (1905–1982), proponent of "objectivism," a philosophy that embraced "rational self-interest" and rejected altruism, religion, and communism as "incompatible with a free society." Drafts of four novels—*We the Living* (1936), *Anthem* (1938), *The Fountainhead* (1943), and *Atlas Shrugged* (1957)—together with a small amount of material pertaining to Rand's newsletter (150 items; 1933–76; bulk 1933–59) form the nucleus of her papers. Small collections also exist for novelists **Marcia Davenport** (4,000 items;

1932–70), **Margaret Landon** (6 items; 1944), **Anne Morrow Lindbergh** (25 items; 1943), and **Elizabeth Madox Roberts** (500 items; 1920–40).

Complementing the papers of women novelists are several collections relating to women playwrights, including **Clare Boothe Luce** (see "Congressional Collections" above). Sixty-three volumes of diaries, love letters exchanged with her fiancé, and drafts of her plays make up the papers of playwright and peace advocate Olivia Cushing Andersen (1871–1917), sister-in-law of **Hendrik Christian Andersen** (12,000 items; 1844–1940; bulk 1880–1920). **Paul Field Sifton** and his wife **Claire G. Sifton** (1897–1980) collaborated on several literary and theatrical works, but the most appealing part of their papers (25,500 items; 1912–80) are Claire's diaries, which span the time from her junior high school days in Kansas City to her retirement in Mexico. They contain detailed descriptions of college life in the 1915–16 period, thoughts of a young working woman in New York in the early 1920s, the concerns of a government official's wife in late New Deal Washington, and interesting philosophical observations of a senior citizen spending her retirement in Maine and Mexico.

Transfers from the Copyright Office account for several collections of women's plays. Actress **Mae West** (1893–1992) submitted for copyright registration at least thirteen unpublished plays that she wrote between 1921 and 1964, including "The Hussy," "Sex," and "Diamond Lil." Social worker and reformer **Rose Pastor Stokes** (1879–1933) also submitted plays for copyright (5 items; 1913–15), as did **Djuna Barnes** (1 item; n.d.), **Barbara Garson** (1 item; 1966), and **Ruth Saint Denis** (2 items; 1905). Additional playscripts are likely to join these as the product of the division's ongoing effort to microfilm copyright submissions and retain selected originals as part of the **Library of Congress Copyright Office Manuscript Plays** Collection.

Joining the division's ranks of novelists and playwrights are several important women poets, foremost among them **Edna St. Vincent Millay** (1892–1950) and **Muriel Rukeyser** (1913–1980), both of whom were as well known for their political activities as for their literary achievements. The Library first began acquiring Millay's papers (32,625 items; 1892–1963; bulk 1921–44) shortly after the Pulitzer Prize–winner's death in 1950. Included are the original manuscript for Millay's long poem "Renascence," which brought the young poet her first public acclaim in 1912; correspondence from numerous friends and associates such as Sara Teasdale, Georgia O'Keeffe, and Vita Sackville-West; and items relating to Millay's protest of the 1927 trial and execution of anarchists Nicola Sacco and Bartolomeo Vanzetti, her defense of civil liberties, and her concern for the rise of totalitarianism in the 1930s.

Muriel Rukeyser followed in Millay's footsteps—from Vassar College to a lifetime of liberal and humanitarian causes. In 1932, she covered for the proletarian *Student Review* the controversial second trial of the Scottsboro Boys (nine black teenagers wrongly convicted of raping two white women) and was arrested after associating with black reporters during the proceedings. With the publication of Rukeyser's first volume of poetry in 1935, Louis Untermeyer hailed her as "the most inventive and challenging poet" of her generation. She later wrote about the Spanish civil war, published a disturbing account of West Virginia miners dying of silicosis, and in the 1950s to 1970s lent her name in support of dissident Korean poet Kim Chi Ha, anti-Vietnam War protests, and the emerging women's movement. Her large collection (30,000 items; 1882–1980; bulk 1936–79) includes literary and political files as well as correspondence with family and friends such as Elizabeth Bishop, Carson McCullers, Marianne Moore, Katherine Anne Porter, May Sarton, and Alice Walker. Other poets whose papers are in the division include **Elisabeth DuPuy** (200 items; 1895–1928), **Louise Imogen Guiney** (1,500 items; 1884–1916), and **Louise Chandler Moulton** (9,000 items; 1852–1908).

Women poets, novelists, and playwrights are also represented in the papers (2,000 items; 1876–1969; bulk 1908–38) of musician and philanthropist **Marian MacDowell** (1857–1956) and in the records of the **MacDowell Colony** (35,000 items; 1869–1970; bulk 1945–68), an artists' retreat in Peterborough, New Hampshire, which she founded in 1908 in memory of her husband, composer Edward A. MacDowell (see "The House that Marian Built" in this volume). **Helen Keller** (1880–1968) saved among her papers (2,000 items; 1908–54) manuscripts by authors who were blind. Files relating to Jessie Fauset, Eslanda Robeson, and other African American writers may be found in the records of the **Harmon Foundation** (37,800 items; 1913–67; bulk 1925–33), established in 1922 to acquaint the public with the work of black artists and writers and to recognize the achievement of blacks in the arts, business, science, religion, and race relations.

Included in the Records of the **United States**

Work Projects Administration (409,000 items; 1524–1947; bulk 1935–42) are more than three hundred thousand documents relating to the Federal Writers' Project (FWP), a New Deal work relief initiative that provided jobs to unemployed writers and other white-collar workers who could qualify as writers or editors.[23] Among the women employed by the FWP were several who later achieved national literary prominence, including Zora Neale Hurston, May Swensen, Mari Thomasi, and Margaret Walker. More than half of the FWP records relate to the *American Guide* program, which generated a series of travel guides providing the basic history of each state. Also carried out were projects relating to Folklore, Social-Ethnic Studies, Negro Studies, and Ex-Slave Narratives, as well as special, smaller studies such as one on food preparation and consumption—"America Eats"—and one titled "The Lexicon of Trade Jargon," which covers various occupations, including many dominated by women.

Much of the FWP material consists of field reports, oral history transcripts, and unpublished draft essays, which are a treasure trove of information on women, family life, slavery, work, and racial and ethnic customs in the United States. The data were collected in the 1930s, but they capture memories of informants from the mid-nineteenth century forward and preserve oral traditions that date to even earlier generations. Thousands of life stories were recorded with the aim of celebrating the country's multiculturalism and countering the rise of fascism sweeping Europe at the time. A quick search of the Folklore Project uncovers life histories of an Irish maid from Massachusetts, a woman textile worker in North Carolina, and a Vermont farm wife. These and many others have been reproduced on the Library's Web site.[24]

Among the male writers who worked for the FWP was the future National Book Award–winner **Ralph Ellison,** author of the now-classic *Invisible Man* (1952). Ellison's personal papers (46,100 items; 1890–1996; bulk 1933–90) are held by the Library. They include the papers of his wife, Fanny McConnell Ellison (b. 1912), pertaining to her work for the American Medical Center for Burma and her contributions as one of the founders of the Negro People's Theatre in Chicago. Other collections of male novelists and poets are also rich sources of information for women's historians. Women writers Gertrude Atherton, Sarah Orne Jewett, and Edith Wharton corresponded with western novelist **Owen Wister,** whose papers (26,130 items; 1829–1966) also include those of his grandmother, actress Fanny Kemble (1809–1893); his mother, author Sarah Butler Wister (1835–1908), who wrote *Worthy Women of Our First Century* (1877); and his wife, civic reformer Mary Channing Wister (1869–1913).

Poet and Librarian of Congress **Archibald MacLeish** (20,000 items; 1907–81; 1925–70) corresponded with some of the most important literary and political women of the twentieth century, including Mary McLeod Bethune, Pearl S. Buck, Helen Hayes, Dorothy Parker, and Irita Van Doren. Leading women writers and editors are also represented in the papers of poet and psychiatrist **Merrill Moore** (131,750 items; 1904–79; bulk 1928–57), poet **Karl Jay Shapiro** (2,300 items; 1939–68), and crime fiction novelist and screenwriter **James M. Cain** (30,000 items; 1901–78; bulk 1925–78). Cain's papers also contain letters of his wives, including his third wife, silent screen movie star Aileen Pringle (1895–1989), and his fourth wife, opera singer Florence Macbeth Cain (1891–1966).

Collections of male editors, literary critics, and publishers are equally valuable sources for researching women writers ranging from Emily Dickinson and Charlotte Perkins Gilman to Anaïs Nin and Susan Sontag. Among the most promising in this category are the papers of **Horace and Anne Montgomerie Traubel** (75,250 items; 1824–1979; bulk 1883–1947); **Joseph Warren Beach** (8,200 items; 1891–1955); **Benjamin Holt Ticknor** (3,000 items; 1595–1935; bulk 1850–1920); **B. W. Huebsch** (10,500 items; 1893–1964); **Ken McCormick** (60,000 items; 1882–1992; bulk 1910–92), and **Huntington Cairns** (58,450 items; 1780–1984; bulk 1925–84).

In 1931, political reporter **Ruby A. Black** (1896–1957) told a radio audience that she had experienced less sexism from the politicians and government officials who were her sources than from her male counterparts in the profession: "It is years, usually, before a woman is admitted to the fraternity . . ., years before other newspaper men give her tips and ask her for information in the way they trade with their male colleagues."[25] Historians eager to explore the connections between women, journalism, and politics should turn not only to Black's papers (35,000 items; 1916–61; bulk 1933–45), which cover her career as a part-time United Press correspondent, manager of her own news bureau, and biographer of Eleanor Roosevelt, but to many of the division's other journalism collections as well. (See also chapter 2.) Black's friend and colleague, newspaper columnist **May Craig** (1889?-1975), assembled a collection of papers (12,000 items; 1929–75) concerning her career as a reporter, radio broadcaster, and foreign war correspondent. As an active member of the Women's National Press Club, Craig shared Black's interest in women's rights and also championed children's education and other reforms. Like Black and Craig, **Bess Furman** (1894–1969) also covered the Roosevelt White House and became good friends with the first lady. During her more than forty years with the Associated Press and *New York Times,* Furman wrote about presidential wives, equal rights for women, and women in politics. Her collection (47,000 items; 1728–1967; bulk 1900–1966) includes correspondence with Grace Abbott, Helen Gahagan Douglas, Oveta Culp Hobby, Ruth Bryan Owen Rohde, Frances Perkins, and several first ladies.

One of the division's most important journalism collections is also a particularly strong source for women's history. The **Reid Family** Papers (232,000 items; 1795–1970) document the involvement of both Elisabeth Mills Reid (1858–1931) and her daughter-in-law Helen Rogers Reid (1882–1970) in the operation of the *New York Tribune* (later the *New York Herald-Tribune*). Elisabeth Reid closely followed her husband's career when he was managing editor and owner of the paper. After their son Ogden took control of the business, she wrote him and his wife Helen extensive letters concerning the paper's editorial policy and daily operations. Helen Reid had started as the paper's advertising editor in 1918 and eventually became president and chairman of the board. Like her in-laws, she too corresponded with the foremost women journalists and political figures of the period, and her papers make up the bulk of the Reid Family collection. Both Helen and Elisabeth were active philanthropists, with Elisabeth engaging in work with the American Red Cross, Bellevue Hospital, and Trudeau Sanitarium, whereas Helen supported various colleges and universities, the Fresh Air Fund, and women's suffrage.

Complementing the Reid collection are the papers of **Irita Taylor Van Doren** (1891–1966) who served as the *New York Herald-Tribune*'s longtime literary editor from 1926 to 1963. Van Doren corresponded with many famous women authors, such as Pearl S. Buck, Agatha Christie, and Mabel Dodge Luhan, and collected files of their original manuscripts, articles, and book reviews (4,360 items; 1920–66). Other Van Doren papers may be found in the records of the ***American Scholar*** (70,500 items; 1926–88; bulk 1944–88), on whose editorial board she served during the 1940s and 1950s, along with Ruth Benedict, Ada Louise Comstock, Margaret Mead, and Mary K. Simkhovitch, all of whom are represented in the journal's records.

Mary Bainbridge Hayden's journalism career, especially her coverage of Herbert Hoover's presidential campaign of 1928, is documented in the papers of her father **Edward Everett Hayden** (11,000 items; 1817–1965; bulk 1879–1932). A few papers of suffragist and journalist Mary Isabella Cadwallader are included with those of her husband **Sylvanus Cadwallader** (250 items; 1818–1904; bulk 1862–98), and the papers of lawyer and editor **Louis Freeland Post** (600 items; 1864–1939; bulk 1900–1922) contain articles, poems, and letters of Post's second wife, Alice Thacher Post (1853–1947), who established and edited the *Chicago Public* with him.

From 1912 until her death, **Gertrude Battles Lane** (1874–1941) edited the *Woman's Home Companion,* one of the most popular ladies' magazines of its time, with an estimated circulation of three million in 1938. Her collection consists almost entirely of correspondence (220 items; 1915–35), including letters from Jane Addams, Carrie Chapman Catt, Edna Ferber, and Ida M. Tarbell. Teacher, feminist, and Democratic Party leader **Marion Glass Banister** (d. 1951) was editor and publisher of the *Washingtonian* magazine from 1929 to 1933, before becoming assistant treasurer of the United States. Her small collection (1,500 items; 1933–51) contains correspondence and items relating to the Democratic National Committee. Boston *Globe* and New York *Times Herald* journalist **Dorothy Godfrey Wayman** (1893–1975) donated a collection (6,000 items; 1862–1971) documenting her newspaper career, her research on Edward Sylvester Morse and others, and her interests in Catholicism and religious matters in Asia.

Several collections relate to women's involvement with the *Washington Post.* **Evalyn Walsh McLean** (1886–1947), the daughter of millionaire Thomas F. Walsh, married into the McLean family, which owned the newspaper. She became the grande dame of Washington society in the first half of the twentieth century. Her papers (45,000 items; 1874–1948) document her much-publicized divorce, various libel suits, her involvement in the Lindbergh kidnapping case and Teapot Dome scandal, and her ownership of the Hope diamond. They also concern the Walsh family's Colorado mining interests and the McLean fam-

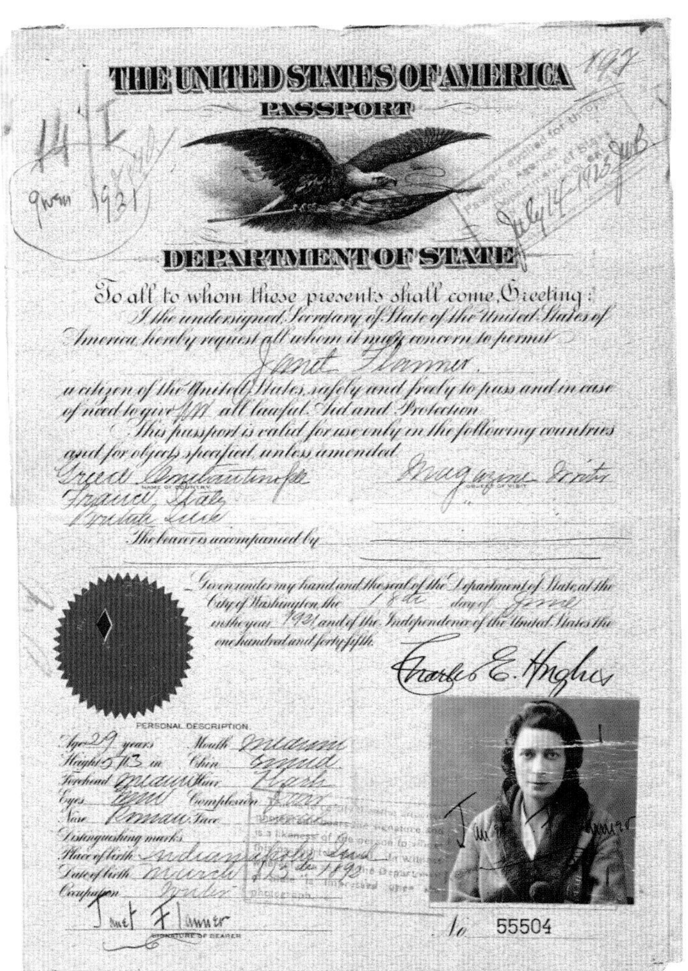

THE UNITED STATES OF AMERICA

PASSPORT

DEPARTMENT OF STATE

To all to whom these presents shall come, Greeting:

I the undersigned Secretary of State of the United States of America hereby request all whom it may concern to permit Janet Flanner, a citizen of the United States, safely and freely to pass and in case of need to give all lawful Aid and Protection.

This passport is valid for use only in the following countries and for objects specified, unless amended

The bearer is accompanied by

Given under my hand and the seal of the Department of State at the City of Washington the 18th day of June in the year 1921 and of the Independence of the United States the one hundred and forty fifth.

Charles E. Hughes

PERSONAL DESCRIPTION

Age 29 years

Height 5 ft 3 in

Place of birth Indianapolis Ind

Date of birth March 13th 1892

Occupation writer

Janet Flanner

SIGNATURE OF BEARER

No. 55504

Passport, 1921. Papers of Janet Flanner and Solita Solano (container 18). Manuscript Division. LC-MS-47084-3.

With this passport in hand in 1921, Janet Flanner (1892–1978) left her Greenwich Village literary life behind and embarked on what was to become a fifty-year career as one of the country's most influential foreign correspondents. Recently divorced and traveling with writer Solita Solano (1881–1975), with whom she would maintain a longtime intimate relationship, Flanner visited mainland Greece, the British Isles, and Italy before settling in France, where in 1925 she became the Paris correspondent for Harold Wallace Ross's recently launched magazine *The New Yorker.* Through her witty and informative "Letter from Paris" columns, written under the pseudonym Genêt, Flanner kept her American audience informed of the latest cultural and political happenings in France and throughout Europe.

ily's publishing operations. An interview and other materials about McLean appear in the papers of *Washington Post* society editor **Hope Ridings Miller** (800 items; 1887–1998; bulk 1934–90), who worked for the newspaper in the 1940s, edited *Diplomat* magazine in the 1950s and 1960s, and wrote several books on the architecture and social life of the capital city.

In 1933, the Meyer family purchased the *Washington Post,* and aspects of the newspaper business may be traced in the papers of both **Agnes Elizabeth Ernst Meyer** (1887–1970) and her husband **Eugene Meyer** (78,500 items; 1819–1970). Agnes's papers (70,000 items; 1907–70) document her life as an author, literary and art critic, social reformer, and philanthropist. Included are notes from her student days at Barnard College, diaries detailing life in Washington, D.C., in the 1920s, and family correspondence with her parents, husband, and children, including daughter Katharine Meyer Graham. Agnes was instrumental in lobbying for the creation of a cabinet-level department of health, education, and welfare, and her papers contain materials on that topic and on her work with the President's Commission on the Status of Women and the National Citizens Commission for the Support of the Public Schools. Additional correspondence with Agnes Meyer, Helen Rogers Reid, and other newspaperwomen may also be found in the papers of *St. Louis Post-Dispatch* publisher **Joseph Pulitzer** (67,500 items; 1897–1958; bulk 1925–55).

Dubbed "the first lady of the black press" for her pioneering coverage of civil rights, the Vietnam War, and international affairs for the *Chicago Daily Defender* and the *Afro-American* newspapers, **Ethel L. Payne** (1911–1991) was also the first black woman commentator on network television. A few months after Payne's death in 1991, the Manuscript Division acquired a collection (15,500 items; 1857–1991; bulk 1973–91) documenting her journalism career and her involvement in the civil rights movement and protests against South African apartheid.

Janet Flanner (1892–1978), who wrote under the pseudonym Genêt, and her longtime companion **Solita Solano** (1888–1975) were among the American journalists, writers, and literary editors who settled in Paris, France, in the twenties. They covered international affairs for *The New Yorker* and other American publishers. Their papers, known as the Flanner-Solano collection (3,000 items; 1870–1976; bulk 1955–75), provide a window into the literary and intellectual life of Paris and New York during the first half of the twentieth century. They counted among their friends and acquaintances prominent women such as Berenice Abbott, Margaret Anderson, Djuna Barnes, Kay Boyle, Nancy Cunard, Anita Loos, Carson McCullers, Gertrude Stein, and Alice B. Toklas. Additional papers, relating primarily to the last decade of Flanner's career and her lesbian relationship with editor **Natalia Danesi Murray** (1901–1994), may be found in a separate Flanner-

Murray collection (4,500 items; 1940–84), which includes the selections Murray published in *Darlinghissima: Letters to a Friend* (1985).

As seen in the earlier discussion about **Frederick Douglass** (see "Reform" above), the collections of male journalists and newspaper publishers often contain subject files, correspondence, and family papers relevant to women's history. Although not herself a journalist, **Margaret Bayard Smith** (1778–1844) was married to one—Samuel Harrison Smith, editor of the *National Intelligencer*. By virtue of her husband's career and her own intellect and social skills, Smith enjoyed the reputation of being one of Washington's most prominent women and one of the keenest observers of the city's early political and social life, a talent reflected in her papers (3,600 items; 1789–1874; bulk 1796–1840). A similar twentieth-century example might be the papers of **Gilbert A. Harrison** (4,200 items; 1902–78; bulk 1960–75), editor and publisher of the *New Republic* and president of Liveright Publishing Company. Not only do his papers contain correspondence and subject files for prominent women such as Anita McCormick Blaine, Meg Greenfield, Lillian Hellman, Mary McGrory, and Gertrude Stein, but they also include the papers of his wife, Nancy Blaine Harrison, relating to her activities in North Carolina in the 1940s as an organizer for the Textile Workers Union of America.

Fine and Performing Arts

Examples of women's artistic expression in the Manuscript Division range from an anonymous hand-painted Shaker greeting card to the innovative furniture designs of celebrated artist Ray Eames. The work of women sculptors is especially well represented, beginning with the career of nineteenth-century artist **Vinnie Ream** (1847–1914), who as a young teenager sculpted a bust of Abraham Lincoln while he met with petitioners visiting his White House office. She later created the statue of Lincoln that now stands in the U.S. Capitol. Her papers (2,500 items; 1853–1937; bulk 1853–1914) relate primarily to her career and her marriage to army lieutenant Richard Leveridge Hoxie, but they also touch upon racial conditions after the Civil War and social life in Washington, D.C., during Reconstruction. Also located in the U.S. Capitol is the controversial statue of women's rights leaders Susan B. Anthony, Lucretia Mott, and Elizabeth Cady Stanton. Derisively called "Three Women in a Bathtub" by its critics, this women's suffrage memorial was created by feminist sculptor **Adelaide Johnson** (1859–1955) under commission to the National Woman's Party (NWP). Photographs and documentation about the sculpture may be found in Johnson's papers (40,000 items; 1873–1947) as well as in the NWP records (see "Women's Suffrage" above). The work of sculptor Helene Sardeau (1899–1969) may be researched in the papers of her husband, muralist **George Biddle** (3,500 items; 1863–1973; bulk 1916–73), and that of Margaret French Cresson (1889–1973) and Brenda Putnam (1890–1975) in the papers of their respective fathers, sculptor **Daniel Chester French** (23,000 items; 1850–1968) and Librarian of Congress **Herbert Putnam** (8,000 items; 1783–1958; bulk 1899–1939).

Although the work of women photographers, architects, and other visual artists is usually best researched by consulting the collections in the Library's Prints and Photographs Division (see chapter 6), one Manuscript Division holding deserves special mention. **Frances Benjamin Johnston** (1864–1952) began as a photographer of national figures and events. She later excelled in garden photography and became known for compiling a remarkable photographic record of southern colonial architecture. All aspects of her career are reflected in her papers (19,000 items; 1855–1954; bulk 1890–1945), including her business partnership with Mattie Edwards Hewitt and her contributions to the emerging role of women in the photographic profession. Additional Johnston correspondence may be found in other division collections, including the papers of architect **Waddy Wood** (2,400 items; 1885–1941; bulk 1913–35), who was involved in the design of several buildings in the nation's capital relating to women, notably the Young Women's Christian Association building, All States Hotel for Women Government Employees, and National Training School for Girls.

Architects **Cass Gilbert** (9,000 items; 1841–1961), **Montgomery C. Meigs** (11,000 items; 1799–1968; bulk 1849–92), **Louis Skidmore** (2,000 items; 1908–76), and **William Thornton** (3,400 items; 1741–50) also all retained papers relating to female family members or colleagues. Thornton's papers are especially noteworthy because they include correspondence of his wife **Anna Maria Brodeau Thornton** (1775?–1865), whose own collection of diaries and notebooks (7 volumes; 1793–1863; gap 1816–27) is considered one of the best sources on the social life of Washington, D.C., from the late eighteenth through mid-nineteenth centuries.

In addition to their work in sculpture and photography, women also influenced American art as painters, illustrators, critics, and dealers. Marguerite Thompson Zorach (1887–1968) was a

Vinnie Ream. Photographer unknown. Biographical File. Prints and Photographs Division. LC-USZ62-10284.

While helping to support her family as a sixteen-year-old Post Office Department clerk, Vinnie Ream (1847–1914) decided to change course and pursue a sculpting career under the tutelage of Washington, D.C., artist Clark Mills, whose studio in the basement of the U.S. Capitol attracted a steady string of senators and representatives. Within a very short time, the ambitious and charming Ream had begun to cultivate Mills's clientele, sculpting busts of several congressmen and gaining others as lifelong champions who later helped her win two important and controversial congressional commissions—the marble statue of Abraham Lincoln in the U.S. Capitol, which she began shortly after the president's assassination when she was only nineteen, and the bronze of Admiral David Farragut dedicated in 1881 in Washington's Farragut Square. Her supporters also intervened on her behalf to convince President Lincoln to allow her to sculpt this bust of him, on which she worked for five months while he conducted other business in his White House office.

painter and weaver who married sculptor **William Zorach** (14,000 items; 1822–1974; bulk 1930–68) in 1912. Their daughter Dahlov Zorach Ipcar (b. 1917) also became a painter and writer, and her letters to them are part of the collection, as are letters from art dealer Edith Gregor Halpert, who was William Zorach's agent. The careers of artists **Gertrude Quastler** (825 items; 1895–1965; bulk 1940–63) and **Caroline Mytinger** (150 items; 1942–46) are documented by small collections. Biographical files, exhibition catalogs, application forms, and other material relating to Caroline Alston, Selma Burke, Blanche Byerley, Katherine Gardner, Lois Mailou Jones, Laura Warine, and other African American artists are in the records of the **Harmon Foundation** (see "Literature and Journalism" above).

A recently acquired collection documents the multifaceted careers of artist and designer **Ray Eames** (1912–1988) and her husband, architect and designer **Charles Eames.** Manuscripts (131,400 items; 1885–1988; bulk 1965–88) from the collection include biographical material, correspondence, research files, scripts, catalogs, drawings, and financial records relating to the Eameses' pioneering furniture designs (including their well-known "potato chip chair"), exhibition designs, and films for corporate and government bodies. Ray Eames's years at the Bennett School in Millbrook, New York, and her studies with Hans Hofmann are reflected in the family papers. Other materials from the Charles and Ray Eames collection are found in the Prints and Photographs Division (see page 211) and the Motion Picture and Recorded Sound Division.

One of the division's earliest sources of information on actresses is the **Robert Merry** collection (50 items; 1792–1850), containing engravings, clippings, and notes relating to Merry's wife, actress Ann Brunton Merry (1769–1808), and playbills, 1801–17, from several Philadelphia theaters, which list the names of several actresses. Researchers interested in women's theatrical endeavors in the mid-to-late nineteenth century have more sources to mine. Complementing the papers of **Fanny Kemble** (1809–1893) in the **Owen Wister** collection (see "Literature and Journalism" above), is a separate group of the actress's papers (75 items; 1829–74) containing correspondence relating to her 1849 divorce from southern plantation owner Pierce Butler, whose ownership of slaves she found abhorrent, and two volumes of material she used for her 1835 *Journal of a Residence in America,* which was critical of American social life and customs.

Shakespearean actress **Charlotte Cushman** (1816–1876) enjoyed a successful theatrical career both in the United States and abroad. Her collection of correspondence, annotated scripts, and reviews (10,000 items; 1824–1941; bulk 1861–75) chiefly concerns theatrical matters, including a benefit tour for the U.S. Sanitary Commission in 1863. For much of the 1850s through the 1870s, Cushman lived in semiretirement in London and Rome, and her correspondence from that period records the activities of Americans abroad and their reactions to the Civil War and Abraham Lincoln's assassination. From 1857 until her death, Cushman's constant companion was American sculptor Emma Stebbins (1815–1882), whose correspondence also appears in the collection. Additional Cushman items may be found in the research papers (1,750 items; 1830–1960) of educator **Jennie Lorenz** (1886–1962), who wrote a master's thesis on the actress.

Actress **Laura Keene** (1826–1873), best known for her performance in *Our American Cousin* the night Lincoln was assassinated, was also a theater manager, and her papers (107 items; 1855–85) contain clippings about that fateful night at Ford's Theater as well as documents reflecting the business side of theatrical ventures. The collection of army officer **F. W. Lander** (1,250 items; 1836–94; bulk 1849–62) includes the papers of his wife, Jean Davenport Lander (1829–1903), relating to her career as an actress in Europe, North America, and the Caribbean. Her correspondents include Harriet Lane, Julia Marlowe, and Anna Cora Ritchie. Marlowe (1866–1950) is also represented by more than one hundred letters in the papers of author and journalist **Charles Edward Russell** (12,000 items; 1864–1941; bulk 1900–1930). At the turn of the century, both **Anna E. Dickinson** (see "Reform" above) and **Minnie Maddern Fiske** (1865–1932) blended their acting careers with their interests in reform. An outspoken critic of cruelty to animals, Fiske denounced bullfighting, use of aigrette feathers on hats, and fur-trapping. Her papers (18,000 items; 1884–1932) reflect these concerns and provide a picture of an accomplished actress, director, and producer who defiantly bucked the theatrical trusts of the period.

Twentieth-century stage actresses are equally well represented in the division. Small collections document the careers of **Maude Adams** (1872–1953), the immensely popular actress who later became a lighting designer (19 items; 1925–56); legendary Russian-born stage and film actress **Alla Nazimova** (1879–1945), who was considered the foremost interpreter of Henrik Ibsen's dramas (1,400 items; 1877–1988); and Russian-born actress and cinematic designer **Natacha Rambova** (1897–1966), who married Rudolph Valentino (210 items; 1955–65).

Providing high-quality stage productions at affordable prices to working Americans was an important goal of actress and producer **Eva Le Gallienne** (1899–1991), whose recently acquired collection (9,000 items; 1875–1993; bulk 1916–83) documents her profound influence on American theater as an actress, director, translator, teacher of young actors, and founder and promoter of repertory theater in this country. Le Gallienne had great admiration for actresses Sarah Bernhardt and Eleonora Duse, who are represented in her papers, as are her former partners Marion Gunnar Evenson, actress Josephine Hutchinson, and actress **Margaret Webster** (1905–1972). Like Le Gallienne, Webster was a director and producer as well as an actress. Her papers (7,000 items; 1837–1974; bulk 1937–70), including especially candid letters to her mother, relate to her career and her research on two family biographies, *The Same Only Different* (1969) and *Don't Put Your Daughter on the Stage* (1972), which focus on her parents, May Whitty and Benjamin Webster of the British stage. Other topics include Webster's involvement with Le Gallienne and Cheryl Crawford in the American Repertory Theater in New York, her interest in experimental theater with Marweb Productions, a Shakespearean company, and her associations with Lynn Fontanne and Sybil Thorndike. Two other supporters of American repertory theater were stage and screen actors **Jessica Tandy** (1909–1994) and husband **Hume Cronyn** whose papers (98,800 items; 1885–1994; bulk 1935–93) reflect their long careers and marriage.

Years before Tandy embarked on a film career, other pioneering actresses had already begun to make their mark on that medium, including **May Robson** (1858–1942), **Miriam Cooper** (1891–1976), **Lillian Gish** (1893–1993), and **Ruth Gordon** (1896–1985). Cooper's papers (300 items; 1915–76) concern her marriage to actor and director Raoul Walsh and her work with D. W. Griffith in *Birth of a Nation* and *Intolerance.* Highlights of

Gish's papers (8,750 items; 1920–73) are several annotated film scripts and nearly four hundred letters relating to her activities on behalf of the America First Committee. Gordon's papers (6,000 items; 1924–69) concern her dual careers as an actress and playwright and include correspondence from many writers and Hollywood leading ladies such as Claudette Colbert, Edna Ferber, Gertrude Lawrence, Vivien Leigh, Anita Loos, Clare Boothe Luce, Mary Martin, and Rebecca West. Three collections of television and radio scripts—**Sid Caesar** (2,000 items; 1950–63), **General Foods Corporation Radio Script Collection** (150 items; 1932–49), and **Fred Allen** (404 items; 1932–51)—contain texts of commercials aimed at women and document the work of writers Selma Diamond and Lucille Kallen and actresses Imogene Coca, Janet Blair, Nanette Fabray, and Talullah Bankhead.

As with most topics and types of collections explored in this chapter, documents of interest to women's historians may also be found in the papers of men who were active in the theater and film business. A good example of this are the papers of **Vincent Price** (60,000 items; 1883–1992; bulk 1932–92), which concern his acting career as well as his accomplishments as a gourmet cook, art collector, and critic. As an art consultant for Sears, Roebuck and Company, he generated numerous files relating not only to women artists but also to home fashion accessories, housewares, and other items typically designed for and purchased by women. Other files relate to Charlotte Cooper, Barbara O'Neill, and the Miss America Pageant, and correspondents include his wives—actress Edith Barrett (1906–1977), costume designer Mary Grant Price (b. 1917?), and actress Coral Browne (1913–1991).

From the papers of film actors and presidents to suffragists and poets, the Library's manuscript collections offer a rich and varied avenue for studying the history of women in the United States from the colonial period to the present day. Included are the papers of the famous and the unknown—of women who achieved prominence in their own right and those whose lives we learn about from sources hidden among the papers of celebrated men. From these manuscript materials, we can piece together a picture of American womanhood that covers both the personal and the political, the private and the public side of women's lives. We gain from these sources innumerable stories of women's courage and achievements as well as of their failures and disappointments. Nothing can quite match the thrill and immediacy of reading in a woman's own words and in her own handwriting what she thought and what she did. Sometimes these writings are eloquent and sometimes uninspired, but they all help reveal the women that came before us as real people, who individually and collectively shaped the course of our nation.

This chapter provides but a brief overview of women's history sources held among the Manuscript Division's fifty-three million items and the major tools for accessing them. It covers ten major collecting strengths of the division and touches on various aspects of women's lives, including family relationships, health issues, education, reform efforts, political involvement, legal struggles, literary and artistic achievements, and military and government service. Some of the collections cited as well as other related papers are easily located in the Library of Congress Online Catalog. Other holdings may be discovered by browsing division finding aids and by consulting the specialized guides mentioned throughout the chapter. Many more sources await the researcher who is willing to dig deep into the actual collections, opening countless boxes and folders and reading page upon page of manuscripts.

Be sure to equip yourself beforehand with the names of people, places, organizations, and events relating to your research topic. Also consult with the reference librarians and subject specialists in the Manuscript Division, both before your visit, to check on possible access restrictions and the availability of off-site collections, and after your arrival, for tips about collections and research strategies. The division has answered Mary Ritter Beard's call to preserve and provide access to documents by and about women. It is our hope that our researchers answer her call to write, and rewrite, women's history.

With thanks for their support, I would like to acknowledge the academic advisers; editors Sara Day and Evelyn Sinclair; Library colleagues Sheridan Harvey and Barbara Orbach Natanson; and Manuscript Division staff members Leonard C. Bruno, Connie L. Cartledge, James H. Hutson, Laura J. Kells, David Wigdor, and Mary M. Wolfskill for reviewing and commenting on earlier drafts of this chapter.

Theodor de Bry. Adam and Eve in America. Engraving in Thomas Hariot, A Briefe and True Report of . . . Virginia *(Frankfurt, 1590; F229. H27 Rosenwald Coll). Rare Book and Special Collections Division. LC-USZC4–5347.*

Eve, a European maiden with the anatomically awkward body type familiar from Northern European engravings by such artists as Albrecht Dürer, looks knowingly over her shoulder as she reaches for the fatal apple indicated by the she-demon-serpent entwined at the center of the tree of knowledge, while Adam gazes guilelessly heavenward. In the background are the consequences of her action—Adam tills the soil while Eve mothers Cain in a makeshift shelter. In Eve: The History of an Idea *(1984), John Phillips describes his impression from studying many pictures of Eve conversing with her snake-woman adviser: "the artist is governed by a male dread of conspiring females, the fear of the witches' coven" (p. 62).*

Behold Columbia's empire rise,
On Freedom's solid base to stand;
Supported by propitious skies,
And seal'd by her deliverer's hand.

"A Federal Song," *Albany* (New York) *Journal,* August 4, 1788

I would give my daughters every accomplishment which I thought proper, and to crown all, I would early accustom them to habits of industry, and order; . . . they should be enabled to procure for themselves the necessaries of life, independence should be placed within their grasp, and I would teach them to "reverence themselves."

[Judith Sargent Murray,] "The Gleaner No. XV," *Massachusetts Magazine* 5 (August 1793): 461[1]

American women's ongoing struggle to capture and define their own varying realities has been shaped by western societies' changing attitudes and ideas about gender roles, race, religion, and politics. Reflecting these changing ideologies are the female allegorical representations and visual stereotypes that have in fact helped to limit women's roles in America. From the first illustrations made by Europeans of the American continent's native women to the patriotic model devised for white, middle class women in the late eighteenth century, visual and textual collections of the Library of Congress may be uniquely suited to throw light on the sometimes crude, sometimes subtle shadings of motive behind the early imaging of American women. A trio of engravings—two made in Europe and one in the brand new United States of America—showing the allegorical image of American women, respectively, as sinful Eve, as Indian queen and princess, and as neoclassical Liberty figure, reflects this evolution.

In 1590, Flemish engraver and publisher Theodor de Bry opened part one of *America,* his illustrated compilation of early travel accounts describing European encounters with the strange peoples in the mysterious "new found lands" across the Atlantic, with his engraving of Adam and Eve and the serpent.[2] Thus the old stereotype of the formerly blessed couple cast out into the wilderness through the perfidy of original woman was transposed to an imagined America, the New Eden. De Bry, an ardent Protestant who never traveled to America, was influenced by European iconographical, cultural, and religious tradition, particularly in his depictions of

Cartouche. From Henry Popple, A Map of the British Empire in America with the French and Spanish settlements adjacent thereto *(London, 1733; G1105.P6 1733 Vault). Geography and Map Division.*

The tropical Indian queen surveys her world from above the map title. Surrounded by a palm tree, an alligator, a parrot, and a monkey, holding an arrow, and with her foot placed firmly on a severed human head, she announces her South American origins. To the right, her daughter, the Indian princess, represents the British Colonies in North America. With a protective arm around a small child and separated from her warrior by the title, she glances up at her mother but gestures toward a port scene (not shown) where European gentlemen supervise the unloading of a ship, symbolic of trade.

Edward Savage. Liberty. In the form of the Goddess of Youth; giving Support to the Bald Eagle. *Stipple engraving,1796. Popular Graphic Arts Collection (PGA–Savage–Liberty [C Size]). Prints and Photographs Division. LC-USZ62–15369.*

A buxom young woman in a windblown diaphanous dress and garlanded with flowers offers a feeding cup to a swooping eagle, symbol of the proud new nation. Floating in the sky are the liberty cap mounted on the pole of the American flag. Under her right foot Liberty tramples implements of English tyranny, including chains, scepter, key, and medal.

women. The remainder of de Bry's plates in this volume, despite his tendency to Europeanize drawings made from life, illustrate the lifestyle of the native peoples living on Roanoke Island when the first British settlers arrived in what they called Virginia. Eyewitness and chronicler Thomas Hariot tells us at one point in the text that these peoples believed that "woman was made first,"[3] and subsequent plates show women participating as apparent equals in the impressive economy and ceremony of tribal life.

Nearly 150 years later, Indian women—mother and daughter or, alternatively, queen and princess—had become established as symbols of America, the first for the Western Hemisphere (North and South America), the second for the British colonies in North America. Both dominate the cartouche (the ornamental frame to a map title) of Henry Popple's *Map of the British Empire in America* (1733). European artists—all male—had turned real and capable Indian women into prurient icons of a new civilization; the "queen" rests a foot on a human head, evidence of highly disturbing behavior.

The third engraving, a handsome rendering of the neoclassical Liberty figure, by American artist Edward Savage, made a few years after the ratification of the U.S. Constitution, represents the young nation struggling to reemphasize the ideals on which it was founded. With the concept of freedom permeating American political and social philosophy and propaganda, who or what did the new country's leaders choose to represent the concepts of nationhood and civic virtue? Abandoned for now was the iconic Indian woman. Instead, a beautiful, young, white, classicized female was invented as an emblem of national values and republican motherhood.

De Bry's work can be seen in original editions found in the extraordinary Rosenwald Collection held in the Rare Book and Special Collections Division of the Library of Congress and in

Theodor de Bry. Florida Indians planting beans of maize. Engraving after a watercolor by Jacques Le Moyne de Morgues, 1564. From de Bry, Brevis narratio eorum quae in Florida Americae *[America. pt. 2 Latin] (Frankfurt, 1591; G159.B7 Rosenwald Coll RBSC), plate 21. Rare Book and Special Collections Division. LC-USZ62-31869.*

De Bry and Le Moyne show a division of agricultural labor between the sexes: the universally young and attractive Timucua women with incongruous blond and curly locks and modest moss skirts perform the less physically demanding task of planting the maize while the men, who are perhaps more realistically depicted, till the soil. The baskets and implements are all European types with the exception of the digging stick. Father Joseph Lafitau only slightly modified this same engraving for his 1724 account of the Iroquois, even though he described farming as being purely women's work.

numerous later editions in the Library's General Collections.[4] Woman as symbol or allegory of nationhood, patriotism, and civic and moral virtue—and of sexual temptation, immorality, and wilful or unruly conduct—can also be seen in countless examples of images made before 1800—and in a deluge thereafter—in the Library's vast collections. These engravings, etchings, and woodcuts are ubiquitous, whether presented as fine prints, map cartouches, political cartoons, and newspaper mastheads or as illustrations in journals and magazines, on broadsides, paper currency, or stock and benevolent society membership certificates. With the advent of the new national government, designs for the decoration of the U.S. Capitol and other public buildings and monuments came forth, rife with neoclassical females.[5] These visual images are buttressed by standards for women expounded, often allegorically, in sermons and advice literature, and, later, in articles and novels (see chapters 1 and 4). Following the generalized female chronologically through North America's history shows how she has been recruited for every manifestation of propaganda and satire, particularly at times of political uncertainty and challenges to the status quo.[6]

It was de Bry's engravings, not the watercolors made from real life, that influenced European artists for at least two hundred years. Perhaps most influential as models for iconic images and stereotypes of Indian women were his engravings for Hans Staden's account of his year-long trials as a captive and threatened meal of Brazil's Tupinamba tribe. For this new edition, part 3 of *America,* de Bry made forty-five engravings based on woodcuts in Staden's original 1557 account, many of which sensationalized the central role of women in the cannibalism of their enemies, particularly the Portuguese (as in the background illustration here), and the preparation of stomach-emptying alcoholic brews.[7] Influenced by Staden's account, and that of Amerigo Vespucci—whose baptismal name, feminized, was placed on the first map of the Western Hemisphere—other artists had begun to represent the unfamiliar continent as a naked Indian maiden in an exotic landscape.[8] They pictured her with severed heads and other gruesome detritus of the alleged cannibalism of the Tupinamba. America, wild and scantily clad, now joined the symbols for her sophisticated sister continents of Europe, Africa, and Asia.[9] For those who were contemplating founding religious settlements in America, these images were evidence—along with many accounts of native females' sexual licentiousness—that Eve, the embodiment of original sin, was already running amok in the new lands.[10]

The imaging of America's natives had begun with the purely imaginary woodcuts illustrat-

Theodor de Bry. Their Manner of praying with Rattles about the Fire. *Engraving after a watercolor by John White. From Thomas Hariot,* A Briefe and True Report of . . . Virginia *(Frankfurt, 1590; F229 .H27 1590 Rosenwald Coll RBSC), plate 17. Rare Book and Special Collections Division. LC-USZ62–54017.*

John White. Indians round a Fire. *Photograph of a watercolor drawing in the British Museum. Graphics File. Prints and Photographs Division. LC-USZ62–571.*

De Bry's description for this engraving, based on Hariot's text, begins: "When they have escaped any great danger by sea or land or returned from the war, as a token of joy they make a great fire about which the men and women sit together, holding a certain fruit in their hands like a round pumpkin or a gourd . . . ." Among the additions that de Bry made to John White's drawing were the two standing and conversing figures on the left, one of them female, and the foreground and background details. The Prints and Photographs Division holds reproductions and negatives for many of John White's watercolor drawings.

ing a 1494 edition of Columbus's famous printed letter reporting his "discovery."[11] A few woodcuts illustrating sixteenth-century travel accounts and histories depicted Indians of Brazil and the Caribbean engaged in daily activities, but the reality of native lives in North America remained a matter of speculation until de Bry included his own engravings with travel accounts that he published in the order in which he acquired them. He based his engravings of the Timucua Indians—first published in 1591 as part 2 of *America*—on artist Jacques Le Moyne de Morgues's watercolors made in 1564 in northeast Florida.[12] Le Moyne, the first professional artist to work in the territory that would become the United States, had accompanied French Huguenot leader René de Laudonnière on an expedition to found a settlement. All but one of his watercolors have been lost but, judging by the remaining example, de Bry made remarkably few changes in designs that depicted native life through a European lens. Timucua women, however, are shown actively involved with men in work and ceremony—planting the fields (see opposite), loading and transporting baskets with corn and fruits, and worshiping a column left by a previous French expedition.[13]

John White's apparently more ethnographically accurate watercolors of southeastern Algonquian peoples, made twenty years later than the Florida designs, were actually the first to be engraved and published by de Bry.[14] Here, women are shown participating in ceremonial occasions, posing proudly and individually for their portraits as wives and leading citizens of the Algonquian towns of Secotan or Pomeiock, and involved in daily activities, such as a self-confident young woman "sitting at meate" with her husband.

Looking for the women in these images reminds us that, although we may learn much from them about the reality of Indian women's lives during the encounter period, the images reflect the artist's—and particularly the engraver's—own prejudices, preconceptions, and misconceptions. The creator's point of view is central to the interpretation of any historical document, including visual images. Comparison of the Virginia engravings with the original watercolors, most of which have survived, shows that de Bry altered the faces, particularly the women's, making them conform to European ideas of beauty and attractiveness; sometimes removed the tattoos shown in the White watercolors; adjusted poses and physiques—Botticelli's "Three Graces" appear in one of de Bry's versions of ceremonial scenes (plate 18, White: LC-USZ62-572; de Bry: LC-USZ62-40055); added pastoral landscapes, plants, and animals; and "corrected" the Indian artifacts.[15]

During the period of European colonial settlement of America, the colonists' image of their new country derived from their home countries. Travel and missionary accounts continued to depict Indian customs, lifestyles, and, increasingly, territorial conflicts with white settlers.[16] It was not until well toward the end of the eighteenth century, however, several generations after the arrival of the first European settlers in New England and along the mid-Atlantic coast, that American artists and engravers, conscious of their newly separate nationality, began to build a substantial visual record of American life and cultural and political attitudes. Although printing presses had been established in the British colonies by the mid-seventeenth century—and even earlier in the Spanish colonies, the economy and the ideological climate were not yet ripe for the making or printing of images in colonial America. The earliest printed portraits made in America in the early eighteenth century were of men, including a mezzotint of the Congregational minister Cotton Mather, an authoritarian with strong views on women's roles.[17]

Despite the fact that women had shared with men the religious per-

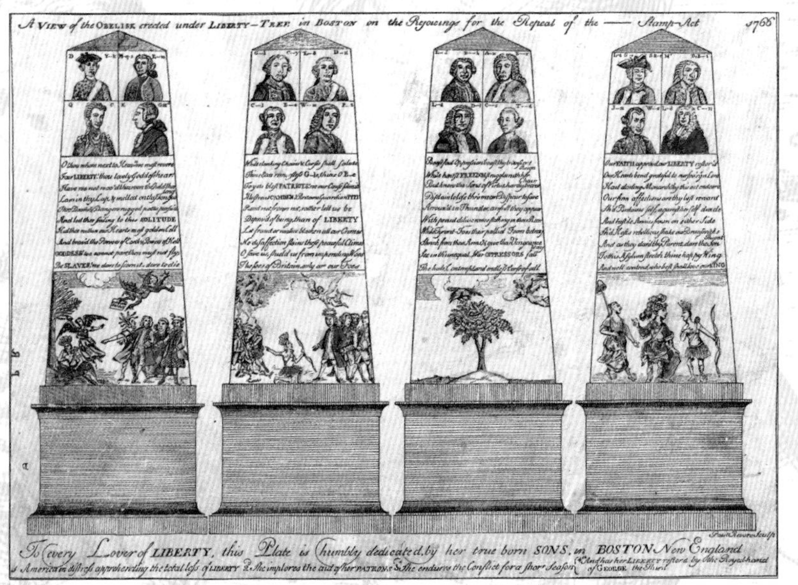

Paul Revere. View of the Obelisk erected under Liberty-tree in Boston on the Rejoicings for the Repeal of the . . . Stamp Act 1766. *Etching with watercolor. Boston, 1766; restrike printed 1839 or later. Popular Graphic Arts Collection (PGA—Revere—View of the obelisk [A size]). Prints and Photographs Division. LC-USZC4-4599 (color); LC-USZ62-22385 (black and white).*

Paul Revere. Masthead engraving with Liberty figure for the Massachusetts Spy, or, Thomas's Boston Journal, *July 7, 1774. Newspaper and Current Periodical Room. LC-USZ62-7984.*

Paul Revere's schematic rendering of the illuminated obelisk erected on Boston Common to celebrate the repeal of the Stamp Act includes the Liberty figure on two sides; three of the panels also include the Indian princess. By the time British soldiers had occupied Boston, however, Liberty had become the American symbol for revolution. The British remained wedded to the Indian princess as the battle of the cartoons was engaged.

Scipio Moorhead. "Phillis Wheatley, Negro Servant to Mr. John Wheatley, of Boston." Frontispiece engraving to Wheatley's Poems on Various Subjects, Religious and Moral *(London: Printed for A. Bell, 1773; PS866.W5 1773 RBSC). Rare Book and Special Collections Division. LC-USZC4-5316 (color); LC-USZ62-40054 (black and white).*

On the other end of the spectrum from "cookie-cutter" imagery to denote African American slaves, and perhaps indicating early abolitionist sentiments as well as the poet's brilliance, Phillis Wheatley was the subject of a rare printed image of an individual female slave—or, indeed, of any individual woman in America. Wheatley was brought to Boston from Africa as a small child, was given a liberal education by her owners, and was shown working on a poem—pensive and refined, and yet still identified as a "Negro Servant"—in the frontispiece to her Poems. *The tension between reality and symbol is manifest in images of African Americans.*

secutions and economic depressions that had driven them to settle British North America, European immigrants—with the notable exception of Quakers—believed explicitly in women's inferiority, intellectually, spiritually, and legally. Students of American women's history, including nineteenth-century suffrage leaders, have remarked on the difference in attitudes toward European women, who, through the *feme coverte* tradition of English common law governing married women, could neither own property in their own right nor make decisions about their children independently of their husbands (see chapter 3), and the apparent sharing of power and division of labor between women and men in many Indian tribes.[18] In the matrilineal Iroquois Five Nations, for example, the household and land up to the forest's edge were the women's domain, giving them economic heft and authority in their tribe, and older women had the right to nominate the council of elders and depose chiefs.[19] Men's work—war, trading, hunting, and international relations—was generally carried out in the forest.

Another factor in the retardation of American-made imagery was that the Protestant sects that came to America tended to shun graven images. As people of the Word, they relied on the sermons of ministers or church elders for definitions and allegories of ideal or dangerous womanhood. Dissidents such as Anne Hutchinson, Mary Dyer, and other "disorderly women," like Eve, were often demonized, and put to trial, executed, or banished.[20] Women who fulfilled traditional roles as good wives were idealized by the Puritan community.[21] Although women's essential contributions as managers of the domestic economy were more valued in the struggling colonies than they might have been in England, men were imbued with a fear of assertive women that had its roots in Judeo-Christian doctrine.[22] By contrast, religious icons were central to the Spanish *conversión* of Indians to Christianity—specifically Catholicism—in the Southwest between the seventeenth and early nineteenth centuries. Symbols of the Madonna, the metaphysical image of the Mother Church—especially the ubiquitous Virgin of Guadalupe—and female saints were there revered and held up as exemplars of ideal womanhood. Catholic women generally remained in their submissive place, however, and outspoken, immoral, or otherwise unconventional women risked being singled out for punishment by the Spanish Inquisition.[23]

During the seventeenth century, New England colonists intermittently suffered devastating losses from territorial wars with Northeastern Indian tribes and frontier attacks, while the Indians themselves were decimated by war and disease. Ironically, it was often white women—or men writing in their name—who published accounts of their captivity and the murder of their children by vicious savages who mocked white settlers.[24] These descriptions became an influential force in the creation of the American antithesis of the noble savage image promulgated by Europeans. In the meantime, European mapmakers were depicting America in cartouches as an increasingly noble Indian queen, with the trappings of natural wealth and Caribbean culture.[25] As noted earlier, the symbol was initially based on the native women of South and Central America because those areas of the Western Hemisphere were the first to be described. As England began to reap the benefits from trade with its increasingly prosperous colonies in North America in the early eighteenth century, mapmakers began to differentiate and use a separate symbol for those colonies, an Indian princess pictured before a seaport. This evolution from the queen-as-continent to the colonial princess can be traced in many different map cartouches found on the Geography and Map Division's rare maps (see chapter 7).

The casting of women as universal abstractions for civic virtue and geographical spaces in Europe originated with the classical republics of Greece and Rome, whose political and intellectual elite assigned lofty ideals to womankind while excluding real women from the public and political realm. Marina Warner asks how it is possible to equate Aristotle's claim that woman is a defective male, considered by Greek law to be incapable of running her own finances or bearing witness in a court of law, with the fact that ideals of civic virtue were expressed in the feminine. The answer to this paradox, she says, was to render the female form as generic and universal, removed from all connection to individuality, whereas the male form retained individuality even when it was used to express a generalized idea.[26]

As intellectuals and artists inspired the renaissance of classical ideals in Europe in the fifteenth through sixteenth centuries, a long tradition of symbolic imagery became standardized, along with more recent innovations, in a series of emblem books and dictionaries. Among these, the most influential were Cesare Ripa's *Iconologia* (from 1603) and George Richardson's *Iconology or a Collection of Emblematical Figures* (1779, found in the Rosenwald Collection), based on Ripa's compositions and published in time to ride the tide of neoclassicism.[27]

European mapmakers made ample use of the emblem books, but the books were also at hand for political and intellectual leaders, artists, journalists, printers, or anyone else in search of effective ways to express revolutionary ideas to a largely illiterate populace as America be-

"The able Doctor, or America Swallowing the Bitter Draught." Etching. From the London Magazine, *May 1, 1774. British Cartoon Collection (PC 1–5226 [A size]). Prints and Photographs Division. LC-USZC4-5289 (color); LC-USZ61-77 (black and white).*

Prime Minister Lord North, author of the Boston Port Bill, forces the "Intolerable Acts," or tea, down the throat of America, a vulnerable Indian woman whose arms are restrained by Lord Chief Justice Mansfield, while Lord Sandwich, a notorious womanizer, pins down her feet and peers up her skirt. Behind them, Mother Britannia weeps helplessly. This British cartoon was quickly copied and distributed by Paul Revere.

Philip Dawes. A Society of Patriotic Ladies, at Edenton in North Carolina. *Mezzotint. London, March 25, 1775. British Cartoon Collection (PC 1–5284B [A size]). Prints and Photographs Division. LC-USZC4-4617 (color); LC-USZ62-12711 (black and white).*

*Considering the important role that women played in supporting the boycott of English goods and in raising funds and providing supplies for the revolutionary army, the dearth of printed imagery of real white women contrasts strikingly with the serried ranks of allegorical women. An exception—in that it depicts individualized, if imagined and caricatured, women from varying social backgrounds, including a slave woman—is a rare British cartoon that satirizes the fifty-one "patriotic ladies" of Edenton, North Carolina, in their attempt to endorse the nonimportation association resolves of 1774. Their depiction as ugly or foolish probably owes more to their allegiance to the colonial cause than it does to their gender. As Linda Kerber has remarked, for many American women, the signing of a petition—virtually unknown before the 1770s—was their first political act (*Women of the Republic: Intellect and Ideology in Revolutionary America *[1980], 41).*

gan to loosen "her" bonds with England and England battled to hold onto "her" rich offspring. Following the Stamp Act of 1765, Boston craftsman Paul Revere taught himself the art of engraving and began to produce a number of propagandistic cartoons in support of the American colonies' protest against taxation without representation. Several of these can be seen in the historical prints collections in the Prints and Photographs Division. Revere is credited with introducing the Britannia figure with liberty cap and pole as a symbol of the American rebellion, which the Sons of Liberty—still British subjects—were quick to adopt (see page 180).[28] The Liberty/Britannia figure soon became part of the iconography of the American Revolution.[29]

Switching to fashionable and lofty neoclassical imagery allowed American leaders to avoid associating the newly independent American colonies with now threatening indigenous tribes.[30] Some of the most powerful Indian tribes on the northwest frontier had seized the opportunity to ally with the British and ravage frontier settlements. Europe's "noble savage" again became the colonists' enemy. Even so, the positive equation of Indians with freedom may have prompted the Sons of Liberty to dress up as Mohawk Indians for the Boston Tea Party in 1773.

Would the Sons of Liberty have seen the irony, however, if they had been told that the liberty cap and pole had their origins in an ancient Roman ceremony for the manumission of a slave?[31] Freedom was unknown to the African slaves who had been brought to North America to labor for white owners, particularly in the tobacco-growing southern colonies. A jarring juxtaposition in the *Pennsylvania Evening Post* of July 2, 1776, of an advertisement for a runaway slave alongside a brief announcement of the Continental Congress's resolution to declare independence, reminds us that slaves—along with free Euro-American women and Native Americans—were ignored in the Declaration of Independence. Many of the runaway advertisements and broadsides that blazoned "Negroes for Sale," while often providing individual characteristics in the text, were illustrated with crude, cookie-cutter icons representing the actual men, women, and children whose bondage made a mockery of the language of and fight for freedom from the 1760s to the 1780s (by contrast, see Phillis Wheatley, page 181).[32]

While Revere was leading the way in establishing an American school of political cartooning, America's friends in England, particularly the merchant class, supported a storm of political propaganda in the form of allegorical prints as the conflict reached hurricane force. These

America Triumphant and Britannia in Distress. *Etching. Boston, 1782. Popular Graphic Arts Collection (PGA—Unattributed—America Triumphant—A size). Prints and Photographs Division. LC-USZC4-5275 (color); LC-USZ62-45922 (black and white).*

While the peace talks were under way, a Boston printer published a crude allegory, both as a separate print and as the frontispiece to Weatherwise's Town and Country Almanack *of 1782 (AY 201.B7 W5 Am Almanac Coll RBSC), where America is represented by the martial, helmeted Liberty or Britannia figure with cap and pole. She holds out an olive branch to a weeping, bare-headed Britannia, and invites all nations—represented by many ships—to trade with her.*

John Wallis. Cartouche; etching. From The United States of America laid down From the best Authorities *(London, April 3, 1783; G3700.1783.W3 Vault). Geography and Map Division.*

The differences between the cartouches on the map used in the negotiation of the Treaty of Paris (1783) and the one drawn up to show the new, independent territories are revealing. The first, the long used and much published 1755 Mitchell map, shows the lovely Indian queen, with attendants, in a tropical setting. The Wallis map pairs Liberty with George Washington and Wisdom and Justice with Benjamin Franklin. American leaders now wanted symbols that indicated equality and dignity. Thus, generic, universal but white, females and heroic, individualized but white, males became the subject of countless celebratory and memorial designs of the period.

can be seen in pamphlets and magazines in the Rare Book and Special Collections Division and in the British Cartoons collection in the Prints and Photographs Division. The Indian princess remained the preferred English symbol for America, even among her English friends, but she was increasingly shown with the attributes of liberty, alienated from her mother Britannia. In *Britain, America, at Length Be Friends,* from the January 1774 issue of the *London Magazine,* the Indian princess wears a feather bonnet and bears a cornucopia representing natural bounty, but her robes are becoming classicized and the goddess Concord is shown trying to reconcile Britannia and her daughter on the wharf of a busy port (LC-USZ62–45498).[33]

Three months later, however, the same magazine offered the shocking image *The able doctor, or America swallowing the Bitter Draught,* which was also issued as a separate print (see page 182). It was quickly copied and signed by Paul Revere for publication in the June issue of Boston's *Royal American Magazine.*[34] On this occasion, he was apparently more taken by the depiction of America's hapless plight than he was wedded to his own preference for the Liberty figure as symbol of America.

But although Liberty was the seceding colonists' new sign for America, the "daughters of Liberty" themselves had no independent political rights, despite the many calls that were made on their own patriotism before and during the Revolutionary War in the form of boycotting English household goods (see page 183), managing and defending farms and estates in their husbands' absence, and materially supporting the American soldiers.[35] Ideological justification for the effort led by Esther De Berdt Reed, wife of the president of Pennsylvania's supreme executive council, and Benjamin Franklin's daughter Sarah Franklin Bache, to solicit funds for Washington's troops can be seen in the broadside *The Sentiments of an American*

Woman, Philadelphia, June 10, 1780 (RBSC; see endpapers). Declaring that American women were "born for liberty" and that "if the weakness of our Constitution, if opinion and manners did not forbid us to march to glory by the same paths as the Men," they would at least be found equal in their convictions and loyalty to the "Thirteen United Colonies," Reed presented a list of historical role models for politically active women, such as Deborah, Judith, and Esther; the great European queens; and the "Maid of Orleans."[36]

While women's broadsides continued to use such biblical and classical allusions to legitimize real American women's courage under trial, the framers of America's Constitution once again chose to ignore women as an independent political class. Instead, classicized "universal woman" was proffered in a number of different guises—Liberty, Columbia, America, Minerva—in the search for a new, national identity on medals, coins, or public decoration following the establishment of the federal government in 1789, and American women were assigned a new role as the moral upholders of the Union. They should confine themselves, they were told, to the domestic sphere and dedicate themselves to "republican motherhood,"as the nurturers, educators, and moral compasses of a nation of public-spirited citizens.[37] The frontispiece for the 1789 *Columbian Magazine* depicts "the Genius of Foederate America" as a young woman surrounded by the symbols of prosperity and education while Apollo points her way to the Temple of Fame.[38]

Personal ambition and political activism were still frowned on for American women, but the tide was in fact about to turn in favor of their education for a higher purpose, that of national unity, and their long march to establish and claim their own image had begun. The Liberty who nurtures the presumably male bald eagle, or soaring young nationhood, in the Savage print (page 177) seems to have descended from her classical pedestal and to be moving into real life to challenge the barriers of stereotype, satire, social custom, and law.

I wish to thank my coeditors, Evelyn Sinclair and Sheridan Harvey (HSS), Barbara Orbach Natanson (P&P), and Janice Ruth (MSS) on the specialist editorial team, as well as Patricia Molen van Ee (G&M) and Roger Walke (CRS), for their encouragement and advice. Together with members of the scholars' advisory board, they helped me guide the way through the symbols to women's realities.

"America! With Peace and Freedom blest." Frontispiece etching. From the Columbian Magazine, or Monthly Miscellany, *1789 (AP2.A2 U6). Rare Book and Special Collections Division. LC-USZ62-45573.*

America becomes a young white woman enjoying the benefits of prosperity and education now that the war is over. At her side rests her shield, bearing a new national emblem, the eagle. Her liberty cap and pole lean against the palm tree behind her. Apollo with a lyre points to the Temple of Fame and sings to her:

America! With Peace and Freedom blest,
Pant for true Fame, and scorn inglorious rest:
Science invites; urg'd by the Voice divine,
Exert thyself, 'till every Art be thine.

Background Image: Theodor de Bry. "Four women of the tribe take four pieces of the dead body and carry these around a hut while they scream with pleasure." Engraving in de Bry, Americae, *part 3 (Frankfurt, 1593; G159 .B8), p. 86. Rare Book and Special Collections Division. LC-USZ62-45103.*

A woodcut by Hans Staden, an illustration to his chapter "Of their manner of killing and eating their enemies," inspired this gruesome scene by de Bry but seems quite tame by comparison—until you notice the body parts being roasted by the women. De Bry's title for his engraving shows that he embellished his engravings of cannibalism with some of the details from Staden's account, particularly the degree to which the Tupinamba women tormented their prisoners before killing them, their quartering of the bodies, and the pleasure they took in the entire ritual. The terrified, bearded Hans Staden is at top right. (See discussion on page 178.)

6 Prints and Photographs Division

Barbara Orbach Natanson

The holdings of the Prints and Photographs Division document people, events, trends, and artistic and technical creativity that helped to shape the history and culture of the United States. As integral players in the country's history and culture, women, and issues affecting them, are evident everywhere in the division's collections. You find them among the documentary and art photographs; prints; cartoon and other drawings; posters; architecture, design, and engineering documentation; and applied graphic art materials and ephemera such as sheet music, seed packets, and tobacco and patent medicine labels. Collection materials relating to women in American history date from before the American Revolution to the present day. Because photographs make up the bulk of the collections, the holdings are strongest for the period between 1860 and 1970. Although some of the division's collections are strong in coverage of the American West, women do not figure prominently in them. With a few exceptions—notably the Farm Security Administration/Office of War Information Collection and various groups of images relating to Native Americans, discussed below—coverage of women tends to be stronger for the eastern states, to the extent that the geographic location is apparent in the pictorial materials at all.

Dorothea Lange. "Destitute peapickers in California . . ." and "Nipomo, Calif. Mar. 1936. Migrant agricultural worker's family. . . ." (Migrant Mother series). Photographs, March 1936. Farm Security Administration Collection. Prints and Photographs Division. Clockwise: *LC-USF34-9058-C; LC-USF34-9093-C; LC-USF34-9095; LC-USF34-9097-C; LC-USZ62-58355.*

The photograph popularly known as "Migrant Mother" has become an icon of the Great Depression. That compelling image, however, is one of a series of photographs that Dorothea Lange made in February or March of 1936 in Nipomo, California. Seeing the photograph in the context of related images, understanding the purpose for which it was made, and knowing something of the photographer's and subject's views of the occasion amplify our perspectives on the image and, at the same time, suggest that no single meaning can be assigned to it.

Lange made the photographs toward the end of a month's trip photographing migratory farm labor for what was then the Resettlement Administration, later to become the Farm Security Administration. Her work was part of the administration's larger effort to document economic and social distress among the nation's agricultural workers and to advertise the agency's relief programs and the measures it was taking to address underlying causes of the dislocation. In 1960, Lange gave this account of the photographic encounter:

> I saw and approached the hungry and desperate mother, as if drawn by a magnet. I do not remember how I explained my presence or my camera to her, but I do remember she asked me no questions. I made five exposures, working closer and closer from the same direction. I did not ask her name or her history. She told me her age, that she was thirty-two. She said that they had been living on frozen vegetables from the surrounding fields, and birds that the children killed. She had just sold the tires from her car to buy food. There she sat in that lean-to tent with her children huddled around her, and seemed to know that my pictures might help her, and so she helped me. There was a sort of equality about it. (Lange, "The Assignment I'll Never Forget: Migrant Mother," *Popular Photography,* February 1960)

Whatever the woman, Florence Owens Thompson, thought of Lange's actions at the time, she and her children came to regret that Lange ever made the photographs, which they felt permanently colored them with a "Grapes of Wrath" stereotype. Thompson, a Native American from Oklahoma, had already lived in California for a decade when Lange photographed her. The immediate popularity of the image in the press did nothing to alleviate the financial distress that had spurred the family to seek seasonal agricultural work. Contrary to the despairing immobility the famous image seems to embody, however, Thompson was an active participant in farm labor struggles in the 1930s, occasionally serving as an organizer. Her daughter later commented, "She was a very strong woman. She was a leader. I think that's one of the reasons she resented the photo—because it didn't show her in that light" (Geoffrey Dunn, "Photographic License," San Jose *Metro,* January 19–25, 1995, p. 22).

The sheer vastness and variety of Prints and Photographs Division holdings, which comprise an estimated 13.5 million items, make the division a rich resource for researchers in women's history. The collections encompass the kinds of pictorial materials routinely found in historical societies, government archives, and art museums. Unlike many of these institutions, however, the Prints and Photographs Division stands out for its mammoth holdings of visual materials originally created for commercial purposes, including images intended for sale directly to the public or those designed for use in publications or advertising. The Library's relationship to the Copyright Office has contributed greatly to this strength. Starting in the 1870s, artists and publishers who wished to protect their rights in a pictorial work deposited copies of it in the U.S. Copyright Office. By no means did all of the deposited images enter the Library's collections, but hundreds of thousands of visual items were retained and are now part of the division's holdings. Images acquired in this way range from Currier & Ives lithographs, such as the company's 1869 satire on the women's rights campaign, to Napoleon Sarony's portraits of theatrical personality Mary Anderson, to photographs of Native American women made by Edward Curtis for his multivolume work *The North American Indian*. The Prints and Photographs Division has also, over the years, accumulated a wealth of graphic images created for use in magazines, books, and newspapers, as well as vast collections of photographs, referred to as "photo morgues," assembled by news photo agencies and by three major American publications: *Look Magazine, U.S. News & World Report,* and the *New York World-Telegram & Sun* newspaper.

Although images designed for commercial or publication purposes are a particular strength of the collections, pictures of many types and depicting many subjects can be found in the division's holdings, acquired from a great variety of sources. Scattered throughout are images that reflect the activities and proclivities of particular individuals and institutions, largely acquired through transfer from the Manuscript Division. The National Archives and Records Administration is the official repository for records of the federal government, including its visual records, but two renowned collections generated by government agencies, the Farm Security Administration/Office of War Information Collection and the Historic American Buildings Survey/Historic American Engineering Record, have, by historical agreement, come to the Library of Congress. The division's holdings also incorporate fine art prints and photographs (the division does not generally collect paintings) that came in through purchases and generous gifts.

Researchers regularly tap the collections to illustrate publications or to supply visual content for documentary films, educational media projects, and electronic resources. Such projects take advantage of the sometimes dynamic, sometimes humorous, and frequently information-filled content of individual images. Our collecting strengths, however, also support areas of growing interest in historical scholarship, including the representation of women in the United States over time and the role American women have played in communicating about their world in visual terms. All types of research involving the division's holdings, whether the ultimate object is to convey visual information or to interpret trends in representation, are facilitated by an understanding of, first, the source of the particular material being used and, second, the purpose for which it was originally in-

PRINTS AND PHOTOGRAPHS READING ROOM
James Madison Memorial Building, 3rd floor, room LM 337
Hours: Monday through Friday, 8:30 a.m. to 5:00 p.m. Closed weekends and federal holidays.
Address: Prints and Photographs Division, Library of Congress, 101 Independence Avenue, SE, Washington, DC 20540-4730
Telephone: 202 707-6394
Fax: 202 707-6647 (Fax inquiries are treated as letters and answered in order of receipt.)
Web site: <http://www.loc.gov/rr/print/>
Access and use: To make full use of the collections, you must visit in person. Limited service by mail and telephone is also available. Arrangements must be made in advance when patrons expect to view more than fifteen original items from the division's collections of posters, drawings, master photographs, and fine prints (this restriction does not include documentary photographs, the bulk of the division's holdings), when requesting unprocessed or fragile material requiring supervised handling, for visits by a class or study group, or when the number of images required by a project will far exceed average use (e.g., when searching thousands of images for digital publication).

Once you have identified appropriate reproduction numbers, you may order photographic copies of works in the division's collections from the Library's Photoduplication Service (telephone: 202 707-5640). The Library generally does not own rights to material in its collections, and not everything in the holdings is in the public domain. It is the patron's obligation to determine and satisfy copyright or other use restrictions (such as donor restrictions, privacy rights, licensing, or trademarks) when publishing or otherwise distributing materials found in the collections. Staff members will attempt to inform you of restrictions when such information is available, but frequently it is not available.

tended. A picture showing a woman at a stove in order to advertise the virtues of the appliance, for instance, would naturally present a different image of American women than one made the same year with the intention of documenting the limited spread of electricity to rural kitchens.

Rich as the resources of the Prints and Photographs Division are for those researching images relating to women's history, it is important to keep in mind that it is by no means the sole source of imagery in the Library of Congress. Books and periodicals in the General Collections and in other divisions in the Library, such as the Rare Book and Special Collections Division, are rife with illustrations, which can be studied on their own and in the context of the textual material with which they are presented. Custodial divisions other than the Prints and Photographs Division also sometimes house collections of visual materials. For instance, the Manuscript Division sometimes retains photographs and other visual materials associated with the personal papers of an individual or the records of an organization, as does the Music Division. The American Folklife Center features a large body of photographs resulting from various field projects.

Not only are images found embedded in textual materials held elsewhere in the Library, but textual sources in other reading rooms frequently hold the key to making knowledgeable use of Prints and Photographs Division holdings. Researchers who come armed with names, dates, and factual information about the images or image subjects they are seeking will have a better chance of locating images appropriate to their needs. Few of the division's catalogs or indexes systematically list images by the gender, ethnicity, or occupation of their makers or subjects. Someone seeking, for instance, images of nineteenth-century women journalists will need to look under the names of women known to have pursued that profession. A researcher interested in finding images of Mexican American women workers can mine the holdings more thoroughly by coming equipped with information about the regions and occupations in which Mexican American women worked at various points in time. Even after using multiple search strategies—searching by ethnicity, by region, and by occupation—the researcher may find that she or he must still make informed guesses about the ethnicity of women depicted in the collections. It is a truism that creators of visual images accent the visual. Information identifying images is frequently scarce, and written documentation that illuminates the motives and intentions of the image-maker is even rarer. As a consequence, you may need to consult textual materials held in other parts of the Library to aid in the identification and interpretation of images you find in the Prints and Photographs Division. Consulting such sources may also shed light on how the images were used to accompany the news, to advertise products and ideas, or to provide aesthetic pleasure.

USING THE COLLECTIONS

Over the course of the century in which the Prints and Photographs Division has existed, a variety of methods have been developed to provide access to its diverse holdings. *Reading room files*—file cabinets containing a mixture of original and copy images—provide direct access to some materials. Reading room files that may prove most useful for women's history topics are listed here:

- **Biographical File:** Pictures of people, especially posed portraits, as well as their families, homes, and activities, arranged by name;
- **Specific Subjects File:** Photographs of objects, events, activities, and structures, arranged by topical headings. Images relating to women and girls can be found under such varied headings as "Women—Politics and suffrage," "Sports—Rowing," "Children—Playing adults" and "Cowgirls;"
- **Graphics File:** Nonphotographic images, such as prints and drawings, arranged by topic groups, such as "Women's movements" or "Daily life."

Materials that cannot be accessed directly in reading room files are kept in storage areas and can be located by consulting catalogs, indexes, and finding aids. Some images are described in groups, based on their related provenance, subject matter, or format; other images are cataloged individually. Major tools include the following:

- **Prints and Photographs Online Catalog (PPOC):** An ever-increasing proportion of the division's collections can be found through this tool, which provides access to descriptions of groups of materials and single items, sometimes with linked digitized images. You can access PPOC remotely from the Prints and Photographs Reading Room home page (<http://www.loc.gov/rr/print/>), although some images will display only as "thumbnails" (small reference images) to those searching off-site. About 25 percent of the materials found in PPOC can also be found in the Library of Congress Online Catalog and that percentage is expected to grow, but at present the Library-wide

ACCESS METHODS: EVOLVING CONVENTIONS Over the course of its one-hundred-year existence, the Prints and Photographs Division has used a variety of methods for providing access to its holdings, ranging from placing images in file cabinets for direct browsing by researchers to making representations of the original images accessible on computer through sophisticated indexing and digitization schemes. In devising these access methods, staff members have kept in mind researchers' interests in people, places, things, and concepts.

Researchers familiar with cataloging practices in libraries, archives, and museums will recognize that, just as the division holds materials characteristic of all of these kinds of repositories, its access systems have partaken of methods from all three worlds. Collections that have been traditionally valued for their aesthetic and technical qualities, such as fine prints and art photographs, are still, for the most part, accessed through card catalogs that index only the creator of the piece, not its subject matter. In indexing collections of documentary photographs before the age of the computer, on the other hand, subject matter was given greater emphasis than listings for what were often a multiplicity of ill-identified creators. Therefore, the division's access systems do not lead comprehensively to all subjects and artists or, especially, photographers represented in the collections. Indirect methods are sometimes helpful in locating subjects and creators. For collections that are indexed primarily by subject, it may be necessary to search under subjects that an unlisted photographer or artist was known to have covered and to examine the materials themselves for credits or attributions. Conversely, in collections indexed primarily by artist's name, it may be necessary to research artists known to have depicted a particular subject in order to find pictures relating to that topic.

Because of emphasis on subject matter in many of the division's access tools, staff members have, over the years, put considerable effort into devising subject indexing schemes suited to its collections. The division attempts to match the rest of the Library's indexing for names of people, organizations, and places. When it comes to topical terms, however, many of the terms and conventions used in the *Library of Congress Subject Headings* (*LCSH*), or the Red Books, which were originally intended for indexing the subjects of books, are not well suited to pictorial materials. Some commonly depicted concepts, like "Shotgun weddings" or "Children playing in mud," are too specific to be included in that general list. In an effort to fill these gaps, Prints and Photographs Division cataloging specialists extracted the most appropriate terms from *LCSH* and other subject heading lists and supplemented them with additional terms as needed in the course of cataloging. Headings used in several reading room files and card indexes are derived from a preliminary list issued in 1980, *Subject Headings Used in the Library of Congress Prints and Photographs Division*, by Elisabeth W. Betz, which is available in notebooks near the files in which the terms are used, to help researchers identify appropriate headings. A new thesaurus, better suited to the capabilities of computer indexing and adhering to thesaurus guidelines for expressing relationships among terms, was published by the division in 1987 and is continuously updated. The *LC Thesaurus for Graphic Materials I: Subject Terms*, the source of subject terms for most of the collections in the Prints and Photographs Online Catalog, is available from the division's Web site, enabling users to discover additional terms if their initial search terms fail.

Research involving pictorial materials is concerned not only with who made the materials and what they depict, but also with the pictorial processes and formats they employ and the genres they represent. You may wish to concentrate on images produced as "postcards," "fashion plates," or "cartoons," or to focus on a particular type of portraiture, such as "group portraits," or a specific print process, such as "etchings." The *LC Thesaurus for Graphic Materials II: Genre & Physical Characteristic Terms*, also available on the division's Web site, helps indexers and researchers locate terms for such categories of pictorial material. Although these terms appear sporadically in some of the division's older card catalogs, they are most useful for searching material indexed in the online catalog.

catalog does not feature the quantity of digital images PPOC offers. Unless otherwise noted, references to the "online catalog" in this chapter refer to PPOC.

- **Divisional Card Catalog:** The primary access tool for groups of images that are not reflected in the online catalog, this card catalog provides access by subject term (these have varied through time), by geographic heading, and, to a lesser extent, by name of image producer or copyright holder.
- **Card Indexes:** Separate card catalogs list fine prints, posters, and other materials that have been cataloged individually, but access is often limited to a single entry under artist or publisher.
- **Finding Aids:** Catalog records for groups of images sometimes lead researchers to finding aids—either printed lists, card indexes or, occasionally, electronic indexes—that provide greater detail about the contents of the group.

Because of the complexity of these finding tools, it is expected that users of the Prints and Photographs Division will need to consult regularly with reference staff.

SELECTED HOLDINGS

Understanding the context in which someone originally created or collected an image is fundamental to evaluating its content and significance. The division's holdings reflect the wide variety of uses to which pictorial materials traditionally have been put. Some images derive from the world of journalism and some are the results of efforts to document systematically an event, era, or phenomenon, here termed "documentary surveys." Others served to advertise products, activities, or organizations; to educate, entertain and satisfy the need for aesthetic expression; to aid materially in the design of structures or products; or to record the activities and associations of individuals or organizations. Selected holdings useful for the study of women's history and culture will be discussed below in terms of these categories of use, recognizing that there are overlaps among the categories and that a single image may often be put to multiple uses.

Journalism

The division preserves several premier archives of pictorial journalism. These offer you the opportunity to analyze how women were (or were not) represented in events and activities the media considered newsworthy and to reflect on journalistic practices and biases with respect to women.

Graphic Journalism and Illustration

Before the development in the 1880s of efficient means for reproducing photographic images in magazines and, later, newspapers, publishers used drawings to depict events of the day for readers. Even after the photomechanical halftone process made it possible to reproduce photographs in books, magazines, and newspapers, publishers continued to use the work of artists to illustrate feature material, if not the news itself.

Original drawings by artists such as Alfred Waud and Edwin Forbes in the **Civil War Drawing Collection** (1,600 drawings,[1] 1860–65) enable researchers to examine original art work intended for use in illustrated newspapers such as *Harper's Weekly* and *Frank Leslie's Illustrated Newspaper* as the publications attempted to portray this cataclysmic event for the reading public. Women do not appear prolifically in the collection, but online catalog records for the drawings provide access to scenes of African American and white women's activities on the home front and parting from their men; others depict women in military camps and newly freed African American women encamped in Union territory. Access to the collection is primarily through PPOC, where catalog records for the drawings can be retrieved by searching the collection name "Civil War Drawing Collection" in combination with particular subjects or names.

Drawings and sketches in the **Cabinet of American Illustration** (4,000 drawings, 1845–present) afford you the opportunity to examine images produced as illustrations for American books and magazines. Catalog records in PPOC (retrievable through the collection name) with accompanying digital images enable researchers to explore how artists drawing for American publications presented women of many classes and walks of life. The collection includes, for instance, many of Charles Dana Gibson's original drawings from the turn of the century, including his sketches of "Gibson girls," which have been credited with influencing his generation's vision of the ideal woman. While accenting her sinuous beauty, Gibson frequently presented the Gibson girl in satirical situations. The artist's satirical style is particularly apparent in sampling some of his other sketches, such as "Studies in Expression: When Women Are Jurors" (see page 68) which places women of differing ages and economic status side by side in the jury box (CAI—Gibson, no. 23 [C size]); Repro. no. LC-USZ62-46321). Drawings by other artists from the golden age of American illustration, 1890–1920, provide additional visions of women as idealized beauties, as African American "mammies," as courting young women, and more rarely, as workers. In this way, the collection provides a sampling of the range of images of American womanhood that popular literature presented to its readers.

In addition to exploring how women were represented in illustrations, you can tap the collection to examine the work of such women illustrators

CHRONOLOGY OF IMAGE-MAKING PROCESSES: The existence of cave paintings testifies to the fact that the impulse to communicate through pictures accompanied the dawn of humanity. As early as A.D. 55, the Chinese experimented with technologies that expanded the communication potential of pictures by applying ink to seals and then replicating the designs on such surfaces as fabric, wood, and eventually paper. By the turn of the fifteenth century, technologies appeared in Europe for relief printing from wood, which made it possible to reproduce multiple copies of a picture from a single matrix—a woodblock. As the century progressed, further innovation resulted in the development of intaglio printing processes, such as engraving and etching, where the lines in the print are produced by ink transferred from below the printing surface, rather than from what is left in relief on the surface. The commercial potential of image-printing accelerated with the invention in 1798 of still another printing process, *lithography*, which offered a quick and inexpensive crayon-on-stone method of making multiple copies of an image for direct consumption by the public and for use in advertising and in illustrating publications.

Printmaking conveyed an artist's conception of a subject to many people at once. The development of photography in 1839 offered a seeming departure in image-making. The camera operator still had an influence on the resulting picture, but the mechanical process of recording the scene before a camera lens, through the use of light and chemicals, seemed to promise new heights of verisimilitude. By the late nineteenth century, image producers began to merge the two technologies for making multiple copies of images—printing and photography—to speed reproduction and to offer new pictorial effects in the form of, for instance, photolithography (patented in 1858) and halftone photography (first used commercially in magazine illustration in the 1880s). In this chapter, the term *prints* refers to images produced primarily with nonphotographic processes, and *photographs* refers to those using primarily photographic technology.

as Alice Barber Stephens (1858–1932), Charlotte Harding (1873–1951), Elizabeth Shippen Green Elliott (1871–1954), and Rose O'Neill (1874–1944)—artists whose images and pioneering careers merit exploration. O'Neill, for instance, was one of the few women to achieve marked financial success and professional independence in early twentieth-century cartooning. Her work was published in top humorous periodicals of the day, including *Puck, Judge,* and *Life,* many of which had largely male readerships. O'Neill also introduced readers of the *Ladies' Home Journal* to "The Kewpies," cherubic characters that soon became a national craze, generating lucrative "spin-offs" in the form of dolls and other merchandise as well as a syndicated comic strip.

Catalog records for items in the Cabinet of American Illustration frequently include a citation for the published work in which the drawing eventually appeared. This documentation provides a starting point for examining how images were integrated with text and, possibly, how the artist's original conception underwent alteration in later publication stages. Catalog records also frequently include the names of the authors of those textual works, many of whom were women, opening the possibility of exploring dynamics between authors of texts and creators of images. The digital images for this collection act as a reference surrogate. Because of their fragility, the original drawings are seen only by appointment.

Politics have long been a favored topic of the press, conveyed through satirical treatments as well as more ostensibly neutral reporting. The division's **British Cartoons** (10,000 prints, 1621–1832) include visual commentaries on the developing American political consciousness. American women appear in the prints, although determining the degree of their representation is difficult, as access through published and unpublished finding aids and microfilm is primarily by date, with title and some limited subject indexing for prints dating between 1771 and 1832.[2]

In addition to collecting early political prints, the division has maintained a strong focus on more recent types of political satire and comic art, in the forms of editorial cartoon and comic strip drawings. Online records for the **Cartoon Drawings** (9,200 drawings, 1794–1994) and the **Caroline and Erwin Swann Collection of Caricature and Cartoon** (2,000 drawings, 1780–1975) provide entrée to examining the ways in which cartoon artists used images of women metaphorically to comment on political events of the day. The materials also invite exploration of the humorous, sometimes biting ways in which cartoonists dealt with issues that touched on the rights and status of women, such as suffrage, health issues, participation in sports, and paid (and unpaid) labor. The more than one hundred recently acquired drawings for the comic strip "Blondie," for instance, offer evidence of changes—and surprising continuities—in the equality-minded title character's approach to marriage and domestic life between the 1930s and the 1960s. (See page 87.) As another example, a number of cartoons by African American artist Oliver Harrington portray black women putting black men in their place, guiding and chiding their children, and serving as symbols in the struggle for racial justice. The drawings thus offer commentary on relationships between the sexes and the generations within the urban African American community, as well as on race relations in general. As with many of the division's drawings collections, the images and the associated documentation could be used in conjunction with materials available in the Newspaper and Current Periodical Room or in the General Collections to study the editorial and technical practices that newspaper and magazine

Bill Mauldin. "The government has my whole family working on scientific progress. My husband is a jet plane mechanic, my son is a radar technician, and my brother makes rockets." Drawing, ink over pencil, published July 25, 1948. Cartoon Drawings Collection. Prints and Photographs Division. LC-USZ62-126823. Copyright © 1948 Bill Mauldin. Reprinted with permission of Bill Mauldin.

Published in the *New York Star* the very day the Berlin airlift was launched in July 1948, Bill Mauldin's commentary on the Cold War–inspired technology race offered, at the same time, an observation on the ways in which the tasks commonly assigned to women remained unaided by technological progress. Historians writing in recent decades have argued that even when new devices have been developed to assist with housework, the introduction of such technology has increased, rather than decreased the amount of time women spend in maintaining the home.

Frances Benjamin Johnston. Women working in Bureau of Engraving and Printing in Washington, D.C. Photographic print, cyanotype, ca. 1889. Frances Benjamin Johnston Collection. Prints and Photographs Division. LC-USZC4-8151.

Frances Benjamin Johnston made a name for herself with her portraits of socially prominent residents of the nation's capital. Her photojournalistic work sometimes offers glimpses of her interactions with less elite members of society, as in this photograph of women workers at the Bureau of Engraving and Printing circa 1889, which includes one worker who adopts a playful pose, complete with hat.

staffs have employed in reproducing such drawings in their publications.

The Prints and Photographs Division also preserves substantial runs of the illustrated weeklies, *Harper's Weekly* (January 3, 1857–September 6, 1976; P&P holds 1857–1900, although lacking some volumes in that span) and *Frank Leslie's Illustrated Newspaper* (December 15, 1855–June 17, 1922; P&P holds most volumes within this span), as well as the comic weeklies *Puck* (1877–1918; P&P holds many volumes in the span 1878–1917) and *Judge* (1881–1939; P&P holds October 1882 onward). These pictorial publications contain a wealth of imagery indicative of social issues and attitudes of the late nineteenth and early twentieth centuries. The division's copies of these publications, however, are maintained primarily for reproduction and exhibition purposes; microfilm copies of the periodicals are available in the Microform Reading Room for research use.

Photojournalism Collections

The archive of one of America's earliest news photo agencies, the **George Grantham Bain Collection** (100,000 photographic prints and negatives, ca. 1910–22), provides evidence of the many ways in which women made the news in the early decades of the twentieth century. The collection includes hundreds of photos documenting women's suffrage activities (see illustrations pages 33, 36), as well as depictions of immigrant women, women engaging in various sports and physical education activities, recreational activities of upper-class women, women workers striking in the pre–World War I era, and women taking on new roles during that war. Although Bain collected images from publications across the United States that subscribed to his photo service, a large proportion of the photographs were produced under his direction and focus primarily on activities in New York City and, to a lesser extent, the East Coast. Many of the portraits from the collection have been integrated into the division's Biographical File. Other images have been cataloged as groups ("LOTs") in the Divisional Card Catalog.

Frances Benjamin Johnston (1864–1952) was one of the photographers who carried out photographic assignments for Bain's news service. One of her scoops for Bain was to photograph and interview Admiral George Dewey, the "Hero of Manila Bay," aboard his flagship as it rested in the harbor of Naples, Italy, in 1899, after Dewey's naval victory in the Philippines. Since women did not readily obtain invitations to board battleships, Johnston made use of her connections, tracking

Toni Frissell. Nuns clamming on Long Island. Photograph, September 1957. Toni Frissell Collection. Prints and Photographs Division. LC-F9-04-5709-012-07.

Although Toni Frissell became known for her fashion photography, by the 1950s her interest in fashion work was waning and her professional focus shifted to sports photography. In this scene, however, she captured the figures of women who had explicitly rejected fashion and whose "sport" had a practical result.

down Assistant Secretary of the Navy Theodore Roosevelt at his Oyster Bay home and obtaining from him a letter of reference that read, "My dear Admiral Dewey, Miss Johnston is a lady, and whom I personally know. I can vouch for, she does good work, and any promise she makes she will keep."[3]

In addition to running the active Washington, D.C., portrait studio she had launched in 1890, Johnston continued to pursue freelance photojournalism, publishing magazine articles illustrated with her own photographs on topics ranging from coal mining to new methods in education. Turning increasingly to garden and estate photography in the 1910s, Johnston also forged a name for herself in that photographic specialty. Long an advocate for photography as a profession for women, Johnston took on the assignment of representing the work of women photographers in the 1900 Paris Exposition. This advocacy, along with her mastery of a variety of subfields of the photographic profession, earned Johnston the status of a pioneer among women photographers.

The results of Johnston's early forays into photojournalism, along with photographs from other stages of her varied career, family photographs and keepsakes, and images by other women photographers, make up the **Frances Benjamin Johnston Collection** (25,000 items, ca. 1864–1947, bulk 1897–1927). Most of Johnston's images have been grouped by subject matter. Catalog records for the groups are included in both the Divisional Card Catalog and the online catalog, indexed under her name. Women appear in Johnston's photojournalistic coverage of various industries, including box-making (LOT 7512), the Lynn shoe factories (LOT 2913), and activities at the U.S. Mint and the Bureau of Engraving (LOT 8861), and in her coverage of school activities in Washington, D.C., schools (LOT 2749), at Tuskegee Institute (LOT 2962), at Hampton Institute (LOT 11051), and at the United States Indian School at Carlisle, Pennsylvania (LOT 12369). Her portrait work demonstrates her ability to capitalize on her connections to Washington's politically powerful and socially elite, capturing the faces and activities of Washington, D.C., and New York society women (see especially LOT 11735). Associated material held in the Manuscript Division offers further insight into Johnston's life and working methods.

Toni Frissell (1907–1988) began her career as a photojournalist and fashion photographer about the time Frances Benjamin Johnston's was winding down, but she demonstrated a similar versatility in her work as a staff photographer for *Vogue, Harper's Bazaar,* and *Sports Illustrated* and in her publication of several photographically illustrated books, ranging from *A Child's Garden of Verses* (1944) to *The King Ranch, 1939–1944* (1975). She is perhaps best known for her pioneering fashion photography and her informal portraits of the famous and powerful in the United States and Europe, including Winston Churchill, Eleanor Roosevelt, and John F. and Jacqueline Kennedy.

The **Toni Frissell Collection** (340,000 items, ca. 1930–69) includes 270,000 black-and-white negatives, 42,000 color transparencies, and 25,000 enlargement prints, as well as proof sheets, not all of which have been processed for general use. Frissell's own selection of about 1,800 of her best and most representative photographs have been processed for use (LOT 12452) and provide a substantial representation of Frissell's chief interests: children, fashion, families, leisure activities such as eating and drinking, members of American and British upper classes, well-known personalities, and sports. Catalog records, accessible through the collection name, lead to descriptions of this and other processed groups of images, including a substantial portion of Frissell's documentation of World War II military and civilian activities, both in the United States and abroad. Frissell focused in particular on women's contributions during the war, including their Red Cross activities and a 1943 visit by Women's Auxiliary Army Corps (WAAC) director Oveta Culp Hobby to two WAAC facilities.

Frissell is noted for taking fashion photography out of the studio into the outdoors, thus placing an accent on the active woman. She is also known for the imaginative angles, both physical and metaphorical, from which she covered her subjects. She documented women from all walks of life and in all situations, sometimes using them to comment on the human condition. Thus, in the single year of 1957, her work ranged from her quiet portrayal of an elderly African American woman enjoying a barefoot moment fishing in the Tidal Basin in Washington, D.C. (LC-F9-02-5706-053-06), to an intimate portrait of actress Elizabeth Taylor with her husband Mike Todd and their infant daughter (LC-F9-52-5709-52A-26); and from a lyrical depiction of two nuns clamming on Long Island (LC-F9-04-5709-012-07), to a shot of a woman taking a "snooze" on the beach at Waikiki (LC-F9-04-5711-015-22). Frissell's personal papers, which have not yet been prepared for general use, will be transferred to the Manuscript Division when the entire photograph collection has been processed.

Whereas Frissell's photographs exemplify the type of news and fashion photography designed for publication in general interest magazines, the **New York World-Telegram and Sun Newspaper Photograph Collection (NYWTS)** (1,000,000 photographic prints, ca. 1880–1967, bulk 1920–67) offers researchers a rich body of material with which to investigate how this mass circulation newspaper represented women. The collection is divided into a biographical section and a subject/geographical section. Access to both sections is through a lengthy finding aid, which reproduces all of the headings *New York World* staff assigned to the folders in which they filed the images. The collection includes images made by staff photographers, and these images are considered to be in the public domain. More prevalent in the collection, however, are images gathered from commercial studios and wire services, and to publish these, you must first evaluate their rights status. Because the size of the collection has necessitated storing the material off-site, you should be aware that there could be a wait of as long as ten working days before you will be able to view materials you request.

The collection has proven to be a valuable source of images of people (the biographical section of the finding aid occupies fourteen of the seventeen notebooks of folder headings). The single best collection in the division for images of women legislators, it includes press photos of actresses, authors, athletes, other celebrities, and, most well represented of all, people who attracted considerable press notice. The collection features, for example, twenty-one folders of images relating to the career of Amelia Earhart, ranging from the folder labeled rather generally by *New York World* staff, "Earhart, Amelia—Aviatrix. Dead. Flights," which holds twenty-seven photos on this subject, to the folder more precisely labeled, "Earhart, Amelia—Aviatrix. Dead. Welcomes. Paris, France," which contains a single photo. The subject/geographical portion of the file yields intriguing glimpses of women's involvement in the civil rights movement and local, national, and international politics. It also highlights aspects of family life, popular culture, and consumerism, particularly in the 1950s and 1960s. (See page 43.)

The **Look Magazine Photograph Collection** (5,000,000 photographs, 1937–71) is the largest single collection in the division's holdings. It includes both color and black-and-white photographs—published and unpublished—accumulated by the magazine during its thirty-four-year history. Originally designed as a tabloid-type publication, full of sensational coverage, the magazine shifted its focus after World War II under the influence of Fleur Cowles, the wife of the publisher. Advertised as a biweekly for the whole family, *Look* made a concerted effort to appeal to women, particularly in their roles as consumers. One expression of this effort was the regularly featured "For Women Only" section, which highlighted consumer goods and services, frequently of the less conventional sort, such as women's spats and fur bikinis. As this suggests, the magazine blended the frivolous with the serious, not only covering fashion, food, celebrities, and popular culture, but also presenting more probing investigations of the civil rights struggle, health issues, and education.

The magazine's coverage of women celebrities ranging from Lucille Ball to Gloria Steinem yields a wealth of portrait imagery for periods not well represented elsewhere in Prints and Photographs Division holdings. The visual coverage of individuals, both well known and unknown, often follows a "day in the life" approach, picturing a person through a number of her activities. For instance, Ruby Hurley's 1957 tour of National Association for the Advancement of Colored People (NAACP)

Charlotte Brooks. "Fluoridation: Why All the Controversy?" Contact sheet, April 1958. Look Magazine Photograph Collection. Prints and Photographs Division. LC-USZ62-126852.

William Attwood and Charlotte Brooks. One page of a Look *magazine article titled "Fluoridation: Why All the Controversy?"* Look *(June 24, 1958), p. 22. Prints and Photographs Division and General Collections. LC-USZ62-126855.*

To dramatize the debate over the fluoridation of drinking water, a practice that started in1945 to promote dental health, staff writer William Attwood and several photographers, including Charlotte Brooks, focused on strife in New Canaan, Connecticut, over a fluoridation referendum. Dr. Charlotte Brown, the town's health director, became the center of the photographic coverage as Brooks showed her addressing citizens at community meetings, examining patients at her medical practice, and standing in line to cast her vote. Editorial marks made on the original contact sheets by *Look* staff members offer traces of the selection process in progress. The published story illustrates not only what the fluoridation issue was but also how photographs were deployed to tell it.

FLUORIDATION

"Let's vote on it."

For Dr. Charlotte Brown, election day culminated weeks of tension and exasperation. She didn't know whether the people of New Canaan would believe her and their own doctors—or the antifluoridation lecturers. At noon, local politicians told her the vote would be close: a rumor had started in one section of town that fluoridation would make you impotent. In the afternoon, between patients, she used two phones to stir up late voters. By 6 p.m., when the polls closed, she was at the town hall, her letter of resignation in her pocket. Friends tried to reassure her, and A. Leland Glidden, water-company president, said he favored installing fluoridation regardless of how the vote came out. (The antis promised court action if he did.) Her fears turned out to be groundless. When the results were announced—1,513 "yes" and 673 "no"—Charlotte Brown and her fellow doctors discovered that the people of New Canaan trusted them after all.

Carrying one of her children, Dr. Brown is greeted by a well-wisher on way to the polls.

Profluoridationists were encouraged when young couples with children turned up to vote.

Expecting a close vote, Dr. Brown and friends wait tensely at town hall to hear results. Big margin of victory first surprised, then delighted them.

22

branches as the organization's Southeast regional secretary shows her encounters with everyone from a rural farmer to Lena Horne, as well as the more mundane aspects of her life on the road (LOOK—Job 57-7241). The archive exhibits the magazine's emphasis on women caring for their families and working in jobs traditionally occupied by women, such as nursing, teaching, and social work, but it also features women in some nontraditional roles, such as the woman police detective featured in a 1956 story (LOOK—Job 55-4033) and auto test-driver Betty Skelton undergoing exams to become an astronaut in 1959 (LOOK—Job 59-8504). The impact of the conflict in Vietnam on women's lives is reflected in photo assignments showing military wives, as well as those documenting antiwar protests. Other coverages suggest developments affecting women's roles and choices. Several sets of images delve into the availability of birth control. Others explore, more generally, the quality of American middle-class women's lives—a subject tackled, for instance, in the 1958 piece "America's New Middle West: St. Louis Woman" (LOOK—Job 58-7929). One assignment carried out in the early 1970s documented participants in the "Fascinating Womanhood" movement, a response to calls for women's liberation (LOOK—Job 70-5730). Although the magazine directed itself to a middle-class audience and frequently focused on middle-class lifestyles, as early as the 1940s, *Look* attempted to illustrate the culture of America's less economically advantaged citizens, including Native Americans, African Americans, and Puerto Ricans. From the mid-1960s onward, *Look* staff made a concerted effort not only to acknowledge the poverty in which some African Americans lived but also to highlight African Americans' inclusion in American society, with an emphasis on integrated schools and workplaces.

The magazine aimed to inform, but not necessarily to shock its readers. Because the *Look* photo archive includes both published and unpublished images, it is possible to gather evidence about editorial selection practices in examining the materials. For instance, photographer Al Clayton's hard-hitting coverage of the poverty-stricken Pilgrim family in Yazoo County, Mississippi (LOOK—Job 67-3368), numbered in the hundreds of images, of which eight were chosen to illustrate the article "Poverty: The Hungry World of Teresa Pilgrim," (*Look*, December 26, 1967; available on microfilm in the Prints and Photographs Reading Room, as well as in hard copy in the General Collections; AP2.L79).

Look's photography staff was composed primarily of men. Although a number of women did short-term, freelance work for the magazine, Charlotte Brooks (b. 1918) stands out—because she was apparently the only woman to be hired on staff, because of the length of time she worked on the magazine, and because of the sheer volume and variety of her work.

The photographs in the collection are being readied for public use in stages: published and unpublished black-and-white material (mostly reproduced as "contact sheets"—photographic prints that reproduce multiple negatives or 35-millimeter negative strips on a single sheet) and published color images created for issues after 1951 are available; earlier material is still being processed. Catalog records in PPOC enable researchers to retrieve descriptions of "jobs" (groups of images made for a particular assignment) by subject and by the title of the *Look* articles in which images from the job appeared. Despite its lack of caption information or other textual documentation for unpublished images, the Look Magazine Photograph Collection offers potential for exploring how the magazine presented American culture to its readers, and particularly to women readers, in the middle decades of the twentieth century. The magazine gave this rich photo archive to the Library with the understanding that the images should not be used for trade or commercial purposes. Readers are advised to contact the photographer or his or her heirs to seek permission to use materials for other publication purposes.

The division's other major magazine photograph morgue, the **U.S. News & World Report Magazine Photograph Collection (USNWR)** (1,000,000 photographic negatives and 45,000 contact sheets, 1952–86), was associated with a publication less overtly geared to a female audience. Nevertheless, the images cover political events and figures, including civil rights and women's rights marches and demonstrations. They document social and economic trends such as school desegregation, urban and industrial expansion, consumerism, and tourism and depict some popular culture developments, including the incorporation of television into American family life. The collection offers researchers visual documentation for more recent American history that is not comprehensively covered in other Prints and Photographs Division holdings. Housed in the reading room, the collection is organized by "job" number, which provides a rough form of chronological access to the images reproduced in contact sheets. Subject access to the collection is provided by a card index developed by *U.S. News & World Report* staff, with headings under proper names, as well as somewhat variable topical terms such as "People—Families" or "Negroes—Segregation." There are few listings directly under "Women," so researchers must be creative in determining the settings and situations in which they might see women depicted. About 65 percent of the images were made by *U.S. News & World Report* staff photographers and are considered to be in the public domain, but rights for other images may have been retained by the photographer or by his or her heirs.

As a sample of the range of ways in which women appear in the collection, browsing the files for the months of January and February 1962 yields images of a Women's National Press Club dinner for Congress; a woman in rather brief costume modeling with a convertible at an auto show; African American singer Grace Bumbry rehearsing for her performance at the White House; women (and men) attending a Young Republican Leadership training school; women working in the booming aerospace industry in Florida, and shopping or attending high school in the rapidly developing surrounding area; a young woman being admitted to George Washington University; and a woman walking on a dark Washington, D.C., street. The last set of images (LC-U9-7491) demonstrates the research that is sometimes necessary to understand the content and context of images from photojournalism archives, where written documentation is frequently sparse. The caption on the contact sheet folder merely notes that the photographs were made for a "Washington crime story," but it does not indicate whether the woman represented a victim or a perpetrator. The neighboring folder (LC-U9-7490), containing photos from the same assignment, provides little added illumination, as it is captioned simply, "Washington, D.C. after Dark." The published volumes of *U.S. News & World Report* that are accessible in the Prints and Photographs Reading Room enable the researcher to place the image in the context of the accompanying story, which compared crime rates in different cities. The image of the woman appeared as an allusion to citizens' vulnerability to crime, alongside text discussing the capital city's high crime rate at the time. Correspondingly, the images in the U.S. News & World Report Collection offer a different kind of context. As with Look Magazine Collection photographs, the substantial body of unpublished images offers clues to the editorial selection practices of the magazine.

Documentary Surveys

Images made for purposes of publication reflect the desire to document and persuade. Some Prints and Photographs Division collections that were products of documentary survey projects likewise reflect these drives, even when the images they contain were not made expressly for publication purposes. Survey materials reflect a desire on the part of several individuals working collaboratively to provide a systematic record of a time or a phenomenon. These collections number among the division's most popular and widely known collections.

As with the Civil War Drawing Collection, the **Civil War Photographs Collection** (7,000 photographs, 1861–65) does not provide much coverage of women's involvement in this national conflict. But the inclusion of women in scenes of military camp life, in hospitals, and in a few images showing African American families fleeing northward does provide visual clues suggesting the profound ways in which the war affected women's lives and vice versa. Photographs in this collection are often associated with the name of Mathew Brady, although Brady really acted more as an entrepreneur, planning the documentation effort, commissioning other photographers to make the images, and attempting to market the resulting photographic record to the American public (see, for instance, page xxx). About 1,100 of the images are accessible in digital form in PPOC. The remainder are cataloged as LOTs that can be browsed in a reading room file. The division hopes eventually to add them to the online offering.

Less than a century after Mathew Brady and the Civil War photographers set out to record that cataclysmic event, the nation was again in crisis, first from a severe economic downturn and associated agricultural dislocation, followed by world war. President Franklin D. Roosevelt established the Resettlement Administration, later the Farm Security Administration, to assist dislocated farmers. The agency's "Historical Section" aided in this effort by documenting the need for agricultural assistance and recording the results of the agency's efforts to address that need. Under the direction of Roy Stryker, the head of the photographic unit, the documentation effort went further than that. Images in the **Farm Security Administration/Office of War Information (FSA/OWI) Collection** (164,000 black-and-white film negatives, 107,000 black-and-white photographic prints, and 1,610 color transparencies, 1935–44) show Americans at home, at work, and at play, with an emphasis on rural and small-town life and the adverse effects of the Great Depression, the Dust Bowl, and increasing farm mechanization. Some of the most famous images portray displaced people migrating West or to industrial cities in search of work. In its later years, the project documented America's mobilization for World War II.

Because the FSA and OWI photographers concentrated on the daily lives of ordinary people all over the United States, the images offer an unparalleled resource for glimpsing family life, living quarters, personal grooming, paid and unpaid labor, recreational activities, and religious and organizational life during the 1930s and 1940s. Although biographical details on the subjects of the images are seldom available, the collection encompasses many images of African American women, substantial documentation of Hispanic women in the Southwest (see pages 358–59), and women of various other ethnicities. As the photographers shifted from documenting economic and agricultural crisis to promoting the war effort, a concerted effort was made to document the lives of members of various ethnic groups and the entry of women into the workforce. The collection includes the work of several outstanding women photographers, including Dorothea Lange (1895–1965), Esther Bubley (1921–1998), Marion Post Wolcott (1910–1990), and Marjorie Collins (1912–1985), as well as well-known male photographers such as Gordon Parks, Walker Evans, Russell Lee, Jack Delano, John Vachon, Arthur Rothstein, and John Collier. The division also holds the unit's written records. It is not always possible to trace the intentions or working methods of the photographers in these records, since the photographer may never have committed such information to paper or the paper on which it was written may not have been preserved at the unit headquarters. Nevertheless, the written material does provide insight into the operations of the photographic unit in a way that few other photo archives do.

Color transparencies are available as digital images in PPOC; digital images and associated catalog records are regularly added to the catalog for the black-and-white negatives. The more than 100,000 prints made by the FSA/OWI unit from these negatives have been organized first by region of the United States and then by subject matter. Before the prints were filed in this arrangement, they were microfilmed in groups that generally reconstructed a photographer's work on an assignment in a particular location. Viewing these microfilmed LOTs may help place individual images in the context of the story that the photographer was attempting to tell. The written records are also served on microfilm.

The FSA documentation effort was only one of many New Deal–era projects that set out to record aspects of American life and culture. Architectural surveys documented many of the spaces in which women lived, learned, worshiped, and worked. The Carnegie Corporation funded two architectural surveys, beginning in 1929. The **Pictorial Archives of Early American Architecture (PAEAA)** (10,000 photographs, ca. 1930–38) instituted a national campaign to acquire photographic negatives of seventeenth-, eighteenth-, and nineteenth-century buildings in the United States. During its most active period, the PAEAA collected and cataloged approximately ten thousand negatives and photoprints, primarily of structures in the New England and Middle Atlantic states, including images by Frances Benjamin Johnston and others. Johnston canvassed nine southern states in a separate Carnegie-funded project, the **Carnegie Survey of the Architecture of the South** (7,000 photographs, 1933–40), making a systematic record of the early buildings and gardens. She was one of the first to document vernacular building traditions, photographing not only the great mansions of the South but also churches, graveyards, row houses, offices, kitchens, warehouses, mills, shops, farm buildings, and inns. The survey includes numerous shots of interiors and architectural details. Separate collection card indexes provide access to the photographs by location (state/county/local place name).

The **Historic American Buildings Survey/ Historic American Engineering Record (HABS/HAER)** (photographs, measured drawings, and/or textual information for over 35,000 structures and sites, ca. 1933–present) began with a proposal by architect Charles E. Peterson of the National Park Service to put a thousand unemployed architects to work for ten weeks documenting what he called "America's antique buildings." Operating under various administrative authorities for the first two years, HABS became a permanent program of the National Park Service in July 1934. In 1969 the **Historic American Engineering Record** began carrying out systematic documentation of engineering works and industrial sites. Online catalog records summarize the documentation available for each site and offer some access to building types. The catalog records themselves can often provide intriguing clues about successive uses to which buildings have been put, such as the former stable in Des Moines, Iowa, that was converted in 1942 for use as housing for Women's Auxiliary Army Corps volunteers (HABS, IOWA, 77-DESMO,24-N-). Continuing in the tradition of the Carnegie surveys, the documentation covers structures used by the wealthy as well as those of more humble circumstances. Demonstrating both the range of structures surveyed and the variety of materials documenting them are photographs of the La Jolla Women's Club in California (HABS, CAL,37-LA-JOL,1-) and drawings showing the spatial arrangements of a Shaker washhouse in Hancock, Massachusetts (HABS, MASS,2-HANC,14-). It is possible to reconstruct the layout of slave quarters or a plantation schoolhouse at Thornhill Plantation, Greene County, Alabama (HABS, ALA,32-WATSO,1-), or to explore the structures used by Native American inhabitants of Acoma Pueblo, New Mexico (HABS, NM, 31-ACOMP,1-). At least one publication on landmarks relating to women's history has provided references to HABS and HAER documentation, and articles in a 1983 guide to the HABS/HAER collection suggest how the documentation may be used in conjunction with other sources to explore, for instance, the evolution and use of the American kitchen.[4] In general, however, the surveys' rich holdings remain relatively untapped resources for the study of women's history.

An instinct for preserving a record of the built past inspired architectural surveys such as HABS and HAER. Prompted by a somewhat different preservation instinct, photographer Edward S. Curtis embarked at the turn of the century on an effort to document all of the Native American peoples who "still retained to a considerable degree their primitive customs and traditions." In the

Historic American Buildings Survey. Thornhill Plantation, Greene County, Alabama.

Clockwise: *W. A. Hotchkiss, delineator. Site plan. Drawing, ca. 1936. Historic American Buildings Survey. Prints and Photographs Division. HABS AL–238, sheet 1; LC-USZA1-1287.*

W. A. Hotchkiss and Willis E. Jordan, delineators. Elevation and floorplan of housekeeper's cabin. Drawing, ca. 1936. Historic American Buildings Survey. Prints and Photographs Division. HABS AL–238, sheet 15; LC-USZA1-1767.

Alex Bush, photographer. Housekeeper's cabin and present occupant. Photograph, December 30, 1934. Historic American Buildings Survey. Prints and Photographs Division. HABS ALA 32-WATSO, 1–26.

Developed as a cotton plantation in the early 1830s by James Thornton, Alabama's first secretary of state, Thornhill extended over 2,600 acres and by 1860 employed 156 slaves. About a third of the slaves lived in quarters behind the Thornton residence. The site plan, measured drawings, and photographs made by Historic American Buildings Survey staff in the 1930s provide clues to the daily workings of the plantation. Photographs include the part of the yard known as the "wash place," where laundering activities took place, and the housekeeper's cabin, seen here with its contemporary occupant.

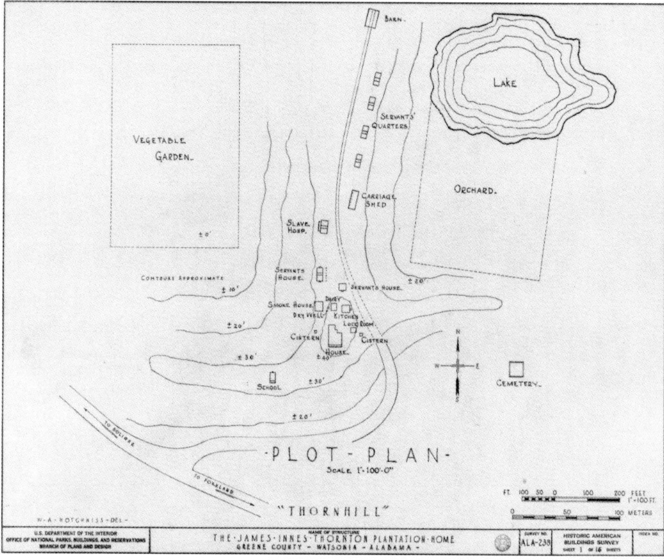

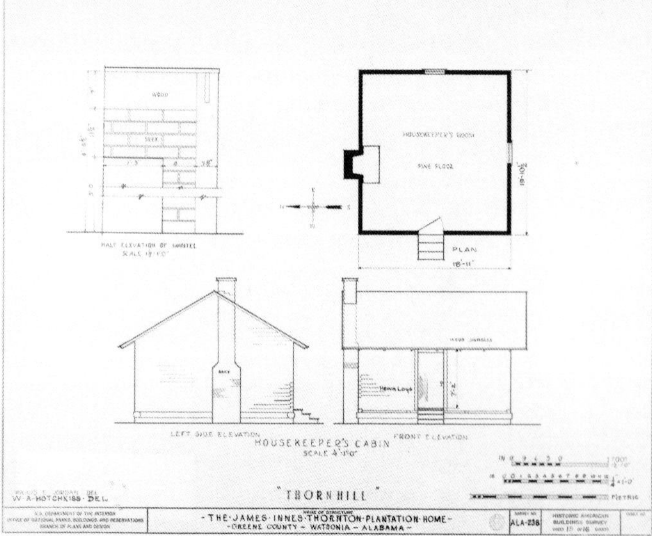

course of a thirty-year project, Curtis documented more than eighty tribes. Numerous commentators have pointed out how Curtis manipulated his subjects and their surroundings to produce a romanticized vision of a Native American past, often eliminating any acknowledgment of the ways in which modern Euro-American culture had already reshaped Native American life. The **Edward Curtis Collection** (2,400 photographic prints, 1899–1929) consists primarily of photographic prints that Curtis deposited for copyright in the course of preparing his twenty-volume work *The North American Indian*, including many views not published in the book. The prints offer plentiful, often detailed portrayals of Native American women and their activities, inviting exploration not only of the subject matter of the photographs but of how Curtis chose to represent his subjects in light of his own objectives and assumptions.[5] (See, for example, the illustration on page xxiv.) The images have been organized by tribe into twenty-two LOTs (LOT 12310–12331) indexed online and in the Divisional Card Catalog. Reprint volumes of *The North American Indian* (New York, Johnson Reprint Corp., 1970; E77.C98) kept in the division's reference book collection, provide an additional avenue of access to the images; the original edition of the publication, with its photogravure illustrations, is housed in the Rare Book and Special Collections Division.

Advertising and Propaganda

Those with wares to sell or propaganda to purvey have long tapped the potential that first printmaking and then photography provided for inexpensive and rapid dissemination of images. Although written language is seldom completely absent from broadsides, posters, and other advertising media, the imagery used on such materials was designed to catch the eye and communicate in a manner that often conveyed several messages at once. The juxtaposition of words and images, originally intended to pique viewers' interest, can also point to new avenues for research. Items in the Prints and Photographs Division's unparalleled poster collection advertise events, products, and ideas ranging from theatrical performances to recruitment for war work, from household goods to women's liberation. Graphic ephemera such as pictorial package labels suggest the ways in which an industrializing consumer culture associated women and women's concerns with particular products. Photographs were sometimes used to perform a similar function. Mostly acquired through copyright deposit, such images are scattered throughout the collections, usually minus the advertising copy that formed a part of the final product.

Posters

The invention of lithography spurred the development of the modern poster in the nineteenth century. Beginning in the 1890s, poster design flourished, as artists began to work in the medium. Women were early contributors to this form of applied graphic art. The division's **Artist Posters** series (85,000 posters; mid-1800s–present) highlights the work of poster artists from the United States and elsewhere, including the nineteenth-century work of Ethel Reed (b. 1874) and Blanche McManus (b. 1869) and sprinklings of later work by Jessie Willcox Smith (1863–1935), Anna Milo Upjohn (1869–1951), Neysa McMein (1890–1949), Florence Lundborg (1871–1945), Dorothy Waugh (b. 1896), and Martha Sawyers (b. 1902).[6] Posters created in the 1960s, 1970s, and 1980s by Muriel Cooper (1924–1994), Jacqueline Casey (b. 1927), and April Greiman (b. 1948) help bring the collection up to date. Comprising some of the outstanding pieces of poster design from the efflorescence of the medium in the 1890s to more contemporary works, the collection also provides a cross section of design conventions used in posters produced to advertise everything from laundry soap to labor organizing and from radiators to reading. A card index provides access to artists' names. A supplementary card index provides access to many of the posters by their promotional goal, although considerable browsing may be required to determine which campaigns related to women's concerns or portrayed women. As an aid to browsing, a microfilm made in 1973 reproduces the posters in order by designer.

The **Performing Arts Posters** (2,100 posters, 1840s–1930s) incorporates posters advertising burlesque, minstrel, vaudeville, operetta, and magic shows as well as "legitimate" theater. With their depictions of such luminaries as Anna Held and Fanny Rice, the posters provide an avenue for exploring both the role women played in the entertainments themselves, and the ways in which their images were used to lure prospective audiences to the shows. Records from the divisional online catalog provide access by title and type of show, poster producer, topics such as "Mothers," and "Servants," as well as to the names of particular theater companies and entertainers. A researcher hunting for images of African American singer Sissieretta Jones, for instance, could discover through a name search an 1899 poster featuring a portrait of her and advertising her as "The

Strobridge Lith. Co. Adam Forepaugh & Sells Brothers Enormous Shows Combined. *Poster, color lithograph, 1896. Circus Posters. Prints and Photographs Division. LC-USZC4-930.*

The notion of the "New Woman" emerged in the final two decades of the nineteenth century. Representing an ideal of independence, the archetypal new woman was single, white, educated, athletic, and progressive. Signaling society's ambivalence about this developing ideal, she was often portrayed as manly or licentious in visual and other media. This circus poster expresses some of the ambiguity surrounding the New Woman. It heralded her while at the same time suggesting that she occupied the circus ring as a clown, a scantily clad equestrienne, and a tuxedoed ringmaster.

Black Patti . . . the greatest singer of her race" (POS—TH—POR .J67, no. 1 [C size]; repro. no. LC-USZC4-5164). (See illustration page xxi.)

Circus Posters (600 posters, 1840–present) likewise depict stars from a particular entertainment arena, such as Barnum and Bailey stars Isabella Butler and Rose Meers. One poster proclaims Meers to be the "Greatest Living Lady Rider—Entirely original in dress, style and action, engaged at a salary of $100.00 per day" (POS—Circus—Barnum & Bailey 1897, no. 9, [D size]; Repro. no. LC-USZ62-24078). A card index organized by circus company provides access to the posters. Photographic reproductions of many of the posters can be found in the division's "Specific Subjects—Graphics" file, under the heading "Circus & Shows."

Reflecting the advent of a new entertainment technology, the division's collection of **Motion Picture Posters** (6,000 posters, 1896–present) encompasses thousands of posters and is particularly strong for films of the 1940s and 1950s. The breadth of the collection supports investigation of such topics as the evolving depiction of women in posters advertising Westerns, ranging from the poster for *The Rustler's Reformation,* a 1913 release from Selig Polyscope Company (POS—MOT. PIC.—1913 .R88, no. 1 [C size]) to the poster for *Two-Gun Lady,* which was issued more than forty years later (POS—MOT. PIC.—1955 .T96, no. 1 [C size]). Card indexes provide access to film titles, dates, stars, and directors; occasionally the cards describe what the posters depict. A binder containing microfilm strips reproducing posters dating from the 1890s to the 1940s enables researchers to preview a portion of the items in the collection. Recently acquired posters are not listed in the card index, nor are they reproduced in the binder. Advance arrangements are required to see uncataloged posters. The Prints and Photographs Division's film posters and pictorial lobby cards complement similar materials held in the Motion Picture Reading Room.

Among the original silk-screened **Work Projects Administration (WPA) Posters** (900 posters, 1936–43) produced by various branches of the WPA, there are several that address women directly, promoting prenatal care, advertising employment opportunities, and offering advice about health and child-rearing matters. Among posters about cancer prevention is one designed by Alex Kallenberg in the mid-1930s advocating early detection of breast and uterine cancer and reminding women that cancer claims more women than men (POS—WPA—NY .K34, no. 1 [C size]; Repro. no. LC-USZC2-1009). Women artists contributed to the WPA poster effort, Katherine Milhous (1894–1977) and Vera Bock (b. 1905) prominent among them. Online catalog records with digitized images and card catalogs arranged by state, artist, and title provide access to the collection.

Posters were put into service during both World

Alfred Palmer. "This girl in a glass house is putting finishing touches on the bombardier nose section of a B-17F navy bomber, Long Beach, Calif. She's one of many capable women workers in the Douglas Aircraft Company plant . . . ." Made for the Office of War Information. Color slide, October 1942. Office of War Information Collection. Prints and Photographs Division. LC-USW361-212.

Office of War Information Division of Public Inquiries. The More Women at Work, the Sooner We Win! Women Are Needed Also As: Farm Workers, Typists, Salespeople, Waitresses, Bus Drivers . . . : See Your Local U.S. Employment Service. *Poster, 1943. World War II Posters. Prints and Photographs Division. LC-USZC4-5600.*

Alfred Palmer's photograph for the Office of War Information during World War II offered little visual information about this war worker's actual work process, focusing, instead, on her attractive features and prominently displayed wedding ring. The photographic focus clearly filled government propaganda needs, as it was used in a poster designed to recruit women into the wartime workforce.

War I and World War II to gain women's participation in bond drives, conservation efforts, war work, and the military itself. Images of women were also used to enjoin men to strive for victory. The division's **World War I Posters** (300 posters, ca. 1914–18) and **World War II Posters** (1,000 posters, ca. 1940–45) include posters made by the U.S. government and by private industry. They can be viewed on microfilm, arranged by the "promotional goal" of the poster. (Online catalog records and digitized images for the World War I posters are planned.) Images and text both offer insight on ideals that were held up to the American public and how women figured into them. Sometimes the acknowledgment of women's capabilities under the exigencies of war is backhanded, at best, as in the poster that declares, "Good Work, Sister: We Never Figured You Could Do a Man-Sized Job!" (POS—WWII—US .J49 1944 [C size]; Repro. no. LC-USZC4-5597).

The war posters generally express official messages of government and industry. In contrast, the propaganda ("prop art") posters collected by Gary Yanker that form the **Yanker Poster Collection** (3,500 posters, 1927–80; bulk 1965–80) often reflect less mainstream values. Nearly half of the Yanker posters were produced in the United States. Reflecting a period of upheaval in American politics and society, the political and social messages frequently express the views of causes and organizations that, at least at the time, were considered radical in nature. Posters by groups that have gained prominence, such as the National Organization for Women (NOW), as well as less well-known groups such as "Another Mother for Peace," and "East Bay Women for Peace," demonstrate women's public participation in efforts to better their own position in society and to address international social and political concerns. Posters gathered from countries outside the United States provide a comparative glimpse of women's involvement in political movements abroad, as well as reaction to events and developments in the United States in general.

Online catalog records provide access by the

International Ladies' Garment Workers' Union. If Union Families Don't Look for the Union Label, Who Will? *Poster, between 1965 and 1980. Yanker Poster Collection. Prints and Photographs Division. LC-USZC4-8146. With permission of UNITE.*

This poster made an appeal to women to back unionized labor in their roles as consumers as well as union members.

names of organizations and poster designers (when the designer was noted on the poster), and by subject matter. It is possible to retrieve, for instance, eighteen posters on the subject of birth control, thirty-two on the subject of sexism, eleven that reflect the organizing efforts of women garment workers, and twenty-two works of the Women's Graphics Collective.

Graphic Ephemera

While posters announced the availability of products or services and pronounced on issues of the day, Americans' graphic universe was also populated by the colorful packaging increasingly used to market commercial goods. The development of cheap color lithography applied to inexpensive, machine-produced paper made the production of various kinds of labels and small advertisements possible. The growth of American commerce and urban centers encouraged their use. The division's rich holdings of **product labels** (700 items, 1840s–80s), especially tobacco and patent medicine labels, which were acquired through copyright deposit, reflect this commercial development and invite analysis of the connections between the marketing of particular products, their intended customer base, and the nature of the imagery used in the product's packaging.

It has been argued, for instance, that manufacturers provided lavish, often ingenious, pictorial labeling for luxury goods such as tobacco and wine, aiming to appeal to the potential purchaser's yearning for elegance and for self-indulgence. By the 1870s, tobacco art had developed along two lines: labels reflecting events of the day, such as the expansion of the frontier and women's quest for emancipation, and a more sensual school, emphasizing the female figure in a variety of settings.[7] The labels also depict celebrities of the day, including popular actresses and singers. The division's tobacco labels (LOT 10618) and patent medicine labels (LOT 10632) have been sorted into categories according to the subjects they depict. The Divisional Card Catalog shelflist (where groups are listed by their LOT numbers) indicates the categories, but a certain amount of intuition is needed to select those where women are likely to be depicted. The topics seldom mention women explicitly but do describe scenes in which women might be expected to be represented, such as "Allegories," "Bicycles and bicycling," or "Daily life and activities." Other advertising labels (LOTs 10661–10771) have been organized according to the product advertised, from beer, chewing gum, and cosmetics to condensed milk, sewing machines, and yeast. The arrangement, again, can be scanned in the Divisional Card Catalog shelflist. Although researchers have, to a certain extent, mined the product labels for illustration and for research on representation of racial and ethnic groups, they remain fertile territory for scholarly exploration, particularly with respect to the connections between gender representation, commerce, and consumption.

Sheet music covers (1,500 items, ca. 1820s–1900s) were another product of the nineteenth century that made heavy use of imagery to attract purchasers. Supplementing the content of the music and lyrics, the pictorial covers convey information about gender conventions and ideals. The Music Division holds a large collection of sheet music with covers intact (see chapter 8). The Prints and Photographs Division holds a substantial collection of sheet music covers (LOT 10615), occasionally with the music still attached. As with the tobacco and patent medicine labels, the music covers have been sorted into categories according to the theme of the cover illustration, with the arrangement listed in the Divisional Card Catalog shelflist. Not surprisingly, portraits of popular singers abound, but comic and romantic songs also featured illustrations intended to match the mood of the music.

The Business and Art of Making Pictures

Posters and advertising labels are examples of art put into service to market ideas and products. But pictures were, themselves, products marketed to an expanding consumer base. The Prints and Photographs Division's collections support the study of image-making as a business—how image makers created pictures directly for consumption by the public. Archives of photographic firms and studios reflect the application of photographic technology, almost from its inception, to fueling consumer interest in the likenesses it could produce. Collections highlighting particular photographic formats illuminate the rapid proliferation of a variety of photographic product lines. The division's collection of historical prints demonstrates the ways in which print publishers, at the same time, used nonphotographic technologies for reproducing images in order to feed and further stimulate consumer demand for pictures.

The business of making pictures is not easily separated from the creation of pictures for art's sake, however. The products of commercial photo studios and print publishers highlight the marriage of aesthetics and commerce. Although the division has historically made a distinction between prints and photographs mass-produced for sale to a broad market and those produced for the fine art market, the distinctions do not always hold up in practice. Both photographs and prints have traditionally provided a relatively inexpensive, democratic means of bringing art to the masses; both have also earned reputations as special forms of aesthetic expression, savored by the elite.

Photographic Production

Daguerreotypes (725 items, 1839–64), which represent the division's earliest photographic holdings, demonstrate the blending of commerce and aesthetics. The process invented by Louis-Jacques-Mandé Daguerre in France in 1839 created a highly detailed image on a sheet of copper plated with a thin coat of silver. American photographers quickly capitalized on this new invention. Daguerreotypists in major cities invited celebrities and political figures to their studios in the hopes of obtaining a likeness for display in their windows and reception areas. They encouraged the public to visit their galleries, which were like museums, in the hope that these visitors would pay to be photographed as well. In this way, daguerreotypes brought portraiture to the middle classes.

The majority of the division's daguerreotypes are portraits, including 384 items credited to Mathew

Charles Currier. Portrait of an elderly woman. Photograph, ca. 1900. Charles Currier Collection. Prints and Photographs Division. LC-C801-41.

Charles Currier was noted for his sensitive portraiture and his ability to endow the banal with unsuspected qualities. This portrait exhibits some of those skills while raising questions about the sitter: who was she and what role did she play in constructing this depiction, complete with prominently featured crutches?

Brady's studio, the largest collection of Brady studio daguerreotypes in existence. Overall, the corpus of daguerreotypes may suggest the greater visibility of males in the public sphere in the nineteenth century, but the collection includes both some notable images of women and some images collected by notable women. The earliest known photograph of Mary Todd Lincoln (DAG no. 1223), as well as a portrait of women's rights advocate Lucy Stone (DAG no. 1201), appear in the collection, for instance. The Library has also made a point of collecting rare occupational portraits, including an evocative portrait of an unidentified woman sitting beside a sewing machine, ca. 1853 (DAG no. 1204).

Many other daguerreotypes came to the Library with the manuscript collections of prominent Americans and document women from elite circumstances, including members of the Alexander Graham Bell family, whose depictions were included in the Grosvenor family papers, Walt Whitman's mother, from the Charles E. Feinberg collection, and members of Frances Benjamin Johnston's family. Images such as these invite reflection on what women's dress and their poses suggest about the ways in which they, their families, and the photographer wished to present them for posterity. Among the most unusual of the daguerreotypes are those from the American Colonization Society Records, which document African American emigration to Liberia (see chapter 5). The thirty portraits of Liberian government officials and other colonists include two women, one of whom, Jane Roberts, was the wife of the first president of Liberia (DAG no. 1001). The daguerreotypes can be searched and viewed in the division's online catalog.

Portraits and other images by professional photographers from the post-daguerreotype era can be found scattered throughout the division's collections, inviting exploration of the manner in which photographers' clients, who were largely of the middle class, and the photographer collaborated to convey idealized versions of their physical features and their lifestyles. Examining the output of a single photographer affords researchers evidence with which to investigate the role the camera operator may have played in this transaction. For instance, photographs made by Boston-based photographer **Charles Currier** (500 photos, 1887–1910) provide a glimpse into the homes and recreations of upper-class families in that region (LOT 11337). Currier's interior views of clients' dwellings offer a detailed picture of the Victorian home and furnishings. His work also provides sparse but intriguing glimpses of women working in factories and an almshouse (whether the latter were residents or paid workers remains unclear from the very generally captioned images).

Frances Benjamin Johnston's portraiture provides expansive coverage, particularly of Washington's elite set, much as her architectural and garden photography later did for the environments frequented by members of the upper class. One of Johnston's innovations, in fact, was to photograph individuals in the comfort of their homes, rather than in a strictly studio setting. Arnold Genthe, well known for his photographs of San Francisco's Chinatown (which feature some images of Chinese women and children, as illustrated on page xiv) and the aftermath of the city's 1906 earthquake, also maintained active portrait studios,

M. F. Weaver, copyright holder. Annual "Bathing Girl Parade," Balboa Beach, Cal., June 20, 1920. *Panoramic photograph, gelatin silver, 1920. Panoramic Photographs. Prints and Photographs Division. LC-USZC4-8150.*

P. T. Barnum initiated photographic beauty contests in the United States in the 1880s. Despite outcries regarding the morality of such displays, mass-circulation newspapers quickly adopted them as a marketing device. By 1920, shows of independence by women—in fashion as well as politics—had become more commonplace, and a number of resorts had instituted beauty pageants as a way to attract tourists. This California parade, held just two months before women gained the right to vote, featured beauties sporting a variety of bathing costumes, including one participant for whom walking was probably a recent accomplishment.

first in San Francisco and, after 1911, in New York. He captured the visages of socially prominent women in both cities. The portraits and other images in the **Arnold Genthe Collection** (16,800 photos, 1896–1942) can be searched and viewed in PPOC. Likewise available through the division's online catalog are **Carl Van Vechten's** studio portraits of people involved in the arts, including many associated with the Harlem Renaissance (1,300 photographs, 1927–64).

Some commercial photographers produced images of individuals not for the individuals' own use but to sell as ethnographic documentation of foreign or "exotic" peoples. A recent project to catalog groups of images relating to Native Americans demonstrated how many commercial firms embarked on such efforts in the late nineteenth and early twentieth centuries. As with the well-known Curtis photographs, the images frequently focus on women and their activities. The recently produced catalog records describing the groups are found in both the Library of Congress and Prints and Photographs online catalogs. A finding aid, entitled "Indians of North America: A Guide to LOTs" provides a convenient listing of all the groups, both those that were recently cataloged and those cataloged earlier and listed in the Divisional Card Catalog.

Images in the **Detroit Publishing Company Collection** (25,000 negatives, 20,000 photographic prints, 2,900 transparencies, 1880s–1930) offer insight on the commerce in images at a completely different scale of production from the individual studio or commercial photographer. Launched as a photographic publishing firm in the late 1890s by two Detroit businessmen, William A. Livingstone Jr. and Edwin H. Husher, the company purchased the negatives of a number of photographers. Its success, however, was, in large part determined by the participation of accomplished American landscape photographer William Henry Jackson, who joined the firm in 1897. Catalogs published by the company, found in the division's reference collection, provide documentation regarding the images and formats the firm offered to the public and the prices originally charged for them. The collection emphasizes the types of scenes consumers might have wished to frame and hang on their walls or to send to friends as postcards. It provides valuable clues to popular art works of the day that featured women, as well as to sites familiar to women of the leisure class, such as the "S.S. Dakota, Ladies' reception room" (LC-D4-22206). Besides marketing images to individual consumers, it appears that the company photographed industrial plants and commercial firms, such as the National Cash Register Company and the advertising firm of the Whitney Warner Publishing Company, for corporate use. These images reflect the increasing presence of women in offices and manufacturing plants at the turn of the century. Online records and images provide access to the negatives and some color prints and transparencies; additional groups of photographic prints are indexed in the Divisional Card Catalog.

Among the many formats the Detroit Publishing Company experimented with were panoramic views, a photographic format that was to gain popularity around the turn of the century. **Panoramic photographs** (4,200 photos, 1851–1981; bulk 1880–1930) typically have a length that is at least twice as long as the panorama's width, making them ideal for depicting wide expanses of landscape and large groups. Postcards and magazines reproduced panoramas as advertisements for real estate and for the promotion of the tourist industry, but they were also popular as portrait souvenirs for people attending conventions and other events. The collection reflects the growing popularity of beauty contests in the 1920s, documents some women's colleges, and suggests women's relative visibility or invisibility in various types of religious and political organizations.

Whiting View Company. Getting Her Hair Banged *and* Getting His Hair Banged. *Stereographs, 1900. Prints and Photographs Division. LC-USZC4-8148 and LC-USZC4-8149.*

This pair of turn-of-the-century stereographs offered a takeoff not only of modish hairstyles but also, as with many of the stereographs designed to be humorous, of relations between the sexes. Many such stereographs depicted a philandering male making free with an unreluctant servant girl or, as in this case, with a more captive victim.

Cityscapes and views of city life give some sense of women's presence and interactions in public places (or lack thereof) during the period, while rural landscapes give one a feel for the settings in which many women, particularly before 1920, spent their days. The panoramic photographs have been digitized and can be retrieved through the online catalog.

Panoramic photographs represented an attempt to market photographic images in a format that was novel and conveyed visual information in a particular way. Stereographs and card photographs, which proliferated from the 1860s through the 1910s, represent a similar drive toward novelty. Stereographs consist of a pair of images, usually photographs, which are placed side-by-side. When looked at through a special viewer, they appear to be a single three-dimensional image. These were used as parlor entertainment and as educational tools starting in the 1850s.

The division's collection of **Stereographs** (200,000 items, 1880s–1930s) was acquired largely by copyright deposit. Publishers frequently issued stereographs in sets or series, some of which presaged the development of the early motion picture in telling stories with simple plots and few words. The images also document rural and urban scenes and present humorous and sentimental vignettes. Given their content and varied uses in the home and classroom, the stereographs invite investigation of recreational habits, educational practices, and popular commentary on manners and customs in the decades surrounding the turn of the century. A number of stereographs, for instance, comment humorously on courtship, marriage, and domestic life. Images that record industrial scenes, agricultural activities, and recreational life provide a view of women's presence (or absence) in these settings. Stereographs were also used for portraiture. The division's collections include stereographic portraits of Clara Barton at work at her desk; pensive views of poet and journalist Ella Wheeler Wilcox; what appear to be memorial portraits of temperance leader Frances E. Willard, published two years after her death; and a portrait of Native American "Adeline, Princess of Seattle," published in 1896, reputedly her 100th year (all in STEREO BIOG FILE). Some stereographs are available in a reading room file divided into four sections: Subjects, U.S. and Foreign Geographical, Biographical, and Presidential. Other stereographs that clearly form a group have been cataloged as LOTs; descriptions are found in the

Divisional Card Catalog or, for more recently cataloged groups, in PPOC.

Other types of card-mounted photographs proliferated as keepsakes, beginning in the 1850s. Cartes-de-visite and cabinet cards were two small-format card photographs used to reproduce individual and family studio photographs, as well as portraits of celebrities. The larger "imperial" cards were more often used to present theatrical portraits of actresses in costume. The division does not have a card photograph collection as such, but such images are sprinkled throughout the holdings, particularly in personal and family collections (see below).

While photography firms and studios experimented with formats, settings, and props in order to appeal to a broad audience, photographers producing for the fine art market also explored various styles and effects. Although the line between the two realms of photographic production is often difficult to fix, the division has set aside photographic prints and portfolios of great aesthetic, technical, or historic importance in its individually cataloged **Photographs** collection (3,500 photographs, 1842–present). The collection features both notable works by women photographers and works focusing on women as subjects. A card catalog provides access by photographers' names, such as Eva Watson-Schütze (1867–1935), Imogen Cunningham (1883–1976), or Rosalind Solomon (b. 1930). It gives brief descriptions of, for instance, Doris Ulmann's (1884?–1934) photographs of the rural South and Gertrude Käsebier's (1852–1934) allegorical images of women. The catalog also lists Laura Gilpin's (1891–1979) portraits of Native Americans and various celebrities, as well as work she did in the Southwest and in Central America. Within the collection of photographers' portfolios, there is a large variety of work by American women: Berenice Abbott's (1898–1991) New York City buildings, Lisette Model's (1901–1983) spontaneous street portraits, Diane Arbus's (1923–1971) people at the fringes of society, Barbara Brooks Morgan's (1900–1992) modern dancers, the light and color effects achieved by Dorothea Kehaya (b. 1925), and Marilyn Bridges's (b. 1948) aerial photography. Subject access to the material is limited. Researchers seeking fine art photographs depicting women do best to identify photographers whose work is of interest and then check the card catalog to see if work by that photographer is represented in the collections. Because of the fragility of some of the photographic prints, advance arrangements may be required for viewing some original images.

Print Production

Just as the nineteenth century saw the proliferation of photographs for display in people's homes, the marketing of popular prints to adorn the walls of middle-class homes also flourished. The Currier and Ives firm, for instance, advertised its wares under the slogan "Works of art to brighten the home within the reach of all." In its **Popular Graphic Arts (PGA) Collection** (40,000 prints, ca. 1750–1910), the division has a substantial body of these types of prints, mostly acquired through copyright deposit. Currier and Ives prints, as well as lithographs and chromolithography by other prominent firms such as Prang and Strobridge, can be researched by publisher's name in the Popular Graphic Arts card catalog. The division's **Graphics File** (see reading room files, under "Using the Collections") provides the primary subject access to a substantial selection of the prints (as well as to nonphotographic material in other collections), enabling researchers to retrieve prints that comment on women's dress and gender roles, as well as those that simply idealize women in their roles as wives and mothers or as decorative "objects." Although many of the prints were designed for home decoration, quite a few appear to have been intended for advertising purposes. (See, for example, the illustration on page xxii.) Like the advertising labels discussed above, they can reveal how women's images were incorporated into the marketing of products and ideas.

Not only did the copyright deposit program bring the array of prints found in the Popular Graphic Arts Collection to the Library, but it also bolstered the division's substantial holdings of nineteenth-century etchings, which were incorporated into the **Fine Prints Collection** (100,000 items, ca. 1480s–present), joining a rich assemblage of prints deriving from two major bequests. In 1898, Gertrude M. Hubbard donated an important group of Old Masters and nineteenth-century prints, as well as funds that were used to build the Fine Prints Collection further.

In 1926, Joseph and Elizabeth Robins Pennell, who had long collaborated in promoting the art of printmaking, exhibited similar generosity (see chapter 4 for more about the Pennell's contributions). They contributed to the division Joseph Pennell's own prints, as well as works by other artists, and established a fund that has proven vital to the division's collecting efforts. The earliest prints in the Fine Prints Collection are European in origin, but a major strength of the collection is in American prints from the 1870s to the 1950s, as well as more contemporary works from the 1980s onward. In addition to purchases and gifts, the division holds a substantial number of prints produced under the auspices of the Works Progress Administration (later known as the Work Projects Administration).

Prints have been referred to as the "democratic art" because they provide a means of making works of art widely available. As with some of the other popular art media, such as posters and book and magazine illustrations, prints have historically been a democratic medium in the sense that they early offered a field in which women artists could flourish. The study and practice of art in traditional public arenas such as guilds, academies, and studios remained off-limits to most women until the mid-nineteenth century. Around that time, art schools began extending admission to female students, bringing increasing numbers of women creators into the mainstream of the art world. The division's holdings reflect this history. The Fine Prints Collection offers researchers examples of works by nineteenth- and early twentieth-century American artists such as Mary Nimmo Moran (1842–1899), Mary Cassatt (1844–1926), Bertha Boynton Lum (1869–1954), Helen Hyde (1868–1919), and Edna Boies Hopkins (1872–1937).[8] The work of twentieth-century women printmakers constitutes a particular strength, reflecting their contributions to major art historical styles, including social realism, regionalism, and abstract expressionism. The names Isabel Bishop (1902–1988), Peggy Bacon (1895–1987), Jolán Gross-Bettelheim (1900–1972), Clare Veronica Hope Leighton (1898 or 1899–1989), Elizabeth Catlett (b. 1915), Mariana Yampolsky (b. 1925), Sylvia Wald (b. 1915), Helen Frankenthaler (b. 1928), Carmen Lomas Garza (b. 1948), Jaune Quick-to-See-Smith (b. 1940), Jennifer Bartlett (b. 1941), Alison Saar (b. 1956), Vija Celmins (b. 1939), Yong Soon Min (b. 1953), and Lesley Dill (b. 1950) represent a small sampling of the women artists whose work is found in the Fine Prints Collection. Selections by the Pennell Committee enable the division to continue to develop its holdings of prints by women and minority artists. The recent acquisition of the Ben and Beatrice Goldstein Foundation Collection has also enriched the division's holdings of works by women printmakers. (As with other collections that have not yet been prepared for public service, access to the Goldstein materials and to the work of a few of the other women mentioned above is by special, advance arrangement.)

In addition to documenting the work of women artists, the Fine Prints Collection reflects an ongoing interest in women as subject matter. Throughout the history of Western art, women have claimed attention in two particular respects: as representatives of idealized beauty and as symbols of motherhood. Many of Mary Cassatt's best-known works, for instance, deal with these themes, while also reflecting her interest in Japanese aesthetics. Other prints in the collection document aspects of women's experience ranging beyond figure studies or maternal themes. Two examples from the World War II era are Jolán

Mary Cassatt. Gathering Fruit. *Color drypoint and aquatint, ca. 1895. Fine Prints. Prints and Photographs Division. LC-USZC4-1577.*

Mary Cassatt (1844–1926) was the only American artist and one of the few women among the core group of French Impressionists. This print is one of a series of works by Cassatt that relate closely to her commissioned mural for the Chicago World's Columbian Exposition in 1893 on the theme of the "Modern Woman." The original mural (which now survives only in photographic reproductions) was composed of three allegorical scenes titled *Arts, Music, Dancing; Young Women Plucking the Fruits of Knowledge or Science;* and *Young Girls Pursuing Fame. Gathering Fruit* is based on the mural's central panel showing women and young girls harvesting fruit in an orchard—a symbolic gathering and sharing of the "fruits of knowledge." Here, Cassatt emphasizes the idea of passing knowledge down to the next generation.

Gross-Bettelheim's *Home Front,* the Czech-born artist's industrialist twist on the American icon "Rosie the Riveter," which renders the defense workers as anthropomorphic elements of the machines on which they work (FP—XX—Gross-Bettelheim [J.], no. 3 [B size]; Repro. no. LC-USZ62-87989) and Caroline Durieux's (1896–1989) depiction of Bourbon Street entertainers in wartime New Orleans (FP—XX—D910, no. 4 [A size]; Repro. no. LC-USZ62-88026/LC-USZC2-3688).

A published catalog, *American Prints in the Library of Congress* (Baltimore: Johns Hopkins Press, 1970; NE505.A47), provides a listing of some twelve thousand prints by American artists cataloged through about 1966. A card catalog, organized first by century and, thereunder, by artist, provides access to the full collection. As with the individually cataloged Photographs Collection, subject access to the Fine Prints Collection is very limited. *American Prints in the Library of Congress* does include an index by broad topic (e.g., "Mythology") and by names of places and people represented in the prints. Items for which photography has been requested are indexed by subject in the division's biographical and subject indexes and, more recently, in the online catalog. Books and articles discussing the work of particular fine print artists and catalogues raisonnés for individual artists may help identify printmakers whose works are of interest from the point of view of subject matter or style.

Design Collections

Visual images play an instrumental role in the design process, and the division's holdings include a rich array of drawings and plans that reflect this process, principally with regard to buildings, but also in the development of objects and vehicles. As noted above, architectural and engineering drawings may offer insights into the environments women inhabited—the spaces designed specifically for their use, as well as the spaces that were not designed to accommodate women. Outside of the HABS/HAER measured drawings of already built structures (see Documentary Surveys, above), the division's greatest strength in terms of architectural drawings is in the original designs contained in its **Architecture, Design, and Engineering Drawings** (38,500 drawings, 1600–1989, bulk 1880–1940). Most of these drawings relate to Washington, D.C., sites and architects, and they include plans for shopping centers and apartment houses as well as for more monumental structures. Women's names rarely appear as architects and designers in this collection, perhaps because the work of women designers went uncredited by the firms for which they worked.

The collection does include several interior designs by Maria Ramona Drayer (b. 1920), some structures designed by Mary Craig (1889–1964), and designs for several sculptural works by Vinnie Ream (1847–1914). Browsing the index for "creators" in the catalog records for Architecture, Design, and Engineering Drawings yields additional names of women architects—for example, Katherine Gibbs, Julia Finch Gilbert, Elsa Gidoni (1901–1978), and Verna Cook Salomonsky (later Verna Cook Shipway, 1888?–1978), each of whom was responsible for one or more drawings for commercial or residential structures. The work of more contemporary women designers is reflected in competition drawings for the Vietnam Veterans Memorial, including the winning submission by Maya Ying Lin (b. 1959). Women's participation in the design process is also documented insofar as their names appear as clients for design projects. Among the more familiar clients the collection includes are Mary Lord Harrison (Mrs. Benjamin Harrison), who commissioned drawings for alterations to the White House (ADE—UNIT 2838); Lady Bird Johnson, who had drawings done for several renovation projects during her husband's career in Washington, D.C.; and sculptor Vinnie Ream, who had Thomas M. Plowman draw up plans for a duplex in downtown Washington, D.C. (ADE—UNIT 2900).

As consumers, women have sometimes had an indirect influence on the design of furniture and other utilitarian and decorative objects they put to daily use. The division holds work that shows the direct influence of women designers, most notably Ray Eames (1912–1988) who, with her husband, Charles, had a major impact on American graphic, textile, furniture, architectural, and exhibit design. The mammoth Eames collection, known as **The Work of Charles and Ray Eames** (308,000 color 35mm slides, 220,700 negatives and contact prints, 9,000 architectural drawings, and 100 posters; ca. 1940–78) is currently being organized and cataloged, as are manuscript and film materials held in other divisions of the Library (see chapter 5). The collection has already begun to yield much insight into the creative and business aspects of design work.[9]

Images from Records of Organizations

Because images can be so useful for communicating ideas, for advertising products, and for documenting events, structures, and processes, organizations that have nothing to do with image production frequently assemble images in the course of their work. In many cases, pictorial materials that come to the Library's Manuscript Division along with the records of an organization are transferred to the Prints and Photographs Division for cataloging, housing, and service. As organizations seldom systematically caption the photographs and other images they collect or produce, such visual materials frequently lack identifying information and are best used in conjunction with manuscript records and secondary sources that might help illuminate the context and content of the images. Nevertheless, these bodies of images can be valuable in gaining a sense of the activities and concerns of an organization and suggesting how members of an organization wished to portray its goals and activities to the public (see chapter 5).

Among the Prints and Photographs Division's collections relating to women's organizations are images acquired from the **League of Women Voters** (279 items, 1890–1935, LOTs 5539–5546). Next to the George Grantham Bain Collection, the League of Women Voters collection provides some of the division's strongest holdings relating to women's suffrage, including news photographs collected by the organization (and, probably, its initial parent body, the National American Woman Suffrage Association) and images prepared for use in promotional materials in the 1920s. Images from the **National Women's Trade Union League of America** (NWTUL) (133 items, 1886–1950, LOTs 5793–5799) include individual and group portraits of officers and members, documentation of meetings and conventions, images of sites associated with the league, and photographic copies of images found in periodicals showing women at work, probably used by the NWTUL as illustrative material.

Women's participation in organizations focusing on issues affecting males and females alike is suggested by images in the **Visual Materials from the National Association for the Advancement of Colored People (NAACP) Records** (4,596 items, ca. 1838–1969, bulk 1944–55), which reflect the active role women played in the fight for African American civil rights. The NAACP materials include portraits of officers, images of conferences, documentation of civil rights violations, and portrayals of protest activities. Images by photographer Lewis Hine, acquired with the **National Child Labor Committee** Records (5,000 photos, 1908–21; LOTs 7475–7483), focus on work performed by children (including girls), but include depictions of adult women working in various industries, particularly the conditions under which women engaged in industrial homework, that is, the manufacturing of garments, flowers, and other items in family living quarters, labored. Although the ethnicity of Hine's subjects is not consistently identified in his captions, he photographed members of several immigrant groups, as well as African Americans, in the work, home, and school settings he covered. His sometimes extensive captions (reproduced in a card catalog keyed to the photograph item numbers) often yield clues not only about the ethnicity of his photo subjects, such as their names, but about the conditions under which they worked, their family circumstances, and Hine's own documentary methods. In some cases, the images correspond to image numbers that Hine cited in written reports found in the Manuscript Division.

Most collections generated by organizations, whether transferred from the Manuscript Division or acquired directly by the Prints and Photographs Division, are cited under the organization's name in the Divisional Card Catalog or the Library of Congress and Prints and Photographs online catalogs. References in Manuscript Division finding aids also point users of the records to associated visual materials transferred to the Prints and Photographs Division. (It is important to note, however, that in some instances all or part of the visual material associated with manuscript collections is retained with those collections rather than being transferred.) The division has not had an opportunity to organize and describe all materials transferred to it; individuals must apply for access to materials that are still unprocessed, because extra staff time is required to prepare them for use.

Images from Personal Collections

Just as organizations accumulate images in the course of their activities, so too, do individuals. In many cases where a substantial amount of pictorial material arrives in the Manuscript Division with an individual's personal papers, the images are transferred to the Prints and Photographs Division. As with material from organizational records, such images frequently lack identification, but may be revealing, not only of the individual whose activities and proclivities they reflect, but also of the individual's social milieu. Images found with the **Clara Barton** Papers (600 items, 1863–1946), for instance, include carte-de-visite portraits of families in her social circle. Although not all of the individuals are identified, the images are valuable for the record they provide of styles of studio portraiture depicting members of the upper middle class in the 1860s. Barton's papers also include images documenting relief activities in the United States, Cuba, and Europe, carried out by the Red Cross, the organization with which Barton was so long associated. Images from the **Nannie Helen Burroughs** Papers (550 items, 1910–58) document the students and activities of the school for African American girls that she founded in Washington, D.C., in 1909, including a photo album compiled by one of her students, Alice Smith. The visual material also documents Burroughs's involvement in Baptist philanthropic activities and her missionary activities in Liberia and in Malawi.

Images transferred from the **Margaret Sanger** Papers (63 items, ca. 1900–1965; LOT 13246) document her acquaintances and concerns and picture scattered scenes from her life. The collection includes informal portraits of Sanger, her family, and associates; activities of various birth control advocacy organizations; and photographic views of Hiroshima after the atomic bomb explosion. Images from the **Blackwell Family** Papers (165 items, ca. 1850–1920) depict members of the family as well as women and men prominent in the National American Women Suffrage Association. The materials include lantern slides used in a lecture about the history of women's suffrage. Maud Wood Park used a portion of this lecture in 1939 to commemorate Carrie Chapman Catt's eightieth birthday. (Other Blackwell family im-

Lewis Hine. Mrs. Guadina sewing pants in a room with three children. Photographic print, gelatin silver, February 1912. National Child Labor Committee Collection. Prints and Photographs Division. LC-USZ62-126853.

Lewis Hine's photograph of a woman doing piecework in her home, surrounded by her children, offers visual information on her living circumstances. Hine's caption supplies further details illuminating her situation and his perspectives on it: "Mrs. Guadina, living in a rear house at 231 Mulberry St., N.Y., a dirty, poverty-stricken home, and making a pittance by finishing pants. On the trunk is the work of four days. She was struggling along, (actually weak for want of food) trying to finish this batch of work so she could get the pay. There seemed to be no food in the house and she said the children had had no milk all day. The father is out of work (sells fish) on account of rheumatism. Three small children and another expected soon." It is interesting to note that even in the dire circumstances Hine describes, pictures decorated the walls of the Guadina home.

Postcard, ca. 1910. Nannie Helen Burroughs Papers. Prints and Photographs Division. LC-USZC4-8147.

Typical of the types of visual material found with collections of personal papers, this postcard raises as many questions as it answers. The only identification on the item is the message inscribed on the back, "To Miss Burroughs from Sarah Ellen." Presumably the small girl on the front is the sender, who was probably a student at the National Training School for Girls. The artifact elicits who, what, and when questions, but also raises the more abstract question of why this child was posed or chose to pose herself, almost merging bodily with her Caucasian-featured doll.

ages remain in the Manuscript Division.) The Manuscript Division also transferred to the Prints and Photographs Division visual materials from the papers of **Clare Booth Luce** (3,800 items, ca. 1890–1981), including many photo albums from her ambassadorship in Italy, portraits of Luce and her friends, and a few posters relating to productions of her play *The Women.*

Access to images from personal papers collections is similar to access to those from organizational records. Names of people and organizations prominently represented in the materials are listed in the Divisional Card Catalog or the online catalog. References in Manuscript Division finding aids also point users of the records to associated visual materials transferred to the Prints and Photographs Division, although occasionally some visual items also remain with the personal papers. As with organizations' collections, advance arrangements must be made to view materials that have not yet been processed and cataloged.

Research with historical images, as with other types of historical research, is a painstaking process that involves building on background knowledge of a topic, as well as steady applications of intuition, in order to uncover what are often scattered sources of visual evidence. The evidence must then be sifted and weighed in light of what is known about the makers and the subjects of the images, the technical processes used to produce them, as well as the purpose for which the given image or set of images was intended. Because of the vastness and variety of the Prints and Photographs Division's holdings, researchers will need to exercise both searching and interpretation skills in attempting to illuminate aspects of women's history through visual evidence. In their vastness and variety, as well as in their sometimes intricate interconnections with other types of material the Library of Congress holds, the division's visual materials also stand to reward researchers with the means for enriching our understanding of the role the country's rapidly expanding image production played both in representing American women and in serving as sources of livelihood and creative expression for American women.

I would like to thank the members of the Prints and Photographs Division Reference, Curatorial, Technical Services, and Administrative Sections, many of whom read and commented on earlier versions of this chapter, assisted in locating and interpreting images, or provided cataloging assistance. Particular thanks go to Arden Alexander, Katherine Blood, Sara Duke, Jan Grenci, Mary Ison, Helena Zinkham, editors Sara Day and Evelyn Sinclair, and Library colleagues Sheridan Harvey and Janice Ruth for their comments and assistance.

PICTURE PATHFINDERS

Because of the myriad types of images found in Prints and Photographs Division holdings, many of which have their own form of access, researchers normally end up consulting a variety of tools and collections in investigating any particular topic. The sample pathfinders below are intended to give you a flavor for the variety of ways in which any given topic can be approached in the division's holdings. A search strategy checklist outlining search paths for these and eight additional topic areas within women's history, including Education, Employment and Labor Organizations, and searching for members of racial and ethnic groups, is available as an online reference aid on the Web site. Other than suggested searches in the Prints and Photographs Online Catalog (PPOC), which is available remotely through the division's Web page, the research strategies refer to tools that must be consulted in the reading room. Although they are not exhaustive, the lists point out tools and collections that should not be missed in approaching a topic area. Because of the unique materials in the Prints and Photographs Division and the unique access systems leading to them, reference staff expect you to consult regularly with them as you pursue your research in the collections.

1. PORTRAITS, FASHION, AND THE BODY

At the most rudimentary level, the division's pictorial holdings are valued for their ability to show how something—or someone—looked. Besides showing what a particular individual looked like, portraits can provide clues regarding fashion trends and cultural conventions. Fashion prints, fashion photography, and glamour photographs also shed light on such trends by documenting physical qualities that were held up as standards of beauty, by situating these idealized bodies in idealized settings, and by highlighting innovations or developments that defied convention. Portraits are found among most of the types of materials described in this chapter: the products of photojournalism, advertising images, organizations' records, and personal papers. Likewise, fashion images and more exotic depictions of women's bodies are found in many forms: in copyrighted fashion plates, among the historical prints, in stereographs, and in panoramic documentation of beauty pageants.

- **BIOGRAPHICAL FILE** under names of individuals
- **BIOGRAPHICAL CARD INDEX** under names of individuals
- **PRINTS AND PHOTOGRAPHS ONLINE CATALOG** under names of individuals, headings such as "Bathing beauties," "Beauty contests," "Clothing & dress," "Cosmetics & soap," "Nudes," "Women"
- **SPECIFIC SUBJECTS PHOTO FILE/STEREOGRAPH SUBJECT FILE/ SPECIFIC SUBJECTS INDEX** under headings such as "Advertisements," "Bathing beauties," "Beauty culture," "Clothing and dress," "Glamour photographs," "Hair Styles and hairdressing," "Negro women—Portraits," names of articles of clothing, e.g., "Hats," etc.
- **GRAPHICS FILE:** especially "Fashions" (LOT 4440), "Advertisements" (LOT 4397), and "Maidens, Sentimental" (LOT 4450D)
- **DIVISIONAL CARD CATALOG** under such terms as "Portraits," "Portrait photographs," "Women—", "Clothing and dress," "Fashion," "Costume," "Millinery," "Beauty contests"
- **FSA/OWI COLLECTION:** images emphasizing women's faces and figures are filed under classification numbers beginning with .33 in each of the geographical regions; there is no reliable way to search for portraits, per se, in the online portion of the file, but searching for such words in the record as "woman," "family," and "girl" yields some results.
- **NYWTS:** "Biographical" notebooks for named individuals; Subject/Geographical notebooks under terms such as "Bathing beauties," "Beauty contests—," "Clothing—Women," "Expositions—," and names of articles of clothing, e.g., "Bathing suits," etc.
- **POSTER CARD CATALOGS:** especially, Promotional Goal catalog under "C5—Textiles/Clothing" and 19th Century Advertising Posters under "Clothing"

2. POLITICAL ACTIVITY AND SOCIAL REFORM

Other than the division's substantial documentation of the women's suffrage campaign, images that actually show women engaging in political and social reform work are relatively few and scattered. Representation of some of the causes for which they worked, however, especially the abolition of slavery, the abolition of child labor, civil rights, prohibition, and, to a certain degree, ecology awareness and pacifism, is available in the division's holdings. Little material has so far been found on food or social purity issues. Representation of organizations working for charitable and reform causes can be found in many collections.

- **PRINTS AND PHOTOGRAPHS ONLINE CATALOG** under names of organizations and headings such as "Abolition movement," "Boycotts," "Civil rights," "Child labor," "Demonstrations," "Women's suffrage"
- **SPECIFIC SUBJECTS PHOTO FILE/SPECIFIC SUBJECTS INDEX** under headings such as "Charity and charitable organizations," "Child labor," "Demonstrations," "Negro slavery—Abolition movement," "Temperance," "Women—Politics and suffrage," "Women—Rights of women"
- **GRAPHICS FILE:** especially, "Women's movements" (LOT 4404), "Temperance" (LOT 4441), "Black history" (LOT 4422), "Collective settlements" (LOT 4244)
- **DIVISIONAL CARD CATALOG** under such terms as "Milk hygiene," "Prohibition," "Temperance," "Women—Politics and government"
- **NYWTS** under headings such as "Atomic Energy—Weapons—Protests," "Clubs—," "Foundations—," "Funds—," "Pacifists—," "Racism—," "Settlement houses—," names of organizations and political parties, etc.
- **U.S. NEWS & WORLD REPORT COLLECTION** under terms beginning with "Women" and headings such as "Demonstrations," "Abortion," "Civil Rights," "Negroes—," names of organizations, causes (e.g., ERA), and political parties, etc.
- **POSTER CARD CATALOGS**—especially Promotional Goal catalog, under "A6—Ecology," "F1—National Subgroups," "F31—Minority Advancement groups," "G—Social Welfare, Education, and Economic Policy," "H—Politics and National Ideology," and "J—Foreign Relations and War"

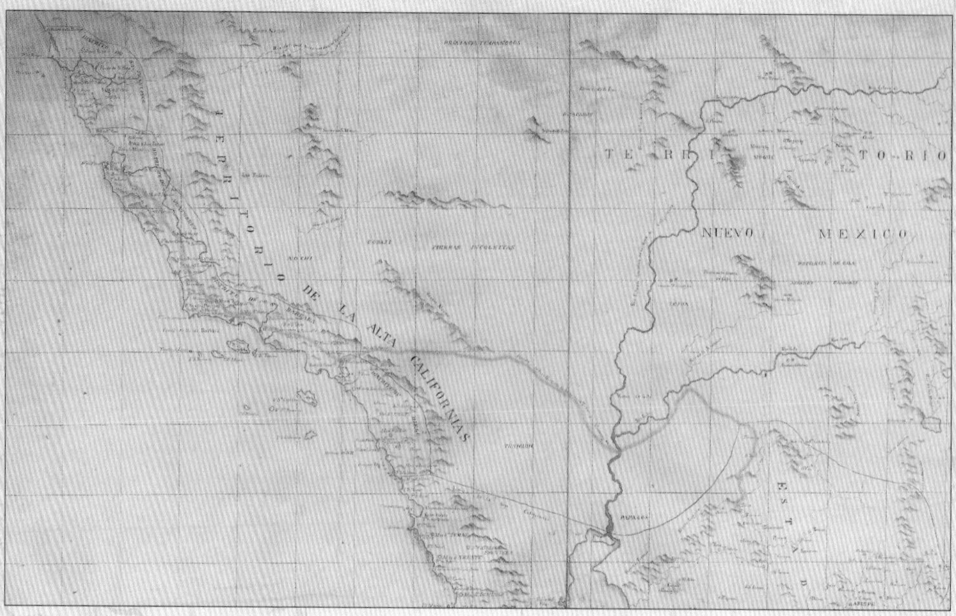

José M. Narvaes. Carta Esferica de los territorios de la alta y baja Californias y estado de Sonora. *Manuscript map, pen and ink and watercolor, 1823 (V4300 1823.N3 TIL Vault). Geography and Map Division.*

The route taken by Anza from Tubac to Monterey in 1776 has been enhanced here in green, on one of the few early Spanish maps to record this information. The map also shows the missions, presidios, towns, haciendas, and rancherias hugging the coastline when California was the northernmost territory of the Spanish-Mexican empire in the Americas. Anglo migration to California's Central Valley had not yet occurred.

American women on the move. The picture that comes to mind for most Anglo-Americans when women are discussed in the context of historical travels to California is that of the overland wagon trains moving westward, peopled by sturdy and daring pioneers who arrived in California after the discovery of gold in 1848. A few might also mention that some of the women came by ship, interrupting their voyage with an arduous trek—on foot or by mule—across the Isthmus of Panama, all the while with small children in tow. Even fewer people are aware that these women were relative latecomers to the Golden State, as California came to be known.

At the time Anglo-Americans began arriving in California in large numbers during the nineteenth century, they were part of the third wave of migration to the Pacific Coast. The first immigrants were Indians who had lived in California ten to fifteen thousand years before the region was visited by Old World explorers.[1] A prevalent myth that the rich land was empty, ripe for colonization, is refuted by recent studies indicating that "at the time of Euro-American contact, California was more densely populated than any area of equal size in North America, north of central Mexico . . . . What is labeled 'wilderness' in today's popular imagination . . . harbored human gathering and hunting sites, burial grounds, work sites, sacred areas, trails, and village sites. Today's wilderness was then human homeland."[2]

Our understanding of the California Indians is limited by the absence of written cultural artifacts, except for a few drawings on cave or canyon walls, and is further hampered by a lack of understanding of the ecology of California's landscape before European contact, which took place over several centuries. A map produced by August Wilhelm Kuchler, *Natural Vegetation of California* (Lawrence, Kans., 1977; G4361.D2 1977 .K8), in the Geography and Map Division, provides the best information available at this time regarding the native vegetation as it existed before the arrival of Spanish explorer Juan Rodríguez Cabrillo in 1542.

What is clear, however, is that the Indians altered the physical environment through planting, pruning, irrigating, and periodically burning vegetation and that Indian women played a major and very specific role in these activities.[3] Approximately five hundred loosely affiliated Indian groups, or "tribelets," have been identified. Although new information about Indian life in California is emerging, the story of the their journeys has yet to be told.[4]

There is, however, an abundance of written source material about the second wave of immigrants who settled the borderlands in the northernmost portion of the Spanish empire. Incursions by the British and Russians, and the fear that others might attempt to claim areas of the North American continent, motivated Spain to create a strong military and human presence along the California coast. Between 1769 and 1821, twenty missions, four presidios (forts), and three civil communities known as pueblos were built, stretching from San Diego to just north of San Francisco.[5]

From the beginning, families were sent to these outposts for the express purpose of increasing the population of Spanish citizens. In addition to the relatively few people who could be considered Hispanic, having been born in Spain or of solely Spanish ancestry, the vast majority of the colonists came from Mexico, where some of their families had lived for at least two generations. Included were many mestizos who were part Native American and part Spanish or Mexican and mulattoes and blacks.[6] California, already populated by multiple Native American cultural groups, with the arrival of these newer immigrants became a model of diversity that continues to the present day.

Among the best documented expeditions in North American history are the two overland journeys led by Juan Bautista de Anza in 1774 and 1775. How colonists from the Spanish provinces of Sinaloa and Sonora in what is now Mexico migrated as families to the San Francisco Bay area—traveling from the Tubac garrison on Sonora's northern frontier; traversing the Sonoran desert, the treacherous Gila and Colorado Rivers, and rugged mountain ranges; and then moving up California's Central Valley—is one of the most amazing and least known stories in American history.[7]

Anza established for the first time an overland route across the desert, connecting established portions of New Spain with the California outposts, six hundred miles of which required blazing a new trail. His first expedition in 1774 transported forty soldiers, twelve women, and several children. By the time he returned to Monterrey, Mexico, to report his success to his superiors, he had covered over two thousand miles.[8]

The opening of the trail, which was maintained by preserving friendly relations with the Indians in its vicinity, and a continuing need for settlers to protect Spanish interests in the region, led to his most stunning success—shepherding 240 men, women, and children, including seven infants under the age of eight months, across the desert and up the California coast.

D. D. Morse. View of San Gabriel, Cal. *Bird's-eye view, n.p.,1893? (G4364.S52A3 1893 .M6). Panoramic Maps 39. Geography and Map Division.*

Father Pedro Font recorded in his diary on Thursday, January 4, that the Anza expedition arrived at the San Gabriel mission after he had said Mass earlier that morning: "The mission of San Gabriel is situated about eight leagues from the sea in a site of most beautiful qualities, with plentiful water and very fine lands. The site is level and open, and is about two leagues from the Sierra Nevada [San Gabriel mountains] to the north, which from the pass of San Carlos we had on our right as we came along. It appears that here ends the snow . . . ." Maria Feliciana Arballo was married in the church and settled in the vicinity of the mission.

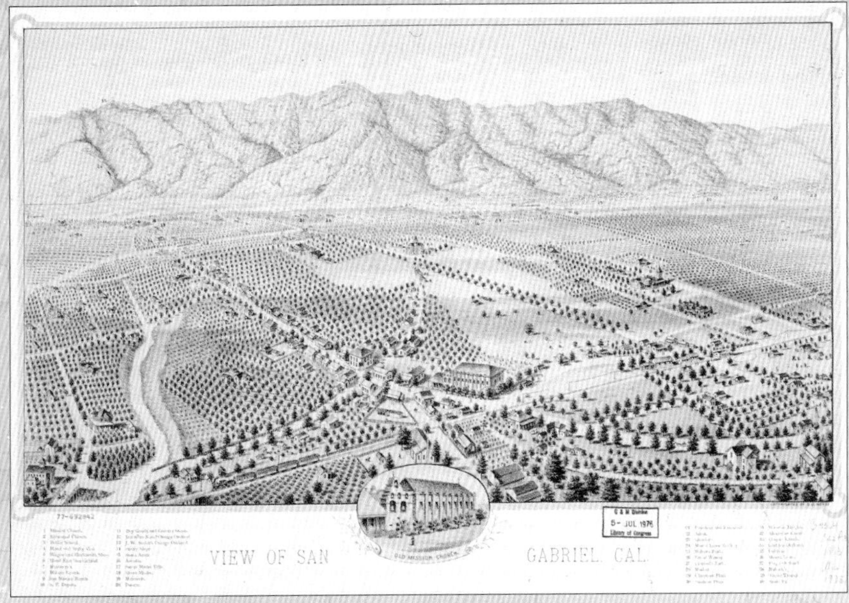

The expedition left Tubac on October 23, 1775. Winter came unusually early that year; it was unseasonably cold with a record-breaking amount of snow and ice and the colonists, used to the warm climate of Mexico, were unprepared for the hardships they faced. Rations were short, finding potable water was difficult, people and livestock sickened, and many of the animals weakened or died.[9]

Despite the adverse conditions, Anza arrived at Monterey, California, with two more people than he had enlisted for the long journey to Alta California, three of whom were born on the trail. He lost only one person the entire trip, a mother of six, Señora Felix, who died in childbirth the first night. All of the rest of the party, including the newborns, survived.[10] Such a successful outcome overland to California was never equaled—before, during, or after the Gold Rush—and had the thirteen diaries penned on his two expeditions been written in English rather than Spanish, Anza would today be known throughout the world as a famous leader and the names of the remarkable women who traveled with him would be remembered.

Although none of the women traveling north from Mexico left written journals of their thoughts, feelings, and experiences on the trail, fascinating vignettes can be extracted from the diaries kept by the men who accompanied them. For example, we know that, because the primary purpose of the 1775 expedition was to populate Spanish California, Anza actively recruited young married couples and that three marriages took place along the way. Recruitment of suitable colonists from among the poorer Mexican families was influenced by the ideal of eighteenth- and nineteenth-century womanhood. Spanish expectations for women were by and large those that crossed national and cultural lines: westering women were to be pious, pure, domestic, and modest, whether they were English, French, or Spanish-Mexican.[11] There were, however, some exceptions to the general patterns of behavior and family composition expected of all women regardless of their social class.

The women who accompanied Anza were primarily from the lower classes of Mexican society. One of them, Maria Feliciana Arballo, who was born in Spain, was only twenty years old when she and her mestizo husband signed on to travel with Anza. In part, the journey to California helped them to escape the rigid class society in established parts of the Spanish empire that denigrated her husband on the basis of color and race. His sudden death did not deter her from insisting that she and her two young daughters be permitted to accompany Anza to California. Perhaps the persuasiveness of her arguments convinced Anza, despite strong

"Jeu des Habitans. de Californie." Lithograph by Norblin after a drawing by Louis [Ludwig Andrevitch] Choris. From Choris, Voyage pittoresque autour du monde, avec des portraits de sauvages d'Amérique. . . *(Paris: Firmin Didot, 1822; G420.K84 C5). Rare Book and Special Collections Division.*

Ludwig Andrevitch Choris, serving as an artist on the Russian Pacific Ocean expedition under Otto von Kotzebue from 1815 to 1818, sketched a group of "Mission Indians" who lived and worked the land at the mission of San Francisco. The women are shown observing a game that may have been played traditionally by California Indian males. Gambling was prohibited by the Franciscans, but some scholars suggest that Indians continued to play these games as a form of resistance to Hispanic authority.

objections from Father Pedro Font, to make an exception to his policy that all women be accompanied by male family members. She and her daughters, one riding in front of her, the other behind, traveled on horseback all the way to California. Once there, she again asserted her independence by leaving the group in San Gabriel, where she entered into a second marriage. The man she chose was also a mestizo soldier.[12]

Apparently Arballo was a high-spirited young woman, because Father Font was repeatedly annoyed with her and with Anza, who had permitted her to go to California against the priest's adamant opposition. He confided in his diary, as translated and published by Herbert Eugene Bolton, that she drank alcohol to excess one evening when the group was celebrating, having completed an arduous portion of the journey. Font noted her unseemly behavior, commenting that the "very bold widow . . . sang some verses which were not at all nice, applauded and cheered by the crowd."[13] She refused to play the submissive and modest role required of women of her time and, by performing in public, she resisted the social controls normally governing Spanish women's actions. She also defied, not once but twice, the class and color constraints of Hispanic culture by marrying common soldiers who were mestizo when she herself was of Spanish birth. In marrying beneath her class and caste, defying her priest's advice, resisting male authority, and acting boldly in the public sphere, she subverted the gender requirements of proper behavior for Hispanic women of her time.[14]

At the highest end of the social spectrum, although not a member of Anza's party, was Eulalia Callis, born in Spain to an influential family. She became the wife of Alta California governor Pedro Fages. Despite her prominent position, she made private matters public in 1785 by openly accusing her husband of infidelity and refusing to sleep with him; in addition, she insisted on returning to Mexico City. The governor denied any wrongdoing and their priest advised her, when she consulted him about a divorce, to drop the matter. She refused to do so,

"Eene waterplaats in Neder Californie" [A watering hole in Lower California] and "Eene Serenade in Uppen Californie" [A serenade in Upper California]. Engravings after drawings by William Redmond Ryan from vols. 1 and 2 of Ryan's Aventuren gedurende een tweejarig verblijf in Californie *(Haarlem: A. C. Kruseman, 1850; F865.R97). Rare Book and Special Collections Division.*

Pictured from an Anglo-Saxon point of view, William Redmond Ryan's drawings for his Personal Adventures in Upper and Lower California, 1848–9: With the Author's Experiences at the Mines *portray Spanish-Mexican-mestizo life romantically rather than realistically.*

"The Winter of 1849." Color engraving by J. H. Baillard after a drawing by Frank Marryat. From Marryat's Mountains and Molehills *(London: Longman, Brown, Green, and Longmans, 1855; F865.M3 1855b). Rare Book and Special Collections Division.*

Women's accounts of life in San Francisco at the time of the California Gold Rush emphasized the many hardships, including a lengthy rainy season and a great deal of mud. As in most boom towns, the buildings pictured here seem to have been thrown up and some appear to be rooming houses. Many of the women who went to California took in boarders and provided services such as washing laundry, ironing, sewing, and baking pies for sale.

and she was punished for her actions by imprisonment, isolation, the continual threat of flogging, and excommunication from the Church. Although her contemporaries were unsympathetic, Callis's actions in retrospect appear to have been motivated by a strong survival instinct for she had endured four pregnancies in six years, buried two of her children, and longed, understandably, to return to a safer and more comfortable life in Mexico City.[15]

Notably successful in exercising her independence was a third woman, Apolinaria Lorenzana, who arrived on the ship *Concepcion* with her widowed mother. In keeping with Spanish norms, which were clearly stated in the context of sending ten female foundlings to California in 1800, Señorita Lorenzana was supposed to marry and bear children to bolster the population of the northern borderlands of the Spanish empire.[16] She never acquiesced in doing either, despite a proposal from a young Californian. Her strategy for avoiding marriage, "because I was not particularly inclined toward that state even though I knew the merits of that sacred institution," was to perform valued work by cooking, nursing, and caring for the Native Americans who lived near the mission. "La Beata" was respected, admired, and loved for her life of service, and thus maintained control of her own sexuality and lived a life of independence, supporting herself by working for the Church. Her efforts resulted in her being one of very few women in California to receive a land grant in her own name.[17]

Source material for studying Anza's expeditions, Spanish California (1769–1821), and the Mexican period (1822–46) is available in a variety of formats at the Library of Congress. Although the original manuscript diaries are in Mexico, with additional copies in the archives of Seville and Madrid, the Manuscript Division has multiple copies of Anza material for those willing to translate them; they can be accessed by using several published and unpublished finding aids.[18] Photographic reproductions of manuscripts and transcripts of the original materials in English and Spanish, bilingual published editions of primary source material, and translations of varying quality of the records associated with Anza are also in the Library's collections.[19] Examples of information related to women's history contained in these works includes census data on the members of the 1775 expedition, including names, ages, marital status, and the number of male and female children per family, and detailed lists of supplies and provisions that Anza procured for each man, woman, and child, including articles of clothing.[20]

In addition to the materials published by Bolton from Spanish and Mexican archives, copious sources supporting studies of women in Pre-Conquest California are available in several

"Encampment at Sac City, Nov. 1849: My Own Tent." Lithograph by G. W. Lewis after a drawing by G. V. Cooper. From J. M. Letts, California Illustrated including a Description of the Panama and Nicaragua Routes by a Returned Californian *(New York: William Holdredge, 1852; F865.L65). Rare Book and Special Collections Division.*

The discovery of gold in California created interest in accounts and drawings, real and imagined, of camp life and the overland journey. J. M. Letts, a shareholder in a New York mining company, is shown sitting in front of his tent in a mining camp in Sacramento City. Letts describes a family he had met the day before in Sutterville, who "had been wandering about since 1845, without having entered a house . . . The children were all natives of the forest except the eldest. They were encamped under a large oak-tree a short distance from the river. The bed was made up on the ground, the sheets of snowy whiteness, the kitchen furniture was well arranged against the root of the tree, the children were building a playhouse of sticks, while the mother was sitting in a 'Boston rocker' reading the Bible, with a Methodist hymn-book in her lap."

"Emigrant Party on the Road to California." Color engraving. Frontispiece to California: Its Past History, Its Present Position, Its Future Prospects *(London, 1850; F865.C14). Rare Book and Special Collections Division.*

An idealized image of the overland trail shows a level, graded pass through rugged mountains. Here the women's colorful dress closely resembles European clothing of the period. In the foreground, a woman cradles an infant in her arms; another holds her child's hand. Besides performing the many domestic chores that fell to them on the overland trail, women were the primary caregivers for their offspring, who had to be watched closely lest they be injured. The overland journals tell of children's deaths from snake bites, drownings, and falls under the wheels of the heavy wagons.

Library of Congress collections. The earliest written observations and visual images of California women were recorded by travelers and traders who visited the area before the Mexican War (1846–48). Contemporary American and foreign published accounts of that period are housed in the Rare Book and Special Collections Division, including works by Frenchman Jean-François de Galaup, comte de La Pérouse, who was there in 1786, and Russian Louis Choris, whose 1822 publication included drawings made in 1816 of California Indians (see page 218).[21]

Life in California: During a Residence of Several Years in that Territory . . . By an American, recorded Alfred Robinson's views of Indian gendered roles. "They [the men] passed their time in play, and roaming about from house to house, dancing and sleeping and this was their only occupation . . . The women were obliged to gather seeds in the fields, prepare them for cooking, and to perform all the meanest offices as well as the most laborious. It was painful in the extreme, to behold them with the infants, hanging upon their shoulders, groping about in search of herbs and seed."[22]

Richard Henry Dana Jr.'s extremely popular *Two Years before the Mast,* published in 1840, included observations that he made in July 1835 while visiting California. His views were influential in shaping American attitudes in the eastern United States toward the Hispanic-mestizo population of the Southwest. "The men are thriftless, proud, and extravagant, and very much given to gaming; and the women have but little education, and a good deal of beauty, and their morality, of course, is none the best; yet the instances of infidelity are much less frequent than one would at first suppose . . . . The women have but little virtue, but then the jealousy of their husbands is extreme and their revenge deadly and almost certain."[23] His writing added to growing expressions of Anglo-Saxon superiority and belief in "Manifest Destiny" in the years leading up to the American conquest of California.

The Geography and Map Division has both contemporary cartographic material, including manuscript maps, and more recent thematic maps showing the extent of the Spanish empire, the routes taken by Anza and other Spanish explorers, the sites of presidios, pueblos, and missions, and the topography and geology of Alta California. Particularly useful for providing orientation to the Spanish Empire in North America is *Mapa, que comprende la Frontera, de los Dominos del Ray . . .* , drawn by Joseph Urruta and Nicolas LaFora in 1769. A large and detailed map, it is the product of the 1766–68 expedition to survey presidios and defenses of northern New Spain, and shows administrative boundaries and selected European and Native American towns and settlements on the eve of the founding of Spain's first colony in Alta California in 1769.[24]

In addition, there are many secondary works devoted to history and culture of the Spanish and Mexican eras of Alta California and individual communities in formats including mono-

Daniel A. Jenks. Camp 100–Humbolt *[sic]* River. *Watercolor and pen-and-ink drawing, 1859. Documentary Drawings. Prints and Photographs Division. LC-USZC4-8872.*

Daniel A. Jenks documented life on the overland trail, basing his drawings on observations that he made as he traveled west in 1859. His views appear much more realistic than the color engraving published in London in 1850, illustrated on page 221. Here the women wear homespun or calico and sunbonnets and the men are not wearing top hats. Instead we see soldiers in uniform cooking their own meals, a modestly dressed young couple engaged in conversation, women tending a cooking fire, a man and woman fetching water from the river, and a man opening his bedroll in a tent. In the background, a man appears to be holding a fishing pole. The drawing depicts the wide variety of activities taking place at the campground along the Humboldt River.

Daniel A. Jenks. North Platte. *Watercolor and pen-and-ink drawing, 185?. Documentary Drawings. Prints and Photographs Division. LC-USZC4-8874.*

Jenks's drawing of covered wagons crossing the Platte River illustrates yet another barrier to those traveling west. River crossings were difficult and dangerous even when they were not flooded. The journals of women recount numerous tragedies such as drownings and the loss of draft animals and possessions while crossing the rivers on the overland trail.

graphs, bibliographies, journal articles, and doctoral dissertations. Subject headings that identify this material include "California–History–to 1846."

The great watershed in California history began with the American conquest of the Mexican province, followed almost immediately by the discovery of gold in 1848, widespread immigration in the rush to the goldfields, and California's admission to the Union in 1850. Socially, economically, and demographically, California became unrecognizable almost overnight as San Francisco changed from a small town to a bustling port (see page 220) and mining camps and villages sprang up all along the eastern slopes of the Sierras.

Demographic information about women is helpful in understanding the magnitude of the social revolution. Census averages by locality are available for the age of married couples, the age difference between married partners, and the number of children per family in 1790, and can be used as a baseline of comparison for the period after 1850. Equally informative are statistics that reveal the relatively large numbers of male to female inhabitants, peaking at a ratio of twelve men to one woman in 1850. The number of foreign-born residents of both sexes also increased dramatically. Defining those born outside the United States (and outside California, before it became a state) as "foreign," the number of foreign women increased from 19 to 28 percent between 1850 and 1860, whereas the figure for men for the same period jumped from 24 to 43 percent.[25]

Both American and foreign immigrants added to the diversity and complexity that already existed in California society. Several mulatto families had traveled to California with Anza, and intermarriage between races was so frequent that the racial classification system in colonial New Spain was highly formalized—including terms such as "castizo" and "morisco." One scholar has noted that "approximately 55 percent of the Spanish-speaking population in California in 1790 was of mixed heritage" and 20 percent may have possessed some African ancestry.[26]

Forty-niners were drawn to the goldfields from all around the globe.[27] Of particular interest —because the Asian population of North America before the Gold Rush was extremely low— are the number of immigrants from China who sailed to Northern California within a narrow time span, creating a unique community there. Relatively few Chinese women immigrated: in 1890, there were 69,382 Chinese men in California and 3,090 women.[28] San Francisco customhouse records for 1852 show that 20,026 Chinese arrived by sea that year; soon thereafter the city's Chinatown included Chinese girls imported for prostitution, many of whom had been sold by impoverished parents or simply stolen off the streets in China.[29]

The vast majority of men and women on the move to California during the Gold Rush, however, came from east of the Mississippi River. Many of them had already relocated once in their lifetimes to the old northwest, leaving for California from small farms in Illinois, Indiana, and Ohio. Others, including Mrs. D. B. Bates, the wife of a sea captain who had three ships burn under her during her voyage around Cape Horn to San Francisco, departed from the eastern seaboard.[30] Those whose journey overland consisted of crossing the Isthmus of Panama wrote in detail about their novel experiences, including riding astride mules, sometimes wearing men's clothing, sleeping on the ground or in Indian huts, and their horror at being served baked monkey for dinner. For some it was an adventure, for others an excruciating ordeal.[31]

Although the story of the trip overland from the east is well known to most, recent scholarship has helped us to understand more about the social and psychological effects of being uprooted from their homes and how life on the trail affected women. Lillian Schlissel has identified and analyzed almost one hundred diaries and journals kept by women moving west in the decades between 1840 and 1870.[32] These sources provide remarkable insight into the lives and values of the authors and how they perceived themselves and the times in which they were living. Many of the titles used when women's diaries were published reflect the perspectives of the writers as well as their hardships and experiences. *To the Land of Gold and Wickedness: The 1848–59 Diary of Lorena L. Hays* (St. Louis, Mo.: Patrice Press, 1988; F593 H36 1988) and *"I Hear the Hogs in My Kitchen": A Woman's View of the Gold Rush* by Mary B. Ballou (New Haven, Conn.: Yale University Press, 1962; F865.B2 1962) are examples.

Both first and subsequent editions of these kinds of publications, including many contemporary reports of life on the overland trail, voyages around Cape Horn or via the Isthmus of Panama, and living conditions in the cities, towns, and goldfields, can be found in the Rare Book and Special Collections Division and in the General Collections, especially in local history and genealogy materials.

The Music Division's sheet music collection contains works such as the well-known "O My Darling Clementine" and the relatively obscure "Emigrant's Dying Child," a particularly poignant piece about a father's loss of first his wife and then two small children on the trail to the goldfields.[33] Newspaper accounts include material on women and life in California and can be found in publications from around the globe. The San Francisco newspapers, particularly *Alta California*, contain news about the political and social life in San Francisco, including reports of events in and around the gold mining towns.

Cartographic materials, contemporary and thematic, provide information about the routes taken by the wagon trains, the places from which the migrants originated, the locations of mining towns and other places in California, and the first official map of the state authorized by the state legislature.

These sources provide different perspectives from which to explore social, economic, and gender-related topics. Most of the works related to the California Gold Rush and the forty-niners can be accessed by using the subject heading "California Gold Discoveries." in the Library of Congress Online Catalog.

In her comprehensive work *Women's Diaries of the Westward Journey*, Schlissel points out that the decision to move west was generally made by male members of the family and was only reluctantly accepted by women. The difference between men and their wives in their willingness to go to California was related to the life cycles of men and women: men were in the most active phases of their lives and were eager to break free and take whatever risk might make them wealthy. If their search for gold proved unsuccessful, they could obtain land and resume farming. The majority of the women, however, were in their childbearing years and at a stage in their lives where they wanted to put down roots and enjoy a sense of community and the company of other women and their families; many went to California reluctantly.[34]

The long journey to California exacerbated tensions in marriages, and women exercised their options in California when it came to seeking divorce. There was a lengthy list of grounds upon which an action could be based, including "natural impotence, minority, adultery, extreme cruelty, habitual intemperance, desertion, willful neglect, consent obtained by force or fraud, and conviction for a felony."[35]

Despite obvious differences between the women who traveled with Anza and the Anglo-American women when it came to divorce, there were many similarities in two waves of migration. Women in both groups experienced birth, miscarriages, and death; few females traveled outside of their family unit; there were hardships, deprivation, and continual exposure to extremes in temperature and weather conditions; and the women were expected to cook, wash the clothing, nurse the sick, and carry and tend to their children.

The degree to which they suffered, however, was dramatically different. Those traveling westward in the mid-nineteenth century lacked the cohesion and leadership found in the Anza expeditions. Attempted shortcuts and turnoffs on the trail resulted in disasters such as the one suffered by the Donner party.[36] In addition, cholera was rampant and the way became lined

George A. Crofutt. American Progress. *Chromolithograph, ca. 1873, after an 1872 painting by John Gast. Popular Graphic Arts Collection. Prints and Photographs Division. LC-USZC4-668.*

"American Progress" is depicted as a light-haired woman, classically dressed, who is leading the Americans west. She guides and protects miners, farmers, covered wagons, railroads, and even a stage coach, displacing Indian families and the buffalo of the Great Plains. She is stringing the transcontinental telegraph cable wire with one hand and holds a book in the other. The concept of Manifest Destiny—the idea that American conquest of the west was a sign of progress, taking civilization and prosperity to unenlightened peoples—provided a rationalization to Americans who displaced the Indians and other people of color who had long lived in California and other parts of the country west of the Mississippi River.

with the graves of those who had died from measles, dysentery, smallpox, and fevers. Infant mortality played a significant role in the loss of life, and contaminated water and spoiled food contributed to the overall misery and deaths of others. One diarist, Cecelia McMillen Adams, morbidly recorded over two hundred grave sites along the trail from Illinois in 1852.[37]

Superior planning, including blazing the trail that was taken and properly equipping the participants, in addition to specific recruitment of persons deemed most suitable for the journey and life on the frontier, were advantages of the Spanish experience over that of Anglo-Americans on the westward trail. While the Anza expedition was a small and relatively cohesive group, the forty-niners were an amorphous collection of thousands of individuals and families that lacked leadership and experience on the difficult journey west. With the exception of the evening when Father Font was critical of Anza's decision to provide liquor for the fandango rather than say prayers of thanksgiving, and the young widow entertained the group with her bawdy song, conflict among the Spanish leaders and rank and file was expressed primarily by writing in personal journals. Compared to the tales of crime and punishment that took place along the trail of the forty-niners, the Anza group was peaceful and well disciplined.[38]

Spanish success in California was short-lived, however, as the outpost of empire fell first to the Mexicans and then to the Americans. In the span of eighty years, the days of Hispanic supremacy were over as the American government implemented Manifest Destiny and solidified its conquest by changing property laws, including those that had enabled women to inherit, own, buy, and sell land, and that permitted them to enjoy the profits made in the course of a marriage through community property. Despite prolonged litigation, most Hispanic landowners eventually lost their holdings, large and small, and the process of marginalization of those not of Anglo ancestry began. Increasingly isolated by language and culture, the people of Spanish and Mexican extraction, and those of African origin, as well as the original Californians—the Native Americans—moved into the economic and social shadows. Perhaps new studies of the earliest residents of the Golden State will return strong, independent women such as Maria Feliciana Arballo, Eulalia Callis, and Apolinaria Lorenzana to their rightful place in a widened mainstream of American history.

I wish to thank the advisory board scholars, especially Vicki Ruiz, for suggestions on sources and interpretation; Rosemary Fry Plakas, Janice Ruth, Harry Katz, Robin Rausch, and Barbara Tenenbaum for searching the Library's collections; John Hébert, for his support; Gene Roberts for digitally enhancing and processing the Narvaes map; Myra A. Laird for bibliographic searching; and editors Evelyn Sinclair and Sara Day.

48
LICKING
Scale 2 Inches to the Mile
BEAVER
TWP.
RICHLAND TWP.
PINEY TWP
TOBY TWP.
PERRY TWP
CANOE RIPPLE
CALLENSBURG BOROUGH
EASTON
REFERENCES
Roads
Lanes
Streams
Houses
Orchards
Stone Quarries
Oil Wells
Coal Banks
EASTON
Scale 400 Feet to one Inch
LICKING TWP.
TO CALLENSBURG 1/2 MILE
TO CLARION 13 1/2 MILE
TO SLIGO 3 1/2 MILES
TO CANOE RIFFLE 3 MILE
Christopher Pfeiffer 10 A
G.W. Spencer
Mrs. Williams
John Reese 10 3/4 A
John Reese
J.B. Miller
George Truly
KOSSUTH P.O.
Scale 330 feet to one inch.
ASHLAND TWP
John Mimm
H.J. Smith Blacksmith Shop

Geography and Map Division

Patricia Molen van Ee

The intersections and mutual influences of "geography" and "gender" are deep and multifarious. Each is, in profound ways, implicated in the construction of the other: geography in its various guises influences the cultural formation of particular genders and gender relations; gender has been deeply influential in the production of "the geographical."
—*Doreen Massey,* Space, Place, and Gender.[1]

The Geography and Map Division acquires, processes, maintains, and provides access to "cartographic materials," which are defined as spatial data that are presented graphically. Traditional formats include single maps, series or set maps, atlases, globes, nautical charts, and three-dimensional maps and terrain models. As of January 2000, there were approximately 4.6 million maps and more than seventy thousand atlases in the division.[2]

The division also collects a wide variety of recent spatial data sets that vary in terms of their accuracy and usefulness and require the use of associated geographic information system (GIS) software packages. Although specialized training is necessary to use these parts of the collection, many recent atlases contain maps that have been made with this kind of material assisted by GIS technology, producing cartographic products which can easily be interpreted by researchers.

Only a small proportion of the Library's retrospective maps and atlases directly address the status of women or their spatial behavior, but the division's traditional resources, previously overlooked by most scholars, are readily available to researchers and contain a wealth of information awaiting discovery.

Some of the most exciting questions being studied by scholars of American women's history can be answered only by the use of cartographic collections. Historical differences between men's and women's spatial behavior and their responses to physical and social environments; the nature and varieties of gender relationships in urban,

Joseph A. Caldwell. Caldwell's Illustrated Historical Combination Atlas of Clarion County, Pennsylvania . . . *(Condit, Ohio: J.A. Caldwell, 1877; G1263.C6 C2 1877) (map, 48; illustration, 92). Geography and Map Division.*

One of the largest houses in Clarion County, Pennsylvania, belonged to the Widow Kribbs, shown in this beautifully colored county landownership atlas dated 1877. Although she owned just fifty acres fronting on Beaver Turnpike, shown in cartographic form in the upper right corner of the map of Licking township, the view of Mrs. Kribbs's farm and the caption describing it alert us to her wealth. We learn that she had eighteen oil wells in her front yard, a source of considerable income. The affluence of the area, owing to the discovery of oil on many county properties, is emphasized by engravings of handsome houses on farms whose loveliness is marred only by the appearance of oil rigs. Other illustrations convey contradictory information about women. Despite their affluence in terms of land holdings, oil wells, buggies drawn by fine horses, and their spectacular dwellings, women in Clarion County are demonstrably less important than men. An image is included that clearly reflects the cultural value placed on male children: a tree appears with the notation that beneath it stood the house that was the birthplace of the first white male child born in the county, with an extensive genealogy of his family. No record exists for the first female child born there. The illustrations also clearly differentiate between male and female activities. Women parade around carrying parasols; men are out buying new buggies. Gendered spaces and activities are revealed and reinforced by the visual material that is used to emphasize the information found on the maps.

suburban, and rural settings; the similarity and differences between men's and women's work and workplaces; the concepts of space and place—central, gendered, public, private, and communal—are but a few of the subjects that not only benefit from the use of cartographic material, but require it. As Doreen Massey, a pioneer in the field of feminist geography has said, "Geography matters!"[3]

Examples of new approaches using traditional materials and reframed questions about geography in the context of gender roles, space, place, and time can be found in the works of Massey, Daphne Spain, John Paul Jones III, Heidi J. Nast, Susan M. Roberts, and Alison Lee, which offer historians exciting perspectives from which to interpret the history of women in America. Although scholars have long recognized that gender relations evolve over time, an important contribution of the feminist geographers to historians has been to point out that gender relations also vary between spaces within similar time frames and in those same spaces over longer periods of time.[4]

The result of these studies is a growing realization that geographic differences—including such characteristics as topography, vegetation, climate, geology, urbanization, transportation networks, power source availability, labor pools, and access and proximity to markets—create different social structures that determine gender roles and behavior. This body of work also demonstrates that interpretation of geographic information is essential not only to the study of gender but also to discussions of broad historical topics such as regionalism, urbanization, industrialization, borderlands, frontiers, migration, immigration, contact zones, and cultural encounters.[5]

Nikolas H. Huffman, in the 1997 compilation *Thresholds in Feminist Geography,* notes that traditionally the fields of geography and cartography have had a masculine bias that has limited the scope of field studies as well as cartographic products produced by these studies. He points to the systematic exclusion of women "which can be seen in the ensuing history of women in cartography, and how masculinity is reflected in maps as images of power, communicating world order as well as world views, and in the virtual silence about women in the disciplinary discourse of academic cartography."[6]

For these reasons, some feminist geographers have been reluctant to use maps as sources. They argue that maps fail to adequately represent women and women's lives and that they are primarily the work of men. They recognize that maps are also products of the prevailing masculine culture, and, as artifacts of that culture, maps are often used as tools of domination and power.

But despite legitimate reservations about the objectivity of maps as reliable sources, significant work is currently being done that indicates that a much larger role has been played by women in the fields of geography and cartography than was previously recognized. Even more important is evidence reflecting the presence of significant amounts of information about women on traditional maps to a far greater degree than has been noted by scholars.

GEOGRAPHY AND MAP DIVISION READING ROOM
James Madison Memorial Building, basement, room LM B01
Hours: Monday through Friday, 8:30 a.m. to 5:00 p.m.
Closed weekends and federal holidays.
Telephone: 202 707-6277
Fax: 202 707-8531
Address: Geography and Map Division, Library of Congress, Madison Building, 101 Independence Avenue, SE, Washington, DC 20540-4650
E-mail: maps@loc.gov (Please include your full name and residential mailing address.)
Web site: <http://www.loc.gov/rr/geogmap>
Access and use: Before you begin research in the Library's cartographic collections, it is essential that you identify a specific geographic area of interest because that is the key to locating material. To gain access to the collections, first obtain a Library of Congress reader identification card and then register with the Geography and Map Division. Additional restrictions apply to the use of rare materials that are kept in the division's vault.

Reference service is provided by mail, e-mail, and fax, but to make full use of the Geography and Map Division's collections and reference services, a personal visit is highly recommended. Limited "quick-copy" photocopying facilities are available in the reading room and a variety of other photoreproduction services can be ordered through the Library's Photoduplication Service. Copyright restrictions are the responsibility of the researcher and are observed in all duplication processes.

Organization of the collections of the Geography and Map Division is maintained in a number of filing systems, generally by format, geographical location, and date. Because there is no simple way to find all of the materials that might prove useful to the researcher, the division's highly experienced reference staff provides invaluable assistance in identifying appropriate resources.

Written reference service is provided for those unable to visit the division. Please be as specific as possible when describing your project; it is imperative that the geographical area be identified and that the subject and scope of the research project and inclusive dates be provided. While the staff is prepared to help locate cartographic material relevant to a study, its primary service is referring users to appropriate source material, rather than conducting research on their behalf.

Close examination of a variety of cartographic material reveals a wealth of information about women's lives that has until recently been overlooked. Many more female landowners' names appear on maps than have previously been noted. Indications of their occupations, the distances that they travel to and from work, and their relative wealth and standing in the community are only a few examples of data that can be found on cartographic materials.

Doreen Massey has illustrated the connections between geography and gender in her publications primarily on the basis of studies of the lives of British women. An example is found in "A Woman's Place," the chapter she wrote with Linda McDowell in *Geography Matters!*[7] In a section entitled "Coal Is Our Life: Whose Life?" she elaborates on the themes of her study. Her research has led her to the conclusion that "danger and drudgery: male solidarity and female oppression—this sums up life. . . . Here the separation of men and women's lives was virtually total: men were the breadwinners, women the domestic labourers, though hardly the 'angels of the house' that featured so large in the middle class Victorian's idealization of women" (p. 129). "For miners' wives almost without exception, and for many of their daughters, unpaid work in the home was the only and time-consuming option" (p. 130). Although men worked in dirty and dangerous coal mines, during their leisure hours they gathered together in the union halls or the local pubs, sharing a sense of community and commonality. Women, however, worked in isolation in their homes, cooking and cleaning for husbands and sons who often worked different shifts and came home dirty. Food preparation around the clock and the constant need to launder work clothes and rid the house of coal dust consumed their time and energy. Women were subordinate to men and unable to work outside the home. Their daily lives were clearly connected to geology, geography, and mining technology.

Although Massey's research was based on work done in Europe, her concepts are applicable to other parts of the world, particularly the United States, which has a close affinity to Great Britain. Geography and technological capabilities make coal mining possible. Where there are mines, the social conditions that Massey describes are likely to be found, although more research into women's lives in coal mining communities of the United States remains to be done. Her analysis of life in agricultural societies and factories using female laborers is also relevant to the history of the United States. Massey and her colleagues have indeed proven that "geography matters!"

Perhaps the most important result of this work is that maps are finally receiving the attention they deserve as *primary* sources for the study of topics in women's history. Use of geographic information and maps in historical studies on topics in American women's history has produced some gratifying initial results. Laurel Thatcher Ulrich's Pulitzer Prize–winning work *A Midwife's Tale: The Life of Martha Ballard, Based on Her Diary, 1785–1812* analyzes subjects such as migration patterns by identifying places of origin of residents settling in a new community in Hallowell, Maine.[8] She also traces the distances traveled in the course of women's daily lives and the proximity of dwellings to each other and to other significant places in and around the community. Maps are then created to illustrate her findings. The importance of cartographic information to her work suggests that other historical studies may come to be evaluated in part on whether and how maps are integrated into the research, analysis, and presentation of the finished product.

USING THE COLLECTIONS

Using maps as sources requires time and effort on the part of the researcher. The staff of the Geography and Map Division provides skilled reference service that is facilitated by catalogs, bibliographies, inventories, and other finding aids. In addition, large portions of some of the most heavily used historical collections are now available online on the Library's American Memory Web site.

Map collections that are part of **American Memory** can be located either from the Geography and Map Division's home page or by going to <http: // memory . loc . gov / ammem / gmdhtml /gmdhome.html>. The collections are listed under a variety of headings: *Cities and Towns* includes the Panoramic Map Collection, dated 1847–1929; *Military Battles and Campaigns* encompasses Civil War Maps, 1861–65 and maps from the era of the American Revolution, 1750–89. American Colonization Society/Liberia Maps, 1830–70 can be found under the heading *Cultural Landscapes;* Railroad Maps, 1828–1900 are filed under *Transportation and Communication;* and a variety of maps dated 1544–1999 are filed under *General Maps.* A multimedia presentation called *African-American Odyssey* includes maps and can be accessed through the "Using the Collection Finder" part of American Memory under *Original Format: Maps.*

Scanned map images make use of special features such as location key maps, indexing systems, and "zoom" capabilities. The compression technology does not eliminate any of the pixels of the original, making it possible for users to enlarge portions of the maps in order to see detail that is invisible to the naked eye on the original item. The navigator window outlines the portion of the map that is included in the enlarged image.

The **MARC Map Collection** consists of the relatively small portion of the map collections for which there are records in the Library of Congress Online Catalog. Most maps *acquired* since 1968 have been made available on the MARC (Machine-Readable Cataloging) database, searchable online with bibliographic access by geographic area, title, author, and subject, as well as by call number. Cataloging records for current acquisitions and the maps included in **American Memory** continue to be added to the automated system.

Library of Congress Subject Headings are used in map cataloging records, but few if any records of interest to historians will be located by using "women" for a subject search. Historical sites related to women, a map showing women and minorities in the 100th Congress, local maps created by the League of Women Voters, and a very small number of miscellaneous maps are identified in this kind of search. More fruitful headings are broad subjects that locate thematic material such as "landownership," "population," "health care," "birth and death rates," and "cancer mortality." Although recent material makes up the bulk of the MARC Map Collection, selected county landownership maps, panoramic maps, historic urban plans, much of the material pertaining to the United States dated prior to 1800, and manuscript maps are also frequently fully cataloged and are in this category.

The MARC Map Collection is arranged by call number, which is determined first by format, followed by geographic area, date, and subject. This collection is a good place to begin a research project because you can do your initial searching in the Library's online catalog before visiting the Geography and Map Division. Though representing only a small portion of the total cartographic resources of the Library, maps searchable online represent a good cross-section of the Geography and Map Division's complete holdings, particularly Americana. Online cataloging records may lead you to other cartographic material for a given place and time period. The full cataloging record for a particular map may also include contents notes that describe some of the information shown on the item.

Most of the **Atlas Collection** is also cataloged, with its records available online. The catalog can be searched by geographic area, title, author, and subject. Unlike searching for maps, in searching for atlases, the term "women" is useful in identifying some of the newer thematic works about women. In addition, there are detailed finding aids available for much of the collection, including the nine-volume reference work *A List of Geographical Atlases in the Library of Congress* (Washington: Library of Congress, 1958–92; Z6028 .U562 1992) by Philip Lee Phillips and Clara Egli LeGear, which contains a partial index to individual plates bound into atlases published before 1968. Most of the atlases that contain useful information for studying women's history are fully cataloged.

The vast majority of maps in the Geography and Map Division are neither cataloged nor classified. Unless they are unusually rare, these maps are found in either the **Title Collection** or the **Set Map Collection.** Both groups of materials are arranged by geographic area and are most efficiently used when the research area and inclusive dates have been carefully defined. Research projects that focus on a particular geographic or political unit such as a state, county, or city are most easily supported by cartographic material.

Individual maps received before 1968, including many of the items of greatest interest to historians, are among the 1.5 million maps in the **Title Collection,** which is sometimes referred to as the "Single Map Collection." Virtually all of the nineteenth-century maps and those received by the Library before the advent of machine-readable cataloging in 1968, make up this category of material. Historians will find cartographic sources filed under "North America," "United States," and the names of regions, individual states, and administrative units such as counties and cities. The holdings are frequently further subdivided by subject, but few, if any, maps are filed under the subject of "women" or "women's history." In addition, there may be several possible filing locations for identical copies of the same item or very similar items, and a variety of additional filing locations for closely related items.

It is important to remember that the quality and quantity of cartographic information that is available vary considerably over place and time. Although rich resources may exist for some locations, other areas—particularly less affluent rural communities—may not be as well represented in the collections simply because fewer maps were made of these places or fewer maps were collected and preserved as a record of them.

The Title Collection includes a wide range of kinds of geographic and cartographic products. Some of the maps are atlas plates or maps that originally were included in monographs or serials but have been removed from their bindings. A significant and often overlooked category of material found in this collection is photoreproduced copies or facsimiles of material held by other repositories either in the United States or abroad.

Access to this collection, which includes some of the division's most heavily used material, is facilitated by many published finding aids and bibliographies. Materials related to the American Revolutionary War era, the Civil War, county landownership, railroads, panoramic maps, literary maps, and maps showing Spanish exploration and settlement in North America are listed and described in excellent bibliographies that are widely available in university and large public libraries.

A vast amount of cartographic information awaits discovery and analysis by diligent researchers. For the most part, however, using the portions of the title collection not covered by published bibliographies requires the assistance of highly trained reference and specialist staff members who are experienced in locating specific kinds of resource material for researchers. Frequently, the staff can suggest items that are particularly useful for specific studies. Although suggestions can be made through correspondence, it is preferable for researchers to visit the reading room in order to determine what material best serves their needs.

Set Maps contain at least ten sheets published at a uniform size, usually drawn at the same scale, that are intended to be portions of a larger map. In general, these maps are medium to large scale and provide much more detailed information than is shown on single maps. Many of the set maps are controlled by index maps that indicate which sheets the Library holds for a given series. Some of the most heavily used maps in this part of the collection are the large-scale topographic maps of the Austro-Hungarian Empire dated circa 1870 to 1914. Frequently used to locate villages and towns that were the homelands of large numbers of Jewish immigrants who came to the United States around the turn of the twentieth century or towns that were "lost" in the Holocaust, these sheets are easily copied from microfilm and can be purchased for reference use at a nominal cost. Similar sets exist for other countries of origin for American immigrants.[9] Detailed set maps for the United States as a whole, as well as for individual states, are also available.

The division holds a variety of **Special Collections** consisting of groups of material that are related to each other and are housed together in the division. Some but not all of these collections are considered to be rare and are kept in the division's vault. Special requirements apply for their use and reproduction, including special handling procedures, additional registration forms, and a surcharge or "rare materials fee" for photoduplication orders. A considerable portion of this material has been cataloged and can be searched online. There are also many alternative and supplementary finding aids for special collections such as the preliminary, unpublished vault shelflist and unpublished inventories and indexes that are available for use in the division reading room. Many rare materials have been photocopied at their original size. Black-and-white copies of these items can be purchased through written reference requests. Full color copies of items that have already been scanned and posted on the Web can be purchased directly from the Photoduplication Service. Researchers can also pay an additional fee to have a particular item scanned to produce a digital file or a copy of the original in a variety of sizes.

The division maintains a small collection of approximately six thousand books in its **Reference Collection,** including about fifty published cartobibliographies related to the Library's map and atlas holdings. In addition to full-length monographs on maps and mapmakers, there is a pamphlet file of articles about specific items in the collections written by division staff members or scholars studying the Library's maps and atlases. An extensive collection of unpublished inventories and indexes is also available.

The reference collection also contains basic works on the subjects of history, geography, and cartography; catalogs related to other major map collections and exhibitions; and two major bibliographies that are particularly helpful for historical researchers. *The Index to Maps in Books and Periodicals by the American Geographical Society, Map Department* (Boston: G.K. Hall, 1968; Z6028.A5) provides access to materials that may be found in other special format divisions of the Library of Congress and in the General Collections. It also gives publication information about individual items housed in the division that may have been removed from other works. *The U.S.*

Serial Set Index and Cartobibliography of Maps, part 14, by Donna P. Koepp (Bethesda, Md.: Congressional Information Service, Inc., 1995; Z1223 .Z9 C65 1975) lists the maps that are found in the Congressional Serial Set that were originally published by the U.S. Senate and House of Representatives as part of their official reports. Subject headings that are useful in searching these works for information about American women are "population," with the subheadings of "sex distribution, U.S.," followed by "foreign born," or "race proportions by gender" and similar demographic terminology.

A large preservation project is in progress that involves removing folded maps from the large Congressional Serial Set volumes from the Law Library. After the maps are flattened and repaired, they are labeled and filed as a collection in the Geography and Map Division.

Another resource is *The Bibliography of Cartography* published by the Library of Congress, Geography and Map Division, in five volumes (Boston: G. K. Hall, 1973; Z6028.U49 1973); and its *First Supplement,* in two volumes published in 1980. This finding aid includes articles about cartography published in a variety of periodicals, listed by author and title. It includes subject headings and more recent articles have been indexed and are in card form, available for use in the division. Its usefulness in finding material about women mapmakers and geographers is considerable if the name of the author writing articles about women is known; unfortunately, the work is not indexed.

A small collection of place-name literature describing how specific locations have come to be named is also included in the division's reference collection. Most of the place-names in the United States have been designated by explorers, early settlers, surveyors, mapmakers, and government officials. Some of these names honor wives, sisters, daughters, or sweethearts who can be identified by using this material. Such works are generally devoted to a single state, although occasionally a volume pertains to a larger geographic area or to certain kinds of names, such as those related to Native Americans. Except for a few items in the pamphlet file, place-name literature is fully cataloged and can be found under the name of the state.

Place-names reflect the history of the area. For example, California, with its Spanish, Mexican, Russian, Native American, and American heritages, reflects the rich variety of sources from which the names of physical and cultural features are named. The town "Benicia," which served as the capital of the state in 1853–54, was named for the wife of General Mariano G. Vallejo, Francisca Benicia. Another California town, called "Marysville," went through several name changes before a group of residents at a town meeting in 1850 finally named it to honor Mary Murphy Covillaud, a survivor of the Donner party, who was also the wife of the principal owner of the townsite.[10]

SELECTED COLLECTIONS

Although certain collections contain richer resources to study American women's history, almost any kind of cartographic material may provide data that can be used for a particular project. The groups of materials listed here are among the most useful to researchers both in terms of the quality and quantity of information that they contain about American women.

Thematic Maps and Atlases

Recent interest in women's history in the context of geographic location has resulted in the creation of thematic maps and atlases that focus on topics related to women. Thematic cartographic material addresses a single topic or closely related topics, illustrating the distribution of that topic or subject. Some of the newer thematic publications are rich sources of information about twentieth-century women. The quality and complexity of these works has greatly increased in the past decade as more systematic approaches have been used with more accurate statistics, and often with the application of GIS technology.[11] In some cases, however, distribution patterns or variations with regard to place can be shown quite effectively with simple line drawings, such as those found in *A Midwife's Tale* (see note 8).

Selected thematic atlases show the promise and products of GIS technology and its effectiveness in conveying information about American women. A stunning example of a thematic atlas using carefully researched recent data that has been analyzed by GIS technology is *The State of Women in the World Atlas* (New York: The Penguin Group, 1997; uncataloged) by Joni Seager. Seager's subjects include women's work, motherhood, female children, the beauty culture, lesbian rights, domestic violence, women in government, poverty, property ownership, education, and the use of contraception. The maps display the spatial distribution for that topic around the world, making it relatively easy to compare various countries and areas of the globe with each other and with the United States. The author uses additional

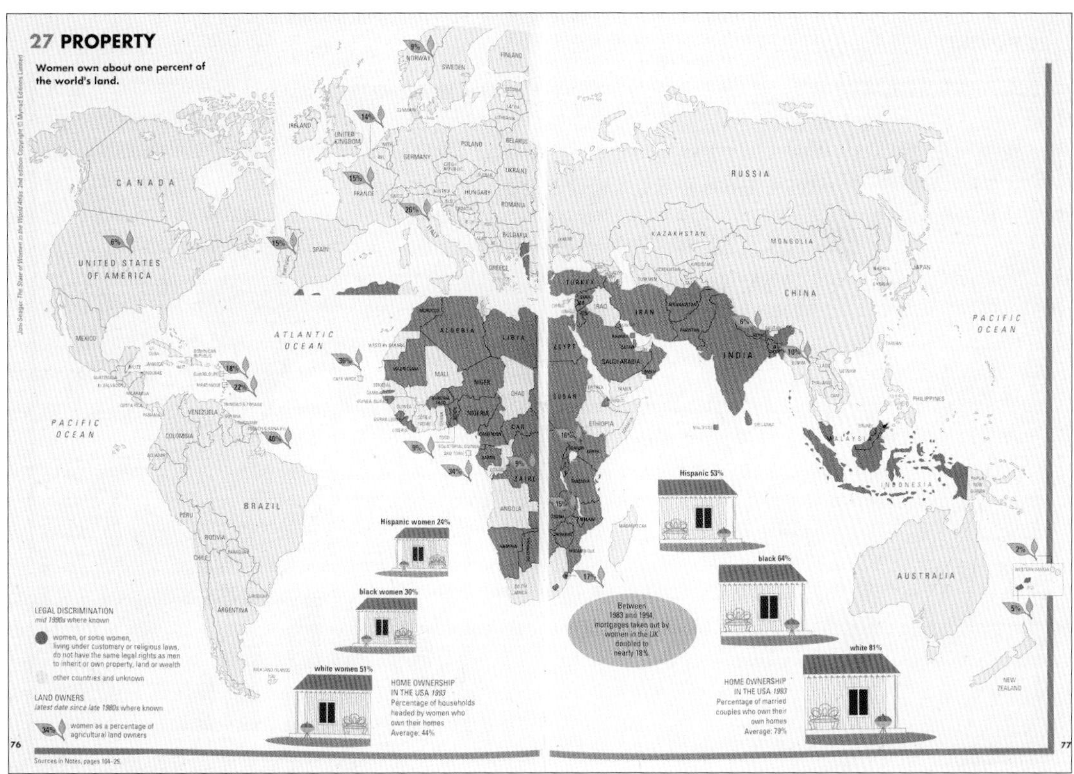

"Property." Plate 27 from The State of Women in the World Atlas *by Joni Seager (New York and London: Penguin Group, 1997; uncataloged). Geography and Map Division. Copyright © Myriad Editions Ltd.*

A map comparing women's limited ownership of land and property around the world is typical of plates appearing in *The State of Women in the World Atlas,* published in 1997. Through maps and graphic comparisons, various aspects of a topic such as this are explored. Most of the plates use additional tables or pictorial material to make comparisons within the United States or to elaborate on how the U.S. data relate to those for the rest of the world.

symbols and statistical information to compare the United States in greater detail to other countries in the world, elaborating on the subject or theme of the map.

In plate 27, "Property," for example, the author states that women own about 1 percent of the world's land (Seager, 76–77). The map compares countries of the world where women can legally own land with those areas where there are customary or religious laws preventing women from inheriting or owning property, land, or wealth on the same basis as men. There is an additional symbol showing the percentage of women who own agricultural land in many countries of the world; at 6 percent, the United States has one of the lowest rates. Detail for the United States on the map shows home ownership in 1993, indicating that of households headed by women, 44 percent own their own homes, whereas 79 percent of married couples own their homes. The pictorial comparison between female-headed households versus married couples is further broken down by race. Only 24 percent of Hispanic female-headed households own their homes, followed by 30 percent for African Americans, and 51 percent for whites. The figures for married homeownership are 53 percent for Hispanics, 64 percent for African Americans, and 81 percent for whites. The volume contains extensive lists of source material used for each of the topics and identifies additional resources for further study. This work provides a model for compiling similar maps illustrating geographical patterns and distribution that can be used to analyze historical trends and change over time.

The Routledge Historical Atlas of Women in America (New York: Routledge, 2000; HQ1410 .P68 2000), edited by Sandra Opdycke, is one of the few thematic atlases specifically designed to address major themes, trends, and topics in American women's history. Taking a geographical and demographic perspective, it uses maps and charts to document the growth of women's social and political rights and reform movements, such as temperance, women's suffrage, abolitionism, contraception, abortion rights, and the Equal Rights Amendment. It is inclusive of groups of women that are sometimes overlooked; for example, it contains material on women living in tenements and the migration of African American women from the South to cities in the North between 1914 and 1925. Although statistical data are the basis for much of its content, it is one of few atlases placing demographic information within the political and social contexts of the past that is solely devoted to American women.

Two recently published atlases about American women that deal primarily with twentieth-century women's history are *The Women's Atlas of the United States* (New York: Facts on File, 1995; G1201.E1 G5 1995) by Timothy H. and Cathy Carroll Fast and *Atlas of American Women* (New York: Macmillan, 1987; G1201.E1 S5 1987) by Barbara Gimla Shortridge. In addition to mapping recent trends and topics, they also suggest ways in which retrospective data can be analyzed in studying earlier time periods.

The Fasts' work is primarily based on 1990 census data, comparing them to past census information. It is divided into sections on demographics, education, employment, health, politics, family, and criminal activity and victims of crime, but few of the plates show change over time. One plate that does show the population of women from 1800 to 1980, with benchmarks for 1850, 1900, and 1950, also indicates states where men outnumber women. The Fasts provide current data and maps on women minorities other than Hispanics, as well as maps focusing specifically on Hispanics. For the latter, there are data on AIDS, education levels, immigration, out-of-wedlock births, poverty, and unemployment. Information on Native Americans includes demographics, education levels, suffrage, numbers of victims of crime, prisoners, and those living in nonfamily households or in nursing homes. For Asian Americans there is information on immigration, demographics, high school graduates, poverty levels, and those living in nursing homes or in prison.

The Women's Atlas provides more categories of data for African Americans than for any other racial group. Information on birth weight, AIDS, correctional officers, number of homicide victims, those living in poverty or on death row, and life expectancy is given; there is also a category for African American women in Congress.

The major source of data for the Shortridge atlas is the 1980 census, but there are additional maps illustrating patterns of change over a longer period of time. Categories of information include data on demographics, the labor force, earnings and income, occupations, education, sports, relationships, pregnancy, health, crime, and politics. Groups are more narrowly defined in the Shortridge atlas than in the Fasts' publication. There is information about elderly women and those dwelling in rural areas. Data on Pacific Islanders, Eskimos and Aleuts, and the foreign born are also included. In general, Shortridge makes comparisons between groups of women, whereas the Fasts primarily compare data between men and women. Used together, these two atlases provide a wealth of information about American women in the late twentieth century.

A new atlas published by the U.S. Centers for Disease Control and Prevention, *Women and Heart Disease: An Atlas of Racial and Ethnic Disparities in Mortality* (Atlanta, Ga.: CDC, [1999?]; G1201.E51 W6 1999), analyzes deaths from 1991 to 1995 by county and race. Between various regions of the country, large disparities exist, but within local areas, the difference between the death rate for white women and those of minorities is also considerable. For the entire country, 370,000 women die annually from heart disease; the death rate for black women is 533 per 100,000 population compared to 388 per 100,000 for white women. Atlas plates highlight these differences.

Another example of a thematic atlas that includes material about women is the *Atlas of American Sport* by John F. Rooney Jr. and Richard Pillsbury (New York: Macmillan Publishing Company, 1992; G1201.E63 R6 1992 fol.). It contains information on participation of women in sports such as gymnastics and swimming between 1970 and 1990. Finding this kind of material is difficult without examining the volume because it is not always evident that the content includes data on women. The best strategy for finding these resources is to locate a theme or themes related to your research topic to use in the subject field—such as "sports"—for a computer catalog search. Other subject headings that may lead you to useful source material are "minorities," "race relations," "ethnic relations," "urban poor," or the more general heading "historical geography."

Statistical Data

Most modern thematic maps and atlases rely heavily on statistical data. The Geography and Map Division has several kinds of data resources, including historical U.S. Census Bureau material. Beginning in 1870, three statistical atlases were produced to illustrate the results of the decennial censuses, all three of which are now available in their entirety on the Geography and Map Web site. *The Statistical Atlas of the United States Based on the Results of the Ninth Census, 1870,* edited by Francis A. Walker (New York: Julius Bien, 1874; G1201.G1 U53 1874), was the first attempt by the Census Office to prepare a cartographic census summary. Unfortunately, only one plate is devoted to population distribution by sex. For the 1880 census, a summary is available in *Scribner's Statistical Atlas of the United States* (New York: Charles Scribner's Sons, 1883; G1201.G1 H4 1883), while a more complete record is available for the 1890 census in *Statistical Atlas of the United States, Based upon the Results of the Eleventh Census,* edited by Henry Gannet (Washington: GPO, 1898; G1201.G1 U53 1898). The latter includes graphs and tables showing age and sex percentages and detailed information on the African American population. Subsequent atlases based on census material were published for the data gathered in 1900, 1910, and 1920.

The most recent census material is considerably more detailed. The Topologically Integrated Geographic Encoding and Referencing (TIGER) System developed for the 1990 census provides a single, fully automated source from which data and cartographic products related to the 1990 census can be derived. The Geography and Map Division holds extensive material, including census tracts and all of the digital data stored in the TIGER files. Additional digital data sets are available for use with geographic information systems to create maps. In-depth reports for some cities and counties, arranged by state, and copies of many of the maps created by the Census Bureau are also housed in the division.

Some of the publications based on this material, both in textual and cartographic formats, show rates of change between censuses over time. The *Atlas of the 1990 Census* (New York: Macmillan Publishing, 1992; G1201.E2 M3 1992) by Mark T. Mattson contains population pyramids by age and sex for 1970, 1980, and 1989; for white, African American, and other races by age and sex for 1989; state populations by gender; births, abortions, and infant mortality by state; and the composition of households, including those with married couples and households headed by females.

Statistical data sets are available on CD-ROM and are sometimes published in conjunction with atlases. An example is the *Dartmouth Atlas of Health Care, 1998* (Chicago: American Hospital Publishing, 1998; G1201.E5 D3 1998), which shows the geographic distribution of health services throughout the United States, including information on mammography and breast-sparing surgery, based on information supplied by health care organizations and the U.S. Census. These kinds of publications allow users to incorporate the data sets into their own research projects.

Other atlases based on census data that are directly related to women's health care issues are *U.S. Cancer Mortality Rates and Trends 1950–1979,* vol. 4, *Maps* (Washington: U.S. Environmental Protection Agency, 1983; G1201.E51 U44 1983), and *The Atlas of U.S. Cancer Mortality*

"Uterine Cancer Rates in South Dakota, by County, 1953–1987." The State Cancer Control Map and Data Program of the National Cancer Institute (*Uncataloged digital data set—inquire at reference desk). Geography and Map Division.*

The State Cancer Control Map and Data Program of the National Cancer Institute, using data from 1953 to 1987, is an example of a GIS software package using statistical data that were developed by the National Institutes of Health. It produces customized maps based on cancer rates for males and females for each state down to the county level. Selected parameters for making this map, which highlights the dramatically high rate of uterine cancer in a single county of South Dakota, were for the state, the type of cancer, and all women. Although the program can differentiate between racial groups, this group of settings reveals that Shannon County stands apart from the rest of the state with regard to uterine cancer. The county is the home of the Pine Ridge Indian Reservation located near the historical site of Wounded Knee. These kinds of maps reveal differences in health status and health care delivery and can be used in making health and environmental policy decisions.

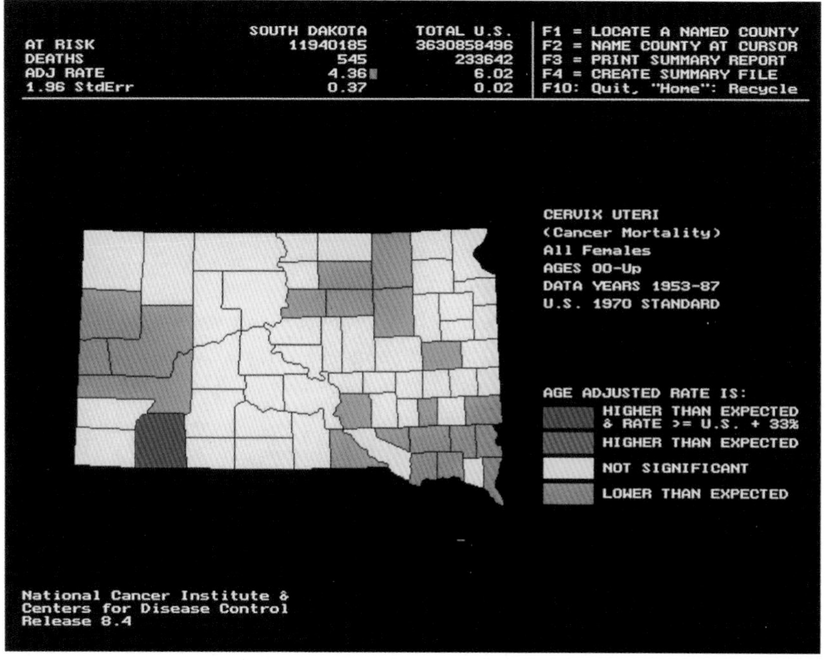

among Nonwhites: 1950–1980 (Bethesda, Md.: NIH; uncataloged). *The State Cancer Control Map and Data Program of the National Cancer Institute,* using data from 1953 to 1987, is a GIS software package and data developed by the National Institutes of Health (NIH). It produces customized maps based on cancer rates for males and females for each state down to the county level (see page 235). Excellent maps based on interpretations of statistics are also published with government reports in the Congressional Serial Set maps, which are indexed in *The U.S. Serial Set Index and Cartobibliography of Maps* (part 14) (see page 232).

The major limitation on the usefulness of the recent thematic cartographic information for historians is that, with the exception of the early Census Bureau atlases and the Routledge historical atlas, most of these publications deal primarily with very recent data. Not only is there a shortage of similar retrospective data in statistical form to compare with it, but if it exists at all, it frequently has been gathered in different ways, making comparisons difficult if not impossible. Generally, retrospective information must be compiled from a variety of sources and modified in order to make statistical analyses valid, which is time consuming and often very difficult.

Recent data can be more easily used by those trained in GIS to analyze changing demographic and spatial patterns to produce colorful and easily interpreted maps for the last decades of the twentieth century. It remains the task of historians, however, to identify and collect relevant information about the past that can be used to re-create historic landscapes and to provide a meaningful analysis of changing patterns over time. The final hurdle is that few historians are sufficiently trained in GIS methodology and geographic concepts to use the abundant new software packages to analyze their data and make maps, so these scholars must seek collaborators with skills to successfully map the results of their research. Joni Seager's attractive and insightful maps (see page 233) are based on her extensive research into data sources, but even she fully acknowledges the assistance of skilled cartographers in producing her impressive atlas.

Landownership Maps and Atlases

Landownership maps and atlases are a particularly rich source of information about women's property, businesses, and relative wealth, also providing insight into family structure. County boundaries define the areas most frequently found among the materials that show landownership. The Library's collections include both maps and atlases that were produced primarily for the purpose of showing landownership, although they also may show how land was used and sometimes indicate changes in land use over time. A variety of other kinds of maps, such as battlefield maps and urban plans, provide landownership and land use information in addition to the primary purpose for which the map was drawn. These maps are not included in the finding aids for county landownership maps and atlases but may be listed and described in other bibliographies and finding aids.

Single sheet maps, often very large in size, are described in *Land Ownership Maps: A Checklist of Nineteenth Century United States County Maps in the Library of Congress* (Washington: Library of Congress, 1967; Z6027.U5 U54). The checklist includes bibliographic descriptions of nearly fifteen hundred maps that were created to show landownership. Landownership material is also available in atlas format, particularly at the county level. The major bibliographic resource for these materials is *United States Atlases: A List of National, State, County, City, and Regional Atlases in the Library of Congress* (New York: Arno Press, 1971; Z881.U5 1971) by Clara Egli LeGear.

Most of the maps and atlases produced primarily to show landownership and business locations were published during the nineteenth century and were financed by selling subscriptions. Where there was not a sufficient financial base to produce a profit for the publisher, who recovered costs by selling subscriptions and advertising space, few of these kinds of maps were produced. Less affluent areas of the United States are therefore not well represented on subscription maps.

The maps often show the size of the real estate holdings of named individuals, an indication of social and economic status in the community. Occupational information concerning women may also be ascertained from indications of land use such as lists of buildings or listed business patrons who provided funds toward the production of the map in exchange for advertising space. Personal names associated with boardinghouses, hotels, general stores, bakeries, and other kinds of businesses requiring the use of a commercial building provide clues to women's occupations. The marital status of the landowner is sometimes indicated by such forms of address as "Mrs.," "Miss," or "Widow." Even in the absence of gender identification, surnames on landownership maps often provide information as to the family name of a woman and show proximity between family residences in the community, helping to trace family and kinship networks.

Sometimes the size of the family can be determined using the frequently appended "Jr.," which appears for males and occasionally for females to indicate parent-child relationships. Illustrations show prominent individuals, family portraits, and the homes of affluent residents. Some maps also show how towns were laid out, naming the larger structures in the town, including women's schools and colleges. Both in terms of landownership and secondary information about land use, these maps show spatial relationships in the area and in the process also provide information about gender-defined spaces at a particular point in time.

An example of such a map is filed in the Title Collection under Connecticut, Fairfield County, 185-?. It is a map of the boroughs of Danbury and Bethel, and one of its beautiful illustrations shows the elegant residence of Mrs. Laura Barnum. Danbury Institute, described as "a family boarding school," is indicated, with a list of its faculty including a Miss H. M. Schenck, who was a music teacher there. Other properties are labeled with such names as Miss Bishop, Mrs. Mygatt, Mrs. Dobbs, and the Widows Hoyt, Wood, Rider, and Smith. Mrs. Stoker and Taylor are listed together as are Clark Smith and Miss Ridge, the home of Mrs. Mills and Miss Barnum, and Mrs. S. W. Bonner and Mrs. Sherwood's School.

These groupings may or may not have meaning beyond the fact that the listed properties were in close proximity to each other and perhaps for that reason the owners' names were connected with an ampersand. If the purpose of using the ampersand was to condense the labels into a smaller space, however, the ampersand is an additional element introduced into a limited space on the map, leaving the question open as to the relationship between the two named individuals in each pair.

The map is typical of a landownership map in the amount of information it contains about women, but the picture of the grand home of Mrs. Barnum is unusual. Relatively few women are indicated as owners of such large dwellings or of the named buildings shown on these maps. Much more work needs to be done, however, to explain some of the groupings listed on the map and to round out the picture of life in this county in the 1850s.

It is possible to trace migration patterns in landownership maps, particularly when immigrants settled in ethnic communities. Germans, Scandinavians, Eastern Europeans, and Asians can be found living in close proximity to one another on some of these maps. For example, there are several Pennsylvania county maps showing enclaves of residents with German surnames, including *Scott's Map of Lancaster County* by Joshua Scott (Philadelphia: James D. Scott, 1855), filed under Pennsylvania, Lancaster County, 1858, in the Title Collection. In addition to ethnic groupings of the landholders, the map also shows how some of the county's land was used, such as indicating the location of a boardinghouse in Columbia township run by Mrs. Elizabeth Wolfe and the "Ladies' Seminary" and grounds.

A few of the county landownership maps and atlases also contain material on racial minorities. *The Standard Atlas of Graham County, Kansas* (Chicago, 1906; G1458.G4 O3 1906) includes the African American town of Nicodemus established in 1877. The town was settled by African Americans who migrated there from Kentucky, and the atlas gives the names of the inhabitants and shows their property. Likewise, "Cherokee Nation, Township 2 North, Range 24 East" from *Township Maps of the Cherokee Nation* (Muskogee, Okla.: Indian Territory Map Company, 1909; G1365.I5 1909) includes the names of many Cherokee landowners. Nancy Parchcorn, Lydia Leaf, Myrtle Morris, Elizabeth Carnes, and Mary Tehee are but a few of the women's names shown on one of the plates.

Although the military was primarily a masculine institution—both in terms of the participants involved in wartime activity and those who produced its cartographic documentation—military maps often convey information about social and economic activities of a place and time. An example is maps in the Civil War collection, especially the relatively large-scale battle plans that contain landownership information, including the names of plantation owners in the South and farmers and entrepreneurs in the North. Often there is information about buildings in the vicinity with some identified as being related to female use, such as women's and girls' seminaries and schools.

Recently a researcher located the birthplace of the legendary African American entrepreneur and philanthropist, Madam C. J. Walker (1867–1919).[12] Walker was born on a plantation directly across the river from the site of the Civil War battle of Vicksburg. The search strategy began with knowledge of the plantation owner's name and its general location and a time period around the era of the Civil War. Documentation on two maps of the seige of Vicksburg shows the plantation on which Walker was born, although there is a slight variation between the two maps in the spelling of the owner's name, one appearing as "Birney," the other as "Burney." The map that most clearly shows this plantation is by George W. Tomlinson, *Tomlinson's Map of Vicksburg, showing all of the surrounding fortifications, batteries, principal plantations, &c.* (Boston: J. Mayer & Co., 1863; Civil War Collection, no. 286). The Civil War Collection, of which it is a part, is mounted on American Memory through the Map Collections site. The finding aid for the collection is *Civil War Maps: An Annotated List of Maps and Atlases in the Library of Congress* (Washington: Library of Congress, 1989; Z6027.U5 L5 1989) by Richard W. Stephenson.

A recently purchased manuscript map of Los Angeles, based on a map from the 1850s, was drawn in 1873 to show the central area of the Mexican pueblo. That same year, the town was resurveyed by the Americans who had seized California during the Mexican War. The Library purchased the map in part because it holds no other early original maps of Los Angeles that show the central part of the city in detail at the time when the area was becoming Anglicized. It is an artifact documenting the meeting of two cultures in an area of the country that at the time was a borderland, just as a new, hybridized culture was developing there (see illustration). In addition, the map records early titles to lots and buildings in the central city which helped Hispanic landowners prove property claims to the satisfaction of the American government, thus enabling them to retain their land and homes after the American conquest. Among those named as owners of city lots were several individuals with female given names, such as "Pilar," "Maria," "Ramona," and "Serafina." These names illustrate an aspect of Spanish law, which allowed married women to retain family property in their own names and to buy and sell land (see chapter 3).

Using the Los Angeles map that was based on information from the 1850s and 1860s and *The First Los Angeles City and County Directory*, originally published in 1872, a researcher can begin to understand the roles played by women during the pueblo era and into the early period of American

A. G. Ruxton, surveyor. "Map of the Old Portion of the City surrounding the Plaza, Showing the Old Plaza Church, Public Square, the First Gas Plant and Adobe Buildings, Los Angeles City." March 12, 1873 (manuscript, n.p.). Geography and Map Division.

Although many maps in the Geography and Map Division indicate property owners of different ethnic origins and give considerable information about them, this map of Los Angeles is unusual in showing a comparatively large number of women owners in a relatively small geographical area. The map is an important resource for studying Hispanic and mestizo women in an urban borderland.

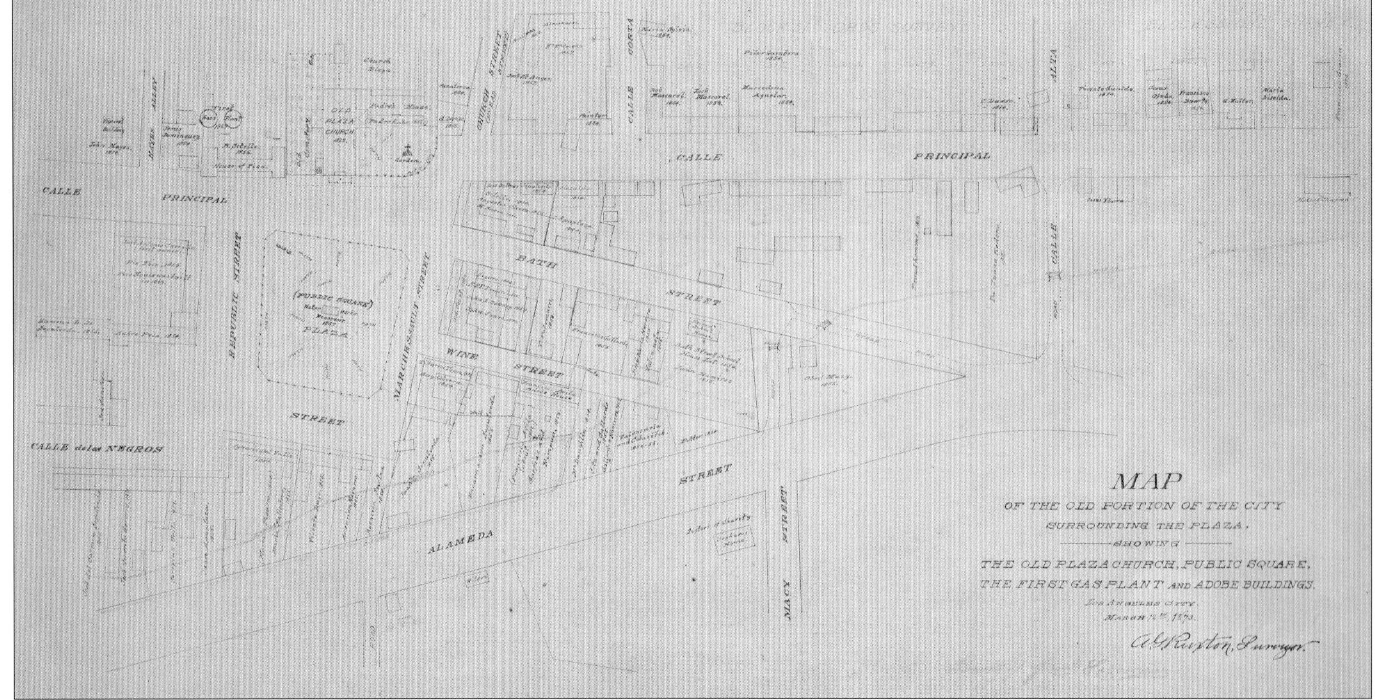

occupation and settlement.[13] The Sisters of Charity convent, which is in close proximity to the orphanage on the map, shows the origin of what later became the Sisters of Charity school for girls and young women advertised in the city directory.

The directory lists a number of women, including many widows, and contains a full-page advertisement for a female nursery-owner who claimed to have the best citrus trees—oranges, lemons, and limes—all grown from seeds that she brought from Nicaragua. Although trees are shown on the map, only one area resembles an orchard, showing trees planted in rows, but its label indicates that the area was used as a cemetery.

Some of the large-scale set maps contain significant amounts of material about women and family life. An example is a series of Hawaiian tax maps, produced by the Taxation Maps Bureau of the Territory of Hawaii in the decade of the 1930s, with a correction sheet done in the 1940s, providing detailed information about Hawaiian landowners (see illustration). Not only are the first and last names given for each of the property holders, male and female, but relationships between husband and wife and lots held by other joint tenants are identified and documented in far greater detail than is available for most other American cities and states.

For the eighteenth century there are understandably fewer primary sources of information on landownership. A few of the maps of the American colonies and the United States dated between 1750 and 1789 that show landownership information are indexed under "cadastral maps" in *Maps and Charts of North America and the West Indies, 1750–1789: A Guide to the Collections in the Library of Congress* (Washington: Library of Congress, 1981; Z6027.N68 U54 1981 GA401), compiled by John R. Sellers and Patricia Molen van Ee.

In addition to the primary sources described, all of which are contemporary historical maps and atlases, a significant amount of secondary source material is available based on a variety of landownership data that have been compiled from original records and presented in map format. An excellent example is Beth Mitchell's landownership map of Fairfax County, *Beginning at a White Oak . . . : Patents and Northern Neck Grants of Fairfax County, Virginia* (Fairfax, Va.: Fairfax County Administrative Services, 1977; F232.F2 M57). The map is based on early land patents showing the names of owners, some of whom are female, for the period from 1651 to 1679. A meticulously researched text explains the information

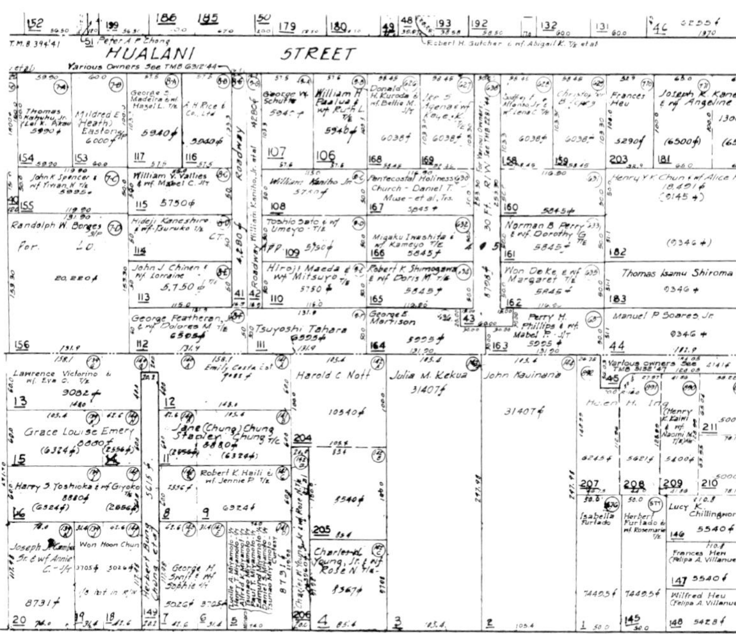

Taxation Maps Bureau Territory of Hawaii. *Tax map (first division, zone 4, section 3, plat 28, sheet 228 [Honolulu],193-; G4381 G47svarH5). Geography and Map Division.*

Portuguese, Chinese, Japanese, Native Hawaiian, and the usual mix of surnames found in other parts of the United States reflect the great diversity of the population of Hawaii. Many women's names appear on this map, some with their maiden names. Emily Costa, Jane (Chung) Chung, Grace Louis Emery, Lucy K. Chillingworth, and Mildred E. (Heath) Easton are named, as well as Lucille Miyamoto, who appears to have inherited property equally with her male siblings who are listed as minor children.

on the map. The site of the modern city of Alexandria was originally part of the patent taken out by Margaret Brent (ca. 1601–1671) in 1651. She was the first woman in the North American colonies to obtain and hold a large land grant in her own name, and she managed her own estate, one of the largest in the county. Brent has the additional distinction of being the first American woman to ask for the right to vote because of her status as a property owner (see chapter 3). Similar reconstructed landownership maps are available for other locations and time periods, generally under the subject heading of "land titles," followed by the place-name. The subject headings for Mitchell's work are "Land titles—Virginia—Fairfax Co." and "Fairfax County (Va.)—Genealogy."

Land Use Maps

Insurance maps, published both as individual sheets and as bound volumes, are a major resource for studying urban land use in the United States in the late nineteenth and into the twentieth century. The Library's collection of Sanborn

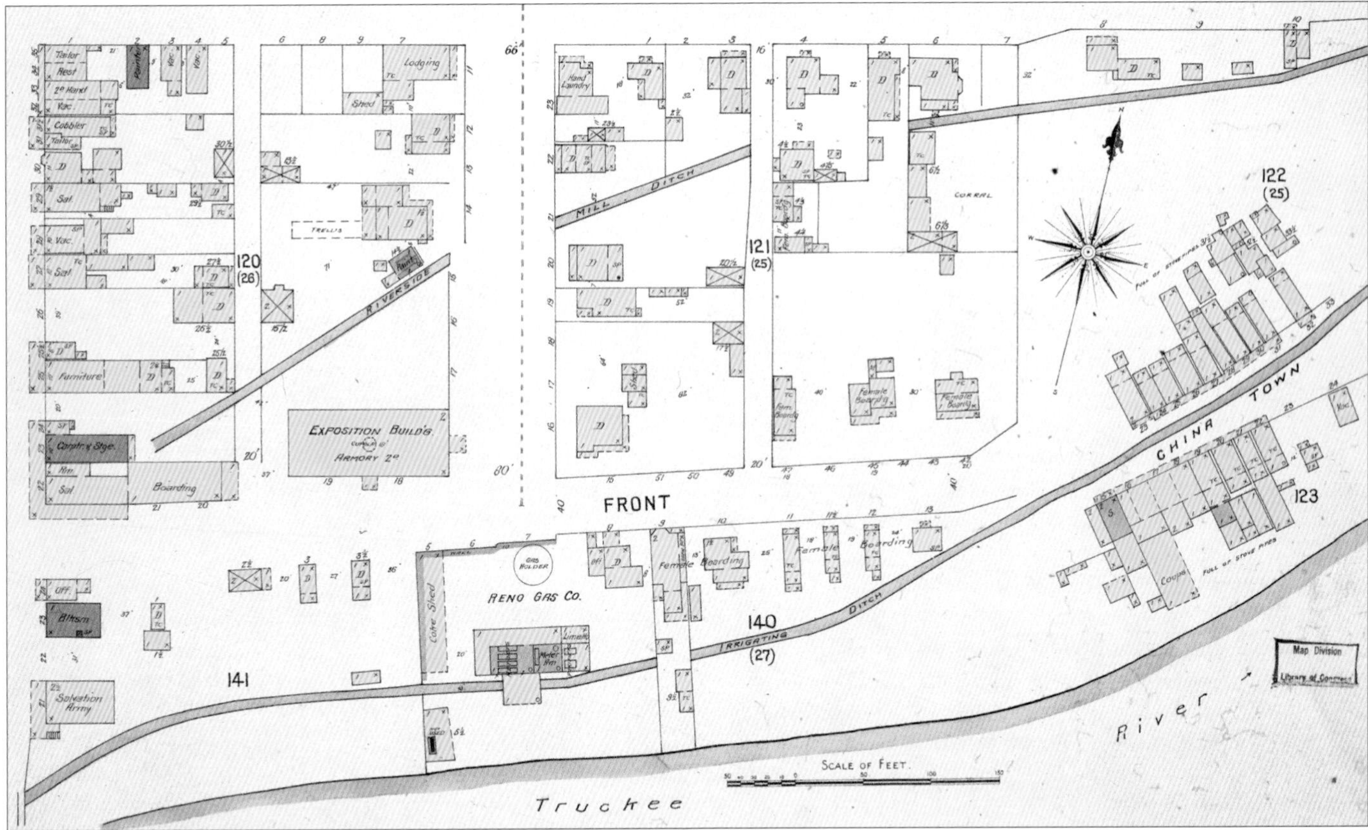

April 1899 Reno Nev. *Sanborn Fire Insurance Map for Reno, Nevada, April 1899 (Sheet no. 5). Geography and Map Division.*

Chinatown, seen in the lower right corner of sheet no. 5 for Reno, Nevada, 1899, is an area of the city associated with activities such as gambling, drinking, and prostitution. The Sanborn Fire Insurance Maps provide sufficient information to define neighborhoods, including residential areas with large homes indicative of relative affluence, and to identify gender-related activities.

Company fire insurance maps of U.S. cities produced between 1867 and the late 1950s consists of approximately 700,000 sheets for 12,000 cities and towns assembled in atlas format. They were acquired from sources that include copyright deposits, transfers from the Bureau of the Census, gifts, and purchases. Their original purpose was to provide data for insurance underwriters estimating potential risks to urban structures when calculating insurance rates. The need for detailed information about the construction materials used for each building, the number of floors in each structure, and the nature of the commercial activity taking place in large buildings resulted in a block-by-block inventory in the densely populated areas of most American cities and towns. Color is used to indicate construction materials for each building. In addition, the maps show individual dwellings and outbuildings and property lines.

Extensively labeled, the maps frequently identify structures such as women's colleges, seminaries, schools, and academies; hospitals for women, including maternity wards; religious structures, including convents, orphanages, and schools; cemeteries; factories and warehouses; and prisons. They show businesses frequented by women such as shops selling dry goods, millinery, or groceries.

Another indication of gendered space is the label "F.B.," an abbreviation for "Female Boarding," and "W'House" or "Ill Fame," contemporary terms for buildings used by prostitutes. These buildings are frequently grouped together forming "Red Light Districts" and are invariably located close to wharves, saw mills, the kinds of factories that primarily employed male workers, warehouses, and saloons, all of which were at that time predominantly male-occupied space.

There are many examples in the insurance map collection documenting the presence of prostitution. *The Fire Map of Honolulu,* published by the Board of Fire Underwriters of the Territory of Hawaii in 1906 (G1534.24.H6 G9 1906 fol.), uses the terms "Ill Fame" and "W'House" for buildings located near a fertilizer plant, pig pens, the Honolulu Gas Works, and petroleum storage tanks, not far from "Prison Road."

Other structures in Honolulu used by women, include the Kawaiaao Seminary and the Kaiulani Home for Girls, the Girls' Reform School, which has a nearby Matrons' Residence, and Mrs. Freeth's Boarding House. Ethnic areas that warrant further study as to whether or not they are associated with women are the Portuguese Kindergarten, a Korean church and school, a Japanese Boarding Stable, and Immigration and Emigration facilities.

The Sanborn Fire Insurance maps for Reno, Nevada, in 1899 show schools, churches, a Young Men's Christian Association building, the Salvation Army building, two foundling and orphan homes, a mental hospital with male and female wards, and a Chinese quarter. Reno's Chinatown included boarding houses, restaurants, saloons, rooming houses, tenements, and gambling places, and had its own physician. It was adjacent to a large area labeled "FB" near the commercial center of the city, in an area with hotels, saloons, garages, and a variety of other businesses (see illustration).

An interesting aspect of the secular grade schools in Reno—Mount Rose School and the McKinley Park Grammar School—is that, although they appear to be coeducational, the school buildings are divided almost equally into two distinct areas, one for "Manual Training," the other for "Domestic Science," which suggests that the sexes occupied different parts of the schoolhouse and studied separate curricula. There is no such division apparent in the Dominican Sisters' Catholic School, which is near the order's convent, or in Mary Dolan's School.

The campus of Nevada State University on sheet 32 of the Reno fire insurance map shows the location of Manzanita Hall girls' dormitory and the girls' dining hall that are close to each other in an otherwise isolated area of the campus. Lincoln Hall, the boys' dormitory, is much closer to the rest of the college buildings and has no separate dining facilities. Steward Hall, near the classroom buildings, has both a kitchen and dining room and may be where the male students dined.

Examination of the Sanborn sheets for Alaska in the 1920s reveals that, despite its name, the Alaska Agricultural College and School of Mines in Fairbanks, which might generally be thought to have solely male students, was undoubtedly coeducational because there is a women's dormitory on the campus. Fairbanks also had a hospital with an adjoining "Nurse's Cottage" and a beauty parlor.

The Sanborn atlas maps of the frontier towns of Cordova, Douglas, Haines, and Juneau, Alaska, dated 1927, show that all had areas of town with groups of buildings labeled as female boardinghouses. They are found near saloons, saw mills and lumberyards, fish canneries, and large commercial structures such as iron works and warehouses. Comparing the Alaskan towns with other mill towns such as Gastonia, North Carolina, reveals that the cotton mill towns that employed large numbers of women were unlikely to have adjacent areas labeled this way. The young women working in the mills appear to have resided in boardinghouses, structures marked "D" for dwelling, and occasionally in tenements. The number of houses of prostitution in a factory city or town seems to have been directly related to the gender of those working in the large industries in those locales.

The highly detailed and systematic mapping used on fire insurance maps makes them an extremely valuable source for studies of urbanization and urban change, including the development of tenements in inner cities that received large numbers of immigrants, industrialization, the growth of suburbs, and the evolution of gender-specific institutions. They also can be used to determine distance traveled by women between their residences and places of employment, including the routes taken by domestic and factory workers to and from work. Factoring in the addresses of close relatives and the location of the churches, schools, and businesses frequented by a particular woman, the scope of her world can be studied. Because of the large scale to which they are drawn and their highly detailed labeling, fire insurance maps are among the best cartographic resources for studying patterns of land use and gendered spaces in urban areas.

Rarely individually cataloged, Sanborn map sheets are controlled by arrangement by city and state. The major finding aid is *Fire Insurance Maps in the Library of Congress: Plans of North American Cities and Towns Produced by the Sanborn Map Company,* a checklist compiled by the Reference and Bibliography Section, Geography and Map Division (Washington: Library of Congress, 1981; Z6026.I7 U54 1981).

In addition to insurance maps, there are other

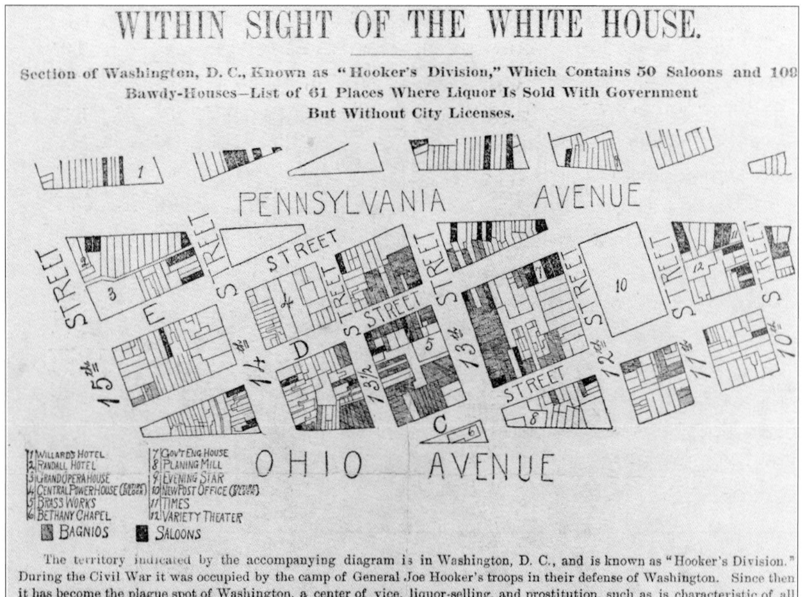

WITHIN SIGHT OF THE WHITE HOUSE.

Section of Washington, D. C., Known as "Hooker's Division," Which Contains 50 Saloons and 109 Bawdy-Houses—List of 61 Places Where Liquor Is Sold With Government But Without City Licenses.

The territory indicated by the accompanying diagram is in Washington, D. C., and is known as "Hooker's Division." During the Civil War it was occupied by the camp of General Joe Hooker's troops in their defense of Washington. Since then it has become the plague spot of Washington, a center of vice, liquor-selling, and prostitution, such as is characteristic of all High-License cities. It is in the very heart of the city, extending along Pennsylvania avenue to the United States treasury. The four daily papers of the city, *Post*, *Star*, *Times*, and *News*, are published in this teritrory. Within its borders are the leading banks, opera-houses, and hotels.

This district alone contains 109 regular houses of prostitution, exclusive of assignation-houses, 31 of which are in the single block surrounded by C, D, 13th and 13½ streets northwest. Besides this there are an even 50 saloons, most of them run directly in connection with bawdy-houses.

Each one of these 109 houses of prostitution sells liquors openly and freely every day, and not a single one pays the $400 local license. There are 61 bawdy-houses in this district which hold Federal permits, while the other 48 pay no license whatever. They not only defy every provision of the High-License law, but they refuse to pay the Government license as well.

Grover Cleveland can sit in his bedroom window at the White House and survey this entire territory. He is within sight and gunshot of each of these 109 dens which defy the laws which he is supposed to execute through his commissioners. The following is a list of 61 persons in this district and their addresses who are selling liquor under Federal permits and who do not pay the $400 High-License:

Kate Anderson, 1431 D, N. W.; Mrs. May Albert, 300 11th; Ray Astor, 406 13th, N. W.; Ida Bronson, 217 10th N. W.; Kate W. Brown, 1208 D; Lulu Burke, 214 11th; Mrs. K. T. Crowley, 313 13th; Nannie Coles, 1207 C; Alice Curry, 1215 C.; Sarah Carter, 325 13th; Maud Conant, 305 13½; Sarah Chesley, 311 13th; Emma Coleman, 309 13th; Maud Duval, 404 13th; Ida Drury, 1222 D, N. W.; Bessie Edmondson, 310 13th; Grace Emerson, 1353 Ohio; Grace Furguson, 1309 C; May Fitzpatrick, 1340 14th; May Fitzgerald; Willie Gilmore, 401 13th; Cora Graham, 401 15th, removed to 1428 C street; Mary Gray, 326 13th, N. W.; Daisy Grey, 321 13th; Annie Hester, 1317 D; Mabel Haynes, 1307 C; Fannie Hill, 314 13½, N. W.; May Howard, 1222 C, N. W.; Jennie Javins, 1225 C, N. W.; Lizzie Jones, 1106 C, N. W.; Kate Lott, 1209 C; Josie Jong, 1315 D, N. W.; Nellie Larue 412 13th; Alice Linden, 312 13th; Mary Milovich, 1313 C; Edith Bertha May, 1304 D; Gertie Peterson, 1357 Ohio; Lou Roberts, 301 13½; Ellen Reynolds, 307 13th; Belle Saville, 1213 C; Gussie Smith, 1214 C; Blanche Mc Coy, 1310 D, N. W.; Ella Monroe, 1433 D, N. W.; Victoria McClellan, 1355 Ohio; Rosie Moore, 1116 C.; Anna Murphy, 1219 C; Dora L. Marion, 326 13, N. W.; Ida Nightingale, 322 13½; Bell Norris, 1424 C, N. W.; Lena Ordway, 1223 D.; Lizzie Peterson, 1309 D.; Sadie Street, 1226 D; Blanche Snow, 1114 C; Miss H. Stewert, 328 13th; Bertie Stokes, 301 13th; Mollie Turner, 305 13th; Minnie Thompson, 1217 C.; Lottie Tilford, 212 11th; Josie West, 1220 C; Nellie Wallace; 1311 C; Eva White, 306 13th.

"Within Sight of the White House." Map from unknown Washington, D.C., newspaper, 1890s (G3851.E625 189-.W5). Geography and Map Division.

The area shown on this map clipped from a District of Columbia newspaper in the 1890s, where General Joe Hooker's troops camped during the Civil War, is referred to as "Hooker's Division."

kinds of maps that provide information on land use and changes in use in gendered spaces. An excellent example is a map that was clipped from a District of Columbia newspaper in the 1890s. Entitled "Within Sight of the White House," its subtitle is "Section of Washington, D.C., Known as 'Hooker's Division,' Which Contains 50 Saloons and 100 Bawdy-Houses—List of 61 Places Where Liquor Is Sold with Government But without City Licenses" (see illustration).

The subject of the map and the accompanying article is the failure of certain establishments to pay local taxes on liquor, and the names of the offending proprietors are listed. One hundred and nine brothels occupy the area shown on the map, which is now known as the Federal Triangle area of Washington, D.C. In the 1890s, it was the center of the city—where the U.S. Treasury, four newspapers, banks, opera houses, and hotels, in addition to the White House, were located. There, too, were 109 businesses where large numbers of women worked as prostitutes. Of the sixty-one named proprietors who did not pay the local tax, no more than four have male given names—Ray Astor, Lou Roberts, Willie Gilmore, and Gussie Smith. It is possible, in fact, that even these four were female, as the names are ambiguous with regard to gender, and judging from the fifty-seven obviously female given names, most of these businesses were run by women. Shown is the area where Joseph Hooker, whom President Lincoln appointed commander of the Army of the Potomac in January 1863, camped with his men. They were referred to as "Hooker's Division," and the name became synonymous with prostitution. An accompanying article indicates that the term "bawdy house" refers to houses of prostitution but not to "houses of assignation," indicating that different social and economic relationships were involved in these establishments.

Panoramic Maps or Birds'-Eye Views

In the years following the Civil War, the panoramic map became a popular cartographic form for portraying American cities. Though generally not drawn to scale, these maps were based on detailed on-site studies and provide an accurate perspective view of landscape features, streets, and buildings of the period. They frequently show individual structures and their use, some of which are identified by gender, including schools and academies, hospitals, and seminaries for women. *Panoramic Maps of Cities in the United States and Canada: A Checklist of Maps in the Collections of the Library of Congress, Geography and Map Division*, 2nd ed. (Washington: Library of Congress, 1984; Z6027.U5 L5 1984), compiled by John R. Hébert and revised by Patrick E. Dempsey, describes and gives the physical location of these views, some of which are housed in the Prints and Photographs Division. All of the images are now available online at <http://lcweb2.loc.gov/ammem/pmhtml/panhome.html>.

Frequently portrayed in the foreground of these decorative prints are male and female figures, sometimes in family groups and always in contemporary dress. The decorative borders of the maps often include engravings showing the larger homes and business structures of the town.

Pictorial Maps

A genre of map that uses illustrations to convey information about geographic locations, pictorial maps are an important but underused resource. Many of these maps are found in the division's single map file under the term "pictorial map" for a geographic area, followed by the date.

A sampling of pictorial maps of the United States dated from 1900 to 1950 reveals an abundance of material about cultural attitudes toward women. More than half of the maps surveyed show at least one female figure, often portrayed stereotypically in activities and settings that reflect social and cultural norms for females. A variety of women from different racial and cultural backgrounds are shown. White women are depicted in familiar roles that include teachers, nurses, bathing beauties, westward-bound pioneers in covered wagons, and southern belles. Native American women are almost always shown performing chores, such as cleaning animal hides, weaving, and making pottery or baskets, usually in close proximity to their tepee homes and often with infants on their backs. African American women are often shown picking cotton, in contrast to only one white woman shown at work in the cotton fields. There is also a dramatic depiction of an African American slave and her child escaping via the underground railroad.

Americans of Negro Lineage by Louise E. Jefferson (New York: Friendship Press, 1946; G370.A5 1946.J4 no.12) shows in great detail the contributions African Americans have made to American society and is one of the few maps in the Library's

Dorothea Dix Lawrence. Folklore Music Map of the United States from the Primer of American Music *[New York: Hagstrom Co., 1946] (Single Map File, "U.S. Pictorial, 1946"). Geography and Map Division. Copyright © Hagstrom Map Company, Inc., NY, Lic. no.: H–2194.*

With the drawings on the *Folklore Music Map* are a few words from the lyrics of the folk song that they illustrate. Bayou ballads, Creole folk songs, early California music, songs of the open range, Louisiana folk music, folk hymns, African American spirituals, and songs for children are included. One of the best maps in the division's collections for illustrating American diversity, this map was drawn by a woman and half of the many sources listed in the bibliography on the map were written by women.

collections to include illustrations of black women as nurses, teachers, housewives, performing artists from the theater, musical, and motion picture industries, musicians, explorers, WAVES and WACS, journalists, and bankers.

Another map rich in detail about women's ethnicity and regional roles was drawn by Dorothea Dix Lawrence. Her *Folklore Music Map of the United States* depicts a multicultural society, with a wide variety of women in traditional dress (see illustration). Black, Hispanic, Cajun, Creole, Native American, and white women dressed in ethnic clothing are shown in close proximity to the areas where these groups lived in the 1940s.

Two manuscript pictorial maps created by the Federal Theatre Project document the tours of actresses Fanny Davenport and Lotta Crabtree, providing sketched portraits of them in costume for their stage appearances and showing illustrations of the theaters where they performed ([Federal Theatre Project: Tours by Famous Actors and Actresses 1865?–1904]. G3701. E645 1904.U Vault).

Also among the pictorial maps are literary maps, which show places associated with authors and their works. Literary and other pictorial maps published within the past thirty years are more likely to have included women and minority authors as subjects than those of earlier periods. *Language of the Land* (Washington: Library of Congress, 1999; Z6026.L57 H66 1999; G1046.E65) by Martha Hopkins and Michael Buscher is one such guide.

Especially valuable to studies of gendered spaces are the detailed manuscript pictorial maps produced by members of the Shaker congregations or, as they called themselves, "families." A religious sect that lived communally and believed in the equality of men and women, the Shakers made simple but elegant drawings depicting the neat, tidy villages in which they lived. Although

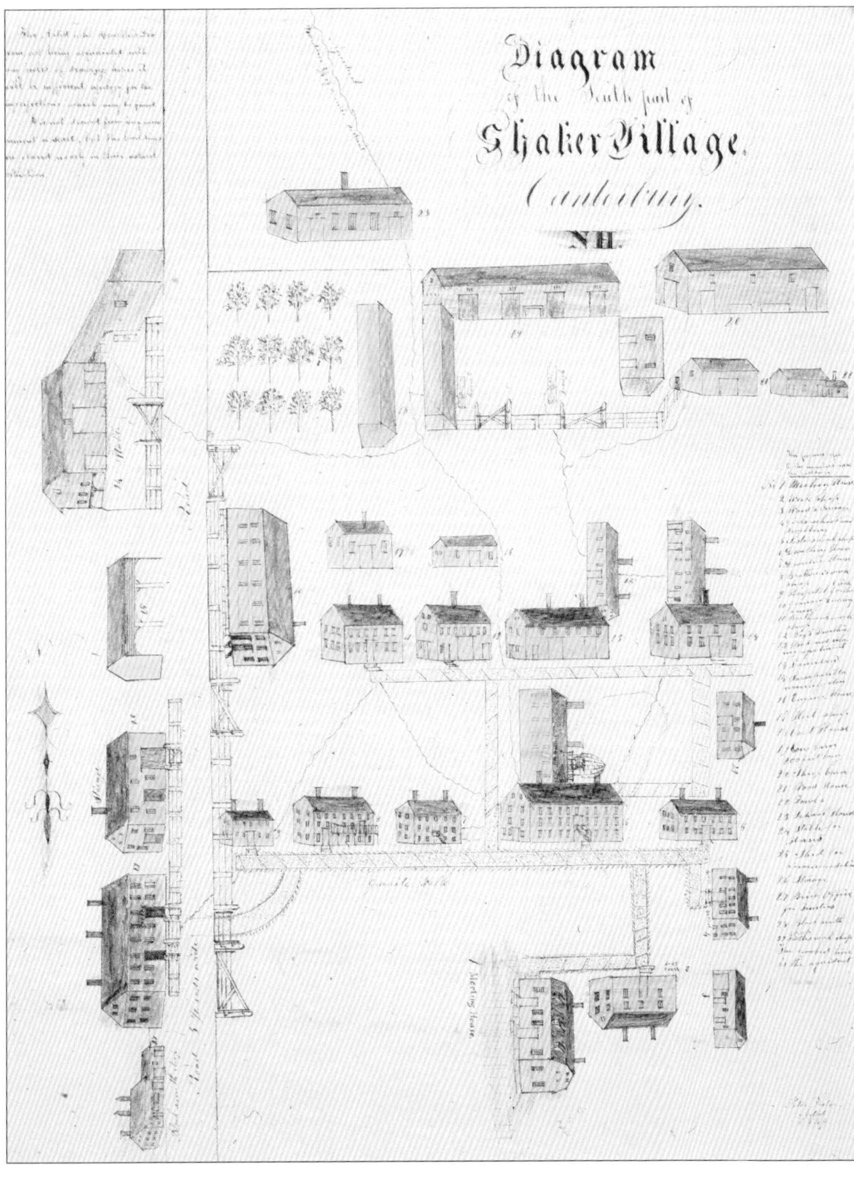

Peter Foster. "Diagram of the South Part of Shaker Village, Canterbury, N.H." Colored manuscript map (Vault; G3744.S5 1849). Geography and Map Division.

Peter Foster, author of the beautifully colored map of part of the Shaker Village of Canterbury, New Hampshire, described his method: "The artist who drew this diagram, not being acquainted with any rules of drawing, hopes it will be sufficient apology for the imperfections which may be found. It is not drawed from any measurement of scale, but the buildings are placed nearly in their natural situation." The image is available online at <http://hdl.loc.gov/loc.gmd/g3744s.ct000129>. Similar drawings exist for Shaker communities in Maine and other parts of the country. See Robert P. Emlen, *Shaker Village Views: Illustrated Maps and Landscape Drawings by Shaker Artists of the Nineteenth Century* (Hanover, N. H.: University Press of New England, 1987; G1201.E423 E7 1987 G&M).

they considered men and women to be equal, the Shakers also believed in celibacy. Except for the church which always had double doors so that the men and women could enter the church on an equal footing, each sex had its own buildings, labeled on the maps, showing where they spent their time and what activities were associated with both space and gender (see illustration).

Graphic Images on Maps

A variety of visual art material appearing on maps provides an additional source of information about women and their roles in society. For example, cartouches—the scroll-shaped frames containing the map's title, author, and publication information—often contain drawings or engravings. Designed as decorative features of the map, and including elaborate figures, scenes, and illustrations related to the map's content, they also reflect cultural perceptions related to place. Cartouches and other drawings on early modern maps frequently depict the prevailing image of the country or continent shown by feminine personifications, often with Europe portrayed as a genteel lady and America as a Native American woman.

The contrast between America and Europe was emphasized by European cartographers such as Joel Gascoyne, whose 1682 map of Carolina shows a bare-breasted, seductive America (G3870 1682.G3 TIL Vault). Perhaps the best-known allegorical image comes from one of the most important maps ever published of America, the John Mitchell map, which was used to draw the boundaries of the newly independent nation (G3300 1755.M56 Vault and later numerous editions). Mitchell's map shows a Native American woman seated above a male figure with symbols of New World richness—corn, lumber, fishing nets, a beaver, and coconut palm trees. The Native American theme on cartouches gradually gave way to a new image of "Liberty," an Anglo-Saxon woman who was often surrounded by symbols of freedom. One of the best known images in this genre can be seen on the 1783 Wallis map of the United States (G3700 1783.W3 Vault). (Both images are available online.) (See "'With Peace and Freedom Blest'" in this volume.)

Advertisements provide additional visual images related to time and place. Twentieth-century road maps published by major oil companies sometimes feature cover art such as the young, attractive woman driving her automobile along the open road, suggesting the growing independence of women (see illustration). A survey of road maps for Michigan, home of the automobile industry, indicates that during the decade of the 1930s more of these "independent women" appeared as artwork on maps than they did during the 1920s and 1940s. Oil company maps of all periods advertise the availability of clean restrooms to women and girls traveling by automobile. Road maps are filed in the Title Collection under the name of the state and the subject "roads"; sometimes they are also found under "gas" or "gasoline."

Shell Road Map: Pennsylvania *(Chicago: H. M. Goushá, 1933). Title Collection. Geography and Map Division. Printed with permission of Shell and Rand McNally.*

As the popularity of the automobile grew during the middle decades of the twentieth century, a new form of map became increasingly available. Primarily distributed by oil companies, road maps were found in almost every car in America. Their graphic designs illustrate life in America, particularly changes in society brought about by the widespread use of the automobile, including the growing independence of women.

Some thematic atlases contain more text, artwork, and photographs than maps. An example is the *Illustrated Atlas of Native American History* (Edison, N.J.: Chartwell Books, Inc., 1999; uncataloged) edited by Samuel Willard Crompton. Although the volume contains many maps, its primary value to scholars is its illustrations. There are photographs of the Cherokee Female Seminary, which was the first institution west of the Mississippi established solely for the education of women, and many illustrations, some taken from maps and government surveying reports. Artistic renditions of Native American life, pictographs, a formal portrait of Pocahontas, and an engraving after John White's drawing of a Florida Native American woman are also found in this work.

A similar atlas entitled *The Historical and Cultural Atlas of African Americans* (New York: Macmillan, 1991; E185.A8 1991) by Molefi K. Asante and Mark T. Mattson includes maps related to the life of Sojourner Truth. Other maps show African American women in the workforce, heads of household, birth rates, an age table for men and women, and the birthplaces of performing artists, including Leontyne Price, Mahalia Jackson, Josephine Baker, Diane McIntyre, Marian Anderson, Lena Horne, Pearl Bailey, and Ruby Dee. The atlas also contains many photographs and illustrations, including a section on women's contributions to abolitionism and examples of advertisements for the sale of slaves, including women and children.

A wide variety of graphic material can be found throughout the collections of the Geography and Map Division. *The Lowery Collection: A Descriptive List of Maps of the Spanish Possessions within the Present Limits of the United States, 1502–1820*, by Woodbury Lowery, edited with notes by Philip Lee Phillips (Washington: GPO, 1912; Z6021.A5 U6), not only provides a list of maps recording Spanish exploration and settlement in North America but also has beautiful, full-color images of women on its title page. Even the verso of World War II maps clipped from newspapers show women's clothing styles and accessories. Locating these resources is often time consuming but can be very rewarding.

WOMEN'S CONTRIBUTIONS TO GEOGRAPHY AND CARTOGRAPHY

Until recently, scant attention has been paid to women's contributions to the fields of geography and cartography. A group of articles by Alice C. Hudson, head of the Map Division of the New York Public Library, and Mary McMichael Ritzlin, a map dealer, has revised the erroneous perception that the fields of geography and cartography were solely the province of men.[14]

Women as Mapmakers

Hudson and her colleagues have systematically studied European and American cartographers and have discovered that women mapmakers have often been overlooked and their work has been unrecognized. They have succeeded in identifying approximately two hundred pre-twentieth-century mapmakers, most of whom worked in Europe. Much of the following discussion on American women cartographers is based on their publications and the database that they are developing on women associated with map creation and publication.

Several well-known historical maps and atlases in the Library's collections were produced by women. For example, Mary Biddle's (n.d.) name appears on the 1762 version of the Scull and Heap Map of Philadelphia as its joint editor with Matthew Clarkson. The oldest child of Nicholas Scull and Abigail Heap, Biddle married at age nineteen and gave birth to ten children. She apparently learned her cartographic skills from other members of her distinguished family, and when she and her husband fell upon hard times, she contributed economically to the family unit by editing this well-known map. The map, *To the Mayor Recorder Aldermen Common Council and Freemen of Philadelphia this plan of the improved part of the city surveyed and laid down by the late Nicholas Scull, Esqr.* . . . (Philadelphia: Matthew Clarkson and Mary Biddle, 1762; G3824.P5 1762 .S3 Vault), was republished a number of times, but this is the only edition that acknowledges Biddle's contribution. Both she and Clarkson are identified on the piece as the map's sellers, another example of the multiple roles women played in the early American map trade.

Although Eliza Colles (b. 1776) died in 1799 at the age of twenty-four, she had already engraved maps for her father, Christopher Colles, the publisher of the first American road atlas. Her name appears on plates 1 and 5 in the *Geographical Ledger and Systematized Atlas* by Christopher Colles of New York (New York: John Buel, 1794; G1201 .P2 C595 1794 Vault).

Women also were map publishers. Esther Lowe of New York published several maps and reissued an encyclopedia while working in New York between 1810 and 1815. Lydia Bailey (1779–1869) of Philadelphia was one of the most prolific of the women printers. She printed engraved maps, one of which appeared in 1830 and was used to illus-

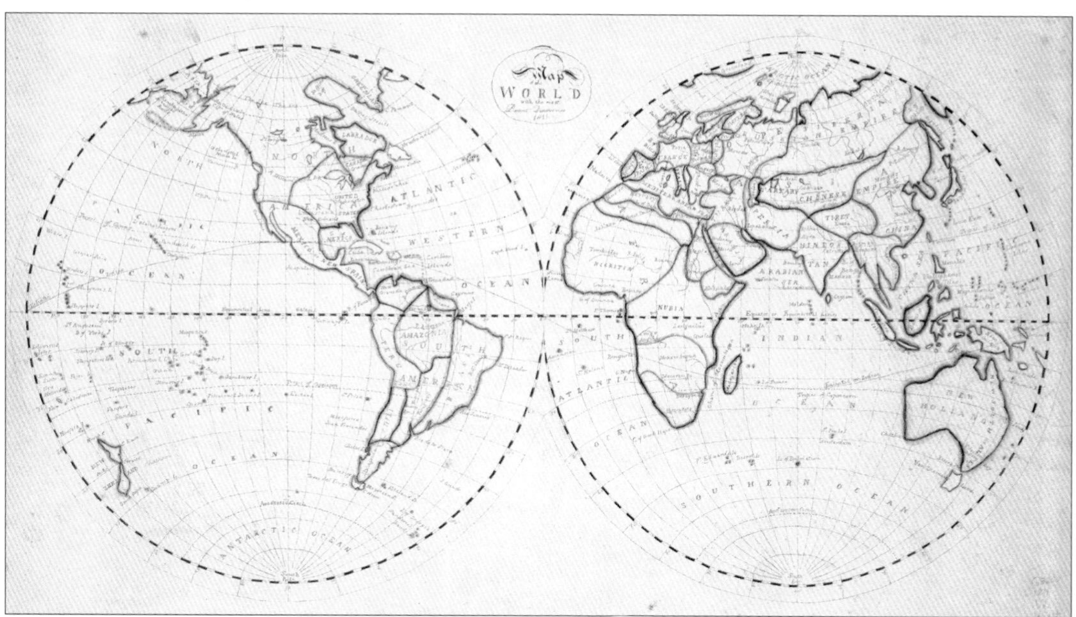

"Map of the world with the most recent discoveries." Manuscript map drawn by Mary Van Schaack of Kinderhook, New York, 1811 (G3200 1811 .V2 Vault). Geography and Map Division.

The Geography and Map Division has in its collections two maps by Mary Van Schaack (n.d.), drawn twenty-two years apart, indicating that world geography was a long-term interest of Van Schaack. The earlier work, a hand-colored manuscript map outlining the countries of the world, is pictured here.

trate a work on internal waterways in the United States. The Farmer family, consisting of the widowed Roxanna (n.d.), her daughter Esther (n.d.), and her two sons, took over the family business after the death of her husband in 1859. An example of Roxanna's work is a railroad map issued in 1862.

Ellen Eliza Fitz (b. 1836), an American working in Canada as a governess, in 1875 obtained a patent for an invention to mount globes. Her innovation mounted the globe so as to show the position of the sun and the length of days, nights, and twilight for the entire year. In her *Hand-Book of the Terrestrial Globe; or, Guide to Fitz's New Method of Mounting and Operating Globes, designed for the Use of Families, Schools, and Academies* (Boston: Ginn Brothers, 1876; General Collections), she explained how it worked. One of Fitz's globes, mounted and operated as she describes, is in the Geography and Map Division.

Even though the number of American women working in the map trade before the twentieth century was small, the works that they produced were of noteworthy quality. Little has been written about twentieth-century American women who may have continued this tradition. As Alice Hudson points out, considerably more research needs to be done in all areas where American women participated in mapmaking. Possible topics include the role of marriage and family patterns in the map trade, a reexamination of the navigational role that Sacagawea played as one of the leaders of the Lewis and Clark Expedition, and why so little is known about the work of twentieth-century women, who seem to have disappeared from the scene after women contributed so richly in earlier eras. Hudson's own contribution to the field has been to heighten awareness of the scope and extent of women's cartographic activities and accomplishments, as well as collecting detailed information on women cartographers.

Women Geographers

A glowing exception to the perceived absence of twentieth-century woman geographers and cartographers is the monumental work of Marie Tharp (b. 1920). The Geography and Map Division is currently processing a large collection that comprises some of the finest work ever produced by a woman cartographer. The Heezen-Tharp Collection, dating from the 1940s to the present, is based on the pioneering work of Bruce C. Heezen and Marie Tharp who were pioneers in exploration and mapping of the ocean floors.

The collection consists of primary data, includ-

Alvaro F. Espinosa (USGS), Wilbur Rinehart (World Data Center), and Marie Tharp (Lamont-Doherty Geological Observatory of Columbia University). Seismicity of the Earth, 1960–1980. *([Washington: Office of Naval Research?], 1981). Tharp Collection (uncataloged). Geography and Map Division. Copyright © 1981 by Marie Tharp and Rebecca M. Espinosa. Used by permission.*

Marie Tharp and Bruce Heezen's work proved that the ocean's Atlantic Ridge extended into the Arctic, went around the tips of both Africa and South America, and joined with similar structures in the Indian and Pacific Oceans, confirming that the Atlantic Ridge is part of a continuous set of ridges existing at the Earth's plate boundaries for over forty thousand miles. The geographers' work supported and confirmed the theory of plate tectonics, explaining earthquakes, volcanic activity, and changing formations on the ocean floors. This example of a base map, *World Ocean Floor Panorama,* originally published in 1977, shows the work of Heezen and Tharp, interpreted for publication by Heinrich Berann, an artist who worked with them over a long period of time. It superimposes new data on the seismicity of the Earth to illustrate clearly how earthquakes follow the Earth's shifting plates.

ing ship tracks and bathymetric soundings, bottom profiles, geologic and hydrologic data, information on gravity and magnetism, earthquake and seismic data, and a variety of water and ocean current data. In addition, secondary data in the collection consist of contour information, province maps, and Tharp's special domain—physiographic diagrams that she drew by hand. Tharp's hand-drawn, original manuscript maps of ocean floors are based on systematic study of each ocean's depths and contours. The maps provide compelling evidence of her contributions to geographic knowledge (see illustration). Rounding out the collection are globes, photographs, undersea cable data, various worksheets, preliminary drawings, and published maps used for points of reference.

In the course of their laborious work, Tharp and Heezen made a remarkable discovery. The Atlantic Ridge had long been known to exist, but what was not known was that there was a valley down its center. It was here that the continental plates were spreading as new material rose from the ridge itself. Dating of the rock proved that the material on both sides of the valley became older as the distance from the valley's center increased. It took Tharp almost a year to convince her male colleague of the accuracy of her findings before he was willing to publicly acknowledge their discovery.[15]

In addition to Tharp, who supported the work of her male colleague, there are legions of twentieth-century women who have worked in various settings as engravers, geographers, and cartographers, particularly in government agencies where individual authorship is seldom acknowledged. Once again, the true extent to which women have participated in the accumulation of knowledge about the earth and who have made maps has been obscured by the erroneous perception that geography and cartography are primarily male disciplines.

Women's Role in Geographic Education

One of the best-known women in the field of geographic education is Emma Hart Willard (1787–1870), who was also an innovative geographer and cartographer. The sixteenth of seventeen children in her family, she was a precocious child who, when hardly out of her teens, became the head of Middlebury Female Academy, a boarding school for girls. In 1821 the school relocated to Troy, New York, and was renamed the Troy Female Seminary. The curriculum taught by Mrs. Willard used maps for lessons in both history and geography. Dissatisfied with the textbooks of the period, she wrote her own, illustrated by one of her students, Elizabeth Sherrill. Willard also collaborated with William Channing Woodbridge in *A System of Universal Geography on the Principles of Comparison and Clarification* (Hartford: Oliver D. Cooke & Co, 1824; 2nd ed., 1827, G1019 .W715 1827), a text that revolutionized the study of geography. Many of her students themselves became geography educators, further disseminating her ideas and influence.

Willard was one of the first geographers to show on maps accurate information pertaining to the distribution and migration of Native Americans in the eastern United States. Rather than using the European concept of boundaries, she recognized and illustrated the mobility of tribes across large geographic areas, acknowledging Native American concepts of space. Her maps also reflect the loose affiliation between independent groups of Native Americans. The Library has many examples of her pioneering work, such as *Locations and Wanderings of the Aboriginal Tribes* from *A Series of Maps to Willard's History of the United States* (New York: White, Gallaher and White, 1828; G1201.S1 W52 1839 Vault).[16] Clearly women have long played a major role in the discipline of geography, paving the way for the recent work of feminist geographers.

Women's Map Collections

Several of the division's special collections were assembled by women and reflect the influence of female collections and collectors. The **Clara Barton** and **Margaret Mead** collections were acquired by the Library along with their manuscript collections. The thirty-six items in the Barton collection were assembled between 1877 and 1903 and are primarily maps of Europe and the United States. The Mead collection is smaller and consists of several sheets from map sets showing her study areas and other maps containing practical information, such as steamship routes, that Mead used for her work in the field.

In contrast, the **Ethel M. Fair** and the **Muriel H. Parry** collections are large, with well over eight hundred maps in each. Detailed finding aids exist for both collections. A card file subject catalog for the Fair Collection (G3701.A5 coll .F3 Fair) includes numerous subject headings but does not have one for "Women." The inventory for the uncataloged Parry Collection provides information about each individual map.

Both Fair and Parry collected pictorial maps, and both collections include a large number of maps made by women. A fascinating aspect of the maps in these collections is the way they convey cartographic information from the point of view of the women who made them. Several maps show women's college campuses—gender-specific space—and interpret the features of the area, often in great detail (see illustration).

There are also large numbers of historical thematic pictorial maps in the two collections. *A Map of Exploration in the Spanish Southwest, 1528 to 1793*, compiled by Joseph J. Hill (Los Angeles: Automobile Club of Southern California, ca. 1931–32; Fair Collection no. C654) depicts the route taken by the Anza party, which traveled overland from Tubac, then in the Mexican province of Sonora, to California in 1775. (See "Women on the Move" in this volume).

Few original contemporary maps match the degree of detailed information about historical events presented in thematic maps based on primary source material. Frequent use of thematic maps in educational settings, particularly in elementary schools where a majority of the teachers are women, may explain why so many of these maps have been created and collected by women.

The **Mary J. Webb Collection** (G4030 coll .W4) acquired in 1941, consists primarily of maps that were traced from original surveys in an effort to establish property rights to early Texas land grants. Copied in the early years of the twentieth century, the maps are listed and described in a finding aid, which in most cases names the original map sources.

The **Janet Green Collection,** given to the Library of Congress by her estate, is a magnificent collection of maps, many of which are both old and rare. It reflects Green's collecting interests, which spanned the globe and included maps from the sixteenth to the twentieth centuries. She was particularly interested in rare historic maps of Virginia. A cross-referenced finding aid arranged by call number of the individual maps in the collection and author is available for use in the division's reading room.

Women and Map Librarianship

Clara Egli LeGear (1896–1994) carried on the bibliographic work begun by the first chief of the Geography and Map Division, Phillip Lee Phillips. Originally hired as a typist, Clara LeGear joined the staff of the Library of Congress in 1914, an affiliation that she maintained until her death in 1994. She mastered all aspects of map librarianship, including cataloging, reference, acquisition, bibliography, and administration. During her

Emma Lee Aderholt and assistants. Bird's Eye View of the Campus of the Woman's College of the University of North Carolina *(Greensboro, N.C.: Jos. J. Stone & Co., n.d.). Fair Collection (no. C433). Geography and Map Division.*

Sponsored by the Home Economics Club, this map of the Woman's College of the University of North Carolina was drawn by Emma Lee Aderholt "and assistants." Its scale is indicated by an inchworm saying, "I'm measuring as fast as I can," a bow to the stereotypically masculine domains of measurements and mathematics. Around the border of the map are illustrations of "then and now" showing how things have changed since the college was founded—where women once rode horses to college, they now travel by automobile, train, boat, or airplane. A scene showing women in caps and gowns notes that their graduation day will be a sad one. The colorful, detailed images show both a sense of humor and a deep attachment to alma mater.

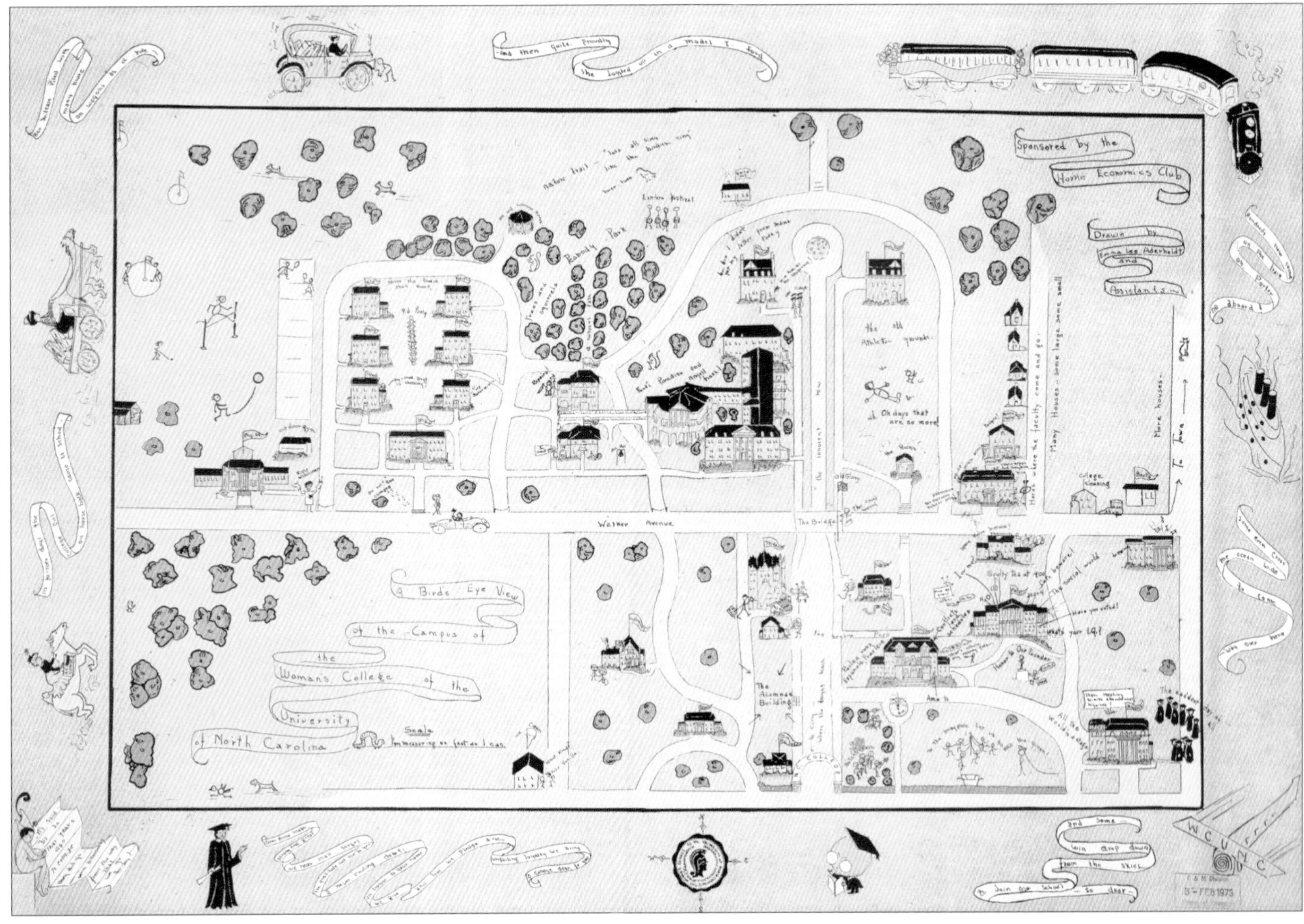

first thirty-five years in the Geography and Map Division, she held positions in cataloging and reference and for four years was assistant division chief. During that time, she completed her education, studying library science, geology, cartography, and editing.

After World War II, LeGear devoted her full attention to writing and publishing bibliographic works in her field. She continued this work into retirement, completing the massive *List of Geographical Atlases in the Library of Congress* shortly before her death (see above).

Mining the collections of the Geography and Map Division in search of information for historical studies related to American women requires creativity, persistence, and patience. For the researcher who is able and willing to invest the necessary time and energy to find and interpret the rich variety of geographical data available, the rewards are considerable. But the Geography and Map Division is only the first place to look for cartographic resources in the Library of Congress. Besides the maps and atlases housed in the Geography and Map Division, cartographic material can also be found in other parts of the Library. Some of the panoramic maps are housed in the Prints and Photographs Division. Rare books containing maps, atlases that are part of special collections, or ephemeral maps are held in the Rare Book and Special Collections Division. Maps from manuscript collections may be stored as integral parts of personal papers or organizational records in the Manuscript Division, if they have not been separated from the manuscript material and transferred to the Geography and Map Division. Many if not most of the Library's thematic maps, containing extremely useful and very specific material for researchers of American women's history, are bound into books, serials, and government documents found in the General Collections or in the Serial and Government Publications Division. Doctoral dissertations available in the Microform Reading Room are another excellent source for cartographic information.

Many Library materials gain deeper meaning when used in conjunction with maps. Travel literature, discussed in chapter 1, is an excellent example of textual material that is greatly enhanced by referring to maps and nautical charts. Foreign-language materials (see chapter 12) are supplemented and enhanced by cartographic information, which is sometimes stored as part of foreign-language collections but more frequently found in the Geography and Map Division. Set maps provide a backdrop for studies of women ethnographers, botanists, and zoologists, photographers, or news reporters. Projects related to women in the military serving overseas are supported by detailed topographic maps, including the series maps of Indochina and Thailand that are frequently requested by Vietnam War veterans (U.S. Army Map Service, 196-; G8020.S50 U5 and U51). A good biography is incomplete without an understanding of the subject's physical and cultural environment that can be provided only by using cartographic resources.

Because bits of relevant data can be so widely distributed not only throughout the collections of the Geography and Map Division but throughout the Library of Congress as a whole, it is important to be properly prepared before coming to the Library. Specific information about place-names, dates, and property owners will enable you to focus on the portions of the cartographic collections that are most likely to yield significant material.

Despite the many challenges involved, scholars of American women's history and all other researchers are warmly welcomed and are encouraged to use the Library's cartographic collections, especially those of the Geography and Map Division. Because cartographic resources have long been underused in historical research as primary source material, the odds are excellent that new information will be discovered that will lead to a more complete understanding of the women in America's past.

I would like to thank my colleagues, cartographic specialists Ronald E. Grim, James A. Flatness, and Gary L. Fitzpatrick for their assistance in identifying source material and recommending items for inclusion; digital conversion coordinator Gene E. Roberts for scanning and processing cartographic images; Gary L. Fitzpatrick for creating a digital map from the National Cancer Institute database; and program assistant Myra A. Laird for compiling bibliographic information and locating material. To the Geography and Map Division's chief, John R. Hébert, I am indebted for his granting me both the time and the independence to write and illustrate the chapter as I envisioned it, and for his wholehearted support of this project.

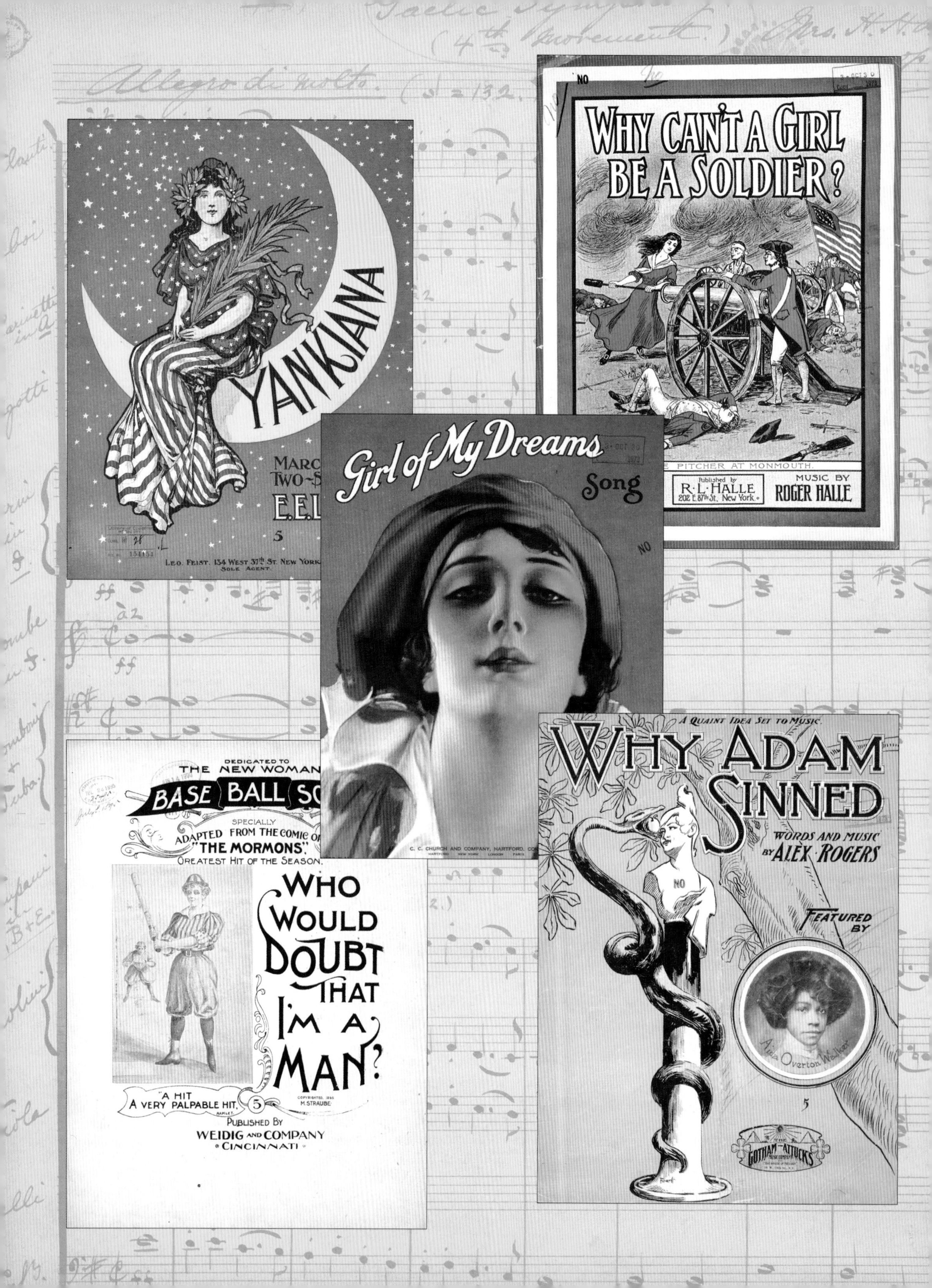

YANKIANA

MARC

TWO-S

E.E.L

5

LEO. FEIST. 134 WEST 37th ST. NEW YORK

SOLE AGENT.

WHY CAN'T A GIRL BE A SOLDIER?

E PITCHER AT MONMOUTH.

Published by R·L·HALLE 202 E. 87th St. New York.

MUSIC BY ROGER HALLE

Girl of My Dreams

Song

C. C. CHURCH AND COMPANY, HARTFORD, CO

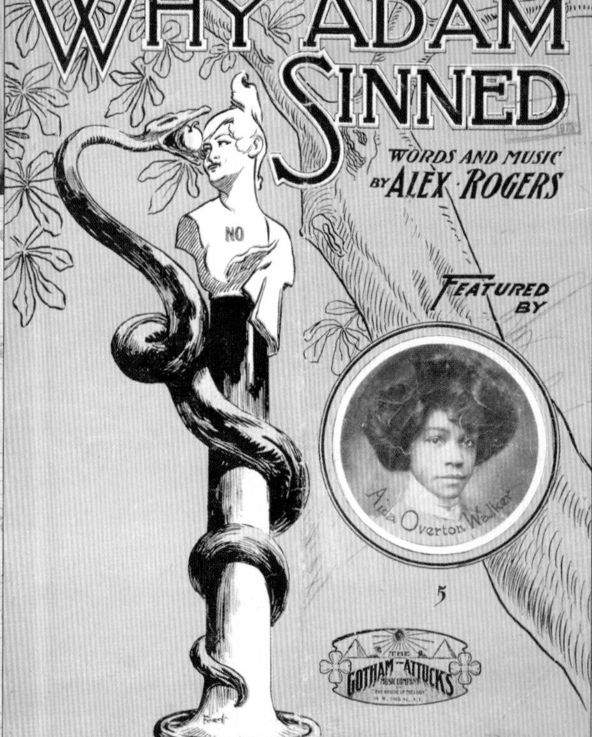

8 Music Division

Robin Rausch

Whether a mother crooning lullabies or an opera diva, a neighborhood piano teacher or a rock star—women have always made music. They compose it, perform it, inspire it, commission it, collect it, and otherwise fill their leisure time in its pursuit. The collections of the Music Division demonstrate women's music making in all its many guises.

It is here that you can find the volume of piano music collected and bound for the private use of Eleanor P. Custis, better known as Nellie Custis, granddaughter of George and Martha Washington (M1.A11 Case vol. 26). One of hundreds of similar volumes compiled by women during the nineteenth century, it contains predominantly pieces by European male composers yet, nonetheless, reflects the role of music in women's lives. Musical accomplishment was a mark of the well-bred woman, and the piano in particular was most often her instrument of choice. Arthur Loesser provides an entertaining history of women's relationship with the piano in his *Men, Women, and Pianos: A Social History* (1954; reprint, New York: Dover Publications, 1990; ML650.L64 1990), another example of what may be found on the Music Division's shelves.

Women's work as composers can be examined through the vast holdings of music scores that contain classically conceived compositions such as Rebecca Clarke's *Sonata for Viola and Piano* (M226.C), as well as popular songs like those of singer and songwriter Joni Mitchell. Countless other songs depict women in lyrics, titles, and cover art. You can find a copy of the sheet music to Helen Reddy's hit "I Am Woman" (M1630.2.B), find out when it was number one on the Billboard charts (the week of December 9, 1972), and look up her famous acceptance speech at the Grammy awards when she thanked God "because She makes everything possible."[1]

Books about women and their relationship to music include biographies of women musicians, ethnomusicological investigations, and histories. The Music Division is the place to come to read Marian Anderson's autobiography, *My Lord, What a Morning* (1956; reprint, Madison: University of Wisconsin Press, 1992; ML420.A6A3 1992), research women's role in American Indian music (*Women in North American Indian Music* [Bloomington, Ind.: Society for Ethnomusicology, 1989; ML3550.W65 1989], edited by Richard Keeling), or find out about women and rock and roll (Lucy O'Brien's *She Bop: The Definitive History of Women in Rock, Pop, and Soul* [New York: Penguin Books, 1996; ML82.O27 1996]).

The special collections of the Music Division include the performing arts of dance and theater as well as music, and they contain the personal papers of many creative women. Researchers can study the compositional process of Ruth Crawford Seeger through her original musical sketches (**Charles and Ruth Crawford Seeger Collection**), look through the scrapbooks of opera star Beverly Sills (**Beverly Sills Collection**), and read the correspondence between Elizabeth Coolidge and Martha Graham discussing the creation of a new American work—a ballet that would ultimately be set to music by Aaron Copland and become the much-loved *Appalachian Spring* (**Elizabeth Sprague Coolidge Collection**).

The music holdings of the Library of Congress

Popular songs portray women in countless ways. Patriotic symbols frequently take female form, as seen on the cover of "Yankiana" (1905) by E. E. Loftis (M28.L), and the archetypal fantasy woman depicted in "Girl of My Dreams" (1920) by Charles and Henry Tobias (Edison Sheet Music Collection) has inspired many a composer. "Why Can't a Girl Be a Soldier?" (1905) by John J. Nilan and Roger Halle (Edison Sheet Music Collection), and "Who Would Doubt That I'm a Man?" (1895), a song by A. F. Groebl (M1508) about a woman baseball player, question stereotypical roles. "Why Adam Sinned" (1910) by Alex Rogers (Edison Sheet Music Collection) offers a new answer to the age-old question: because he didn't have a mother.

are regarded as one of the best music research collections in the world. Estimated at over twelve million items, they are unmatched in their coverage of both classical music and popular music of the United States. They are also strong in European classical music, opera scores and libretti, early imprints of works dealing with music literature and theory, and music periodical literature from the eighteenth century to the present. These collections consist of information sources on paper: the musical notation of scores and books and periodicals about music. Music that is transmitted orally—as is that of many ethnic traditions—is rarely written down as notes on paper. These traditions are best represented in recordings found in the Recorded Sound Section or the American Folklife Center.

The Performing Arts Reading Room is administered by the Music Division and is the access point for all print and manuscript sources whose subject is music, comprising everything in Class M and over five hundred special collections of primary source material in music.[2] The Music Division actively began to collect primary source material in theater and dance in the 1990s. Although presently small in number, these collections are significant—and include the papers of Martha Graham as well as the archives of the Federal Theatre Project. Aside from these special collections, however, the performing arts of theater and dance are represented here only in the small reference collection in the reading room. Most published monographs in dance are found in class GV. Theater monographs are more widely distributed: the majority are in class P and others are found in class N and class T. Material classed in other than class M is in the General Collections and should be requested through the Main Reading Room in the Jefferson Building or the Book Service Desk in the Adams Building. Researchers interested in women and the performing arts should also be aware that there may be material relevant to their study in other divisions. Sound recordings, as noted above, are in the custody of the Motion Picture, Broadcasting, and Recorded Sound Division, which maintains a Recorded Sound Reference Center adjacent to the Performing Arts Reading Room. The Manuscript Division, Prints and Photographs Division, and American Folklife Center also contain collections related to women in the performing arts.

PERFORMING ARTS READING ROOM
James Madison Building, 1st floor, room LM 113
Hours: Monday through Saturday, 8:30 a.m. to 5:00 p.m.
Requests for material may be submitted until 4:15 p.m.
Closed Sunday and federal holidays.
Telephone: 202 707-5507
Fax: 202 707-0621
Address: Music Division, Library of Congress, James Madison Building, 101 Independence Avenue, SE, Washington, DC 20540-4710.
E-mail: mdiv@loc.gov
Web site: <http://www.loc.gov/rr/perform/>
Access and use: The Performing Arts Reading Room is the service point for general collections in music (class M) and special collections in music, theater, and dance. The majority of theater and dance holdings are housed in the Library's General Collections, and may be requested through the Main Reading Room in the Jefferson Building or the Book Service Desk in the Adams Building. The Performing Arts Reading Room is open to all readers of college age and above who have a Library of Congress reader registration card. Although no appointments are necessary, researchers wishing to use special collections are advised to write or telephone before visiting. Collections that are unprocessed, or currently being cataloged, may not be available at a given time. Photocopying restrictions may apply to unpublished material and items in extremely fragile condition. Microfilm is served in place of the original in cases where rare items have been filmed for preservation purposes. Researchers should consult with the librarian on duty if it is necessary to examine the original. In all instances, when a microfilm exists, photocopies must be made from it and not from the original. Additional information on the division's services and facilities may be found on the Music Division's Web site.

USING THE COLLECTIONS

The Music Division has custody of all material in class M, music copyright deposits, and special collections in music, theater, and dance. The class M holdings are organized according to the three major subdivisions of the class M schedule: M for music scores, ML for literature about music, and MT for works on musical instruction and study. (See chapter 1 for a brief discussion of the Library of Congress classification system.) The division's card catalog reflects this organization with separate sections for the M, ML, and MT classes. The scores, or M, section of the card catalog contains bibliographic records for music scores cataloged prior to 1980. It is further subdivided into two alphabetical files, the first for personal names and the second for titles. A separate classed catalog, in call number order, is located at the end of the card catalog and provides subject access to scores. The ML and MT portions of the card catalog contain bibliographic records for books about music cataloged up to 1978. In each of these sections names, titles, and subjects are interfiled. Scores and books about music cataloged after 1980 and 1978, respectively, may be found in the Library of Congress Online Catalog. Searches in the online catalog may be limited by type of material; scores may be specified by selecting "music (printed)" as a search limit. There are, however, bibliographic records for older scores in the online catalog that would be excluded from such a search. If you are unable to locate a piece in either catalog, ask the reference librarian for assistance.[3]

The most important thing to remember when searching for music scores is that the card and online catalogs contain records for less than 20 percent of the Music Division's holdings. Most of the sheet music in the collection is classified only (assigned a classification number but not cataloged) or it is filed by its copyright registration number. To request a search for music by a woman that is not found in the catalogs, you must provide a composer's name and a description or genre of the kind of music sought. A reference librarian will then determine the appropriate call number. The researcher interested in the song repertoire of Carrie Jacobs Bond, for example, could submit a search request for music shelved under the call number M1621.B, where M1621 denotes scores of solo songs with piano accompaniment and .B relates to the composer's surname. Such a search, specifying "all" or "everything" instead of a distinctive title, would retrieve all the songs by Carrie Jacobs Bond classified under this number.

Music copyright deposits are shelved by their copyright registration number. Those that predate 1978 are stored off-site and require two or three days to retrieve. The only bibliographic access to this material is through the catalogs of the Copyright Office. These catalogs are arranged in chronological segments by year of copyright registration: 1870–1897, 1898–1937, 1938–1945, 1946–1954, 1955–1970, and 1971–1977. Since 1978, registrations have been recorded in the online catalog of the Copyright Office (see <http://www.loc.gov/copyright/rb.html>). Entries are filed by title and claimant, which may be the composer or the publisher. The catalogs do not follow library filing rules, nor do they always allow for multiple access points through added entries. Researchers must be diligent in looking under every possible name or title in every possible time period related to their query.

Finding aids are on file in the reading room for special collections in music, theater, and dance that are processed and available for use. Researchers wishing to use special collections are advised to write or call before their visit to confirm the availability of the material they wish to see. At times, even processed collections are unavailable owing to additional processing requirements or conservation needs. Occasionally, individual items may be on exhibit and not accessible. It is the general policy of the Music Division that unprocessed collections are not served. When such unprocessed collections are in some semblance of order, however, it is possible to get special permission to see them. Such permission is granted on a case-by-case basis by the head of the Acquisitions and Processing Section in consultation with the head of the Reader Services Section.

A card index to selected correspondence is kept behind the circulation desk and may be examined upon request. Called the "salmon file," for the color of the card stock on which it is typed, this index covers correspondence in special collections that were processed in the Music Division circa 1965–80. For correspondence in collections processed after 1980, the respective finding aids should be consulted. To find letters written by a particular individual, you must often search beyond that person's personal papers, unless the individual in question was meticulous about keeping copies of the correspondence she or he sent. The Martha Graham Collection, for example, contains little correspondence written by Graham. Many Graham letters are found in other collections, however, notably the Aaron Copland Collection, the Elizabeth Sprague Coolidge Collection, and a file known as Old Music Division Correspondence. These are all indexed in the salmon file.

Unpublished manuscripts, both music and literary, may require written permission from the author or composer, or their estate, before photocopies can be made. The Music Division maintains a permissions file with contact information identifying who holds rights to materials in many of its special collections and will share this information when available. It is ultimately the responsibility of the researcher to determine who holds rights and to obtain permission for use.

MUSIC SCORES

Music scores are an obvious primary source for researchers interested in women composers. That they may also be of use to those whose main focus is not music is less evident. Women appear frequently as the subject of popular song and song lyrics, and sheet music cover art can be an instructive tool for the historian. Both music by women and music about women can be found in abundance in the collections of the Music Division.

In Search of the Woman Composer: Finding Music by Women

When the eminent psychologist Carl E. Seashore published his now-famous article "Why No Great Women Composers?" in 1940, he was continuing a long tradition espousing the inferiority of women in music. As far back as 1880, music critic George P. Upton argued that "it does not seem that woman will ever originate music in its fullest and grandest harmonic forms. She will always be the recipient and interpreter, but there is little hope she will be the creator." Seashore concurred, theorizing that "woman's fundamental urge is to be beautiful, loved, and adored as a person; man's urge is to provide and achieve in a career."[4] Women's defenders frequently mentioned the lack of training available to women and lamented that women were too quick to support men's efforts at their own expense. Pianist Amy Fay (1844–1928) wrote in 1900 that "[w]omen have been too much taken up with helping and encouraging men to place a proper value on their own talent, which they are too prone to underestimate and to think not worth making the most of." And English composer Ethel Smyth (1858–1944), in her *Female Pipings in Eden,* proclaimed "there is not at this present moment (1933) one single middle-aged woman alive who has had the musical education that has fallen to men as a matter of course, without any effort on their part, ever since music was!"[5]

Today the field of women and music is a thriving branch of women's studies. Research has shown that women have been composing music through the ages just as their male counterparts have, and the scores collection at the Library of Congress bears this out. Music scores make up the largest portion of the Music Division collections, and women's works are amply represented. From new editions of chant by Saint Hildegard (1098–1179) and first editions of piano pieces by Amy Beach (1867–1944) to original copyright deposits of songs by blues singer Ma Rainey (1886–1939), the scores collection is rich with the music of women.

Music scores are cataloged and classified according to genre and medium of performance and the composer's name. Although the subject heading "Music by women composers" exists, it is used only when gender is mentioned as a significant aspect of a work. Thus, the *Historical Anthology of Music by Women,* edited by James R. Briscoe (Bloomington: Indiana University Press, 1987; M2.H68 1987), receives this subject heading, but Clara Schumann's *Ausgewählte Klavierwerke* (München: G. Henle, 1987; M22.S393 K6 1987) is assigned only the heading "Piano music". Obviously, the vast majority of pieces by women composers will not be represented by a subject heading that denotes gender.

SEARCH TIPS: Numerous sources are available to assist in locating music by women composers. Aaron Cohen's *International Encyclopedia of Women Composers,* 2nd ed. (New York: Books & Music [USA], 1987; ML105.C7 1987) and *The Norton/Grove Dictionary of Women Composers* (New York: W.W. Norton, 1994; ML105.N66 1994) provide extensive work lists and biographical information. Specialized bibliographies include *American Women Songwriters* by Virginia Grattan (Westport, Conn.: Greenwood Press, 1993; ML106.U3 G73 1993), *Music by Black Women Composers* (Chicago: Center for Black Music Research, 1995; ML128.W7 W35 1995) by Helen Walker-Hill, and numerous bibliographies from the Greenwood Press Music Reference Collection series: Joan Meggett's *Keyboard Music by Women Composers* (Westport, Conn.: Greenwood Press, 1981; ML128.H35 M43), Heidi Boenke's *Flute Music by Women Composers* (Westport, Conn.: Greenwood Press, 1988; ML128.F7 B6 1988), Rose-Marie Johnson's *Violin Music by Women Composers* (Westport, Conn.: Greenwood Press, 1989; ML128.W7J63 1989), Adel Heinrich's *Organ and Harpsichord Music by Women Composers* (Westport, Conn.: Greenwood Press, 1991; ML128.O6 O73 1991), Janna MacAuslan and Kristan Aspen's *Guitar Music by Women Composers* (Westport, Conn.: Greenwood Press, 1997; ML128.G8 M33 1997), and *Piano Music by Black Women Composers* (Westport, Conn.: Greenwood Press, 1992; ML128.P3 W3 1992) by Helen Walker-Hill. Barbara Garvey Jackson's *"Say Can You Deny Me": A Guide to Surviving Music by Women from the 16th through the 18th Centuries* (Fayetteville: University of Arkansas Press, 1994; ML128.W7 J3 1994) is an invaluable union list of music manuscripts and early imprints that includes some of the earliest compositions by American women.

Music copyright deposits are another important source for research. The copyright law of 1870 brought eighty years of copyright records and deposits to the Library of Congress and ensured that all future registrations and deposits would come directly to the Library. Copyright deposits are the reason the music collections are so strong in holdings of music from the United States and account for the extensive number of popular songs. Popular song is less well represented as notes on paper from 1978 on owing to a change in the copyright law that allows music to be submitted for copyright in recorded format. Much popular music is registered this way today and becomes the custody of the Motion Picture, Broadcasting, and Recorded Sound Division. Researching copyright records can be tedious and time consuming (see "Using the Collections" above) but it can reap real rewards. Unpublished manuscripts of African American composer Florence Price (1888–1953) have been discovered in this way, as well as original copyright deposits of songs by blues singer Bessie Smith (1894–1937) and jazz pianist and composer Mary Lou Williams (1910–1981).

Topical Research in Popular Song

A woman's "no" is "yes,"
A woman's "don't" is "do,"
And tho' she says contrary things,
She means the same as you.
—from "A Woman's No! Is Yes!" by J. Walker (1909)

Besides being creators of popular song, women and the roles they inhabit are also often its subject. Popular song research can provide a picture of an era, a rich social commentary on women's lives through the ages. Fashion, hairstyles, and popular trends of a time may be seen in sheet music cover art (see also chapter 6). Current ideas and opinions can also be heard in song titles and lyrics. The bloomer craze, for example, inspired many nineteenth-century songwriters. The cover of "My Sweet Little Bloomer Girl" (1895) (M1622.R), words by H. J. Craig, music by E. D. Roberts, features a photograph of a woman wearing bloomers sitting astride a bicycle. P. H. Van der Weyde weighed in against the new fashion with his "Anti Bloomer Schottisch" (1851) (M1.A12 I vol. 40), which is "respectfully dedicated to the ladies who dislike the bloomer costume and are opposed to its adoption." Motherhood is extolled in "The Hand That Rocks the Cradle Rules the World" (1909) (M1622.H), words by Carroll Fleming, music by Abe Holzmann:

In childhood all our greatest men learned at their mother's knee
The lesson that in after years has set our country free
And made the hearts of tyrants tremble, far across the sea,—
Our battle cry "For Home and Mother" dear.

From the social mores preceding prohibition in "Good-bye, Wild Women, Good-bye!" (1919) (Leo Feist Sheet Music Collection, box 13), words by Howard Johnson and Milton Ager, music by George W. Meyer:

After the country goes dry,
Good-bye, wild women, good-bye!
How on earth do you expect to win 'em?
Unless you get a little bit of good liquor in 'em,
The girlies will start to act shy,
Right after the first of July;
Then ev'ry night you'll see many a sinner,
Taking his own little wifie to dinner,
The minute the country goes dry,
Good-bye, wild women, good-bye!

to the sassy independence of "No One's Fool" (1921) (Leo Feist Sheet Music Collection, box 13), by Phil Furman and Fred Rose:

Why should I let some preacher give me away
When it took me so long to get this way
I'm going to make this world get up and say
"There goes no one's fool!"

popular song provides a unique snapshot of a subject in the context of its age, and often depicts women as seen by men.

Topical research in popular song is challenging because the number of songs in the Library's collections is so great and the subject access to them so limited. This type of material usually falls into the "classified not cataloged" category or is simply filed by copyright registration number.

The classification schedule for music (class M) is only marginally helpful in providing subject access to songs. There are numbers for songs about specific topics that allow a subject search by calling up pieces with that call number. Songs about prominent or notorious people, for example, will be found classified as M1659.5 followed by the first letter of the subject's last name. This is where songs about Amelia Earhart are found (M1659.5.E). Songs about political parties and movements are classified as M1664 (collections) and M1665 (separate songs). For example, woman's suffrage songs are located here under M1664.W8 and M1665.W8. Patriotic societies and organizations have their own song numbers as well and include such groups as the Daughters of the American Revolution (M1676.D3), Daughters of Union Veterans of the Civil War (M1676.D4), Gold Star Mothers (M1676.G6), United Daughters of the Confederacy (M1676 .U7), and the Ladies' Auxiliary (M1676.V42). The classes M1977–M1978 are assigned to songs of special character and arranged topically. Homemakers and housewives, mothers, nurses, secretaries, and women in general are just some of the subjects included within this class. Searching these topical classes, however, should not be considered exhaustive; only about 1 percent of such material finds its way here. Songs that are topical in nature more typically are found under the general number for popular songs and among the copyright deposits. Locating these may require the use of reference sources that index songs by subject, searching titles that begin with a topical term, and the help of a little serendipity.

We'll Show you when we come to Vote
THE GREAT WOMAN'S SUFFRAGE
Vote for Susan B. Anthony For President
For Vice President Mrs. Geo. F. Train
Vote Early and Often
Down with Male Rule
FOR LADIES
FOR GENTS
Ballot Box
Song & Chorus by
FRANK HOWARD.
TOLEDO, O.
Published at W.W. Whitney's "Palace of Music"
AL. JOLSON'S TERRIFIC HIT
WHEN THE GROWN UP LADIES ACT LIKE BABIES
I'VE GOT TO LOVE 'EM THAT'S ALL
Words By Joe Young & Edgar Leslie
Music By Maurice Abrahams.
DEDICATED TO
"THE MOTHERS OF ALL THE BOYS WHO ARE TENTING TONIGHT PREPARING TO FIGHT"
FOR THE GOOD OLD U.S.A.
I'M RAISING MY BOY TO BE A SOLDIER
TO FIGHT FOR THE
·U·S·A·
Words By
LEO J. RYAN
Music By
MRS. LEO J. RYAN
EVERY HIT =A= HOME RUN!
A MOTHER'S PLEA FOR PEACE
I DIDN'T RAISE MY BOY TO BE A SOLDIER
McCORMACK & IRVING
LYRICS BY ALFRED BRYAN
MUSIC BY AL. PIANTADOSI
LEO. FEIST NEW YORK
RESPECTFULLY DEDICATED TO KATHRYN OSTERMANN
THE HAND THAT ROCKS THE CRADLE RULES THE WORLD.
INTRODUCED BY
WORDS BY CARROLL FLEMING
AUTHOR OF "A ROSE WITH A BROKEN STEM"
MUSIC BY ABE HOLZMANN
COMPOSER OF "SMOKY MOKES" "HUNKY DORY" "CALANTHE WALTZES" ETC. ETC.
FEIST & FRANKENTHALER

SEARCH TIPS: Subject indexes to popular song literature are found in *The Great Song Thesaurus* by Roger Lax and Frederick Smith, 2nd ed. (New York: Oxford University Press, 1989; ML128.S3 L4 1989), *A Resource Guide to Themes in Contemporary American Song Lyrics, 1950–1985* by B. Lee Cooper (Westport, Conn.: Greenwood Press, 1986; ML156.4.P6 C66 1986), *The Green Book of Songs by Subject: The Thematic Guide to Popular Music,* by Jeff Green, 4th edition (Nashville, Tenn.: Professional Desk References, 1995; ML156.4.P6G73 1994) and *The Stecheson Classified Song Directory,* by Anthony and Anne Stecheson, (Hollywood, Calif.: Music Industry Press, 1961; ML128.V7 S83). For a brief historical survey of what songs were popular in a given year, *Variety Music Cavalcade,* by Julius Mattfeld, 3rd edition (Englewood Cliffs, N. J.: Prentice-Hall, 1971; ML128.V7 M4 1971) is helpful. Though not a subject index, this volume provides a chronology of vocal and instrumental music popular in the United States from 1620 to 1969.

Subject searching of a limited variety is possible in the title portion of the card catalog for music scores by looking up titles that begin with a specific word. Searching under "woman" or "mother," for example, will locate songs whose titles begin with those words. Since most of the popular song holdings are not represented in this catalog, this type of topical search is of limited use. The same strategy, however, can be used to search copyright records. To search for songs about the suffrage movement, go to the relevant chronological section of the catalog of copyright registrations and search under words like "woman," "suffrage," and "vote." A search of the late nineteenth- and early twentieth-century copyright records reveals many suffrage songs whose titles begin with these words, though undoubtedly there are many more with titles that do not begin with one of these terms. In addition, this search also brought to light several songs on the theme of "A Woman's No! Is Yes!" from this same time period, just one example of the sort of serendipitous find one can make when searching copyright deposits.

Electronic resources such as the World Wide Web have made title keyword searching of sheet music easier. American Memory, a collection of online resources compiled by the Library of Congress National Digital Library program, contains a wealth of performing arts collections. *Music for the Nation: American Sheet Music, 1870–1885* reproduces in digital format more than 47,000 pieces of sheet music registered for copyright during this time. The accompanying essay, "A Decade of Music in America, 1870–79," provides an excellent context for popular song of this era. Also a part of American Memory are *Historic American Sheet Music: 1850–1920* and *African American Sheet Music, 1850–1920,* collaborative efforts with Duke University and Brown University, respectively, featuring selected songs from their collections. All of these digital collections offer keyword title text searching and digitized images of the music itself, including covers and advertisements on back and inside covers. With future plans to add music copyright deposits from 1820 to 1860 and, later, music deposits from the Civil War era, American Memory will eventually provide access to the sheet music of nearly the entire nineteenth century.

Women are called to action in the suffrage song "We'll Show You When We Come to Vote" (1869) by Frank Howard (M1665.W8H), yet infantilized in "When the Grown Up Ladies Act like Babies" (1914) by Joe Young, Edgar Leslie, and Maurice Abrahams (Edison Sheet Music Collection). Mothers figure prominently in popular song, especially during times of war. "I Didn't Raise My Boy to Be a Soldier" (1915) by Alfred Bryan and Al Piantadosi (M1646.P) is countered by the hawkish "I'm Raising My Boy to Be a Soldier to Fight for the U.S.A." (1917) by Leo J. Ryan and Mrs. Leo J. Ryan (M1646.R). "The Hand That Rocks the Cradle Rules the World" (1901) by Carroll Fleming (Leo Feist Sheet Music Collection) is a paean to all mothers whose noble sons, it is assumed, will gladly go forth to battle when their country calls.

RESEARCHING WOMEN AND MUSIC

In addition to music as notes on paper, class M includes class ML, literature about music, and class MT, works of instruction and study. Class MT is a relatively small class and contains books on music education and pedagogy, theory instruction, and musical analyses. Most books dealing with the topic of women and music will be found in class ML: biographies and published letters of women musicians, histories of women in music, and musicological gender studies.

Bibliographies and Subject Headings

Published bibliographies of literature on women and music began to appear in the late 1970s as women's studies programs gained legitimacy. Of particular note among these are Adrienne Fried Block's *Women in American Music* (Westport, Conn.: Greenwood Press, 1979; ML128.W7 B6), which covers colonial times to 1978, and Margaret D. Ericson's *Women and Music: A Selective Annotated Bibliography on Women and Gender Issues in Music, 1987–1992* (New York: G.K. Hall, 1996; ML128.W7 E75 1996). The explosive growth of writing on women and music is evident in this latter work, which requires four hundred pages to cover five years of publications.

Subject access to cataloged monographs on women and music is provided through *Library of Congress Subject Headings* (LCSH). Books about individual musicians may be found by searching personal names as subjects. Subject headings that are qualified by sex or ethnic group, such as "Women composers," "Women musicians," "African American women musicians," or "Women jazz musicians," are used only when the sex or ethnic group is mentioned as a significant aspect of the work. Biographies of Dolly Parton, for example, receive the subject heading "Country musicians—United States—Biography," whereas Mary A. Bufwack and Robert K. Oermann's *Finding Her Voice: The Saga of Women in Country Music* (New York: Henry Holt, 1995; ML3524.B83 1995) receives the subject heading "Women country musicians—United States—Biography" because the fact that the country musicians are women is an integral part of the study.

Gender studies in music may be located by searching under the following subject headings: "Gender identity in music," "Gay musicians," "Homosexuality and music," "Sex in music," and "Feminism and music." Here the subject heading "Gay musicians" includes both gay men and lesbians. A book like *Queering the Pitch: The New Gay and Lesbian Musicology* edited by Philip Brett, Elizabeth Woods, and Gary C. Thomas (New York: Routledge, 1994; ML55.Q44 1993) is assigned the subject heading "Gay musicians," referring to both men and women. And Susan McClary's *Feminine Endings: Music, Gender, and Sexuality* (Minneapolis: University of Minnesota Press, 1991; ML82.M38 1990) is assigned "Feminism and music" and "Sex in music," but not "Gender identity in music" despite the term *gender* in the title. The rules governing subject heading assignment are not always apparent to the end user. Researchers should take note and make use of the large red volumes that make up *Library of Congress Subject Headings,* 19th edition, to locate established headings and related terms (see chapter 1).

Periodicals

Periodicals that deal primarily with music are also classified in the ML class. Those that cover other subjects in addition to music, such as *Rolling Stone,* are shelved in the General Collections, with current issues available in the Newspaper and Current Periodical Reading Room. Music periodical indexes available online include *Music Index* (1979–1999), *International Index to Music Periodicals* (from 1996 forward), *Répertoire International de Littérature Musicale (RILM)* (from 1969 forward, available through FirstSearch), and *Répertoire International de la Presse Musicale (RIPM),* an index of nineteenth-century music periodicals. Print copies of *Music Index* (ML118.M84) provide coverage of music periodicals dating back to 1949. A periodical index card file located at the end of the card catalog provides citations to many older music periodicals not covered in the standard music periodical indexes. Although this card file reflects somewhat idiosyncratic interests of its time and its compilers, it can prove invaluable for locating references to articles that otherwise might never be found. The manually typed or handwritten cards index articles about musical topics from a variety of music periodicals dating from the late nineteenth century to around 1940. A search under "women" reveals more than one hundred cards on topics related to women and music. Here are citations to "The New Woman in Music" from *The Music Student* of 1911–12; "Should We Have Women in Our Symphony Orchestras?" from a 1913 issue of *Jacob's Orchestra Monthly;* and an article by the composer Amy Beach in an issue of *Etude* from 1918 titled "To the Girl Who Wants to Compose."[6]

SPECIAL COLLECTIONS

The special collections in the Music Division represent the creative life of women in myriad ways. Primary source materials tell the story of women composers such as Ruth Crawford Seeger and Carrie Jacobs Bond and such performers as singer Geraldine Farrar and violinist Maud Powell. The entrepreneurial talents of women can be seen in collections like that of the **National Negro Opera Company,** founded and directed by Mary Cardwell Dawson, or the **Edward and Marian MacDowell Collection,** which documents the vision and tenacity of Marian MacDowell, founder of the MacDowell Colony (see "The House that Marian Built," this volume). Especially important to the Library of Congress are those collections resulting from women's patronage.[7] The Music Division is particularly fortunate to be the beneficiary of such support.

The generosity of two remarkable American women, Elizabeth Sprague Coolidge (1864–1953) and Gertrude Clarke Whittall (1867–1965), was instrumental to the formation of the first special collections in music at the Library of Congress. Elizabeth Sprague Coolidge was an ardent supporter of chamber music and, in 1925, established a foundation at the Library of Congress to promote the composition and performance of new chamber works. At the time her endowment was without precedent at the Library and served as a model for those to follow. It funded the construction of the Coolidge Auditorium in the Library of

The Fairy Godmother of Chamber Music: Elizabeth Sprague Coolidge. *Photograph of bronze relief sculpted by Sir Henry Kitson, 1933. Elizabeth Sprague Coolidge Collection. Music Division.*

Elizabeth Sprague Coolidge (1864–1953) distinguished herself as a patron of chamber music long before her generous gifts to the Library of Congress. Beginning in 1918, her Berkshire Festival and corresponding Berkshire Competition promoted the performance and composition of chamber music, establishing an ongoing tradition. Coolidge built a facility for the festival at South Mountain, just outside Pittsfield, Massachusetts. It provided housing for musicians as well as an auditorium, which she called "the Temple." This bronze relief of Coolidge, which hangs in the Temple of Chamber Music at South Mountain, was created by the English sculptor, Sir Henry Kitson, who was her friend and neighbor in Pittsfield.

Congress, an intimate state-of-the-art concert hall that has seen premieres of such works as Igor Stravinsky's *Apollon Musagète* and Aaron Copland's *Appalachian Spring,* both Coolidge commissions. The endowment also supports musicological lectures and commissions new works of chamber music, some by women composers. The resulting collection of commissioned autograph scores and related correspondence is part of the **Elizabeth Sprague Coolidge Collection.** Among composers represented are Rebecca Clarke (1886–1979), Mary Howe (1882–1964), Mél Bonis (Mme Albert Domange) (1858–1937), Clara Wildschut (1906–1950), Vivian Fine (1913–2000), Miriam Gideon (1906–1996), and Sofia Gubaydulina (b. 1931). Mrs. Coolidge was a composer herself and several of her songs and chamber pieces are included in the collection.[8]

Gertrude Clarke Whittall was another patron of the Music Division whose support, although independent of the efforts of Mrs. Coolidge, nonetheless complemented them. In 1935–36 she donated five Stradivari instruments to the Library and established a foundation for maintenance and promotion of their use in concerts. She saw these instruments as belonging to the nation and in 1937 built the Whittall Pavilion, adjacent to the Coolidge Auditorium, for their public display. In 1941 she purchased for the Music Division a collection of music manuscripts and letters by European masters of the eighteenth, nineteenth, and twentieth centuries. The **Gertrude Clarke Whittall Collection** contains works by Haydn, Mendelssohn, Beethoven, Mozart, Brahms, and Schoenberg. These manuscripts also include an autograph score of Clara Schumann's cadenzas to Mozart's Piano Concerto in D minor, K. 466, a few letters of Fanny Mendelssohn Hensel (1805–1847), a facsimile of Hensel's *Das letzte Lied,* and a copy of a prelude for organ by Hensel in the hand of a member of the Mendelssohn family. Her gifts extended beyond the Music Division when, in 1950, she established the Gertrude Clarke Whittall Poetry and Literature Fund in the Library of Congress, which sponsors series of poetry readings, lectures, and dramas. She loved poetry and gave the Library many valuable literary manuscripts in the hand of contemporary poets. Robert Frost, a dear friend of Mrs. Whittall, once wrote to her: "Having you there in Washington is like having seeds of fire on the hearth that only needs a scrap of manuscript for tinder to burst into flame with the first passing breath of inspiration."[9]

Since the acquisition of the Coolidge and Whittall collections, the Music Division has actively pursued collection development of primary source materials. Today there are more than five hundred named special collections varying in size from fewer than a dozen items to more than a half-million. What follows is a selection of special collections that may be of interest to researchers of American women in the performing arts.

Special Collections in Music

The Arsis Press was founded in 1974 by Clara Boone (b. 1927), also known as Lyle de Bohun, to publish and promote music by contemporary women composers. The **Arsis Press Archives** (partially processed, 6 linear feet, 9 containers) contains printer's masters of scores published by the press; correspondence between Clara Boone and various composers, publishers, and business associates; and business trademark papers. Composers published by the press include Mary Jeanne Van Appledorn (b. 1927), Emma Lou Diemer (b. 1927), Anna Larson (b. 1940), Ruth Loman (b. 1930), Vivian Fine (1913–2000), Clara Shore (b. 1954), Ruth Schonthal (b. 1924), Nancy Van De Vate (b. 1930), and Elizabeth Vercoe (b. 1941).[10]

The **Carrie Jacobs Bond Collection** (7 linear feet, 11 containers, approximately 1,050 items) consists of music manuscripts, papers, photographs, and other materials relating to the personal and professional life of American sentimental song composer Carrie Jacobs Bond (1861–1946). Best known for her songs "I Love You Truly" (1901), "A Perfect Day" (1910), and "God Remembers When the World Forgets" (1913), Bond turned entrepreneur and started her own publishing house in 1896 after experiencing great difficulties getting her music published elsewhere. Her song "A Perfect Day" sold over eight million copies of sheet music and five million recordings.

Legendary American soprano Geraldine Farrar (1882–1967) donated her personal papers to the Library in 1954. Other materials acquired through gift and purchase were later added to the collection that documents the stellar career of this remarkable singer. The **Geraldine Farrar Collection** (17 linear feet, 58 containers, approximately 25,000 items) contains music, including compositions by Farrar, correspondence, concert programs, Metropolitan Opera contracts, drafts of her autobiography *Such Sweet Compulsion,* scripts for radio programs, and photographs. Fifty-five phonograph records that were included have been transferred to the Motion Picture, Broadcasting, and Recorded Sound Division.

The **Alma Gluck Collection** (11 scrapbooks) documents the life of the notable American soprano Alma Gluck (1884–1938) with particular emphasis on the years from 1909 to 1917, when she was at her height as a performer and recording artist. Donated by her daughter Marcia Davenport in 1973, the collection includes photographs, annotated music scores, and scrapbooks of performance reviews. The finding aid lists 113 of the 124 recordings she made on the Victor Red Label that are housed in the Motion Picture, Broadcasting, and Recorded Sound Division.

Pianist and composer Helen Hopekirk (1856–1945) was born in Edinburgh, Scotland, and received her musical training in Europe. She made her American debut in 1883 with the Boston Symphony Orchestra, under the management of her husband, the music critic William A. Wilson. In 1897 she accepted a teaching position at the New England Conservatory and became a fixture in the musical life of Boston. Both she and her husband became American citizens in 1918. The **Helen Hopekirk Collection** (6 linear feet, 16 containers) contains her original music manuscripts, scores by other composers inscribed to her, biographical material, and five scrapbooks of press clippings and programs.

Sylvia Fine (1913–1991) was a writer and composer of musical comedy best known for the special material she wrote for her husband, actor and comedian Danny Kaye. The two met in 1939 while working on a Max Liebman production and married the following year. Fine wrote songs for several of Kaye's films, including *The Court Jester* (1956), *The Five Pennies* (1959), *On the Riviera* (1950), and *The Secret Life of Walter Mitty* (1947). In 1975 Fine began a lecture series on musical comedy at Yale University. These lectures later became the basis for *Musical Comedy Tonight,* a series of three television specials produced by Fine in 1979, 1981, and 1985. The **Danny Kaye and Sylvia Fine Kaye Collection** (435 linear feet, 1,079 containers, approximately 96,377 items) contains music, scripts, books, slides, programs, and various research materials related to these shows. Other music manuscripts, printed music, and lyric sheets by Fine are also found in the collection, as well as material relating to the career of Danny Kaye.

Marian MacDowell (1857–1956) was the wife of composer and pianist Edward MacDowell and founded the MacDowell Colony for creative artists in Peterborough, New Hampshire. The essay "The House That Marian Built" in this volume is largely based on material from the **Edward and Marian MacDowell Collection,** and discusses it in some detail.

Leonora Jackson McKim (1880–1969) was one of the first American women to achieve international acclaim as a concert violinist. Mrs. Grover Cleveland was one of her early patrons, enabling her to study in Chicago, Paris, and Berlin. She was decorated by Queen Victoria and performed throughout Europe and the United States with leading orchestras including the London Philharmonic and the Boston Symphony. She retired from performing after her marriage in 1915 to Dr. William Duncan McKim (1855–1935). The McKims were avid supporters of the arts, holding musical programs in their home and collecting a large number of works of art, many of which were donated to the Smithsonian and the Maryland Historical Society after the death of Dr. McKim. The McKim Fund was established in 1970 for the creation and appreciation of music for violin and piano. The fund has commissioned new works for violin and piano by many well-known contemporary composers, including Ellen Taaffe Zwilich (b. 1939), Annie LeBaron (b. 1953), and Daria Semegen (b. 1946).

The **McKim Fund Collection** (21 linear feet, 39 containers, approximately 1,500 items) consists of the personal papers of Leonora Jackson McKim and the holograph music scores of the McKim Fund commissions. Among the personal papers are clippings of performance reviews; programs; posters and other publicity material; photographs, including one of Susan B. Anthony with a Mrs. Gross of Chicago; correspondence; Leonora's music library; and an extensive collection of her writings, including novels, short stories, plays, and poetry in manuscript form.

Loretta C. Manggrum (1896–1992) was a notable composer, teacher, and church musician who became in 1953 the first African American to receive a master's degree from the University of Cincinnati College Conservatory of Music. She composed numerous works for church, including her cantatas *Christ Our Lord* (1953) and *Watch* (1958). The **Loretta Cessor Manggrum Collection** (2 linear feet, 4 containers, approximately 140 items) contains printed and manuscript musical scores, programs, and other biographical materials.

Founded in 1941, the National Negro Opera Company was the creation of Mary Cardwell Dawson (1894–1962). A graduate of the New England Conservatory of Music and Chicago Musical College, Mrs. Dawson managed the company until it ceased with her death in 1962. The **National Negro Opera Company Collection** (27 linear feet, 67 containers) contains financial records, correspondence, photographs, music, programs, and promotional material. Also included are scrapbooks and miscellaneous biographical material of the soprano La Julia Rhea (1908–1992), who performed with the company in 1941. Other notable female singers who performed with the company include Carol Brice (1916–1985), Debria Brown (b. 1932?), Minto Cato (1900–1979), Lillian Evanti (1890–1967), Omega King (1892–1973), Muriel Rahn (1911–1961), and Camilla Williams (b. 1922).

Violin virtuoso Maud Powell (1867–1920) achieved international distinction in her performing career at a time when female solo instrumental performers were rare. She enjoyed the support of her husband, who was also her manager, and continued to perform up until her untimely death at the age of fifty-two. The **Maud Powell Collection** (unprocessed, up to 30 linear feet) consists of the research material compiled for Karen A. Shaffer and Neva Garner Greenwood's biography *Maud Powell: Pioneer American Violinist* (Arlington, Va.: The Maud Powell Foundation; Ames: Iowa State University Press, 1988; ML418.P79S5 1988). Included in the collection are binders containing copies of programs, reviews, advertisements, periodical articles about Maud Powell, research correspondence, and almost six hundred photographs. Maud Powell's 78rpm Victor Red Seal Recordings and audio and video taped interviews of people who knew her will be transferred to the Motion Picture, Broadcasting, and Recorded Sound Division.

The German-born music publisher Arthur P. Schmidt came to America in 1866 and began publishing music in 1877. He was a valuable ally of American composers, many of whom first saw their publications in print under the A.P. Schmidt

Company name. The **Arthur P. Schmidt Company Archives** (212 linear feet, 514 containers) include the records of the company, correspondence with composers, and autograph manuscripts used for the printed editions, many by women composers. Among them, the manuscripts of Amy Beach are of particular note. Other women represented in the collection include Florence Newell Barbour (1866–1946), Marion Bauer (1887–1955), Gena Branscombe (1881–1977), Mabel Daniels (1878–1971), Helen Hopekirk (1856–1945), Lucinda Jewell (1874–?), Margaret Ruthven Lang (1867–1972), Frances McCollin (1892–1960), Edna Rosalind Park, Olga von Radecki (fl. 1882), Anna Priscilla Risher (1875–1946), Clara Kathleen Rogers (1844–1931), and Mildred Weston.[11]

Amy Beach. Gaelic Symphony *(First page of the fourth movement). Holograph, 1896. Arthur P. Schmidt Company Archives, Music Division.* Printed by permission of The MacDowell Colony. Copyright © 2000 The MacDowell Colony.

Symphonic composition was the true test of a composer's worth in the late nineteenth century and largely the domain of male composers. Amy Beach tried her hand at it when she was twenty-seven. Her *Gaelic Symphony,* begun in 1894 and completed two years later, was premiered October 31, 1896, by the Boston Symphony and received much critical acclaim. Beach's biographer Adrienne Fried Block (*Amy Beach: Passionate Victorian* [New York: Oxford University Press, 1998]) devotes an entire chapter to the symphony and quotes composer George Whitefield Chadwick, whose praise for the work included counting Mrs. Beach as "one of the boys."

The **Charles and Ruth Crawford Seeger Collection** (partially processed, estimated up to 40 linear feet) contains the music manuscripts, printed materials, correspondence, and other papers of composer Ruth Crawford Seeger (1901–1953) and her husband, musicologist Charles Seeger. The first woman to receive a Guggenheim Fellowship in Composition, Ruth Crawford Seeger was a respected figure in the American musical avant-garde early in her career. After her marriage, her musical interests turned to folk song when her husband became involved in collecting American folk music. She was highly regarded as a music teacher and maintained a grueling teaching schedule while raising four children. Her transcriptions and arrangements of folk songs are well-known through her *American Folk Songs for Children* (1948; reprint, Garden City, N.Y.: Doubleday, 1980; M1629.S4 A5 1980). The music manuscripts include her original compositions as well as the hundreds of folk song transcriptions and arrangements that she made from recordings in the Archive of American Folk Song at the Library of Congress (see chapter 11). Additional papers acquired from the Seeger family by Judith Tick, author of *Ruth Crawford Seeger: A Composer's Search for American Music* (New York: Oxford University Press, 1997; ML410.S4446 T5 1997), are recent additions to the collection.

The **Beverly Sills Collection** was established in 1992 with an initial gift of forty scrapbooks from the noted American soprano Beverly Sills (b. 1929). Twenty-eight scrapbooks chronicle her life and career, four are devoted solely to her recordings, and eight are devoted to specific topics. They contain clippings, photographs, correspondence, programs, promotional materials, and other items. A brief finding aid to the scrapbooks is available to researchers.

Special Collections in Dance

Franziska Boas (1902–1988) was a pioneering dancer, percussionist, teacher, ethnologist, and dance therapist. The daughter of noted anthropologist Franz Boas, she was, like her father, a committed activist for racial equality and social justice. She worked to teach young people about the value of dance as a means of communication. She pioneered dance as therapy; encouraged students to expand their own creativity through improvisation; combined the study of dance with ethnology;

Alexandra Danilova in The Firebird. *Photograph by Bennett and Pleasant, New York, ca. 1935. Alexandra Danilova Collection. Music Division.*

Ballerina Alexandra Danilova toured America in the 1930s with Colonel Wassily de Basil's Ballets Russes de Monte Carlo. She helped make classical ballet popular in this country for the first time. This portrait, one of over two thousand photographs in the Alexandra Danilova Collection, shows her in the title role of the de Basil production of *The Firebird,* a role she made her own.

Peggy Clark. Set design for Holiday *(act 2) by Philip Barry, ca. 1940. Peggy Clark Collection. Music Division.*

Peggy Clark designed this set (ca. 1940) for an unknown production of Philip Barry's *Holiday.* One of many watercolor set designs in the Music Division's Peggy Clark Collection, it shows a playroom where a New Year's Eve party is about to occur as the scene opens on act 2. The main character, Linda Seton, is not having a good evening, and sits pensively awaiting the arrival of her guests.

and broke down the racial barriers that stood in the way of African Americans wishing to pursue careers in dance.

The **Franziska Boas Collection** (36 linear feet, 95 containers, approximately 13,250 items) consists of choreographic scores, music manuscripts and printed music, her personal and general correspondence, business files, personal files, writings and research by and about Boas, clippings, iconography, miscellaneous items, and audiovisual material. It spans Boas's career, from her academic training at Barnard College through her professional work as a dance teacher, accompanist, therapist, and ethnologist, including documentation of her work as a social activist and as a community educator after her retirement. Audiovisual materials transferred to the Motion Picture, Broadcasting, and Recorded Sound Division include audio tapes of lectures by Boas and film footage of her performances.

Ballerina Alexandra Danilova (1903–1997) was a star attraction with the Ballets Russes de Monte Carlo, whose American tours helped popularize classical ballet in this country during the 1930s and 1940s. She eventually settled in America and became a U.S. citizen in 1946. After her retirement from the stage, Danilova was choreographer for several seasons at the Metropolitan Opera. Respected as a teacher, she gave classes at the School of American Ballet in New York City from 1964 to 1989. The **Alexandra Danilova Collection** (30 linear feet, 46 containers, approximately 4,500 items) contains over two thousand photographs dating from the 1920s to the 1990s, correspondence, writings, including drafts of her autobiography *Choura: The Memoirs of Alexandra Danilova* (1986), programs, press clippings, and awards. Audiovisual materials, which have been transferred to the Motion Picture, Broadcasting, and Recorded Sound Division, include videos of an interview with Dick Cavett in 1978 and the 1989 Kennedy Center Honors at which she was an honoree.

Dancer Gwen Verdon (1925–2000) is best known for her work in the Broadway productions of *Can-Can* (1953), *Damn Yankees* (1955), *New Girl in Town* (1957), *Redhead* (1959), *Sweet Charity* (1966), and *Chicago* (1975). The **Bob Fosse and Gwen Verdon Collection** (133 linear feet, 114 containers, approximately 54,840 items) reflects her close collaboration with choreographer and director Bob Fosse, whom she married in 1960. Extensive production and project files are arranged by show title. Other material pertaining specifically to Gwen Verdon is located in the "Verdon: Career Miscellany" series. Scrapbooks belonging to both Fosse and Verdon chronicle their respective careers with clippings, photographs, and other memorabilia. Audiovisual materials, including record albums, audiotapes, audiocassettes, compact discs, videocassettes, and films, have been transferred to the Motion Picture, Broadcasting, and Recorded Sound Division.

Martha Graham (1894–1991) redefined modern dance in the twentieth century and influenced countless creative artists through her work. Her prodigious repertoire, original dance technique, distinctive theatrical productions, and fruitful artistic collaborations stand as treasures of our nation's cultural heritage. The **Martha Graham Collection** (unprocessed) is strong in its holdings of music scores, many of which are autograph composers' manuscripts annotated with Graham's notes. There are also extensive holdings of photographs of Graham and her company. Other material includes books from her personal library, press clippings, posters, and correspondence.

Hallie Flanagan, director of the WPA Federal Theatre Project. Photograph, ca. 1939. Federal Theatre Project Collection. Music Division.

Hallie Flanagan (1890–1969), who had studied theater production in Europe with a Guggenheim Fellowship, went on to become production assistant to George Pierce Baker at Yale University and then director of the Experimental Theatre at Vassar College. In July 1935, Harry Hopkins appointed her director of the Federal Theatre Project of the Works Progress Administration, where she took on the cause of supporting self-respect and skills of unemployed workers in the theater nationwide.

Special Collections in Theater

The work of Peggy Clark (1915–1996), one of the foremost lighting designers in the American theater, was seen in some of the best-known stage productions of the mid-twentieth century. She worked especially closely with the noted set designer Oliver Smith, creating the lighting for many of his shows and often putting his rough designs into final form to allow actual construction of the sets. Clark worked in all areas of theater: legitimate drama, musical comedy, dance, and opera. She became the first woman to be elected to the board of the union for stage designers, United Scenic Artists. Material in the **Peggy Clark Collection** (unprocessed, estimated up to 200 linear feet) includes lighting plots, color and black-and-white renderings, finished elevations, costume design sketches, and ground plans. Also in the collection are typescripts for plays, notebooks, clippings, photographs, scrapbooks, correspondence, posters, personal notebooks, and color and black-and-white renderings by set designer Oliver Smith.

Part of the Works Progress Administration (WPA), the **Federal Theatre Project** was intended to create jobs for unemployed professionals who were on the public relief rolls in the late 1930s. Women figured prominently among the actors, directors, playwrights, designers, vaudeville artists, stage technicians, and other theater workers who found work under the program, which at one time during its four-year existence employed over twelve thousand people. The collection (522 linear feet, 43 file cabinets, approximately 525,000 items) contains production records for shows staged around the country, a sample of which may be seen on the American Memory Web site as *The New Deal Stage: Selections from the "Federal Theatre Project,"* 1935–1939 (<http://memory.loc.gov/ammem/fedtp/fthome.html>). More than 2,500 play scripts may be found in this collection and approximately 2,000 radio scripts from the Federal Theatre Radio Division which include

William P. Gottlieb. Sarah Vaughan. Photograph, August 1946. William P. Gottlieb/Ira and Leonore S. Gershwin Fund Collection. Copyright © William P. Gottlieb. Music Division.

Singer Sarah Vaughan was one of many female jazz musicians captured on film by photographer William P. Gottlieb. This photo was taken at the Café Society in New York City in August 1946. It can be found on the American Memory Web site *William P. Gottlieb—Photographs from the Golden Age of Jazz.*

programs such as *Women in the Making of America* (1939) and *The Women of the Day* (1936). The administrative records of the Federal Theatre Project contain correspondence, memoranda, and briefings by Hallie Flanagan (1890–1969), national director of the project for its entire existence. A finding aid to the whole collection is available on the American Memory Web site accompanying the presentation *The New Deal Stage.*

Other Special Collections and Primary Source Material

There are literally hundreds of other special collections in the custody of the Music Division that are potential sources for the women's history scholar. A master list is kept in the Performing Arts Reading Room and may be consulted upon request. Collection names in many cases identify those that contain personal papers of women, but in other instances the relevance is not so obvious. **The Modern Music Archives** documents the history of *Modern Music,* the quarterly journal of the League of Composers from 1924 to 1946. Edited by Minna Lederman Daniel (1898–1995), the writings and criticism published in this journal influenced a generation of composers at the forefront of the American musical avant-garde. Photos of singers and opera characters may be found in **The Charles Jahant Collection,** which includes both publicity shots and stills from actual productions. The **U.S. Work Projects Administration Federal Music Project** documents musical life in America during the years of the WPA, roughly 1935–43. Designed to provide jobs for professional musicians on the relief rolls, many of whom were women, the project employed instrumentalists, singers, concert performers, and teachers of music and strove to establish high standards of musicianship and to educate the public through an appreciation of music.

Aside from special collections, there is also primary source material in music that is individually cataloged and designated as rare material. Music manuscripts, letters, and first editions of music scores that are not part of a special collection are cataloged and shelved as "Case," the designation for rare material in the Music Division. Music manuscripts of African American composer Florence Price, for example, are cataloged separately and are not part of a Florence Price Collection.

ONLINE PERFORMING ARTS COLLECTIONS: AMERICAN MEMORY

In addition to the previously mentioned sheet music collections and the Federal Theatre Project selections found among American Memory online resources, there are others that deserve mention. *William P. Gottlieb—Photographs from the Golden Age of Jazz* (<http://memory.loc.gov/ammem/wghtml/wghome.html>) features the work of the noted photographer William Gottlieb and includes photos of some of the great women

"Mother, My Ruin Is Accomplished!" Illustration from Luigi Satori, Modern Dances *(Colleg[e]ville, Indiana: St. Joseph's Printing Office, 1910; GV1741.S3). General Collections.*

The anti-dance literature of the late nineteenth and early twentieth centuries was aimed particularly at women, who were considered at the time to be especially weak and therefore susceptible to their potentially lustful dance partners. The Rt. Rev. Mgr. Don Luigi Satori published a vehement assault on dancing in his *Modern Dances,* in which he equates the waltz with breaking the Sixth Commandment, forbidding adultery. This illustration, taken from that volume, shows a young woman confessing her downfall, presumably brought about by dancing, to her dismayed mother. The full text of this work, along with that of many other dance manuals, may be found on the American Memory Web site *An American Ballroom Companion.*

in jazz: Ella Fitzgerald (1918–1996), Billie Holiday (1915–1959), Lena Horne (b.1917), Sarah Vaughan (1924–1990), Ethel Waters (1896–1977), Mary Lou Williams (1910–1981), and others.

An American Ballroom Companion brings together dance manuals from the General Collections, the Rare Book and Special Collections Division, and the Music Division to form a unique collection that exists only online. Of particular interest here are the anti-dance treatises that warn young women against the immorality of the dance. T. A. Faulkner, famous for his *From the Ballroom to Hell* (1892), writes in the sequel to that volume, *Lure of the Dance* (1916):

> My especial aim at this time is to show that the strength of the so-called "White Slave Traffic" is the dance and the dance halls. Unsophisticated young working-women, simply desiring amusement and recreation after their arduous daily toil, are trapped in these places like flies in a spider's web.[12]

The full text of these treatises and digitized images of them are available on the library's American Memory Web site at <http://memory.loc.gov/ammem/dihtml/dihome.html>.

The Music Division's collections are an invaluable resource for those who study women in the performing arts. Women's contributions to the creative life of our country can be seen through their patronage and their work as composers, performers, entrepreneurs, collectors, and scholars. Music tells the stories of other women as well. The songs women sing, and those that are sung about them, can offer insightful commentary on women's lives. There is great potential for research in the Music Division. Those who are researching all aspects of women's lives will want to discover what lies on its shelves for themselves.

I would like to extend special thanks to my Music Division colleagues Susan Clermont, Ruth Foss, and Wayne Shirley for their helpful comments and suggestions.

Marian Griswold Nevins. Photograph. Edward and Marian MacDowell Collection. Music Division. All photographs from the Edward and Marian MacDowell Collection are reproduced here courtesy of the Estate of Edward and Marian MacDowell.

Marian Griswold Nevins was a serious child and, as eldest daughter, gradually assumed responsibility for running the household after her mother's death. This undated photo was likely taken around 1865, not long before her mother died in childbirth.

> It took long years for me to realize what a different world I would have had, and how narrow my usefulness would have been should this child have lived. Aside from the fact that I know now that some of the happiest moments are those where the husband and wife are brought closer together through the intimate companionship, which is inevitably broken where there are children too, of course, the Colony would never have existed.[1]

Looking back over her long life, Marian MacDowell, the wife of American composer and pianist Edward MacDowell, reflected on the direction it had taken. She gave up a promising future as a pianist to devote herself to her husband's career, insisting that "the fostering of a great creative gift was an infinitely higher mission for her, than interpreting the works of others."[2] Her only child was stillborn, and she lost her beloved Edward after twenty-three years of marriage when he succumbed to a devastating nervous disorder at the age of forty-six. Marian MacDowell was fifty years old when her husband died in 1908. She spent the rest of her life—another forty-eight years—creating the artists' retreat that was his final wish. Returning to the piano after more than twenty years, she became the foremost interpreter of Edward MacDowell's piano music, and traveled across North America playing concerts to benefit the fledgling MacDowell Colony. The last half of her life is synonymous with the birth of the MacDowell Colony, an institution that has left its mark on the cultural landscape of this country and continues to nurture and support creative artists today.

Marian MacDowell's story touches many different collections throughout the Library of Congress. The Music Division is a particularly rich source of information with numerous special collections that contain her correspondence and, more importantly, its Edward and Marian MacDowell Collection which fills 73 boxes and 25 linear feet of shelf space.[3] This collection is divided into three sections: the papers of Edward MacDowell, the papers of Marian MacDowell, and the records of the MacDowell Colony. Marian MacDowell's papers include her unpublished autobiographical writings, which are central to any study of her life. These recollections, source of the opening quote above, include anecdotes from her childhood and recall how she came to study with Edward MacDowell in Germany. They tell of beginnings, Marian's and the colony's, and provide a logical starting place for research into both.

Marian Griswold Nevins was born in 1857, the third of five children born to David H.

Nevins, a Wall Street banker, and his wife, Cornelia L. Perkins. Her mother's death in childbirth left a vivid impression on the eight-year-old Marian, who was chosen to tell her father the news as he returned from a business trip.

> I can remember it as though it were yesterday, sitting in the dining room, we little girls, not quite conscious of the desperation in the minds of my grandmother and the doctor, who was also a relative, as to the return of my father to find what had happened. I heard the carriage come up to the front door and then they all looked at each other with consternation; neither one could dare to go out and meet him. They did not know what an awful thing they did, but knowing the very strong affection my father had for me, they pushed me out into the hall and said, "You have got to tell Father Mother is dead." He came in, looked at me and said, "What is the matter?" I said, "Mother is dead," and he fell as though he had been knocked over the head with a heavy blow.[4]

Marian became the oldest female of the family after her mother's death and assumed an increasingly responsible role in the years that followed. Her aunt Caroline Perkins of South Carolina, a talented musician who came to New York to teach piano, recognized the child's musical gifts and worked with her to develop them. As Marian became more accomplished, she realized that her future depended on study in Europe. No one was taken seriously as a music teacher or performer in America without having studied abroad. She decided to work with Clara Schumann, and, using a modest inheritance she received upon her mother's death, she left with a chaperone for Frankfort-am-Main in 1880.

Madame Schumann was away on concert tour when Marian arrived in Germany and, not wanting to waste time, she inquired of

Marian MacDowell in the woods near the log cabin studio. Photograph, ca. 1898. Edward and Marian MacDowell Collection. Music Division.

Ever aware of her husband's need for a quiet spot in which to compose, Marian had a log cabin studio built for him in the woods on their Peterborough property. This photo, probably taken by Edward MacDowell, shows Marian in front of the cabin which later became the model for the colony studios.

Marian MacDowell (right) and nurse Anna Baetz. Photograph. Ca. 1908–1909. Edward and Marian MacDowell Collection. Music Division.

Marian hired nurse Anna Baetz in 1905, when caring for Edward became too difficult for her alone. The two women became good friends and remained so until Anna's death in 1923. This photo was probably taken around 1908–9. Anna sports a parasol and Marian, who had aggravated an old back injury lifting her ailing husband, leans on a crutch as they pose together on the steps of Hillcrest.

Marian and Edward MacDowell. Photograph, ca. 1905. MacDowell Colony Records. Prints and Photographs Division (unprocessed). LC-USZ62–92627.

This formal portrait of Marian and Edward MacDowell was made around 1905. Edward's final illness is evident in his vacant stare and graying hair, which turned completely white within a year's time. Marian's sure and steady gaze as she leans protectively towards her husband, her hand on his arm, lends a certain poignancy to the photo, one of the last taken of them together.

Joachim Raff, head of the Frankfort Conservatory of Music, who another suitable teacher might be. Raff recommended a brilliant young American, Edward MacDowell, since Marian's conversational ability in German was still somewhat limited. "Of course," Raff remarked, "I am not sure that MacDowell would want to give you lessons." Marian was more certain. "I knew that I was very sure I didn't want to take them," she wrote. She had not come all the way to Europe to study with an American. Edward and Marian both so respected Raff that they agreed to meet. "We were both so indignant at the situation for he didn't want to teach me and I didn't want to have him; but we started in." Upon first hearing her play Edward remarked "You know, you really have quite a lot of talent but you can't play piano one bit." Challenged by his assessment, Marian realized her playing did indeed have technical limitations. She saw that Edward MacDowell might have something to offer as a teacher after all, and began working with him in earnest.[5]

Marian won Edward MacDowell's respect by her hard work and as the two became better acquainted, they grew closer. The death of his friend Joachim Raff and the death of Marian's father deepened their friendship as they turned to each other for consolation and support. When it came time for her to return to America, they realized their feelings for each other and began to talk of marriage. Marian accepted Edward's proposal on one condition: so strongly did she believe in his talent as a composer, she insisted he devote himself to composing and live off her savings for the next five years. He objected strongly, but realizing she was quite serious and would not marry him otherwise, he finally agreed. They were married in Waterford, Connecticut, on July 21, 1884.

Marian MacDowell's dedication to her husband's creative work was evident from the beginning of their life together. It appears, however, that she did not enter into marriage with the knowledge that she would be giving up her own career entirely, for in her memoirs she recalls, "I hadn't been married three months before I knew that I had to make a choice between a husband and a career."[6] She had an uncanny empathy for her husband's need of a quiet place for his composition and, whenever they moved, preoccupied herself with finding him a room of his own. "I had a bad but useful habit," she wrote, "of not consulting my husband. . . . [T]his avoided discussion. It never hurt . . . to follow an impulse, then talk it over with him."[7]

It was in this manner that, in 1896, Marian MacDowell bought Hillcrest, a farm in Peterborough, New Hampshire, for their summer residence. She telegraphed the news to Edward and he wired back the following reply: "All right, in your name, your responsibility."[8] Despite his reservations, Edward MacDowell fell in love with Hillcrest. His wife surprised him after their first summer there by having a log cabin built in the woods near the house. It was here that he found the perfect conditions necessary to pursue his creative work. In this log cabin he wrote his most significant piano works. This studio became the "house of dreams untold" that he versified on the title page of his piano piece "From a Log Cabin," opus 62, number 9. And the opportunity to work undisturbed afforded him by the log cabin studio became his fervent wish for other artists.

In 1904, Edward MacDowell resigned in protest from a position at Columbia University as head of the Music Department over a disagreement with the new president concerning their fine arts curriculum, a new program and one not altogether welcome in academia. It was a traumatic time for the MacDowells; faculty took sides and many grievances were aired in the press. Whatever the medical reason for Edward MacDowell's death, the Columbia episode contributed to his slow mental decline which was marked by periods of dementia. By late 1905, Marian MacDowell could no longer care for her husband by herself, yet she refused to institutionalize him. She hired a nurse, Anna Baetz, to help her look after him and the two women became close friends. Anna left a brief diary excerpt, found in Edward MacDowell's papers, that offers a poignant account of Edward and Marian's devotion to each other. She ultimately curtailed her nursing career and remained with Marian MacDowell for almost eighteen years, the formative years of the colony. When Anna died in 1923, a memorial fund was begun for a studio in her honor. A tribute to Anna Baetz, "the nurse of Edward MacDowell," appears in the June 1926 issue of *The Trained Nurse and Hospital Review.*[9]

During his final illness, Edward MacDowell became obsessed with his dream of an artists' retreat. He wanted other artists, not only musicians, to benefit from the same uninterrupted solitude that he had enjoyed. Marian promised him she would make that happen. In 1907, she transferred the deed of the Peterborough property to the newly formed Edward MacDowell Association, an organization that evolved from a group of prominent names in the creative arts that supported the composer's ideas.

> I was wise enough to realize that there had to be something tangible for people to have back of a venture so that they could believe in what we were trying to do; it was not enough for me to say that I would leave this property to the Association, but it had to belong to them while I was still alive.[10]

After the construction of a large studio, the colony was officially begun that summer with the arrival of Helen Mears (1872–1916), a young sculptor, and her sister Mary Mears (1876–1943), a writer who later published an account of the

Mrs. Edward MacDowell: Piano Recitals of MacDowell Music. *Publicity brochure, ca.1920. Edward and Marian MacDowell Collection. Music Division.*

Marian MacDowell returned to performing after people began asking to hear her play Edward's piano works. This publicity brochure dates from around 1920 when she was actively traveling throughout the United States and Canada to raise money for the colony. She performed in over four hundred programs and was regarded as the foremost interpreter of her husband's music.

colony in the July 1909 issue of *The Craftsman.*[11] Edward did not live to see a second season of colonists. He died January 23, 1908.

Marian MacDowell did not have the financial resources of an Elizabeth Sprague Coolidge or Isabella Stewart Gardner and she knew she was going to have to raise substantial sums if the colony was to survive and grow. She began to speak to local women's groups and music clubs to enlist their help. It was one of these speaking engagements that quite accidentally brought her piano career back to life.

> After I had finished talking and really interested the people, somebody in the audience said, "Won't you play for us?" I laughed and I said I had not played piano for twenty-two years. But she said we don't care how you play but it will be interesting to hear how you play the MacDowell compositions. To my utter amazement they seemed very pleased.[12]

Marian soon realized that as Edward MacDowell's wife and former student, she occupied a unique role as the leading interpreter of his piano music. At the age of fifty she resumed her career as a pianist and, for approximately the next twenty-five years, traveled throughout the United States and Canada, giving between 400 to 500 concerts to raise money for the colony. Her performances and speaking engagements are well documented through the programs and reviews found among her papers in the Music Division's Edward and Marian MacDowell Collection.

In addition to Marian MacDowell's writings, which detail her fund raising efforts and the growth of the colony, the correspondence in the collection is also a rich source of information. Edward MacDowell's papers include letters to his wife from 1880 to1903, and Marian MacDowell's papers contain extensive correspondence with family members, prospective colonists and benefactors, and her long-time companion Nina Maud Richardson, who became her assistant in the late 1920s. Among Marian MacDowell's correspondents one finds the names of Eleanor Roosevelt, Leonard Bernstein, and the esteemed French music pedagogue Nadia Boulanger who wrote the following words of support and encouragement: "it is so wonderful that your devotion turns to help for young people—and that the great memory you are living for, becomes the sign under which a new generation finds herself."[13]

The records of the MacDowell Colony that comprise the third section of the Edward and Marian MacDowell Collection contain Marian MacDowell's working copies of corporate and organizational materials concerning the management of the colony. There are also lists of colonists, clippings about the colony, board meeting minutes, annual reports, and financial documents. There is some duplication of material

Louise Talma composing in her studio at the MacDowell Colony, Peterborough, N.H. Photograph by Bernice B. Perry, March 1947. Modern Music Archives. Music Division.

Composer Louise Talma (1906–1996) worked on her oratorio The Divine Flame *at the MacDowell Colony in 1947, while on her first Guggenheim Fellowship. Here she is shown in Pan's Cottage under the watchful eye of composer Lukas Foss whose photo sits on the piano. A photo of her teacher, Nadia Boulanger, sits on the mantel. Talma inscribed her photo to Minna Lederman, editor of* Modern Music.

Marian MacDowell and pianist Lillian Steuber with the score to Edward MacDowell's Concerto No. 2 for piano and orchestra. *Photograph by Rothschild Photo, 1951. Edward and Marian MacDowell Collection. Music Division.*

Marian MacDowell was the foremost interpreter of Edward MacDowell's piano music during her lifetime and was frequently consulted by other pianists who were performing Edward's music. Here she examines the score to Edward MacDowell's Concerto No. 2 for piano and orchestra *with pianist Lillian Steuber.*

between these records and the Records of the MacDowell Colony located in the Manuscript Division. This latter collection is the more extensive of the two, containing approximately 35,000 items and occupying 33 linear feet. It contains colony records up to 1970 with the bulk of material from 1945–68, a period covering the transitional time from 1946–56, when Marian relinquished her administrative responsibilities to the board of directors of the Edward MacDowell Association.

The Manuscript Division's Records of the MacDowell Colony document the management and administration of the colony and its parent organization, the Edward MacDowell Association. Comprising correspondence, applications for admission, minutes of meetings, reports, legal and financial papers, and miscellany, these records provide a fascinating look at the workings of Marian MacDowell's enterprise. The annual reports of the Edward MacDowell Association are full of information about resident artists, finances, and general colony news. Proceeds from Marian's lecture recitals, which totaled close to $100,000 by 1930, are itemized in early reports—she chose not to have them published in later ones. Among the donors listed, women appear as regular and generous benefactors. Elizabeth Sprague Coolidge gave $31,000 to the general fund of the colony between 1916 and 1935. Estate bequests, predominantly from women, include one from former colonist and composer Amy Beach. While the colony did benefit from large contributions of single individuals, equally important was the support of music clubs and associations across the country. Local MacDowell clubs, the women's music sorority Sigma Alpha Iota, and the National Federation of Music Clubs, all became involved in fund-raising efforts for the colony. Marian MacDowell was well aware of how much of her support came from women. "I hate to admit it," she once said, "but women do most of it. Five music sororities helped me but not one fraternity."[14]

In addition to the Records of the MacDowell Colony, the Manuscript Division also houses its own collection of Marian MacDowell material. Numbering approximately 2,000 items in just under 4 linear feet of shelf space, the Papers of Marian MacDowell relate chiefly to her activities with the MacDowell Colony, particularly during the period 1908–38. The collection is primarily correspondence and includes recommendations for admittance to the colony, requests for time to work at the colony, and Marian MacDowell's letters to Nina Maud Richardson dating from the 1930s.

In 1923, Marian MacDowell was awarded *Pictorial Review*'s $5,000 Annual Achievement Award, a prize given to "the American woman who makes the most valuable contribution to American life during the year." "The one outstanding need in America," the feature article from the March 1925 issue posited, "is a stimulation of the creative impulse."[15] Marian MacDowell and her colony fulfilled that need, providing creative artists an ideal environment

Marian MacDowell at the piano with Nina Maud Richardson. Photograph by C. Walbridge, 1940. Edward and Marian MacDowell Collection. Music Division.

Marian met Nina Maud Richardson in the late 1920s when she went to California to recover from a long illness. She eventually spent her winters in Los Angeles at the home of Nina Maud, who became her close companion and assistant. This formal portrait of the two women was made in 1940, when Marian was in her eighties. It was often said that when she sat down at the piano, her years melted away.

in which to work. By this time the MacDowell Colony had grown to 500 acres and nineteen studios, with two more on the way. Applications for time to work at the colony numbered over 300. Artists were now selected by an admissions committee based on letters of reference, a far cry from earlier years when Marian solicited prospective colonists by invitation.

What made the colony so attractive to artists was not only the solitude and uninterrupted days of creative work, but also the opportunity to interact with artists in other fields. Composer and colonist Aaron Copland recalled how working with artists from all disciplines gave him a new insight into art in America.[16] The early decades of the twentieth century found many American artists struggling to break free from European models, and the colony offered them the freedom to experiment and find their own unique voices. Writers, composers, and visual artists, most in the early stages of their careers and many unknown, were given the gift of time. And there has never been a dearth of women working there. From the Mears sisters in 1907, the rolls of artists who were granted residence at the MacDowell Colony during Marian MacDowell's lifetime included composers Amy Beach, Ruth Crawford, Miriam Gideon, Mary Howe, and Louise Talma; visual artists Bashka Paeff, Lilla Cabot Perry, Elizabeth Sparhawk-Jones, Katharine Beecher Stetson, and Ursula Whitlock; and writers Willa Cather, Julia Peterkin, Leonora Speyer, Sara Teasdale, Margaret Widdemer, and Elinor Wylie. Five of these women were Pulitzer Prize winners.[17]

The success of the MacDowell Colony has been documented in numerous periodical and newspaper articles throughout its existence. Colony coverage in music periodicals abounds. Located in the Music Division's collections, these include Marian's own "MacDowell's Peterborough Idea" from *Musical Quarterly* (18:1932). As the prestige of the colony and its artists grew, feature articles appeared in more mainstream publications such as *Atlantic Monthly, Life, Reader's Digest,* and the *Christian Science Monitor.*[18] When Marian MacDowell's ninety-fifth year was celebrated with an officially proclaimed "Marian MacDowell Day," August 15, 1952, *Time, Newsweek,* and the *New York Times* ran stories.[19] Newspapers and periodicals in particular offer a currency of information that is lacking in the other MacDowell material at the Library. The *Boston Globe,* for example, features two accounts of MacDowell colonists in its issues from 1992. The year 1996 was celebrated as the 100th anniversary of Marian MacDowell's purchase of Hillcrest with a feature article in *American Artist* and a special exhibit of MacDowell Colony artists covered by the *New York Times.*[20]

Marian MacDowell's astonishing longevity added to her remarkable achievements; by the time she entered her tenth decade, she was something of a legend. In the early 1950s she was interviewed for a New York Philharmonic intermission broadcast on CBS radio and for the Voice of America by Telly Sevalas, then a VOA reporter. The MacDowell Colony audio material (LWO 15821) in the Recorded Sound Section contains these interviews as well as one with Marian MacDowell and composer Mary Howe. Early silent film footage of the colony (LWO-20379) and of "Marian MacDowell Day" (FEC 1586) is available for viewing in the Motion Picture and Television Reading Room. In 1954, Marian MacDowell was honored in a Hallmark Hall of Fame special based on her life, *Lady in the Wings* (VBH 0858). This dramatization closes with a brief appearance by the elderly Marian, on the arm of her companion Nina Maud Richardson. It is the only moving image with sound of Marian MacDowell in the Library's collections. Equally rare is the recording of her piano playing found among the recordings of the Works Progress Administration. Recorded around 1942, this 16-inch disc (NCPC 00792) contains a short segment of Edward MacDowell's "Haunted House." She was well into her eighties at the time this recording was made.

Photographs of Marian and Edward MacDowell and the MacDowell Colony are found in several collections. The Prints and Photographs Division's MacDowell Colony material (PR 13 1980:70) consists of a box of miscellaneous photos and three scrapbooks. Currently unprocessed, it is viewable upon special application. Some of the photos are identified, such as one of Marian and Edward dating from around 1905–6 and reproduced here, but many are not. Photographs are also found in the MacDowell collections held by the Music Division and Manuscript Division.

Not to be overlooked are the fruits of the colony artists themselves. Aside from published fiction, nonfiction, and poetry by colony writers in the General Collections, and musical scores and recordings in the Music Division and in the Recorded Sound Section, the Rare Book and Special Collections Division has custody of first editions that were presentation copies to Marian from colony writers. A copy of *The Woman of Andros* (PS3545.I345W6 Copy 3) carries the following inscription: "For Mrs. MacDowell, with the happy indebtedness and affection of Thornton Wilder, March 1930." And a copy of *Death Comes for the Archbishop* (PS3505.A87D4 1927 Copy 2 Rare Bk. Coll.) is signed: "For Mrs. Edward McDowell with my love and admiration Willa Cather, September 27, 1927."

When Marian MacDowell died on August 23, 1956, at the age of ninety-eight, her obituary was carried in newspapers across the country. Literally hundreds of these can be found in the Edward and Marian MacDowell Collection in the Music Division. They consistently identify her as the widow of composer Edward MacDowell and some devote considerable space detailing Edward's accomplishments. One columnist, remarking on this trend, was so bold as to set the record straight: "So far as influence in the arts is concerned," wrote David Felts, of the Urbana, Illinois *Courier*, "Edward MacDowell might be identified as the husband of Marian MacDowell."[21]

Marian MacDowell brought the MacDowell Colony to life and saw it through two world wars, the stock market crash, the Depression, and a hurricane that devastated New England in 1938. She was awarded honorary degrees from the University of New Hampshire, Durham (1930), New Jersey State College for Women (1938), and Middlebury College (1939). In 1940 she received the Pettee Medal from the University of New Hampshire and, in 1941, the Henry Hadley Medal for outstanding service to music. At the age of ninety-two, she was honored by the National Institute of Arts and Letters for her distinguished service in the arts. Yet Marian MacDowell was loath to take credit for the colony, preferring to call herself "one of the help." She summed up her extraordinary achievements quite simply: "I am a very ordinary woman who had an opportunity—and I seized it."[22]

I wish to thank music specialists Susan Clermont and Kevin LaVine for their helpful comments and suggestions, and Robert Saladini, who first brought Marian to my attention and encouraged me to tell her story. Thanks also to Rosemary Hanes (MBRS), Sheridan Harvey (GenColl), Rosemary Fry Plakas (RBSC), and Nancy Seeger (MBRS) for their assistance in locating MacDowell materials in their respective collections.

CBS
CBS

9 Recorded Sound Section

Motion Picture, Broadcasting, and Recorded Sound Division

Nancy J. Seeger

Sound affords us the privilege of experiencing firsthand "Crazy Blues" as sung by Mamie Smith (1883–1946) in 1920—the first vaudeville blues recording by an African American—or a Verdi aria charmingly sung by ten-year-old Beverly Sills on a 1939 *Major Bowes' Amateur Hour* broadcast. A powerfully moving 1939 radio talk on the meaning of American democracy by Mary McLeod Bethune (1875–1955) and a 1930s interview with social worker Jane Addams (1860–1935) about public relief are also available to us as recorded sound.[1] The Motion Picture, Broadcasting, and Recorded Sound Division (MBRS) holds one of the world's largest and most comprehensive collections of sound recordings documenting twentieth-century American women's contributions in a great variety of disciplines and areas of achievement. The collections provide us with an aural gateway through which we can study the most noteworthy and some less well-known American women of the century. These recordings offer an opportunity to study twentieth- and twenty-first-century American women not only through the words and songs of others but, most importantly, through the words and songs of the women themselves.

Since it received its first cylinder recording in 1904 the Library has collected over two million audio and radio broadcast recordings dating from 1890 to the present day and spanning the history of recorded sound technology and broadcasting. Nearly every medium ever used to record sound is represented, from wax cylinders and 78rpm discs to digital compact discs and audiotapes. Diverse media such as wire recordings, aluminum discs, piano rolls, rubber compound discs, and translucent plastic discs also are found in the collections. The collections are predominantly American in scope and include both commercial releases and noncommercial archival recordings, the latter of which are unique, unpublished recordings that are usually the result of personal or corporate activity.

The Library did not begin to collect recordings systematically until 1925. At that time, the Victor Talking Machine Company gave the Library a selection of its phonograph records, prompting other companies to follow suit. The Library initially developed its collections almost solely through gifts from individuals and corporations. To this day, private collectors, performing artists, corporations, and associations contribute their recordings, radio programs, and archives to the Library. In 1972, the deposit of sound recordings became a United States copyright law requirement, providing the Library with another invaluable source for acquiring recordings. Among these copyright deposits are cassettes which offer insight into the thoughts and feelings of the "common American" and present an American musical panorama that cannot be found anywhere else. In addition, the division often receives recordings from the Music or Manuscript Divisions that came into the Library as part of large, multiformat collections, such as the Margaret Mead collection. The recorded sound holdings are rich in published recordings of ethnographic interest, as well as Library of Congress music and literary programs; material from other government agencies; voice transcriptions;

Rosalind Russell (right) and Lurene Tuttle (left) in "The Sisters" on Suspense. *March 16, 1949. Photograph by Wide World. Specific Subjects File. Prints and Photographs Division. LC-USZ62-91912.*

Lurene Tuttle (1907–1986) was one of the hardest-working and most well-respected actors in radio. Politically active in her profession as well, Tuttle became the first woman president of the Los Angeles, California, chapter of the American Federation of Radio Artists. A gifted dialectician, Tuttle played a wide variety of characters in theatrical dramas, as shown here, and in continuing series such as *The Adventures of Sam Spade* and *The Red Skelton Show.* Though she may have lacked the glamour of a Hollywood leading lady, Tuttle thrived in radio, where she relished her meaty roles. As she observed, "I could play opposite Cary Grant or Gary Cooper . . . and on the air I could be the most glamorous, gorgeous, tall, black-haired female you've ever seen. . . . Whatever I wished to be, I could be with my voice."

and popular, folk, jazz, musical theater, and classical music from private sources.

Sometimes content is not of primary importance in a recording. The fact that a recording provides one of the few, perhaps only, opportunities to hear a public person's voice may be of equal interest as is the fascination of hearing variations in oratorical styles, vocal expressions, and language dialects. In an unpublished 1952 recording (LWO 5114), Helen Keller (1880–1968) spoke to Library of Congress employees about the talking books for the blind program. Her speech had to be translated as the words are almost entirely indiscernible. Corinne Roosevelt Robinson (1861–1933) spoke in crisp, patrician tones heard on a 1920 recording (included in the Library's "Compressed" audio collection) in which she supported the Harding-Coolidge presidential ticket. Robinson and her brother Theodore displayed a meticulous and refined way of speaking that may sound affected and strident to Americans today. Margaret Woodrow Wilson (1886–1944), President Woodrow Wilson's daughter who aspired to a career as a singer, recorded a medley of patriotic airs in 1915 with Columbia for the American Red Cross (Columbia A1685). A copy of an 1892 brown wax cylinder reveals a heartfelt message to "every white-ribboned sister" by Isabella (Lady Henry) Somerset (1851–1921), vice president of the World's Woman's Christian Temperance Union.

Sound recording technology and radio broadcasting matured during the twentieth century, developing during the time in American history when women were experiencing major social, political, and cultural changes. Radio programs and sound recordings in the division offer numerous approaches for examining these changes. Take the women's suffrage movement as an example. Through interpretation, dramatization, documentation, and commentary, the movement comes alive in the medium of recorded sound. In the 1910s, woman's suffrage was a topic of ridicule in the humorous talks and songs popular on 78rpm recordings. In "Since My Margaret Became a Suffragette" (Victor 17145), the singer Maurice Burkhardt complained that his Margaret "wears the pants that kill romance." "Schultz on Women's Suffrage" (Victor 16294) featured Frank Kennedy's comical predictions of a future when women would be elected to office. A female street-cleaning department would sprinkle the streets with cologne and decorate the ashcans with ribbons, he grumbled.

Songs, on the other hand, that express the exhilaration and determination of the movement are available today on modern compilation recordings such as *Songs of the Suffragettes* (1958, Folkways FH5281), performed by Elizabeth Knight; and *Hurrah for Woman Suffrage* (1995 copyright deposit, RYF 3942), performed by the Homespun Singers. The suffragists' words are given voice by some of our most expressive actors on Caedmon's *Great American Women's Speeches* (1973, Caedmon TC 2067).

Radio as well has been a rich source of information on women's suffrage. For example, *Women in the Making of America* (1939), a 1930s NBC radio series devoted to dramatizing the cultural and social contributions that women have made throughout the history of the United States, featured programs on many important suffragists, including Lucy Stone (1818–1893), Julia Ward Howe (1819–1910), Angelina Grimké (1805–1879), and Lucretia Mott (1793–1880). Ninety-one-year-old Mabel Vernon (1884?–1975), a suffragist who worked with the National Woman's Party, was interviewed on a 1974 Pacifica Radio broad-

RECORDED SOUND REFERENCE CENTER
James Madison Memorial Building, 1st floor, room LM 113
Hours: Monday through Friday, 8.30 a.m. to 5.00 p.m.
Saturday by appointment. Closed Sunday and federal holidays.
Telephone: 202 707-7833
Fax: 202 707-8464
Address: Recorded Sound Reference Center, Motion Picture, Broadcasting, and Recorded Sound Division, 101 Independence Avenue, SE, Washington, DC 20540-4698
E-mail: rsrc@loc.gov
Web site: <http://www.loc.gov/rr/record>
Access and use: It is not necessary to make appointments to use the Recorded Sound Reference Center during the week. If, however, patrons wish to make listening appointments for Saturday, when the center is closed, they must do so during the week, by Thursday. Listening to recorded sound collections is restricted to those conducting research of a specific nature, leading toward a publicly available work, such as a publication, thesis or dissertation, radio, film, or television production, or a public performance. Listeners are required to describe their project, present a reader identification card, and read and sign a form agreeing that they will abide by the formal rules and regulations for using the reference center. Only materials essential to research are allowed in the reading room. Adjacent to the reference center is the Performing Arts Reading Room, where multipurpose rooms are available for listening to recordings through speakers. The Recorded Sound Reference Center staff will guide patrons through the procedures required to listen to such recordings or to study album covers and other documentation. Copying of recordings is not permitted and tape recorders or equipment may not be taken into the listening area. Patrons may purchase tape copies of recordings from the Library's Recording Laboratory after obtaining written authorization from the rights holders.

cast (RYA 4044). The venerable suffragist Carrie Chapman Catt (1859–1947) appeared several times on the radio to advocate peace and disarmament. In a 1944 broadcast (RWA 6399 B2) of her eighty-fifth birthday celebration, she shared the microphone with Eleanor Roosevelt (1884–1962) and Helen Hayes (1900–1993).

Suffrage is just one of many topics that can be researched in the division's holdings. The following sections of this chapter suggest other research possibilities and strategies by providing access information and descriptions of collections relating to American women's history and culture.

USING THE COLLECTIONS

To reach the Recorded Sound Reference Center, you must pass through the Music Division's Performing Arts Reading Room. This is not an accidental arrangement as the two reading rooms have a complementary relationship and work closely together. The Recorded Sound Reference Center provides access to the recorded music and songs of composers, lyricists, songwriters, and performers that patrons may also research in the Performing Arts Reading Room. Resources in the reading room include books on music, scores, music reference tools, finding aids to the Music Division's archival collections, and other music, dance, and theater-related materials that provide crucial supplemental information to those researching sound recordings. For example, recordings that accompanied the Bob Fosse and Gwen Verdon collection were deposited in MBRS, whereas much of the rest of the materials in the collection, including papers, photographs, and other ephemera, reside in the Music Division (see chapter 8). Other divisions throughout the Library may also have material that pertains to your research project. Researchers should check with reference librarians for information about where to find additional pertinent material.

The Motion Picture, Broadcasting, and Recorded Sound Division has made great progress during the 1990s in improving access to its vast collection of sound recordings. Before 1990 relatively few commercial recordings and practically no archival recordings were fully cataloged. New automated systems and additional staff have enabled the division to begin systematically cataloging more of its collections. Recordings cited throughout the chapter are held in the Motion Picture, Broadcasting, and Recorded Sound Division. Shelf location numbers, whenever they exist, are given for all recordings cited. Dates following radio program titles indicate the years of those broadcasts that the Library holds, not the years during which the programs were broadcast.

It is best to begin researching your topic in the computer databases and card files, but because a significant portion of the Library's sound recordings is not yet fully cataloged, the failure to find a listing there does not necessarily mean that a recording is not held by the Library. The reference staff will assist you in suggesting alternate search strategies and approaches for locating material and for searching different resources, including many that are not described here.

Library of Congress Catalogs and Finding Aids

The online and card catalogs described here provide access to those primarily responsible for a recording, such as composers, authors, actors, speakers, and performers. Searching for a particular person is therefore fairly straightforward. Subject searching is a little more difficult, requiring knowledge of the intricacies of searching by subject, using headings usually derived from *Library of Congress Subject Headings* (*LCSH*). (For more about subject headings, see chapter 1.)

■ The **Library of Congress Online Catalog** contains information about recordings cataloged by the Library from 1951 to the present. These recordings are held in the Library and include mostly commercial and some archival recordings, popular and classical music, the spoken word, and an increasing number of radio broadcasts. Searchable by name, album title, song title, subject or genre (*LCSH* and other sources), label name and number, shelf number, and keyword, the online catalog is the best place to locate more recent commercial music and spoken recordings, particularly compact discs and LPs. It contains data for selected archival collections, including the Library's recordings of its own musical performances, poetry readings, and literary and theatrical events and Columbia University's Brander Matthews Dramatic Museum collection, which features unique recordings of such notable American women as Gertrude Stein (1874–1946), Jane Addams, Willa Cather (1873–1947), and Amelia Earhart (1897–1937). The catalog is also available to researchers outside the reference center through the Library's Web site at <http://www.loc.gov>.

■ The **MBRS Recorded Sound Online Catalog,** or **SONIC (Sound Online Inventory and Catalog),** contains information about recordings cataloged by the Library from the 1980s to the present. There is very little overlap between the holdings recorded here and those found through the Library of Congress Online Catalog. They include commercial and archival recordings, strong holdings of radio broadcasts, popular music, test pressings, and the spoken word. Searchable by name, album title, program title, song title, subject or genre (LCSH and other sources), date, label name and number, shelf number, and keyword, the division's online catalog is the best place to locate radio shows, archival collections, 78rpm discs, and cassettes and 45rpm discs submitted for copyright. It contains over 350,000 bibliographic records and provides access to dozens of archival collections, among which are the NBC Radio collection, *Meet the Press,* National Press Club luncheon speeches, Former Members of Congress oral histories, the Marine Corps Combat Recordings collection, which contains fascinating material on World War II women marines, including interviews, and the Danny Kaye and Sylvia Fine collection. The catalog (SONIC) is available on the Web via the Recorded Sound Reference Center's Web site.

The **Recorded Sound Reference Center Card Catalog Supplement** contains information about recordings inventoried by the Library between 1951 and 1990. These recordings are held in the Library and include mostly archival recordings plus all types of music, the spoken word, and radio broadcasts. The card catalog supplement is searchable by name, title, and subject (LCSH and other types). The division's unique archival collections, which are often difficult to catalog, come from a variety of sources, including individuals, broadcasting networks, and organizations. Staff members rely on this catalog for information on radio broadcasts, special collections, noncommercial pressings, and miscellaneous archival recordings. A below-minimal-level-cataloging card index, the supplement provides little topical access to the material. Yet a search on "women" turned up many pertinent recordings, including dozens of radio broadcasts, a 1960 radio documentary series on the history of women's suffrage called *Women Who Won* (RWD 7915), and a debate on women's liberation between Phyllis Schlafly (b. 1924) and Congresswoman Martha Griffiths (b. 1912) (RZA 0760). A radio broadcast (RWA 3069) of the 1938 Wimbledon women's singles tennis match between Helen Jacobs (1908–1997) and Helen Wills Moody (1905–1998) is also listed there, as is a recording of Pope John Paul II at the 1979 Mass on the Mall in Washington, D.C., where he spoke on abortion, marriage, and family (RZA 0781).

The **Copyright History Monograph Database** contains information about recordings received by the Copyright Office from 1978 to the present, particularly music and spoken word commercial recordings. These recordings may or may not be held in the division and the bibliographic records are searchable by claimant name, by album title, and often by song title. All sound recordings registered for copyright since 1978 are listed in the Copyright History Monograph (COHM) database, which is also available on the Library of Congress Web site. The division does not retain all of these recordings. Recordings that are selected for the collections are cataloged and can be found by consulting the Library and divisional catalogs described above. Audio cassettes and 45rpm discs submitted for copyright and retained by the division are cataloged in the division's online catalog, SONIC, which provides limited subject access (using LCSH).

Recordings that are not retained by the division are sent to off-site storage and are accessible only through the COHM database. The reference staff will assist you in locating items not retained for the collections by the division. Copyright deposits from 1972 to 1977 are listed in a printed index called the *Catalog of Copyright Entries: Sound Recordings,* available in the Recorded Sound Reference Center.

For years, composers and songwriters were required to deposit sheet music, lead sheets, or other written transcripts of their music in applying for copyright. When the copyright law changed in 1978, claimants could instead submit recordings of their musical works. As a result, the Library receives thousands of copyright recordings every year—some by established performers, others recorded at home in someone's basement. The change in the law allowed amateur musicians and performers to share their opinions in musical form on social issues such as abortion and women's rights. "The Ballad of Anita Hill" (1991 copyright deposit, RYD 1817), sung by Sally Chappell; Tania Wahl's composition "Ride, Sally Ride!" (1983 copyright deposit, RYG 4601) in honor of the first American woman in space, astronaut Sally Ride (b. 1951); and Lindy Gravelle's feminist tune "We've Come a Long Way, Ladies" (1992 copyright deposit, RYC 2714) are all in this collection.

Copyright deposits may reveal the early musical stirrings of future recording stars. The division has dozens of copyright recordings submitted in the mid-1980s by a young musician and songwriter named Ellen Amos. One 1978 recording features the fifteen-year-old Amos performing with the band Contraband. By the early 1990s she was garnering attention and building a following as Tori Amos (b. 1963). Now she fills concert halls and sings eloquently of concerns and issues that speak directly to women of her generation.

National and International Catalogs

Several important catalogs contain bibliographic information for audio recordings held by the Library of Congress, as well as thousands of national and international libraries and archives. These invaluable resources enable you to augment and expand your research beyond the confines of the Library of Congress. In addition, these catalogs may help in locating uncataloged commercial recordings at the Library of Congress by supplying label names and issue numbers which are needed for manual shelf-checks.

The **OCLC Online Union Catalog** is a bibliographic utility created in the 1960s to which thousands of libraries contribute. It includes records for commercial and archival recordings as well as all kinds of music and the spoken word. These recordings may or may not be held by the division, and the records are searchable by name, album title, song title, subject, date, label name and number, and keyword. OCLC is available through university libraries, often through a public interface.

The **SilverPlatter Music Library CD-ROM** contains records for only those music recordings that have been cataloged on OCLC from the mid-1960s to the present. These are mostly commercial recordings—although some are archival. All types of music are included and the recordings may or may not be in the Library's recorded sound collections. These records are searchable by name, album title, song title, subject, date, label name and number, and keyword. This catalog is available only in the reference center.

The **Rigler and Deutsch Index** to 78rpm recordings held in five libraries, including the Library of Congress, indexes commercial recordings of all kinds of music and the spoken word. The recordings may or may not be in the division and the index is searchable by name, song title, and label name and number. This index is also available through RLIN (see below).

The **RLIN Bibliographic Database** is a bibliographic utility created in the 1970s to which over 160 cultural, academic, and scientific organizations contribute. It includes both commercial and archival recordings of all kinds of music and the spoken word, which may or may not be held by the division. The database is searchable by name, album title, song title, subject, date, label name and number, and keyword. RLIN is available at many university libraries, often through a public interface.

Reference Works

Published discographies are extremely useful resources in the field of recorded sound. They are descriptive lists of recordings by such categories as label, performer or artist, composer, or genre. They cover primarily commercial recordings of various musical genres. It is important to bear in mind, however, that the recordings listed in the various discographies found in the reference center are not necessarily held in the division. You must search for particular recordings in the various Library and divisional catalogs to determine their availability within the division.

Three discographies in the Recorded Sound Reference Center are particularly relevant to the study of American women composers and performers. *Women Composers: A Discography* by Jane Frasier (Detroit: Information Coordinators, 1983; ML156.4.W6 F7 1983) and *The International Discography of Women Composers,* compiled by Aaron I. Cohen (Westport, Conn.: Greenwood Press, 1984; ML156.4.W6 C6 1984), are guides to classical music recordings written by women composers. Only the first volume (covering letters A–F) of *The Encyclopaedia of Gay and Lesbian Recordings* (Amsterdam: J. McLaren, 1989; ML156.4.G4 M2 1989) has been published, and it may be the only existing annotated discography that includes information on performers from the lesbian and feminist music scene.

Another very important resource is the *Ladyslipper Catalog and Resource Guide of Music by Women* (Durham, N.C.: Ladyslipper, Inc., 1976–), which is available only in the reference center. For twenty years this triennial, annotated publication has provided information about musical and literary recordings by women artists, including musicians, writers, composers, and comics. The catalog is organized by categories such as women's spirituality, gospel music, classical music, drumming/percussion, comedy, and the spoken word. Within these categories, artists are arranged alphabetically by their first names.

The division shelves many of its commercial releases numerically by recording company (for some media, this system is gradually being changed to a shelf number arrangement). Among the best guides to the collections, therefore, are the many record manufacturers' or other trade catalogs on file in the reference center, or listed there and shelved in the Music Division. These are descriptive lists of commercial recordings for various musical genres. Once a label and number are located, a search can be made for the recording. Note, however, that the presence of a manufacturer's catalog in the division does not indicate that all of the recordings it lists will be in the Library's collections.

SELECTED COLLECTIONS

For the purposes of researching women's history and culture, the recorded sound collections can be considered as forming roughly four broad areas: radio broadcasts, music recordings, recordings of dramatic and literary performances, and recordings of the spoken word. Obviously, considerable overlap exists among the four groupings—radio broadcasts encompass both music and the spoken word, and dramas are frequently broadcast on the radio. Such an arrangement allows us to highlight nonmusic, unpublished collections that have come to the Library of Congress from individuals, organizations, or associations.

Radio

The Library of Congress holds the largest and most important collection of radio broadcasts in the United States. Spanning the mid-1920s through the present day, these broadcasts include all types of radio genres—comedy, drama, public affairs, propaganda, interviews, news, and musical variety. Among more than five hundred thousand radio programs are many containing information about American women's history and culture. The radio collection comprises many "special collections," donations from radio networks, performers, writers, and producers. The two largest of these are the **National Broadcasting Company (NBC) collection** and the **Armed Forces Radio and Television Service (AFRTS) collection.** Dozens of collections are devoted to a single performer—often donated by that performer—or a particular company. Broadcasts by Arthur Godfrey and singer Jessica Dragonette (1910–1980), soap operas and variety programs sponsored by General Foods Corporation, and programs by interviewer Larry King are among these. Others concern anthropologist Margaret Mead (1901–1978), the poetry and literature series *New Letters on the Air,* the *Original Amateur Hour,* Phil and Evelyn Spitalny's All-Girl Orchestra, and soprano Helen Traubel (1899–1972). These radio broadcasts, which offer several different paths for studying American women, are a largely underused resource.

Much is already known about the legendary women performers, comedians, and actors who have had their own shows or appeared as guests on the radio, but such stars as Judy Canova (1916–1983), Marian Jordan (1897–1961) of *Fibber McGee and Molly,* Gracie Allen (1902–1964), and Eve Arden (1912–1990) represent only a fraction of the female stars found in the Library's collections. Perhaps all of the major newsmakers of the day in all professions have appeared on the radio—Mamie Eisenhower (1896–1979), Bess Truman (1885–1982), birth control advocate Margaret Sanger (1879–1966), pilot Amelia Earhart (1897–1937), athlete Babe Didrikson Zaharias (1911–1956), writer and folklorist Zora Neale Hurston (1891–1960), and religious leader Aimee Semple McPherson (1890–1944), whose skillful use of the radio made her one of the most famous evangelists of her time, are among them. The ubiquitous Eleanor Roosevelt, who was an extremely effective communicator on the radio and used this skill to great political and social advantage, can be heard on hundreds of broadcasts.

Other once-influential radio personalities, such as Mary Margaret McBride (1899–1976), are not as well known today (see illustration, page 290, and the introduction to this volume). Originally employed as a print journalist, McBride hosted an extremely popular daily radio program during the late 1930s, the 1940s, and the 1950s. Her audience was composed mainly of women.[2] Her show mixed spontaneous interviews with notable guests, many of whom were women, and useful information with a heavy dose of advertising targeted at women. Topics discussed on her show included prostitution, unwed mothers, marriage in the modern world, and pioneering women. The program offered an alternative to the afternoon soap operas and demonstrated that women's interests ranged beyond cleaning tips and recipes. McBride maintained complete editorial and commercial control over her program and in doing so made lasting changes in the style of radio talk shows.

The **Cynthia Lowry/Mary Margaret McBride collection** at the Library of Congress includes over twelve hundred hours of interview programs and related broadcasts. All phases of

McBride's radio career, from 1935 to the 1970s, are represented. Access to the collection is available through the division's online database, SONIC, where you can search by guest name or date of broadcast.

Beyond the Microphone

From radio's earliest pre-network days, women worked in almost every capacity, both at the microphone and behind the scenes. Women have been among radio's most imaginative and productive writers and producers. Eva vom Baur Hansl (1888?–1978), a journalist who worked with several different broadcasting organizations, produced such educational programs as *Women in the Making of America* (1939), a Federal Radio Theatre project written by Jane Ashman (n.d.); *Gallant American Women* (1939–40); and *Womanpower* (1942). Virginia Safford Lynne (n.d.) and Ruth Adams Knight (1898–1974) wrote for, among other programs, *The Great Gildersleeve* (1941–49, 1952–57, 1966) and *Those We Love* (1942, 1944), respectively. Writers Ann Barley (n.d.) and Ruth Barth (n.d.) contributed to the docudrama series *March of Time* (1937–39, 1941–45). Helen Mack (1913–1986) directed *The Saint* (1950–51) and *The Alan Young Show* (1944–47, 1949–50). In 1930, actress-turned-writer Edith Meiser (1898–1993) persuaded NBC to produce *Sherlock Holmes* (1939–40), which she had adapted for radio from the original stories. She continued to work on the series as script editor, writer, and adapter through the late 1940s.[3]

Beginning in the 1930s, women dominated daytime programming both as creators and as listeners. Radio programs aimed at women's perceived needs and interests filled the airwaves between 9:00 a.m. and 6:00 p.m. Programs dealing with topics such as cooking, childcare, health, fashion, civic news, and women's business news competed with soap operas and light musical programs for women's attention. As a means of sharing information about common problems and issues and offering encouraging messages, these programs enabled homemakers to communicate indirectly with one another.

The rise of the radio soap opera in the mid-1930s demonstrated just how powerful the female audience could be. Before that time little research went into program development for the daytime lineup, which was made up of "throw-away hours" and therefore considered unworthy of much attention. The popularity of the soap opera and the serial drama proved that daytime radio had a devoted audience and could be extremely profitable for sponsors whose products would appeal to these listeners. The number of serials burgeoned to such a degree that in the spring of 1941 a women's serial could be heard during all but a single quarter-hour between the hours of 10:00 a.m. and 6:00 p.m.[4]

The importance of the radio soap opera to American women cannot be overemphasized. Indeed, according to Muriel G. Cantor and Suzanne Pingree, "soap operas, more than any other genre,

Allen Prescott of the radio program Wife Saver. *Publicity photograph from Prescott's personal scrapbook. Recorded Sound Reference Center, Motion Picture, Broadcasting, and Recorded Sound Division.*

Five mornings a week, from 1932 to 1942, Allen Prescott, host of the program *Wife Saver,* greeted his faithful audience of housewives with a cheery, "Hello, girls." Prescott, who sometimes received as many as five hundred letters a week from women all over the country, solved some of life's more mundane problems by offering such homey advice and household tips as how to get meat out of the can, where to store hats, and how to make new silk stockings last longer. Prescott's signature sign-off, "Mrs. Housewife, I hope there's nothing burning," typifies his droll delivery.

have reflected the economic and social conditions under which they were produced. Individualistic values are interspersed with problems and suffering most likely to be encountered by women . . . regardless of their similarity and diversity as to subjects, soap operas are about women and their place in the social world."[5] And during the golden age of the radio soap operas that social world for the most part revolved around the home.

> The soaps offered the homebound listener a dramatization of the conflict she might be expected to have in her own mind about the nature of men, marriage, and the woman's role. And they suggested that they might have useful answers to such questions [as were heard in a soap opera introduction], "To hold a man's love, what should a young wife be? . . . Should she place her home and her children above all else? . . . These are some of the questions the modern woman faces . . . when a girl marries."[6]

Anne Hummert (1905–1996), Irna Phillips (1901–1973), and Elaine Sterne Carrington (1892–1958) were three of the most creative and prolific women writing soap operas during the genre's heyday on the radio. Anne Hummert and her husband Frank, often credited with perfecting the soap opera formula, supervised a stable of writers who wrote dialogue from sketches provided by Anne Hummert.[7] Some of their more famous programs were *Stella Dallas* (1937–55), *John's Other Wife* (1936–42), and *Young Widder Brown* (1938–56). In 1937, Irna Phillips, who actually wrote most of her own scripts, created *Guiding Light* (1942, 1944–46), one of the longest-running soap operas. The fact that *Guiding Light* made a successful transfer to television is a testament to the writer's skills, foresight, and imagination. Phillips was a pioneer who created many techniques—cliff-hangers, organ bridges between scenes, and characters appearing concurrently in different serials—that are taken for granted in soaps today.[8] Elaine Sterne Carrington was a successful short story writer in the 1920s before her switch to radio. She is known for her realistic dialogue, which she wrote herself, and for strong characterizations.[9] Of her soap operas, the Library holds *Pepper Young's Family* (1932–59) and *When a Girl Marries* (1939–55).

Homemaker or talk shows, educational programs, and variety shows were some of the most popular daytime genres produced for and by women. Alma Kitchell (1893–1997) and Nellie Revell (1872–1958) both had talk shows that provided women with pertinent news, information, advice, gossip, and topical discussions, and the Library holds a selection of their shows from the 1930s and 1940s. Isabel Manning Hewson hosted *Morning Market Basket* (1940, 1942), a consumer information show for women. Nutritionist and chef Mary Lee Taylor tried out recipes and shared tips on shopping and cooking. Her program *The Mary Lee Taylor Show* (1948–49) was the longest running cooking program on radio. *Pickens Party* (1951–52), starring Jane Pickens (1908–1992) and her sisters, featured musical variety and light entertainment.

Women took the lead in creating and producing educational and entertainment programs for children. Madge Tucker (b. 1900), who headed up NBC's children's programming department, produced the children's show *Coast-to-Coast on a Bus* (1937–41). Helen Walpole (b. 1911) and Margaret Leaf (1909?–1988) wrote *Adventures in Reading* (1939–40), an educational series for children. Dr. Katharine Lenroot (1891–1982), head of the United States Children's Bureau, hosted two programs on child rearing, *The Child Grows Up* (1938–40) and *Children in Wartime* (1942), the

David Bransky for the U.S. Office for Emergency Management. Barbara Jean Wong and Walter Pidgeon on Three-Thirds of a Nation. *Photograph, June 1942. Specific Subjects File. Prints and Photographs Division. LC-USZ62-77813.*

Once known as the "Chinese Shirley Temple," Barbara Jean Wong (1924–1999) was the first Asian American to appear regularly on network radio drama and comedy programs. Specializing in "little girl" parts even as a young adult, Wong played young Judy Barton, one of the main characters on the very popular children's program *The Cinnamon Bear,* and Amos's daughter Arbadella in *Amos 'n Andy.* Here she shares the mike with Walter Pidgeon as they offer information on the War Production Board's progress in wool production. She later became an elementary school teacher and community activist for local women's clubs and Chinese American organizations.

latter of which examined the effects of war on children. Madge Tucker directed and Jean Peterson wrote for *Our Barn* (1936–41), a children's storytelling program.

The division's radio collections are an especially valuable source for studying the lives of American women during the Second World War. Radio during that time served many functions for women both at home and abroad. The comedies and entertainment programs provided an escape mechanism by which women on both fronts could escape the realities of war. It was also an excellent communicating device that helped bolster confidence, reminding women at home why their family members were off fighting a war. Most important, radio was used to recruit middle-class white women into wartime service, thereby expanding their previously rather limited realm of experience. The Office of War Information (OWI) launched the "Womanpower" campaign in 1942. In addition, OWI's *American Women Speak* (1942–43) and *Women Can Take It* (1942) told women's stories, described their contributions to the war effort, and praised them for jobs well done. Oveta Culp Hobby (1905–1995), commander of the Women's Army Corps (earlier called Women's Army Auxiliary Corps, or WAACs), often appeared on the radio describing the role of women in wartime (1944 broadcast, RWA 6883 B1). To mark her 1943 appearance on the program *The Pause That Refreshes on the Air,* the host, Andre Kostelanetz, included a choral rendition of Lt. Ruby J. Douglas's "The WAAC Is a Soldier Too" (LWO 5855 R31A1).

The great depth and breadth of the Library's radio holdings allow us to observe evolving societal attitudes toward women and assumptions about them. To use the division's radio collections for such research, you will first need to consult primary and secondary sources in other divisions for topics and programs of interest; then you can search the Library and divisional catalogs described earlier to locate programs held by the Library.

Although it is impossible to cover all of the radio collections in this guide, a few of the largest collections will be described here in terms of content, cataloging, and access. Reference staff members can assist you in finding and examining smaller radio collections.

National Broadcasting Company (NBC) Radio Collection

The NBC Radio collection, one of the largest single collections of broadcast recordings (150,000 discs) in the United States, was donated to the Library in 1978. The collection contains all genres of radio from the early 1930s through the late 1960s, including comedy, drama, public affairs, musical variety, sports, news, information, and international shortwave broadcasts. Everything through 1953, plus a selection of programs after 1953, has been preserved and is cataloged on the division's online catalog, SONIC, which contains over 68,000 NBC bibliographic records and permits searching by program title, name, date, genre, keyword, shelf number, and some subjects. An inventory (brief catalog records) of the remainder of the collection can be consulted in the reference center. The publication *Radio Broadcasts in the Library of Congress, 1924–1941* (Washington: Library of Congress, 1982; Z663.36.R32 1982) and the recorded sound card catalog supplement also provide some access to NBC programs.

NBC broadcasts offer listeners examples of America's golden age of radio broadcasting on nearly a daily level. They present a gold mine of material just waiting to be tapped by researchers in their quest for information on American women's history and culture. Not only did NBC programs feature many of the major women comedians, actors, and performers of the day, they also featured programs about women, their history, and the issues that concerned them. Practically all the major women newsmakers of the day appeared on radio. Women worked behind the scenes at NBC as writers, producers, directors, musicians, and newscasters. Programs and advertisements that were expressly created for the female audience offer insight into women's lives and perceptions of them.

In addition to the daytime programming that was so important to women listeners, the NBC Collection contains pertinent evening and special programs created or written by women, such as those who wrote the light dramas *Grand Central Station* (1940–42)—Mary Brinker Post (b. 1906), Dena Reed (1903–1986), and others—and *Grand Marquee* (1946–47)—Virginia Safford Lynne. Gertrude Berg (1899–1966) was another such author, whose semiautobiographical *House of Glass* (1935) told the story of the Glass family, who ran a small hotel in the Catskills.

Respected women journalists and reporters such as Dorothy Thompson (1893–1961), Helen Hiett (1931–1961), and Pauline Frederick (1908–1990) worked on several NBC news and special broadcasts. Hiett was one of the first female foreign correspondents for NBC. A 1930s series called *Women in the News* (1937–39) featured noteworthy women of the day. Dozens of programs

Frederic March and Hazel Scott (at the piano) on the National Urban League's Salute to Freedom, *NBC Radio. Photograph, March 18, 1944. National Urban League, Vocational Opportunity Campaign scrapbook (part 1, series 7). Manuscript Division. LC–MS–40774–2.*

Among the many social changes brought about by World War II was a shift in the way the nation saw African Americans. African Americans began to be treated with somewhat more respect in radio broadcasts. Radio shows advocating "ethnic unity and interracial solidarity" became more common. In this broadcast, sponsored by the National Urban League for Social Service among Negroes, tribute is paid to African American service personnel. Appearing later on the show, H. V. Kaltenborn spoke about the army nurse corps and about Evelyn Samuels, a young African American woman from Brooklyn who received a grade of 99 on her civil service exam—the highest rating achieved by any of the 6,000 women who took the exam.

sponsored by various Democratic and Republican Party organizations dealt with women's issues and featured prominent women. In 1940, Rose Kennedy (1890–1995) spoke on President Franklin Roosevelt's "road to peace" before the Democratic National Conference Women's Division (RWB 5424 A2). The Women's National Republican Club offered a 1948 program (RWB 8844 B2) with Alma Kitchell, Irene Dunne (1904–1990), and Edith Willkie (1890?–1978), wife of Wendell Willkie.

NBC employed many women comedians who were popular during radio's golden age, including Jane Ace (1905–1974), Fanny Brice (1891–1951), Lucille Ball (1911–1989), Penny Singleton (1908–1952), and Billie Burke (1885–1970).

Because topical access is limited, you should have a fairly good idea of particular names or NBC programs that interest you. Prior research and advance preparation will save time and make searching the collections easier. Discographic access to the NBC Radio collection is not yet comprehensive, so the best available source of information about the content of the discs is the card catalog compiled by NBC for nearly forty years and other files and documentation that came with the collection. The NBC catalog and files combined are the single most complete written record of American broadcasting content in the collections of the Library of Congress.

SEARCH TIPS: After searching NBC programs in the division's recorded sound online catalog, or SONIC, you should consult the NBC Collection Resources.

1. The **History files** cover the mid-1920s through the late 1940s. For these files, a computerized inventory is available on the Recorded Sound Reference Center's Web site.

2. The **Log books** list daily programs and cover the period 1922–55.

3. The **Master books** document programs and include scripts, ad and news copy, and musical contents from 1922 to 1984.

4. The **Index card catalog** is a comprehensive index to network programs and includes entries for credits and plots. The catalog is divided into five separate parts: program analysis cards; an index to performers and guests; a title segment listing adaptations of literary works by title of the original work; an index to all NBC news and public affairs broadcasts dealing with World War II; and an index of programs broadcast from service bases, radio plays on the war, and shows with war-related topics. The entire program analysis card index covers the period 1930–60. The sustaining program section contains a yearly index to "women's programs" such as *Women's Patriotic Conference on National Defense* (1939) (RWA 4304 A3–4), *Gold Star Mothers* (1941) (LWO 12873 53A1), *Federation of Business and Professional Women* (1937, 1941–42), *Wife Saver* (1939–41, 1945, 1947), and *Florence Hale's Radio Column* (1937–39).

Meet the Press Collection

Meet the Press, the NBC News program that is still going strong today, began on the radio in 1945. It was not until 1948, however, that the first woman appeared on the show. She was Martha Taft (1891–1958), wife of Senator Robert A. Taft, an activist for the League of Women Voters, and at the time one of the most quoted women in the country. Other women who appeared early on in the program include Vivien Kellems (1896–1975), a fiery businesswoman known for her battles against the federal tax system's discriminatory practices against single people; Elizabeth Bentley (1908–1963), a former Communist Party member and spy who later collaborated with the FBI; and Judge Dorothy Kenyon (1888–1972), an influential force in the struggle for women's rights and social reform. This collection is a treasure trove of appearances by just about every notable American woman from the past fifty years, including Eleanor Roosevelt, Margaret Chase Smith (1897–1995), Geraldine Ferraro (b. 1935), Elizabeth Dole (b. 1936), Congresswoman Edna Kelly (1906–1997), and journalist and political activist India Edwards (1895–1990).

The Library holds most of the *Meet the Press* radio broadcasts, plus audio recordings of the television broadcasts that began in 1949. The entire audio collection spans the period from 1945 to 1984. Programs can be searched by name and date in SONIC, but subject searching is quite limited. In addition, an interdivisional online finding aid is currently being created that will allow researchers to access the sound material as well as the rest of the Library's *Meet the Press* material in the Manuscript Division; Prints and Photographs Division; Moving Image Section of the Motion Picture, Broadcasting, and Recorded Sound Division; and the General Collections.

National Public Radio (NPR) Collection

National Public Radio, a noncommercial radio network, produces its own programming and uses programming supplied by member stations, made by noncommercial networks outside the United States, or made by independent producers. In 1976, NPR started giving the Library its arts, cultural, and performance programming tapes dating back to its inception in 1971. (The news and public affairs programs broadcast by NPR are not

Patricia Roberts Harris and Lawrence E. Spivak on NBC's Meet the Press. *Photograph by Reni Newsphotos, October 24, 1971. Lawrence E. Spivak Collection. Prints and Photographs Division. LC-USZ62-126797.*

Lawyer, educator, diplomat, and cabinet officer, Patricia Roberts Harris (1924–1985) was an active and visible force in American politics for twenty years. When she was appointed ambassador to Luxembourg in 1965, she was the first black woman to serve in such a capacity. The Library's holdings include Harris's appearances on *Meet the Press* and before the National Press Club and recordings pertaining to her 1982 unsuccessful run for mayor of the District of Columbia against first-term mayor Marion Barry.

held by the Library but instead are housed at the National Archives and Records Administration.) Tapes are transferred to the Library five to ten years after their initial broadcast. The Library's collection consists of over 25,000 reels of live jazz festivals, opera, symphonic music, chamber music, folk and bluegrass music, radio dramas, game shows, interviews, and poetry.

Featuring a wide variety of women artists who have made their mark on the cultural scene over the past thirty years, this collection includes appearances by Asian American filmmaker Christine Choy (b. 1954), actress France Nuyen (b. 1939), and Hispanic American writer Julia Alvarez (b. 1950). Marian McPartland (b. 1920), Fiona Ritchie (b. 1960), and Mary Cliff exhibit their prodigious musical knowledge as hosts for NPR programs. Women instrumentalists, feminism and women's art, and women in orchestras are some of the topics that have been discussed. The program *Woman's Work* (1980) features primarily classical music written and performed by women.

The NPR collection, which has been cataloged by NPR, is accessible only in the reference center in SONIC. It is searchable by personal and corporate name, program title, subject, keyword, and genre.

WOR Collection

Another major radio collection that recently has been acquired by the Library of Congress is that of WOR-AM, New York City. In 1984 RKO General, Inc., donated the complete archives of the flagship station of the Mutual Broadcasting Network. This collection offers thousands of hours of programming (ca. 15,000 discs), and, like the NBC collection, contains a diverse array of genres, including news, documentaries, musical variety, dramas, comedies, soap operas, quiz shows, and information.

The *Martha Deane* show, one of the first talk shows for women and a precursor to Mary Margaret McBride's show, is included in the collection (Martha Deane programs can also be found in the Cynthia Lowry/Mary Margaret McBride and NBC collections, and span—including those in all three collections—the period from about 1934 to 1953). McBride was actually the first of several different women to play the grandmotherly character. Even after McBride left to start her own show, *Martha Deane* continued to be very popular into the 1970s.

Columnist Dorothy Kilgallen (1913–1965) and model and movie star Jinx Falkenburg (b. 1919), both part of husband-wife radio teams, appeared with their spouses on breakfast shows during which they conducted interviews, dished up the latest Broadway gossip, and discussed current events.

The manuscript portion of the WOR donation is currently being processed by the division for use by the public. Of particular interest are scripts and papers relating to writer and producer Phillips H. Lord's programs, including *Gang Busters* (1937–53), which featured crime stories based on

Mary Margaret McBride. Photograph, 1941. New York World-Telegram and Sun Collection. Prints and Photographs Division. LC-USZ62-114727.

Mary Margaret McBride (1899–1976) was a powerful force in radio during the latter part of the 1930s, throughout the 1940s, and into the 1950s. With a daily audience of almost six million—most of whom were women—McBride's talk show featured interviews with scores of prominent people from all walks of life. Guests enjoyed McBride's unique, informal style of interviewing, which made them comfortable and encouraged a more open exchange. McBride took a strong interest in the products she endorsed, personally testing every one before she promoted it on the air. She received numerous awards and citations for her salesmanship, including being named one of the "Twelve Master Salesmen" in 1952—the only radio personality and woman included on the list. The Library holds hundreds of McBride's radio programs from all phases of her career.

FBI files, and *Policewoman* (1946–47), which was based on the life of New York City policewoman Mary Sullivan. The archive also includes scripts for many of the radio adaptations of books by Kathleen Norris (1880–1966).

The WOR broadcasts are searchable by program title, name, genre, and date in SONIC.

Pacifica Radio Archive

Pacifica Radio is the nation's first listener-supported, community-based radio network. Since 1949 the network has pursued its mission to promote cultural diversity and pluralistic community expression. Just over a hundred cassettes representing 1960s, 1970s, and 1980s Pacifica Radio programming form a small but important collection of radio shows that feature thought-provoking stories not aired on mainstream, commercial networks. Topics that are pertinent to the study of American women, such as prostitution (RYA 4163), women alcoholics (RYA 3943), women's social networks (RYA 3918), the women's music scene (RYA 4112), and lesbianism (RYA 4162) are addressed. *Women of Color, Voices of Resistance* (RYA 8636) broadcasts the songs and poetry of American minority women such as Babette Vasquez (n.d.) and Miya Iwataki (b. 1944). Interviews with many women, including Maya Angelou (b. 1928) (RYA 3938), singer and songwriter Holly Near (b. 1949) (RYA 3932), and Sister Ita Ford (1940–1980), who was interviewed just before she was murdered in El Salvador (RYA 3922), are available as well.

The entire collection has been cataloged on the Library's online catalog, which provides full access, by name, by subject, and by program title.

Columbia Broadcasting System (CBS) Collection

The CBS Collection actually contains two collections: complete twenty-four-hour programming for two full weeks (May 13–26, 1957) from Washington, D.C., affiliate station WTOP; and selected CBS current affairs and news broadcasts from the 1960s. The CBS material includes press conferences with Presidents John F. Kennedy and Lyndon B. Johnson, coverage of space flights, civil rights and sports events, the 1964 Olympics, United Nations Security Council meetings, and broadcasts on China and Vietnam. With further examination of these broadcasts, information pertinent to the history of women will surely be discovered.

The CBS material is indexed by title in the recorded sound catalog supplement. A paper finding aid with general information about the collection is also available.

Armed Forces Radio and Television Service (AFRTS) Collection

The Armed Forces Radio and Television Service provides radio (and television) programs to service members and families overseas. It obtains informational and entertainment radio programs from commercial networks and syndicators or specially produces them and distributes them to stations and outlets around the globe. The Library has over 300,000 AFRTS electrical transcription discs from 1942, when the organization began as the Armed Forces Radio Service (AFRS), through 1998 when the service stopped distributing hard copies of its programming. Hundreds of musical, educational, and dramatic programs are included in the collection, but news broadcasts and local programs are not.

The biggest names in Hollywood and Broadway recorded for AFRS during the war years, including female stars such as Lena Horne, Doris Day (b. 1924), Rita Hayworth (1918–1987), Betty Grable (1916–1973), Linda Darnell (1921–1965), Jo Stafford (b. 1918), Billie Holiday (1915–1959), and Peggy Lee (b. 1920). In the early 1940s, when radio station WCVX sent a questionnaire to civilians and troops asking for, among other things, their five favorite female singers, the following came out on top in the overwhelming response from the troops: Dinah Shore (1917–1994), Kate Smith (1907–1986), Ginny Simms (1915–1994), Frances Langford (1913–1997), and Helen O'Connell (1920–1993), all of whom are heard on AFRTS broadcasts.

The program *Jubilee* (1943–53), featuring African American performers, broke the color barrier and created an opportunity for African Americans to appear on the popular AFRS variety show *Command Performance* (1942–ca. 1951). *G.I. Journal* (1943–45) and *Mail Call* (1942–49), popular musical variety programs, showcased many well-known female performers. In addition to entertainment, *G.I. Journal* broadcast information on the activities of service personnel throughout the world.

Two extremely popular women disc jockeys were heard over the AFRTS airwaves during two different wars. During World War II, *G.I. Jive* featured "G.I. Jill," the armed services answer to Tokyo Rose, whose broadcasts in the Pacific for the Japanese military were designed to demoralize American troops. Jill was portrayed by Martha Wilkerson (1918–1999), a young mother who had worked with the Office of War Information. Her combination of music and friendly conversation reminded the troops of their girls back home, and she became a particular favorite of Allied troops around the world. Aspiring movie actress Chris Noel (b. 1941) hosted the AFRTS radio program *A Date with Chris,* which ran throughout most of the conflict in Vietnam. Her appealing style and attractiveness made her an instant hit with American troops. She began touring South Vietnam as an AFRTS goodwill ambassador and was so effective in boosting morale that the North Vietnamese offered a $10,000 reward for her assassination.[10]

A partial inventory of AFRTS titles held on sixteen-inch (pre-1959) discs is available. The division is undertaking a full inventory of the AFRTS collection, which will be made available through the division's online catalog, SONIC, providing title and episode number, and in many cases, performers and song titles.

BIBLIOGRAPHY: Seven published indexes to selected AFRTS programs are available in the reference center.

Kiner, Larry F., and Harry Mackenzie. *Basic Musical Library.* "P" Series, 1–1000. New York: Greenwood Press, 1990; ML156.4.P6 K56 1990.

An index to the first part of the popular music series of the Basic Musical Library and provides name, series number, and song title indexes.

Lotz, Rainer E. *The AFR&TS (Gold Label) Transcription Library: A Label Listing.* Menden: Der Jazzfreund, 1978; ML156.4.P6 L67 Case.

Includes indexes by title, artist, and type of music.

——— and Ulrich Neuert. *The AFRS "Jubilee" Transcription Programs: An Exploratory Discography.* Frankfurt (Main): Ruecker, 1985; ML156.4 .J3L68 1985.

Offers a chronological list of *Jubilee* programs with name and song title indexes. The authors claim that *Jubilee* "provides the most representative recorded coverage of black jazz in the United States during World War II and the immediate post-War years."[11]

Mackenzie, Harry. *AFRS Downbeat Series: Working Draft.* Zephyrhills, Fla.: Joyce Record Club, 1986; ML156.4.B5 M3 1986.

Provides show number and artist indexes for the series that eventually became a disc jockey show. Anita O'Day (b. 1919) and Kay Starr (b. 1922) were among the many women who appeared on the program.

———, comp. *Command Performance, USA!: A Discography.* Westport, Conn.: Greenwood Press, 1996; ML156.4.P6 C64 1996.

Provides a chronological listing of this very popular program, including names of performers, musical groups and hosts, an alphabetical index to names, and a chronological listing for *Mail Call* and *G.I. Journal.*

———, comp. *The Directory of the Armed Forces Radio Service Series.* Westport, Conn.: Greenwood Press, 1999; ML156.2.M27 1999.

An attempt to list all of the AFRS series. Includes sample AFRS issues under each series. Contains indexes to series and artists.

Mackenzie, Harry, and Lothar Polomski, comps. *One Night Stand Series, 1–1001.* New York: Greenwood Press, 1991; ML156.4.P6 M253 1991.

A guide to the program that began in 1943 and featured a wide variety of bands, including a band led by Mildred Bailey (1906–1951).

U.S. Office of War Information (OWI) Collection

Soon after World War II several thousand instantaneous lacquer discs representing propaganda broadcasts made by the U.S. Office of War Information were transferred to the Library of Congress. Most of this collection has since been copied onto tape and is available to researchers. In addition to over eight thousand programs in English, the collection includes broadcasts in many other languages. It features domestic and foreign news, entertainment, information, and propaganda broadcasts from 1942 through 1945.

The OWI made a concerted effort to recruit women into wartime service at home. Programs

John Philip Falter. "It's a Woman's War Too! Join the WAVES." Color lithograph, poster, 1942. Artists Posters. Prints and Photographs Division. LC-USZC4-1856.

During World War II, radio played a major role in the recruitment of women into wartime service, especially on the domestic front. Women heard radio appeals that offered the following logical reasoning: "If you can run a vacuum cleaner, you can run a machine in a factory." Women who chose to serve their country in the military were put to work in almost every activity short of combat. The U.S. Navy, in particular, was quite innovative in capitalizing on women's particular skills, including their potential for communications work, as suggested by this poster of a uniformed woman operating a radio.

such as *Place of Women in War* (LWO 5554 GR18 7B7–8A1), *Women's Part in the War* (LWO 5554 GR 8 19A2), and *Women's Contribution to the War Effort* (LWO 5833 GR 34 18A3), all from 1942, are examples of programs that sought to convince women that it was their patriotic duty to apply for wartime work. Yet, as Michelle Hilmes points out in her book on American broadcasting, "all of these appeals were directed at the class of women whose lives permitted a solely domestic role, leaving many working-class and black women outside the boundaries of developing feminist address."[12]

There are OWI reports on the activities of the Women's Army Auxiliary Corps (WAACS) and the Women's Naval Reserve (WAVES). Other programs focus on women from a particular industry, city, or culture, for example, *Women in Railroading* (LWO 5833 GR19 10A8), *Detroit Woman War Worker* (LWO 5833 GR38 5B2), and *Spirit of '43* (LWO 5833 GR42 1A4-B3). The last deals with African American women at war. Stars such as Ethel Merman (1909–1984), Billie Burke, and Patrice Munsel (b. 1925) appeared on OWI broadcasts to help build morale and raise spirits.

The OWI collection is cataloged in SONIC and can be searched by name, program title, genre, date, and subject.

Voice of America (VOA) Collection

The Voice of America is one of the largest newsgathering organizations in the world. A division of the OWI, it has presented music, as well as news and information, to millions across the globe since 1942. The Voice of America collection at the Library of Congress (spanning the years 1945–88) comprises over fifty thousand recordings of arts, culture, and music performances recorded by the VOA for overseas broadcast. This collection features recordings of live musical performances, many unique, by the Boston Symphony Orchestra, the Metropolitan Opera, and the New York Philharmonic. The works of many great women performers and composers are heard on these broadcasts, including opera stars Marian Anderson (1897–1993), Leontyne Price (b. 1927), and Eleanor Steber (1914–1990); American pianist and harpsichordist Rosalyn Tureck (b. 1914); and American composer Mary Howe (1882–1964). A database inventory searchable by series name is available for the VOA collection.

In addition, hundreds of musical artists have been interviewed over the past fifty years by the VOA. Conductor and pianist Antonia Brico (1902–1989), conductor Sarah Caldwell (b. 1928), composer and pianist Margaret Garwood (b. 1927), and singer Eartha Kitt (b. 1928) are just a few of those interviewed. These interviews have been cataloged and can be searched individually by name or collectively as "Voice of America Music Library Collection (Library of Congress)" in the Library's online catalog.

The VOA collection also contains recordings of the Newport Jazz and Folk Festivals. The Newport Jazz Festival features many great female jazz and pop artists, including Ella Fitzgerald (1918–1996), Billie Holiday, Dinah Washington (1924–1963), and Mahalia Jackson (1911–1972). Helen Humes (1913–1981), Nina Simone (b. 1933), Roberta Flack (b. 1939), Abbey Lincoln (b. 1930), Carmen McRae (1922–1994), Dionne Warwick (b. 1941), Tina Turner (b. 1938), Sarah Vaughan (1924–1990), and Maxine Sullivan (1911–1987) were also recorded at these festivals, as was alto saxophonist Vi Redd (b. 1928), who has been called the best female jazz musician since Mary Lou Williams. The Newport Jazz Festival recordings are cataloged in the division's online catalog, SONIC, and are searchable by name, song title, performing group, and date. The inventory to the Newport Folk Festival will also be made available through the Library of Congress's online catalog.

British Broadcasting Corporation (BBC) Sound Archive Collection

The Library is the sole repository of the BBC Collection (1888–1980s) in the Western Hemisphere. Numbering over six thousand LPs, the collection contains a selection of the most important recordings of current affairs and cultural radio programs made by the BBC during the course of its existence. Virtually every major twentieth-century political figure is heard on these recordings. Although obviously primarily British in scope, this collection contains programs on American topics and personalities as well. First ladies Nancy Reagan (b. 1923), Pat Nixon (1912–1993), and Rosalynn Carter (b. 1927) speak on several programs. American women from varied walks of life who appeared on broadcasts include singer Mary Travers (b. 1936), actress Shirley MacLaine (b. 1934), evangelist Ruth Carter Stapleton (1929–1983), Princess Grace (1929–1982), politician Shirley Chisholm (b. 1924), and feminist author Betty Friedan (b. 1921).

Microfiche and paper indexes to the collection offer name, subject (e.g., "gynaecology," "abortion," and "marriage"), keyword, and program title access. The program *Woman's Hour,* for which there are dozens of entries in the index, often features notable American women and addresses a wide range of topics pertaining to American

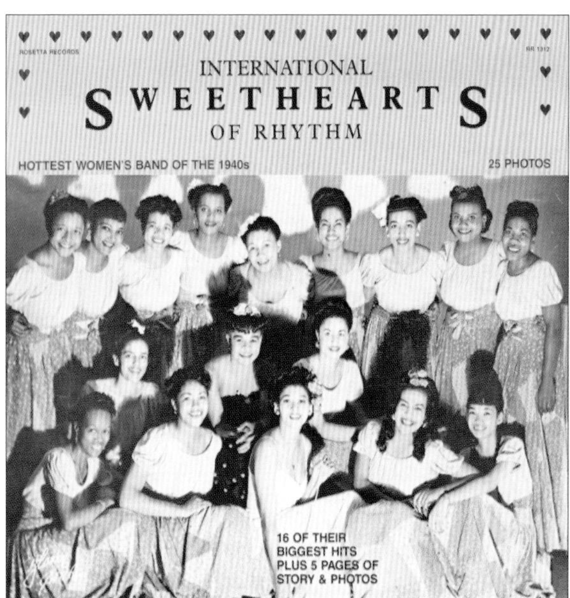

Album jackets. Jane Ira Bloom: Modern Drama *(1987, Columbia FC 40755), courtesy of Columbia Records;* Are You Ready for Phyllis Diller? *(1962, Verve V-15031);* International Sweethearts of Rhythm *(1984, Rosetta Records RR 1302), courtesy of Rosetta Records; and (Buffy Sainte-Marie)* Native North American Child: An Odyssey *(1974, Vanguard VSD-79340) and* Big Mama Thornton: Mama's Pride *(1975, Vanguard VPC 40001), both courtesy of Vanguard Records, a Welk Music Group Company. Recorded Sound Reference Center, Motion Picture, Broadcasting, and Recorded Sound Division.*

The Motion Picture, Broadcasting, and Recorded Sound Division holds an astonishing array of recordings by American women performers. Almost every conceivable genre is represented, including those shown here—jazz, comedy, blues, folk, and big band—in almost every imaginable sound medium.

women. Any with a cataloging number beginning with "LP" may be in the Library's collections.

Music Recordings

Women performers have been recorded since the earliest days of radio broadcasting and sound recording. The breadth of the division's music recordings is so extensive, encompassing a century of radio broadcasting and sound recording and including almost all musical genres, that it is possible to give only a few examples of American women performers represented in the collections. The division's particular strengths are in operatic recordings, chamber music, and American music of all types—classical, popular, jazz, blues, folk, country, and gospel.

The first woman to achieve widespread acclaim as a professional recording star was Ada Jones (1873–1922), who was called "the first lady of the phonograph." With her clear, strong voice and excellent diction, Jones was one of the first women to successfully record on commercial cylinders and discs. Her repertoire included dialect sketches, conversational duets, and comic songs. She and two other great vaudeville and musical comedy performers, Blanche Ring (1871–1961) and Nora Bayes (1880–1928), though now generally forgotten, can be heard on these early commercial sound recordings.

Trumpet virtuoso Edna White (1892–1992), one of the few female instrumentalists in the early days of recording, is featured in a fascinating audio interview (RYA 0001) about her recording career with Thomas Edison. Eva Taylor (1896–1977), billed as "queen of the blues," was another early Edison artist whose recordings are in the collection.

The acquisition in 1992 of the **Altshuler collection** of nearly 250,000 78rpm discs of American jazz and pre-World War II popular music significantly expanded the division's offerings in jazz and blues. Bessie Smith (1894–1937), Mildred Bailey (1907–1951), Clara Smith (1894–1935), Edna White, and Bertha "Chippie" Hill (1905–1950) are just a few of the women who are heard in this collection. Many women performers are also featured on rare 78rpm "race records," a term that companies used in the 1920s, 1930s, and 1940s to describe recordings made for the African American market. An inventory of the Altshuler collection, combined with several other more recently acquired collections, is searchable by name, song title, and label name and number in SONIC.

Other collections that feature many of the great female jazz, pop, and blues vocalists and instrumentalists are the previously discussed **AFRTS collection,** which contains rare, otherwise unissued performances; the **NBC Radio collection,** which also contains unpublished musical broadcasts; the Newport Jazz Festival recordings that are part of the **Voice of America collection;** and the **Wally Heider collection** of big band and West Coast jazz.

Opera and classical music have been popular from the very beginning of sound recording. The

Geraldine Farrar listening to herself on the Victrola, and as Madame Butterfly. Advertisement for Victor Talking Machine Co., Camden, N.J., from the Red Book Magazine *(Chicago: Red Book Corp., March 1914; AP2.R28). Graphics File. Prints and Photographs Division. LC-USZ62-108223.*

Metropolitan Opera diva Geraldine Farrar (1882–1967), with her beauty, lively temperament, and magnetic stage presence, was one of the most celebrated American singing stars during the golden age of opera (ca. 1890–1910). W. J. Henderson of the *New York Sun* called her legion of female fans "Gerryflappers," describing a typical fan as "a girl about flapper age who has created in her own half-baked mind a goddess which she names Geraldine Farrar." Among the many recorded treasures that are part of the Geraldine Farrar collection are several rare, unissued test pressings.

division has an outstanding collection of opera performances from the acoustic recording era featuring many of the top women opera singers of the day. The **John Secrist collection** comprises hundreds of commercial operatic music releases from 1902 to 1925, including many rareties. Private collections belonging to opera divas **Geraldine Farrar** (1882–1967), **Rosa Ponselle** (1897–1981), **Alma Gluck** (1884–1938), and **Helen Traubel** (1899–1972) have significantly enhanced the division's opera holdings. The **Robert Orchard collection** of live opera recordings includes recordings of otherwise unavailable operas such as Mary E. Caldwell's (b.1909) children's operas *A Gift of Song* and *Night of the Star* (both on RXB 9962).

Violinist **Maud Powell** (1867–1920), dubbed a "Victor immortal," was chosen by the record company in 1904 to be the first solo instrumentalist to record for its newly inaugurated celebrity artist series. The division has every 78rpm recording made by this influential artist, a gift of the Maud Powell Foundation.

Since 1925, the Music Division of the Library of Congress has presented a series of chamber music concerts that have featured some of the best American women performers in the country. Since 1940, most of these concerts have been recorded and the tapes held in the Motion Picture, Broadcasting, and Recorded Sound Division. Performers Leontyne Price, Dawn Upshaw (b. 1960), Phyllis Curtin (b. 1921), and other classical music vocalists and instrumentalists can be heard on these history-making recordings. These concerts and musical events are fully cataloged in the Library's online catalog, where they are searchable by name, program title, title of musical works performed, and some Library of Congress subject headings.

SEARCH TIPS: Women and women's issues have long been the subject of musical works. It is possible to unearth specific songs that deal with women, their history, and their culture, but it takes some time and planning. As usual, it is best to start with specific performers, composers, song titles, or record labels, but that is not always necessary. Recordings of the feminist anthem "I Am Woman" by Helen Reddy (b. 1941) are easy to find, whereas it is more difficult to find songs about specific topics, such as domestic violence or divorce. Several reference books that may help you in finding songs of interest include discographies, where starting with a name or song title is helpful. *Blues & Gospel Records, 1890–1943* (Oxford: Clarendon Press, 1997; ML156.4.B6 D59 1997), for instance, lists titles with a distinctively African American musical style recorded between the years 1890 and 1943. It is arranged alphabetically by performer or group, and under each performer is a chronological list of his or her performances up until 1943. An index to song titles is included. The song "Mama Whip, Mama Spank, If Daddy Don't Come Home" by Lucille Hegamin (1894–1970) (Arto 9058) can be found under either song title or Hegamin. *The Green Book of Songs by Subject: The Thematic Guide to Popular Music* by Jeff Green (Nashville, Tenn.: Professional Desk References, 1995; ML156.4.P6 G73 1994) is one of the few books that provides topical access to songs. Organized alphabetically by subject category, within which appropriate song titles with the artists who performed them are listed, it concentrates on popular subjects and emphasizes singles and album tracks released by American companies from 1900 to 1994. It includes the category "Women: General," with *see also* references from "Mothers" and "Women's Names" and *see* references from "Girls" and "Ladies." The "Women's Names" category begins with Abigail Beecher and ends with "The Ballad of John and Yoko." Other relevant categories include "Children," "Divorce," "Marriage," "Fight" (including domestic violence), "Feminism," "Prostitutes," "Homosexuality" (including lesbianism), and "Cowboys" (including cowgirls). *Phonolog* (not cataloged but available in the reference center) is a loose-leaf source book that lists recorded pop and classical music releases that are currently available. It has an alphabetically arranged section of pop song titles, including composer and artist names. The Library of Congress is unusual in holding a complete run of *Phonolog* from 1948 to the present.

Song titles are keyword searchable in both the Library's and the division's online catalogs. You also can perform a more precise search by addressing your query to the exact area in the bibliographic record that contains song titles, such as "title field," "contents note," or "name/title field."

SUBJECT HEADINGS: Several Library of Congress subject headings can be used to find music by or for women. "Feminist music" applies to music about feminism and women's rights. The heading "Women's music" is used for musical works composed, performed, and produced by and for women and often associated with the lesbian feminist movement in the United States. Musical works about women are entered under "Women–Songs and music." To find collections of musical works composed by women search under "Music by women composers" and "Music by African American women composers."

The division's musical recording collections continue to grow, owing both to record companies' compliance with copyright laws that require commercial sound recording deposits and to acquisition activities that build the collections of historical, commercial recordings and expand the unique archival collections.

Drama and Literature Recordings

Drama, literature, and poetry come alive on sound recordings where words, characters, and dramatic situations are given voice by some of the twentieth century's greatest interpreters. Many commercial recordings and archival collections feature great American women writers, poets, actors, and playwrights. America's literary heritage from the past fifty years is displayed in a unique Library of Congress collection called the **Archive of Recorded Poetry and Literature.** Begun in 1943, the archive features literary readings by hundreds of poets, authors, dramatists, and actors, includ-

ing countless American women. The nation's first female consultant in poetry, Louise Bogan (1897–1970), was recorded for the archive, as were Rita Dove (b. 1952), the first woman named poet laureate, Audre Lorde (1934–1992), Marianne Moore (1887–1972), Sylvia Plath (1932–1963), and Adrienne Rich (b. 1929), to name but a few.

The archive also includes dramatizations, such as a one-woman drama re-creating the life of pro-women's suffrage lecturer Anna Dickinson (1842–1932), an American folktale called *Heritage* about the women in Abraham Lincoln's life, and a portrait of playwright Lorraine Hansberry (1930–1965) in her own words. Such programs, which the Library is still producing today, offer invaluable opportunities to hear the literary world's best women writers. The collection is searchable through the Library's online catalog by name, program title, title of literary work, and Library of Congress subject headings, such as "American drama," "American poetry," "monologues," and the like.

Many commercial recordings held by the Library feature the work of great American actresses or women writers. Agnes Moorehead (1906–1974) interpreted prose and poetry and shared personal stories on the recording *The Lavender Lady* (Quinto QR-100), which contains excerpts from her 1968 live show. She is also featured on several radio dramatizations for AFRTS, including a 1974 adaptation of *King Lear* (AFRTS RU50–4, 3B). Pat Carroll (b. 1927), who is known as much for her dramatic roles as for her comedic talents, stars in the one-woman show *Gertrude Stein, Gertrude Stein, Gertrude Stein,* recorded in 1980 for Caedmon (Caedmon TRS 367). The Library holds a recorded copy of the 1987 opera *Nixon in China* (Elektra/Nonesuch 979177–1), which has a libretto written by Alice Goodman.

A multitude of dramas produced for radio include those written expressly for radio and those that have been adapted for broadcast from other sources. The NBC series *Gallant American Women* (1939–40) presented historical dramas on dozens of women in all areas of accomplishment. Women as teachers, pioneer women, ladies of the press, mothers of presidents, women of letters, and women in medicine, science, nursing, and aviation are some of the topics featured. *Brown Women in White* (RWB 9829 B1) is a 1949 NBC drama on black nurses. Other examples are *Now Is the Time,* a 1944 drama on women serving in the military (RWA 8651 B2–3), and *Here's to the Family,* a broadcast about mixed marriages (1949, RWB 8884 B3–4).

The most efficient way to locate plays, poetry, monologues, and literary recitations is to search by specific name of author or performer or by title of the work in the Library's online catalog and the various divisional catalogs. Occasionally, specific subject headings are assigned to literary and dramatic works, but because this is not a consistent practice, searching under broad genre headings is likely to prove more helpful.

The Spoken Word

The division's collections are further enriched by personal and professional collections that have come to the Library of Congress from a variety of notable women. Instead of providing straightforward accounts of their lives through interviews, oral histories, or talks (although the collections may indeed contain such things), these collections might reveal information about the subjects in subtler, less direct ways, through telephone conversations, personal messages, dictations, or items from their professional lives such as lectures or field recordings. Many of these types of materials were acquired as part of personal collections received by the Manuscript and Music Divisions (see also chapters 5 and 8). **Ethel L. Payne** (1911–1991), African American journalist and social activist, reported on the conflict in Vietnam and was involved in many causes related to Africa and

Janet Flanner broadcasting on the program Listen: The Women. *Photograph, 1944. Janet Flanner-Solita Solano Collection. Prints and Photographs Division. LC-USZ62-112975.*

Known for the clarity, precision, and wit of her "Letters from Paris" for the *New Yorker* magazine, Janet Flanner is less well known for the weekly radio broadcasts she made during the months following the liberation of Paris in 1944. The Motion Picture, Broadcasting, and Recorded Sound Division's holdings include seven of these broadcasts from 1945 in which Flanner shared her observations about the effects that political issues have on private lives. Never very comfortable with the constraints of having to distill her thoughts into ten-minute broadcasts, Flanner at the end of the war returned to the medium in which she excelled, the printed word.

developing countries in other parts of the world. Her collection contains speeches by many of the important people she encountered, her interviews with them, and her reports from the field. The multifaceted **Jeannette Piccard** (1895–1981), whose pursuits ranged from aerospace consultant, to wife, to Episcopal priest, left speeches, memoirs, and even meditations in her collection of spoken word recordings. Although **Janet Flanner** (1892–1978) does not add biographical information in speaking aloud, her collection does display Flanner's incisive and insightful reportage and commentary in a series of 1945 radio broadcasts from France. Many of the songs that **Sylvia Fine Kaye** (1913–1991) wrote for Broadway and other artistic media are contained on archival recordings from the **Danny Kaye and Sylvia Fine collection.** The **Bob Fosse and Gwen Verdon collection** offers interviews, cast albums, rehearsal tapes, and audio from television appearances that document the life and work of dancer **Gwen Verdon** (1925–2000). **Barbaralee Diamonstein-Spielvogel,** a teacher, writer, and television interviewer and producer, gave the Library a collection of interviews with contemporary artists, architects, designers, and curators that significantly enhances the Library's primary source material in the visual arts (see chapter 10). Poet **Marcella DuPont** (1903–1985) and literary agent **Lucy Kroll** (1909–1997) also contributed their collections of sound materials to the Library.

Researchers interested in women who have served in the U.S. Congress will find material scattered throughout many collections. Two collections in particular, however, though rather limited in scope, feature the activities, history, and thoughts of some of these women. Unedited audio and video of the **U.S. House of Representatives floor debates** from February 1979 through December 1985 offer a glimpse into congressional activity (after January 1986 the proceedings are on video). Congresswomen who served during this time, such as Geraldine Ferraro, Barbara Mikulski (b. 1936), and Mary Rose Oakar (b. 1940) are heard in action in these debates. Issues relating to women during this time include legislation on the use of funds for abortions, the Domestic Violence Prevention Program, and a bill to ensure that infant formulas contain proper nutrients. This collection is searchable in SONIC by date only, so it is necessary to consult the *Congressional Record* indexes (see chapter 1) to locate subjects, names, and dates of interest. In the 1970s an organization called the Association of Former Members of Congress, Inc., began to record oral histories of individuals who served in Congress. **The Association of Former Members of Congress Oral History Collection** counts ten women among its subjects and includes not only the taped interviews but transcripts of the interviews, which reside in the Manuscript Division and on microform (Microfiche 82/100 MicRR). Martha Griffiths (b. 1912) (RYA 1064–1073), who was instrumental in getting the Equal Rights Amendment through Congress in 1972, and Edith Green (1910–1987) (RYA 1244–1251), called by Senator Mark Hatfield "the most powerful woman ever to serve in Congress," who wrote the Equal Pay Act of 1963, both were interviewed for this project. This collection is accessible by name and date, through SONIC.

One excellent resource for information on many of the major women newsmakers of the past fifty

Senator Maurine B. Neuberger (D-Ore.). Washington, D.C., August 7, 1962. Photograph by Marion S. Trikosko. U.S. News & World Report Collection. Prints and Photographs Division. LC-U9-8293.

Maurine B. Neuberger (1907–2000), only the third woman elected to a full term in the U.S. Senate (1961–67), championed many progressive causes, particularly in the areas of health, education, and consumer reform. She began her political career as a representative in the Oregon state legislature alongside her husband, Senator Richard L. Neuberger, who at the time was a state senator. She reasoned, "I decided that I might as well be speaking for my sex in the House of Representatives as knitting socks and sweaters while I watched Dick in the Senate gallery." An oral history with Neuberger conducted by the Association of Former Members of Congress, Inc., is available in the Recorded Sound Reference Center.

years is the **National Association for the Advancement of Colored People (NAACP) collection** (see chapters 5 and 6), which includes recordings of convention activities, broadcasts, and interviews with many of the men and women who were important movers and shakers of the civil rights movement. It spans the most tumultuous and progressive years of the movement, from 1956 through 1977. Among the prominent women whose voices are heard in this collection are civil rights activist Daisy Bates (1914–1999), who led the effort to test the Supreme Court ruling against segregation in Little Rock, Arkansas in 1957; social worker Dorothy Height (b. 1912), president of the National Council of Negro Women; Judge Constance Baker Motley (b. 1921); and lawyer and civil rights leader Margaret Bush Wilson (b. 1919). A collection-level bibliographic record is available in the Library's online catalog, where it provides access to some of the individuals heard on the recordings. A complete list of those heard in this collection is available in paper form in the reference center.

The National Press Club, another rich resource, began privately recording its luncheon speakers series in 1952. The **National Press Club Luncheon Speakers collection** contains a wide-ranging series of informal talks followed by question-and-answer sessions. The club's guest list has been a veritable Who's Who of newsworthy women from roughly the past fifty years, including Bella Abzug (1920–1998) (LWO 8217 513), Shirley Chisholm (RXA 1406), Elizabeth Dole (RXA 6260), Coretta Scott King (b. 1927) (RYC 46, RSS 13039), and Gloria Steinem (b. 1934) (RXA 1506–1508, RXA 6274). This collection is cataloged in SONIC, where it is searchable by name of guest, date, and sometimes subject.

The **Vital History cassettes** series contains interviews, press conferences, and special events recorded by CBS News from 1970 to 1982. Several shows in the series deal with women's issues or contain interviews with notable women. For example, three generations of the Peabody family of Massachusetts—Mary Peabody (1891–1981), civil rights activist; Marietta Tree (1917–1991), first woman ambassador to the United Nations; and Frances FitzGerald (b. 1940), author of *Fire in the Lake* (1972), the Pulitzer Prize–winning book on Vietnam—are interviewed for the series (RZA 0768). Eleanor McGovern (b. 1921) talks about her role in the 1972 presidential campaign (RZA 0758), and Sandra Day O'Connor (b. 1930) discusses her nomination to the Supreme Court in 1981 (RZA 0786). Clare Boothe Luce (1903–1987), Congresswoman Barbara Jordan (1936–1996), and Governor Ella Grasso (b. 1919) are also participants. Feminism is a popular topic of discussion: author Marilyn French (b. 1929) gave a talk in 1980 on "making room for women" (RZA 0782); Betty Friedan spoke on women's liberation at the 1971 opening session of the National Women's Political Caucus (RZA 0753); and Elaine Heffner (b. 1926) talked about mothering after feminism. Other topics include psychoanalysis and feminism, the Equal Rights Amendment, and the working woman. These cassettes are accessible by name, title, and subject in the Library's online catalog.

One of the most fascinating and eclectic collections in the division is the **Brander Matthews Dramatic Museum collection** in which you will find almost every example of the spoken word. A series of private, experimental, and radio broadcast recordings made at Columbia University, principally during the 1930s, the Brander Matthews collection comprises a wide range of spoken arts, including documentaries, speeches, interviews, and prose and poetry readings. Representative women include Anna Roosevelt Dall (1906–1975), daughter of Franklin D. and Eleanor Roosevelt; actress Cornelia Otis Skinner (1901–1979); writer Fannie Hurst (1889–1968); and poets Harriet Monroe (1860–1936) and Edna St. Vincent Millay (1892–1950), reading their own poetry. This collection can be searched by name, literary title, keyword, and subject in the Library's online catalog.

Recordings serve multiple roles in that they record, comment on, and interpret history and culture. They are themselves the products and artifacts of that history. The vast recorded sound and radio collections at the Library of Congress offer unique insights and rich rewards for those researching American women from the twentieth century on. We hope that this chapter has conveyed the many different ways in which sound recordings and radio broadcasts can enhance and enliven your research.

For their encouragement, support, and patience during all phases of this project, I would like to thank Samuel Brylawski, Bryan Cornell, Eugene DeAnna, Alan Gevinson, Edwin Matthias, and Brian Taves. My particular gratitude goes to Jan McKee, whose invaluable research on women in radio, with a particular focus on the Library's collections, is the source for much of the information found in this chapter.

REMOVED
TO
174
FOX

10 Moving Image Section

Motion Picture, Broadcasting, and Recorded Sound Division

Rosemary Hanes with Brian Taves

From the crude beginnings of cinema produced at Thomas Edison's Black Maria studio to the computer-enhanced effects created at George Lucas's Industrial Light & Magic, the Library of Congress holds the most comprehensive collections of American film and television materials in the world. The Motion Picture, Broadcasting, and Recorded Sound Division (MBRS) houses more than half a million moving image items, including feature films, shorts, serials, newsreels, cartoons, documentaries, educational films, television programs, and commercials.

In the 1901 film *What Happened on Twenty-Third Street, New York* (FLA 4947), a couple is walking down a sidewalk when the woman steps on a grate and the escaping air blows her ankle-length dress up to her knees. Fifty years later and thirty blocks to the north, another couple walked over a subway grate in a movie. With *The Seven Year Itch* (1955, FGB 0012–0023), the image of Marilyn Monroe's thighs exposed under her billowing skirt entered American popular culture. The Library's motion picture and broadcasting collections provide the opportunity to document not only how women's roles and their depictions have changed throughout the past hundred years, but also how much has remained the same.

Women have been represented as every conceivable stereotype in the movies: waif, vamp, girl-next-door, femme fatale, Madonna, whore, shopgirl, career woman, gold digger, wisecracking girlfriend, dumb blonde, self-sacrificing mother, and perfect wife. Although individual film archives may have the collections of particular filmmakers, studios, or performers, the Library's strength lies in the span of its holdings. The development of almost any subject or theme can be traced here. With enough time and effort, a researcher could follow the evolution of a number of character types: from America's Sweetheart, Mary Pickford, to Drew Barrymore's Cinderella character in *Ever After* (1998, CGC 7486–7491); from Clara Bow's "It" girl to Elizabeth Taylor's party girl in *Butterfield 8* (1960, FGB 3617–3623); from Theda Bara's vamp to Sharon Stone's man-eater in *Basic Instinct* (1992, DAA 2526); or from the perils of Pearl White to the travails of Sigourney Weaver in *Alien* (1979, DAA 0334).

The Library of Congress began collecting motion pictures in 1893 when an Edison kinetoscope was deposited for copyright. Although there was no provision in the copyright law for motion pictures until 1912, early film producers printed their movies on paper rolls and sent them to the Library of Congress as still photographs. In 1912, the copyright law established motion pictures as a distinct form, but the Library chose not to house the flammable nitrate film in use at the time and returned all works to the claimants, retaining only descriptive printed material relating to the films. This practice changed in 1942, when, recognizing the importance of motion pictures and the need to preserve them as a historical record, the Library requested the return of selected works and, to fill the gap between 1912 and 1942, pursued gift collections and donations from studios, institutions, and private collectors.

In 1949 the Library began collecting television programs. The Library's television archive comprises an eclectic group offering a broad but uneven view of television broadcasting history. The industry's failure to make kinescope recordings of

What Happened on Twenty-Third Street, New York City. *Frame enlargement. Edison, 1901. Paper Print Collection (LC1933). Moving Image Section, Motion Picture, Broadcasting, and Recorded Sound Division.*

Besides "actualities" of bustling city streets and scenic views of natural beauty, audiences at the turn of the twentieth century were treated to staged films made on location. The street scene *What Happened on Twenty-Third Street, New York City* (1901) offers the unexpected view of a woman's legs in a shot that predates the legendary image of Marilyn Monroe's billowing skirt by half a century. Both are examples of a fundamental appeal of the cinema—displaying the woman as sex object.

much early live television, and the division's practice of selectively retaining copyright deposits because of the initial underestimation of the medium's significance, have resulted in scant holdings of certain popular series and full runs of others. Beginning in 1966, the Library's policy was changed to keep all network documentaries and telefeatures and large samplings of entertainment series and other types of programming. The process has continued to expand in recent years as even more copyright deposits have been selected for the collections, as gifts of television programs not registered for copyright protection have been encouraged, and as funds have been made available for purchases.

The division also has custody of printed descriptive materials received as a part of the copyright registration process. These copyright descriptions can include continuities of the dialogue and action of a film taken directly from the screen, pressbooks, plot synopses, or credit lists. Such written material is especially valuable when the original film or television program is no longer extant. The division also holds motion picture advertising and other paper ephemera.

MOTION PICTURE AND TELEVISION READING ROOM
James Madison Memorial Building, 3rd floor, room LM 336
Hours: Monday through Friday, 8:30 a.m. to 5:00 p.m.
Closed weekends and federal holidays.
Telephone: 202-707-8572
Fax: 202-707-2371
Address: Moving Image Section, Motion Picture, Broadcasting, and Recorded Sound Division, 101 Independence Avenue, SE, Washington, DC 20540-4690
E-mail: mpref@loc.gov
Web site: <http://www.loc.gov/rr/mopic>
Access and use: Viewing facilities, available without charge, are provided for those doing research of a specific nature leading toward a publicly available work such as a dissertation, publication, or film or television production. Graduate students and undergraduates in advanced classes wishing to screen films should first obtain letters from their professors endorsing their individual research projects. All viewing is by advance appointment. Because most of our collections are stored in remote locations, you can expect an average wait of ten days after requesting a film before it is available for viewing. Viewers submitting lengthy title lists to be searched by our reference staff should expect a wait of three to four weeks. Materials in the moving image collections are not available for rental. Copies of works not restricted by copyright or by provisions of gift or transfer, and in sound physical condition, may be purchased through the division's Public Services Office. You will find additional information on the division's services and facilities on the Motion Picture and Television Reading Room Web site.

A high percentage of the moving image material held by the Library has been collected in original production formats that are now obsolete and require preservation or copying to modern viewing formats before the works can be made available to researchers. The Motion Picture and Television Reading Room strives to meet all requests for viewing copies in a timely manner, but you should be aware that limited preservation funds and the difficulties inherent in preserving and restoring obsolete film and video materials may add significantly to the time required to produce access copies. Under special circumstances, researchers may be required to pay a portion of preservation costs. Contact the division in advance of a research visit for further information regarding access to such materials.

USING THE COLLECTIONS

The Library's rich and varied array of fiction and nonfiction film and television holdings offer scholars unparalleled treasures. The size, scope, and nature of the collections, however, lead to difficulties in providing comprehensive bibliographic control. The majority of the moving image materials have not been fully cataloged and are accessible primarily by title. Identifying films and videos by subject usually requires a number of strategies, including keyword searching of the division's various manual and online catalogs, searching the vertical files, and compiling title lists from secondary sources such as reference works, monographs, and periodicals. The reference staff will assist you in suggesting search strategies. The following sections highlight relevant collections, useful reference sources, and various means of access.

Catalogs and Finding Aids

The primary tools for identifying materials in our collections and for creating filmographies include the following catalogs and guides which are available in the Motion Picture and Television Reading Room:

- The **Film and Television Catalog** is a card catalog of moving image materials, most of which are available for viewing. Approximately 120,000 cards, arranged by title, provide shelf location number and basic physical description. Miscellaneous card files arranged at the end of the title file include the Directors File, an incomplete listing by director of feature films, and the Newsreel Catalog, a list of holdings of American newsreels selected as copyright deposits, 1942–1967. The catalog was closed in 1986.

- The **Library of Congress Online Catalog** contains cataloging records created by the division since 1986 and is searchable by virtually any keyword in the entry. Only a small percentage of motion pictures or television broadcasts have been cataloged using Library of Congress subject headings. To gain access to the online catalog, see the Library of Congress Web site at <http://www.loc.gov> (as described in "Using the Library of Congress").

MAVIS, an online database, contains specialized inventory and tracking records for certain of the division's nitrate, safety, and video holdings. Only items that have been preserved as safety reference prints or video viewing copies can be screened. MAVIS is currently available only in the reading room.

The **Dictionary Catalog** contains cards for safety films cataloged from the late 1950s to the early 1970s. It provides additional access points by added entry and subject heading. Converted records for these films are also available in the Library's online catalog, where they are identified as "[from old catalog]" records.

Early Motion Pictures: The Paper Print Collection in the Library of Congress (Washington: Library of Congress, 1985; Z663.36.E27) describes paper print holdings (see page 305).

The George Kleine Collection of Early Motion Pictures in the Library of Congress: A Catalog (Washington: Library of Congress, 1980; Z663.36 .G46) describes 456 motion pictures produced primarily in the United States and Italy between 1898 and 1926 (see page 307).

The Theodore Roosevelt Association Film Collection: A Catalog (Washington: Library of Congress, 1986; Z663.36.T47 1986) describes 318 films released between 1897 and 1934 that focus on the life and times of Theodore Roosevelt.

Three Decades of Television: A Catalog of Television Programs Acquired by the Library of Congress, 1949–1979 (Washington: Library of Congress, 1989; Z663.36.A13 1989), a book catalog of programs produced for broadcast television and acquired by the Library before the end of 1979, includes over 14,000 series, serials, telefeatures, specials, and documentaries; daytime and prime-time programs; network, DuMont, and syndicated broadcasts; and educational material from NET and PBS.

Finding Aids and **Resource Guides** have been created by the division's reference staff to assist researchers in locating items on various popular topics. Of special interest for women's issues are the guides on "Women's Suffrage," "Labor," and "Discovery and Exploration."

Research Methodology

Approximately 80 percent of the films made before 1930 are no longer extant, but the silent film researcher can improve the odds of locating surviving films by compiling as comprehensive a filmography as possible from secondary sources. The division's monograph collections are often the best starting point for research, especially for the scholar without a film history background. For instance, examples of the voyeuristic films of the turn of the twentieth century are provided in Judith Mayne's *The Woman at the Keyhole: Feminism and Women's Cinema* (Bloomington: Indiana University Press, 1990; PN1995.9.W6M36 1990) and Lauren Rabinovitz's *For the Love of Pleasure: Women, Movies, and Culture in Turn-of-the-Century Chicago* (New Brunswick, N.J.: Rutgers University Press, 1998; PN1995.9.W6R33 1998). Kay Sloan's *The Loud Silents: Origins of the Social Problem Film* (Urbana: University of Illinois Press, 1988; PN1995.9.S62S58 1988) and Kevin Brownlow's *Behind the Mask of Innocence* (New York: Knopf, 1990; PN1995.75.B68 1990) do the same for the social problem films of the Progressive era. Reference books, such as the American Film Institute catalog series (PN1998.A57), provide subject indexing to fiction films that is often lacking in the MBRS catalogs.

In many cases, paper sources may be the only surviving artifacts of a motion picture. The often invaluable copyright descriptions offer a unique source of documentation on moving images from 1912 to the present. At the start of the twentieth century, motion picture trade publications provided reviews, synopses, advertisements, and still images, including coverage of films not copyrighted. For example, *Moving Picture World* gives the following description of *When Women Vote* (1907): "The henpecked husband shines her shoes, brushes her coat, and out she goes to attend the woman's suffrage meeting. . . . Mr. O'Brien would like to get a divorce but such cannot be obtained when women vote."[1] An advertisement for *Fighting Suffragettes* (1909) states, "Just the right picture to show in these stirring times, as it shows the woman how much better it is to stay at home. Teach your audience this lesson."[2]

The Motion Picture and Television Reading Room has an excellent collection of trade magazines, including *Moving Picture World* (1907–27), the *Motion Picture News* (1911–30), and *Motogra-*

phy (1911–18). Indexing is limited for these periodicals, but partial access can be found through such sources as the American Film Institute catalogs, *An Index to Short and Feature Film Reviews in the Moving Picture World: The Early Years, 1907–1915* (Westport, Conn.: Greenwood Press, 1995; Z5784.M9D33 1995), and *The Film Index: A Bibliography* (New York: Arno Press, 1966; Z5784 .M9W75). The most rewarding finds may result from simply browsing through the trade journals one page at a time.

The survival rate for films produced after 1930 is much higher, but the strategy of using secondary sources to create title lists is much the same as for the silent era. The American Film Institute catalogs continue to provide subject indexing to the feature films of the 1930s, 1940s, and 1960s. There are dozens of filmographies dealing with a wide range of subjects, including the depiction in film of ethnic groups (see *Contemporary Hollywood's Negative Hispanic Image: An Interpretive Filmography, 1956–1993* by Alfred Charles Richard [Westport, Conn.: Greenwood Press, 1994; PN1995.9.L37R54 1994]); character types (see *Prostitution in Hollywood Films* by James Robert Parish [Jefferson, N.C.: McFarland & Co., 1992; PN1995.9.P76P37 1992]); and women (see *Working Women on the Hollywood Screen: A Filmography* by Carolyn L. Galerstein [New York: Garland Publishing, 1989; PN1995.9.W6G34 1989]). The reading room reference collection includes a number of CD-ROMs dedicated to film research, such as *Reel Women: The Untold Story* (New York: Enteractive, 1996), and provides access to motion picture databases and Web sites, including STAR (American Film Institute database of surviving American silent films) and the Internet Movie Database at <http://imdb.com>.

SELECTED COLLECTIONS

This section surveys motion pictures, television, and non-broadcast performance videos, emphasizing the portrayal of women in film and television and their roles in front of and behind the camera. We highlight selected collections, illustrating the extraordinary scope and variety of the moving image materials available for the study of American women's history and culture at the Library of Congress.

Motion Pictures

The Library's motion picture holdings include films of countless actresses of every rank and caliber, including Lillian Gish, Marion Davies, Greta Garbo, Shirley Temple, Joan Crawford, Lupe Velez, Barbara Stanwyck, Thelma Ritter, Audrey Hepburn, Doris Day, Pam Grier, Jane Fonda, Alfre Woodard, Meryl Streep, Julia Roberts, and Jennifer Lopez. For various generations, these names evoke the range of personas that have been the staples of motion picture genres throughout cinema history. These personas, however, often presented a double-edged sword. Many stars were trapped in the image created by the types of roles that made them popular, often limiting their range of opportunities. An archetypal example is

Anna May Wong. Publicity still. Paramount Publix Corp., ca. 1931. Stills collection. Moving Image Section, Motion Picture, Broadcasting and Recorded Sound Division.

Anna May Wong, the first woman of Chinese ancestry to become a star of the American cinema, was a top-billed player in some sixty movies over a period of twenty years. Wong embodied a beauty that was new to Hollywood films and beguiled American spectators, who accepted her whether playing hero, villain, or victim. Studio publicity focused on her ethnicity and exoticism as the key to her allure and to her screen persona.

Mary Pickford, who found herself forever identified with an innocent-little-girl image that impeded her desire for more mature roles.

Actresses of color often found that stereotyping reduced them to stock characters—the African American maid, the Asian dragon lady, or the Latin spitfire. Although a few minority actresses managed to break out of the confines of supporting parts into starring roles, typecasting severely limited their options. The Mexican actress Dolores Del Rio (1905–1983) achieved stardom when she appeared in films such as *What Price Glory?* (1926, FDA 7809–7811) and *The Bad One* (1930, FEB 1551–1558), but by 1942 her career in Hollywood was in decline. She returned to Mexico, where she became one of her country's leading box-office attractions. Anna May Wong (1905–1961), the first Asian American female star in Hollywood, often found herself in small "atmospheric" character parts, as in *The Thief of Bagdad* (1924, DAA 3137). Although Wong received occasional lead parts, notably in *Daughter of Shanghai* (1937, FEB 1131–1137), she usually played a supporting role while major Chinese characters were played by white actresses, such as Myrna Loy or Luise Rainer. Dorothy Dandridge (1923–1965) built on the success enjoyed by earlier African American leading ladies—such as Nina Mae McKinney and Lena Horne—to become the first black performer to receive an Academy Award nomination in a leading role for her work in *Carmen Jones* (1954, FGA 1800–1812). She continued to appear in such films as *Island in the Sun* (1957, FGA 5578–5591) and *Porgy and Bess* (1959, VBG 3184–3186). In the early 1960s, however, she found Hollywood unwilling "to construct star vehicles, fearful that audiences would not pay to see a black leading lady."[3]

To introduce the reader to the Library's motion picture collections, the holdings are organized here into three general time periods: the silent era, the studio era, and the post-studio era. The boundaries between sections are fluid, and there are multiple research strategies for projects that fall within a single grouping.

The Silent Era

At the close of the nineteenth century, a means of capturing and presenting moving pictures was developed at the Edison laboratories in New Jersey. After a brief period of experimentation, these early filmmakers turned to vaudeville, burlesque, and other forms of mass entertainment both for their subject matter and for their performers. On March 10, 1894, when production began on the twenty-eighth kinetoscope—a film viewed through a peep-hole cabinet—a Spanish dancer became the first woman to appear in an Edison film. *Carmencita* (FGC 8611–8612) was soon followed by numerous risqué films featuring exotic dancers—like *Turkish Dance, Ella Lola* (1898, FLA 4361)—and scantily clad women, as seen in *Trapeze Disrobing Act* (1901, FLA 4917).

As the commercial exploitation of the kinetoscope grew, filmmakers realized they needed to produce films that appealed to an audience that included middle-class women. The **Hendricks Collection** provides a sampling of films produced with this audience in mind, including *Annie Oakley* (1894), where Oakley demonstrated her marksmanship, *Imperial Japanese Dance* (1894), with its Kyoto dance performance, and the famous May Irwin-John Rice *Kiss* (1896). At the same time, the public exhibition of films of boxers, wrestlers, blacksmiths, barber shops, cockfights, and voyeurism allowed women access to a masculine world from which they were usually excluded.[4]

Motion pictures continued to evolve as cameras were taken out of the studios and filmmakers began shooting scenes of everyday life—as in *Women of the Ghetto Bathing* (1902, FLA 4373), scenic views of urban and rural landscapes—like *Panoramic View of Niagara Falls* (1899, FLA 3523), or current events—for instance, *Parade of Women Delegates; World's Fair* (1904, FLA 4812). Such films became known as actualities. Filmmakers also made re-creations of topical events, such as the sinking of the *Maine* and boxing matches. Temperance leader Carry Nation's (1846–1911) "joint-smashing" of the Carey Hotel Bar in Wichita, Kansas, was reenacted for the camera in *Kansas Saloon Smashers* (1901, FLA 4194) and *Unidentified Coffeyville Historical Society, no.1: Carry Nation* (ca. 1905, FEA 7974).

During the first decade of the twentieth century, filmmakers began developing narrative patterns. They enhanced plot and character and used plot conventions and genres, such as comedy, melodrama, crime, costume, social problem, and western. Soon these fiction films, rather than the actualities, dominated the market.

The **Paper Print Collection** (3,000 films, 1894–1915) is the cornerstone of the historic film holdings available in the Motion Picture and Television Reading Room, providing an excellent overview of the development of both American actuality and narrative films. Images range from girls taking time checks or taping coils in the Westinghouse Works factory in East Pittsburgh

(*Westinghouse Works,* 1904, FLA 5896–5897) to girls at play (*Girls' Acrobatic Feats,* 1898?, FLA 3506). They show the fashions of 1903 as worn by middle-class women on the bustling streets of New York in *At the Foot of the Flatiron* (FLA 4963), as well as the attire of newly arrived immigrants in *Emigrants* [i.e., *immigrants*] *Landing at Ellis Island* (FLA 4605).

Melodramas depicted the fate of young women who succumbed to temptation. In *The Downward Path* (1900, FLA 4010–4014), a girl who runs away from home ends up dancing in a disreputable saloon and finally commits suicide. *The Fate of the Artist's Model* (1903, FLA 4614–4618) shows a young woman and her baby who are abandoned by her artist lover. There are numerous voyeuristic films in which the camera is set as if in the audience of a vaudeville theater. In *Peeping Tom in the Dressing Room* (1905, FLA 3917), a man watches through a keyhole as a buxom woman dresses. Discovered, the Peeping Tom is brought into the dressing room, where chorus girls beat him with powder puffs. In *Pouting Model* (1901, FLA 3797), curtains open to disclose an aged man sitting on a chair and a nude young girl with her head turned toward the wall as if crying. Early examples of several genre films with a feminine twist can also be found in the Paper Print Collection. A female police operative attempts to save a girl kidnapped by Chinese white slavers in the crime film *The Fatal Hour* (1908, FLA 5373) and a horsewoman saves her lover from being hanged in the western *The Girl from Montana* (1907, FLA 5046).

Motion picture performers who acted in story films were originally anonymous. Because of the popularity of certain players, however, producers

Left: From Show Girl to Burlesque Queen. *Frame enlargements. Camera: A. E. Weed. AM&B, 1903. Paper Print Collection (LC549). Moving Image Section, Motion Picture, Broadcasting, and Recorded Sound Division.*

Opposite page: Birth of the Pearl. *Frame enlargements. Camera: F. S. Armitage. AM&B, 1901. Paper Print Collection (LC1318). Moving Image Section, Motion Picture, Broadcasting, and Recorded Sound Division.*

Early cinematic efforts incorporated traditions from many forms of mass entertainment, including the theater, vaudeville, burlesque, and the circus. Whether low rent or highbrow, numerous early films feature young women in risqué poses or situations. *From Show Girl to Burlesque Queen* (1903) titillates and frustrates as its star begins to undress in front of the camera, only to duck behind a screen before all is revealed. The art tableau is used in *The Birth of the Pearl* (1901) to provide a provocative view of the female body.

began to identify them in newspaper articles, in advertising, and finally, in on-screen credits, thus giving birth to the movie star. Among the paper prints are films of the very first movie stars, including Florence Lawrence (1886–1938), Lillian Gish (1896–1993), Mabel Normand (1894–1930), Mae Marsh (1895–1968), Blanche Sweet (1895–1986), and Mary Pickford (1892–1979).

The book catalog *Early Motion Pictures: The Paper Print Collection in the Library of Congress* is arranged alphabetically by title with an index including subject categories, place-names, personal names, genres, and company names. Films related to women can be found under headings such as "Socially significant themes," "Peep show," and "Dance."

Purchased from the estate of a film industry entrepreneur, the 456 films in the **George Kleine Collection** span the years from 1896 to 1926, and include dramas, comedies, actualities, and educational films. Public events staged by American suffragists and captured by newsreel cameras are presented in such films as *Franchise Parade, Tarrytown, N.Y.* (1915, FLA 1514), and *Suffrage Parade, New York City* (1915, FLA 1848). Narrative films in the collection include *Deliverance* (1919, FLA 1996–1997) starring Helen Keller (1880–1968) in a dramatization of her life; the melodrama *Heart of a Waif* (1915, FEA 4740) featuring twelve-year-old Clare Boothe Luce (1903–1987); and *The Tiger's Coat* (1920, FLA 1865–1869), with photographer Tina Modotti (1896–1942).

A genre of particular interest to historians is the social problem film of the silent era. These films dramatized societal ills and concerns such as prostitution, women's suffrage, and birth control. *Children of Eve* (1915, FLA 1423–1427) is a child labor melodrama that calls for improved working conditions after a factory fire. Comedy was used both to support and lampoon social causes. In *The Politicians* (1915, FLA 1734–1738), a female detective and a suffragette chief of police thwart the schemes of two dishonest politicians, whereas *The Sufferin Baby* (1915, FLA 1847) shows the comic misadventures of a suffragist's husband who is left to mind their child. Ten comedy shorts in the James Montgomery Flagg's Girls You Know series (1918) present various popular images of young women, such as *The Bride* (FLA 1398), *The Good Sport* (FLA 1533), *The Man Eater* (FLA 1642), *The Spoiled Girl* (FLA 1831), and *The Stenog* (FLA 1801). These films can be found by searching the subject index provided in *The George Kleine Collection of Early Motion Pictures in the Library of Congress* and in the online cata-

Little Lord Fauntleroy. *Directors: Alfred E. Green and Jack Pickford. Camera: Charles Rosher. Scenario: Bernard McConville. Cast: Mary Pickford, Claude Gillingwater, Joseph Dowling, Francis Marion. Lobby card. Mary Pickford Co., 1921. Dwight Cleveland Lobby Card Collection (unprocessed). Prints and Photographs Division. LC–USZC4–8145.*

Mary Pickford (1892–1979) took on a dual role in the 1921 version of *Little Lord Fauntleroy,* playing both the title character and his mother (here with Francis Marion). Although playing a boy, Pickford again embodied an audience favorite: the plucky, honest, sometimes mischievous youth, who wins the affection of even the most hard-hearted adults. Pickford's third and most important role took place off screen, where, as producer, she supervised all aspects of the making of the film. A scene from the film and movie advertising art were typically shown together on lobby cards such as this.

log, by searching under headings such as "Child labor—Drama," "Women—Suffrage—Drama," and "Weddings—Drama."

The 318 films released between 1897 and 1934 that make up the **Theodore Roosevelt Collection** focus on Roosevelt and his life and times but also include many prominent women, especially those in the suffrage movement. The index to the Roosevelt catalog lists Margaret Hill McCarter, Sarah Bernhardt, Helen Rogers Reid, Harriet B. Laidlaw, Elizabeth Ogden Brower Wood, Cornelia Bryce Pinchot, Florence Kling Harding, Edith Wilson, Corinne Roosevelt Robinson, Elizabeth A. Bryce, Geraldine Farrar, Sallie White Bolling, and Helen Herron Taft.

There is no better example of the silent movie star than Mary Pickford. An internationally renowned actress, Pickford was also one of the world's most successful businesswomen and a motion picture producer who achieved control over all aspects of her films. The **Mary Pickford Collection** (100 films) consists of print and preprint materials sampling her entire film career, beginning with *Her First Biscuits* in 1909 (FLA 5434) and ending with her last film, *Secrets* (preprint), in 1933. Several movies in which Pickford collaborated with one of the most successful screenwriters in Hollywood, Frances Marion (1888–1973), are also part of this collection, including a film Marion directed, *Love Light* (1921, VBG 2406–2407).

The films of other popular female silent stars are found in the **Raymond Rohauer Collection** (350 films), including Norma and Constance Talmadge. Norma (1893–1957) specialized in melodrama, and Constance (1898–1973) carved out a distinguished career in sophisticated comedy. Talmadge films in the Rohauer Collection include *Sawdust and Salome* (1914, FEA 5091), *Heart of Wetona* (1918, FEC 1680–1685), *A Daughter of Two Worlds* (1920, FGE 8654–8656), *The Woman Gives* (1920, FGE 9134–9136), and *Her Sister from Paris* (1925, FGE 7281–7284). Also in the Rohauer Collection are rare silent feature films and early sound shorts with performers such as Fanny Brice (1891–1951), Anna Pavlova (1881–1931), and Agnes de Mille (1905–1993).

The motion picture serial—action melodramas that were presented one chapter at a time in weekly installments over the course of several months, with each episode ending with a cliff-hanger—was introduced to American audiences in 1912. Female performers dominated the genre throughout the silent era. Pearl White in *The Perils of Pauline* (1914) set the pattern, as serial heroines leaped onto speeding trains, raced through flames, dived off bridges, and faced threatening buzz saws, all without stunt doubles. The **Public Archives of Canada/Dawson City Collection** has an extensive array of serials that feature women as spies, Robin Hood figures, telegraph operators, railroad professionals, and master thieves, played by such actresses as Pearl White in *Pearl of the Army* (1916–17), Helen Holmes in *Hazards of Helen* (1915), and Marie Walcamp in *The Red Ace* (1917–18). Also included are *Lucille Love* (1914) and *The Girl of Mystery* (1914), starring and written by Grace Cunard, and *The Purple Mask* (1917), which Cunard also directed. Cataloging records are available in the Library's online catalog.

Ephemeral films encompass a wide range of commercial and amateur motion pictures, including advertising and promotional films, educational films, and home movies. The division has examples of early advertising films hawking products for women or using women's sex appeal to sell products to men. *Warner's Corsets* (191-?, FEB 7678) is a fictionalized story of "Warner's fashionable rust-proof corsets, guaranteed not to rust, break or tear." *Buy an Electric Refrigerator* (1926?, FEB 7784) is a product commercial and *Admiral Cigarette* (1897, FLA 4367) features an attractive girl in a striking costume who hands cigarettes to a group of men. *From Cabin to Castle* (ca. 1930, FEB 4440–4442) is believed to be a promotional piece with still shots and footage of African American entrepreneur Madame C. J. Walker (1867–1919), her daughter A'lelia Walker, and employees at work in her cosmetics manufacturing company.

The Timber Queen: Episode No. 11, The Runaway Engine. *Director: Fred Jackson. Screenplay: Bertram Millhauser. Cast: Ruth Roland, Bruce Gordon, Val Paul, Leo Willis. Lobby card. Ruth Roland Serials/Pathé, 1922. Dwight Cleveland Lobby Card Collection (unprocessed). Prints and Photographs Division. LC–USZ62–126851.*

Women were among the most popular serial action stars in the early days of the cinema. Battling dastardly villains each week, actresses such as Pearl White, Helen Holmes, and Marie Walcamp performed their own stunts, in the face of countless perilous situations, managing hair-raising escapes from fires, floods, explosions, runaway trains, and mill saws just in the nick of time. Serial queen Ruth Roland is seen here in yet another knock-down fight with an unscrupulous opponent.

Educational films were intended primarily to instruct and inform and were shown in nontheatrical settings, mainly classrooms. *The Truth about the Liberty Motor* (1919, nitrate), produced by Ford Motor Company, combines promotional and educational functions in a film about women war workers during the First World War. This picture demonstrates that "after a few lessons, she is just as capable a mechanic as her brother who has gone to France." *Social Hygiene for Women* (FEB 4183), produced by the American Social Hygiene Association in 1920, was used to illustrate lectures to women regarding reproductive organs and covering facts about gonorrhea and syphilis.

Family, friends, and vacation locales are the typical subjects found in home movies. The division's amateur film collections include those of prominent American women, such as **Evalyn Walsh McLean** (1886–1947), a leader in the social life of Washington, D.C., from the 1910s to her death, and **Agnes E. Meyer** (1887–1970), author and social reformer, and her husband Eugene Meyer, editor and publisher of the *Washington Post*. The Meyer films, shot in the 1920s, include footage of two of their children, Katharine Meyer Graham (Mrs. Philip L. Graham) and Elizabeth Meyer Lorentz (Mrs. Pare Lorentz).

Before the film industry became a big business, women were involved in nearly every aspect of production. Writer Lizzie Francke has quoted screenwriter Beulah Marie Dix (1898–1973) on this point: "It was all very informal, in those early days. There were no unions. Anybody on the set did anything he or she was called upon to do. I've walked on as an extra, I've tended lights (I've never shifted scenery) and anybody not doing anything else wrote down the director's notes on the script . . . I also spent a good deal of time in the cutting room." As Francke remarked, "In such a relatively egalitarian atmosphere women seemed destined to become equal partners with men in this new industry."[5] The Library holds films created by many of these pioneering filmmakers, including works by Gene Gauntier (1891–1966), Helen Gardner (1885–1968), Mabel Normand (1894–1930), Cleo Madison (1883–1964), Grace Cunard (1893–1967), Julia Crawford Ivers (d. 1930), Ruth Ann Baldwin, and Dorothy Davenport Reid (1895–1977).

The first person believed to have directed a narrative film is Alice Guy (later known as Guy-Blaché, 1873–1968). In 1896, Guy was secretary to Léon Gaumont, whose French photography company was expanding to include the sale of a motion picture camera. Guy asked permission to make a story film to demonstrate the new device. Gaumont agreed, but only if the project did not interfere with her secretarial duties. Within a year, Guy was head of Gaumont film production; and by the time of her emigration to the United States in 1907, she had produced (often directing) about 400 short films.

In America, she formed her own film studio, Solax (1910–14), where, as president and chief director, she supervised the production of more than 300 movies. In 1913, Guy concentrated on making longer films, eventually directing 22 feature films. Her career spanned the evolution of film from embryonic one-reelers to sophisticated feature films that touched on topics such as marriage, divorce, and gender identity. Only a fraction of the films directed by Guy survive. Of the three extant features she made, the Library has an incomplete copy of one, *The Ocean Waif* (1916, FBC 1466). Several of Guy's surviving short films, including *Algie the Miner* (1912, FEB 7679), *Canned Harmony* (1912, FAA 1916), *The Sewer* (1912, FGE 5155), *Matrimony's Speed Limit* (1913, FAB 1473), and *A House Divided* (1913, FEA 5257), are in the Library's collections.

THIS IS THE NEW FALL STYLE IN CAMERA "MEN"

Stagg photo.

Meaning, the style you could fall for. Nor is this a masquerade get-up. Margery Ordway, regular, professional, licensed, union crank-turner at Camp Morosco, has gone into camera work as nonchalantly as other girls take up stenography, nursing, husband-stalking.

"This is the new style in fall camera 'men.'" Photoplay Magazine, *October 1916, p.103 (PN1993.P5). Photograph. Moving Image Section, Motion Picture, Broadcasting, and Recorded Sound Division.*

The potential for women to participate in the motion picture industry during the silent era is suggested in this 1916 picture from the popular fan magazine *Photoplay.* Although the caption emphasizes the traditional gender expectation, it also demonstrated that women were not excluded from this usually male profession. "Margery Ordway, regular, professional, licensed, union crank-turner at Camp Morosco, has gone into camera work as nonchalantly as other girls take up stenography, nursing, husband-stalking."

Before embarking on a film career, Lois Weber (1882?–1939) had already toured as a child prodigy concert pianist, worked as a missionary in Pittsburgh, and appeared on the stage. In 1908, she joined the Gaumont studio in New York City, where she wrote, directed, and acted in motion pictures. Weber eventually moved to Hollywood, where she became Universal Studio's highest-paid director in 1916. In 1917, she formed her own production company and continued to make films that reflected her moral stand on important social issues. She had addressed birth control and abortion in *Where Are My Children?* (1916, VBK 2378), capital punishment in *The People vs. Joe Doe*

(1916), and drug addiction in *Hop, the Devil's Brew* (1916). Her later films included a realistic drama of married life, *Too Wise Wives* (1921, FEA 7930–7935), and a treatment of the problems of ordinary people, *The Blot* (1921, FCA 7932–7933). Additional holdings are listed in the Directors File.

Women were also employed in a wide range of other activities behind the camera. They worked as costume designers, readers, script girls, film cutters, editors, set designers, and casting directors. Perhaps most significantly, as Cari Beauchamp has noted, "during the teens, 1920s, and early 1930s, almost one quarter of the screenwriters in Hollywood were women. Half of all the films copyrighted between 1911 and 1925 were written by women."[6] The work of many of the major women screenwriters in Hollywood, some of whom also directed, can be found in the division's holdings, including films of Anita Loos (1893–1981), June Mathis (1892–1927), Frances Marion (1887–1973), Jeanie Macpherson (1884–1946), Ida May Park (1885?–1954), Bess Meredyth (1890–1969), Elinor Glyn (1864–1943), Lenore Coffee (1897–1984), and Jane Murfin (1893–1955). (See also *What Women Wrote: Scenarios, 1912–1926;* microfilm 89/2007, available in the Microform Reading Room, for access to dozens of screenplays written by women.)

Even by the 1920s, filmmaking was not simply for professionals; it was possible for amateur filmmakers to produce fiction films for exhibition, whether for private audiences or in venues such as churches, schools, and community centers. Eloyce Patrick King Gist (1892–1974) used such venues to show films to the African American community. An independent business woman in the 1920s, Gist became involved with husband James Gist's filmmaking endeavors. She rewrote and re-edited his production, *Hell Bound Train* (ca. 1929–30) and, along with James, produced, wrote, and directed *Verdict Not Guilty* (ca. 1930–33). The films in the **Eloyce Gist Collection** dramatize religious themes using casts of nonprofessional black actors. The movies were so widely shown that they literally fell apart along the splices and were received by the Library in hundreds of short fragments. Currently, only video copies of the out-of-sequence fragments for the two films are available for viewing (VBM 5130–5132). New 16mm prints will be made once the proper continuities for the films are determined. Correspondence regarding the films has been copied from the Manuscript Division's NAACP Records (box I. C-299—Subject File: Films and Plays-General—1924–33) and is available in the Gist vertical file in the Motion Picture and Television Reading Room.

The Studio Era

Today a moviegoer's ticket buys access to a feature film and a few promotional trailers. Before the 1960s, however, filmgoers were often treated to a double bill of feature films, including the main attraction and a "B" film, newsreels, and other short subjects. The Library's collections allow the researcher to study the whole of this cinematic experience, which reached its apotheosis in the studio era—a period from the 1920s to the 1950s when a handful of Hollywood companies dominated the production, distribution, and exhibition of American films. Motion pictures from the studio era are scattered throughout the division's collections. The largest holdings are found in the Copyright Collection and in gift collections from major studios. The collections of Columbia, Disney, Paramount, RKO, Universal, and Warner Bros. films include over ten thousand features and shorts produced during that era. Although reference copies are available for some of these materials, the majority of the studio deposits consist of preprint elements (such as negatives and finegrain master positives) that are not available for viewing. In addition, the division has supplemented its Copyright and Studio Collections with purchases of 16mm television prints, videos, laser discs, and DVDs.

In the studio era, companies began producing some fifty feature films annually, with hundreds of major movies in release during any given year. These pictures covered a wide range of topics and touched on many issues relating to women, including the position of women in the workplace, the role of family, and the social expectations for women. Incidental comments about women and reflections of contemporary attitudes toward them can be found throughout the output of the filmmaking industry. It was also true, however, then as now, that filmmakers frequently dealt with matters directly related to women in certain types of productions.

During the classical Hollywood era, the prolific quantity of motion pictures became organized into specific genres, whose basic content could be recognized by audiences, exhibitors, and producers in a relatively predictable way. Each genre was defined by certain types of subject matter different from the other genres. Another factor forcing films into formulaic patterns was the strengthening of the Production Code, which regulated the content of Hollywood scripts. The code had the effect of minimizing or eliminating from films potentially controversial issues relating to women and their position in society—including divorce, premarital sex, or out-of-wedlock births.

Genres constructed specifically to appeal to female audiences included a class of pictures known as "women's films," addressing issues supposedly of concern primarily to female viewers. These encompassed the melodrama, family, and romance formulas. Known colloquially as "tear-jerkers" or "weepies," these films often concentrated on a female character and her tribulations. Self-sacrifice, self-abnegation, and choices relating to career, family, or romantic partner were often key plot elements.

The "maternal melodrama" centers on a mother who, because of the dictates of society, gives up her child in order to ensure him or her a better life. In *Stella Dallas* (1937, DAA 0954), a girl from the lower classes, Stella, marries a rising businessman, Stephen Dallas. They have a daughter, but soon their class differences cause Stephen to leave. Stella raises their daughter Laurel until she discovers that her vulgar behavior embarrasses Laurel. Pretending her daughter is a burden, Stella sends Laurel to live with Stephen's new family. Some years later, as Laurel is marrying a prominent young man, Stella stands on a sidewalk, satisfied to be watching the ceremony through a window. Other films in this vein are *Blonde Venus* (1932, DAA 3155), *To Each His Own* (1946, FCA 3590–3592), and *A Child Is Born* (1940, FGE 3887–3891).

The "fallen woman" melodrama often features a sympathetic woman who commits adultery or engages in premarital sex and must pay the consequences either by dying or suffering nobly to prove her essential goodness. Set in a variety of times and locales, fallen woman films include *Camille* (1937, VBD 8448–8449), *Waterloo Bridge* (1940, DAA 2443), *Letter from an Unknown Woman* (1948, DAA 2183), and *The Rains of Ranchipur* (1955, FGA 9092–9103). Other films involve the choice a woman must make between social conventions and independence. For example, in *Jezebel* (1938, DAA 0835), headstrong Julie Morris (Bette Davis) will not buckle under to her proper fiancé and so loses him to another woman. In *Woman of the Year* (1942, FGE 7615–7620), renowned foreign correspondent Tess Harding (Katharine Hepburn) believes she must play down her career and learn how to cook if she wants to keep her new husband. *All That Heaven Allows* (1955, CGC 5087–5091) attacks the stifling conformity of suburban life in the story of Cary Scott (Jane Wyman), who is pressured to give up the younger man she loves.

The **Mertz** and **Zouary Collections** provide myriad examples of the low budget films produced by Poverty Row studios that were a prolific part of the movie-going experience of the 1930s to the 1950s but are little remembered today. Alongside the mythic goddesses of the silver screen, researchers at the Library can find similar formulas in films with lesser-known players, such as Aileen Pringle starring in *Love Past Thirty* (Monarch Productions, 1934, FCB 3834–3835), Martha Tilton in *Swing Hostess* (PRC Pictures, 1944, FCB 3290–3291), Elyse Knox in *Forgotten Women* (Monogram, 1949, FCB 3492–3493), and Penny Edwards in *Missing Women* (Republic, 1951, FBC 6142–6143). Zouary titles are cataloged in the Library's online catalog.

Although the first film programs comprised a number of brief films, the length of movies steadily increased until features became the main attraction. By the studio era, shorts were relegated to a supporting function in an evening's entertainment. Short subjects encompassed a wide range of genres, including newsreel, travelogue, musical, sports, documentary, novelty, and animation.

Newsreels—works containing a variety of news footage, ranging in content from lifestyles to international events—began to be released theatrically in the United States in 1911, with the last newsreels appearing in the 1960s. The Library has scattered collections of newsreel footage from the silent era received through gift and deposit, including the coverage of suffrage parades and prominent women. Stories intended for a female audience often centered on fashion and beauty, such as "What a Fashion Decrees—Newest of Spring Styles in Milady's Dainty Headgear," *International News, vol. 2, no. 4* (1919, FAA 1315) and "The Art of 'Dolling Up' Taught to Working Girls," *Unidentified Cromwell, no. 5: Newsclips* (192-?, FEA 8062).

The division's largest collection of newsreels was received through copyright deposit. Beginning in 1942, the Library selected various issues of *Movietone News, News of the Day, Paramount News,* and *Universal Newsreel* for inclusion in the archive. These holdings are listed in a card file by title of newsreel, volume, and issue number. There is no subject access to the content of these newsreels through the division's catalogs. It is generally necessary to know the date of an event, and then to search by date through the copyright descriptions or trade magazines to pinpoint a particular newsreel by volume and issue number.

Also received through copyright are films that re-edited earlier newsreel footage and added new commentary, such as *Almanac Newsreel* and *The Greatest Headlines of the Century*. Subject access to these films is available through the Dictionary Catalog and entries marked "[from old catalog]" in the Library's online catalog. Among these series is footage of the major women newsmakers of the day, such as Eleanor Roosevelt and Ethel Rosenberg; aviators Amelia Earhart, Helen Richey, and Jacqueline Cochran; and sports champions Helen Wills, Babe Didrikson Zaharias, and Maureen Connelly. A very incomplete run of *The March of Time* can be found in the Film and Television Catalog. One of them, *White-Collar Girls* (1948, FGD 3646), investigates the problems besetting the career girl in her search for success.

Repeating the example of the earliest movies, experimental sound films featured variety performers to demonstrate the new technology. DeForest Phonofilms and Vitaphone shorts are among the division's holdings of early sound shorts covering a wide range of popular performers of the day. Opera star Rosa Raisa, nightclub hostess Texas Guinan, impressionist Venita Gould, vaudevillian and former soubrette Fannie Ward, and Ziegfeld beauty and singer Miss Bobby Folsom can all be seen in these short films.

Female animated characters from the sound era run the gamut from the genteel representations of the dainty Minnie Mouse and the even mousier Olive Oyl to the suggestive renderings of the naughty Betty Boop and the blatantly sexual beings in the cartoons of Tex Avery, as in *Red Hot Riding Hood* (1943) and *Swing Shift Cinderella* (1945). In addition to scattered holdings of Disney and Popeye cartoons, the division has the compilations *The Compleat Tex Avery* (DAA 2249) and *Betty Boop* (VAF 2503–2510).

The **Harry Wright Collection** (1,245 films) has a wealth of short subject material related to women. In *Mother Melodies* (193?, FAB 8373), popular tunes are given highly sentimental renderings. "My Mother's Rosary," for instance, shows a mother counting her baby's fingers and toes. One of the curiosities uncovered in *Walter Futters' Curiosities* 2 (1930, FAB 8186) is the introduction of a diaper service in New York City. *Popular Science Excerpt: Kitchen Gadgets* (1936, FAB 9026) demonstrates new items for the housewife in making breakfast, including a device to keep bacon from wrinkling as it cooks. *Feminine Fitness* (1929, FAB 8642) shows the "fair collegians" of Wellesley College participating in various sports for class credits. In *Red Republic* (1934, FAB 9186), famed photographer Margaret Bourke-White is shown traveling through Russia. *Front Line Women* (1941, FAB 8177), made shortly before Pearl Harbor, describes the role of women in war. Cartoons range from Ub Iwerks's *Mary's Little Lamb* (1935, FAB 8740), based on the popu-

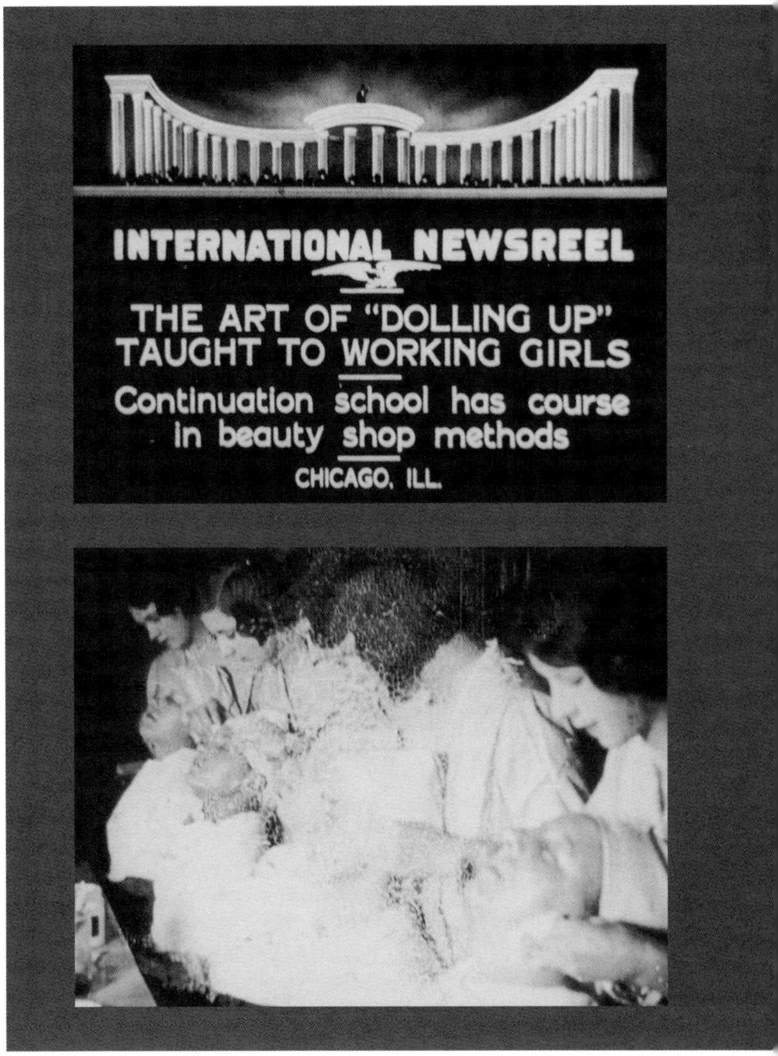

"International Newsreel: The Art of 'Dolling Up' Taught to Working Girls." Frame enlargements. Hearst, 192-?. From Unidentified Cromwell No. 5: Newsclips *(FEA 8062). Moving Image Section, Motion Picture, Broadcasting, and Recorded Sound Division.*

Current events covered by newsreel cameras included wars, natural disasters, views of prominent people, and sports highlights. Much of the material was more mundane, however, including baby shows, parades, and zoo animals, with fashion and beauty among the typical topics aimed at the female audience. The decomposition apparent in the frame enlargement was caused by nitrate deterioration in the original film print.

lar fable, to *Gags and Gals* (1936, FBC 6583), which animates Jefferson Machamer's infamous drawings of well-endowed young women, often in the midst of being chased by their bosses.

Films made to instruct and inform can quickly become obsolete for their originally intended purpose. A film like *All My Babies, a Midwife's Own Story* (1953, FBA 0042–0044), which was made to train African American midwives in rural Georgia, is dated as a teaching tool but remains timeless as a record of childbirth and the living conditions of the people involved.

Other outdated educational films are valuable to historians as a reflection of the accepted social attitudes, values, and mores of their time, often revealing sexual biases and stereotypes presented by teachers and other professionals. For example, *Psychology I: How Men and Women Differ* (1957, FCA 3857) features Dr. Edwin G. Boring of Harvard University giving a now unintentionally humorous explanation of the psychological differences between the sexes. *Molested* (1965, FBA 5518) advises teenage girls that carelessness in dress, dancing, and other activities can imperil their safety.

The division holds *To New Horizons: Ephemeral Films, 1931–1945* and *You Can't Get There from Here: Ephemeral Films, 1946–1960* (VAB 0085–0086), video compilations of a host of promotional and educational films that have taken on new meanings. *Relax* (1937) shows how to improve "*her* efficiency in the office"; *Are You Popular?* (1947) "warns that nice girls don't"; and *The Relaxed Wife* (1957) promotes the use of tranquilizers.

Not Wanted. *Camera: Henry Freulich. Directors: Elmer Clifton and Ida Lupino (uncredited). Screenplay: Paul Jarrico and Ida Lupino. Cast: Sally Forrest, Keefe Brasselle, Leo Penn, Dorothy Adams. Lobby card. Emerald Productions, Inc., 1949. Lobby card collection (box C-11). Moving Image Section, Motion Picture, Broadcasting, and Recorded Sound Division.*

Not Wanted (1949) was the first of a series of films in which longtime star Ida Lupino moved behind the camera to make low-budget films emphasizing women's issues—in this case, unwanted pregnancy. Lupino, the co-scripter and producer, took over the direction of the film from the ailing Elmer Clifton during its production. This was the beginning of a new career as director that Lupino would continue in movies and television for the next twenty years.

As positions became specialized and codified during the studio era, unions were formed, creative decisions were made by production heads, and the women who had flourished behind the camera were shut out of positions of power and prestige. Women remained in lesser positions, such as editors, but the ranks of women directors and producers were decimated. The days when a secretary could become a director overnight disappeared forever.

Dorothy Arzner (1900–1979), Ida Lupino (1918–1995) , and Virginia Van Upp (1902–1970) were among the handful of women in Hollywood who directed or produced during the decades of the thirties, forties, and fifties. Beginning in 1919, Arzner worked up the ranks from script department stenographer to script clerk to film cutter to film editor to screenwriter. She directed her first film, *Fashions for Women,* in 1927 and continued to direct until 1943. Her best-known films held at the Library are *Dance, Girl, Dance* (1940, VBG 6839–6840) and *Christopher Strong* (1933, FEA 4461–4469). Ida Lupino, an actress through the 1930s and 1940s, considered herself "the poor man's Bette Davis" and wanted to expand into other areas. Working as a producer for the first time in 1949 on the film *Not Wanted* (FBA 3577–3584), Lupino took over directing duties when the original director fell ill. She continued to produce and direct motion pictures and television programs thereafter. Lupino films found at the Library include *The Hitch-Hiker* (1953, FGF 0256–0258) and *The Trouble with Angels* (1966, FGB 9470–9475). Virginia Van Upp began as a child actress in silent films and also rose through the ranks to become executive producer at Columbia Pictures in 1945. Films she produced include *Cover Girl* (1944, FCA 1986–1988), *Together Again* (1944, FCA 3600–3602), *Gilda* (1946, FGE 5411–5416), and *Here Comes the Groom* (1951, FGA 4954–4965).

A few American women filmmakers worked outside the Hollywood system. Maya Deren (1917–1961), "the mother of underground film," started making experimental shorts, such as *Meshes of the Afternoon, At Land,* and *Meditation on Violence* (VAC 0246), in the 1940s, at a time when there were no channels of distribution and exhibition for avant-garde works. She advertised her work to universities, art schools, and museums and eventually found outlets in some public theaters. Establishing the Creative Film Foundation, Deren helped paved the way for other independent filmmakers. Shirley Clarke (1919–1997), whose films include *Skyscraper* (1959, FEA 1343–1344) and *The Cool World* (1963, FCB 1701–1703), was one of the first recipients of a grant from Deren's foundation. Deren and Clarke were in the forefront of independent filmmakers who challenged the restrictions placed on women directors and producers.

Women professionals from various fields of endeavor used film in their work. The **Margaret Mead Collection** consists largely of field footage taken on expeditions in Bali and Papua New Guinea from 1936 to 1965 in which noted anthropologist Dr. Margaret Mead (1901–1978) participated. The collection also contains field footage in which Mead was not a participant, including work by Jane Belo, Zora Neale Hurston, and Maya Deren; footage of Mead and her family; footage of Mead lecturing; classroom films taken by Mead's students at Columbia University; and documentaries related to anthropology, some of which included Mead's participation.

The Zora Neale Hurston (1903–1960) material in the Mead Collection consists of several rolls of film footage. The earliest footage is material shot by Hurston in Florida in 1928 and 1929. There is also ethnographic footage filmed in South Carolina from a project headed by Jane Belo. Although Hurston did not act as cinematographer, she served as on-site project director and at times appears in the footage. There are also a few reels of Haitian footage shot by Maya Deren. These materials can be used in conjunction with the Mead papers in the Manuscript Division (see chapter 5).

Mary Marvin Breckinridge Patterson (b. 1905) has been a photographer, documentary filmmaker, community activist, broadcast journalist, and wife of a career diplomat. The **Mrs. Jefferson Patterson Collection** of some 200 items comprises films made by Patterson, home movies, and miscellaneous works relating to the Patterson family. After serving as a volunteer courier for the Frontier Nursing Service (FNS) in Appalachian Kentucky in 1928, Patterson made a documentary promoting the work of the service. *The Forgotten Frontier* (1930, FAA 5886–5890) addresses the problems of the people of Appalachia and highlights the self-reliant women of the nursing service. She went on to make the documentaries *The Ruins of Zimbabwe, Rhodesia* (1932, VBJ 4851) and *A School for Natives, South Africa* (1932, VBJ 6149). Patterson's *Chichen-Itza, the Ancient Mayan Mecca of Yucatan* (1930, VBJ 4850) is the first professional film of that archaeological site and *She Goes to Vassar* (1931, VBK 9367) depicts a student's arrival on campus. A collection-level record can be found in the Library's online cata-

December 5, 1925 National Tie-Up and Exploitation Section Page 29

DON'T FORGET *HER*

The Importance of Putting Your Campaign With the Women Can Not Be Overstressed

IN EVERY exploitation campaign, it would be financial suicide to leave the women folk out of consideration. They are the ones who go to the movies the most, and they are the ones that give the youngsters the pennies needed to attend your matinees.

Sell them on the idea that they and their young ones ought to see the pictures, and you are fairly sure of a good house.

Take up the speculation there is current at the present time regarding the solidity of the bobbed-hair fashion. It looks as though it may lose its popularity, and that the long tresses will soon be in vogue again.

Mr. Exhibitor, you as a man, can hardly appreciate the extreme importance of this fact to women. Why, an earthquake would be relegated to second page news if some famous actress were suddenly to say that bobbed hair is passe.

Play up the poster that is shown to right of this column. Place it in all the beauty parlors, but remember that it will be used in these places only as an excuse for the management of the parlor to issue propaganda to counteract any movement towards long hair.

Gloves and Bags

Any ladies wear shop will welcome the opportunity to use the two stills shown below in a window display of women's gloves and bags. Also note, in the still to the left, how prominently the black bead necklace is worn. This can be utilized in a novelty store tie-up.

Bobbies!
Watch for your laurels!
There is talk of bringing back long tresses again.
How do you like these in
"The Scarlet Streak"
EVERY MONDAY
STRAND THEATRE

IN making up posters such as shown above, keep in mind the color scheme. In all cases, the words "The Scarlet Streak" must be in red. And wherever possible, the window display around the poster should carry out the same idea by having red as the dominant color. It is these little touches that add so much to displays—enough to take them out of the ordinary.

The Scarlet Streak. *Henry McRae. Cast: Jack Daugherty, Lola Todd, Virginia Ainsworth, Albert J. Smith, Al Prisco. Universal Pictures Corporation. Advertising guide ("National Tie-Up and Exploitation Section"), from* Exhibitor's Trade Review *(PN1993.E85), December 5, 1925, p. 29. Moving Image Section, Motion Picture, Broadcasting, and Recorded Sound Division.*

From the beginnings of cinema through the 1970s, studio publicity emphasized attracting female audiences through the appeal of fashions. Advertising and promotional advice and materials on this theme were given to exhibitors to use in theater lobbies, to interest local newspapers, and to distribute to area businesses. Exploitation campaigns outlined in pressbooks and trade publications—exemplified in the exhortation "Don't forget *her*"—reminded exhibitors that "it would be financial suicide to leave the women folk out of consideration." To draw women to the multi-chapter serial "The Scarlet Streak" (1925), theater owners were urged to spotlight the hairstyle and accessories featured in the films.

log and item-level records are in MAVIS. Associated materials can be found in the Manuscript, Prints and Photographs, and Recorded Sound reading rooms.

The Post-Studio Era

From the late 1940s, Hollywood faced two threats to its hegemony, the court-ordered breakup of the studios' exhibition monopoly and the steady loss of audiences to television. With fewer ticket sales, the studios made fewer movies. By the 1960s, the studio system with its huge production facilities and long-term contract personnel came to an end. Films addressing women's concerns continued to be made, but they were often harder to fund, distribute, and exhibit within the changing Hollywood economy. When the eroding Production Code was replaced by the ratings system, however, filmmakers were given the freedom to treat social and political themes in more mature and original ways.

The Library's collections of American feature films received through copyright deposit are exceptionally strong for this period. Movies that could be classified as women's pictures—such as *Alice Doesn't Live Here Anymore* (1974, FGC 8517–8522), *Norma Rae* (1979, DAA 0571), *Terms of Endearment* (1983, DAA 0641), *Places in the Heart* (1984, DAA 0906), *Sleepless in Seattle* (1993, CGB 8668–8673), and *The First Wives Club* (1996, CGC 4150–4155)—are well represented in the division's holdings. Harkening back to the days of silent serials, women appropriated the role of action heroes in many contemporary films, among them *Alien* (1979, DAA 0334), *The Terminator* (1984, CGA 5932–5937), and *Thelma and Louise* (1991, CGB 7631–7637), but more often they appeared as appendages to male stars.

Advances made by women in contemporary America have not meant the end of formulaic representations of women through blatant stereotypes in motion pictures. As recently as *Pretty Woman* (1990, CGB 1603–1608), *Mighty Aphrodite* (1995, DAA 3270), and *Leaving Las Vegas* (1995, DAA 3229), the cliché of the "hooker with a heart of gold" has been a central characterization. Unlike previous generations from Lillian Gish to Katharine Hepburn, the careers of contemporary women stars suffer in comparison to their male counterparts. Today's actresses are generally paid less, find fewer challenging roles, and their lifespans as romantic leads fade long before those of such aging lotharios as Warren Beatty and Jack Nicholson.

With the breakdown of the studio system, however, women were able to forge careers as directors once again. Ranging from exploitation films to independent productions to Hollywood extravaganzas, the Library's holdings include works from such women feature film directors as Stephanie Rothman (b. 1936), Joan Micklin Silver (b. 1935), Joan Tewkesbury (b. 1936), Claudia

Weill (b. 1947), Joyce Chopra (b. 1938), Amy Heckerling (b. 1954), Martha Coolidge (b. 1946), Barbra Streisand (b. 1942), Susan Seidelman (b. 1952), Penny Marshall (b. 1942), Nancy Savoca (b. 1959), Tamra Davis (n.d.), Penelope Spheeris (b. 1945), Julie Dash (b. 1952), Allison Anders (b. 1954), Nora Ephron (b. 1941), Jodie Foster (b. 1962), Mimi Leder (b. 1952), and Betty Thomas (b. 1947). Records for films by these directors are available in the Library's online catalog.

Documentary filmmaking was and continues to be an important outlet for women directors. Liane Brandon (b. 1939) explores the concepts of beauty and self-image in her film *Betty Tells Her Story* (1972, FBB 7142). Barbara Kopple (b. 1946) spent four years in the coalfields of Kentucky covering the events surrounding a miner's strike in the Academy Award–winning documentary *Harlan County, U.S.A* (1976, FDA 6321–6323). Director Lee Grant (b. 1927) documents the case of eight women in Willmar, Minnesota, who went on strike because of job discrimination in *The Willmar 8* (1982, FDA 6917). Greta Schiller (b. 1954) and Andrea Weiss (b. 1956) made *International Sweethearts of Rhythm, America's Hottest All-Girl Band* (1986, VBF 5502), which examines the role of women and minorities through the story of a multiracial all-girl band formed during World War II.

Television

In 1950 only 9 percent of American households had a television set, but by 1960 the figure had reached 90 percent. Despite the ubiquity of television in American life, serious study of television, its history, and its effects is comparatively new. Whereas film studies literature is rich in the area of gender-related issues, only a fraction of such scholarship can be found for television. The collections at the Library of Congress provide ample opportunities for researchers who wish to fill this gap in the literature.

As mentioned above, the Library's television selection practices have been uneven through the years. Browsing through *Three Decades of Television: A Catalog of Television Programs Acquired by the Library of Congress, 1949–1979,* the researcher will find only a handful of episodes listed for *I Love Lucy* (1951–1957), *Our Miss Brooks* (1952–1956), *Oh! Susanna* (1956–1959), and *The Donna Reed Show* (1958–1966). As the commercial potential for older series was realized, however, many programs were deposited for copyright years after their initial broadcast. For example, thirty-five episodes of *Oh! Susanna/The Gale Storm Show* were registered for copyright in 1987 and selected for the archive. In 1982, a similar number of episodes of *I Love Lucy* were received as gifts.

As with motion pictures, television programs of all types can be invaluable resources in examining the spectrum of issues relating to women. Researchers may be particularly interested in the division's sizable holdings of situation comedies featuring central female characters, such as *Petticoat Junction* (1963–70), *I Dream of Jeannie* (1965–70), *That Girl* (1966–71), *Julia* (1968–71), *The Mary Tyler Moore Show* (1970–77), *Maude* (1972–78), *One Day at a Time* (1975–84), *Mary Hartman, Mary Hartman* (1976–77), *Laverne and Shirley* (1976–83), and *Facts of Life* (1979–88). Episodes of *Designing Women* (1986–93), *Roseanne* (1988–97), *Murphy Brown* (1988–98), *All American Girl* (1994–95), *Cybill* (1995–98), *Moesha* (1996–), *Ally McBeal* (1997–), and *Sex and the City* (1998–) bring the collection more up to date. Weekly dramatic series with leading female roles in the division's copyright collection include *Peyton Place* (1964–69), *The Big Valley* (1965–69), *Little House on the Prairie* (1974–82), *Police Woman* (1974–78), *Charlie's Angels* (1976–81), *Wonder Woman* (1976–79), *Family* (1976–80), *Dynasty* (1981–89), *Cagney and Lacy* (1982–88), *Sisters* (1990–96), *My So Called Life* (1994–95), *Xena: Warrior Princess* (1995–), *Buffy, the Vampire Slayer* (1997–), and *Providence* (1999–).

Dozens of made-for-television movies deal with social, medical, and political problems that were once the realm of feature films. Civil rights, battered wives, and incest are explored, respectively, in *The Autobiography of Miss Jane Pittman* (1974, FBC 2831–2834), *The Burning Bed* (1984, VAD 6366), and *Something about Amelia* (1984, FDA 8445–8446). Breast cancer is the subject of *First You Cry* (1981, VBD 6577–6578) and abortion is the focus of *Roe vs. Wade* (1989, VBH 0033–0034). Alcohol and substance abuse are treated in *The Betty Ford Story* (1987, FDA 8498–8499).

Daytime programming received through copyright deposit includes two episodes of *Home* (additional kinescope episodes of which are found in the NBC Collection), a series aimed at the American housewife. Designed as an extension to the *Today* show, *Home* (1954–57) offers coverage of fashion and beauty, food, gardening, home repair, and family affairs. The Library holds thirteen episodes of the syndicated talk show *For You . . . Black Woman* (1977–78) centering on the interests and concerns of African American women. *Three Decades of Television,* published by the Library of Congress in 1989, lists only a handful of daytime game shows and soap operas, including a single program each of *The Hidden Treasure Show* (1957), *Another World* (1978), and *The Doctors* (1978). During the early 1980s, however, copyright deposit holdings of soap operas increased dramatically with the selections of significant runs of *All My Children, General Hospital, One Life to Live,* and *Ryan's Hope.*

The division's holdings of television news and documentary programming are of special interest to historians of women's place in America. *Wide Wide World: A Woman's Story* (1957, FDA 9351–9352) features a discussion of the role of women in American society, politics, and the arts with Helen Keller, Senator Margaret Chase Smith, Margaret Mead, Eleanor Roosevelt, Marian Anderson, and author Kathryn Hulme. *Woman!* (1959–1960), a loosely organized series of documentaries, analyzes different issues of importance to the modern woman. Episodes in the collection include *Do They Marry Too Young?* (FCA 3804–3805), *Is the American Woman Losing Her Femininity?* (FCA 1620–1621), and *The Lonely Years* (FCA 3806–3807).

Television responded to women's changing concerns. The emerging women's liberation movement in America, for instance, was examined in *The American Woman in the 20th Century* (1963, FDA 3698), showing the expanding roles of women in the United States. A few years later this issue was revisited in the *CBS News Special: An Essay on Women* (1967, FCA 5202). *Now: Women's Liberation* (1970, FBB 1050) compares and contrasts various groups within the women's liberation movement. *The American Parade: We, the Women* (1974, FBB 2551–2552) surveys the position of women in American history beginning with the settlers and continuing to the debate concerning ERA. *Woman Alive!* (1974, VDA 0045) profiles the feminist movement, and *NBC News Special Report: Women like Us* (1979, VBB 2806) examines the options available to American women. After the movement made serious strides in this country, it was time to consider what it all meant to men. In 1981, the new CBS daytime program *Up to the Minute* dealt with this subject in the five-part *The Effects of Feminism on Men* (VBC 7848–7852).

The **NBC Collection** consists of 10,000 programs, mostly in the form of kinescopes broadcast between 1948 and 1977. Highlights of the collection featuring women include scattered holdings of *Today with Mrs. Roosevelt* (1950–51), *The Dinah Shore Show* (1951–62), *Home* (1954–57), *Miss America Pageant* (1967–78), *Modern Romances* (1954–58), *Queen for a Day* (1956–60), *Purex Specials for Women* (1960–63), and *The Shari Lewis Show* (1960–63). Also covered are daytime programs for the early years of television not well represented in the copyright collection, such as game shows, soap operas, and children's shows.

The **NET collections** (National Educational Television, the precursor to PBS), acquired at different times and from different sources, comprise 16mm prints of some 550 titles, preprint materials for approximately 10,000 programs, and 8,500 master films and videotapes. The Library continues to acquire a broad range of public television through **PBS**'s ongoing gift of programs. At this time, the division has received approximately 24,000 master videotapes and 16mm films. Public television programs broadcast during the 1960s and 1970s aimed at a female audience include *Erica* on needlepoint and quilting, *Exploring the Crafts, Sewing Skills, Woman,* and *Parent Effectiveness. The French Chef, International Cookbook, Joyce Chen Cooks,* and *Vegetable Soup* focus on food and cooking. The majority of these collections consists of kinescopes, preprint materials, and film and video masters that are not available for screening at this time.

Researchers can find television commercials scattered throughout the division's holdings, as individual copyright deposits—*Vanderbilt Fragrance: A Splendor You Feel* (1984, VBC 5844)—in miscellaneous gift collections—*Exquisite Form Bra Television Commercial: Crown Jewel Collection* (195–?, FAA 9523)—and in compilations—*U.S. Television Commercials Festival: 1972 Awards* (FDA 2763). Others are included as a part of television programs. *Omnibus,* for instance, includes commercials for the Scott Paper Company, Kelvinator appliances, and Norcross Greeting Cards shown during the programs. Since about 1987, commercials have been cataloged in the Library's online catalog beginning with the generic term "[Television commercial—]," followed by the name of the product or sponsor and, when known, the title of the commercial.

The **Karr Collection,** 1,928 commercials produced during the 1960s and early 1970s, is rich in representation of American life, often depicting topics and issues that characterize the period, including the women's movement and the sexual revolution. Included are commercials for appliances, girdles, lingerie, silk stockings, support stockings, dolls, baby food, frozen and prepared

Left: The Donna Reed Show. *Donna Reed and Patty Petersen. Photograph. Todon-Briskin in association with Screen Gems. ABC, 1958–66. "The Donna Reed Show" courtesy of Columbia TriStar Television.*

Right: Roseanne. *Roseanne and Laurie Metcalf. Photograph by Viacom for Casey-Werner, ABC, 1988–97. Stills collection. Moving Image Section, Motion Picture, Broadcasting, and Recorded Sound Division. With the permission of The Carsey-Werner Company, LLC.*

Television's portrayal of motherhood in situation comedies serves as a mirror to the times. Donna Stone (*right*), the solid, middle-class mom with her crisp, perfectly groomed appearance in *The Donna Reed Show,* reflected the American ideal of wholesomeness prized in the 1950s. Post-Vietnam and post-Watergate America found the working-class, raucous Roseanne Conner (*right*) in *Roseanne* a more accurate depiction of motherhood in freer but more turbulent times.

foods, air fresheners, laundry detergents, mops, pain relievers, hair products, perfumes, cosmetics, and skin care products. A finding aid to this collection is available on the Motion Picture and Television Reading Room Web site and in hard copy in the reading room. Finding aids also exist for the **Dartmouth College Collection** of approximately 500 commercials made by Robert Lawrence Productions during the period from 1952 to 1963 and the **Robert R. Gitt Collection** of 363 commercials made during the early 1970s.

Lucille Ball (1911–1989) is the first name that comes to mind when thinking about women pioneers in television. Unfortunately, she is often the only name that comes to mind. A discussion of the role of women in early television is presented in a thin volume by Cary O'Dell, *Women Pioneers in Television: Biographies of Fifteen Industry Leaders* (Jefferson, N.C.: McFarland, 1997; PN 1992.8 .W65 O34 1997). In it O'Dell addresses Ball's outstanding comedic and business achievements, which include cofounding Desilu Productions and becoming the first woman president of a major Hollywood studio. But he also identifies other significant women in the history of television.

Mildred Freed Alberg (1921–1984) began her career as a typist and rose to become executive producer of Hallmark Hall of Fame. Programs produced by Alberg include *Macbeth* (1954, FDA 9427–9428), *Man and Superman* (1956, VBO 7324–7325), and *Little Moon of Alban* (1958, VBO 7322–7323). Lucy Jarvis (n.d.) is an Emmy award–winning documentary producer of such programs as *The Louvre: A Golden Prison* (1964, VAB 8158), *Who Shall Live?* (1965, FDA 0353), and *NBC White Paper: Cry Help!* (1970, FDA 0755–0756). Lela Swift (n.d.) and Ida Lupino were among the first few women who directed in television. Swift was the only woman to direct weekly, live, prime-time dramatic anthologies. She moved to daytime soap operas, such as *Dark Shadows* (see the Library's online catalog). Lupino directed westerns, crime shows, dramas, and situation comedies, including *The Untouchables: The Man in the Cooler* (1963, FDA 4457), *Mr. Novak: Day in the Year* (1964, VBK 5047), and *Bewitched: A Is for Aardvark* (1965, FBB 5470). From 1950 to 1954, Lucille Kallen (b. 1925?) was the sole woman writer on *Your Show of Shows* and she later wrote for the *Bell Telephone Hour* (both cataloged online).

These women led the way for the many others who made their careers in television as writers, producers, and directors. Among them are Gloria Monty (*General Hospital*), Linda Bloodworth-Thomason (*Designing Women* and *Evening Shade*), Carol Black (*Wonder Years*), Marcy Carsey (*Roseanne*), Diane English (*Murphy Brown*), Susan Harris (*Golden Girls*), and Suzanne de Passe (*Lonesome Dove*).

Barbaralee Diamonstein-Spielvogel (n.d.) is a writer, television interviewer and producer, educator, and community activist for cultural affairs. Her interests include architecture, decorative arts, performing arts, and historic preservation, and her collection comprises interview shows and other works that focus on the arts. Women she interviewed between 1976 and 1986 include Betty Comden, Louise Nevelson, Charlotte Curtis, Grace Glueck, Kitty Carlisle, Diane Waldman, Connie Morella, Isabel Bishop, Alice Neel, and Marian McPartland.

Readings, Lectures, and the Performing Arts

The Motion Picture, Broadcasting, and Recorded Sound Division maintains a collection of videotapes, beginning in the 1970s, of special programs held at the Library of Congress. Known as the **LC Performance Collection,** it consists largely of poetry readings and features such acclaimed women poets as Anne Sexton (1972, VAA 4591), Maya Angelou (1984, VBG 4072), Jane Kenyon (1988, VBF 3433–3434), Rita Dove (1993, VBL 0647–0648), and Ana Castillo (1994, VBM 1209–1210). PEN fiction award-winner Helen Norris (1993, VBK 2416–1417) and novelists Ursula K. Le Guin (1974, VAA 4644) and Joyce Carol Oates (1975, VAA 4903) have also given readings at the Library. The collection includes keynote addresses and talks by notable women in public life and academia, including Shirley Chisholm (1989, VBF 9251–9252), Sandra Day O'Connor (1993, VBK 2406), and Evelyn Higginbotham (1998, VBO 7618). Music and dance performances

PATHFINDER: BARBARA JORDAN

A compelling example of the wealth of moving images that can be found for one individual is provided by **Barbara Jordan** (1936–1996). This politician, educator, social activist, and notable African American leader came to prominence in the age of television. Searching for pieces of Jordan's life in MBRS provides an example of strategies that can be used to locate television footage.

Searching Barbara Jordan's name in the division's card catalogs locates appearances on *The Dick Cavett Show* (1979, VBC 8833) and *Ben Wattenberg's 1980* (VBM 7168). The Library's online catalog retrieves moving image records for the Watergate documentary *Summer of Judgment—The Impeachment Hearings* (1984, VAA 0618) and identifies a four-part series, *Who's Keeping Score* (1981, VBC 9821–9823; VBC 9840), with Jordan participating in the examination of the pros and cons of minimum-competency testing in American schools. The initial search of the division's catalogs has uncovered valuable but incomplete results.

The search can be continued using the in-house inventories for *Meet the Press* and NET/PBS, unpublished documentation for NBC programming, and the division's publication *Three Decades of Television.* Because of the lack of subject access to most of the Library's moving image materials, a key strategy is creating a title list from secondary sources available in the reading room. Commercially published works are consulted, such as *Special Edition: A Guide to Network Television Documentary Series and Special News Reports, 1955–1979* (Metuchen, N.J.: Scarecrow Press, 1987; PN 1992.8.D6.E56 1987) and *Television News Index and Abstracts* (Nashville, Tenn.: Vanderbilt Television News Archives, 1968–95; AI3.T44; 1968–present on the Web at <http://tvnews.vanderbilt.edu>), as well as online catalogs and CD-ROMs, including *FirstSearch, MediaSearch,* and *Variety's Video Directory Plus.* These sources yield a list of dozens of Barbara Jordan's appearances on television and in educational videos. A return to the division's catalogs using these titles retrieves from the collections holdings of the complete Watergate Impeachment Hearings, two profiles on *Sixty Minutes* (VBA 1380, VBA 5059), the keynote speeches delivered at the Democratic National Convention in 1976 (VAG 5504) and 1992 (VAD 9755), a 1981 inaugural address (VAE 7528–7529), the Bill Moyers' program *Facing Evil* (1988, VBI 8236–8237), two appearances on *Meet the Press* (1976, VBA 7721; 1987, VBH 1500), an *NBC White Paper: The American Presidency* (1979, VBB 2810–2811), and coverage of Barbara Jordan in several network evening news broadcasts.

include programs by flutist Sandra Miller (1998, VXA 7888–7889), harpsichordist Irina Rees (1998, VXA 7918–7919), and the Baroque Music Masters (1976, VAA 4925).

The **NEA/Martha Graham Collection** of forty-four videotapes and one 35mm film documents the ballets and dance techniques of modern dance pioneer Martha Graham (1894–1991). Three ballets for which Graham created three perspectives—a performance recording, a full rehearsal of the work, and a segment demonstrating specific Graham techniques employed in that performance—are *Cave of the Heart* (1986–89, VAB 6288–6290), *Errand into the Maze* (1985–89, VAB6207–6209), and *Acts of Light* (1989?, VAB 6814–6815). Other titles are available through the Library's online catalog.

A single chapter cannot answer every question, touch upon every type of moving image, or mention every relevant collection of film and video in the area of women's history and culture. Our aim instead has been to provide basic information on access systems and research methods and to highlight a sampling of the films and television programs in the Library of Congress. Although some projects may require only a search of the online catalog, most researchers will need to consult with the reference staff of the Motion Picture and Television Reading Room to successfully explore the varied and vast holdings of the Library's moving image collections.

Keynote address by Representative Barbara Jordan, Democratic National Convention, July 12, 1976. Photograph by Warren K. Leffler. U.S. News & World Report, *July 11–12, 1976. U.S. News & World Report Collection. Prints and Photographs Division. LC-U9-32937, frame 32A-33.*

Television was instrumental in bringing Barbara Jordan into national prominence as a member of the House Judiciary Committee during the coverage of the Richard Nixon impeachment hearings in 1974. The broadcasts brought her passion, incisive thinking, and brilliant oratory into homes throughout the country and led, in 1976, to her becoming the first African American woman to give the keynote speech at a Democratic National Convention. Here she is addressing that convention in 1976.

Thanks to our colleagues Barbara Humphrys, Cooper C. Graham, Patrick Loughney, and Mike Mashon for their contributions to this chapter. We are grateful to Constance J. Balides, of Tulane University, for her comments, suggestions, and encouragement.

11 American Folklife Center

James Hardin

The creative work of innumerable women is represented in the Archive of Folk Culture at the American Folklife Center—a national repository for ethnographic materials documenting the traditional expressive culture of ordinary people doing artful things in the course of their daily lives.

The American Folklife Center is charged by Congress to "preserve and present American folklife," and researchers using the Folk Archive to investigate women's history will make two happy discoveries. First, material pertaining to women is extensive and may be found in nearly all of the archive's approximately three thousand collections; and, second, women are represented in the collections as central players in the expressive culture of everyday life.

Included in the congressional legislation that created the American Folklife Center in 1976 (Public Law 94–201) is a definition of American folklife: "the traditional, expressive, shared culture of various groups in the United States: familial, ethnic, occupational, religious, and regional." Although there are organizations and groups within the American social fabric that are made up specifically of women, the traditional life and culture of women within family, ethnic group, religion, and region are inseparable from the larger whole. Folklife embraces family life and daily routine, material culture, celebrations and rituals, story and song, foodways, and more. The documentation of these subjects reflects women's ingenuity, creativity, humor, strength, hopes, joys, trials, and sorrows. And, frequently, it is women who are the chief bearers of tradition, those who have the responsibility for carrying on the cultural forms of a group from one generation to the next.

The Archive of Folk Culture, which became part of the American Folklife Center in 1978, was established in the Library's Music Division in 1928 as the Archive of American Folk Song. The folk songs collected by the first head of the archive, Robert W. Gordon, have been augmented over the years by many other collectors, both men and women, working in the employ of the Library of Congress, as employees of other federal agencies and organizations, or as private individuals. The collections are now international in scope; encompass a wide range of traditional knowledge, custom, music, dance, art, and craft; and include material from many of the world's ethnic, religious, occupational, social, and regional groups.

But the archive is best known for its collections from the United States and is the de facto national folk archive. Contained therein, for example, are the classic recordings of African American and Anglo-American folk music recorded in the field by John and Alan Lomax in the 1930s and early 1940s. Although most of these recordings are of men, there are many fine performances by women, including Emma L. Dusenbury (1862–1941) of Mena, Arkansas, one of the country's best singers of traditional ballads, and "Aunt" Molly Jackson (1880–1960), who recorded in Eastern Kentucky and is known for her songs of protest against the hazardous working conditions suffered by coal miners. Equally important is the large collection of American Indian song and spoken word, used regularly by tribal leaders and scholars for the purposes of language retention and cultural conservation. Although most of the performers were men, a major portion of this material was

Fannie Lee Teals with her red, white, and blue American Revolution Bicentennial quilt, 1977. Photograph by Beverly J. Robinson. South-Central Georgia Folklife Project. American Folklife Center. (6-17617-29a)

Although the American Folklife Center does not collect artifacts, it does collect the documentation of folk art objects and numerous other forms of traditional expression. There are no quilts in the Archive of Folk Culture, but its many photographs of quilts, along with recordings of women talking about the making of quilts, document this folk art.

recorded in the field by women, using wax-cylinder machines and other recording technologies (see "Women Collectors" below). There are also unique recordings of ex-slaves narrating their pre-emancipation experiences, including moving accounts by women. Providing valuable insights into their respective periods are documentary recordings of multi-ethnic American music, culture, and life made during the New Deal era, and materials pertaining to the folk song revival of the 1940s through the 1960s. Over the past several decades, beginning in 1977, American Folklife Center staff members have conducted field documentation projects in many regions of the country. The materials from these projects touch on many aspects of American life.

FOLKLIFE READING ROOM
Thomas Jefferson Building, ground floor, room LJ G49
Hours: Monday through Friday, 8:30 a.m. to 5:00 p.m.
Closed weekends and federal holidays.
Telephone: 202 707-5510
Fax: 202 707-2076
Address: American Folklife Center, Library of Congress,
101 Independence Avenue, SE, Washington, DC 20540-4610
E-mail: folklife@loc.gov
Web site: <http://www.loc.gov/folklife>
Access and use: The Folklife Reading Room is the access point for the ethnographic collections of the Archive of Folk Culture and for a reference collection of approximately four thousand books, indexes, and periodicals. A Library of Congress reader identification card is required. Appointments are recommended for groups of more than three people, and advance notice is advised for requests to listen to unpublished field recordings or to use large collections. It will be essential to consult the reference staff for assistance in locating information on women's history and culture. Because the collections are so rich in these areas and because information on women is embedded in collections generally organized by subject or region, and spread throughout them, you should be prepared to define the particular topic of your study as carefully as possible. The signature research activity in the Folklife Reading Room involves listening to reference tape copies of field recordings, and there are several listening stations for this purpose. Reference staff will instruct you in the use of the tape machines.

Patrons may request copies of manuscript, photographic, and recorded materials in person or by fax, e-mail, or postal mail. The American Folklife Center fully honors the rights of those whose performances and creative expressions are documented in the collections, and permissions issues will arise for most phonoduplication and some photoduplication requests. Order forms, billing information, and notification of necessary permissions will be provided. After permissions are obtained (where applicable), such orders are filled by the Library's Recording Laboratory and other duplicating services.

Although the collections were not created in such a way as to highlight themes specific to the study of women's history and culture, all include documentation about women. It may be helpful to think of the material in four different ways. Documented in the collections are:

1 Cultural activities that have been traditionally—although not exclusively—practiced by women, such as foodways, quilting, or certain

Agnes Vanderburg and Kay Young on the Flathead Reservation, Northwestern Montana, 1979. Photograph by Michael Crummett. Montana Folklife Survey. American Folklife Center. (MT9-MC3-15)

Agnes Vanderburg, a teacher of traditional skills at a heritage camp for children, pit-roasting camas roots at her camp on the Flathead Reservation in northwestern Montana in 1979, while folklorist Kay Young records her commentary. The American Folklife Center holds the largest and most diverse collection in the world of sound recordings documenting American Indian music and spoken word, from the 1890s to the present day. Most of the recordings feature men performers, but many of them were made by women ethnographers. Folklife specialists at the center maintain close contact with Indian communities, which use the collections regularly for matters pertaining to cultural—especially language—retention. Several of the contemporary collections include documentation of pow-wows, which are tribal and pan-tribal social gatherings. Women and children figure more prominently in these collections than in the earlier materials.

Myrtle B. Wilkinson playing tenor banjo, Turlock, California, 1939. Photographer unknown. California Folk Music Project. American Folklife Center. (AFC 1940/001:PO51)

Myrtle B. Wilkinson accompanied fiddler Mrs. Ben Scott with her tenor banjo, as they played a medley of Anglo-American tunes in Turlock, California, in 1939. The Folklife Center's Archive of Folk Culture houses about three thousand ethnographic field collections, many of which were made by individual folklorists, ethnomusicologists, or inspired amateurs with a particular mission or interest. In the case of the California Folk Music Project, Sidney Robertson Cowell recorded a variety of ethnic music from Northern California for the Works Progress Administration.

Josephine Martellaro of Pueblo, Colorado, with the Saint Joseph's Day table she created at her home in 1990. Photograph by Myron Wood. Italian-Americans in the West Project. American Folklife Center. (IAW-MW-C001-13)

Women are often regarded as tradition-bearers within their respective communities. One tradition maintained by women in the Italian American community of Pueblo, Colorado, derives from a centuries-old tradition on the famine-plagued island of Sicily. According to the story, Sicilian peasants prayed to Saint Joseph, the island's patron saint, to end the famine and suffering that was their lot. When their prayers were answered, the poor people of the island offered up in thanksgiving their most prized possession—food. Brought to Pueblo in the 1890s, the tradition has evolved into large, open-house events that feature tables laden with food, such as this one, photographed in 1990. Today, the tables are prepared to thank Saint Joseph for his assistance in helping families through all sorts of difficult times.

Dressmaker Elsa Mantilla and a beauty pageant contestant, Woodridge, New Jersey, 1994. Photograph by Martha Cooper. "Working in Paterson" Folklife Project. American Folklife Center. (WIP-MC-C008-20)

Latina dressmaker Elsa Mantilla adjusts one of the dresses she has made for a contestant at the annual banquet and beauty pageant sponsored by the Dominicans of New Jersey, held at "The Fiesta," in Woodridge. A 1994 Folklife Center field project based in Paterson, New Jersey, documented the traditions surrounding work in this industrial city—traditions found in both its factories and its homes. A number of the women interviewed for the project had exploited skills traditionally associated with home life, such as cooking and sewing, for the sake of gainful employment.

religious festivals. Folklife Center field projects are especially rich in material documenting the creative expressions of both everyday life and seasonal holidays and celebrations.

2 Performances by women—such as singing, dancing, and storytelling—for formal or informal audiences.

3 Representations of women, as depicted by men or women, in songs, stories, and folk art, for example.

4 Ethnographic field collections that have been made, organized, and commented upon by women.

The Archive of Folk Culture contains unpublished, multiformat, ethnographic, field documentary collections. A single collection might include sound recordings, photographs, videotapes, manuscript materials, and printed ephemera such as fliers, brochures, and newspaper articles. The Folk Archive is organized by collection rather than by format in order to preserve the unity of each collection. For example, in researching the Saint Joseph's Day Table tradition, as practiced in Pueblo, Colorado—an elaborate display of food and a community event staged as a thanks offering to the saint—you can view photographs, listen to spoken-word interviews, and read the comments of a field-worker participating in the Folklife Center's Italian-Americans in the West Project. Thus, you will be able to reconstruct, to some extent, the field-worker's intentions and experiences.

As a rule, the Folklife Center does not collect artifacts, but one item is an interesting exception. The archive contains the yellow ribbon that Penne Laingen tied around an old oak tree in her front yard in 1979, for her husband, Bruce, the former acting ambassador to Iran, who was being held hostage at the time. That act symbolized her determination to be reunited with her husband and stimulated a new incarnation of a folk custom that swept the country. The archive contains documentation and information about this symbolic display of ribbons.

In 1978, when the Archive of Folk Culture became part of the American Folklife Center, the archive held about a half million items. By the time of the Folklife Center's twenty-fifth anniversary, in 2001, the archive had grown to about two million items. Much of that growth can be attributed to the field surveys and documentation projects conducted by the Folklife Center in the intervening years. Continuing the tradition begun by archive heads Robert W. Gordon and John and Alan Lomax, the center has actively pursued a program of field documentation in many regions of the country.

These projects, often involving teams of folklorists and other cultural specialists, have resulted in large collections of documentary material—hundreds of hours of sound recordings, thousands of photographs, and thousands of pages of field notes. Some have had particular themes—such as land use in the New Jersey Pine Barrens, Acadian culture in northern Maine, Italian American culture in the West, or occupational culture in Paterson, New Jersey. Others are surveys of folklife in a particular place. Women figure in a central way in all of these documentation projects.

Although the Folklife Reading Room provides access to the many collections in the Archive of Folk Culture, almost every division of the Library contains significant folk cultural resources. The four thousand books available in the Folklife Reading Room for the convenience of the readers researching folklife topics represent only a small selection from the Library's General Collections.

Folklife researchers will also find materials of interest in, for example, the Area Studies divisions; the Local History and Genealogy Reading Room; the Manuscript Division; the Prints and Photographs Division; the Motion Picture, Broadcasting, and Recorded Sound Division; the Music Division; and the Rare Book and Special Collections Division, all described in this guide.

The history of women in Western and other societies, particularly in the nineteenth and twentieth centuries, has included a struggle to break free of traditional roles. Both men and women commonly experience a conflict between individual impulse and desire, on the one hand, and social roles and conventions on the other. That conflict is frequently reflected in folk song, which has long chronicled the roles of women, in areas ranging from love and courtship to women's suffrage, and has been used to protest hateful social conditions, as in the well-known African American spirituals. Many songs and ballads, comic and tragic, portray women who are determined, boastful, or rebellious.

However the individual impulse might manifest itself, individual practitioners of traditional or conventional forms—sometimes known, sometime anonymous—have produced remarkable examples of the cultural expressions that have endured within a particular cultural group for many generations. Singers, fiddlers, boatbuilders, masons, and weavers, as well as pottery-makers, quiltmakers, basket-makers, and a multitude of other "makers," have created beautiful things for use in everyday life and have found individual satisfaction in passing on the forms inherited from previous generations. These expressions of traditional culture provide vivid glimpses into the hearts and minds of a people. They deserve our attention.

USING THE COLLECTIONS

In the Folklife Reading Room, you will find a sampling of the many works on folk music, folklore, ethnomusicology, oral history, and material culture available in the Library's General Collections. Here you may use standard publications and a sizable collection of magazines, newsletters, posters, and other ephemera. Unpublished theses and dissertations, as well as published bibliographies and directories, are also available.

Folk Archive collection material is organized by AFS (Archive of Folk Song) and AFC (Archive of Folk Culture) numbers. The earlier system, AFS, assigned numbers to individual items, in the beginning usually individual songs. Beginning in the 1980s, a new system was devised to assign AFC numbers and dates to collections as a whole. Collection storage areas are not open to readers, and all material will be retrieved by reference staff.

You will find that a number of reference tools available in the Folklife Reading Room are particularly helpful. These include finding aids, collection guides, subject files, and card catalogs:

Folklife finding aids are cross-collection guides to particular subjects. The Folklife Center hopes to have a finding aid for each state, and many are now available. In addition, there are finding aids for such topics as Zora Neale Hurston, Mexico, Puerto Rico, Slave Narratives, and World War II.

Collection guides provide detailed descriptions of fully processed collections.

The **subject-files,** consisting of largely ephemeral material, have grown over the years in response to reader requests for information and now include thousands of folders. There are entries for American Indian tribes, by tribal name, and for many folk song titles, two of the most frequently researched topics in the reading room. Other titles of interest to women's history and culture specialists include Calamity Jane, Double Dutch, Fairy Tales, Festivals, Folk Dance, Gay and Lesbian Folklore, Gospel Music, May Pole, Medicine, Midwife, Needlework, Paper Cutting, Sacred Harp, Suffrage, Wedding Customs, Witchcraft, Women's Army Corps Songs, and Women's Mill Songs.

The **corporate-subject files** include ephemeral material on individuals, organizations, festivals, exhibits, and so forth.

Several **card catalogs** provide information on various collections. One lists primarily English-language field recordings, 1933 to 1950, and is organized by title, performer, and geographic region. An AFS Collection card catalog is organized by collection title, collection number, and subject. Although this catalog can be useful, it is incomplete.

Folklife Center publications frequently list, describe, or illuminate Folklife Center collections. Examples include the quarterly *Folklife Center News* (1977–); the five volumes of *Folklife Annual* (1985–90); illustrated books from many of the center's field documentation projects—such as *Old Ties, New Attachments: Italian-American Folklife in the West* (Washington: Library of Congress, 1992; F596. 3.I8 T54 1992) and *Ethnic Heritage and Language Schools in America* (Washington: Library of Congress, 1988; LC3802.E74

1988); and the published field recordings in the Library of Congress's landmark series Folk Music of the United States. Splendid performances by women playing instruments and singing solo or in groups are featured on these recordings.

Reference aids are bibliographies and directories on selected topics. These are no longer produced and many are out-of-date, but some may be useful. Examples of topics available include Autoharp, Ballad, Carter Family, Folk Dance, Dulcimer, Protest Songs, Shape-note Singing, and Women and Folk Music.

Computer searches are possible in the reading room, with the assistance of the reference staff, and the American Folklife Center's own database, AskSam, is keyword searchable for some collections. The Library of Congress is developing a new bibliographic database that provides the Folklife Center with the opportunity to catalog multiformat collections. Some written records for folklife collections are available through the Library of Congress Online Catalog. These records link to the finding aids for each collection, so researchers may read about each collection in detail.

Collections Available on the World Wide Web

In cooperation with the Library's National Digital Library Program, the Folklife Center is putting whole collections online for use by readers with access to the Internet. The Folklife Center's Web site, which includes a range of publications, information, and links to other sites of interest, may be reached at <http://www.loc.gov/folklife>. Several collections containing material on women's history and culture are currently available:

California Gold: Northern California Folk Music from the Thirties, based on the collection made for the Works Progress Administration (WPA) by

Mr. and Mrs. Frank Pipkin being recorded by Charles Todd (left) *at the Shafter Migratory Labor Camp, Shafter, California, 1940. Photograph by Robert Hemmig. Charles L. Todd and Robert Sonkin Migrant-Worker Collection. American Folklife Center.* (*AFC 1985/001:P9-p1*)

Much can be discovered or surmised by studying the faces and postures of the man and woman featured in this photograph, Mr. and Mrs. Frank Pipkin. Life has been difficult, but they have endured. Like many "Okies" who left the Dust Bowl, these people, one suspects, hoped for a new life in California. Behind the Pipkins, musicians stand ready, either to accompany Mrs. Pipkin or to play on their own, because these are people who know how to make their own entertainment, whether telling stories, playing the fiddle, or organizing Saturday night dances. Charles Todd, the man at the recording machine (*left*), that day in 1940, wrote that Mrs. Pipkin was a gold mine of Old English ballads, and that many thought of her as the prototype for "Ma Joad" in *The Grapes of Wrath.* John Steinbeck was in the labor camps doing research for his great novel at the same time that Todd was there.

Right: *Basque ranch wife Delfina Zatica in her kitchen with her grandchildren, Paradise Valley, Nevada, 1978. Photograph by Carl Fleischhauer. Paradise Valley Folklife Project. American Folklife Center.* (PFP-CF-4-19379-9a)

Below right: *Carrie Severt milks a cow one-handed at her farm in Alleghany County, North Carolina. Photograph by Terry Eiler, 1978. Blue Ridge Parkway Folklife Project. American Folklife Center.* (BR8-TE-96)

On farms and ranches across the country, the division of labor often has been determined by gender roles. Among traditional duties of farmwives and ranchwives are food preparation, housekeeping, and child-rearing. Folklife Center collections from many regions document these daily activities, as well as family relations in general and the central role that women play in the activities of family and community life. Women tend vegetable gardens, chickens, and small livestock associated with the household economy. They help out with the milking and seasonally demanding tasks associated with the harvest.

Sidney Robertson Cowell (see below), includes sound recordings, still photographs, drawings, and manuscripts documenting the musical traditions of a variety of European ethnic and English- and Spanish-speaking communities in California. It comprises 35 hours of folk music recorded in twelve languages by 185 musicians. Among the musicians are Mrs. Francisco Etcheverry and her children singing Basque songs from the Spanish Navarre, and Mary McPhee singing Gaelic songs from the Hebrides, Scotland.

Voices from the Dust Bowl: The Charles L. Todd and Robert Sonkin Migrant Worker Collection consists of approximately 18 hours of audio recordings, 28 graphic images, and 1.5 linear feet of print material, including administrative correspondence, field notes, recording logs, song text transcriptions, dust jackets from the recording discs, news clippings, publications, and ephemera. Among those interviewed by Charles Todd at the Shafter Migratory Labor Camp in Shafter, California, was Mrs. Frank Pipkin, who was "a gold mine" of Old English ballads.

Hispano Music and Culture of the Northern Rio Grande: The Juan B. Rael Collection presents religious and secular music of Spanish-speaking residents of rural northern New Mexico and southern Colorado. In 1940, Juan Rael documented *alabados* (hymns), folk drama, wedding songs, and dance tunes, by making recordings in Alamosa, Manassa, and Antonito, Colorado; and in Cerro and Arroyo Hondo, New Mexico (see also chapter 12).

Buckaroos in Paradise: Ranching Culture in Northern Nevada, 1945–1982 consists of 41 motion pictures and 28 sound recordings, including motion-picture footage from 1945 to 1965 by Leslie Stewart, owner of the Ninety-Six Ranch. An archive of 2,400 still photographs, along with audio and video selections, portrays the people, sites, and traditions of other ranches and the larger community, which is home to people of Anglo-American, Italian, German, Basque, Swiss, Northern Paiute, and Chinese heritage. The presentation includes interviews with Martha Arriola, a ranch cook, who compares meals she prepared on the farm in her native Germany with those she prepares on the ranches of Paradise Valley.

Quilts and Quiltmaking in America presents material from two American Folklife Center collections, the Blue Ridge Parkway Folklife Project Collections (1978) and the Lands' End All-American Quilt Contest Collection (1992, 1994, and 1996). Together these collections provide a glimpse of the diverse quilting traditions in America. The quilt documentation from the Blue Ridge Parkway Folklife Project, conducted by the Folklife Center in cooperation with the National Park Service, includes photographs of, and recorded interviews with, six women quiltmakers in Appalachian North Carolina and Virginia. These materials document quilts and quilting within the context of daily life and reflect a range of backgrounds, motivations, and aesthetic sensibilities. The materials presented from the Lands' End All-American Quilt Contest Collection include images of approximately 180 winning quilts from across the United States, illustrating a range of patterns and materials.

The John and Ruby Lomax 1939 Southern States Recording Trip includes nearly 700 sound recordings, as well as field notes, dust jackets, and manuscripts documenting a three-month, 6,502-mile trip through the southern United States, which began March 31, 1939, in Port Aransas, Texas. During the trip, John Avery Lomax, honorary consultant and curator of the Archive of American Folk Song, and his wife, Ruby Terrill Lomax, recorded approximately 25 hours of folk music from more than 300 performers. These recordings represent a broad spectrum of traditional musical styles, including ballads, blues, children's songs, cowboy songs, fiddle tunes, field hollers, lullabies, play-party songs, religious dramas, spirituals, and work songs. Ruby Lomax was the author of nearly all written documentation relating to the collection. She also cataloged the contents of each disc and operated the Presto recording machine while John instructed and encouraged the performers.

Florida Folklife from the WPA Collections, 1937–1942 presents folk songs and folktales in many languages from a variety of cultural communities throughout Florida: African American, Arabic, Bahamian, British American, Cuban, Greek, Italian, Minorcan, Seminole, and Slavic. The material was recorded by Robert Cook, Herbert Halpert, Zora Neale Hurston, Stetson Kennedy, Alton Morris, and others. Hurston also performed during several recording sessions, as did a number of other women, singing, in particular, children's songs and spirituals.

Zora Neale Hurston (1901–1960), originally from Eatonville, Florida, was already a published novelist and folklorist when she took a job with the Federal Writers' Project in Florida. Hurston served as an important contact in the African American community and wrote a project plan entitled "Proposed Recording Expedition into the Floridas" for Dr. Carita Doggett Corse, state director of the Florida Federal Writers' Project. Songs she performed include "Mama Don't Want No Peas, No Rice," a song from Nassau, the Bahama Islands, sung at jumping dances and fire dances. This song, she said, "is about a woman that wanted to stay drunk all the time, and her husband is really complaining about it. He's explaining to the neighbors what's the matter with his wife and why they don't get along better." Nineteen of Hurston's performances can be heard on this presentation (see also page 331).

Women Collectors

The remarkable folk song collector Sidney Robertson Cowell (1903–1995) described herself as a woman who "travelled 300,000 miles alone with her dog and recording machine, in 15 states; she wore out 3 cars and made several thousand recordings, all of them in the Archive of American Folksong at the Library of Congress in Washington. . . . Fortunately the government kept her travelling for several years in regions whose folklore was unexplored, so she was able to continue with what she still considers the most fascinating pursuit possible in our day."[1]

Women were among the earliest collectors of ethnographic materials in this country and around the world. The most famous is probably the anthropologist Margaret Mead (1901–1978), whose papers, films, recordings, and photographs are in the Library's Manuscript (see chapter 5) and Motion Picture, Broadcasting and Recorded Sound Divisions (see chapter 10), but Mead's career is by no means unique.Women collectors at the beginning of the twentieth century were pioneers in the field of ethnographic documentation and traveled to places where they encountered situations that were unusual for women at that time. Their field notes and correspondence provide commentaries on their experiences. By conducting research in the field, these women were venturing into scholarly territory previously occupied almost exclusively by men.

For example, Alice Cunningham Fletcher (1838–1923), Frances Densmore, Helen Heffron Roberts (1888–1985), and Laura Boulton made large and significant collections of American Indian song and spoken word that are now part of the Archive of Folk Culture.[2] Roberts also made recordings in the Caribbean: "Missy, you shore am God! You am the Lord Himself!" cried one startled old man in Jamaica in 1920, when she played back his recorded voice on the Edison phonograph machine.

Sidney Robertson copying California Folk Music Project recordings for the Library of Congress in the WPA project office, Berkeley, California, early 1939. Photographer unknown. California Folk Music Project Collection. American Folklife Center. (AFC 1940/001:P001)

Field-worker Nancy Nusz photographs oysterman Cletus Anderson, Apalachicola, Florida, November 1986. Photograph by David Taylor. Florida Maritime Project. American Folklife Center.(FMP 86-BDT025-6)

Throughout the twentieth century, women played a central role in the ethnographic documentation of culture, working with many cultural groups in the United States and around the world. Women folklorists continue that tradition today, carrying out their own fieldwork and participating in team-based field projects like those sponsored by the American Folklife Center. Many of the collections in the Archive of Folk Culture were wholly or in part created by women.

Women whose collections are part of the Archive of Folk Culture include **Frances Densmore** (1867–1957), one of the most prolific collectors of wax-cylinder recordings documenting American Indian song and spoken word. She gathered more than twenty-five hundred recordings from members of forty tribes between 1907 and the early 1940s. Densmore worked intensely with Library staff members on the production of published recordings drawn from her cylinder material, and abundant correspondence is available from this cooperative effort.

Ethnomusicologist **Laura Boulton** (1899–1980) participated in over twenty expeditions in her effort to document the music of various world cultures. Recording on five continents, chiefly from the 1930s through the 1960s, she assembled a collection that is particularly rich in the traditional vocal music of Canada, Africa, Southeast Asia, American Indians, and Eskimos. Many of Boulton's field recordings were presented to the Library of Congress by Columbia University in 1973.

In 1935, folklorist and writer **Zora Neale Hurston** and New York University professor **Mary Elizabeth Barnicle** (1891–1978) joined forces with Alan Lomax, a field-worker for the Library's Archive of American Folk-Song, to document African American song traditions in Georgia, Florida, and the Bahamas. Their field research explored the relationship between the music they recorded and antecedents from Africa and pre-emancipation America. A finding aid for Zora Neale Hurston is available.

From 1938 to 1940, **Sidney Robertson Cowell** organized and directed a California Work Projects Administration project designed to survey musical traditions in northern California. The result was the WPA California Folk Music Project, available online as *California Gold: Northern California Folk Music from the Thirties.* The collection includes material from many different ethnic groups, with vocal and instrumental performances by women and recordings of folk songs

Henrietta Yurchenco (right) and an unidentified woman, John's Island, South Carolina, ca. 1970. Photograph by David Lewiston. Henrietta Yurchenco Collection. American Folklife Center.

Henrietta Yurchenco speaks with an African American woman in front of a Methodist church that served as a focus for some of her work on John's Island, South Carolina, in the 1970s. Over the years, Yurchenco has made major donations, including audio recordings, manuscripts, and photographs documenting the folklife of African Americans who speak Gullah, to the Archive of Folk Culture.

about women. Cowell went on to do ethnographic documentation for many years—on the Pacific Coast, in the Ozarks and in the Appalachians, in the Great Lakes states, and in Pennsylvania, New York, and Maine.

Henrietta Yurchenco (b. 1916), professor emerita of the City College of New York, began fieldwork in 1942 in Mexico and Guatemala, where she recorded traditional music in Indian communities. In 1953, she began work in the western and central provinces of Spain, in the Balearic Islands, and later in Morocco. She studied women's songs in Galicia, Spain, and conducted fieldwork in Puerto Rico, South Carolina, and Ireland.

An artist and social documentarian, **Eleanor Dickinson** (b. 1931) was born in Knoxville, Tennessee, and raised within the traditions of the Southern Baptist Church. Trained as an artist, she began to draw participants in Baptist revival meetings in 1967. Later she also took photographs and recorded what she saw and heard at meetings in Knoxville and in other parts of Tennessee and Kentucky. Under the sponsorship of the Corcoran Gallery of Art in Washington, D.C., an exhibit of her work *Revival!* toured the country. One hundred of her drawings are in the Library's Prints and Photographs Division, but until they are cataloged, researchers must apply for access. Most of her recordings (and other material from her documentary excursions) are in the Archive of Folk Culture.

Vida Chenoweth (b. 1928), professor emerita of music at Wheaton College, has done extensive fieldwork in Papua New Guinea among the Usarufa. She is in the process of donating to the Folklife Center a large collection of audio and visual recordings, manuscripts, and photographs representing musical traditions from a variety of cultures around the world.

SELECTED COLLECTIONS

Looking more closely at some of the collections of the American Folklife Center may suggest research topics to students of women's history and culture. From the center's collections of American folk song to the rich windfall from the Library's Bicentennial Local Legacies project to its field documentation projects, there is scarcely a region of the country whose customs cannot be examined here.

American Folk Song

Although "American Folk Song" is not the title of a collection, the Archive of Folk Culture includes premier collections of this genre, which is rich in gender-specific themes. Beginning in 1928, and for nearly fifty years, folk song and folk music were the focus of many collectors who both worked at the archive and contributed to its collections. The Library's Recording Laboratory was established in the 1940s to make these field recordings available to the public, and the series that resulted, Folk Music of the United States, is legendary.

Noted already are the songs collected by Sidney Robertson Cowell for the WPA California Folk Music Collection and religious and secular music of northern New Mexico and southern Colorado collected by Juan B. Rael. The collections also hold songs portraying women in a negative way, as in a number of misogynistic and scatological songs performed at the Library of Congress by Jelly Roll Morton in 1938 and recorded by Alan Lomax.

The texts of folk songs provide a wealth of cultural data on men's attitudes toward women and on women's attitudes toward men and toward themselves. Examples from the center's large collection of Anglo-American ballads include "The House Carpenter," in which a young woman is lured away from her husband and baby by the entreaties of a romantic (sometimes demonic) lover:

"If you'll forsake your house carpenter,
And come and go with me,
I'll take you where the grass grows green,
To the lands on the banks of the sea."

She went 'n' picked up her sweet little babe
And kissed it one, two, three,
Saying, "Stay at home with your papa dear,
And keep him good company."

"The Farmer's Curst Wife," another such ballad, tells the story of a scolding wife whose husband offers no resistence when the Devil comes and carries her away. But the woman makes such a nuisance of herself in Hell that the Devil brings her back:

This is what a woman can do:
She can outdo the Devil and her old man too.

There's one advantage women have over men:
They can go to Hell and come back again.

A sentimentally romantic treatment of love and death is portrayed in the famous ballad "Barbara Allen," which ends with traditional symbolism:

Sweet William died on a Saturday night,
And Barbry died a Sunday.
Their parents died for the love of the two;
They was buried on a Easter Monday.

A white rose grew on William's grave,
A red rose grew on Barbry's;
They twined and they twined in a true-lover's knot,
A-warnin' young people to marry.

Ex-Slave Narratives

In the 1930s, researchers working in the South for the Federal Writers' Project sought out and interviewed former slaves and documented their words in writing. The interviewers spoke with hundreds of elderly people about their experiences of slavery. These accounts of day-to-day life give voice to the individual men and women who suffered and endured during a dark and troubling period of American history. At about the same time, folklorists such as Zora Neale Hurston, Mary Elizabeth Barnicle, Alan Lomax, John and Ruby Lomax, and John Henry Faulk were making recordings of former slaves, often as part of general collecting expeditions. The bulk of the Federal Writers' Project Collection transcriptions of interviews and photographs are in the Manuscript Division. The Folklife Center has about six hours of sound recordings, which are particularly moving for having captured the voices of the speakers. A recent publication provides a sampling of both the interviews and the sound recordings, along with a valuable introduction on the historical background and meaning of the collection. See *Remembering Slavery: African Americans Talk about Their Personal Experiences of Slavery and Emancipation,* edited by Ira Berlin et al. (New York: The New Press, 1998).

In one recording, made in Hempstead, Texas, by John Henry Faulk in 1941, Laura Smalley, a former slave on a Brazos Bottom plantation, describes a cruel beating inflicted upon a woman as a punishment:

But they taken that ol' woman, poor ol' woman, carried her in the peach orchard, an' whipped her. An' you know, jus' tied her han' this-a-way, you know, 'roun' the peach orchard tree. I can member that just as well, look like to me I can, and 'roun' the tree an' whipped her. You know she couldn' do nothing but jus' kick her feet, you know, jus' kick her feet. But the, they, they jus' had her clothes off down to her wais', you know. They didn' have her plum naked, but they had her clothes down to her waist. An' every now an' then they'd whip her, you know, an' then snuff the pipe out on her you know, jus' snuff pipe out on her. (AFS 5496 A and B).

Folk Music Revival

The Folk Archive includes recordings and other material from the National Folk Festival, an annual event now coordinated by the National Council for the Traditional Arts (NCTA) of Silver Spring, Maryland. The festival, first held in St. Louis, Missouri, in 1934, sought the help of folklorists, anthropologists, and other field-workers to identify and present authentic folk performers. The National Folk Festival, which has been staged in many different cities, has been a model for other such events and has presented the most notable of folk virtuosos, from many ethnic traditions—British, Irish, Native American, African, Hispanic, Asian, and European. The archive collections include material from the early years and the present day.

The Folk Archive also houses a major collection

of recorded music and other material concerning the "folk revival" that occurred in the 1950s and 1960s, when many college students learned to play the guitar and the coffeehouse was a favorite social venue. The spirit of that movement changed radically with the war in Vietnam, as did so many other things, but musicians of all sorts continued to trace their roots to folk music and its popularizers. Many performers associated with the folk revival are women, both as individuals, such as folksinger and musician Jean Ritchie, and as members of groups, such as Ronnie Gilbert of the Weavers. Some perform music they learned in the traditional manner, in their families and communities; others perform new compositions in a traditional style, or traditional music they have learned in nontraditional ways—for instance, by listening to Library of Congress field recordings.

Duncan Emrich Autograph Album Collection

The Duncan Emrich Autograph Album Collection comprises twenty autograph albums and ephemera dating from the turn of the twentieth century, compiled by Duncan Emrich, head of the Archive of Folk-Song, 1955–56. The albums were sent to the archive in response to Emrich's request for such material on the *NBC Weekend* radio program. The albums, from several families in Iowa, represent the German and Anglo-American tradition, practiced in this country principally by young women, that dates back to the fifteenth century. In one album, black and leather-bound, embossed with gold and silver patterns, Fannie R. Hale has collected the sentiments of her friends, both male and female. One inscription, perhaps from a suitor, reads: "That you may attain the perfect heights of merited success in your chosen life work and mould your character by the models of your highest ideas in art is the wish of / Your Sincere Friend J.E. Bromwell Jr Marion [Iowa] Aug 30th 1881." A collection guide is available online.

The Local Legacies Project Collection

The Local Legacies project was launched by the Librarian of Congress as a major component of the Library of Congress's Bicentennial, which was celebrated on April 24, 2000. The Library invited members of Congress to identify grassroots traditions and activities from every state and congressional district, document them in photographs, sound and video recordings, and manuscripts, and send a portion of that documentation to the Library of Congress for inclusion in the Archive of Folk Culture. The resulting collection provides a snapshot of traditional community life in America at the turn of the twenty-first century.

Project guidelines defined a local legacy as "a traditional activity, event, or area of creativity that merits being documented for future generations." The project staff hoped for representative or signature events and activities that characterized the local communities. Approximately thirteen hundred projects were nominated by 412 members of Congress. At the time of the May 23, 2000, reception at the Library for Local Legacies participants, more than a thousand had been sent in. Projects included a Chinese New Year's parade in Portland, Oregon; the burning of an effigy of "Old Man Gloom" in Sante Fe, New Mexico; Sacred Harp singing in rural Georgia; the National Storytelling festival in Jonesborough, Tennessee; Nebraskaland Days in Wilber, Nebraska; the California Strawberry Festival in Ventura County; the Bolder Boulder ten-kilometer Memorial Day Run in Boulder, Colorado; arts and crafts from Puerto Rico; Native American dancers from several states, and many more.

Of particular interest to scholars of women's history and culture are the parades, festivals, and other community celebrations that pervade the collection. Many include beauty queens and beauty pageants, ethnic food preparation, costumes, and other activities and displays that represent the traditional roles of women in particular communities. A brief description and sample photograph has been prepared for each Local Legacies project and made available online. From the American Folklife Center's home page at <http://www.loc.gov/folklife>, go to Local Legacies Project, and then click on Project Listing. Projects are listed by state.

Field Documentation Projects

The Folklife Center has conducted field documentation projects and cultural surveys in the following cities, states, and regions: Chicago, Illinois (1977); South Central Georgia (1977); the Blue Ridge Parkway, Virginia and North Carolina (1978); Nevada (1978–82); Rhode Island (1979); Montana (1979); the Pinelands National Reserve, New Jersey (1983); Utah (1985); Lowell, Massachusetts (1987–88); the western states of California, Colorado, Nevada, Utah, and Washington (1989–91); Maine (1991–92); West Virginia (1991–92; 1994–98); and Paterson, New Jersey (1994).

These projects have resulted in large collections of documentary material: photographs, in black and white and in color; recordings; field notes; and ephemeral printed material pertaining to particular events, local customs, or family traditions studied. Several of the more recent projects can be searched through the Library of Congress Online Catalog. For others, there are logs created by the individual field-workers. The photographic materials from these projects of the past twenty-five years are extensive. Research tools include photographic logs for identifying particular subjects, contact sheets for surveying black-and-white images, and a light table for viewing color slides.

Researchers interested in the contemporary practice of women's folklore should consult Folklife Center reference librarians for information on pertinent material. Project collections frequently have accompanying publications, and most have been described in *Folklife Center News*. Even when the project or survey has a particular focus—such as land use, occupational culture, or ethnic traditions—the documentation covers a complex of cultural traditions that involve women in many ways.

The **Chicago Ethnic Arts Project** (1977) documented traditions within the city's homes and informal neighborhood meeting places in about thirty ethnic communities. The collection includes material on women's musical performances, quiltmaking, and needlework. In one recorded interview, artist Faith Bickerstaff describes the important link between grandparents and grandchildren: "my grandmother, in her last days . . . her eyes were failing. So the lace, the handwork, was her art . . . Which is why she taught me. She felt it was important. And if I can keep it alive, I believe, that if she were alive, she would be quite pleased."

The **South Central Georgia** (1977) and **Blue Ridge Parkway Folklife Projects** (1778) are rich in documentation of quiltmaking, foodways, religious practices, and other aspects of domestic and community life. For example, food-drying as a form of preservation along the Blue Ridge is documented in photographs and recorded interviews. In the past, a drying shed might have been used, but field-workers found contemporary practitioners using the automobile: thinly sliced apple

Mary Higeko Hamano teaches the traditional art of Japanese flower arranging, Chicago, June 1977. Photograph by Jonas Dovydenas. Chicago Ethnic Arts Project. American Folklife Center. (B50891-24)

Particular folk art expressions are often associated with ethnic groups and are a vital part of their ethnic identity. Through teaching ikebana, the art of flower arranging, Mary Higeko Hamano brought some sense of traditional Japanese identity to her community in Chicago. Ethnic communities are often at pains to see that their folk art traditions are carried on from one generation to the next.

Girls on a float in the Columbus Day parade, San Francisco, California, October 8, 1989. Photograph by Ken Light. Italian-Americans in the West Project. American Folklife Center. (IAW-KL-C115-4)

In a Columbus Day parade in San Francisco, on October 8, 1989, Italian American girls dressed as angels ride on a festival float created by the Società de la Madonna del Lume. The many strategies for passing on folk traditions from one generation to the next include traditions practiced at home as well as community events such as this parade. Children learn by observing their parents, by performing chores, or by playing assigned roles within a festival or celebration. Religious festivals and beauty pageants are components of many community celebrations across the United States.

wedges were arranged on dashboards or placed on rear shelves to dry in the sun shining through the windows. And field-worker Geraldine Johnson interviewed Ruth Newman, of Galax, Virginia, a locally known cook and poet. Both her poems and her recipes are included in the Blue Ridge collection. *Blue Ridge Harvest: A Region's Folklife in Photographs,* edited by Lyntha Scott Eiler, Terry Eiler, and Carl Fleischhauer (Washington: Library of Congress, 1981), offers a sampling of black-and-white photographs from the project. The online presentation *Quilts and Quiltmaking in America* includes photographs and interviews made during the Blue Ridge Project.

The **Lowell Folklife Project** in Massachusetts (1987–88) examined the way successive ethnic communities established identity within particular urban neighborhoods and spaces. In the nineteenth century, huge textile mills were established in Lowell, which was known as "spindle city," and many women migrated from surrounding rural areas to work in them. Since that time, waves of immigrants, from Irish to Southeast Asian, have sought to work and raise their families in Lowell. Project documentation includes, for example, Cambodian wedding traditions, women factory workers, and Hispanic festivals.

Adaptations to America was one of the themes examined by project field-workers. Narong Hul complained that the younger children of her community "have a tendency" to adopt American rather than Cambodian ways, which creates arguments in families. Children point out that "the American way" is often cheaper and faster than the traditional way. At home, the Huls eat both Cambodian and American foods. "We don't drink water anymore, we drink Coke," says Narong (LFP MB-R008). Theresa Theobald was interviewed about the symbolic importance of food, and the French Canadian talked about variations in her family's recipes for pea soup. "I had some pea soup at the folk festival and as far as I'm concerned it was nothing like what I make. It was totally different. I like mine better" (LFP MB-RO14). Maria Cunha reported that increasing numbers of women from the Portuguese community were choosing to enter professional careers, which is often difficult for the traditional community to accept—there is still prevalent the attitude that the wife belongs at home and should not be seen in public with any man but her husband. She says she is teaching her child to "wait on themselves," even though her mother and her mother's generation waited on their husbands and children (LFP BF-AO13).

The **Ethnic Heritage and Language Schools in America Project** (1982) surveyed the role of twenty ethnic schools around the country in language and culture preservation. Schools surveyed included a Cambodian school in Houston, Texas; an Islamic school in Seattle, Washington; a Korean school in Silver Spring, Maryland; a Polish school in Chicago; a German-Russian ethnic studies program in Strasburg, North Dakota; a Greek school in Buffalo, New York; a Czech school in Cedar Rapids, Iowa; and a Hupa language school in Hoopa Valley, California. Many of the classes were taught by women. See *Ethnic Heritage and Language Schools in America,* edited by Elena Bradunas and Brett Topping (Washington: Library of Congress, 1988).

The **Maine Acadian Folklife Survey** (1991–92) identified a wide range of ongoing Acadian traditions of French settlers in northern Maine and surveyed the organizations, institutions, and individuals engaged in conserving and celebrating Acadian cultural heritage. Collection materials include documentation of women's participation in Acadian music, dance, and storytelling; Acadian foodways; French language retention; farming; maple sugaring; religious beliefs; oral history; the annual Acadian festival; and the preservation of historic buildings and sites.

One of the local legends documented by researchers tells the story of Tante Blanche. According to oral tradition, the harvest of 1796 was ruined in the fields by an early snow. By the turn of the year 1797, famine hit the Acadian communities along the St. John River. During this time of hardship, Marguerite-Blanche Thibodeau performed many remarkable acts of charity. Wearing snowshoes, she brought clothing and provisions to people suffering from hunger and cold. Tante Blanche, as she was known, became legendary for her selflessness. She is memorialized at the Tante Blanche Museum in St. David, which was created by the Madawaska Historical Society.

The **Italian-Americans in the West Project,** which began in 1989, was developed as part of the Library's contribution to the commemoration of the Columbus Quincentenary. The American Folklife Center conducted a study of Italian American life and culture in five western states: California, Colorado, Nevada, Utah, and Washington. Field-workers focused on occupations such as fishing, farming, mining, and wine-making but also studied the way food traditions, celebration, and family and religious life shape community culture.

Field-worker Paula Manini documented the

Sister Mary Abdi talking over homework assignments with Rohymah Toulas and Lanya Abdul-jabbar at the Islamic School in Seattle, Washington, 1982. Photograph by Susan Dwyer-Shick. Ethnic Heritage and Language Schools in America Project. American Folklife Center. (ES82-197518-1-34A)

Although folklife traditions are often learned in informal settings, many ethnic communities in the United States have found it necessary to establish formal language-training schools in order to ensure that children learn this most important component of their cultural heritage. In 1982, the American Folklife Center conducted a national survey of these schools to discover how widespread the practice was, identified and studied twenty schools, and published profiles of them. Often, it was women who taught in the schools.

Jelina Cubic at the Kalkstein Silk Mills, Paterson, New Jersey, 1994. Photograph by Martha Cooper. "Working in Paterson" Project. American Folklife Center. (WIP-MC-C021-7)

In the 1900s, young women were engaged to work in the silk mills in Paterson, New Jersey. Founded as a corporation in 1792 by Alexander Hamilton and the Society for the Promotion of Useful Manufactures, the city holds the distinction of being the nation's first planned industrial area. When the American Folklife Center conducted its field documentary project "Working in Paterson" in 1994, researchers interviewed a number of former women textile workers about their experiences and visited a silk factory where women are still working the machines.

Saint Joseph's Day Table tradition in Pueblo, Colorado, a religious tradition brought from Sicily that has evolved into a celebration of food and community open house. Philip Notarianni interviewed the Nick family, of Price, Utah, about traditions brought from Italy, although some family members wanted to talk about the American ways they were eager to adopt. Helen D'Ambrosio and Kerry Nick Fister were the singing cowgirls "Tex and Ted" in the 1930s. "We were absolutely cowboy crazy. That is, cowboy music," Kerry Fister told field-workers. Italian field-worker Paolo Tavarelli interviewed Jean Conrotto Burr of the A. Conrotto Winery, Gilroy, California. Jean and her sister Jermaine, along with their husbands, carry on their family's wine-making business. And project photographer Ken Light documented the 1989 Columbus Day celebration in San Francisco, during which the members of the Società de la Madonna del Lume march down Columbus Street ahead of a float carrying an image of the saint. For a collection of scholarly essays on the project, see *Old Ties, New Attachments: Italian-American Folklife in the West,* edited by David A. Taylor and John Alexander Williams (Washington: Library of Congress, 1992).

In the 1900s, young girls worked in the silk mills in Paterson, New Jersey, the nation's first planned industrial area. In cooperation with the Mid-Atlantic Regional Office of the National Park Service, the Folklife Center developed the **Working in Paterson** folklife project to examine many aspects of occupational culture. Project director David Taylor interviewed a number of former textile workers about their experiences, including labor union activist Marianna Costa. Costa recalled the long hours that her mother put in at her job at National Dye and Printing in East Paterson and that her father put in as a construction worker:

> My mother left for work at 6:30 and she didn't come back until 6:00 at night. It was a long day between transportation and a ten-hour work day. She was away almost twelve hours. [My father] would leave at about 7:00, and he was doing construction . . . And he would get back at 5:00—an hour before she did—because of the transportation. He had a bicycle, so he was able to do better time. And she had to walk to a bus and walk the distance back home.[3]

Marianna Costa began working in a dye house in 1932, and she told David Taylor about her participation in a textile workers' strike in 1933, at a time when she knew practically nothing about organized labor:

> I didn't even get the full comprehension, but I went with them. I wasn't going to stay alone in the plant. I went with them and we walked from the Riverside section to the Turn Hall, which was quite a walk. . . . And, anyway, when we got there, there were organizers that were trying to establish an organization to speak to the crowd and say, "You got to stay out. You have a right to organize. You can do better than what you're getting. And the idea is to be firm, stay together, and we'll see what we can do for you."[4]

Field-worker Susan Levitas interviewed workers at Sweet Potato Pie, Inc., and Easter Benson, owner of the E and A Soul Food Restaurant. Benson had no idea of running a restaurant when she opened a candy store across the street from her house, a modest shop without a name, which she operated at odd hours in addition to working her regular job. She began to add items to her menu, increased her hours of operation, and soon found herself with a thriving restaurant business featuring African American "soul food." In a city with few African American women who are business owners, says Susan Levitas, Easter Benson has turned a traditionally female skill into a successful enterprise.

Center folklorist Mary Hufford visited southern West Virginia over a period of several years, from 1991 to 1998, and has assembled a large collection of documentary material for the **Appalachian Forest Folklife Project** and the **Coal River Folklife Project.** Hufford was interested in the relationship between land use and local customs, and, in particular, the idea of the commons—forested areas open to all for the practice of traditional ways. Hufford has organized a National Digital Library Program online presentation based on her research. The collections include many interviews, with both men and women, individually and in groups, about the growing and harvesting of ginseng, home decoration for Halloween and Christmas, quilting, baby showers, women in the mines, canning, gardening, and the annual ramp supper. Hufford also documented female camaraderie at a local gathering spot called the "Ramp House," named for the wild, fragrant member of the onion family, native to the region, that is part of local culture and tradition. The women had come together to drink tea and coffee and prepare for the 1997 ramp supper at the Delbert Free Will Baptist Church: "We sit in a circle and clean ramps and talk," said Delores Workman. "It's a lot of fun. I love my ramp circle."

Working with field notes, photo logs, contact sheets, and tape recording machines may be an unusual form of research for many scholars of women's history and culture. But for those interested in the everyday lives of ordinary women—urban and rural, both newly arrived and long-time residents of the United States—the field project collections of the American Folklife Center should prove to be well worth the time and trouble.

Contributing to this chapter were Judith Gray, Joseph C. Hickerson, Ann Hoog, Alan Jabbour, Catherine Hiebert Kerst (an early member of the Library's Women's History Resource Group), and David Taylor.

IL PROGRESSO  ITALO-AMERICANO

10 PAGINE

First Italian Daily Newspaper in the United States — ESTABLISHED IN 1880 — Office: 42 Duane Street

CONSOLIDATED WITH THE Cristoforo Colombo

TELEPHONES: Editorial Room: 3470 Worth. Business Dept.: 3471 Worth. Address: P. O. Box 1320, N. Y.

10 PAGINE

ANNO XXXII. — No. 74. Cav. C. BARSOTTI, Direttore. UN SOLDO la copia. NEW YORK, MARTEDI' 28 MARZO 1911 Numero arretrato 5 SOLDI IL TEMPO D'OGGI: Bello

RECENTISSIME DALL'ITALIA

Servizio diretto di cablogrammi al "Progresso"

(L'ufficio del "Progresso" in Roma è in via dei Serpenti n. 44)

Dal Campidoglio la parola del Re ricorda l'Unita' d'Italia e apre le grandi feste di Roma

IL CAMPANONE DEL CAMPIDOGLIO INIZIA LA GIORNATA PATRIOTTICA.

ROMA, 27. — La capitale s'è svegliata stamane mentre il campanone del Campidoglio suonava a distesa.

Già a mezzanotte il cannone aveva tuonato da Castel Sant'Angelo, annunziando il primo minuto della grande giornata.

Tutte le case sono imbandierate; per le vie è tutta una gloria di bandiere, di orifiamme, di simboli patriottici. Le mura sono tappezzate di manifesti: il sindaco Nathan ha annunziato la celebrazione con nobilissime parole.

L'entusiasmo della popolazione è vivissimo.

IN CAMPIDOGLIO

La cerimonia reale in Campidoglio riveste una solennità grandiosa, imponente e traboccante di sentimento patriottico.

Prima delle ore 10 tutte le adiacenze del Campidoglio si affollano: favorita da una bella giornata, quasi tutta la popolazione s'è riversata nelle vie. Moltissime le signore con le coccarde tricolori; i bambini poi hanno tutti delle bandierine. Assai grande il numero degli ufficiali nelle loro brillanti uniformi.

Per le vie circolano musiche e fanfare.

Il sindaco Nathan, gli assessori e i consiglieri sono già in Campidoglio dalle ore 9.

I Reduci dalle Patrie Battaglie fanno il loro servizio a sommo della scalinata.

Le autorità civili e militari arrivano alla spicciolata, ricevute dal Sindaco e dagli assessori.

L'ARRIVO DEI MINISTRI E DEGLI ALTI DIGNITARI

La folla applaude all'arrivo delle rappresentanze della Camera dei Deputati e del Senato del Regno. Sono al completo gli uffici di presidenza delle due Camere e le commissioni per gli indirizzi che i due rami del Parlamento offriranno al Re.

Alle dieci e un quarto giunge il Presidente del Consiglio on. Luzzatti. Lo seguono gli altri ministri e i sottosegretari di Stato.

Poi mano mano giungono senatori, deputati, magistrati, autorità amministrative. Assai rimarcato è l'arrivo degli Ambasciatori e dei Plenipotenziari accreditati presso il Quirinale.

GIUNGONO I SOVRANI

Quando giungono i Sovrani, in berlina di gala, preceduti dai battistrada e dai corazzieri, la folla che si addensa intorno al Campidoglio, è immensa.

Le musiche intuonano l'inno reale, e la folla applaude con calore e con slancio indescrivibile.

Il Re saluta: la Regina affascinante di grazia, china ripetutamente la testa e sorride.

I Sovrani vengono ricevuti dal Sindaco Nathan, dai Ministri, dalle alte autorità, mentre il campanone del Campidoglio suona a distesa, e tuona il cannone da Castel Sant'Angelo.

Dalle berline di Corte scendono il Duca di Genova, il Duca d'Aosta, il Conte di Torino e gli alti dignitari di Corte.

PARLA IL RE

I Sovrani vengono accompagnati nell'aula senatoria dove ha luogo la cerimonia solenne.

I reali seggono in un trono sontuoso; intorno a loro i principi, i ministri, il sindaco e la Giunta. Ad un lato i membri del corpo diplomatico, in uniforme. Dall'altra i senatori e i deputati. Più in là i sindaci delle città di Italia.

L'aula è pienissima. Il momento è d'una solennità commovente.

Quando il Re si leva per parlare tutti sorgono in piedi.

Il Sovrano, accentando con energia e con vigore le frasi pronunzia un breve discorso, ricordando il voto del Parlamento Subalpino, e inneggiando a Roma, legittima capitale del Regno d'Italia.

Un'ovazione saluta le parole del Sovrano.

GLI INDIRIZZI DELLE CAMERE E IL SALUTO DI NATHAN

Il Presidente Manfredi legge l'indirizzo del Senato del Regno — redatto da S. E. Finali — e il Presidente Marcora legge l'indirizzo della Camera dei deputati.

Infine il Sindaco Nathan saluta i Sovrani. Una grande ovazione succede alle parole di Nathan.

IL RITORNO

Il ritorno dei Sovrani alla Reggia ha dato luogo ad una nuova festosissima manifestazione.

I Sovrani hanno dovuto affacciarsi ai balconi del Quirinale, per rispondere ai saluti della folla plaudente.

L'ESPOSIZIONE DI BELLE ARTI INAUGURATA.

Nel pomeriggio ha avuto luogo, alla presenza dei Sovrani, l'inaugurazione dell'Esposizione Internazionale di Belle Arti a Vigna Cartoni.

Alla cerimonia hanno assistito gli ambasciatori e le alte autorità.

Hanno parlato il conte Enrico Rospa di San Martino, Presidente del Comitato, il senatore Secondo Frola, il ministro degli Esteri marchese Di San Giuliano e l'ambasciatore di Francia, Barrère, ch'è decano del corpo diplomatico.

La mostra ha ottenuto un grandioso successo.

I Sovrani — nel rientrare alla Reggia — sono stati acclamatissimi.

RICEVIMENTO IN CAMPIDOGLIO

Questa sera vi sarà ricevimento di gala in Campidoglio, con l'intervento del corpo diplomatico.

La capitale sarà illuminata, e vi saranno molte feste popolari.

IL CINQUANTENARIO NEL REGNO

ROMA, 27. — La data odierna è stata commemorata con entusiasmo in tutte le città del Regno.

UNA CAROVANA NAZIONALE UNIVERSITARIA

ROMA, 27. — Le associazioni universitarie di Roma e di Torino, hanno organizzata una carovana nazionale universitaria la quale, partendo da Torino, andrà a deporre sulle tombe di Cavour a Santena, di Mazzini a Genova, di Garibaldi a Caprera e di Vittorio Emanuele II a Roma, una corona votiva romana di quercia e d'alloro.

Fatto così atto di omaggio e di devozione alla memoria degli uomini che meglio contribuirono alla redenzione del Regno d'Italia, e idealmente chiuso questo loro tributo di memore affetto tra i nomi delle due città che del moto nazionale furono l'una iniziatrice e culla, l'altra meta agognata e gloriosa, gli studenti italiani accenderanno una lampada votiva alla tomba di Dante a Ravenna.

Da quì la carovana tornerà a Torino dove si scioglierà.

L'amnistia

ROMA, 27. — S'è pubblicato oggi il decreto dell'amnistia concessa dal Re pel Cinquantenario.

L'amnistia comprende: — i reati di stampa; i reati di istigazione a delinquere; i reati avvenuti durante gli ultimi scioperi e conflitti di lavoro, e i reati disciplinari.

L'amnistia comprende anche i disertori e renitenti di leva, ai quali si impone di regolare la loro posizione in consolato, coll'obbligo del rimpatrio e del servizio militare entro il dicembre del 1912.

ANCHE OGGI LA NOSTRA INTERA TERZA PAGINA E' DEDICATA ALL'ESPOSIZIONE DI ROMA, APERTA IERI DAL RE.

La crisi ministeriale

BISSOLATI RIFIUTA RECISAMENTE DI ENTRARE NEL GABINETTO.

ROMA, 27. — La crisi che pareva risolta, si riapre nuovamente con la recisa rinunzia dell'on. Leonida Bissolati ad entrare nel Gabinetto Giolitti.

L'on. Bissolati ha scritto all'onor. Giolitti una lettera che taglia corto ad ogni discussione.

Il deputato socialista dice, tra l'altro, che "si troverebbe imbarazzato dal complicato cerimoniale del potere".

Tuttavia egli promette di aiutare l'on. Giolitti nell'espletamento del suo nuovo programma a base democratica.

A questa decisione dell'on. Bissolati non è estranea la riunione tenuta ieri dal gruppo parlamentare Socialista, nella quale prevalsero opinioni assolutamente contrarie all'entrata dei socialisti al governo.

GIOLITTI LAVORA

Sembra che al posto dell'on. Bissolati all'Agricoltura sarebbe destinato l'on. Pozzi, e che Facta — come già fissato definitivamente — rimarrebbe alle Finanze.

L'on. Giolitti ha conferito con questi due parlamentari e con gli onorevoli SACCHI, CREDARO e DI SAN GIULIANO.

La "Tribuna" dice stasera che le liste pubblicate finora non hanno base di verità.

Milano tributa solenni funerali al col. Missori

MILANO, 27. — Ieri l'altro si spense il colonnello Giuseppe Missori, uno degli eroi della camicia rossa che Garibaldi ebbe dilettissimo.

Il compianto è stato vivissimo. Tutta la stampa commemora l'illustre estinto.

Oggi hanno avuto luogo i funerali che sono riusciti straordinariamente solenni. Una folla immensa accompagnava la salma.

Elezioni politiche

MILANO, 27. — Nell'elezione che ebbe luogo ieri nel secondo collegio, per la successione dell'on. Greppi, fu eletto DELLA POLA.

SUSA, 27. — Nell'elezione per la successione dell'on. Richard, è stato proclamato il ballottaggio tra BOUVIER e VIGLIONGO.

Municipio disciolto

ROMA, 27. — E' stato pubblicato il decreto che scioglie il consiglio comunale di RUVO DI PUGLIA.

Paterno' radiato dai ruoli dell'esercito

ROMA, 27. — Il consiglio di disciplina ha radiato dai ruoli dell'esercito il barone Vincenzo Spedalotto di Paternò, barone dell'Ungo, uccisore della contessa Giulia Trigona.

Terremoto e vittime a Reggio Calabria

REGGIO CALABRIA, 27. — Una scossa di terremoto ha fatto crollare il capannone in costruzione, destinato a sede della Camera di Commercio.

Sotto i rottami sono rimasti varii operai.

Sono stati estratti in gravissimo stato: — FILIPPO DE BLASIO — DOMENICO ARCHINA — DOMENICO SCALA — ANTONIO D'AGOSTINO — GIORDANO SALVATORE.

L'on. Boselli lascia la presidenza della "Dante Alighieri,,

TORINO, 27. — Dopo una vivacissima assemblea della "Dante Alighieri" l'on. Paolo Boselli ha rassegnato le dimissioni da Presidente della Società.

L'arresto di un brigante

SALERNO, 27. — Telegrafano da Nocera Inferiore che è stato colà arrestato il brigante GIACINTO MURINO, camuffato da frate elemosiniere.

PROCESSO CUOCOLO

L'INDIFFENZA DEI VITERBESI

VITERBO, 27 - Mentre tutto il mondo si occupa di questo processo, i Viterbesi si mantengono assolutamente indifferenti e dimostrano all'evidenza che questo processo non li interessa nè punto nè poco. Nella città medioevale, così immutata e incorrotta nella compagine silenziosa delle sue case stemmate, dei suoi archi, delle sue chiese, delle sue logge, delle sue torri, nessun segno di avvenimenti inconsueti.

Eppure si poteva credere che un processo simile fosse per mettere a soqquadro l'intera città; ma che? Viterbo è città di buon senso: essa non s'è neppure scomposta. Ciò fa onore ai bravi Viterbesi.

In verità nei centri commerciali, al caffè Schienardi, nella farmacia della piazza delle Erbe, si sente parlare un po' del processo; ma gli interlocutori non sono Viterbesi: sono quasi tutti napoletani, testimoni nel processo, o parenti degli imputati.

Domani si riprenderà il dibattimento. Come sapete il sabato, la domenica naturalmente, ed il lunedì non hanno luogo le udienze.

Anche la traduzione degli accusati dalle carceri di Santa Maria in Gradi alla Corte di Assise, che nei primi giorni ha dato luogo a scene di viva curiosità, ora si compie come un fatto normale della vita quotidiana viterbese. Del resto la traduzione si effettua in modo da eludere quella folla di curiosi sfaccendati che si raccoglie tutte le mattine e tutte le sere in piazza Fontana Grande, al passaggio dei pesanti furgoni. Ma è impossibile a chiunque vedere gli accusati, che sono fatti discendere nel cortile del Tribunale comunicante per un breve tratto di corridoio colla camera di sicurezza della Corte di Assise. I carrozzoni al loro arrivo sono circondati da un forte numero di carabinieri e guardie, mentre altri carabinieri impediscono l'accesso ai locali giudiziari a chiunque non sia munito di uno speciale permesso.

Fuori la porta è stato messo un picchetto armato del 60.o fanteria.

Dopo la ramanzina ricevuta dal presidente comm. Bianchi, nella giornata in cui giunse in ritardo, la prima ad arrivare alla Corte è l'im-

(Continua in 2.a pagina)

Leggete in ottava pagina la fine della Deposizione completa di GENNARO ABBATEMAGGIO

LE TRAGEDIE DEL LAVORO

Centoquarantacinque vite periscono nell'incendio di Washington Place

Particolari terrificanti -- Diecine di operaie, le vesti in fiamme, si lanciano dalle finestre dell'ottavo piano e si sfracellano sulla via -- L'eroismo dei nostri connazionali rifulge ancora una volta -- Le sottoscrizioni per le vittime.

L'ultima tappa del calvario...

LE VITTIME ITALIANE FINORA IDENTIFICATE

B

BENENTI FRANCESCA, di circa 17 anni, indirizzo sconosciuto: il nome ottenuto dalla busta di paga.
BENENTI VINCENZA, di 22 anni, residente al n. 17 Marion st.
BRUNETTI LAURA, di 17 anni, residente al n. 160 Columbia street, Brooklyn.

C

CAPUTO ALBINA, di 20 anni, residente al n. 81 Degraw street, Brooklyn.
CARUSO FRANCESCA, di 20 anni, residente al n. 21 New Bowery.
CIRRITO ROSA, di anni 18, residente al n. 135 Cherry st.
COLLETTI ANNA, di anni 30 residente al n. 410 E. 13.a strada.
CARLESI JOSEPHINA, di anni 31 residente al n. 502 E. 12.a strada

F

FRANCHI TINA, di anni 17, residente al n. 342 E. 11.a strada.

G

GRASSO ROSA, di anni 16 residente al n. 172 Thompson st.

L

L'ABBATE ANNA, di 16 anni, abitante al n. 509 E. 13.a strada.

M

MAIALE BERTINA, di anni 18, residente al n. 135 Sullivan street.
MALTESE LENA, di anni 21, residente al n. 35 Second Avenue.
MALTESE ROSINA, di anni 14 residente al n. 35 Second Avenue.
MARCIANO MICHELE, di anni 25, residente al n. 272 Bleecker st.
MIRAGLIA MARIA, di anni 27, residente al n. 227 E. 28.a strada.

N

NICOLESCI NICOLINA, di anni 21, residente al 410 E. 13.a strada.

P

PASQUALETTO ANTONIETTA, di anni 16, abitante al n. 509 E. 13.a strada.
PRATO MILLIE, di anni 24, residente al n. 93 Macdougal street.

S

SARACINO TESSIE, di anni 20 residente al n. 118 E. 119.a strada.
SARACINO SERAFINA, di anni 25, residente al n. 118 E. 119.a st.
SENINILIO ANNA, di anni 30, domiciliata al n. 471 Ralph ave., Brooklyn.

T

TERRANOVA CLOTILDE, di anni 26, residente al n. 106 President street, Brooklyn.
TORTORELLA ISABELLA, di anni 17, residente al n. 116 Thompson street.

U

ULLO MARY, di anni 26, residente al n. 437 E. 20.a strada.
UZZO CARRIE, di anni 22, domiciliata al n. 1990 Second avenue.

V

VIVIANI BESSIE, di anni 15, residente al n. 81 Chrystie street.

IL DOVERE CHE S'IMPONE

La Colonia lavoratrice di Nuova York — e così dicendo intendiamo parlare di tutti, di tutti i connazionali — sosterà di lavorare, compatta, nelle ore in cui le salme carbonizzate delle misere figlie del lavoro dovranno attraversare le vie per essere portate al camposanto.

Vogliamo lunghi cortei, interminabili, appresso alle vittime; vogliamo che il dolore che ha spezzato il cuore si legga sui volti di tutti; vogliamo che la mesta processione, nel suo silenzio solenne, significhi allo straniero la protesta che l'Umanità leva irretrattabile verso il crudele abbandono con cui le vite degli ospiti d'America — le vite di quanti sono i fattori della prosperità di questo mondo — sono lasciate all'abbraccio della Morte.

Tante creature di nostro sangue vogliono questo estremo omaggio di bontà e di fraternità. Morirono con la disperazione nel cuore, col nome delle loro mamme sulle labbra, chiamarono aiuto nella favella della loro patria, col terrore folle negli occhi che avevano un momento prima mille fulgori di gioia, mille sorrisi di speranze; si precipitarono nelle voragini delle fiamme, nel vuoto, si congiunsero insieme nell'amplesso mortale mormorando nell'agonia inenarrabile il nome di Dio!

Si sospenda ogni lavoro al passare dei cortei funerarii e l'anima si raccolga nella preghiera. Quale altro ufficio pietoso — una volta che il destino si compì così terribile — noi dobbiamo alle vittime?

Tutta la nostra tenerezza alla memoria dei morti; tutto l'augurioso voto di guarigione ai feriti superstiti; tutte le buone parole di conforto vadano alle famiglie che non sentiranno più il respiro delle loro creature!

Parole di conforto; ma che siano anche di promessa. Non scendano nella profondità delle zolle le bare che avremo infiorato e irrorate di lagrime, senza aver detto a noi stessi che devono vendicarsi i sacrificati.

✝ ✝ ✝

Ecco: non è sufficiente che le autorità cittadine conducano le loro inchieste; quella amministrativa per un verso e quella giudiziaria per l'altra. Per noi occorre una terza inchiesta; e dev'essere questa condotta, senza badare a spese, senza debolezza veruna, dall'autorità consolare preposta alla tutela dei sudditi italiani.

Il Consolato ha le più ampie facoltà di investigare intorno alle cause immediate e remote dell'ecatombe; presso di sè ha un ufficio legale che serve appunto a tutelare i connazionali nei casi d'infortunio; sta poi, a fianco ad esso, un ispettorato d'emigrazione le cui mansioni dovrebbero esser volte al medesimo scopo.

Senza preoccuparsi menomamente di conflitti, senza ricorrere ad accomodamenti, senza abbandonarsi a concessioni ed amità che suonerebbe vigliaccheria, la inchiesta consolare deve procedere diritta verso la dimostrazione ampia e precisa di tutte le responsabilità, sia dei padroni del laboratorio-trappola SIA DELLE AUTORITA' AMERICANE CHE SI SONO RESE, DIRETTAMENTE O INDIRETTAMENTE, COLPOSE DI AVER LASCIATO MANO LIBERA AI PADRONI STESSI DI TENERE IL VASTO CASAMENTO PRIVO DEI PIU' ELEMENTARI MEZZI PRECAUZIONALI.

Non abbiamo ragione, oggi, di supporre che le inchieste degli americani non debbano procedere con rigore e non debbano condurre a conclusioni severe. L'opinione pubblica è insorta: da ogni parte si levano clamori di proteste: si domanda l'esemplare punizione dei colpevoli e la giustizia pei morti. L'America si coprirebbe di vergogna inaudita negando loro la vendetta!

Però... si tratta di vittime di nazionalità straniera: cessate le prime emozioni del tristissimo evento, sopraggiunge l'oblio. Una triste esperienza abbiamo noi italiani delle abitudini di questo paese!

Comunque — si agisca nel modo più soddisfacente di questo mondo nelle investigazioni da parte americana, a far paga la nostra coscienza OCCORRE CHE L'INCHIESTA DEL CONSOLE D'ITALIA COINCIDA PERFETTAMENTE CON LE ALTRE.

Considerazioni di vario carattere potranno scaturire dall'identità o meno di tutte le inchieste; ma la principale risultanza dell'opera dell'autorità tutelare nostra deve significare CHE L'ITALIA UFFICIALE SA TENERE IL SUO POSTO NEL DIFENDERE LA VITA E LA LIBERTA' DEI SUDDITI ALL'ESTERO.

La carne dell'operaio italiano finora è stata considerata in America come da macello, materiale grezzo da "paking-houses".

EBBENE — E' ORA CHE QUESTO SINISTRO MACABRO PREGIUDIZIO FINISCA!

Noi abbiamo il diritto di sapere se il suddito italiano all'estero — l'operaio che l'America domanda alla nostra terra perchè più lavoro n'ottiene e meno lo paga — venga protetto dalla legge e se, una volta che la legge esiste, essa la si applichi. Quando non dovesse la constatazione della colpa singola o collettiva condurre all'equo risarcimento dei danni materiali, sono i diritti dell'umanità che devono essere riaffermati e sostenuti.

✝ ✝ ✝

Noi domandiamo alle autorità italiane di compiere il loro dovere.

Le vittime non sono state ancora composte e inchiodate nelle assi; il pianto stilla da tutti gli occhi; avida è l'invocazione di giustizia!

Sarà compiuto quel dovere? Vorremmo non dubitarne.

Perchè con profondo accoramento, con indicibile disgusto dobbiamo constatare che nella tragica notte, mentre i cadaveri si ammucchiavano sui marciapiedi, insanguinati di Washington Place — quando le autorità italiane, che, per le notizie avute dai giornali della sera, si sarebbero dovute trovare sul posto a raccogliere i primi elementi, i più preziosi, dell'inchiesta che invochiamo, — l'Ispettore d'emigrazione che trae stipendio dalla massa raccolta con la tassa degli emigranti, e qui risiede a scopo di protezione — si recava ad un ballo di "Mi-carème" nel travestimento di Arlecchino!

L'incendio del laboratorio della Triangle Shirt Waist Company, a Washington Place, angolo di Greene street — di cui demmo notizia nel giornale di domenica — assunse in breve tempo le proporzioni di disastro immane.

Diamo qui appresso i particolari più minuti della catastrofe terrificante.

Le vittime sono

CENTOQUARANTACINQUE

Nell'ecatombe sono periti molti nostri connazionali.

PREDIZIONE AVVERATA

La predizione fatta da mr. Croker capo del servizio dei pompieri in New York il giorno 27 novembre dell'anno scorso allorchè in Newark un incendio immane distruggeva completamente una fabbrica e consacrava alla morte centinaia di poveri lavoratori, si avverò sabato sera in New York nel laboratorio della Triangle Waist Company sita all'angolo di Greene St. e Washington Place, di proprietà di Isaac Harris e Max Blanck. "New York, disse allora mr. Croker non tarderà certo a registrare qualche incendio forse anche più spaventevole di questo. Vi sono in New York dei fabbricati in cui il pericolo è facilissimo come in quello di Newark. Ciò che occorre assolutamente è una legge che imponga l'impianto delle scale di salvataggio in tutti gli edifici destinati all'opera manufacturiera".

Queste parole mr. Croker le richiamò sabato alla memoria del pubblico allorchè si trovò tra le rovine ancora fumanti di quell'edificio quasi completamente sprovvisto di scale di salvataggio.

L'essersi avverata la sua predizione in un modo così orribile costituirà un elemento prezioso nella ricerca delle responsabilità.

L'INIZIO E LA CAUSA DELL'INCENDIO

La "Triangle Waist Company" aveva impiegato al lavoro circa 600 donne e 100 uomini.

Lieti tutti del ricevuto compenso della fatica settimanale e pregodendo nel loro cuore i divertimenti del giorno festivo che si annunziava sereno e tepido come un vero giorno di primavera inoltrata, così stavano aspettando il segnale dell'uscita. Erano le 4.40, allorchè invece del segnale allegro dell'uscita si udì il primo allarme del fuoco, seguito dalle grida e dalla confusione delle operaie che si accalcavano nelle sale del lavoro, cercando la via di fuga tra gli stretti sentieri delle macchine allineate fitte come in un magazzino di vendita.

L'incendio si sviluppò all'ottavo piano, e dalle investigazioni fatte dall'autorità è risultato ch'esso ebbe origine, dall'accendersi improvviso di un serbatoio di benzina che si usava per iscaldare i ferri da stirare nella sala della rifinitura. L'accensione parve esser provocata da una sigaretta lanciata imprudentemente ancora accesa vicino al recipiente.

LE PRIME SCENE

La prima scena di terrore fu superiore ad ogni immaginativa. Il grido di allarme richiamò subito alla memoria delle operaie che quella costruzione non aveva scale di salvataggio e che non vi era per loro altro scampo che l'ascensore. Esso però allora non funzionava. Si precipitarono allora per una scaletta, ma giunte ad un altro punto le fiamme le respinsero indietro. Non restava loro altra ancora di salvataggio che un'altra via alla morte e questa esse scelsero immantinente gettandosi dalle finestre nella strada. L'orrore della morte per fuoco era troppo grande.

L'altezza da cui si gettarono era di 100 piedi. La prima a sfracellarsi sul lastricato di Greene st. fu una ragazzina, a lei seguirono subito molte altre. La folla che già erasi accalcata nella via gridava: non vi gettate giù! ma il consiglio trovava ostacolo nell'orribile dilemma, o bruciare o saltare dalla finestra. Quelle che non ebbero il coraggio d'incontrare una morte meno orribile di quella per il fuoco, perirono tra le fiamme ai sono piano. Esse erano cinquanta.

Samuel Bernstein, foreman del laboratorio, e Max Rothberg, ...

(Continua in 7.a pagina)

Il baratro in cui perirono molte povere operaie

12 Area Studies Collections

Peggy K. Pearlstein and Barbara A. Tenenbaum

Vais broit . . . azoyfil vayse penitslekh frish broit far alemen.
Mayne oygen tsinden zikh on mit hunger.

White bread, so many small slices of fresh, white bread for all of us.
My eyes lit up with hunger.[1]

From its very beginnings, the Library of Congress has collected works in foreign languages. Today the Library's book collections number more than eighteen million volumes. Half of these are works written in languages other than English, representing about 450 different languages and 35 scripts. In many instances, the Library is considered to be the best repository outside the country of origin for Western-language books, periodicals, and other materials about a particular culture. Its non-roman-script-language collections are generally the largest and most extensive in the world outside of the countries where those languages are spoken. Foreign-language items published in the United States form yet another substantial segment of the Library's collections.

The Library's foreign-language collections and adjunct sources on different cultural groups are an important and often untapped resource for study of the origins and development of women's history in the United States. This chapter suggests ways for researchers to avail themselves of the many opportunities afforded by these materials throughout the Library of Congress.

The African and Middle Eastern Reading Room (AMED), the Asian Reading Room (AD), the European Reading Room (EurRR), and the Hispanic Reading Room (HISP), collectively known as the "Area Studies" reading rooms, provide the primary gateways to the Library's foreign-language materials and culture groups. Each contains a specialized reference collection that is open to researchers. Each reading room is staffed with its own area specialists and reference librarians. Their linguistic proficiency and subject expertise enable them to provide valuable assistance to scholars and to the general public concerning a great variety of cultural communities. Because of their broad knowledge about a culture, the area specialists and reference librarians can also guide researchers to other reading rooms that contain special format material, such as films or sound recordings, on certain groups and individuals. The accompanying charts shows how to access items that are in both roman- and non-roman-script languages and in different formats.

It should be noted that research on particular cultural groups can be enriched by knowledge of their places of settlement, prevalent occupations, and forms of cultural expression. This is particularly relevant in searching special-format collections where materials may not have been indexed consistently by the ethnic group represented in them.

The experiences of women from several different cultures, regions, and time periods can be highlighted by the following examples from the Library's collections. Those described below are not limited to custodial items in Area Studies, but represent the myriad print and nonprint media found throughout the Library. Our hope is to suggest previously unexplored channels that can enlarge our understanding of United States women's history similar to the approach taken in two topical resource guides already published by the Library of Congress, *Many Nations: A Library of Congress Resource Guide for the Study of Indian and Alaska Native Peoples of the United States* and *The African-American Mosaic: A Library of Con-*

"Le Tragedie del Lavoro." Il Progresso Italo-Americano, *March 28, 1911 (News MF 2297). Serial and Government Publications Division.*

On March 25, 1911, a fire swept through the Triangle Shirtwaist Company, an anti-union shop in Greenwich Village. One hundred and forty-six employees lost their lives in one of the worst industrial disasters in the history of New York City. Most of these workers were recent Jewish female immigrants; others were young Italian immigrant women. The huge public outcry and wave of sympathy for working women led to the eventual establishment of a Factory Investigating Commission, which was instrumental in drafting new factory legislation that mandated improved working and safety conditions. A list of the names of the Italian women who had been identified as victims of the fire appears on the front page of the Italian-language New York City daily *Il Progresso Italo-Americano,* next to the sketch of a victim.

gress Resource Guide for the Study of Black History and Culture.[2]

The Library's abundant collections of memoir literature, autobiographies, interviews, and oral histories in several languages and formats provide a corpus of firsthand information for learning about women's experiences and lives. Among those who did not have to emigrate to become American was Fabiola Cabeza de Baca Gilbert. In her memoir of her family and community, *We Fed Them Cactus* (1954; 1994), she chronicles the evolution of Hispanics in New Mexico at the end of the nineteenth century. A half-century later, an oral history interview titled "Yoshi Mary Tashima: Evacuation to Santa Anita Assembly Center" discusses a woman's ordeal in an internment camp for Japanese Americans during World War II. More recently, Monique Ugbaja, a newly arrived immigrant, records in *In the Secret Place: The Ordeal of an African First Wife in America* (1996) the contemporary difficulties of broken homes and divorce.[3]

The Library's comprehensive collection of foreign-language newspapers and periodicals published abroad constitutes a useful tool for understanding how other peoples view and interpret events in this country bearing on women's history. For instance, on September 20, 1920, the Tokyo-based Japanese newspaper *Asahi Shinbun* (uncataloged, Orien Japan) spotlighted the success of the women's suffrage movement when it reported that Tennessee, the last state necessary, had ratified the constitutional amendment that gave women the right to vote in the United States. *Fu nü tsa chih/Fu nü za zhi* (The ladies journal, 6:3) (HQ1104.F8 Orien China), a monthly periodical published in Shanghai, China, similarly announced to its readers in 1920 that the Nineteenth Amendment granting suffrage to women in the United States had become a law.

Immigrant and ethnic newspapers issued in this country are a fertile source for discerning the varieties of women's experiences and endeavors. *Al-Hudá* (Guidance) (1898–, microfilm 2351 Arab, Near East), a New York Arabic-language newspaper, recorded in its pages the activities of the Syrian Ladies Aid Society of Boston during the 1910s. The New York Yiddish-language newspaper *Forverts* (Jewish daily forward) (1897–; microfilm, Hebr) and the Italian-language newspaper *Il Progresso Italo-Americano* (1880–1989; News MF 2297, N&CPR) headlined on each of their front pages the names of the 146 young Jewish and Italian female garment workers who died tragically in the fire at the Triangle Shirtwaist Company sweatshop in New York City on March 25, 1911.

Front cover. Rah-e-Zendegi, *no. 742, May 19, 1995 (AP95.P3 R34 Pers). Near East Section, African and Middle Eastern Division. Courtesy of Rah-e-Zendegi.*

The largest Iranian population outside of Iran resides in Los Angeles, California. The vast majority of Iranian emigrants left their country immediately before or just after the 1979 revolution. With the official establishment of a conservative Islamic republic after the revolution, Iranian women have had to adhere to a strictly enforced dress code there. The Farsi text on the cover of this issue of *Rah-e-Zendegi* describes a woman who left Iran and who is now wearing fashionable and revealing Western clothing. When the woman pictured in the upper left-hand corner returned to her homeland, she was required to appear in public dressed modestly, covering herself completely except for her hands and face.

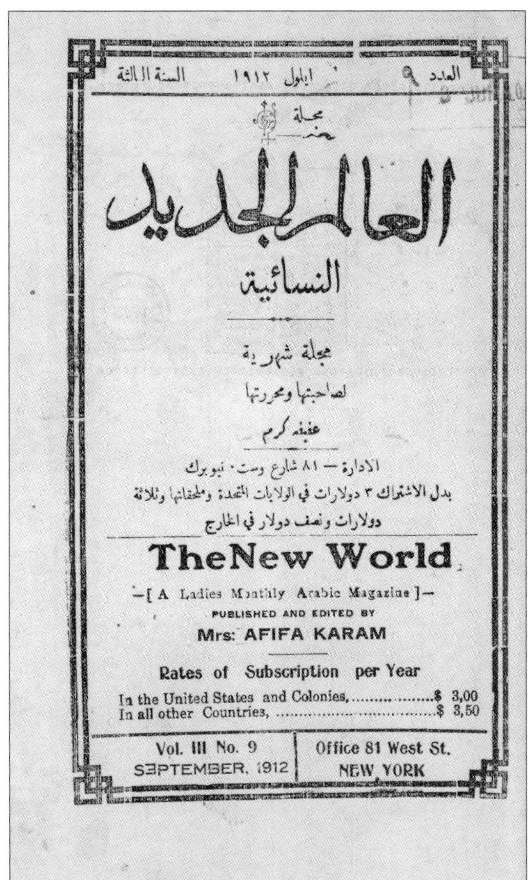

العدد ٩ ايلول ١٩١٢ السنة الثالثة

مجلة

العالم الجديد

النسائية

مجلة شهرية

لصاحبتها ومحررتها

عفيفه كرم

الادارة — ٨١ شارع وست · نيويرك

بدل الاشتراك ٣ دولارات في الولايات المتحدة وملحقاتها وثلاثة دولارات ونصف دولار في الخارج

The New World

—[A Ladies Monthly Arabic Magazine]—

PUBLISHED AND EDITED BY

Mrs. AFIFA KARAM

Rates of Subscription per Year

In the United States and Colonies, ...$ 3,00
In all other Countries, ...$ 3,50

Vol. III No. 9 SEPTEMBER, 1912 | Office 81 West St. NEW YORK

Front cover. Al-ʻĀlam al-jadīd [al-nisaʼīyah] *(The New World [A Ladies Monthly Arabic Magazine]) 3:9 (September 1912) (New York, N.Y.; AP95.A6 A495 Orien Arab). Near Eastern Section, African and Middle Eastern Division.*

The first Arabic-language journal about women published in the United States beginning in 1910, was edited and published by the Lebanese-born ʻAfīfah Karam (1883–1924), who was married at the age of fourteen and emigrated to New York that same year. After becoming interested in journalism and both Arabic and American literature, Karam established this journal. An author and translator, she is considered among the pioneers of those who served the cause of women's advancement through their writings.

Hai Hellēnidēs en Amerikē *(Portraits of Greek women in the United States) (New York: Ethnikos Kēryx, 1923; E184.G7 E8), unpaged. General Collections.*

The *Ethnikos Kēryx* (National herald), a Greek-language newspaper in New York City, held a beauty contest for Greek American women in 1923. The contestants submitted photographs, assembled in this album, to be judged by the newspaper's readers voting by means of a detachable ballot on the back of the album. The winner was to receive a gold crown worth $250.

Rich sources for the study of women in the United States are the publications of women themselves. *Głos Polek* (The Polish women's voice) (1902–; LC has vols. 12–14, 1921–23, and vols. 72–75, 1977–80, incomplete; HQ1104.G5 fol, GenColl), the important Polish-American women's journal that began in Chicago at the turn of the century, and *Zarja* (The dawn) (1928–; LC has vol. 14, 1942–vol. 59, 1987, incomplete; AP58 .S55 Z3 GenColl), the twentieth-century official publication of the Slovenian Women's Union of America, printed in Joliet, Illinois, are two examples of this genre. One of the most recent periodicals for newcomers is *Rah-e-Zendegi* (The way of life) (1979–; LC has 1981–; uncataloged, Near East), a Farsi-language monthly published in Los Angeles, California, home for a large group of Iranian Americans. *Rah-e-Zendegi,* whose publisher is female, is devoted to preserving Iranian culture and identity, especially through the use of Farsi. Yet it describes, filters, and even promotes customs of modern American women. Here, full-color advertisements bring the newest commercial enticements of America both to recent arrivals and to more established members of the Iranian community in the United States.

AREA STUDIES READING ROOMS		REFERENCE SERVICES	LANGUAGES AND SCRIPTS	BOOKS
African & Middle Eastern Division (AMED) Reading Room Thomas Jefferson Building 2nd floor, room LJ 220 **Hours:** Monday through Friday 8:30 a.m. to 5:00 p.m. **Tel:** 202 707-4188 **Fax:** 202 252-3180 **Address:** Library of Congress 101 Independence Avenue, SE Washington, DC 20540-4820 **E-mail:** amed@loc.gov **Web site:** <http://www.loc.gov/rr/amed>	**African Section**	Sub-Saharan Africa (African American reference services are available in the Main Reading Room.)	Afrikaans, Amharic, Arabic, Chichewa, French, Kinyarwanda, Malagasy, Ndebele, Northern Sotho, Portuguese, Rundi, Somali, Sotho, Spanish, Swahili, Swazi, Tsonga, Tswana, Venda, Xhosa, Zulu, and other languages of sub-Saharan Africa	Africana books in all languages are part of the General Collections and may be requested for use in the AMED Reading Room, Main Reading Room, or Science and Business Reading Room.
	Hebraic Section	Israel, Ancient Near East, Diaspora Jewry	Hebrew, Yiddish, Ladino, Judeo-Arabic, Aramaic, Syriac, Coptic, languages of Ethiopia and Eritrea	Books and manuscripts in Hebrew script and related vernacular languages must be requested and used in the AMED Reading Room.
	Near East Section	Islam, Arab World (including North Africa), Turkey, Iran, Afghanistan, Malta, Central Asia, Caucasus	Thirty-five languages, primarily Arabic, Persian, Turkish, Armenian, Georgian	Books and manuscripts in Arabic script and related vernacular languages must be requested and used in the AMED Reading Room.
Asian Division (AD) Reading Room Thomas Jefferson Building Ist floor, room LJ150 **Hours:** Monday through Friday 8:30 a.m. to 5:00 p.m. **Tel:** 202 707-5426 **Fax:** 202 707-1724 **Address:** Library of Congress 101 Independence Avenue, SE Washington, DC 20540-4810 **E-mail:** asian@loc.gov **Web site:** <http://www.loc.gov/rr/asian>	**Chinese Section**	South Asian subcontinent and Southeast Asia to China, Korea, and Japan	Chinese, Manchu, Mongol, Moso (Naxi)	Books and manuscripts in Chinese script must be requested and used in the AD Reading Room.
	Japanese Section	Japan	Japanese	Books and manuscripts in Japanese script must be requested and used in the AD Reading Room.
	Korean Section	Korea	Korean	Books and manuscripts in Korean script must be requested and used in the AD Reading Room.
	Southern Asia Section	South and Southeast Asia	Languages of Bangladesh, Bhutan, Brunei, Burma, Cambodia, India, Indonesia, Laos, Malaysia, Nepal, Pakistan, Singapore, Sri Lanka, Thailand, the Philippines, Tibet, Vietnam, Pacific Islands	Books and manuscripts in South Asian scripts must be requested and used in the AD Reading Room.
European Division (EUR) Reading Room Thomas Jefferson Building 2nd floor, room LJ 250 **Hours:** Monday through Friday 8:30 a.m. to 5:00 p.m. **Tel:** 202 707-4515 **Fax:** 202 707-8482 **Address:** Library of Congress 101 Independence Avenue, SE Washington, DC 20540-4830 **E-mail:** eurref@loc.gov **Web site:** <http://www.loc.gov/rr/european>		Europe (Reference services for the United Kingdom and Ireland are available in the Main Reading Room. Luso-Hispanic reference services are available in the Hispanic Reading Room.)	Czech and Slovak, Dutch, French, German, Hungarian, Icelandic and Faroese, Italian, Polish, and Russian, South Slavic, and Ukrainian	Books in all languages are part of the General Collections. They may be requested for use in the European Reading Room, Main Reading Room, or Science and Business Reading Room.
Hispanic Division (HISP) Reading Room Thomas Jefferson Building 2nd floor, room LJ 240 **Hours:** Monday through Friday 8:30 a.m. to 5:00 p.m. **Tel:** 202 707-5397 **Fax:** 202 707-2005 **Address:** Library of Congress 101 Independence Avenue, SE Washington, DC 20540-4850 **E-mail:** hispref@loc.gov **Web site:** <http://www.loc.gov/rr/hispanic>		Caribbean, Latin America, Iberia; Latinos in the United States; peoples of Portuguese or Spanish heritage in Africa, Asia, Oceania; peoples influenced by Luso-Hispanic culture	Spanish, Portuguese, Dutch, French, Arabic, German, Catalan, Galician	Books in all languages are part of the General Collections and may be requested for use in the Hispanic Reading Room, Main Reading Room, or Science and Business Reading Room.

HOW TO ACCESS FOREIGN-LANGUAGE MATERIAL

PERIODICALS	NEWSPAPERS	MICROFORM MATERIAL	SPECIAL MATERIALS
Current unbound periodicals must be requested and used in the Newspaper and Current Periodical Room. Bound periodicals are part of the General Collections and may be requested for use in the AMED Reading Room, Main Reading Room, or Science and Business Reading Room.	Newspapers in all languages must be requested and used in the Newspaper and Current Periodical Room.	Microform for Africana must be requested and used in the Microform Reading Room.	With some exceptions, special materials such as photographs, sound recordings, films, etc., are in special collections reading rooms. They are available subject to the hours and restrictions of those reading rooms.
Periodicals in Hebrew script and related languages must be requested and used in the AMED Reading Room.	Newspapers in Hebrew script and related languages must be requested and used in the AMED Reading Room.	Microform in Hebrew script and related languages must be requested and used in the AMED Reading Room.	
Periodicals in Arabic script and related vernacular languages must be requested and used in the AMED Reading Room.	Newspapers in Arabic script and related vernacular languages must be requested and used in the AMED Reading Room.	Microform in Arabic script and related languages must be requested and used in the AMED Reading Room.	
Periodicals in Chinese script must be requested and used in the AD Reading Room.	Newspapers in Chinese script must be requested and used in the AD Reading Room.	Microform in Chinese script must be requested and used in the AD Reading Room.	With some exceptions, special materials such as photographs, sound recordings, films, etc., are in special collections reading rooms. They are available subject to the hours and restrictions of those reading rooms.
Periodicals in Japanese script must be requested and used in the AD Reading Room.	Newspapers in Japanese script must be requested and used in the AD Reading Room.	Microform in Japanese script must be requested and used in the AD Reading Room.	
Periodicals in Korean script must be requested and used in the AD Reading Room.	Newspapers in Korean script must be requested and used in the AD Reading Room.	Microform in Korean script must be requested and used in the AD Reading Room.	
Periodicals in South Asian scripts must be requested and used in the AD Reading Room.	Newspapers in South Asian scripts must be requested and used in the AD Reading Room.	Microform in South Asian scripts must be requested and used in the AD Reading Room.	
Current unbound periodicals except for those in Russian/Slavic languages must be requested and used in the Newspaper and Current Periodical Room. Bound periodicals are part of the General Collections and may be requested for use in the EUR Reading Room, Main Reading Room, or Science and Business Reading Room.	Newspapers except for those in Russian/Slavic languages must be requested and used in the Newspaper and Current Periodical Room.	Microform material in all languages must be requested and used in the Microform Reading Room.	With some exceptions, special materials such as photographs, sound recordings, films, etc., are in special collections reading rooms. They are available subject to the hours and restrictions of those reading rooms.
Current unbound periodicals in all languages must be requested and used in the Newspaper and Current Periodical Room. Bound periodicals are part of the General Collections and may be requested for use in the HISP Reading Room, Main Reading Room, or Science and Business Reading Room.	Luso-Hispanic and Caribbean newspapers must be requested and used in the Newspaper and Current Periodical Room.	Microform material in all languages must be requested and used in the Microform Reading Room.	With some exceptions, special materials such as photographs, sound recordings, or films are in special collections reading rooms. They are available subject to the hours and restrictions of those reading rooms.

The Library's special-format divisions also provide numerous opportunities to research the lives of women from different backgrounds, some of whom are current immigrants and others of whom are fourth- and fifth-generation Americans. For example, *With Silk Wings—Asian American Women at Work: Four Women* (Lone Ding Vox Productions, 1983, VBC 3836, MBRS), a series of four films that focus on the challenges and conflicts of adjusting to a new culture, is available for viewing in the Motion Picture and Television Reading Room (chapter 10). Polish-born American actress Helena Modjeska appears in photographs in the Prints and Photographs Division, and several letters from her can be read in the Manuscript Division. Lastly, the Thomas Čapek Collection of Material Relating to Czechoslovakia and Czech Americans, also located in the Manuscript Division, has a photograph, bibliography, and sketch of the life of Čapek's wife and collaborator, Anne Vostroveský Čapek.

BIBLIOGRAPHY:

A Comprehensive Bibliography for the Study of American Minorities. 2 vols. New York: New York University Press, 1976. Z1361.E4 M529, MRR Alc., EurRR.

Gale Encyclopedia of Multicultural America. 3 vols. Detroit: Gale Group, 2000. E184.A1 G14 2000, MRR Alc.

Harvard Encyclopedia of American Ethnic Groups. Cambridge: Belknap Press of Harvard University, 1980. E184.A1 H35, MRR Alc., EurRR, N&CPR, HispRef, LH&G.

USING AREA STUDIES COLLECTIONS

To maximize your opportunities to mine the riches of the Library's foreign-language materials, you should consult the reference librarians and area specialists in the Area Studies reading rooms. Refer frequently to the chart at the beginning of this chapter to clarify the sometimes confusing custodial assignment of items throughout the Library. You will also find the chapters "Using the Library of Congress" and "The General Collections," especially the sections on Library of Congress Subject Headings, very helpful for understanding how the Library is structured so that you can locate source material in all of the collections. Specific search strategies are discussed more thoroughly in the two case studies on Jewish women and Latinas below.

A SELECTED FOCUS

This chapter will highlight materials and how to access them for just two of the many cultural communities covered by Area Studies collections: American Jewish women and Latina women. Previously, the Library has published guides to its collections for the study of Indian and Alaska native peoples of the United States and for the study of African American history and culture (see above). American Jewish women and Latina women highlight the religious and ethnic pluralism of the United States. The Hispanic community constitutes the largest and the fastest-growing minority cohort of the population today. In addition, a focus on these two groups of women demonstrates how doing research at the Library in a non-roman vernacular-script language such as Yiddish, spoken by the majority of Eastern European Jewish women immigrants in the latter part of the nineteenth century and well into the twentieth, or in a Western foreign language such as Spanish, spoken by Latinas, can enrich research through the use of multiple language sources. Since location of items in the Library is determined by format as well as by subject and language, examples of resources concerning these two groups of women come from several collections and can be found in various specialized reading rooms. Appearing as they do in the final chapter of this guide, the examples that follow reemphasize the interdisciplinary nature of research on women in general and emphasize in particular the importance of looking at the Library's collections across all of the reading rooms in order to plumb most thoroughly the depths of resources available. Keep in mind that the two groups selected are only examples; you can use the methods described below to research women from other backgrounds. In doing so, it is very likely that you will uncover unexpected aspects of women's history in the United States.

AMERICAN JEWISH WOMEN

Jewish women first arrived in North America in 1654 when a boatload of refugees—four women, six men, and thirteen children—fleeing Dutch Brazil after its reconquest by the Portuguese, landed in New Amsterdam, now New York City. Most of the refugees, known as Sephardim, the descendants of Jews expelled from Spain and Portugal in 1492 and 1497, respectively, returned to Holland or sailed for the West Indies or Surinam when they were unable to maintain a viable community of their own in New Amsterdam. Nevertheless, by the eve of the American Revolution, about twenty-five hundred Jews were in the American colonies, many of them merchant families clustered in six eastern port cities. It was another two generations, and with a steady infusion of immigrants, before Jewish communal life in New York and the other cities became firmly established.

Protest against child labor in a labor parade. Photograph, 1909. George Grantham Bain Collection (LOT 10876-2). Prints and Photographs Division. LC-USZ62-22198.

Wearing "Abolish Child Slavery" banners in English and Yiddish, with one clearly carrying an American flag, these two girls were very likely participants in a labor parade held in New York City on May 1, 1909. Many of the Jewish immigrants who worked in the garment industry in New York City—where women made up a significant proportion of the industry's workforce—believed that to create a new order of society, labor needed to be organized. American Jewish women fought both in the rank and file and as central figures in labor groups to eradicate a variety of social injustices through government legislation for the protection especially of women and children.

In this period, the typical Jewish woman, sometimes herself a seamstress, was the wife of a craftsman or storekeeper. Perhaps involved in the family business, she most likely kept a home where the dietary laws were observed. Almost always literate, an important skill in helping in a family enterprise, these women were barely visible in early American Jewish communal and religious life and publications. Public Judaism was reserved for males. Women expressed their religion in the home as the keepers of the spiritual legacy and then publicly as the founders of associations like the first Female Hebrew Benevolent Society established in 1819 or the first Hebrew Sunday School dating from 1838, both in Philadelphia.

An exception—like poet Emma Lazarus—was writer Penina Moise, who lived in Charleston, South Carolina, her entire life. Moise wrote 180 of the 210 hymns that appear in *Hymns Written for the Use of Hebrew Congregations* ([n.p.] [1856] BM679.E5 H8 1856 GenColl).

Toward the end of the nineteenth century, middle-class women played an increasingly active role in philanthropic life, both Jewish and gentile, while upholding the "cult of true womanhood." They embodied the role of pure and pious homemakers who stressed the ethical, rather than the ritual and ceremonial. In the twentieth century, the new American Jewish woman, primarily of German descent, sought higher education, other ways to express her Judaism, and solutions to the challenges of the progressive era. The National Council of Jewish Women, founded by Hannah G. Solomon (1858–1942) at the World's Parliament of Religions in Chicago in 1893, created mission schools and settlement houses and provided aid for newly arrived Jewish immigrant women and children (see chapter 5). Between 1881 and 1921 more than two million Jewish immigrants came to the United States, most often in family units.

By 1920, Jewish women of Eastern European heritage and their American-born children outnumbered Central European Jewish immigrants and their native American Jewish children by five to one. Concentrated in the large urban centers, hundreds of thousands of these female immigrants made a living in the garment industry and sweatshops, as reflected in the photographs and field reports of reformer Lewis Hines (see chapter 6). Among their daughters who took advantage of public schools and higher education, many became teachers and others be-came physicians, dentists, or lawyers. Other first-generation Jewish women became union leaders and political radicals. Five playscripts written by Socialist reformer, lecturer, and labor agitator Rose Pastor Stokes (1879–1933), who was on the staff of the New York *Yidishes tageblatt* (Jewish daily news) (1888–1929, title varies; microfilm, Hebr) are in the Manuscript Division as well as a collection of sixteen items from social worker Pauline Goldmark (1874–1962), who was an executive of the New York office of the National Consumers' League. Rose Schneiderman (1882–1972), Jewish labor organizer, socialist, and suffragist, became president of the National Women's Trade Union League of America from 1927 to 1947 and went on to serve in government positions for the cause of labor. Emma Goldman (1869–1940), the outstanding woman radical in the Jewish community who spoke out against social injustice for half a century, helped edit an anarchist journal. She is the best-known Jewish woman represented in the Anarchism Collection and in the anarchism materials in the Paul Avrich Collection (RBSC). Deported to Russia with others during the 1919 Red Scare in America, she fled the Soviet regime and lived in exile in Canada. Upon her death, however, the United States government allowed her to be buried in Chicago, close to the graves of the men executed in 1886 for the Haymarket killings (see chapter 4).[4] Political activist Mollie Steimer (1897–1980) is represented in the Paul Avrich Collection as well. The stage and screen also attracted Jewish women to the spotlight, first as stars of the Yiddish theater and film and then on the national scene.

Still, marriage was all-important to most American Jewish women, and careers outside the home for middle-class women were not the norm. The lives of Jewish homemakers were filled with child rearing, local female mutual aid societies, and involvement in religious life, primarily through synagogue auxiliaries and national Jewish women's groups like Hadassah, a Zionist organization, or the National Council of Jewish Women.

American Jewish women began to find new voices at the same time that Americans responded to Betty Friedan's *The Feminine Mystique,* which appeared in 1963. Some participated in campus upheavals, civil rights marches, and protests against the war in Vietnam. The women's liberation movement also appealed to many American Jewish women. They entered the Reform and Conservative rabbinate and sought parity with men in religious life, while Orthodox women began to learn traditional texts generally reserved for men. Today Jewish women are academic scholars, politicians, Nobel Prize–winners, and astronauts. The Manuscript Division, for example (see chapter 5), holds the papers of political philosopher, writer, and lecturer Hannah Arendt (1906–1975), who wrote widely on Jewish affairs and totalitarianism and on the Jewish response to the Holocaust, and of current Supreme Court Justice Ruth Bader Ginsburg (b. 1933). The Manuscript Division also has in its custody the original transcripts of interviews carried out in the last years of the Depression, which included interviews with Jewish women. Some of these can be read on the Library's American Memory Web site under the title *American Life Histories: Manuscripts from the Federal Writers' Project, 1936–1940.*

Currently, the Jewish population of the United States numbers close to six million individuals. Jewish women in this cohort continue to adapt to change and challenge even as they seek new ways to maintain their Jewish identities. Sources on these women are abundant throughout the Library of Congress and may be found as part of collections discussed in this and other chapters, through catalog searches by individual name or organization, and through the use of selected reference tools that yield relevant information. In all cases, the immensity and range of the Library's resources can be used, as perhaps nowhere else, to synthesize an understanding of American Jewish women within the broader society.

Search Strategies

The following section contains strategies for use of the catalogs, provides a brief list of reference sources and tools, and suggests types of materials found in selected reading rooms that will yield information on the history and lifestyles of American Jewish women. Similar sources exist in the Library of Congress for research about women of other groups.

There is no single catalog that lists all of the Hebrew-language material in the Library of Congress. Most titles, including all of those cataloged since 1981, are represented in the Library's online catalog as transliterations, and the lack of vernacular script can make it difficult to locate authors and titles because of spelling changes. Researchers can check Hebrew, Yiddish, and Ladino (the spoken and written language of Jews of Spanish origin) script titles and also romanized authors' names and subject headings (current only to 1981) in the card catalogs in the African and Middle Eastern Division Reading Room to determine if the Library holds an item. These card catalogs also contain entries, by short title only, for items that remain uncataloged and do not appear in the online database.

Records for all Judaica subject books in non-Hebrew script are in the Library's online catalog, and these materials are part of the General Collections, except for classes K (Law) and M (Music). Judaica materials in distinctive formats such as Yiddish film or Ladino sound recordings can be accessed in the Library's special-format reading rooms. Not all of these items appear in the online catalog, but they can be located through the use of local files in those reading rooms.

The varying levels of bibliographic access and the array of catalogs that represent the Hebraic and Judaic holdings of the Library of Congress often make it difficult to grasp the Library's complete holdings on a particular subject. It is important to consult with an area specialist or a reference librarian in the Hebraic Section for assistance.

A good place to begin research is with two biographical titles, based on earlier biographical sources, that provide sweeping and comprehensive information on individual American Jews.

The Concise Dictionary of American Jewish Biography, edited by Jacob Rader Marcus, in two volumes (Brooklyn, N.Y.: Carlson Publishing, 1994; E184.J5 C653 1994, Hebr Ref), alphabetically lists twenty-four thousand brief biographies of American Jews, including those of more than two thousand women. Each entry lists the sources used in researching it. Readers should check this reference work first to determine which earlier general and special American Jewish biographical works and Jewish encyclopedias to search.

Jewish Women in America: An Historical Encyclopedia, edited by Paula Hyman and Deborah Dash Moore, also two volumes (New York: Routledge, 1998; DS115.2.J49 1997, MRR Biog, Hebr Ref), is an award-winning reference work, indispensable to anyone interested in the history of American Jewish women. It contains eight hundred individual biographies and one hundred topical essays integrated into one alphabetical sequence. Complete bibliographic citations are provided for all entries. Essay topics range from assessments of immigration and assimilation in specific time periods to histories of individual women's organizations to surveys of the role of women in Jewish and American culture. "A Classified List of Biographical Entries" at the end of volume 2 provides an index to Jewish women's participation in specific fields of endeavor such as art, education, and politics. The second volume also includes a broad bibliographic essay, "An Annotated Bibliographic Guide to Archival Resources on the History of Jewish Women in America." An online version is available through the Women's Studies Library at the University of Wisconsin. The annotated bibliography cites other useful bibliographies, including Ann Masnik's *The Jewish Woman: An Annotated Selected Bibliography, 1986–1993: With 1994–1995 Recent Titles List* (New York: Biblio Press, 1996; Z7963.J4 C36 1987 Suppl.; MRR Alc).

BIBLIOGRAPHY:

Antler, Joyce. *The Journey Home: Jewish Women and the American Century.* New York: Free Press, 1997. E184.36.W64 A57 1997 GenColl.

Baum, Charlotte, Paula Hyman, and Sonya Michel. *The Jewish Woman in America.* New York: Dial Press, 1976. E184.J5 B37 1976 GenColl, Hebr Ref.

Glanz, Rudolph. *The Jewish Woman in America: Two Female Immigrant Generations, 1820–1929.* 2 vols. New York: Ktav, 1976; E184.J5 G493 1976 GenColl.

Hyman, Paula. *Gender and Assimilation in Modern Jewish History: The Roles and Representation of Women.* Seattle: University of Washington, 1995. DS148.H93 1995 GenColl.

Kohn, Gary J., comp. *The Jewish Experience: A Guide to Manuscript Sources in the Library of Congress.* Cincinnati, Ohio: American Jewish Archives, 1986. Z6373.U5 K64 1986 MSS, Hebr Ref.

Marcus, Jacob R. *American Jewish Woman, 1654–1980* and *The American Jewish Woman: A Documentary History.* New York: Ktav, and Cincinnati: American Jewish Archives, 1981. HQ1172.M37 (and Suppl) GenColl, MRR Alc, Hebr Ref.

SAMPLE LCSH: Jewish women—United States; Jewish women—Bibliography.

Selected Sources

This section will cover several groups of material—newspapers and periodicals, community publications, and cookbooks that include Yiddish and English sources. A fourth category focuses on Yiddish material.

Newspapers and Periodicals

The Jewish press in the United States has appeared primarily in English and Yiddish but has also sustained publications in Hebrew, German, Ladino, and Russian. No single catalog or list represents the Library's holdings of the Jewish press. Readers must consult both the online catalogs and the Hebraic section catalogs located in the African and Middle Eastern Reading Room. In addition, readers should consult with the appropriate area specialist and reference librarians in order to definitively ascertain the status of specific titles (see chapter 2 for more information about newspapers and how to locate them).

The major nineteenth-century American Jewish newspaper was the *Israelite* (later known as *American Israelite*) founded by Reform rabbi Isaac M. Wise (1854–; AP92.A55 fol GenColl, LC has 1854–1945 and current issues in hard copy, incomplete; News MF 3131, N&CPR). Characteristic of the Anglo-Jewish press, it offered local, national, and international news, editorials, feature articles, and general serialized fiction. Ellen Price Wood's *Lady Adelaide's Oath* (1877) and Amelia Edward's *Debenham's Vow* (1879) were two fictional works presented in serialized form. In the twentieth century, Jewish communal weeklies such as the Philadelphia *Jewish Exponent* (1887–; AP92.J5 fol GenColl; LC has 1917–44 and current issues in hard copy, incomplete; microfilm [o] 94/4593 MicRR) added more local news. Their reports on synagogues, their auxiliary sisterhoods and religious schools, and their coverage of benevolent organizations and local chapters of national Jewish women's groups have provided an important source for the study of women and culture. *Deborah* (1855–1903, title varies; AP93.D5 fol GenColl; LC has 1876–1900 in hard copy; News MF 3131, N&CPR), the German-language weekly (and then monthly) supplement to the *Israelite,* was the most notable publication created to serve the German-Jewish immigrants who arrived in the United States in increasing numbers in the mid-nineteenth century. Its focus was on a female readership interested in the home, school, and community.

Yiddish-language newspapers have been the largest and most influential arm of the Jewish press. The golden age of Yiddish journalism peaked in 1915–16 when five dailies in New York City alone boasted a circulation of 500,000 readers—many of whom were women. The Hebraic Section holds microform of the major American Yiddish newspapers that expressed the new immigrants' idealistic yearnings even as they moved headlong into full citizenship. In addition to national and international news, the papers devoted considerable space to labor issues—especially strikes in the garment industry, which employed a

Front cover. Der Idisher froyen zshurnal *(The Jewish woman's home journal), August 1922. (New York, N.Y.; HQ1172.I35 Hebr). Hebraic Section, African and Middle Eastern Division.*

An editorial in the April 1922 inaugural issue of the monthly illustrated magazine *Der Idisher froyen zshurnal* stated that the journal's focus would be on the "Americanization of the immigrant as well as the Americanization of the parent." Through the journal's retention of the Yiddish language to interpret modern culture, the editors hoped to acquaint young Eastern European Jewish women and their mothers with their newly adopted land and with the spirit of its institutions. Articles on child-rearing and home decor and an advice column on love, courtship, and marriage were bracketed by full-page advertisements for consumer goods that, in the words of historian Jenna Weissman Joselit, "whetted the immigrant's appetite as much as they shaped it."

great number of women—and to efforts to improve the conditions of all workers. From 1923 to 1927, during a period of rivalry with communists, the anarchist group within the International Ladies' Garment Workers' Union and the Amalgamated Clothing Workers of America published the Yiddish-language newspaper *Der Yunyon arbayter* (The union worker) (1925–27, HD6515.C6 Y86, RBSC). *Di Fraye arbeter shtime* (The free voice of labor) (1890–1977, HX821.F65 Avrich Coll RBSC; microfilm, Hebr), the Yiddish-language anarchist monthly, provided a forum for female writers and poets. Archival materials about it, as well as the records of the anarchist farm colonies in New Jersey, comprising mostly Jews, a number of them women, can be found in the Rare Book and Special Collections Division.

Among the New York Yiddish dailies, the foremost newspaper that supported both social activism and Americanization was the *Forverts* (Jewish daily forward) (1897–; AMED retains current issues in hard copy; microfilm, Hebr), published for more than a century in New York City. The most widely read feature, the "Bintel Brief" (Bundle of letters), was a daily personal advice column that began in 1906 to give immigrants the opportunity to pour out their hearts about their problems with husbands, wives, in-laws, children, poverty, and work, responding with advice. One newly wed American-born woman wrote to ask if she should leave her Russian-born husband because her friends scoffed at his being a "greenhorn" and she was beginning to think like them. The editor assured her that her bridegroom would learn American history and literature as well as her friends and be a better American than they.[5] Today, Yiddish readers in New York, many of them survivors of the Holocaust and observant Orthodox, can subscribe to *Di Tsaytung* (1988–; LC retains current issues in hard copy; microfilm, Hebr) and *Der Algemeyner zshurnal* [*Algemeiner Journal*] (1972–; LC retains current issues in hard copy; microfilm, Hebr).

Owing to a fresh readership, the small Hebrew press in the United States, most notable for *ha-Do'ar* (1922–; DS101.D6 Hebr), a weekly that first appeared in 1922, has generated new publications in recent decades. The Hebrew-language New York newspaper *Yisrael Shelanu* (1979–; DS101 .Y48, LC retains current issues in hard copy; microfilm, Hebr) is geared to the 200,000 Israelis who now live in this country. Its "Ezrat Nashim" (the term for the women's gallery in the synagogue) section offers recipes, shopping tips, and biblical commentary. A newspaper that appeals mainly to traditional Jews, *Yated Ne'eman* (1989–; LC retains current issues in hard copy; microfilm, Hebr), began publication in Monsey, New York, in 1989. Among its features in the "Home and Family" section are "Mother to Mother" and "Letters to Bubby" (or letters to grandmother) columns.

Front cover. Eve, *November 1936 (Eve Publishing Corporation, New York; AP92. E8). General Collections.*

Eve, a short-lived journal for the American Jewish woman, submitted a questionnaire to men and women leaders in public opinion and politics about whether a woman would be president of the United States. The response, in the lead article in this issue, from the sixty-six men and twenty-one women who replied, was a resounding "Yes." Those polled in 1936 thought it could happen in the next generation. At the same time, publisher Paul Ward Brody's editorial celebrates the most important and prestigious woman's job—that "of the presiding hostess of an American home, the central point of civilization. Without her arts and skills and graces, civilization, we venture to assert, would collapse."

The first independent Jewish women's journal in the United States was the *American Jewess* (1895–99; AP92.A6 GenColl; microfilm 51565), an outgrowth of the activism generated by late nineteenth-century middle-class German-Jewish club women, particularly those associated with the newly founded National Council of Jewish Women. This organization created the *Jewish Woman* (1921–31; E184.J5 J65 GenColl), and regional sections of the group published their own monthly and annual publications. Organs of other Jewish women's groups in the Library's collections, although holdings for them are not complete, include those of Hadassah, Na'amat (formerly Pioneer Women), and Jewish Women International (formerly B'nai B'rith Women). Additional independent journals include *Der Idisher froyen zshurnal* (Jewish woman's home journal) (1922–23; HQ1172.I35 Hebr), *Di Idishe heym* [Di Yiddishe Heim] (The Jewish home) (1958–; BM198.I33 Hebr), *Lilith: The Independent Jewish Women's Magazine* (1976–; BM729.W6 L54 GenColl), and *Bridges: A Journal for Jewish Feminists and Our Friends* (1990–; WMLC 91/933 GenColl, N&CPR), a twice-yearly anthology that seeks to make connections among lesbian, gay, antiracist, and working class Jewish women's movements.

Various specialized published indexes provide some access to articles, book reviews, obituaries, and bibliographies in select Jewish journals. Online databases, available on-site in the Library's reading rooms, are a newer source for indexes. The Periodical Contents Index (PCI) provides the tables of contents for several dozen Jewish periodicals. The *Project Muse* database makes full-text available for many current journals, including *American Jewish History*.

BIBLIOGRAPHY:

Goren, Arthur. "The Jewish Press." In *The Ethnic Press in the United States*, edited by Sally M. Miller, 203–28. Westport, Conn.: Greenwood Press, 1987. PN4882.E84 1987, MRR Alc, EurRR, N&CPR.

This volume provides dates and titles for newspapers for many different groups.

Index to the American Jewish Year Book. Vols. 1–50. New York: American Jewish Committee, n.d. E184.J5 A6 Hebr Ref.

Index to the Publications of the American Jewish Historical Society. Vols. 1–20. Baltimore: American Jewish Historical Society, 1914. E184.J5 A5 Hebr Ref.

An Index to Publications of the American Jewish Historical Society. Vols. 21–50. Brooklyn, N.Y.: Carlson Publishing, 1994. E184.3.I56 1994, Hebr Ref.

Kaganoff, Nathan M. *Judaica Americana: An Annotated Bibliography of Publications from 1960–1990.* 2 vols. Brooklyn, N.Y.: Carlson Publishing, 1995. Z6373.U5 K34 1995, Hebr Ref, MRR Alc.

Koppel, Lenore Pfeffer, ed. *Index to Jewish Periodicals.* Cleveland Heights, Ohio, 1964–. Z6367.I5 MRR Alc., Hebr Ref.

Marcus, Jacob Rader, ed. *An Index to Scientific Articles on American Jewish History.* Cincinnati, Ohio: American Jewish Archives, and New York: Ktav, 1971. Z6372. M35 Hebr Ref.

Bibliography continued

Zafren, Herbert C., ed. *Jewish Newspapers and Periodicals on Microfilm: Available at the American Jewish Periodical Center.* Cincinnati: The Center, 1984. Z6367.H48 1984, Hebr Ref.

SAMPLE LCSH: Jewish women—Periodicals; Women in Judaism—Periodicals; Jews—Periodicals; Jews—Newspapers.

Community, Institutional, and Synagogue Publications

A variety of Jewish organizations, such as mutual aid societies, synagogues, educational institutions, and community organizations, have produced publications that can be used to document the activities of women. These publications, often with illustrations and lists of workers, are also helpful to genealogists working on family histories. Jewish women enthusiastically volunteered their services to organizations whose goals centered around home, community, and education.

Landsmanshaftn, Jewish beneficent societies that were formed by immigrants who came to the United States from the same village, town, or city of Eastern Europe, aided indigent, sick, and bereaved fellow Jews. Such a society would also support literary clubs, hold fund-raising galas, and issue annual and commemorative reports and journals. These publications contain information on women or women's activities and serve to illustrate ways in which women participated in both acculturation and maintenance of cultural ties. The Yiddish- and English-language *Byalistoker leben* (an added title page notes that it celebrates the "Fortieth Anniversary of the Bialystoker Bikur Cholim of Brooklyn") edited by Luis Palter ([Brooklyn]: Byalistoker biker hoylim fun Bruklin, 1937; F128.9.J5 B95 1937 Hebr), for example, contains a report and photographs on the ladies' auxiliary of this organization to aid the sick. *Poylish Idn/Poilisher Yid* (Polish Jews), an annual edited by Z. Tygel (1870–1947) and later Abraham Goldberg (1933–42; New York: American Federation of Polish Jews; title varies, E184.J5 P6 Hebr), contains brief reports about Ezra, the network of women's auxiliaries of the Federation of Polish Jews in America.

Synagogue histories are a helpful source for information on women's activities in an organization's sisterhood, its religious school, and the eventual governance of the institution itself. There are more than 1,200 monographs, pamphlets, and articles that give histories of synagogues and Jewish communities in the United States, of which at least 300 are in the Library's collections. New histories continually appear, and women are increasingly credited as authors. Gerry Cristol's *A Light in the Prairie: Temple Emanu-El of Dallas, 1872–1997* (Fort Worth: Texas Christian University, 1998; BM225.D35 E49 1998 GenColl) is representative. The Ladies Hebrew Benevolent Association of newly formed Dallas Temple Emanu-El sprang up in 1875 to ensure regular services and a religious education for children. The proceeds from a series of fund-raisers and "entertainments" permitted women to purchase a lot to build a future synagogue building.

A community history such as Carolyn Gray LeMaster's *A Corner of the Tapestry: A History of the Jewish Experience in Arkansas, 1820s–1990s* (Fayetteville: University of Arkansas Press, 1994; F420.J5 L46 1994 GenColl) presents a broad sweep of the Jewish life of the entire state, including even the smallest towns. "The distaff side" is a section discussing organizational activity and giving brief personal biographies of women. From North Little Rock, we learn, for example, about Gertrude Green (1884–1970), who served with the Volunteer Services of the American Red Cross in France during World War I and became a national representative of the Women's Overseas Service League, traveling nationwide on the organization's behalf.

BIBLIOGRAPHY:

Kliger, Hannah, ed. *Jewish Hometown Associations and Family Circles in New York: The WPA Yiddish Writers' Group Study.* Bloomington: Indiana University Press, 1992. F128.9.J5 J574 1992 GenColl.

Korros, Alexandra Shecket, and Jonathan D. Sarna. *American Synagogue History: A Bibliography and State-of-the Field Survey.* New York: Markus Wiener Publishing, 1988. Z6373.U5 K67 1988 LH&G, GenColl.

SAMPLE LCSH: Jews—[name of state]**—Societies, etc.; Immigrants—**[name of state]**—Societies, etc.; Jews—**[name of state]—[name of town]**—History; Synagogues—United States.**

Cookbooks

Jewish cookery offers readers a variety of ways to study Jewish traditions and home life, especially as they are shaped by women through their culinary efforts. Cooking was women's domain in a Jewish household and most cookbooks were intended for women and written by them. The Library's collection of several hundred Jewish cookbooks includes the first one known to have been published in the United States, Mrs. Esther Levy's *Jewish Cookery Book, on Principles of Economy, Adapted for Jewish Housekeepers, with the Addition of Many Useful Medicinal Recipes, and Other Valuable Information, Relative to Housekeeping and Domestic Management* (Garden Grove, Calif.: Pholiota Press, 1982, TX724.L4 GenColl; Philadelphia: W.S. Turner, 1871; RBSC). A Jewish calendar listing feasts and the special instructions for preparing for the Passover holiday document literacy among middle- and upper-middle-class Jewish women of that period to whom the cookbook was addressed and the attempt to impart to them a basic knowledge of Jewish customs. Hinde Amchanitzki's *Lehr-bukh vi azoy tsu kokhen un baken* (Textbook on how to cook and bake) (New York: S. Druckerman, 1901; TX724.A47 Hebr) is the first Yiddish cookbook published in this country. Like most, but not all, other Jewish cookbooks, both of these books contain recipes that are *kosher,* a Hebrew word meaning ritually proper or fit to be used. Jewish cookbooks usually contain sections that specify what foods can be used in cooking and instructions on setting up and keeping a kosher kitchen. Food columns that appear in the Anglo-Jewish, Yiddish, and Hebrew press and in specialty periodicals discuss keeping kosher, provide recipes, and include advertisements that give a picture of Jewish foodways. An early example of this genre is the Organized Kashruth Company's *Kosher Food Guide* (New York, n.d.; BM710.K67 GenColl). Its stated purpose was to be a "guide to the observant Jewish woman desiring to uphold the traditional dietary laws." Some 48,000 Jewish homes received its inaugural issue in 1935.

A generation later, food-writer Joan Nathan expanded her award-winning book *Jewish Cooking in America* (New York: Alfred A. Knopf, 1998; TX724.N368 1998 GenColl) into twenty-six half-hour programs by the same name televised by Public Broadcasting Service stations (uncataloged, MBRS). Nathan's book and television series, both replete with interviews, early photographs, and advertisements, document the authentic culinary and cultural practices of Jews past and present in which women have played such a prominent role.

BIBLIOGRAPHY:

Abusch-Magder, Ruth. "Cookbooks." In *Jewish Women in America: An Historical Encyclopedia,* ed. Hyman and Moore, 1:281–87. 1997.

Nathan, Joan. "Food." In ibid. 1:460–64.

(See also cookbooks in chapters 1 and 4).

SAMPLE LCSH: Cookery, Jewish; Jews—Dietary laws; Jews—United States—Social life and customs.

Yiddish Materials Documenting Artistic Expression

In tandem with the large influx of Eastern European immigrants to the United States at the end of the nineteenth century, Yiddish theater in America blossomed and flourished. The audi-

Chantshe in Amerika. *From the operetta* Chantshe in Amerika. *Music by Joseph M. Rumshisky, lyrics by Isidore Lillian. (New York, N.Y.: Hebrew Publishing Company, 1913; copr. no. E305266, March 4/8, 1913, MUS, Hebr). Music Division and Hebraic Section, African and Middle Eastern Division.*

Yiddish actress Bessie Thomashefsky (1873–1962) appears in men's clothing on this sheet music cover from the operetta *Chantshe in Amerika* (1913). The musical concerns an immigrant girl Chantshe/Khantshe, who takes on a male identity so she can drive an automobile. The lyrics, "What a lady is Chantshe. They laughed at her, but now she is admired. She's a suffragette, and is for women's rights and independence," expressed many women's continuing desires for enfranchisement and equality and fueled their efforts in that direction.

ences that packed the theaters—the majority of whom were women—mainly on New York City's Lower East Side, thrilled to the operettas, melodramas, comedies, and musicals written, produced, and emotionally portrayed by their fellow Yiddish-speaking immigrants.

The Hebraic Section has custody of about 1,200 Yiddish American play manuscripts that were deposited for copyright at the Library in the first half of the twentieth century. Among more than two dozen women playwrights represented is Sara Adler (1858–1953), whose husband Jacob Adler was the foremost actor of the Yiddish stage at the beginning of the twentieth century. Lucy Lang (1884–1962) and sisters Rose Shomer Bachelis (1882–1966) and Miriam Shomer Zunser (1882–1951) are also represented. Many of the plays they (and some of the men) wrote concern love, marriage, divorce, family life, and the struggles to balance the options of becoming an assimilated American versus retaining one's tradition. The inquiring and persistent researcher of the history of women's health issues in this country will be rewarded upon finding that two of these Yiddish plays, Harry Kalmanowitz's "Geburth Kontrol, oder, Rassen zelbstmord (Birth Control or Race Sucide [*sic*])" and Chicagoan S. Grossman's "Di Flikhten fun a froy in geburt kontrol) (A woman's duty in birth control)" were written in 1916, the year that Margaret Sanger opened the first birth control clinic, which was located on the Lower East Side of New York City (see chapter 5). Seventy-seven of these Yiddish plays can be found on the Library's American Memory Web site; two of the plays were written by women. In 1913, Dr. Ida Badenes-Rovinsky, a physician, journalist, and playwright, wrote the comedy-drama "Dem Doktors refue: a drama in 4 akten (The doctor's remedy)." In 1919, Lizzie Schreiman completed the drama "Di Mekhutonim fin gan heydn *[!]* (Relatives of the Garden of Eden)."

First active in Yiddish vaudeville and theater,

many American Jewish women went on to appear in motion pictures and on television or behind the scenes in both these media. The vast scope of the Library's film collections enables the researcher to examine the phenomenon of female Jewish cinema and television stars in the industry, their experiences as Jews, and the ways in which Jewish women have been portrayed and by whom. One subset of the Library's collection in the Motion Picture, Broadcasting, and Recorded Sound Division (MBRS) consists of more than a dozen Yiddish films, including for example, *Vu iz mayn kind* (Where is my child) (FPC 0292–0299 MBRS), starring Celia Adler, Anna Lillien, and Blanche Bernstein, in 1937. *A brivele der mamen* (A letter to mother) (VAF 1760 M/B/RS) is a video reproduction of an early Yiddish film set in Polish Ukraine and New York City that traces the breakup of a family owing to the stresses of the First World War, poverty, and the immense challenges of immigrant life. A combination of comedy and drama, the work focuses on the efforts of one Jewish mother to keep her family together.

Also deposited for copyright at the Library of Congress in the first half of the twentieth century were some 3,400 Yiddish song sheets. Housed in the Music Division, some of these are kept in duplicate copies in the Hebraic Section as well. More than eighty-five women have been credited as publishers, composers, arrangers, and lyricists of these songs. They include Mary Adler, Friede Belov (Weber), Celia Boodkin (Drobkin), Nellie Casman, Pauline Fellman, Ida Gittleman, Jennie Goldstein, Aliza Greenblatt, Molly Picon, and Esther Zweig. Many of the songs are about the home, love, marriage, children, and work. "Di fayer korbunes" (The fire victims) (Copr. no. E265489; Aug. 24/28, 1911 MUS) expresses the

Lynne Avadenka. An Only Kid *(Huntington Woods, Mich.: Land Marks Press, 1990; BM 670.H28 A9 1990 Hebr Cage). Copy 41 of a limited letterpress edition of 75. Hebraic Section, African and Middle Eastern Division. Courtesy of Lynne Avadenka.*

An artist, a printmaker, and a calligrapher, Lynne Avadenka created this version of "Had Gadya," the last and one of the most beloved songs in the Haggadah, the book read on the holiday of Passover in the context of family gatherings and festive meals. "Had gadya" ("an only kid") are the first two words of the song. Allegorically, the song describes successive nations that seek, one after another, to devour and destroy the Jewish people. Finally, God ends the escalating violent cycle, bringing peace. Avadenka suggests in her commentary that "Had Gadya" might also be a song of personal redemption, where one rises beyond fear and doubt to create a life for oneself, guided by deeds of loving kindness. The cover paper of this work is made of cotton rag and goat hair.

anguish felt by the Jewish community after the deaths of 146 young women, most of whom were Jewish, in the fire at the non-union Triangle Shirtwaist Company on New York City's Lower East Side on March 25, 1911. The sheet music cover shows a building in flames, with women at the windows or jumping to the ground. In examples such as this, the iconography of the Yiddish sheet music offers a special visual dimension to the understanding of the history of American Jewish women.

The Ruth Rubin collection, held in the Archive of Folk Song in the American Folklife Center, consists of field recordings of Jewish folklore made by the New York folklorist from the 1940s to the 1960s. Ruth Rubin interviewed female as well as male performers in the United States, Canada, Britain, and Israel. Yiddish art songs that reflected immigrant life and songs created by Soviet Jews in the 1920s and the 1930s form part of the collection. A concordance lists the 126 tapes.

Jewish female performers ably crossed over from the stage to the media of recorded sound and broadcasting beginning in the second decade of the twentieth century. The Library holds, for example, several test pressings of "Eili, Eili" (NC26B 00413, NCPB 00302, NCPB 00224), a Yiddish ballad originally written in 1896 for Sophie Karp, star of Yiddish revues and Bowery theaters on the Lower East Side of New York City, and made more popular by Yiddish actress Bertha Kalisch. When Cantor Yosele Rosenblatt began to include it in his concerts and recordings, the hymn then became synonymous with male singers.

Researchers can also locate in the Recorded Sound Reference Center Yiddish actress Stella Adler's 1944 appeal to voters on NBC radio (Adler, who energized the study of acting in America, lived from 1901 to 1992), as well as NBC radio shows of actresses Gertrude Berg (1899–1966) (of *Mollie Goldberg* fame) and Fanny Brice (1891–1951) (in *Baby Snooks*). Brice also appears on the *Mail Call* show of the Armed Forces Radio and Television Service transcription disc collection.

Most of the nearly fourteen hundred commercial phonograph discs in the Benedict Stambler Archive of Recorded Jewish Music in the Recorded Sound Reference Center are recordings of well-known American and European cantors of the first four decades of the twentieth century. A sampling of performances by Yiddish comedians, singers, and popular musicians is available in the archive as well. Among these are recordings by diva and folksinger Isa Kremer (1887–1956) and by singer Miriam Kressyn (1911–1996), who was also a songwriter, translator, radio announcer, news analyst, and teacher.

BIBLIOGRAPHY:

Baker, Zachary, comp. "The Lawrence Marwick Collection of Copyrighted Yiddish Plays at the Library of Congress." Unpublished. Hebr

Erens, Patricia. *The Jew in American Cinema.* Bloomington: Indiana University Press, 1984. PN1995.9.J46 E7 Hebr Ref, GenColl.

Goldberg, Judith N. *Laughter through Tears: The Yiddish Cinema.* Rutherford, N.J.: Farleigh Dickinson University, 1983 PN1995. 9.Y54 G6 1983 Hebr Ref, GenColl.

Heskes, Irene, comp. *Yiddish American Popular Songs, 1895 to 1950: A Catalog Based on the Lawrence Marwick Roster of Copyright Entries.* Washington: Library of Congress, 1992. ML128.J4 H49 1992, Hebr Ref, MUS, MRR Alc, AFC, PARR.

Lyman, Darryl. *Great Jews in Music.* Middle Village, N.Y.: J. David Publishers, 1986. ML385.L95 1986 Hebr Ref, PARR.

Rubin, Ruth. *Voices of a People: Yiddish Folk Song.* New York: T. Yoseloff [1964]. ML3776.R77 1964 Hebr Ref, PARR.

Sandrow, Nahma. *Vagabond Stars: A World History of Yiddish Theater.* Syracuse: Syracuse University Press, 1977. PN3035.S25 Hebr Ref.

SAMPLE LCSH: Jews—United States—Music; Songs, Yiddish—United States; Theater, Yiddish—United States; Jewish theater—United States; Yiddish drama; Motion pictures—Yiddish; Jews in motion pictures; Jews—Folk songs, Yiddish; Songs, Yiddish; Klezmer music.

Since their first arrival in this country more than three hundred and fifty years ago, Jewish women have given voice to their words and actions. In every area of life, from the literary to the artistic to the political, they have at times both acculturated to the society around them and actively maintained their cultural heritage. The next section of this chapter describes some of the varied collections, again scattered throughout the Library of Congress, that reflect the experience of Latinas as they have moved through the social, political, and economic realms of the United States and made their imprint on its climate and culture beginning with their arrival a century earlier than Jewish women. These back-to-back case studies demonstrate the Library's different collection strengths and the variety of special materials for both groups of women. Research on women from other backgrounds can benefit by applying all of the methods described in both case studies.

LATINAS

Although many believe that Latinas, women of Latin American heritage in the United States, only recently arrived, thousands trace their ancestry in territories that became part of the United States back to the sixteenth, seventeenth, and

Bill Hughes. "'La Tules' [Gertrudis Barceló] Dealing Monte in Her Santa Fe Gambling House." Illustration for Walter Briggs et al., "Venal or Virtuous? The Lady They Called La Tules," New Mexico Magazine *49:3 (March/April 1971; F791.N3), 8–9. General Collections.*

An evening of cards at the gambling salon of María Gertrudis Barceló, known as "La Tules," the richest woman in Santa Fe during the 1840s, is imagined by this artist. La Tules is shown, as in Susan Shelby Magoffin's description, as "a stately dame of a certain age, the possessor of . . . that shrewd sense and fascinating manner necessary to allure the wayward, inexperienced youth to the hall of final ruin" (*Down the Santa Fe Trail and into Mexico: The Diary of Susan Shelby Magoffin, 1846–1847*). In reality, Gertrudis Barceló was born in Sonora, Mexico, learned to read and write, and married into an old New Mexico family in 1823 when four or five months pregnant. When she died in 1852, she willed three houses to family members as well as livestock and cash. She also gave money to the church and to city officials for charitable use.

eighteenth centuries, well before the great waves of European and Asian immigrants. Indeed, the first Latinas were born in Saint Augustine, Florida, after its settlement by Spaniards in 1565. When missionaries founded the Nombre de Dios Mission there in 1566, female members of the Timucua-speaking Indian nobility like Chief Doña María were converted to Christianity and married Spanish soldiers, in her case Clemente Bernal. On April 2, 1606, the mission held a service of confirmation for 200 Indians, 200 Spaniards, and Doña María and her children in the church in Saint Augustine.

Since then, the extent of Latina settlement in the United States has broadened considerably. From 1598 to 1810, Spanish explorers, missionaries, and settlers built communities in present-day Texas, Louisiana, New Mexico, Colorado, Arizona, and California and explored all the way up to Alaska. These areas became part of the Provincias Internas, the northern frontier of the Viceroyalty of New Spain. For example, Spanish-born María Feliciana Arballo and her *mestizo* husband were scheduled to make the trek from Tubac in present-day Arizona to Southern California with Juan Bautista de Anza in 1775. When her husband died before the trip began, Arballo won the right to travel with her two daughters. She eventually left the Anza party in San Gabriel, California, where she married a soldier. (For more on Arballo, see the essay "Women on the Move" in this volume.)

It is difficult to find direct evidence of women from the sources for this period, even in a culture whose members retain their mother's lineage as a second last name. Nevertheless, historians know that countless women among the descendants of the original settlers, the Indians who lived with them, and others who had joined them were indispensable in the establishment and maintenance of their communities. Women labored under often difficult circumstances, particularly when other colonizing powers or indigenous peoples like the Comanches and the Apaches attacked their homes. Some evidence of the influence of Latinas during these times can be gleaned from such manuscript and microfilm collections in the Manuscript Division of the Library of Congress as the Spanish Archives of New Mexico (1621–1821), the Santa Barbara Mission Collection (1768–1844), and the East Florida Papers (1737–1858). In 1820, the United States absorbed Spanish Florida; the following year, when Mexico gained its independence from Spain, the communities of the Provincias Internas chose to stay with Mexico rather than become independent themselves.

These communities continued to develop during the years between Mexican independence in 1821 and the Mexican-American War in 1846–48. As soon as Mexico became independent from Spain, settlers from the United States (Anglos) emigrated to Texas, still part of Mexico, to settle on large tracts of rich land the government offered at bargain prices to populate the territory. The most famous woman of the period, María Gertrudis Barceló (known as "La Tules"), started her first gambling casino in the Ortiz Mountains of New Mexico in 1825. In 1836 the Anglos living in Texas defeated the Mexican army and proclaimed themselves independent. Meanwhile, La Tules opened a casino in Santa Fe under the protection of Governor Manuel Armijo, catering to Anglo traders on the Santa Fe Trail and local residents alike. Over time she became a folkloric heroine and was mentioned in Federal Writers' Project interviews (see chapter 5) nearly a century later. In 1845 the Lone Star Republic, as the Anglos in Texas called their state, decided to join the United States, setting the stage for the Mexican-American War, which broke out the following year. When the fighting began, the other areas of the Provincias Internas became fair game, so that following the victory of the United States in 1848, the northern nation had conquered not just Texas, but California, Arizona, New Mexico, and parts of Colorado, Utah, and Oklahoma.

U.S. control soon led to alterations in legal systems, official language, education, and a constellation of social and economic mores. James McHall Jones, delegate to the California Constitutional Convention of 1849 and later judge of Southern California, confided to his mother in the first of his *Two Letters . . . .*, dated August 26, 1849 (San Francisco: Grabhorn Press, 1948, p. 8; F865.J75 Rare Book), that his knowledge of Spanish in the now-Anglo territory would give him a real advantage when "There will be titles annulled, judgments reversed, property seized (and) I'll have a whole fist in the pie." Women who lived under Spanish and then Mexican sovereignty owned property in their own name even after marriage, held a 50 percent stake in whatever the spouses managed to accumulate during their life together, and had the right to make wills, a privilege that had only begun to be granted during the 1840s in the rest of the United States (see chapter 3). Although law codes in the new territories appeared to reflect Spanish practice, historians must look at other evidence to see what happened when justice was administered in English to people who knew only Spanish. These new Latinas suffered in other ways as well. In the 1850s, the pregnant Josefa Segovia became the first woman hanged in California for having killed an Anglo who had assaulted her. In 1862 Chipita

Dorothea Lange. "Mexicans at the U.S. immigration station." El Paso, Texas, June 1938. Photograph. Farm Security Administration Collection. Prints and Photographs Division. LC-USF34-018215-E.

This photograph taken by Dorothea Lange at the El Paso, Texas, Immigration Station in June 1938 reveals a world of emotions. The woman with the white hat and pearls, decked out in her Sunday best, seems much more eager to go north than does the older señora in the middle wearing a house dress and a wary expression, perhaps fearful of the camera's gaze and of her future. As historian Vicki Ruiz notes in *From Out of the Shadows: Mexican Women in Twentieth-Century America,* El Paso was the Ellis Island for Mexican immigration. The community there grew from 8,748 in 1900 to almost 70,000 by 1930.

Rodríguez, convicted for murdering an Anglo horse trader, became the only woman hanged in the state of Texas, despite the lack of any direct evidence linking her to the crime. Some Latinas spoke up about the two-fold discrimination they suffered as women and as people of Latin American descent. María Amparo Ruiz de Burton (1832–1895) published anonymously (although a Library of Congress cataloger penciled in her name on the catalog card) the first novel written and published in English by a Latina. Her book *Who Would Have Thought It?* (Philadelphia: J.B. Lippincott & Co., 1872; PZ3.B9545 W GenColl) offered a bitter critique of U.S. racism while supporting women's suffrage.

Latinas played an important role in fostering the Cuban and Puerto Rican independence movements. In New York, Emilia Casanova de Villaverde (1832–1897) established the Liga de Hijas de Cuba (League of Daughters of Cuba) in the 1870s. Descriptions of the league's sessions can be found in the anonymously written *Apuntes biográficos de Emilia Casanova de Villaverde* (New York, 1874; F1785.C33 GenColl). After Cubans were defeated in their first war of independence against Spain (1868–78), more than one hundred thousand emigrated to the United States. According to the *Memoirs of Bernardo Vega* (New York: Monthly Review Press, 1984; F128.9.P85 V4313 1984 GenColl), before the next war, Cuban and Puerto Rican women founded additional clubs such as Mercedes de Verona at 235 East 75th Street in Manhattan and Hijas de la Libertad (Daughters of Liberty) at 1115 Herkimer Street in Brooklyn. In 1895 Cubans began their second war of liberation, which sparked the Spanish-American War. Following the U.S. victory in 1898, the island of Puerto Rico, first explored by the Spanish in 1503, became a commonwealth of the United States, and in 1917 Puerto Ricans became U.S. citizens. Cuba, too, became increasingly aligned with the U.S. economy and social customs during this period.

From 1910 to 1930, more than a million Mexicans came to the United States to escape from the Mexican Revolution, or to join neighbors and other family members who had already made the trek northward, and settled where plentiful and financially rewarding jobs in mines, railroads, and farms held the promise of a better life. Some of these women and their descendants were pictured in the 1930s and 1940s by the photographers of the Farm Security Administration whose work is found in the Prints and Photographs Division (see chapter 6), and others spoke to interviewers from the Federal Writers' Project whose texts are housed in the Manuscript Division (see chapter 5). At the same time, Puerto Rican and Cuban women worked long hours for extremely poor pay in the tobacco industry in Tampa and New York. Under the leadership of Luisa Capetillo (1879–1922) and others, women demanded that the males-only Unión de Tabaqueros (Union of Tobacco Workers) represent them as well. Capetillo once ran a boardinghouse on 22nd Street and Eighth Avenue in Manhattan, where she regaled her lodgers with revolutionary and anarchist speeches. Some of her collected writings appear in *Amor y anarquía: Los escritos de Luisa Capetillo,* edited by Julio Ramos (Río Piedras, Puerto Rico: Ediciones Huracán, 1992; HQ1523.C372 1992 GenColl Overflow).

By 1926 Latinas in Los Angeles had founded La Sociedad de Madres Mexicanas (the Society of

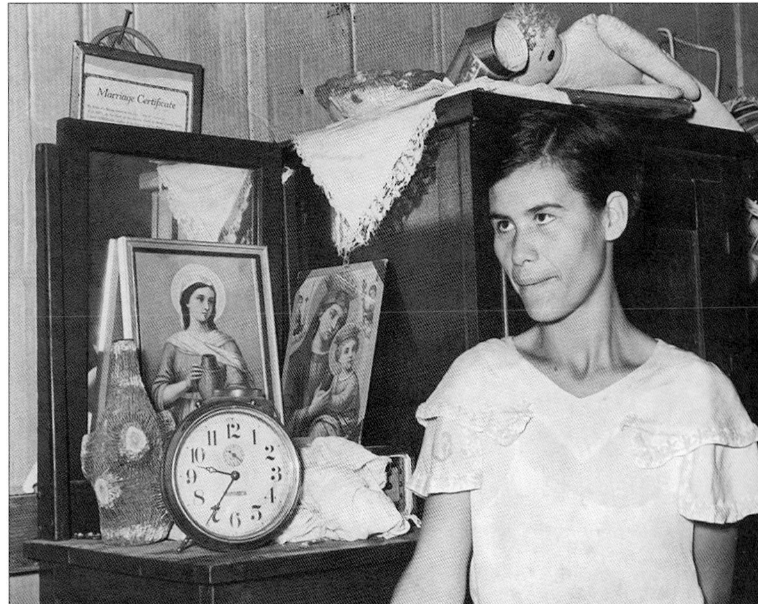

Russell Lee. "San Antonio, Texas, March 1939, Mexican woman standing in front of a bureau." Photograph. Farm Security Administration Collection. Prints and Photographs Division. LC-USF34-32467-D.

If the stages of acculturation could be depicted, this photograph of an anonymous Mexican woman in San Antonio, Texas, perhaps afraid to smile, taken standing in front of her dresser in March 1939, might be a graphic illustration of how that phenomenon works. The pride of place, even before a mirror, is given to holy pictures of the Virgin and Child and Saint Mary Magdalen with her jar, or urn, and a standard Hispanic-style candle. Yet standing cheek by jowl with these religious items is the large alarm clock telling the woman when her child or children (as signaled by the small wicker stroller and the large doll) had to be in school and she at work. Finally, the largest concession to her new life—her marriage certificate in English—is nailed to the wooden slabs of the wall.

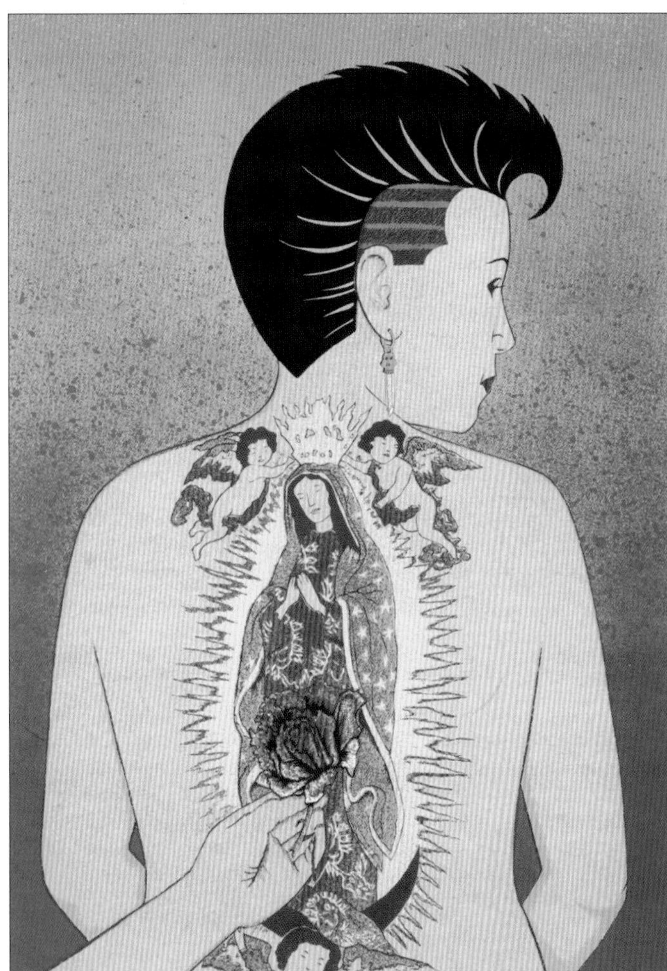

Ester Hernández. La Ofrenda II. *Screenprint, 1990. Fine Prints (unprocessed). Prints and Photographs Division. LC-USZC4-8201. Copyright © 1990. Courtesy of the artist.*

Since the 1960s, Mexican American women have been creating a new identity for themselves as "Chicanas," committed to pursuing full equality as both women and Latinas. In "La Ofrenda" (The offering), Ester Hernández updates the traditional sixteenth-century image of the apparition of the Virgin of Guadalupe, an iconic figure for both Mexicans and Mexican Americans. In her rendering, the Virgin reveals herself on the back of a thoroughly modern, high-tech Chicana of indigenous ancestry, illustrating symbolically how Latinas literally bear their cultural identities with them as they deal with the contemporary world.

Mexican Mothers), a civil rights group that raised money to pay for the defense of Latinos charged with crimes. In 1929 Alonso Perales organized what would become the League of United Latin American Citizens (LULAC) in South Texas, the first national Mexican American group to fight for civil rights. That same year, María and Pedro Hernández, also activists in the region, left the new group because it focused almost exclusively on improving men's lives and founded the Orden de Caballeros de América (Order of the Knights of America), the first to espouse a feminist perspective. Condemnations of LULAC's sexist stance written by Alice Dickerson Montemayor (always known to LULAC as Mrs. F. I. Montemayor) of Laredo, Texas, appear in the *LULAC News* in the 1930s.

On April 28–30, 1939, Luisa Moreno (1907–1992), whose long experience with labor struggles had given her contacts throughout the Latino community, founded El Congreso de Pueblos que Hablan Española (the Spanish-Speaking Peoples Congress), the first national organization of all Latinos.

Many immigrants who came to the United States throughout the twentieth century experienced great dislocation and loneliness. The Puerto Rican poet Julia de Burgos (1914–1953) wrote three volumes of poetic reflections on the inherent tension between an island upbringing and exile in the Nuyorican (New York) setting. Others, like the folklorist Pura Belpré (1899–1982), considered the first Puerto Rican librarian in the New York public library system, and Lillian López (b. 1925), also a pioneering librarian, founded many organizations dedicated to preserving the island's heritage for children growing up on the mainland. Their life in the New York of the 1930s and 1940s is vividly remembered in "Reminiscences of Two Turned-On Librarians" by López and Belpré in *Puerto Rican Perspectives*, edited by Edward Mapp (Metuchen, N.J.: Scarecrow Press, 1974; E184.P85 M36 GenColl). During the late 1940s and 1950s, Puerto Ricans relocated to the United States in much greater numbers. In 1961 teacher and activist Antonia Pantoja (b. 1922) created a new group, ASPIRA (Aspire), to assist Puerto Rican children to go on to higher education.

During the 1960s hundreds of thousands of Cubans emigrated to Puerto Rico and the U.S. mainland, settling mostly in Florida and the East Coast, to escape from the Cuban Revolution. That same decade witnessed the growth of the civil rights movement when many Mexican American women activists who wanted to emphasize their dual Indian and Spanish heritage began calling themselves Chicanas to demonstrate their commitment to the struggle for racial, ethnic, and gender equality. This identity is brilliantly represented in the screenprints of Ester Hernández (b. 1944), ten of which are held in the Prints and Photographs Division. Many members of that group still identify themselves as Chicanas, while others continue to prefer the term "Mexican American" or "Mexicana." Similarly, Puerto Rican women committed to similar causes used the term "Boricua," derived from the Native American name for the island. Women of Hispanic heritage in New Mexico use the term "Hispana," whereas those in Texas describe themselves as "Tejanas."

According to the 1999 U.S. Census, by the last decade of the twentieth century some 180,000 Mexicans were arriving in the United States each year, forming the largest single group of immigrants. Mexican American women were the most significant Latina population in the country by far, numbering, according to census estimates, 10,058,000, making up 7.24 percent of the total number of women in the United States. According to the census, living in the United States at that time were 712,000 Cuban American women, or 0.51 percent of all women counted, and 1,602,000 Puerto Rican women, or 1.3 percent of all U.S. women. The three-volume *Gale Encyclopedia of Multicultural America,* edited by Robert von Dassanowsky and Jeffrey Lehman, 2nd ed. (Gale Group: Detroit, Michigan, 2000; E184 .A1 G14 2000), further subdivides Latinas into groups ranging from Argentine Americans to Salvadoran Americans, and it includes both Portuguese and Spanish Americans from the Iberian peninsula.[6]

BIBLIOGRAPHY:

Clayton, Lawrence A., ed. *The Hispanic Experience in North America: Sources for Study in the United States.* Columbus: Ohio State University Press, 1992. E184.S7 H57 1992 HISP Ref.

Kanellos, Nicolás, and Claudio Esteva-Fabregat. *Handbook of Hispanic Cultures in the United States.* 4 vols. Houston: Arte Público Press; 1994. E184.S75 H365, 1993 HISP Ref, MRR Alc.

Matos Rodríguez, Félix V., and Linda C. Delgado, eds. *Puerto Rican Women's History: New Perspectives.* New York and London: M.E.Sharpe, 1998. HQ1522.P84 1998 GenColl.

Ruiz, Vicki L. *From Out of the Shadows: Mexican Women in Twentieth Century America.* New York: Oxford University Press, 1998. E184.M5 R86 1998 GenColl.

Stoner, K. Lynn. *Cuban and Cuban-American Women: An Annotated Bibliography.* Wilmington, Del.: Scholarly Resources, 2000. Z7964 C85 S76 2000 MRR Alc.

Using the Collections

The Hispanic Division, with its excellent staff of reference librarians and subject specialists, is the first stop for researchers interested in finding both primary and secondary sources concerning Latinas in English and in foreign languages. The division has a useful collection of general reference works in several languages. The staff can also advise new researchers about specialists in other divisions, some of whose materials will be described below.

Another cluster of sources can be found by accessing the Hispanic Division's Web site at <http://www.loc.gov/rr/hispanic>. There you can find links to American Memory's *Puerto Rico at the Modern Age; Spain, the United States, and the American Frontier: Historias paralelas; The World of 1898: The Spanish American War;* and many more sites.

One unique source, *The Handbook of Latin American Studies* (*HLAS*), is produced in the Hispanic Division. Beginning in 1935, *HLAS* contains annotations of works in the humanities and the social sciences published in a variety of languages. Although its main focus is on Latin America per se, its annotations include material on migration to the United States, historical information from 1492 to the present, and comparisons between Latinas and populations still residing in the home country. Its database can be found at <http://lcweb2.loc.gov/hlas>.

SAMPLE LCSH: Hispanic American women; Cuban American women; Mexican American women; Puerto Rican women.

Selected Collections

The Hispanic Division itself does not have custody of any materials except for the Archive of Hispanic Literature on Tape, described more fully below, and substantial pamphlet files on Latin America and Iberia. (Almost 15,000 such pamphlets, dated 1802–1992, are available on microfilm, MicRR.) The search strategies for the breadth of topics about Latinas (or any other subject) in the General Collections at the Library of Congress often involves visits to the reading rooms of other divisions.

Audiotapes

In 1943 the Hispanic Division established the Archive of Hispanic Literature on Tape (AHLOT). The archive contains the recordings of more than 640 authors from Spain and Portugal, as well as Latin America, the Caribbean, and those who live in the United States. These authors usually read from their works and often comment on their lives and the sources for their writings. The Hispanic Division is the only place where researchers can consult these recordings. The basic finding aid for recordings from 1943 to 1972 is *The Archive of Hispanic Literature on Tape: A Descriptive Guide* by Francisco Aguilera and Georgette Magassy Dorn (Washington: Library of Congress, 1974; Z1609.L7 U54 1974). The researcher seeking information about more recent readings can find it by accessing the Hispanic Division's home page. The archive includes recordings of such Latinas as Chilean-born novelist Isabel Allende (b. 1942), playwright and novelist Denise Chávez (b. 1948), and poet and novelist Ana Castillo (b. 1954). Among Cuban American women recorded are the historian and sociologist Lydia Cabrera (1899–1991), novelist and playwright Julieta Campos (b. 1932), psychologist Lourdes Casal (1938–1981), literary magazine editor Belkis Cuza Malé (b. 1942), biographer and children's writer Hilda Perera Díaz (b. 1926), poet Juana Rosa Pita (b. 1939), and feminist poet and critic Eliana Rivero (b. 1940). Prominent women from Puerto Rico include novelist Rosario Ferré (b. 1938), professor and writer of children's literature Ester Feliciano Mendoza (b. 1917), poet and essayist Laura Gallego (b. 1924), poet Violeta López Suria (b. 1926), scholar and poet Concha Meléndez (1895–1983), folklorist and poet Marigloria Palma (pseudonym of Gloria María Pagan Ferrer, b. 1921), lawyer and literary critic Nilita Vientós Gastón (1903–1989), and short story writer and poet Carmelina Vizcarrondo de Quiñones (1906–1983). On October 16, 1995, Chicana poet Sandra Cisneros (b. 1954) recorded her work for the Archive of Recorded Poetry and Literature, maintained by the Library's Poetry Office (RWD 6205 <Rec Sound>).

SAMPLE LCSH: Authors, Cuban—20th century—interviews; Mexican American authors—20th century—interviews. Also searchable by the name of recorded author.

Manuscripts

The Manuscript Division holds microfilm and photocopies of archival and manuscript collections held in archives throughout the United States and abroad. For example, "Spanish Archives of New Mexico (1621–1821)" on twenty-two reels of microfilm includes the official documents of the central and local government then under Spanish control. The East Florida Papers (65,000 items; 1737–1858) has marriage licenses for 1785–1803 as well as proceedings from the town council of Saint Augustine from 1812 to 1821. In 1905, the Library established a Foreign Copying Program that brought together many types of reproductions—hand-copied, photostats and photocopies, and microform—from the millions of pages found in archives from around the world. The copies and films from the Archivo General de la Nación of Mexico are excellent sources for the Latina past. Manuscripts filmed at the Archivo Histórico Nacional and the Archivo General de Indias in Spain are also fruitful sources for researchers interested in searching for the context of women's lives during the period of Spanish colonial rule in what has become the United States. An excellent guide to these materials is found in *The Hispanic World, 1492–1898/El Mundo Hispánico, 1492–1898: A Guide to the Photoreproduced Manuscripts from Spain in the Collections of the United States, Guam, and Puerto Rico*, edited by Guadalupe Jiménez Codinach (Washington: Library of Congress, 1994; Z663.32.H54 1994 MRR Alc). See also chapter 5.

Film Materials

Images of Latinas in films can be seen in the Motion Picture and Television Reading Room. Eighteen viewable films of Dolores Del Río (1905–1983), from *What Price Glory* (1926; FDA 7809–7811) to *More Than a Miracle* (1967; FGC 398–403), are found in the Library's collections, including works that were produced and filmed in Mexico, Spain, and Argentina. The collections also contain more than twenty films of Lupe Vélez (1908–1944), "the Mexican Spitfire," filmed in the United States, ranging from *Wolf Song* (1929; FBA 9216–9219) to *Mexican Spitfire at Sea* (1942; FDB 0545–0546). Researchers who wish to consult Mexican researcher Angel Miquel's unpublished finding aid in Spanish to silent movies and other films starring Latinas in the Library's collections should ask the reference staff in the Motion Picture and Television Reading Room or in the Hispanic Division Reading Room.

Films made by Latinos themselves include those films scholars might expect to find, such as *Selena* (1997, CGC6715–6721), the biographical motion picture of the Tejana singing sensation, Selena Pérez, who had a massive following in the Spanish language community before her untimely death. The much rarer film, *A Tribute to Selena* (1995, VAE 7536), produced by Robert Rodríguez Rodd, is also in the collections. Several episodes of the mainstream television program *Wonder Woman*, starring Lynda Carter (Lynda Jean Cordoba Carter) (FDA 4887–4889), and Public Television's *A Mexican-American Family* (FBB 1779) represent television programming that casts more light on our subject.

The Motion Picture, Broadcasting, and Recorded Sound Division (chapter 10) also contains rare scrapbooks maintained by Dorothy Blum of popular actresses in the 1930s and 1940s. One of these examples from the Dorothy Blum Scrapbook Collection is a tribute to Dolores Del Río and contains clippings showing how her studio publicist attempted to present the Mexican-born actress. According to one article, she had become so American that she could no longer eat Mexican food. Blum also kept a scrapbook with articles and pictures relating to Lupe Vélez's career. When Vélez appeared in the film *Wolf Song* with Gary Cooper, the publicity featured questions about their real life romance. Later a feature article talked about her trading kisses for cash and preferring older men. Although typical of the fodder prepared by studio publicists, such publicity served to reinforce stereotypes.

The MBRS vertical files contain some additional material about such stars. In the AFI–Des Moines Still Collection, the researcher can find

Rita Moreno and members of the "Sharks" in West Side Story, *1961. Photograph. New York World Telegram and Sun Collection. Prints and Photographs Division. LC-USZ62-116064. Copyright © 1961 United Artists Pictures Inc. All Rights Reserved. Courtesy of MGM CLIP+STILL.*

Rita Moreno (b.1931) as Anita was photographed singing "America" in the movie version of *West Side Story* (1961). Reflecting the young lyricist Stephen Sondheim's understanding of Puerto Rican life in New York in the 1950s, Anita and the other women argued that life in America was better for women ("Lots of new housing with more space") while "Bernardo" (George Chakiris) and the men countered with reminders of the discrimination they found ("Lots of doors slamming in our face"). Perhaps it had not occurred to Sondheim that Latinas too suffered discrimination in New York. Moreno is the only actress to have won an Academy Award, a Tony Award, a Grammy Award, and two Emmy Awards.

Rita Hayworth in Cover Girl, *1944. Color lithograph, poster. Motion Picture Posters. Prints and Photographs Division. LC-USZC4-5015. "Cover Girl" copyright © 1944, renewed 1972 Columbia Pictures Industries, Inc. All Rights Reserved. Courtesy of Columbia Pictures.*

In her early films, Margarita Carmen Cansino, billed as "Rita Cansino," played seductive *cantina* dancers in the cowboy movies known as the "Three Mesquiteers" films (using the mesquite plant in a pun on the three musketeers). In 1937 she sang "La Cucaracha" ("the cockroach," and slang for marijuana) in *Hit the Saddle.* That year, she changed her name to Rita Hayworth and became one of the sexiest of Hollywood's beauties. In fact, *Cover Girl* was inspired by all the covers graced by Rita Hayworth and other stars like Betty Grable. When Hayworth appeared as a "cover girl" for the *Life* magazine issued on August 11, 1941, the demand for that issue was so great that by 1946 more than five million copies had been printed.

photographs of Rita Hayworth (Margarita Carmen Cansino) dancing in Des Moines, Iowa, in December 1940 or selling war bonds in 1944.

BIBLIOGRAPHY:

Keller, Gary D. *Hispanics and United States Film: An Overview and Handbook.* Tempe, Arizona: Bilingual Review/Press, 1994. PN1995.9.L37 K46 1994.

Noriega, Chon A., ed. *Chicanos and Film: Representation and Resistance.* Minneapolis: University of Minnesota Press, 1992. PN1995.9.M49 C49 1992 GenColl.

Reyes, Luis, and Peter Rubie. *Hispanics in Hollywood: 100 Years in Film and Television.* Hollywood, Calif.: Lone Eagle Press, 2000. PN1995.9.H47 R49 2000 GenColl.

Rodriguez, Clara E., ed. *Latin Looks: Images of Latinas and Latinos in the U.S. Media.* Boulder, Colo.: Westview Press, 1997. P94.5.H582 U65 1997 GenColl.

SAMPLE LCSH: Hispanic Americans in motion pictures; Hispanic Americans on television; Hispanic American actors.

Copyright

When authors apply for copyright of their creative efforts by filing an application, paying a fee, and supplying the Library with two copies of the specified work, these materials enrich the Library's collections in many areas, including books, maps, films, recorded sound, television broadcasting, and sheet music. The copyright deposit records are interesting in themselves and researchers need only go to room 459 of the Madison Building to consult them firsthand. From 1978, all copyrights have been recorded online, but for earlier submissions, the researcher needs to search a specific author in the card files that are arranged by years, specifically 1898–1937, 1938–45, 1946–54, 1955–70, 1971–77, as well as the online entries. Although historically copyrights have been held mostly by large companies, still the catalog cards are full of useful information. It takes just a few moments to locate Vikki Carr's first recording in Spanish in 1972 or to see that Linda Ronstadt started writing songs in Spanish as early as July 1976, with "Lo siento mi vida" (I'm sorry my love/darling). Copyright also applies to performances. The Cuban American salsa goddess Celia Cruz (b. 1924) has thirty recordings listed online and the co-creator of the Miami Sound Machine, Gloria Estefan (b. 1957), has well over one hundred, in addition to the songs she has written.

Newspapers

The Newspaper and Current Periodical Reading Room (see chapter 2) holds many current and historic Latino newspapers. The collection includes *El Diario/La Prensa* (New York City, 1963–; News MF2396) with its "La Reina de Reinas" (The queen of queens) beauty contests sponsored by the newspaper; its ads for secretarial schools complete with blond images; and its horoscope column "Es Hoy su Cumpleaños?" (Is today your birthday?) by Stella. The newspaper also features the column "Marginalia" by Luisa Quintero; clothing patterns pictured on a blonde little girl; and articles with pictures of such notable Latinas as Irma Vidal Santaella, president of the Comisión Nacional Hispánica de Asesoramiento Económico (National Hispanic Commission of Business Consultants). *La Opinión* (Los Angeles, 1981 News MF2240) includes features on child development, recipes from Mexican states, paper dolls for children, a "Conozca Sus Derechos" (Know your rights) column, and an unsubtle juxtaposition of the "Belleza total" (Total beauty) column by Yolanda Aguilar side by side with the wedding announcements section. The Library also holds a complete run of *Diario las Américas* (Miami, 1953–; News MF 1026), and *El Latino* (Washington, D.C., News MF 3111). Twenty more titles are indexed in the subscription database *Ethnic NewsWatch*.

Research on Latinas, however, should hardly be limited to the Spanish-language press. The Library's extensive holdings of major newspapers include the journal of record of most state capitals, as well as vehicles of national scope such as the *New York Times*, *Washington Post*, *Miami Herald*, and *Los Angeles Times*. These newspapers provide important information on the interaction between the Latino community and the general community, including local news, classified advertisements, and feature sections.

Celia Cruz and Ray Barretto. Ritmo en el Corazón *(1988, Fania Records JM 651). Recorded Sound Reference Center, Motion Picture, Broadcasting, and Recorded Sound Division. Courtesy of Fania Records.*

Born in Cuba in 1924, Celia Cruz, the long-reigning queen of the Afro-Cuban music known as salsa, studied at Havana's Conservatory of Music and began her singing career on Havana radio in the late 1940s. In 1950 she joined the legendary group Sonora Matancera and toured extensively from 1951 to 1959. She gave her first performance in the United States in 1962, three years after the Cuban revolution. Here she is shown in full costume with conga virtuoso Ray Barretto, on her album *Ritmo en el Corazón,* which won a Grammy Award in 1988. Barretto is just one of many partners, who include such legends as Machito, Tito Puente, Johnny Pacheco, and Willie Colón. During her career, Cruz has recorded more than eighty albums, over twenty of which went gold, and has received more than a hundred awards, including a star on Hollywood Boulevard and recognition from the National Endowment for the Arts. She has been an inspiration for generations of performers, including the musical team of Gloria and Emilio Estefan.

BIBLIOGRAPHY:

Grove, Pearce S., Becky J. Barnett, and Sandra J. Hansen, eds. *New Mexico Newspapers: A Comprehensive Guide to Bibliographical Entries and Locations.* Albuquerque: University of New Mexico Press, 1975. Z6952.N55 G75 GenColl, N&CPR.

Kanellos, Nicolás, and Helvetia Martell. *Hispanic Periodicals in the United States, Origins to 1960.* Houston: Arte Público Press, 1999. Z6953.5.S66 K36 2000 GenColl, HISP Ref.

Rodríguez, América. *Making Latino News: Race, Language, Class.* Thousand Oaks, Calif.: Sage Publications, 1999. PN4888.H57 R63 1999.

Journals and Newsletters

The Library holds a substantial array of Latino publications for both the general public and for scholars. Current issues can be consulted in the Newspaper and Current Periodical Reading

Room (chapter 2), but back issues are usually found bound in the General Collections (chapter 1). *Nuestro: The Magazine for Latinos* (E184.S75 N83 GenColl), *La Luz* (E184.S75 L88 GenColl), *LATINA Style* (E184.S75 L39 GenColl), *La Herencia del Norte* (uncataloged), *Hispanic Business* (HF3000.H57 GenColl), and *Hispanic Review of Business* (HD2346.U5 H57 GenColl) all contain articles that reflect Latinas' interests in themselves and in their quest for a better life. You will find in the Library's collections an excellent group of journals, including *Linden Lane* ([0] 87/723 MicRR), *El Fortín de la Trocha* (E184.C77 F67 GenColl), *Revista Chicano-Riqueña* (PS508.M4 R47 GenColl), *De Colores: Journal of Chicano Expression and Thought* (PS508.M4 D4 GenColl), *Aztlán: International Journal of Chicano Studies Research* (E184.M5 A98 GenColl), and *La Palabra: Revista de Literatura Chicana* (1979–85; PQ7070.A27a GenColl), to list just a few.

For researchers seeking to track women's issues and their impact through the years, a good source is the wide range of newsletters issued by Hispanic American volunteer organizations. Many are found in the Chicano Studies Library Serial Collection (uncataloged), a group of periodicals of all sorts dating from 1855, available on 426 reels of microfilm. The Library also holds various newsletters, ranging from *Legislative Update* (KF4757.5 .L38 L34 Law), prepared by the National Council of La Raza, to *Somos Primos* (uncataloged), the organ of the Society of Hispanic Historical and Ancestral Research.

SAMPLE LCSH: Mexican Americans—Periodicals.

Maps

Latinas can show up in many places where perhaps they might not be expected. Researchers with imagination and ingenuity are sometimes rewarded by finding them on historical maps. An excellent guide to these maps is *The Luso-Hispanic World in Maps: A Selective Guide to the Manuscript Maps to 1900 in the Collections of the Library of Congress,* edited by John R. Hébert and Anthony P. Mullan (Washington: Library of Congress, 1999; Z6027.S72 L43 1999 GenColl; also online at <www.loc.gov/rr/geogmap/activ.html>. For example, when Vicente Sebastián Pintado fashioned his official map of Spanish New Orleans and vicinity in 1795–96, a map in continuous use until at least 1873, he designated who owned property within the city limits and Bayou Saint John. On this map (*Map of New Orleans and Vicinity,* by Pintado and Carlos Trudeau, Havana, 1819 [1804]; G4014.N5 G46 1819 .P Vault G&M), Pintado noted a sizeable parcel belonging to "La Negra Rachon," perhaps an Afro-Latina of means.

Sanborn Fire Insurance Maps supply a wealth of detail about the locations of important structures within numerous U.S. towns and cities. If you look at the maps produced for New Mexico, you will discover that in 1886 the Sisters of Loredo in Santa Fe had a wooden convent and academy. By 1898 the convent had become known as the Loretto Convent and Academy and included a girls' dormitory. At the same time, Saint Vincent's Academy also had a girls' school dormitory. In Albuquerque, you can locate a Spanish Seventh Day Adventist Church made of concrete in 1950, as well as one wooden structure housing the Catholic Teachers College, and another used by the Saint Therese Roman Catholic Church and Sisters' Home.

The Geography and Map Division (see chapter 7) also houses more general maps, such as the United States Bureau of the Census map *Spanish Origin Persons as a Percent of Total Population by Counties of the United States,* 1970 (G3701.E1 1970 .U55) and *American Geographic approved mapa del mexicano americano* (G4051.S1 1976 .A5).

SAMPLE LCSH: Mexican Americans—West (U.S.)—Maps; West (U.S.)—History—Maps.

Photographs

If you are researching specific Latinas, you may be tempted to make a beeline to the Biographical File in the Prints and Photographs Division (see chapter 6), believing it to be a quick way to find illustrations for monographs or articles. Other collections, however, hold rich caches of material depicting Latinas. The New York World-Telegram and Sun Newspaper Photograph Collection, for example, contains images of Latinas listed by name, from the singer and activist Joan Baez (b. 1941) to tennis champ Rosemary Casals (b. 1948), as well as the actress and comedienne Imogene Coca (b. 1908) and ballerina Lupe Serrano (b. 1930). The division's other photojournalism collections offer pictorial information about general movements of Latinas. For instance, the card index for the U.S. News & World Report Magazine Photograph Collection features listings for "Cuba, refugees," "Cubans in Miami," and "Cuban Exiles." Searching under areas of the country where many Latinas have settled points to a few additional groups of photo documentation. For example, the heading "United States—Florida—Miami" provides a listing for the "Cuba

Raid Ban Story," which includes images taken in chain stores that catered to Cubanas, in Cubano neighborhoods in Miami, and scenes of refugees in relief lines in April 1963 (see LC-U9-9524, frame 35). Searching for records in the Look Magazine Photograph Collection in the Prints and Photographs Online Catalog (PPOC) (<http://www.loc.gov/rr/print/catalog.html>) using the term "Mexican Americans" locates Maurice Terrell's 1958 images depicting the daily life of Mona Silva and her family in Torrence, California (LOOK–Job 58-4323 and LOOK–Job 58-7810).

In the 1930s and 1940s, photographers working for the Farm Security Administration and later the Office of War Information documented many aspects of daily life in the United States. Included in the group of 164,000 negatives and 75,000 prints are wonderful clues to Latina life, particularly in the Southwest. Many of the photographs document small towns like Las Trampas in Taos County, New Mexico, in 1943. The photographer concentrated on the mayor of the town, Juan López, and his family, providing warm details of everyday activities as he, his wife, and their children went about their chores on the farm (LOT 869). A wealth of information emerges from photographs of San Antonio, Texas, including images of housing and cemeteries. Good times were not neglected and photographs show Charro Days, a celebration of horsemanship, in Brownsville, Texas (LOT 36).

Researchers will find clues to more pictorial resources by searching the Prints and Photographs Online Catalog and referring to chapter 6. Your search will suggest the variety of visual formats in which Latinas have been represented, from fine screenprints by Ester Hernández and Carmen Lomas Garza (b. 1948) to turn-of-the-century stereographs showing women hoeing sugar cane.

Princess at a Puerto Rican festival in Lowell, Massachusetts, 1987. Photograph by Mario Montaño. Lowell Folklife Project. American Folklife Center. (LFP-MM-C007-20)

Beauty pageants are a part of many community celebrations across the United States. They are popular with the media, and newspapers have often used them as a way to boost circulation. Here the "princess" of an open-air Puerto Rican festival in Lowell, Massachusetts, in 1987 sits on her rattan throne on a stage, protected from the elements by an orange canopy.

Folk Songs and Folklife

The Archive of Folk Culture within the American Folklife Center of the Library of Congress (see also chapter 11) has field recordings of songs, music, and narratives that open windows upon selected images and contributions of Latinas. In April 1999, the American Folklife Center put *Hispano Music and Culture of the Northern Rio Grande: The Juan B. Rael Collection* online as part of the American Memory Web site at <http://memory.loc.gov/ammem/rghtml/rghome.html>. Recorded in 1940 by Juan Bautista Rael of Stanford University, the collection contains examples of the religious and secular music of Hispanic Northern New Mexico and Southern Colorado including a march performed by Ernestina Anaya of Rio Arroyo Hondo, New Mexico, and "Voy para Belén" (I go to Bethlehem) sung by Rosabel Espinosa of Antonito, Colorado.

Complementing the Rael collection are four volumes of the *J.D. Robb Collection of Folk Music Texts* (Albuquerque: University of New Mexico Press, 1972; PQ7078.N4 R6 1972 AFC) located in the center's reading room containing transcriptions of the texts of folk songs from New Mexico. Some of the songs present women as symbolic figures, objects of desire, wives, mothers, victims, and saints. Sixty-five tapes of Hispanic Southwestern music (AFS 15459–15523) join another twenty-two records of Spanish American folk songs that Robb recorded in New Mexico in 1944 and 1948 (AFS 6144–6151 and 9610–9628 respectively). The Folklife Center documented the personal devotions of Latinas when it conducted a field documentary project in Lowell, Massachusetts, in 1987 and found Puerto Ricans there preparing for religious festivals. "Puerto Rico Recordings in the Archive of Folk Culture" (finding aid no. 12, LCFA, August 1993) details recordings of Puerto Ricans on the island and in the continental United States held by the Archive of Folk Culture. The center also can make available film of a live concert of Tejana singing sensation Lydia Mendoza (b. 1918), "the Lark of the Border," who recorded more than two hundred singles during her career. Mendoza has become an iconic figure among Chicanas as seen in the screenprint portrait by Ester Hernández in the Fine Prints Collection in the Prints and Photographs Division.

As part of the Bicentennial celebration of the Library of Congress in 2000, the Folklife Center, together with members of Congress, created the Local Legacies project to collect new materials on folkways in the United States. Descriptions of these materials, which can be accessed at <http://www.loc.gov/bicentennial/legacies.html>, include such folkways as Paula Rodríguez demonstrating her straw applique techniques in New Mexico.

The Federal Writers' Project papers, 1936–39, held in the Manuscript Division provide an interesting documentary record of folklore in both rural and urban areas. Items from New Mexico, for example, discuss Christmas customs and fiestas, the growing disuse of the typical Spanish shawl, *el tapalo,* observations of wedding feasts, and even mention the legendary figure of "La Tules," also known as María Gertrudis Barceló (see above).

Federal Writers' Project writers Genevieve Chapin and Lorin W. Brown collected and translated proverbs and folktales (see container A641) with earthy advice, such as "En casa de muger [*sic*] rica ella manda y ella grita" (In the house where the wife has brought the money, she is the chief and wears the breeches) or "Más vale fea con gracia que linda sin ella" (The homely girl possessed of grace [graciousness] is better than the beauty lacking it). Here too, the researcher can find the first in a series of reports on witchcraft and the occult among the Latino population (container A645). For example, in the legend of Tia Toña in 1895 or the Witch of Arroyo Hondo as related by Marcos Váldez to project writer Reyes N. Martinez, members of the community saw a ball of fire rising out of Tia Toña's chimney, a sure sign of a witch, and followed it to a coven of dancing witches. On other nights she ran a gambling operation and prepared food. Balls of light also appear in an account of witchery among Mexican Americans in Hall City, Nebraska, written by Wilbur Cummings (see container A749). A woman named "Bruja" (witch) supposedly had the powers to become invisible and to remove her eyes and replace them with cat's eyes. She could see at night and fly about like a firefly, invisible except for a tiny light field, as she sucked the blood of infants for sustenance.

SAMPLE LCSH: Folk songs, Spanish—[name of state or **United States**]; **Tejano music; Conjunto music; Hispanic Americans—Music; Mexican Americans—**[name of state or **United States**]**—Music; Folk dance music—**[name of state or **United States**]; **Alabados.**

Cookbooks

The Katherine Golden Bitting Collection on Gastronomy in the Rare Book and Special Collections Division (see chapter 4) contains approximately forty-five hundred volumes devoted to food handling, preparation, and cooking. In terms of literature featuring Latina cooking, the collection holds books written by Latinas and non-Latinas that purportedly represented their food. Quite a few of these were sponsored by the Gebhardt Chili Powder Company of San Antonio, Texas, as a way to teach potential customers how to use their spices. Among them are *Mexican Cookery for American Homes* (San Antonio: Gebhardt Chili Powder Company, 1923; TX716.M4 M494 1923) and Frances P. Belle's *A California Cookbook: An Unusual Collection of Spanish Dishes and Tropical California Foods* (Chicago: Regan Publishing, 1925; TX715.B45). In these volumes the word "Spanish" is used interchangeably with "Mexican," but either way a recipe for a Spanish omelet without potatoes sheds doubt on their authenticity.

In her cookbook *Early California Hospitality:*

The Cookery Customs of Spanish California with Authentic Recipes and Menus of the Period (Glendale: Arthur H. Clark, 1938; TX715P127), Ana Bégué de Packman, secretary of the Historical Society of Southern California and custodian of the Casa Figueroa, tried to compensate for these travesties with recipes for corn and wheat tortillas, burritos, and two separate ways of making *pozole* (stew with meat and hominy). She dedicated her book to "my hardy and illustrious ancestors: Don Francisco Reyes, soldado de *cuera* (founder of Spanish frontier forts), who first trod the soil of Alta California with Padre Junípero Serra; and Don Maximo Alanis, who assisted in founding the pueblo of Los Angeles and was the original grantee of Rancho San José de Buenos Aires now known as Westwood Hills."

Genealogical Research

When Latinas want to search for ancestors both in the United States and abroad, they should first turn to the finding aid *Hispanic Migration and Genealogy: Selected Titles at the Library of Congress* by Lee Douglas (forthcoming), a compilation of over three hundred works that facilitate the construction of a family tree. Another very important source is the *Diccionario Heráldico y Genealógico de Apellidos Españoles y Americanos* by Alberto and Arturo García Carraffa (Madrid: Impr. de A. Marzo, 1919–<1963>; CR2142.G3). The eighty-eight volumes of this work contain a list of over 15,000 names and genealogical histories for Spanish and Spanish American families. An automated list of names for each volume can be found in the section of the Hispanic Division's Web site devoted to "Other Reading Rooms" at "Genealogy" or directly at <www.loc.gov/rr/hispanic/hbrowse/geneal/index_gc.html>. Additional works on Latina genealogy include Fernando R. de Castro y de Cárdenas, *Genealogía, Heráldica e Historia de Nuestras Familias* (Miami, Florida: Ediciones Universal, 1989; CS222.C37 1989), an excellent source for Cubanas wanting to trace their families back to the island. If you visit the Local History and Genealogy Reading Room, you will be able to access the genealogical database *Ancestry* <www.ancestry.com> free of charge. Within the Library, researchers can log onto the Biography and Genealogy Master Index under "Electronic Research Tools."

Latinas have continuously contributed to the making of what became the United States. Nevertheless important figures have yet to be identified as Latinas, and still others remain anonymous even today. As this listing of selected collections demonstrates, the Library of Congress offers many opportunities for researchers to uncover the lives of Latinas and give voice to their deeds and dreams.

From their very earliest settlements in territory that would ultimately become the United States, Latinas, Jewish women, and many more helped weave the fabric of American society. Their steady influx in the nineteenth and twentieth centuries continued to add color and texture to the nation's evolving design. Uncovering the words and actions of women and their families through the assistance of the staff of the Area Studies divisions and using the foreign-language collections and the special-format collections at the Library of Congress will help you tap into some of the origins of women's history across the land. Such broad-based research enhances our understanding of the multilayered and gendered dimensions of American culture.

At the same time, foreign-language materials test common wisdom about the nature of colonization, the interplay of the dominant society with the "other," and generalizations concerning the factors that serve to construct culture. Continuing research usually reveals that women cannot be reduced to any single set of characteristics or fully described by any one image. The experiences of individual women in each generation add additional layers to their basic identities, as shaped by race, class, genes, and gender. Perhaps what is most remarkable is women's strength in the face of new and persistent challenges. Although not every answer can be found in the Library's foreign-language collections, its documents are certain to lead us in new directions and prompt different insightful responses. In doing so, they will undoubtedly help create a new vision of our past.

Individuals who helped in writing this chapter include Helen Fedor (EUR), Judy Liu (AD), Yoko Akiba (Japanese), Hoa Nguyen (Vietnamese), Ibrahim Pourhadi (Farsi), George Kovtun (Czech), Fentahun Tiruneh (Amharic), John Topping (Greek), and Fawzi Tadros and Mary Jane Deeb (Arabic). Helpful in all ways were Georgette Dorn, chief of the Hispanic Division, Beverly Gray, chief of the African and Middle Eastern Division, and Michael Grunberger, head of the Hebraic Section. Thanks also to Vicki Ruiz, Arizona State University, Pamela Nadell, American University, and Shuly Rubin Schwartz, Jewish Theological Seminary of America, who read earlier drafts.

Russell Lee, "Taos, New Mexico. July, 1940. Spanish-American people at the fiesta." *Farm Security Administration Collection. Prints and Photographs Division. LC-USF33-12863-M4.*

Three New Mexican girls await their turn to perform during the July 1940 fiesta in Taos. Their costumes exemplify different aspects of the life they might expect to lead as adults. The child at the extreme right is dressed as a rancher's wife, with her vest, long skirt, and frilly white blouse. The girl in the middle is ready to attend Mass in an elaborate lace mantilla. Finally, the wailing child seeking comfort in a father's arms is the housewife, wearing a plainer dress and ordinary jewelry. Russell Lee took the photograph as part of his series on the "Spanish-American story," just at a moment when the traditions of many of the rural Hispanic communities began to be irrevocably changed by the need to modernize for World War II.

Abbreviations

AD	Asian Division or Asian Reading Room
AFC	American Folklife Center
AREA	Area Studies Collections
AMED	African and Middle Eastern Division or African and Middle Eastern Reading Room
BusRR	Business Reading Room
CCC	Computer Catalog Center
COP	U.S. Copyright Office
CRS	Congressional Research Service
EUR	European Division
EurRR	European Reading Room
G&M	Geography and Map Division or Geography and Map Reading Room
GenColl	General Collections
Hebr	Hebraic Section
Hebr Cage	Hebraic Section rare materials
Hebr Ref	Hebraic reference collections
HISP	Hispanic Division
HISP Ref	Hispanic Division Reference Section
HSS	Humanities and Social Sciences Division
LAW	Law Library
LA	Library of Congress Adams Building
LC	Library of Congress
LCOC	Library of Congress Online Catalog
LCSH	Library of Congress subject headings
LCSH	*Library of Congress Subject Headings*
LH&G	Local History and Genealogy Reading Room
LJ	Library of Congress Jefferson Building
LM	Library of Congress Madison Building
MBRS	Motion Picture, Broadcasting, and Recorded Sound Division
MCAT	Main Card Catalog
MicRR	Microform Reading Room
MRR	Main Reading Room
MRR Alc	Main Reading Room alcoves
MRR Biog	Main Reading Room biography alcoves
MRR Ref Desk	Main Reading Room reference desk area
MSS	Manuscript Division
MUS	Music Division
N&CPR	Newspaper and Current Periodical Room
News MF	Newspaper microfilm
PAO	Public Affairs Office
PARR	Performing Arts Reading Room
P&P	Prints and Photographs Division or Prints and Photographs Reading Room
PPOC	Prints and Photographs Online Catalog
RBSC	Rare Book and Special Collections Division or Rare Book and Special Collections Division Reading Room
Rare Book Ref	Rare Book and Special Collections Division reference collections
SciRR	Science Reading Room
SER	Serial and Government Publications Division
ST&B	Science, Technology, and Business Division or Science and Business Reading Room (*see* BusRR and SciRR, abbreviations used in this book)

Studio Saunterings

By Louis Reeves Harrison

IN approaching a studio or an office you may find yourself dealing with a raw specimen of humanity at the outset—you can make up your mind there and then that you will come upon some half-baked ones further on. And the contrary is true. If you are treated with courtesy and consideration from the outset, as I was when I sauntered over to the Solax studio at Flushing, you can count upon it that some one of enlightenment and superior breeding is high in control of affairs. In this case, the head of the business, the originator of it, the capitalist, the art director, the chief working director, is a refined French woman, Madame Alice Blache.

This is woman's era, and Madame Blache is helping to prove it without making any fuss at all. She only favors universal suffrage when satisfied that women are ready for it, and she is so modest about what she has done in the Gaumont and Solax companies that I had to depend upon others for any details relating to her remarkable career in the production of moving pictures. Modesty is the most endearing quality woman ever shows to man, egotism being his specialty and most pronounced characteristic, and along with it the head of the Solax Company exhibits a delightful composure of manner under all circumstances, no matter how trying. The average business man imagines that he enhances his importance by exhibiting that enemy of politeness, haste, as if the tremendous responsibility of making a living kept him in a state of constant high pressure.

I have been in studios where there was no inherent lack of appreciation of the value of publicity, but those in control assume that old you'll-have-to-excuse-me air, as though a momentary diversion of energy would cause the entire commercial structure to collapse, and those men of small ability to meet contingencies are the first to complain that they are never able to attract attention. At the Solax, I was personally conducted by gentle-mannered Levine, editor of "The Magnet," and so well treated from start to finish that my work became a pleasure. Levine realized that I was not at the studio as an individual, but as the representative of the only periodical generally regarded as an established authority on moving pictures in this country. He is a live wire.

From Levine, and from others, I learned that Madame Alice Blache became associated with the Gaumont Company very early in the game, when Mr. Gaumont was absorbed with the scientific department of production or merely engaged in photographing moving objects. She *inaugurated* the presentation of little plays on the screen by that company some sixteen or seventeen years ago, operating the camera, writing or adapting the photodramas, setting the scenes and handling the actors. I had an opportunity to see how efficient she was in her diversity of roles before the day was over and was amazed at her skill, especially in directing the action of a complicated scene. She came to this country in 1907—her husband then being general manager of the Gaumont Com-

Madame Blache Rehearsing Cast in "Fra Diavolo."

Notes

INTRODUCTION

1. Virginia Woolf, *A Room of One's Own* (New York: Harcourt, Brace, and World, 1929; PN471.W6 1929a), 25–26.
2. Linda Gordon, *U.S. Women's History* (Washington: American Historical Association, 1997), 2.
3. "Gerda Lerner on the Future of Our Past," interview by Catharine R. Stimpson, *Ms.*(HQ1101.M55) 10 (September 1981): 94, 95.
4. Gordon, *U.S. Women's History*, 5.
5. In the short space of this introduction, it is not possible to provide a summary of the content of American women's history, although some of the key topics and concerns will be touched on. Readers desiring a general overview of the field or discussion of central topics and themes should consult the bibliography of major works at the end of this introduction, as well as bibliographical material presented in individual chapters.
6. Historians use the term "second-wave feminism" to refer to the activism of the 1960s and 1970s, in contrast to the suffrage movement, the so-called first wave of women's activism.
7. Linda K. Kerber, "Gender," in Anthony Molho and Gordon Wood, eds., *Imagined Histories: American Historians Interpret the Past* (Princeton, N.J.: Princeton University Press, 1998; D13.5 U6 I657 1998), 41.
8. Carroll Smith-Rosenberg, "The Female World of Love and Ritual," in *Disorderly Conduct: Visions of Gender in Victorian America* (New York: Knopf, 1985; HQ1419.S58 1985), 53. The essay originally appeared in the first issue of *Signs: Journal of Women in Culture and Society,* (HQ1101.S5). The journal's beginning in 1975 was itself a noteworthy marker of the professionalization of the field. Other important journals founded in these years included *Feminist Studies:* (HQ1101.F46) and *Frontiers.*
9. Quoted in Karen Anderson, *Changing Woman: A History of Racial Ethnic Women in Modern America* (New York: Oxford University Press, 1996; E184.A1 A673 1996), 16.
10. Joan Wallach Scott, "Gender: A Useful Tool of Historical Analysis," *American Historical Review* (E171.A57) 91 (December 1986): 1,053–75.
11. Karen Anderson, *Teaching Gender in U.S. History* (Washington: American Historical Association, 1997), 3.
12. Quoted in Vicki L. Ruiz and Ellen Carol DuBois, eds., *Unequal Sisters: A Multicultural Reader in U.S. Women's History*, 3rd ed. (New York: Routledge, 2000; HQ1410.U54 2000 Overflow), xii.

1 THE GENERAL COLLECTIONS

Unless otherwise indicated, all titles cited in these notes for chapter 1 are shelved in the General Collections of the Library of Congress.

1. Sofia M. Loebinger, "Suffragism, Not Feminism," *American Suffragette* (Official Organ of the National Progressive Woman Suffrage Union; JK1880.A6), December 1909, 3.
2. American Antiquarian Society, ed., *Early American Imprints, 1639–1800* [microform], 22,000 microfiches (New York: Readex, 1981–82; Microfiche 85/431; MicRR guide no. Z1215.S495 MicRR). *Early American Imprints, 1801–1819* [microform], ca. 40,480 microfiches (New York: Readex, 1985–93; Microfiche 90/7049; MicRR guide nos. Z1215.S48 and Z1215.N58 1983).
3. Gretchen M. Bataille and Kathleen M. Sands, *American Indian Women: A Guide to Research* (New York: Garland, 1991; Z1209.2.N67 B36 1991 MRR Alc).
4. Aviva Cantor, *The Jewish Woman, 1900–1985: A Bibliography,* 2nd ed. (Fresh Meadows, N.Y.: Biblio Press, 1987; Z7963.J4 C36 1987 MRR Alc, AMED–Hebr; supplement, 1986–93).
5. Francesco Cordasco, *The Immigrant Woman in North America: An Annotated Bibliography of Selected References* (Metuchen, N.J.: Scarecrow Press, 1985; Z7964.U49 C67 1985 MRR Alc).
6. Dolores J. Maggiore, *Lesbianism: An Annotated Bibliography and Guide to the Literature, 1976–1991* (Metuchen, N.J.: Scarecrow Press, 1992; Z7164.S42 M34 1992 MRR Alc).
7. Monroe Nathan Work, comp., *A Bibliography of the Negro in Africa and America* (1928; reprint, New York: Octagon Books, 1965; Z1361.N39 W8 1965 MRR Alc, LH&G).
8. Sara M. Evans, *Born for Liberty: A History of Women in America* (New York: The Free Press, 1989; HQ1410.E83 1989).
9. Eleanor Flexner and Ellen Fitzpatrick, *Century of Struggle: The Woman's Rights Movement in the United States,* enlarged ed. (Cambridge, Mass.: Belknap Press of Harvard University Press, 1996; HQ1410.F6 1996 MRR Alc).
10. Félix V. Matos Rodríguez, *Women and Urban Change in San Juan, Puerto Rico, 1820–1868* (Gainesville: University Press of Florida, 1999; HQ1525.S26 M38 1999).
11. Katherine Osburn, *Southern Ute Women: Autonomy and Assimilation on the Reservation, 1887–1934* (Albuquerque: University of New Mexico Press, 1998; E99.U8 O83 1998).
12. *History of Women* [microform], 1,248 reels (New Haven, Conn.: Research Publications, 1975–79; Microfilm 51565; MicRR guide no. 47).
13. *The Gerritsen Collection of Women's History* [microform], 17,556 microfiche and 241 reels (Glen Rock, N.J.: Microfilming Corp. of America, 1975; Microfiche (w) 82/12; MicRR guide no. HQ1121.G43 1983, MRR Alc).

Louis Reeves Harrison. "Studio Saunterings." Moving Picture World, *June 12, 1915, p. 1,007 (PN1993.M88). Photograph. Moving Image Section, Motion Picture, Broadcasting, and Recorded Sound Division.*

Not only unheralded but completely unknown to all but the most persistent film historians, the accomplishments of pioneering women filmmakers of the silent era have only recently received widespread recognition. Alice Guy-Blaché, acknowledged as the director of the first narrative film, is shown as she rehearses her cast on the set of *Fra Diavolo,* in a shot from a contemporary film trade journal.

14. See note 2.

15. *The Henry A. Schmidt Photography Collection* [microform], 10 microfiches (Albuquerque: University of New Mexico, Center for Southwest Research, 1990; Microfiche 94/2152; MicRR guide no. 344).

16. *Witchcraft in New England* [microform], 3 microfilm reels (Wooster, Ohio: Bell & Howell; Ann Arbor, Mich.: University Microfilms International, distributor, [1980?]; Microfilm 89/9006; MicRR guide no. 272).

17. *Congressional Record* (Washington: U.S. Government Printing Office, with various titles, 1789–; KF35 MRR Alc, MicRR, LAW; 1989– at <http://thomas.loc.gov/>) (February 21, 1955), 101: 1840. Many important early congressional documents, including the early equivalents of the *Congressional Record* and Senate and House journals, have been digitized and are available at the address given in this note.

18. Esther Katz and Anita Rapone, eds., *Women's Experience in America: An Historical Anthology* (New Brunswick, N.J.: Transaction Books, 1980; HQ1410.W67).

19. Christine Bose, Roslyn Feldberg, and Natalie Sokoloff, eds., *Hidden Aspects of Women's Work* (New York: Praeger, 1987; HD6060.5.U5 H53 1987).

20. Susan Cardinale, comp., *Anthologies by and about Women: An Analytical Index* (Westport, Conn.: Greenwood Press, 1982; HQ1111.C35 1982 MRR Alc).

21. Sara Brownmiller and Ruth Dickstein, *An Index to Women's Studies Anthologies: Research across the Disciplines, 1980–1984* and *1985–1989* (New York: G.K. Hall, 1994,1996; HQ1180.B76 1994 and 1996 MRR Alc).

22. For Margaret Sanger's works, see several advertisements in *To-day's Housewife* (1924; TX1.T6).

23. The magazine had several different publishers and titles: *Calling All Girls* (1941–50, 1956–66), *Senior Prom* (1949–51), *Polly Pigtails' Magazine for Girls* (1953–55), *Young Miss* (1966–85), and *YM* (1985–); incomplete, AP201.C18 and AP201.C2.

24. *Mass Transportation: City Transit's Industry-wide Magazine* (1935–59, TF701.M3), May 1944, 134.

25. Letter, November 29, 1862, "Civil War Letters of Brigadier General William Ward Orme—1862–1866," *Journal of the Illinois State Historical Society* (July 1930, 246–315; F536.I18), at p. 262.

26. *Washington and Georgetown Directory* (Washington, 1853, no call number), 123; and list of businesses in 1863 directory. Most city directories published before 1936 are available in the Microform Reading Room.

27. R. N. T., *Memoir of Mary Whitall* (Philadelphia: Printed for the family [by Grant & Faires], 1885; CT275.W5314 M4), 1.

28. Samuel K. Jennings, *The Married Lady's Companion; or, Poor Man's Friend* (1808; reprint, New York: Arno, 1972; RG121.J45 1972), 19.

29. An American Lady, *Ladies' Vase: or, Polite Manual for Young Ladies* (Lowell: N. L. Dayton, 1843; BJ1681.L3), 116.

30. Lucy Larcom, *An Idyl of Work* (Boston: Osgood, 1875; PS2222.I5), 26, 138.

31. Yoshiko Uchida, *Journey to Topaz: A Story of the Japanese-American Evacuation* (New York: Scribner's Sons, 1971; PZ7.U25. Jo), 85.

32. Ibid., viii.

33. *The Journal of Mrs. Mary Ringo: A Diary of Her Trip across the Great Plains in 1864* (Santa Ana, Calif.: Privately printed, 1956; F594.R58), 20. After burying her husband, she and her five children traveled five more miles before stopping for the night.

34. Eva Antonia Wilbur-Cruce, *A Beautiful, Cruel Country* (Tucson: University of Arizona Press, 1987; F811.W67 1987), 177.

35. Alexis de Tocqueville, *Democracy in America*, 2 vols. (New York: Vintage Books, 1990; JK216.T7; 1835–40 ed., RBSC), 2: 214.

36. Harriet Martineau, *Society in America*, 2nd ed., 2 vols. (New York: Saunders and Otley, 1837; E165.M392), 2: 226.

37. *Spirit of Missions*, January 1873, 79 (Episcopalian; BV2575.A1 S7. LC holds 1837–1973). A brief name and subject index exists for 1836–1900 (BV2575.A1 S724 1977).

38. *Woman's Work for Woman and Our Mission Field*, July 1886, 154 (Presbyterian; BV2612.W8. LC holds 1885–1924, incomplete; 1885–1924, microfiche 82/12, P215).

39. XX [*sic*] De La Banta, *De la Banta's Advice to Ladies Concerning Beauty* (Chicago: S. Junkin, 1878; RA778.D3), 288.

40. George Washington Burnap, *The Sphere and Duties of Woman*, 3rd ed. (Baltimore: J. Murphy, 1848; HQ1221.B92), 46.

41. *The Young Husband's Book; A Manual of the Duties, Moral, Religious, and Domestic, Imposed by the Relations of Married Life* (Philadelphia: Lindsay and Blakiston, 1843; HQ756.Y7 1843), 15.

42. Henry Davenport Northrop, *The College of Life* (Chicago: Chicago Publication and Lithograph Co.,1895; AG105.N848), 23, 153.

43. Pye Henry Chavasse, *Chavasse's Advice to a Mother on the Management of Her Children*, 15th ed. (New York: George Routledge & Sons, 1898; RJ61.C53 1898a; earlier eds. in RBSC), 3.

44. Daniel Clarke Eddy, *The Young Man's Friend*, New Series (Boston: Graves and Young, 1865; BJ1671.E2 1865), 93.

45. Norton Hughes Jonathan, *Guide Book for the Young Man about Town* (Philadelphia: J.C. Winston Co., 1948; BJ1855.J6 1948), 229.

46. Jhan and June Robbins, "Why Young Mothers Feel Trapped," in *Why Young Mothers Feel Trapped*, edited by Robert Stein (New York: Trident Press, 1965; HQ759.R45), 5.

47. E. Marea, *The Wife's Manual, Containing Advice and Valuable Instruction for Married Women and Those Anticipating Marriage* (Cortland, N.Y.: [n.p.], 1896; HQ46.M32), 3.

48. Grace Reese Adkins, *The Sex Life of Girls and Young Women* (Cincinnati: Standard Publishing Company, 1919; HQ51.A3 Overflow), 9.

49. Leslie J. Swabacker, *Letters to My Daughter* (Chicago: Atwood & Knight, 1926; HQ51.S88), 81.

50. Amy G. Ayer, ed., *Facts for Ladies* (Chicago: A.G. Ayer, 1890; RG121.A89), 218.

51. John Harvey Kellog, *Plain Facts about Sexual Life* (Battle Creek, Mich.: Office of the Health Reformer,1877; RG121.K3 1877), 160, 293.

52. Catharine E. Beecher, *A Treatise on Domestic Economy, for the Use of Young Ladies at Home, and at School*, rev. [3rd] ed. (New York: Harper, 1848; TX145.B41 1848), 33, the first edition, 1841, is in RBSC, and the 1850 edition in MicRR.

53. Anna Parmly Paret, ed., *Harper's Handy-Book for Girls* (New York: Harper & Brothers, 1910; GV1201.P3), xiii–xiv.

54. Elizabeth Sloan Chesser, *From Girlhood to Womanhood* (New York: Funk & Wagnalls, 1914; HQ51.C5), 115.

55. Interview of Lizzie Atkins, published in *The American Slave: A Composite Autobiography*. Supplement, series 2, vol.2 of Texas Narratives, part 1 (Westport, Conn.: Greenwood Press, 1979; E444.A45 suppl. 2), 98. Original transcript in MSS.

56. *Outdoor Baseball for Girls and Women* (New York: American Sports Publishing Co., 1930; GV877.A55), 9.

57. George Stillman Hillard and Loomis J. Campbell, *The Franklin Second Reader* (New York: Taintor Brothers, Merrill & Co., 1873; PE1117.F742), 60.

58. Lois G. Nemec, *School Friends*, Democracy Series Revised (New York: Macmillan, 1951; PE1117.D46 Primer), 11–12.

59. Vassar College, *Catalogue* (Poughkeepsie, N.Y.), 1865 (LD7176), 34–35, 38.

60. *Girls Industrial College Bulletin* (Denton, Tex.), August 1903 (LD7251 .D4494), 34.

MARCHING FOR THE VOTE

1. *New York Evening Journal*, March 4, 1913, p. 3 (N&CPR).

2. *Suffrage Parade*, Senate Hearing, March 6–17, 1913, p. 70 (JK1888 1913b GenColl; MicRR; RBSC NAWSA; LAW).

3. There is disagreement about the number of marchers. The *New York Times*, March 4, 1913, p. 4 (N&CPR), said 5,000. Inez Haynes Irwin, *The Story of the Woman's Party* (New York: Harcourt, Brace and Co., 1921; JK1901 .I7 GenColl), 29, says 8,000. Doris Stevens, *Jailed for Freedom* (New York: Boni and Liveright, 1920; JK1901.S85 GenColl), 22, says 10,000.

4. Procession details from throughout the *Official Program: Woman Suf-*

frage Procession (MSS, P&P, RBSC, MicRR); the quotation is from p. 2. The Library's copies of the program have different numbers of pages. All citations in this essay are from the copy in the Rare Book and Special Collections Division.

5. *Suffrage Parade,* 27, 68, 70.

6. Ibid., 94.

7. Ibid., 70, 59, 329.

8. *Chicago Tribune,* March 4, 1913, p. 2 (N&CPR).

9. *Washington Post,* March 4, 1913, p. 10 (N&CPR).

10. *Suffrage Parade,* testimony of Secretary Stimson, 120.

11. For a full description of the Allegory, with descriptions of costumes, props, and music, see the *Official Program* (RBSC), pp. 14, 16. The records of the National Woman's Party (MSS) contain more than fifteen hundred items relating to the parade and its aftermath. All of the parade's many logistical details are documented, including efforts to recruit organizers, secure speakers, obtain permits, assemble the programs, invite members of Congress, and more.

12. *New York Times,* March 4, 1913, p. 4 (N&CPR).

13. Carrie Chapman Catt and Nettie Rogers Shuler, *Woman Suffrage and Politics: The Inner Story of the Suffrage Movement* (1926 RBSC NAWSA; reprint, Seattle: University of Washington Press, 1969; JK1896.C3 1969 GenColl), 242. Irwin, *The Story,* 30, and Stevens, *Jailed for Freedom,* 21, both say it was Wilson himself who asked the question as he drove through empty streets to his hotel. Presidential inaugurations were held on March 4 until the Twentieth Amendment (1933) changed the date to January 20.

14. Eleanor Flexner and Ellen Fitzpatrick, *Century of Struggle: The Woman's Rights Movement in the United States,* enl. ed. (Cambridge, Mass.: Belknap Press of Harvard University Press, 1996; HQ1410.F6 1996 GenColl), 255.

15. *National Party Platforms,* compiled by Donald Bruce Johnson, rev. ed., 2 vols. (Urbana, Ill.: University of Illinois Press, 1978; JK2255.J64 1978 GenColl), 1:176.

16. Irwin, *The Story,* 8–11.

17. Catt and Shuler, *Woman Suffrage and Politics,* 241.

18. Irwin, *The Story,* 18.

19. Ibid., 19.

20. *Historical Statistics of the United States, Colonial Times to 1970* (Washington: U.S. Government Printing Office, 1975; HA202.B87 1975 MRR Ref Desk and other locations), 1:168.

21. National American Woman Suffrage Association, *Forty-fifth Annual Report* (New York: NAWSA, 1913; JK1881.N28 45th 1913 GenColl), 67.

22. *Votes for Women Inaugural Parade,* broadside, National Woman's Party, Records, Group I, box 14, "NWP Leaflets and Broadsides" (MSS).

23. *Woman Voter and the Newsletter,* 4:3 (March 1913), p. 10 (JK1880 .W55 GenColl).

24. Ibid., p. 10.

25. The Library of Congress has preserved a print of the film, but unfortunately no known copies of the sound recording survive. *Votes for Women,* AFI/Tayler Collection (FEA 9595), Thomas A. Edison, Inc., 1913; 1 reel, 368 ft., si., originally produced with sound recording on a cylinder; (the LC copy lacks the cylinder), 35mm ref. print (MBRS). *Variety,* April 11, 1913, p. 6 (microfilm 03722, MicRR, MBRS).

26. Officers of the National American Woman Suffrage Association to The Honorable Woodrow Wilson, February 12, 1913, in the National Woman's Party Records, Group I, box 2, "February 11–13, 1913." This letter states that it was to be "borne" by the hikers to Wilson, but the presence of the signed original in the National Woman's Party Records indicates that it was never delivered. There is no copy in the Woodrow Wilson Papers (MSS). Although they did not present the letter, the suffragists did indeed focus their attention on President Wilson, and when he refused to join their cause, they began to picket the White House. Silent women holding banners stood outside the president's home every day, twenty-four hours a day, for eight months. The pickets endured taunts, arrests, and imprisonment but never faltered. It was still to take until January 1918 before Wilson joined the suffrage bandwagon.

27. *Woman Voter and the Newsletter,* 4:3 (March 1913), p. 10.

28. Stevens, *Jailed for Freedom,* 23. Anna Howard Shaw, president of NAWSA, complained that Paul's group had not told her of the meeting and so she did not attend (Ida Husted Harper, Scrapbooks, XI [JK1899.H4 RBSC], p. 31). Alice Paul and her Washington supporters were soon to establish their own, independent suffrage party, the National Woman's Party, to work solely on the passage of a constitutional amendment.

29. *Woman's Journal and Suffrage News,* March 8, 1913, p. 1 (RBSC–NAWSA, MicRR).

30. *New York Tribune,* March 8, 1913, p. 3 (N&CPR); Harper, Scrapbook, XI (RBSC), p. 28.

31. NAWSA, *Forty-fifth Annual Report,* 17.

32. *New York Evening Journal,* March 3, 1913, p. 3 (N&CPR).

33. Three photographs of the procession and the cover of the official program can be seen on the Library's Web site <http://www.loc.gov/rr/print /076_vfw.html>.

34. Both cartoons were reproduced in *Cartoons Magazine,* 3:4 (April 1913), p. 216 (LC-USZ62–55985 P&P).

35. Many cartoons appear in newspapers, books, and articles in the General Collections and N&CPR. *Life* (1883–1936; AP101.L6 GenColl) is a rich source. For a collection of suffrage cartoons, see Alice Sheppard, *Cartooning for Suffrage* (Albuquerque: University of New Mexico Press, 1994; NC1425.S54 1994 GenColl).

36. *Yidishes Tageblatt,* March 4, 1913, p. 8 (AMED-Hebr).

37. Robert S. Gallagher, "I Was Arrested, of Course," *American Heritage,* 25:2 (February 1974), p. 20 (E171.A43 GenColl).

38. Ibid., 20.

39. See the records of the National Woman's Party (Group I, boxes 1–3) for correspondence on the role of African American women in the parade (MSS). See also *Crisis,* 5:6 (April 1913), p. 267; reprint ed. (New York: Negro Universities Press, 1969; E185.5.C9 GenColl). For Wells-Barnett, see the *Chicago Tribune,* March 4, 1913, p. 2 (N&CPR). Additional sources of material on African American women and the march include the records of the National Woman's Party and NAWSA (both in MSS).

2 SERIAL AND GOVERNMENT PUBLICATIONS DIVISION

1. Ralph G. Martin, *Cissy* (New York: Simon and Schuster, 1979; CT275 .P42 M37), 338.

2. Collection policy statements and overviews are available in the Library's Web site at <http://www.loc.gov/acq/devpol>.

3. Lloyd Wendt, *Chicago Tribune: The Rise of a Great American Newspaper* (Chicago: Rand McNally and Company, 1979; PN4899.C4 T87 N&CPR), 574–75, 665–66. Wendt gives extensive coverage to Schultz.

4. Titles covering the newspaper field can be found in periodical directories such as *Ulrich's International Periodical Directory, Standard Periodicals Directory,* and the *Serials Directory,* usually under the heading "journalism."

5. "Mrs. Jennie June Croly, Something of the Work of the First Newspaper and Club Woman—Farewell Reception to Her," *New York Times,* March 11, 1900, p. 17, c. 5.

6. *Washington Herald* (News MF 1011), October 12, 1931, pp. 1, 12. Besides adding "Largest Morning Circulation in the Nation's Capital" above the masthead, Patterson also printed a full-page advertisement announcing the achievement.

7. George C. Crager, "In Indian Guise," *New York World* (News MF 1363), February 1, 1891, p. 20. Theresa H. Dean, "He Was a Daring Man," *Chicago Herald* (News MF 2133), February 5, 1891, p. 9. Crager credited himself with visiting a hostile Sioux camp disguised as an Indian to interview Chief Two Strike. Dean exposed his story as a fabrication and rather satirically noted the excessive firepower carried by all the eastern reporters: "it looked to me as if the only people at the reservation who seemed to be at all conscious of danger were the newspaper men."

8. The terms "sob sisters" and "weeping willies" originated in 1907 at the Harry Thaw murder trial when a male colleague scorned the emotion-charged coverage that women reporters had provided.

9. Cover story, *Time,* June 12, 1939.

10. Frances Davis, *A Fearful Innocence* (Kent, Ohio: Kent State University Press, 1981; PN4874.D37 A298), 148, 156.

11. Nellie Bly's first-person series about her experiences at Blackwell's Island, "Behind Asylum Bars," appeared in the October 9, 1887, issue of the *New York World* (p. 25).

12. Promotional information for *Standard Periodical Directory,* 2000 edition, from Oxbridge Communication, Inc., <http://www.mediafinder.com/>.

13. "The Black List of States," *Louisville Courier-Journal* (News MF 1158), March 27, 1895.

14. "An Editorial Triumvirate," *Milwaukee Journal* (News MF 1533), February 23, 1895, p. 4.

15. Ann Colbert, "Philanthropy in the Newsroom: Women's Editions of Newspapers, 1894–1896," *Journalism History* 22, no. 3 (autumn 1996: 90–99.

16. *Samir Husni's Guide to New Consumer Magazines* (New York: Oxbridge Communications, 1998; Z6951.S32).

17. Magazine Publishers of America, "Average Circulation for Top 100 ABC Magazines, 2000," *Fact Sheet: Circulation,* <http://www.magazine.org/resources/fact_sheets/cs2_9_01.html>.

18. Lee Server, *Danger Is My Business* (San Francisco: Chronicle Books, 1993; PN4878.5.S47 1993 N&CPR), 19.

3 LAW LIBRARY OF CONGRESS

1. The right of dower was a share of real and personal property owned by husbands during marriage that was designated for the support of widows. The dower was necessary because societal restraints denied women the right to provide for their own financial security.

2. Mary A. Greene, LL.B., *The Woman's Manual of Law* (New York: Silver, Burdett and Company, 1902; KF387.G7), iii.

3. Jurisdictions are areas of authority and can be either a geographic area in which a court has power or the types of cases it has power to hear. *Black's Law Dictionary,* 6th edition (St. Paul, Minn.: West Publishing Co., 1990; KF156 .B53 1990), 766. Jurisdiction refers to federal or state lawmaking and enforcement power.

4. Federal preemption is a doctrine adopted by the U.S. Supreme Court holding that certain matters are of such national, as opposed to local, character that in them federal laws preempt or take precedence over state laws. States may not pass a law inconsistent with the federal law (*Black's Law Dictionary,* 5th ed., 1060).

5. Generally, the laws passed by state legislative bodies are called session laws, but they can have different names depending on the state: "public acts" or "laws" are both used.

6. *Landmark Briefs and Arguments of the Supreme Court of the United States: Constitutional Law* (Bethesda, Md.: University Publications of America, 1975– ; KF101.8.K87). This ongoing publication reprints the records, briefs, and arguments for selected major constitutional decisions.

7. The Law Library of Congress has an extensive collection of digest volumes. Each year the *General Digest* covering state and federal decisions is published. Each ten years the *General Digest* is compiled into a *Decennial Digest. The American Digest, 1658–1896, Century Edition* is the earliest of these. *The First Decennial Digest* includes cases from 1897 to 1906.

8. The Law Library owns a photostatic copy of the 1648 edition. According to the note included in the photostat reproduction of the earliest Massachusetts Code, "The existence of this, the first printed collection of the Laws of Massachusetts Bay, has long been known, but this is the only copy that has come to light. After many years of fruitless search it was discovered in 1906 in a small private library in England. No other book has been more earnestly sought for than this; . . ." —Church.

9. *The General Laws and Liberties of the Massachusetts Colony in New-England, Revised and Reprinted, by Order of the General Court Holden at Boston, May 15th, 1672* (London, 1675; LAW United States Massachusetts 2 1672), 42.

10. *An Abridgement of the Publick Laws of Virginia in Force and Use June 10, 1720* (London: F. Fayram and J. Clarke, 1722; LAW <United States Virginia 1 (Jefferson Coll.) No. 151>).

11. *Trial of Rev. Joy Hamlet Fairchild* (Boston, 1845; BX5960.O6 A2).

12. Morris Cohen, *Bibliography of Early American Law: Criminal Trials,* no. 12772, 542 (Law<Trials (A & E) "Kinney">).

13. Interestingly, the dower right was usually one-third of the husband's estate. Although most states repealed dower rights early in the twentieth century, most modern intestate laws (inheritance without wills) likewise give women one-third of their husbands' estates.

14. Private examinations—where wives were questioned out of the presence of their husbands—were held by court magistrates. The statements were recorded and used to determine if the wife had been coerced into signing the documents conveyancing the property to another person.

15. *Catlin v. Ware,* 9 *Tyng* 218 (1812) (Massachusetts).

16. This is a parallel citation. The court decision can be found in the *New Mexico Reports* and *Pacific Reporter,* 2nd Series. Only the citation differs, although the regional reporter may be annotated. The *Pacific Reporter* is a regional reporting series that publishes court decisions from a group of states. Other states whose decisions it includes are Arizona, Utah, Oklahoma, Kansas, Colorado, Wyoming, Montana, Idaho, Nevada, Oregon, California, and Washington.

17. *McDonald v. Senn,* 53 N.M. 198, 204 P.2d 990, 1002.

18. James H. Deering, ed., *The Civil Code of the State of California,* title 1, section 159 (San Francisco: Bancroft-Whitney Co., 1927; KFC30.5.D4 C56 1927), 62.

19. *The Civil Code of the State of California,* 1872 (Sacramento, 1872; KFC30. A233 1872), 55.

20. Theodore H. Hittell, *General Laws of the State of California, from 1850 to 1864, Inclusive* (San Francisco: Bancroft-Whitney, 1865; KFC30 1865 .A32), 1:516.

21. Hittell, 41.

22. Gustavus Schmidt, *The Civil Law of Spain and Mexico,* Art. 43 (New Orleans: Thomas Rea, 1851; Law Mexico 7 Schm), 12.

23. Deering, 62.

24. Hittell, 516

25. *Lewis v. Lewis,* 18 *Cal.* 654, 655 (1861) (KFC45 .A2).

26. *Jones v. Porters,* 2 *Virginia Colonial Decisions* 93 (1740) [Law<Virginia (Colon) 5>].

27. *The Laws & Acts of the General Assembly for Their Majesties Province of New-York, 1691* (New York: William Bradford, Printer to Their Majesties King William & Queen Mary, 1694), 18.

28. *Barnes' Lessee v. Irwin,* 2 *U. S.* (2 *Dallas*) 199 (1793). The earliest decisions published in the *United States Reports* were decisions of the Pennsylvania Supreme Court. The decisions of the United States Supreme Court began to be published after 1790. *Barnes' Lessee* was a decision by the Pennsylvania Supreme Court.

29. Richard H. Chused, "Married Women's Property Law: 1800–1850," *Georgetown Law Journal* 71 (1983): 1,359, 1,366.

30. 1848 *New York Laws* 307, ch. 200.

31. Joan Hoff-Wilson, *Law, Gender, and Injustice: A Legal History of U. S. Women* (New York: New York University Press, 1991; KF4758.H64 1990), 128.

32. *The Homestead Act of 1862,* c. 75, 12 *Stat.* 392.

33. Constitution of California of 1849, Article XI, section 14, pp. 328, 412 (KFC679.C6 1895).

34. *The Revised Statutes of Texas, 1879,* Title XXXVII, Art. 2181, 320; Title L, 412 (Austin: State Printing Office, 1887; LAW Texas 2 1879).

35. Three indentured servants—John Punch, James Gregory, and Victor—ran away and were recaptured. James Gregory and Victor, both white, were given "thirty stripes" and an additional four years of servitude, whereas John Punch, a Negro, was sentenced to serve the remainder of his life. Helen Tunnicliff Catterall, ed., *Judicial Cases concerning American Slavery and the Negro,* 5 vols. (1926; reprint, New York: Octagon Books, 1968; KF4545.S5 C3 1968), 1: 77.

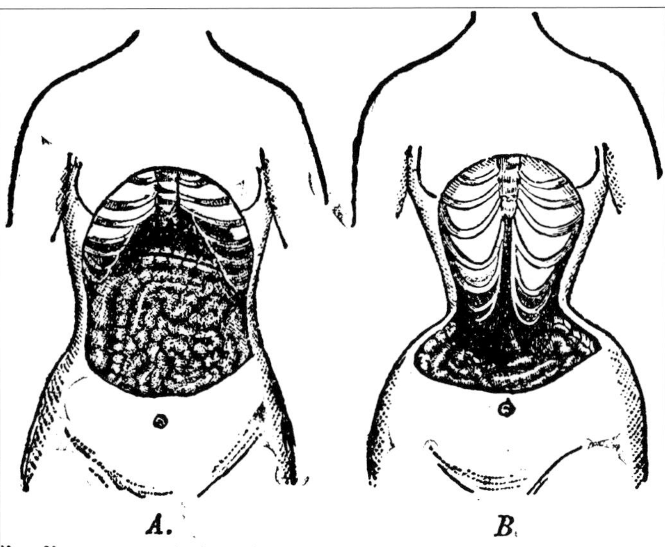

"Nature versus Corsets, Illustrated." *John W. Gibson and wife, Golden Thoughts on Chastity and Procreation (Toronto, Ont., and Naperville, Ill.: J.L. Nichols & Co., 1903; HQ31.G44), 107. General Collections.*

Although women's magazines of the last decades of the nineteenth century are full of advertisements urging women to purchase new and better corsets—women could choose corsets specially designed for bicycling or even select a "suffrage corset"—advice literature and medical literature had for many years warned of the dangers to female health and reproductive ability that could result from tight-lacing. This image appears in the chapter "Looking toward Marriage—Essentials," where the text states plainly that "Any article of dress that confines the body, that prevents freedom of motion, that compresses the vital organs, is harmful, unhealthful and should never be tolerated by a sensible woman" (p. 106). Corsets were rarely worn by lower class women, and by 1900 they were on the wane altogether.

36. Act CII, *Laws of Virginia,* March, 1661–2 (Hening, *Statutes at Large,* 2: 116–17).

37. Act VI, *Laws of Virginia,* December, 1662 (Hening, *Statutes at Large,* 2: 167).

38. Act XII, *Laws of Virginia,* December 1662 (Hening, *Statutes at Large,* 2: 170).

39. *Celia, a Slave* is a narrative account of such a criminal trial, where a slave woman was tried for the murder of her owner, found guilty, and sentenced to be hanged. Robert Newsom, age sixty, had purchased Celia, age fourteen, to be his live-in mistress. Five years later, she asked him to discontinue sexual relations with her until after the birth of their second child. He refused and she killed him by beating him with a piece of wood and burned his body in her fireplace. She could not testify on her own behalf because that would have meant bringing evidence against a white person. Melton A. McLaurin, *Celia, a Slave* (Athens: University of Georgia Press, 1991; KF223.C43 M34 1991).

40. Catterall, 77.

41. Act XVI, *Laws of Virginia,* April 1691 (*Hening's Statutes at Large,* 3:87). This section of the law with its amendments remained in force until the U.S. Supreme Court ruled the law unconstitutional in *Loving v. Virginia,* 388 U.S. 1 (1967).

42. *Laws of Maryland,* chap. XIII (May 1717), 140.

43. Karen B. Morello, *The Invisible Bar: The Woman Lawyer in America 1638 to the Present* (New York: Random House, 1986; KF299 .W6 M67 1986), 8.

44. See note 39.

45. Life estate is an estate whose duration is limited to the life of the party holding it, or some other person. Life interest is a claim or interest in real or personal property, not amounting to ownership, and limited by a term of life, either the lifetime of the person in whom the right is vested or that of another (*Black's Law Dictionary,* 5th ed., 1979, 833).

46. *The Fugitive Slave Act of 1850* required citizens to assist in the return of escaped slaves to their owners (chap. LX, 9 *Stat.* 462 [1850]).

47. Debra Newman Ham, ed., *The African American Odyssey* (Washington: Library of Congress, 1998; Z1361.N39 L47 1993), 54, 50.

48. Morello, 1.

49. J. Clay Smith, ed., *Rebels in Law: Voices in History of Black Women Lawyers* (Ann Arbor: University of Michigan Press, 1998; KF299.A35 R43 1998), 2.

50. *Bradwell v. Illinois,* 84 U. S. (16 *Wall.*) 130 (1873).

51. United States Constitution, Amendment XIV, §1.

52. *Bradwell v. Illinois,* 84 U.S. (16 *Wall.*) 130, 141 (1873).

53. *In re Lockwood,* 154 U.S. 116, 117 (1893).

54. Morello, 12.

55. Smith, ed., *Rebels in Law,* 9.

56. Lelia J. Robinson, L.L.B., "Women Lawyers in the United States," *The Green Bag* (1890), 2:10.

57. *Hishon v. King & Spalding,* 104 *S.Ct.* 2229 (1984). Elizabeth Anderson Hishon filed a Title VII sex-based discrimination suit against King & Spalding, her law firm, when she did not receive a partnership offer. The U.S. Supreme Court reversed and remanded the decision that denied her claim under Title VII.

58. *General Laws, Memorials, and Resolutions of the Territory of Wyoming,* c. 31 (1869), 371.

59. *Congressional Record,* 62nd Congress, 2nd Session (1912). App. 193.

60. New Jersey Constitution of 1776, in William F. Swindler, ed., *Sources and Documents of United States Constitutions,* 10 vols. (Dobbs Ferry, N.Y.: Oceana Publications, 1973–79; KF4530.S94), 6:450.

61. New Jersey Constitution of 1844, ibid., 454.

62. *Anthony v. United States,* 24 *F. Cases* 829 (1873).

63. *Minor v. Happersett,* 88 *U.S.* (21 *Wall.*) 162, 178 (1874).

64. *Congressional Record,* 62nd Congress, 2nd Session, 1912, App. 190.

65. Brief for Defendant in Error, *Muller v. Oregon,* 208 U.S. 412 (1908), commonly called the "Brandeis Brief."

66. *Revised Laws of Massachusetts,* ch. 106, §24 (1902). Reprinted in *Landmark Briefs and Arguments of the Supreme Court of the United States: Constitutional Law,* vol. 16 (Arlington, Va.: University Publications of America, 1975), 66.

67. 208 U.S. 412 (1908).

68. The Brandeis Brief was highly influential in swaying the high court's opinion. It combined more than one hundred pages of sociological data on the negative effects of long hours of work on women's health and reproductive capabilities gathered from several countries with fewer than five pages of legal argument. *Landmark Briefs and Arguments of the Supreme Court,* vol. 16, 63.

69. *Acts of Congress Affecting the District of Columbia from December 3, 1917, to March 4, 1919–2nd and 3rd Sessions, 65th Congress* (KFD1225.A213), 23:519, 523.

70. Freedom-of-contract doctrine was a common law concept that held the ability at will to make, or abstain from making, a binding obligation enforced by the sanctions at the law. It included the right to contract about one's affairs, including the right to make contracts of employment, and to obtain the best terms one can as the result of private bargaining, as well as the corresponding right to accept a contract proposed.

71. 261 U.S. 525 (1923).

72. *West Coast Hotel Co. v. Parrish*, 300 U.S. 379 (1937).

73. *Pub. L.* 88–352, *Title VII*, 78 *Stat.* 241.

74. *Pub. L.* 88–352, *Title VII*, section 703, 78 *Stat.* 241, 255.

75. *Meritor Savings Bank v. Mechelle Vinson*, 106 *S.Ct.* 2399, 2405 (1986).

76. 28 C.F.R. 42 (2000). Regulations promulgated by an administrative agency are cited based on their locations in the *Federal Register* (61 FR 34730, July 3, 1996) and in the *Code of Federal Regulations*. The policy for Equal Employment Opportunity within the Department of Justice can be found in volume 61 of the *Federal Register* on page 34730. The same regulations can be found in its codified format at 28 C.F.R. 42 (2000), which is read, "Title 28 of the Code of Federal Regulations, part 42, in the 2000 edition."

77. Bound federal bills, starting with the 16th Congress, are part of the Law Library of Congress collections.

78. The Law Library has the entire range of debates occurring on the floor of the House and Senate, beginning with the *Annals of Congress* (1789–1824) and including the *Register of Debates* (1824–37), the *Congressional Globe* (1838–73), and the *Congressional Record* (1873–).

79. 110 *Congressional Record* (88th Congress, 2nd Session, 1964), 2,577.

80. An act supplementary to the acts in relation to immigration, ch. 141, section 3, 18 *Stat.* 477 (1875).

81. An act to regulate the immigration of aliens into the United States, ch. 1012, section 3, 32 *Stat.* 1213, 1214 (1903).

82. An Act to amend an Act entitled "An Act to regulate the immigration of aliens into the United States, approved February twentieth, nineteen hundred and seven," ch. 128, section 3, 36 *Stat.* 263, 264 (1910).

83. The Mann Act, ch. 395, 36 *Stat.* 825 (1910).

84. Staff of the House Committee on the Judiciary, 100th Congress, 2d Session, *Grounds for Exclusion of Aliens under the Immigration and Nationality Act: Historical Background and Analysis*, 11 (Comm. Print 1988).

THE LONG ROAD TO EQUALITY

1. The American Nurses' Association was one of the supporters of ERAmerica, the campaign organization founded to administer the final push through to ratification. ERAmerica Records, box 112, MSS.

2. Sandra R. Gregg and Bill Peterson, "End of ERA Battle," B-1 and B-2, *Washington Post,* July 1, 1982. All newspaper microfilm is found in the Newspaper and Current Periodical Room (N&CPR).

3. Katy Butler and Glennda Chui, "Deadline Passes: 1000 Women at S.F. Vigil for the ERA," *San Francisco Chronicle,* July 1, 1982, p. 7.

4. Quoted in Barbara Ehrenreich, *The Hearts of Men: American Dreams and the Flight from Commitment* (Garden City, N.Y.: Doubleday, 1983; HQ1090.E36 1983 GenColl), 145.

5. Elisabeth Bumiller, "Schlafly's Gala Goodbye to ERA," *Washington Post,* July 1, 1982, p. C-1. In her article "Victory is Bittersweet for Architect of Amendment's Downfall," *New York Times* reporter Lynn Rosellini reported that Phyllis Schlafly was now committing her 50,000-member Eagle Forum to campaigns against sex education, against a nuclear freeze, and to rid school texts of feminist influence (July 1, 1982, p. A12).

6. Introduced in the 92nd Congress as H.J.Res. 208. See *U.S. Statutes at Large,* 92nd vol. 86, 1973, 1523. LAW.

7. Susan Ware, *Holding Their Own: American Women in the 1930s* (Boston: G.K. Hall & Co., 1982; HQ1420.W33 1982 GenColl), 110.

8. Cynthia Harrison, "Prelude to Feminism: Women's Organizations, the Federal Government and the Rise of the Women's Movement, 1942 to 1968." (Ph.D. diss., Columbia University, 1982; MicRR), 131. Published as *On Account of Sex: The Politics of Women's Issues, 1945–1968* (Berkeley: University of California Press, 1988; HQ1236.5.U6 H37 1988 GenColl).

9. Edith Mayo and Jerry K. Frye, "The ERA: Postmortem of a Failure in Political Communication," in *Rights of Passage: The Past and Future of the ERA,* Joan Hoff-Wilson, ed. (Bloomington: Indiana University Press, 1986; KF4758.R54 1986 LAW), 82.

10. The President's Commission on the Status of Women was established under Executive Order 10980, 26 Fed. Reg. 12059, on December 14, 1961. The commission's purpose was to assess the progress of women in the United States and to make recommendations for "removing barriers to the full realization of women's basic rights." An excellent collection of the commission's reports is held by the Library in the General Collections. See United States, President's Commission on the Status of Women, *American Women: The Report of the President's Commission on the Status of Women and Other Publications of the Commission* (New York: Scribner, 1965; HQ1420.A52 1965 GenColl). Five other presidential commissions or committees on women were created following the Kennedy administration: one each under Presidents Johnson, Nixon, and Ford and two under President Carter. For an account of the commissions, see Irene Tinker, ed., *Women in Washington: Advocates for Public Policy* (Beverly Hills: Sage Publications, 1983; HQ1236.W638 1983 GenColl), 21–44. For commentaries on sex discrimination in education and employment in this period, see U.S. Congress, House Committee on Education and Labor, Special Subcommittee on Education, *Discrimination against Women, Hearings, 91st Congress, 2nd sess.* (Washington: GPO, 1970; KF27.E336 1970 LAW). This committee was headed by Rep. Edith Green, whose reminiscences of her long, activist career can be found in the Association of Former Members of Congress Oral History Collection on tape (MBRS), in transcript (MSS), and on microform (MicRR).

11. Sound cassette (29 min.), "The ERA in America," National Public Radio, Washington, D.C., 1981 (RYA 7666 MBRS).

12. Mary P. Ryan, *Womanhood in America: From Colonial Times to the Present.* (Irvine: University of California, 1983; HQ1410.R9 1983 GenColl), 308. During the economic and social upheavals of the 1930s, many women were appointed to influential positions in the government, leading to impressive gains for women as policy-makers, but this generation did not establish forward links for the next feminist effort, and they were divided over the Equal Rights Amendment. For a discussion of feminists under the Roosevelt Administration, see Susan Ware, *Holding Their Own.*

13. Once the proposed amendment was before the Congress and the states, the Court cited this factor as a reason for noninterference. Gilbert Steiner, *Constitutional Inequality: The Political Fortunes of the Equal Rights Amendment* (Washington: The Brookings Institution, 1985; KF4758.S73 1985 LAW), 37–40.

14. PCSW, *American Women,* 45.

15. Support of abortion rights was on NOW's second plank. As Betty Friedan recalled, "the Equal Rights Amendment and abortion were and are the two gut issues of the women's movement essential to real security–and equality and human dignity–for all women, whether they work outside or inside the home." Betty Friedan, *It Changed My Life: Writings on the Women's Movement* (New York: Random House, 1976; HQ1413.F75 A34 1976 Gen Coll), 84.

16. A discharge petition is a device used to remove a proposed measure from a legislative committee to which it has been assigned. It has rarely been successful since half the total membership of the House or Senate, plus one, must approve. However, in this instance, the requisite signatures were obtained in five weeks. The papers of Emanuel Celler are held by the Library's Manuscript Division. The Association of Former Members of Congress Oral History Collection includes Representative Griffiths' reminiscences of the ERA (taped interview in MBRS [RYA 1064–1073] and transcript in MSS and on microform [microfiche 82/100 MicRR]).

17. *U.S. Congressional Record,* 91st Congress, vol. 116, part 21, August 10–14, 1970, 27999 (LAW; MRR Alc). Replying to Griffiths' opening statement, Emanuel Celler opposed the motion to discharge the Judiciary Committee on HR 264: "What we are being asked to do is to vote on a constitutional amendment, the consequences of which are unexamined, its meaning nondefined, and its risks uncalculated . . . ever since Adam gave up his rib to make a woman, throughout the ages we have learned that physical, emotional, psychological and social differences exist and dare not be disregarded . . . The adoption of a blunderbuss amendment would erase existing protective female legislation with the most disastrous consequences" (28000–28001).

18. Senator Ervin delivered his speech against the ERA on the floor of the Senate on August 21, 1970. Note in particular his section on "Functional

Differences between Men and Women." *U.S. Congressional Record*. 91st Cong. Vol. 116, part 22 (August 17–31, 1970), 29670. Ervin subsequently offered a copy of his speech in evidence at the Hearings before the Senate Judiciary Committee, noting "On Friday, August 21, 1970, I made a speech in the Senate on the House-passed equal rights amendment, which I called a potential destructive and self-defeating blunderbuss. I borrowed that description from a Law Review article by Prof. Leo Kanowitz, professor of law at the University of New Mexico." *Equal Rights 1970: Hearings on S.J. Res. 61 and S.J. Res. 231 before the Senate Comm. on the Judiciary*, 91st Cong. (1970). Testimony of Senator Sam J. Ervin Jr., North Carolina (Washington; KF26.J8 1970d LAW; MRR Alc), 1–28.

19. Mathews and De Hart, *Sex, Gender, and the Politics of ERA*, 36. The heavy use of speeches and writings by Sam Ervin in anti-ERA literature can be seen in the run of the *Phyllis Schlafly Newsletter* in box 124 of ERAmerica Records, Manuscript Division, and in Schlafly's book *The Power of the Positive Woman* (New Rochelle, N.Y.: Arlington House Publishers, 1977; HQ1426.S33 GenColl), reissued with an additional opening chapter as *The Power of the Christian Woman* (Cincinnati, Ohio: Standard Publishing, 1981; HQ1426.S33 1981 GenColl).

20. The AFL-CIO's chief lobbyist continued to speak of the "potentially destructive impact" of the ERA on women's protective legislation in the Senate hearings. Steiner, *Constitutional Inequality*, 21. See the relevant portion of the testimony by Myra K. Wolfgang, vice president, Hotel and Restaurant Employees and Bartenders International, AFL-CIO, in behalf of Michigan Women's Commission in *Equal Rights 1970: Hearings on S.J. Res. 61 and S.J. Res. 231*, 30–45.

21. The first eight months in the ERA ratification process moved quickly, with twenty-two states ratifying by Thanksgiving 1972. Eight more states ratified between January and March 22, 1973, but no more that year; three in 1974; one in 1975; and one in 1977, a total of thirty-five. Steiner, *Constitutional Inequality*, 55.

22. Tape recording of National Press Club Luncheon, January 24, 1972 (RXA 1506, MBRS).

23. Steiner, *Constitutional Inequality*, 57–58. Mathews and De Hart, *Sex, Gender, and the Politics of ERA*, 51. Sam Ervin's opinions and style, as well as the attitudes and arguments of proponents and opponents, can be seen in the video *Who Will Protect the Family?*, a 1982 PBS feature on the unsuccessful struggle for ERA ratification in North Carolina (VBC 7099, MBRS).

24. Steiner, *Constitutional Inequality*, 63, 65.

25. A complete collection of IWY conference reports are found in the General Collections. See, for instance, *Report of the World Conference of the International Women's Year, 19 June-2 July 1975* (New York: United Nations, 1976; HQ1106 1975 .R46 GenColl) and *International Women's Year World Conference Documents Index* (New York: UNIFO Publishers, 1975; HQ1106 1975 .I57 MicRR).

26. See United States, National Commission on the Observance of International Women's Year, *To Form a More Perfect Union . . . Justice for American Women* (Washington: GPO, 1976; HQ1426.U55 1975 GenColl).

27. Rebecca Klatch,"Women against Feminism," in *A History of Our Time: Readings on Postwar America*. Edited by William H. Chafe and Harvard Sitkoff (New York: Oxford University Press, 1999; E742.H57 1999 GenColl), 224–25, and the *Phyllis Schlafly Report*, May and August 1977. ERAmerica Records, box 124, MSS.

28. Asking the question "What's Wrong with 'Equal Rights' for Women?", Phyllis Schlafly first attacked the ERA and "women libbers" in the *Phyllis Schlafly Newsletter* of February 1972 (ERAmerica Records, box 124, folder marked "STOP ERA and Phyllis Schlafly Report," MSS). Following a spirited defense of traditional family values and American women's privileged position in American society, she alleged that the ERA would make women subject to the draft and that married women would lose their rights to support for themselves and their children from their husbands, as well as alimony in the case of divorce. The following year (May 3, 1973), Martha Griffiths attempted to answer some of Schlafly's arguments in a Vital History series point-counterpoint interview (RZA 760, no. 1, side A, MBRS). Schlafly's views were also discussed on the *Larry King Show* the day after the defeat of the ERA, July 1, 1982, when she declared that, despite laws requiring equitable treatment of working women, "the career most women want is marriage, home, husband, and children." (RYA 5277, MBRS).

29. The records of ERAmerica were acquired by the Library of Congress in 1982.

30. ERAmerica Records, box 6, MSS.

31. As quoted by Lynn Rosellini, "Victory Is Bittersweet for Architect of Amendment's Downfall," *New York Times*, July 1, 1982, A12. N&CPR.

32. Examples included in the ERAmerica records were Jill Newman, "The ERA—What It Would Really Do," *Women's Day*, November 1979, and

Currier & Ives. Age of Brass: Or the Triumphs of Woman's Rights *and* Age of Iron: Man As He Expects to Be. *Lithographs, 1869. Popular Graphic Arts Collection. Prints and Photographs Division. LC-USZC2-1921 and LC-USZC2-1922.*

The year these companion prints were copyrighted, 1869, may well have seemed a watershed year for those observing the evolving status of women. The American Woman Suffrage Association, founded by Lucy Stone and her husband, Henry Blackwell, and the National Woman Suffrage Association, founded by Elizabeth Cady Stanton and Susan B. Anthony, embarked on their separate approaches to achieving women's suffrage. Thousands of women who entered the workforce during the Civil War continued to work outside the home, as recognized by Stanton's establishment of the Working Woman's Association in 1868. Meanwhile, Catharine E. Beecher and her sister, Harriet Beecher Stowe, in their work *The American Woman's Home* (1869), railed at the growing popularity of conveniences such as store-bought bread. The Currier & Ives firm—which itself employed women as artists and colorists—issued this pair of prints as satirical commentary on the women's rights movement and the threat it appeared to pose to traditional gender roles.

Mary Schnack, "ERA: What It Will (Won't) Do for Working Women," *Working Woman's Magazine*, November 1979. Many other articles both for and against passage of the ERA can be identified using periodical indexes (see chapter 1).

33. The Roper Organization, *The 1985 Virginia Slims American Women's Opinion Poll: A Study* (New York: Roper, 1985; HQ1420.A17 1986 GenColl), 16.

34. These included: The Comprehensive Health Manpower Act of 1971, prohibiting use of federal funds for health programs which discriminate on the basis of sex in admissions to professional schools; Title IX of the Education Amendments of 1972, prohibiting sex discrimination in educational programs and activities; the Equal Employment Opportunity Act of 1972, extending coverage of Title VII of the 1964 Civil Rights Act (banning sex discrimination) to employees of federal, state, and local governments, educational institutions, and any business or union with more than fifteen employees; the Housing and Community Development Act of 1974, prohibiting sex discrimination in housing and credit and requiring lenders to consider the combined incomes of husbands and wives in extending mortgage credit; the Equal Credit Opportunity Act of 1974, prohibiting discrimination based on sex or marital status in any credit transaction; the Small Business Act Amendments of 1974, prohibiting discrimination on the basis of sex or marital status in programs for loans and guarantees administered by the Small Business Administration; the Civil Service Reform Act of 1978, prohibiting discrimination in the federal civil service on the basis of sex; the Equal Rights Amendment (Proposed); and the Extension of the Deadline for the Ratification of the Equal Rights Amendment.

35. Mathews and De Hart, *Sex, Gender, and the Politics of ERA*, viii, describe the suspect category test's application to sex discrimination. To use the Ginsburg papers, which are restricted, it is necessary to apply for the donor's permission through the Manuscript Division.

36. Sue Thomas and Clyde Wilcox, eds., *Women and Elective Office* (New York: Oxford University Press, 1998; HQ1391.U5 W63 1998 GenColl), 2.

37. Ibid., 130–49.

4 RARE BOOK AND SPECIAL COLLECTIONS DIVISION

1. Anne Bradstreet, *The Tenth Muse Lately Sprung up in America* (Boston: John Foster, 1678; PS711.S4 1678 Am Imp), prologue, stanza 5.

2. Giles Avery, *Sketches of Shakers and Shakerism* (Albany, N.Y.: Weed, Parsons, 1883; BX9771.A9 1883), 2.

3. Martha J. Anderson, *Social Life and Vegetarianism* (Mt. Lebanon, N.Y. 1893; BX9789.C7 A53 1893), 2.

4. In the May 26, 1870, issue of *The Revolution*, Anthony announced her decision to step down as sole proprietor so that she might devote more time to lecturing for the suffrage cause. *The Revolution* continued under new management until February 1872.

5. For a fuller discussion of this collection, see Leonard N. Beck, "The Library of Susan B. Anthony," *Quarterly Journal of the Library of Congress* 32 (October 1975): 324–35.

6. In this controversial essay Elizabeth Cady Stanton indicts the Bible and the Christian Church for degrading women by perpetuating the myth of women's inferiority and rightful subjection to men and for cultivating self-sacrifice rather than inspiring self-respect. She blamed canon law for "plunging woman into absolute slavery"(p.12) and contended that "there is nothing more pathetic in all history than the hopeless resignation of woman to the outrages she has been taught to believe are ordained of God" (p. 20). Stanton encouraged women to turn their enthusiasm toward public issues and patriotism.

5 MANUSCRIPT DIVISION

1. Abigail Adams to Elizabeth Shaw, July 19, 1799, container 1, Elizabeth S. Shaw Family Papers, Manuscript Division, Library of Congress.

2. Robert Reinhold, "H.U.D. Nominee Says She Is One of the Poor:

We are assembled here, this evening, for the purpose of discussing the question of American Slavery: — — The startling fact that there are in these United States, under the sanction of this professedly Christian, Republican Government, nearly Four Millions of human beings now clanking the chains of Slavery. — Four Millions of Men and Women and children, who are owned like horses and cattle, — and bought and sold in the Market. — Four Millions of thinking, acting, conscious beings, like ourselves, driven to unpaid toil, from the rising to the setting of the Sun, through the weary

Susan B. Anthony. "Make the Slave's Case Our Own," ca. 1859, holograph speech. Susan B. Anthony Papers (container 7). Manuscript Division. LC-MS-11049-1.

Many early women's rights advocates, including Susan B. Anthony (1820–1906), came to the suffrage movement by way of the temperance and abolitionist causes. In their struggle to free the slaves, women recognized their own secondary status and developed the political consciousness and skills that enabled them to challenge women's inequality. In this speech from 1859, written when she was the principal New York agent for William Lloyd Garrison's American Anti-Slavery Society, Anthony urged her audience to "make the slave's case our own." Although she never considered herself a good speaker, Anthony tirelessly traveled throughout the state delivering antislavery speeches while at the same time escalating her campaign for women's rights, a dual mission that caused controversy within the abolitionist ranks and that foreshadowed her break with the society after the Civil War when it refused to protest the exclusion of women from the Fourteenth Amendment.

Mrs. Harris Tells Hearing She Links Herself with Underprivileged," *New York Times*, January 11, 1977, A22.

3. Elizabeth Blackwell to Baroness Anne Milbanke Byron, March 4, 1851, container 55, Blackwell Family Papers, Manuscript Division, Library of Congress.

4. Mary Ritter Beard, "World Center for Women's Archives" pamphlet, ca. 1939, container 172, Margaret Sanger Papers, Manuscript Division, Library of Congress.

5. Clara Barton to Mary S. Logan, June 16, 1911, container 73, Clara Barton Papers, Manuscript Division, Library of Congress.

6. For African American and Native American history, see the preceding

volumes in this series: Debra Newman Ham, ed., *The African-American Mosaic: A Library of Congress Resource Guide for the Study of Black History and Culture* (Washington: Library of Congress, 1993; Z1361.N39 L47 1993) and Patrick Frazier, ed., *Many Nations: A Library of Congress Resource Guide for the Study of Indian and Alaska Native Peoples of the United States* (Washington: Library of Congress, 1996; Z1209.2.U5 L53 1996). Those interested in Jewish American source material should consult Gary J. Kohn, comp., *The Jewish Experience: A Guide to Manuscript Sources in the Library of Congress* (Cincinnati: American Jewish Archives, 1986; Z6373.U5 K64 1986). Other printed guides focus on countries or geographical regions other than the United States, but they occasionally cite manuscript collections that contain material about immigrants from those areas. Examples include G. Raymond Nunn, ed., *Asia and Oceania: A Guide to Archival and Manuscript Sources in the United States* (New York: Mansell, 1985; Z3001.A78 1985); Aloha South, ed., *Guide to Non-Federal Archives and Manuscripts in the United States Relating to Africa* (New York: H. Zell Publishers, 1989; CD3002.S68 1989); and the Woodrow Wilson Center for Scholars multivolume series Scholars' Guides to Washington, D.C., 1977 to date (volumes published thus far relate to Africa, Asia, the Caribbean, Europe, Latin America, Russia, and the Mid-East; different call numbers for each volume).

7. The Library of Congress NUCMC Office Web site at <www.lcweb.loc.gov/coll/nucmc/> provides a free Z39.50 gateway to RLIN AMC (the Research Libraries Information Network Archival and Mixed Collections file), a database of more than 500,000 bibliographic records to archival collections in the United States and abroad, including NUCMC catalog records created since 1986/87. Also useful for locating manuscript materials throughout the United States is the subscription-only database Archives USA at <http://archives.chadwyck.com>, which includes the entire NUCMC catalog file of 84,000 records created since 1959, and the Research Libraries Group Archival Resources at <http://www.rlg.org/arr/index.html>, a union database of archival finding aids. Internet workstations throughout the Library of Congress reading rooms provide researchers with free access to these databases.

8. Roos's collection descriptions and appendixes proved an invaluable resource for this author in organizing and drafting this current survey of the division's collections.

9. A special women's history issue (October 1975) of the *Quarterly Journal of the Library of Congress* included Anita Lonnes Nolen's "The Feminine Presence: Women's Papers in the Manuscript Division," which briefly describes the most important collections acquired up to that time.

10. Elizabeth Cady Stanton, "On the Social, Educational, Religious, and Political Position of Women in America," June 25, 1883, speech delivered at Princess Hall, London, England, container 6, Elizabeth Cady Stanton Papers, Manuscript Division, Library of Congress.

11. Margaret Bayard Smith, commonplace book, ca. 1804, container 1, Margaret Bayard Smith Papers, Manuscript Division, Library of Congress.

12. For additional information on the incredibly diverse and important manuscript collection assembled by Marian S. Carson, which includes a number of interesting documents relating to women's education, occupations, avocations, reform efforts, and clubs, see the recently published *Gathering History: The Marian S. Carson Collection of Americana*, ed. Sara Day (Washington: Library of Congress, 1999; Z1201.G38 1999). See also the discussion of the Carson collection in chapter 4 of this volume.

13. C. A. Logan to Mary S. Logan, November 27, 1881, container 6, John Alexander Logan Family Papers, Manuscript Division, Library of Congress.

14. Many of these sources are described in *Civil War Manuscripts: A Guide to Collections in the Manuscript Division of the Library of Congress*, compiled by John R. Sellers (Washington: Library of Congress, 1986; Z1242.L48 1986).

15. Other plantation books documenting the sale or work of women slaves may be found in the papers of Robert Carter, William B. Randolph, Edward Frost, James Henry Hammond, Roger Jones, and the Sterritt Family.

16. Manuscript Division specialist John J. McDonough documented the significance of these familial exchanges in the Library of Congress exhibition *My Dear Wife: Letters from Members of Congress to Their Spouses, 1791–1944*, which ran from September 1990 through January 1991. A copy of the printed item list for this exhibition is available in the Manuscript Reading Room reference file.

17. For letters written by Continental Congress delegates, see the exhaustive, twenty-six-volume documentary edition *Letters of Delegates to Congress, 1774–1789*, edited by Paul H. Smith (Washington: Library of Congress, 1976–2000; JK1033.L47). Volume 26 is a cumulative index.

18. Job Pierson to Clarissa Pierson, February 12, 1833, container 2, Job Pierson Papers, Manuscript Division, Library of Congress.

19. "J. K. Stout, Pioneering Judge in Pennsylvania, Is Dead at 79," *New York Times*, August 24, 1998, Obituaries, A15.

20. Some of these whaling collections are described in a forthcoming guide by division specialist John J. McDonough, *And God Created Whales: Whales and Whaling in the Manuscript Collections of the Library of Congress* (Washington: Library of Congress, forthcoming).

21. See *American Women and the U.S. Armed Forces: A Guide to the Records of Military Agencies in the National Archives Relating to American Women*, compiled by Charlotte Palmer Seeley; revised by Virginia C. Purdy and Robert Gruber (Washington: National Archives and Records Administration, 1992; U21.75.S44 1992).

22. Ira Eaker to Mrs. Dorothy Dell Kelly, March 13, 1944, container I:11, Ira Eaker Papers, Manuscript Division, Library of Congress.

23. The other one hundred thousand documents relate to the Historical Records Survey (HRS), a WPA project to inventory state and local records. Of possible interest to women's historians in the HRS material are transcripts of Mormon life histories and diaries relating to family life in Utah.

24. See "American Life Histories: Manuscripts from the Federal Writers' Project, 1936–1940," at <http://memory.loc.gov/ammem/wpaintro/wpahome.html.>

25. Ruby A. Black interview, Ruby A. Black Papers, Manuscript Division, Library of Congress, as quoted in *Library of Congress Acquisitions: Manuscript Division, 1984* (Washington: Library of Congress, 1986), 30.

"WITH PEACE AND FREEDOM BLEST"

1. Quoted in Linda Kerber, *Women of the Republic: Intellect and Ideology in Revolutionary America* (Chapel Hill: University of North Carolina Press, 1980; HQ1418.K47 GenColl), 205.

2. Thomas Hariot, *A Briefe and True Report of . . . Virginia* (Frankfurt, 1590; F229.H27 1590 Rosenwald Coll item 723 RBSC). De Bry published this edition in four languages–Latin, English, French, and German. For the entire compilation, see Theodor de Bry, *Historia Americae sive Novi Orbis* (Frankfurt, 1624; G159.B7 Rosenwald Coll item 1309 RBSC).

3. "For mankind they say a woman was made first, which by the working of one of the goddes, conceiued and brought foorth children: And in such sort they say they had their beginning." Hariot, *A Briefe and True Report . . .*, De Bry's 1590 edition with an introduction by Paul Hulton (New York: Dover Publications, 1972; F229.H27 1972 GenColl), 25.

4. A census of the editions of de Bry's works found in the Rosenwald Collection appears in *A Catalog of the Gifts of Lessing J. Rosenwald* (Washington: Library of Congress, 1977; Z881.U5 1977 RBSC, MRR Alc, G&M), 236–39.

5. See Pamela Scott, *Temple of Liberty: Building the Capitol for a New Nation* (New York: Oxford University Press with the Library of Congress, 1995; NA4412.W18 S37 1995 GenColl), 9–17, 108–11.

6. See in particular E. McClung Fleming, "The American Image as Indian Princess, 1765–1783," *Winterthur Portfolio* 2 (1965), 65–81 (N9.W52 GenColl), and "From Indian Princess to Greek Goddess: The American Image, 1783–1815," ibid., 3 (1966), 37–66.

7. Hans Staden's enormously popular account of his trials among the Tupinamba Indians as well as his woodcuts can be seen in *The True History of His Captivity*, 1557, translated and edited by Malcolm Letts (London: George Routledge & Sons, 1928; F2528.S753 Gen Coll).

8. Amerigo Vespucci's *Mundus novus* (Paris, 1503–4?; facsim., Paris:

Fontaine, n.d.; Strassburg: J.H.E. Heitz, 1903; E125.V5 V523 RBSC, GenColl). In the classical tradition, cartographer Martin Waldseemüller gave the feminized version of Vespucci's baptismal name to the vast new continent. Earlier Spanish explorers believed, as Columbus did, that the continent was part of eastern Asia, referring to it as the Indies.

9. The new continent began to be represented as a naked Indian maiden with severed heads and other signs of cannibalism as early as 1575. See Clare Le Corbeiller, "Miss America and Her Sisters: Personifications of the Four Parts of the World," *Metropolitan Museum of Art Bulletin*, April 1961 (N610.A4 GenColl), and Hugh Honour, *The New Golden Land: European Images of America from the Discoveries to the Present Time* (New York: Pantheon Books, 1975; N8214.5.U6 H58 1975 GenColl).

10. This indictment of women's sensuality was embedded in the Eve stereotype, the sexual interpretation of the Fall. *Malleus maleficarum,* the crudely misogynistic and dangerous Dominican treatise on witchcraft published in about 1486, asserted that "all witchcraft comes from carnal lust, which in women is insatiable. . . . Wherefore for the sake of fulfilling their lusts they consort even with devils." John Phillips, *Eve: The History of an Idea* (San Francisco: Harper & Row, 1984; BS580.E85 P48 1984 GenColl), 62–70.

11. "Insula hyspana," in Carlo Verardi, *Historia Baetica* ([Basel], 1494; Incun. 1494.V47 Voll H15942 RBSC).

12. De Bry had intended to publish Le Moyne's account of Laudonnière's ill-fated Huguenot colony in Florida as the first part of his *America* for, as he said in the foreword to the *Virginia* plates, the Florida account "should bee first sett foorthe because yt was discouuered by the Frencheman longe befor the discuerye of Virginia." De Bry said in a brief notice in his *Florida* that he had acquired Le Moyne's drawings from his widow after his death in 1587.

13. The only surviving watercolor by Jacques Le Moyne de Morgues, showing the Timucua Indians worshiping a column, was rediscovered at a French chateau in 1901 and is now at the New York Public Library. It shows that de Bry's translation to a copper plate is remarkably precise and that Le Moyne had already Europeanized the women worshipers.

14. Hariot, *A Briefe and True Report* (1590). See note 2. British maritime editor Richard Hakluyt probably persuaded de Bry, when he came to London in 1588 to buy some paintings by French artist Jacques Le Moyne, to publish Hariot's and John White's work first, maybe because White's patron, Sir Walter Raleigh, had offered financial support to promote the *Virginia* volume. Paul Hulton, *America 1585: The Complete Drawings of John White* (Chapel Hill: University of North Carolina Press and British Museum Publications, 1984; NC242.W53 A4 1984 GenColl), 17.

15. W. John Faupel has juxtaposed reproductions of the watercolors with the relevant engravings and provides a convincing analysis of the changes made by de Bry. Faupel, *A Brief and True Report of the New Found Land of Virginia: A Study of the De Bry Engravings* (East Grinstead, West Sussex, England: Antique Atlas Publications, 1989; G159.B8 F38 1989 GenColl).

16. Of particular interest is Father Joseph François Lafitau's *Moeurs des Sauvages Amériquains, comparées aux Moeurs des premiers temps* (Paris, 1724; E58.L16 RBSC, MicRR) in which he draws heavily on earlier accounts and illustrations of American Indians, including de Bry's, to make comparisons with peoples of the classical and preclassical world, or "primitive times." His most original work comes from his observations of the Iroquois, among whom he lived as a Jesuit missionary. According to William N. Fenton and Elizabeth L. Moore, in their translation of Lafitau's classic work and exhaustive examination of his sources (*Customs of the American Indians Compared with the Customs of Primitive Times,* 2 vols. [Toronto: Champlain Society, 1974–77; E58. L1613 GenColl]), Lafitau was the first to describe the importance of women in Iroquoian tribal life in a chapter on the origin of the peoples of America (1: 69–70). In a section on the Iroquois creation myth, he shows the similarities between the biblical story of the expulsion from Paradise and the Iroquois legend of a woman who is cast out of the heavens for being too easily seduced by one of the original six men on earth and becomes the mother of two children who fight one another (1:81–84). William Sturtevant contributed a chapter on "The Sources of Lafitau's American Illustrations"(1:271–97), many of which he traced to de Bry's engravings.

17. *Cottonus Matherus S. theologiae doctor regia societatis Londone. . . .*, 1727. Mezzotint by Peter Pelham, 1728 (restrike, 1860; FP—XVIII—P383, no.1). P&P. LC-USZC4–4597. As members of the newly prosperous merchant and landed classes began to acquire the material evidence of their success during the eighteenth century, their wives, dressed in the height of London or Paris elegance, were themselves depicted as status symbols in painted portraits (these are not collected by the Library).

18. Sara M. Evans, *Born for Liberty: A History of Women in America* (New York: The Free Press, 1989; HQ1410.E83 1989 GenColl),11, 22. Under French civil law adopted by Spain, Spanish colonial women were allowed to own land but in other ways were regarded no differently from other European women (see chapter 3).

19. Father Joseph François Lafitau's early eighteenth-century observations on the importance of women in the Iroquois tribe (see note 16) are confirmed and elaborated on in William C. Sturtevant, gen. ed., *Handbook of North American Indians* (Washington: Smithsonian Institution, 1978–98; E77.H25 MRR Alc), vol. 15, *Northeast,* 309.

20. See Carol F. Karlsen, *The Devil in the Shape of a Woman: Witchcraft in Colonial New England* (New York: W. W. Norton & Company, 1987; BF1576.K37 1987 GenColl), 179–80. Cotton Mather, of the eminent Mather dynasty of Puritan minister-leaders in New England, demonstrated his own psychological ambivalence toward women's behavior and role in 1692 in *The Wonders of the Invisible World: Being an Account of the Tryals of Several VVitches, Lately Excuted in New-England* ([Boston, London]: Printed . . . for John Dunton, 1693; BF1575 .M54 1693b RBSC), his justification for the Salem witchcraft trials and executions, and, the same year, in *Ornaments for the Daughters of Zion* (reprint of the 3rd ed., 1741; Delmar, N.Y.: Scholars' Facsimiles & Reprints, 1978; BV4527.M27 1978) described models of pious womanhood for women to emulate.

21. This is the central thesis of another classic, Laurel Thatcher Ulrich's *Good Wives: Image and Reality in the Lives of Women in Northern New England, 1650–1750* (New York: Oxford University Press, 1983; HQ1438.A11 U42 1983 GenColl).

22. Phillips, *Eve,* 95.

23. See in particular the story of Sor Maria de Jesús de Agreda, who, in the 1620s, when not yet twenty years old, was seen on several occasions to levitate following Communion at her remote convent in Spain. She reported that she was carried by angels to preach to Indian tribes in today's New Mexico although she never left her convent. After Franciscan missionaries brought back to Spain testimony by Indians that they had been converted by a beautiful lady in blue, Sor Maria became a focus of the Inquisition. Mary E. Giles, ed., *Women in the Inquisition: Spain and the New World* (Baltimore and London: Johns Hopkins University Press, 1999; BX1735.W59 1999 GenColl), 155–70.

24. Examples of captivity narratives can be found in the Rare Book and Special Collections Division (see chapter 4), the General Collections, and the Microform Reading Room.

25. Numerous examples can be seen in Donald H. Cresswell, comp., *The American Revolution in Drawings and Prints: A Checklist of 1765–1790 Graphics in the Library of Congress* (Washington: Library of Congress, 1975; E209.U54 1974 P&P, MRRAlc, G&M, GenColl).

26. Marina Warner, *Monuments & Maidens: The Allegory of the Female Form* (New York: Atheneum, 1985; NX650.F45 W3 1985 GenColl), 64. Thus, Uncle Sam and Brother Jonathan, the male symbols for America, were designed to typify the average American, whereas Liberty and Britannia obviously do not typify the average American or English woman (see p. 12).

27. George Richardson's *Iconology; or, A Collection of Emblematical Figures,* 2 vols. (London: Printed by G. Scott,1779; N7740.R515 Rosenwald Coll RBSC; reprint ed., New York: Garland Pub., 1979; N7740.R515 1979 GenColl), Richardson stated in his introduction that the source of images for abstract ideas and qualities drawn from classical myths and saints calendars was exhausted. He wanted to expand the range of the standard repertoire for new times, to aid modern artists by incorporating Poussin's and Raphael's innovations and new concepts such as "Democracy," "Liberty," and "America." Martha Banta, *Imaging American Women: Idea and Ideals in Cultural History* (New York: Columbia University Press, 1987; NX652.W6 B36 1987

GenColl), 412. Richardson's work includes an Indian woman as America, "The fourth and last part of the world . . ." (*Iconology*, vol. 1, fig. 6).

28. John Higham explains that Britannia was shown with the attributes of liberty in England before that symbol was adopted by the rebellious American colonists, and then Americanized following the Declaration of Independence (Higham, "Indian Princess and Roman Goddess: The First Female Symbols of America," *Proceedings of the American Antiquarian Society* 1990, 59–61 (E172.A35 GenColl). See Cresswell, *American Revolution in Drawings and Prints*, 638, for an etching by G. B. Cipriani after a drawing by F. Bartolozzi of such a Britannia, originally published in William Bollan, *Continued Corruption, Standing Armies, and Popular Contents Considered* (London: Printed by J. Almon, 1768; E211.B68).

29. See for instance, Pierre Eugène du Simitière's design for the title page of the 1775 issue of the *Pennsylvania Magazine* (AP2.A2 P4 RBSC) showing the goddess America with the implements of liberty and war (Cresswell, *American Revolution in Drawings and Prints*, 691; LC-USZ62–45557). The following year, as independence was declared, du Simitière proposed a design for the U.S. seal with a standing Liberty figure.

30. Highham, "Indian Princess," 24.

31. See Yvonne Korsak, "The Liberty Cap as a Revolutionary Symbol in America and France," *Smithsonian Studies in American Art* 1:2 (Fall 1987), 53 (N6505.S56 GenColl).

32. The *Pennsylvania Evening Post* of July 2, 1776, is available in the Newspaper and Current Periodical Room. Some copies of original newspaper advertisements in the Serial Division collections and broadsides from the Rare Book and Special Collections Division can be studied in the Prints and Photographs Division (LOT 4422A: LC-USZ62–10293,-10474,-16876). See Barbara E. Lacey, "Visual Images of Blacks in Early American Imprints," *William and Mary Quarterly*, 3d series, 53:1 (January 1996) (F221 .W71 GenColl).

33. *Britain, America, at Length Be Friends*, from the *London Magazine*, January 1774 (microfilm 01105, reel 205; Cresswell, *American Revolution in Drawings and Prints*, 662; LC-USZ62–45498). This allegorical image can be contrasted with the active trading image of male Indians presenting goods for barter to merchants in the cartouche for *Pensylvania Nova Jersey es Nova York* in Tobias Lotter, *Atlas Géographique* (Nuremberg, 1778; Cresswell, *American Revolution in Drawings and Prints*, 743; G1015.L7 1778 Vault G&M; LC-USZ62–46069).

34. Microfilm 01103, reel 26 AP; Cresswell, *American Revolution in Drawings and Prints*, 664; LC-USZ62–39592.

35. Other examples of women's patriotic activism before and during the Revolutionary War can be followed in newspapers, broadsides, and letters of the period, e.g, a *Boston Evening Post*, February 12, 1770, report that more than three hundred "Mistresses of Families" had promised "*totally* to abstain from the Use of TEA" (no. 1794, page 4) (N&CPR). See Kerber, *Women of the Republic*, chap. 2, "'Women Invited to War': Sacrifice and Survival," 33–67, for many other examples.

36. See endpapers and Kerber, *Women of the Republic*, 104.

37. Ibid., 228–31. For the first time, it was made overtly clear that a "woman's place" was in the home, the beginning of the cult of domesticity.

38. See Carroll Smith Rosenberg, "Dis-Covering the Subject of the 'Great Constitutional Discussion,' 1786–1789," *Journal of American History* 79 (December 1992), 841–73 (E171.J87 GenColl), for an analysis of the complex ideology behind new allegorical representations of America, particularly those in *Columbian Magazine, or Monthly Miscellany* (AP2.A2 U6 RBSC, Microfilm 01103, no. 11 AP MicRR).

6 PRINTS AND PHOTOGRAPHS DIVISION

1. In general, figures for quantities of material in specific collections are approximate.

2. British Museum Department of Prints and Drawings, *Catalogue of Prints and Drawings in the British Museum: Division I. Political and Personal Satires* (London: Trustees of the British Museum, 1870–1954?; NE55.L7 A3); "British Political and Social Cartoons, 1655–1832: A Checklist of the Cartoons in the Prints and Photographs Division of the Library of Congress Which Are Not in the Published Catalogs of the British Museum (London)," compiled by Elena Gonzalez Millie (Washington: Prints and Photographs Division, 1968; NC1470.M4).

3. Pete Daniel and Raymond Smock, *A Talent for Detail: The Photographs of Miss Frances Benjamin Johnston, 1889–1910* (New York: Harmony Books, 1974; TR140.J64 A34 1974), 57–58.

4. Marion Tinling, *Women Remembered: A Guide to Landmarks of Women's History in the United States* (New York: Greenwood Press, 1986; E159.T56 1986); Rodris Roth, "Recording a Room: The Kitchen," in *Historic America: Buildings, Structures, and Sites Recorded by the Historic American Buildings Survey and the Historic American Engineering Record*, edited by C. Ford Peatross and Alicia Stamm (Washington: Library of Congress, 1983; NA705.H53), 107–25.

5. A selection of the Curtis photographs focusing on women is offered in *Heart of the Circle: Photographs by Edward S. Curtis of Native American Women*, edited by Sara Day (San Francisco: Pomegranate Artbooks, in association with Library of Congress, 1997; E89.C87 1997).

6. For a discussion of women poster artists' participation in the World War I propaganda effort, tapping examples from Library of Congress collections, see Elena Millie and Jan Grenci, "Columbia Calls," *Affiche* 14 (1995): 66–71.

7. Renata V. Shaw, "Nineteenth Century Tobacco Label Art," in *Graphic Sampler*, comp. Renata V. Shaw (Washington: Library of Congress, 1979; NE400.G7), 139–65.

8. Published studies that tap Library of Congress collections include: Mary Evans O'Keefe Gravalos and Carol Pulin, *Bertha Lum* (Washington: Smithsonian Institution Press, 1991; NE1112.L86 G73 1990) and Tim Mason and Lynn Mason, *Helen Hyde* (Washington: Smithsonian Institution Press, 1991; NE539.H9 M37 1991).

9. Several books provide insight into the work of Charles and Ray Eames, including Donald Albrecht et al., *The Work of Charles and Ray Eames: A Legacy of Invention* (New York: Harry N. Abrams in association with the Library of Congress and the Vitra Design Museum, 1997; NK1535.E25 W67 1997) and John Neuhart, Marilyn Neuhart and Ray Eames, *Eames Design: The Work of the Office of Charles and Ray Eames* (New York: Harry N. Abrams, 1989; NK1535.E25 N48 1989).

WOMEN ON THE MOVE

1. For a comprehensive study of the lives of California Indians prior to contact with European cultures and for a detailed bibliography, see Ramón Gutiérrez and Richard J. Orsi, eds., *Contested Eden: California before the Gold Rush*. California History Sesquicentennial Series, no. 1 (Berkeley: University of California Press, 1998; F864.C735 1998 GenColl).

2. Ibid., 14. See also Stephen A. Flanders, *Atlas of American Migration* (New York: Facts on File, 1998; G1201.E27 F5 1998 G&M), 30.

3. Ibid., 16. In their essay "A World of Balance and Plenty," pp. 12–47, in the same source, M. Kat Anderson, Michael G. Barbour, and Valerie Whitworth spell out in more detail women's roles in maintaining the balance of nature and using gardening techniques to provide for their needs. See especially p. 41, footnote 15.

4. See Albert L. Hurtado, *Indian Survival on the California Frontier* (New Haven: Yale University Press, 1988; E78.C15 H87 1988) and Victoria Brady, Sarah Crowe, and Lyn Reese, "Resist! Survival Tactics of Indian Women," *California History* 63:2 (Spring 1984), 140–51 (F856.C24).

5. "Spanish Missions, Presidios, and Pueblos to 1824," map, in Gutiérrez and Orsi, *Contested Eden*, 207

6. Quintard Taylor, *In Search of the Racial Frontier: African Americans in the American West, 1528–1990* (New York: Norton, 1998; E185.925.T39 1998), 30–52.

7. Jacob N. Bowman and Robert F. Heizer, *Anza and the Northwest Frontier of New Spain* (Los Angeles: Southwest Museum, 1967; F869.L8 S65 no. 20), 14 (map), 97. More detailed information helpful in exploring the

Library's holdings documenting these expeditions is given in notes 8, 18, and 20 below.

8. Herbert Eugene Bolton, *Anza's California Expeditions,* 5 vols. (New York: Russell & Russell, 1966; F864.B68 1966 GenColl; Berkeley: University of California Press, 1930; F864.B68). Volumes 2–5 contain translations from original Spanish manuscripts edited by Bolton of correspondence, narratives by Francisco Palóu and José Joaguín Moraga, and diaries of Anza, Father Pedro Font, Juan Diaz, Francisco Tomás Hermenegildo Garcés, Francisco Palóu, and Thomas Eixarch.

9. Ibid., vol. 1, *An Outpost of Empire,* 247.

10. Ibid.

11. Vicki Ruiz, e-mail, August 1, 2000.

12. Susanna Bryant Dakin, *Rose, or Rose Thorn? Three Women of Spanish California* (Berkeley, Calif.: Friends of the Bancroft Library, 1963), 10.

13. Bolton, vol. 1, 312–13, and vol. 4, *Font's Complete Diary of the Second Anza Expedition,* 138.

14. Antonio I. Castañeda, "Engendering the History of Alta California, 1769–1845," in Gutiérrez and Orsi, *Contested Eden,* 246. See also Dakin, *Rose, or Rose Thorn?,* 1–11.

15. Castañeda, "Engendering the History," in Gutiérrez and Orsi, *Contested Eden,* 246–48, and Dakin, *Rose, or Rose Thorn?,* 12–24.

16. Castañeda, "Engendering the History," in Gutiérrez and Orsi, *Contested Eden,* 249.

17. Doyce B. Nunis Jr., ed., *Women in the Life of Southern California* (Los Angeles: Historical Society of Southern California, 1996; HQ1438.C2 W67 1996 GenColl), xii.

18. These works include Charles Edward Chapman, *Catalogue of Materials in the Archivo General de Indias for the History of the Pacific Coast and the American Southwest* (1919; reprint: Millwood, N.Y.: Kraus Reprint Co., 1974; CD1859.S3 C62 1974 GenColl). Since 1905 the Library of Congress has systematically supplemented its original manuscript sources by securing transcriptions, photostatic copies, or microfilm of manuscripts and archives relating to U.S. history that are located in foreign repositories. These reproductions are housed in the Manuscript Division and are described in various published and unpublished finding aids. Of specific interest to readers of this essay are the unpublished checklists titled "Foreign Copying Project–Spain" and "Foreign Copying Project–Spain and Latin America." In addition to the reproductions acquired directly by the Library and described in these two guides, the Manuscript Division also holds two other collections of Spanish-related materials assembled by private individuals, Woodbury Lowery and James Alexander Robertson. Of particular note are the "Manuscripts, California, 1588–1800" in the Lowery Collection, container 18. Translated material from the Anza overland journeys is reprinted in the five-volume set of Herbert Eugene Bolton's *Anza's California Expeditions,* along with his idiosyncratic interpretations of the various references to women.

19. Books related to the Anza expedition to California can be found by doing a guided keyword search on the Library's online catalog using "Anza" *and* "California."

20. Donald T. Garate, *Captain Juan Bautista de Anza–Correspondence–on Various Subjects, 1775: Transcribed, Translated, and Indexed (with Commentary Notes): Archivo General de la Nacion, Provincias Internas 237, Section 3* (San Leandro, Calif.: Los Californianos, 1995; cataloging in process). This compilation includes photocopies of the original documents and transcripts of each with an English translation. The list of supplies and provisions can be found in Bowman and Heizer, *Anza and the Northwest Frontier of New Spain,*132–36.

21. Jean-François de Galaup, comte de La Pérouse, *Relation abrégée du voyage de La Pérouse pendant les années 1785, 1786, 1787, et 1788* (Leipzig, 1799; G420.L213 RBSC), which includes the first drawings of life in Spanish California, and Louis Choris, *Voyage pittoresque autour du monde, avec des portraits de sauvages d'Amérique. . . .* (Paris: Firmin Didot, 1822; G420 .K84 C5 RBSC), with its plates of Indians in and surrounding the Spanish missions.

22. Alfred Robinson, *Life in California: During a Residence of Several Years in that Territory . . . By an American [Alfred Robinson], translated from the original Spanish Manuscript* (New York: Wiley and Putnam, 1846; F864.R65 RBSC).

23. Richard Henry Dana Jr., *Two Years before the Mast* (New York: Harper & Brothers, 1840; AC1.H4 no.127 RBSC).

24. *Mapa, que comprende la Frontera, de los Dominos del Rey . . . ,* drawn by José de Urrutia and Nicolas de la Fora in 1769 (G4410 1769 .U Vault) can be found on the Library's Web site, available in four sections, a through d, at *http://hdl.loc.gov/loc.gmd/g4410.ct000539.* See John R. Hébert and Anthony P. Mullan, *The Luso-Hispanic World in Maps: A Selective Guide to Manuscript Maps to 1900 in the Collections of the Library of Congress* (Washington: Library of Congress,1999; Z6027.S72 L43 1999), 51, item 91. See also *Maps Showing Explorers' Routes, Trails, and Early Roads in the United States: An Annotated List,* compiled by Richard S. Ladd (Washington: Library of Congress, 1962; Z6027.U5 U56 G&M, MRR Alc, LH&G) and *The Lowery Collection: A Descriptive List of Maps of the Spanish Possessions within the present Limits of the United States, 1502–1820,* by Woodbury Lowery, edited with notes by Philip Lee Phillips (Washington: Library of Congress, 1912; Z6021.A5 U6).

25. Nunis, ed., *Women in the Life,* 5–71.

26. Taylor, *In Search of the Racial Frontier,* 32, where he cites Jack Forbes, *Afro-Americans in the Far West* (Berkeley, Calif., 1969).

27. For example, see Edwin A. Beilharz and Carlos U. López, trans. and eds., *We Were 49ers!: Chilean Accounts of the California Gold Rush* (Pasadena, Calif.: Ward Ritchie Press, 1976; F865.W37 GenColl).

28. Christiana Fischer, "Women in California in the Early 1850s," in Nunis, ed., *Women in the Life,* 41–71.

29. Jo Ann Levy, *They Saw the Elephant: Women in the California Gold Rush* (Hamden, Conn.: Archon Books, 1990; F865.L67 1990 GenColl), 153. Levy relates the stories of two recorded Chinese prostitutes, Lee Lan and Ah Toy, both of whom had been taken to San Francisco from Canton.

30. Mrs. D. B. Bates, *Incidents on Land and Water, or Four Years on the Pacific Coast* (Boston: J. French & Co., 1857; F865.B3 GenColl).

31. Levy, *They Saw the Elephant,* 32–47.

32. A list of ninety-six journals and diaries kept on the overland trail appears in Lillian Schlissel's *Women's Diaries of the Westward Journey* (New York: Schocken Books, 1982, F593.W65 1982 GenColl). The preponderance of source material, textual and graphic, is related to the overland journeys of women in the 1840s and later.

33. "Emigrant's Dying Child," by Major G. W. Patten, U.S. Army. Music Composed with a Piano Accompaniment by an Amateur (Cleveland: S. Brainard's Sons, 1853). Edison Sheet Music Collection. Music Division.

34. Schlissel, *Women's Diaries,* 14.

35. Levy, *They Saw the Elephant,* 188.

36. Schlissel, *Women's Diaries,* 46.

37. Ibid., 112–13.

38. See John Phillip Reid, *Law for the Elephant: Property and Social Behavior on the Overland Trail* (San Marino, Calif.: Huntington Library, 1997; KF366.R43 1997 LAW) and Reid, *Policing the Elephant: Crime, Punishment, and Social Behavior on the Overland Trail* (San Marino, Calif.: Huntington Library, 1997; HV9955.W4 R45 1997 GenColl).

7 GEOGRAPHY AND MAP DIVISION

1. Doreen B. Massey, *Space, Place, and Gender* (Minneapolis: University of Minnesota Press, 1994; GF95.M37 1994), 177.

2. The totals have been adjusted to account for collection growth since the publication of *The Library of Congress Geography and Maps: An Illustrated Guide,* compiled by Ralph E. Ehrenberg (Washington: Library of Congress, 1996; Z6028.L52 1996). The entire guide is available on the Geography and Map Web site at <http://www.loc.gov/rr/geogmap/guide>.

3. Doreen B. Massey, *Spatial Divisions of Labor: Social Structures and the Geography of Production,* 2nd ed. (New York: Methuen, Inc., 1995; HC256.5 .M396 1995), 51. See also Doreen B. Massey and John Allen, eds. *Geography Matters!* (Cambridge: Cambridge University Press, 1984; G116.G48 1984).

4. Among the best recent works in feminist geography are Massey: *Spa-*

tial Divisions of Labor (1995); *Space, Place, and Gender* (1994); and, with John Allen, *Geography Matters!* (1984). Massey's early work, edited with P. W. J. Batey, was *Alternative Frameworks for Analysis* (London: Pion Limited, 1977). Daphne Spain's work includes *Gendered Spaces* (Chapel Hill: University of North Carolina Press, 1992). Spain's collaborative works include: Daphne Spain, John Reid, and Larry Long, *Housing Successions among Blacks and Whites in Cities and Suburbs* (Washington: U.S. Department of Commerce, 1980), Shirley Bradway Laska and Daphne Spain, eds., *Back to the City: Issues in Neighborhood Renovation* (New York: Pergamon Press, 1980), and Suzanne M. Bianchi and Daphne Spain, *American Women in Transition* (New York: Russell Sage Foundation, 1986). Other important works include: John Paul Jones III, Heidi J. Nast, and Susan M. Roberts, eds., *Thresholds in Feminist Geography* (Lanham, Md.: Rowman & Littlefield Publishers, Inc., 1997), and Susan Stanford Friedman, *Mappings: Feminism and the Cultural Geographies of Encounter* (Princeton: Princeton University Press, 1998).

5. John Allen, Doreen Massey, and Allan Cochrane, *Rethinking the Region* (London: Routledge, 1998), and works listed in note 4.

6. Nikolas H. Huffman in Jones, Nast, and Roberts, eds., *Thresholds.*

7. Doreen Massey and Linda McDowell, "A Woman's Place," in Massey and Allen, *Geography Matters!*, 128–47.

8. Laurel Thatcher Ulrich, *A Midwife's Tale* (New York: Vintage Books, 1991; F29.H15U47 1991). See pages 15, 26, 41, 78, 128, 166, 228, 268, 289, 321, and 330.

9. For Jewish immigrants, see Austria-Hungry, ca. 1870–1914 (G6480 s75 .A8). For Italian immigrants, see ca. 1880–1914 (G6710 s100 .I8).

10. Erwin G. Gudde, *California Place Names* (Berkeley: University of California Press, 1998; F859.G79), 26, 194. See also George R. Stewart, *American Place-names: A Concise and Selective Dictionary for the Continental United States* (New York: Oxford University Press, 1970; E155 .S79).

11. Geographic Information Systems are software packages that analyze and arrange layers of data into a map format.

12. A'Lelia Perry Bundles, *Madam C. J. Walker* (New York: Chelsea House Publishers, 1991; HD9970.5.C672 W353 1990).

13. Reproduced in facsimile with an introduction by Ward Ritchie and early commentaries by J. M. Guinn (Ward Ritchie Press, 1963).

14. Alice Hudson, "Pre-Twentieth Century Women in Cartography–Who Are the Groundbreakers?" *International Cartographic Association Conference Proceedings,* August 14–21, 1999, 401–6; and "Pre-Twentieth Century Women Mapmakers," *Meridian* (Chicago: American Library Association, Map and Geography Round Table, no. 1, 1989), 29–33. Mary McMichael Ritzlin, "Women's Contributions to North American Cartography: Four Profiles," *Meridian* (Chicago: American Library Association, Map and Geography Round Table, no. 2, 1989), 5–16; and "The Role of Women in the Development of Cartography," *AB Bookman's Weekly,* June 9, 1986, 2709–13.

15. This information is based on an unpublished paper delivered by Tharp at the joint meeting of the Philip Lee Phillips Society (a friends' group of the Geography and Map Division) and the California Map Society, in San Marino, California, April 2000, and a June 2000 interview with Gary W. North, who is processing her collection.

16. Willard's innovative map illustrating the wanderings of Native American tribes appears in *Many Nations: A Library of Congress Resource Guide for the Study of Indian and Alaska Native Peoples of the United States,* edited by Patrick Frazier (Washington: Library of Congress, 1996; Z1209.2.U5 L53 1996), 220.

Maya Ying Lin. Vietnam Veterans Memorial competition drawing. Drawing on paper mounted on board, mixed media, color, 1980 or 1981. Architecture, Design, and Engineering Drawings. Prints and Photographs Division. LC-USZC4-4915.

Maya Lin's winning design for the Vietnam Veterans' Memorial began as a student project at Yale University's School of Architecture. The twenty-one-year-old, who was a child when most of the lives she was memorializing were lost, included with this plan and perspective of the proposed memorial a written description of her vision of how the memorial would communicate "the sense of overwhelming numbers, while unifying those individuals into a whole. For this memorial is meant not as a monument to the individual, but rather as a memorial to the men and women who died during the war as a whole."

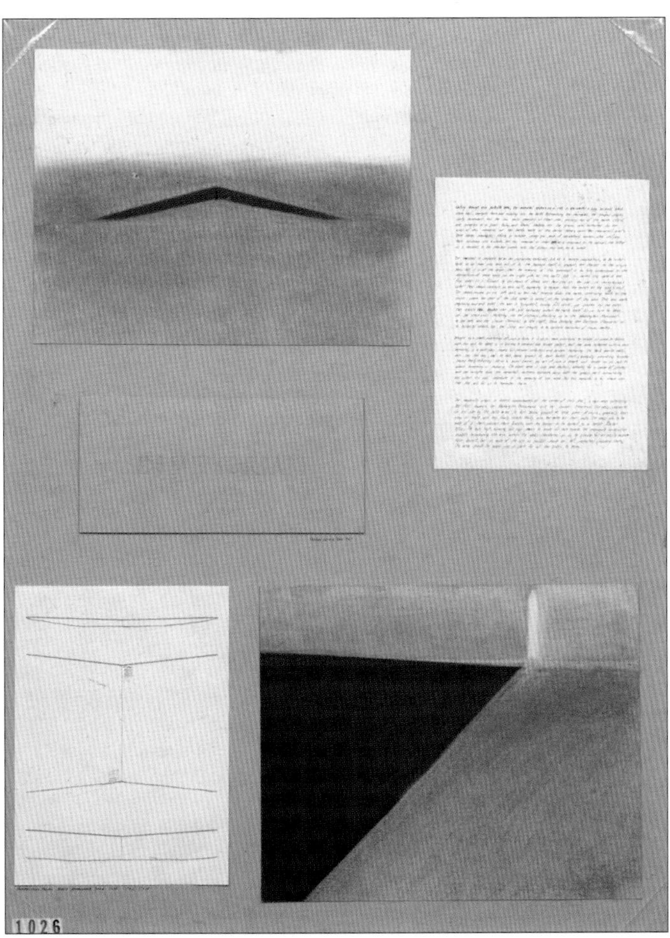

8 MUSIC DIVISION

1. Fred Bronson, *The Billboard Book of Number One Hits* (New York: Billboard Publications, 1988; ML156.4.P6 B76 1988).

2. For an in-depth study of the history of music at the Library of Congress, see Gillian B. Anderson, "Putting the Experience of the World at the Nation's Command: Music at the Library of Congress, 1800–1917," *Journal of the American Musicological Society* 42, no. 1 (1989), 108–49.

3. A useful case study highlighting the problems of locating scores at the Library of Congress may be found in Irving Lowens, "The Library of Congress and Gustave Satter: A Cautionary Tale," *Journal of the American Musicological Society* 18, no. 1 (1965), 73–77.

4. Carl E. Seashore, "Why No Great Women Composers?" *Music Educators Journal,* March 1940: 21, 88; and George P. Upton, *Woman in Music* (Boston: James R. Osgood, 1880).

5. Amy Fay, "Women and Music," *Music* [Chicago] 18 (October 1900): 506; and Ethel Smyth, *Female Pipings in Eden* (London: Peter Davies, 1934), 12.

6. Further information on this periodical index may be found in Gillian B. Anderson, "Unpublished Periodical Indexes at the Library of Congress and elsewhere in the United States of America," *Fontes Artis Musicae* 31, no. 1 (January–March 1984): 54–60.

7. For a thorough discussion of women's contributions as patrons of music in America, see Ralph P. Locke and Cyrilla Barr, eds., *Cultivating Music in America: Women Patrons and Activists since 1860* (Berkeley: University of California Press, 1997).

8. For further information on Mrs. Coolidge, see Cyrilla Barr, *Elizabeth Sprague Coolidge: American Patron of Music* (New York: Schirmer Books, 1998). Barr is also the author of *The Coolidge Legacy* (Washington: Library of Congress, 1997), available from the Music Division upon request.

9. Robert Frost, letter to Mrs. Whittall, April 12, 1961. This letter is from a specially bound volume of letters of tribute to Mrs. Whittall presented to her on May 3, 1961, by Librarian of Congress L. Quincy Mumford in celebration of the tenth anniversary of the Whittall Poetry and Literature Fund. Library of Congress Archives, Manuscript Division.

10. For a history of the Arsis Press by its founder, see Clara Lyle Boone, "Women Composers' Upbeat: Arsis Press," in *The Musical Woman: An International Perspective,* vol. 1, 1983, ed. Judith Lang Zaimont, Catherine Overhauser, and Jane Gottlieb (Westport, Conn.: Greenwood Press, 1984), 98–104.

11. Adrienne Fried Block discusses Arthur P. Schmidt's support of women composers in "Arthur P. Schmidt, Music Publisher and Champion of American Women Composers," in *The Musical Woman: An International Perspective,* vol. 2, 1984–1985, ed. Judith Lang Zaimont, Catherine Overhauser, and Jane Gottlieb (Westport, Conn.: Greenwood Press, 1987), 145–76.

12. Thomas A. Faulkner, *Lure of the Dance* (Los Angeles: T. A. Faulkner, 1916), 10.

THE HOUSE THAT MARIAN BUILT

1. "Writings about Edward A. MacDowell: Biographical," unnumbered pages, box 39, folder 14, Edward and Marian MacDowell Collection, MUS.

2. "Mrs. Edward MacDowell" publicity brochure, box 57, folder 1, Edward and Marian MacDowell Collection, MUS.

3. The Music Division's "salmon file," an index to correspondence in special collections, lists seventeen special collections that contain letters of Marian MacDowell. For information on how to locate these and other correspondence, consult the section "Using the Collections" in chapter 8 on the Music Division.

4. "Writings: Autobiographical," page I-9, box 39, folder 6, Edward and Marian MacDowell Collection, MUS.

5. Ibid., pages I-43 through I-44.

6. "Writings: Autobiographical," unnumbered pages, box 39, folder 7, Edward and Marian MacDowell Collection, MUS.

7. "Writings: Autobiographical," page I-114a, box 39, folder 6, Edward and Marian MacDowell Collection, MUS.

8. "Writings about MacDowell Colony," page II-82, box 40, folder 5, Edward and Marian MacDowell Collection, MUS.

9. The library's holdings of the *Trained Nurse and Hospital Review* do not include the June 1926 issue, but a copy of the article is located with the diary excerpt in box 1 of the Edward and Marian MacDowell Collection, MUS.

10. "Writings about MacDowell Colony," page II-31, box 40, folder 5, Edward and Marian MacDowell Collection, MUS.

11. Mary Mears, "The Work and Home of Edward MacDowell, Musician," *The Craftsman* 16 (July 1909; N1.C87 GenColl).

12. "Writings: Autobiographical," page I-122, box 39, folder 6, Edward and Marian MacDowell Collection, MUS.

13. Nadia Boulanger to Mrs. MacDowell, no date, box 42, Edward and Marian MacDowell Collection, MUS.

14. Edward MacDowell Association annual reports, box 72, Records of the MacDowell Colony, MSS; Paul V. Beckley, "Mrs. MacDowell Honored Today for Art Colony," *New York Herald Tribune,* August 15, 1952, box 79, Records of the MacDowell Colony, MSS.

15. Ida Clyde Clarke, "Mrs. Edward MacDowell and Her Great Work for America," *Pictorial Review* (March 1925; TT500.P6 GenColl; microfilm 01104 reel 1487–88 MicRR), 100.

16. Interview with Aaron Copland during intermission of a New York Philharmonic broadcast, May 5, 1957. MacDowell Colony audio material (LWO 15821), Recorded Sound Section, MBRS.

17. "A List of the Artists who have been granted residence at the MacDowell Colony (1910–1953)," box 72, Records of the MacDowell Colony, MSS.

18. See Rollo Walter Brown, "Mrs. MacDowell and Her Colony," *Atlantic Monthly* (July 1949; AP2.A8 GenColl; microfilm 03388 MicRR); "Life Visits the MacDowell Colony," *Life* (August 23, 1948); Jerome Beatty, "Pilot on the Glory Road," *Reader's Digest* (October 1937); Pearl Strachan Hurd, "Artists' Winter Haven," *Christian Science Monitor* (February 4, 1956). N&CPR.

19. *Time* (August 25, 1952); "Peterborough Paean," *Newsweek* (August 25, 1952; AP2.N6772 GenColl; microfilm 01125 MicRR); Olin Downes, "Colony of the Arts," *New York Times,* Sunday, August 24, 1952. N&CPR.

20. Anthony Tommasini, "A Studio of One's Own: MacDowell Memories," *Boston Globe,* 23 February 1992, sec. B; D. Quincy Whitney, "MacDowell Colony: A Place of the Heart for Poet Vaeth," *Boston Globe,* August 9, 1992, sec. NH; "MacDowell Colony Celebration," *American Artist* (July 1996); Grace Glueck, "Fruitful Months in the Country," *New York Times,* January 31,1997, late New York edition, sec. C. N&CPR.

21. David Felts' Column, Urbana, Illinois, *Courier,* August 29, 1956. Box 39, Edward and Marian MacDowell Collection, MUS.

22. *The Peterborough Transcript,* Thursday, August 21, 1952. Box 79, Records of the MacDowell Colony, MSS.

Imitation of Life. *Director: John M. Stahl. Camera: Merritt Gerstad. Screenplay: William Hurlbut. Cast: Claudette Colbert, Warren William, Louise Beavers, Rochelle Hudson, Fredi Washington. Lobby card. Universal Pictures, 1934. Dwight Cleveland Lobby Card Collection (unprocessed). Prints and Photographs Division. LC-USZC4–8144*

Imitation of Life exemplifies a woman's film staple: the self-sacrificing mother. The movie tells of two single mothers and their daughters, with the families sharing experiences as their children grow to adulthood. Claudette Colbert, seen here with Rochelle Hudson as her daughter, is a successful businesswoman. Her fortune is based upon a recipe given to her by her maid and best friend, played by Louise Beavers, a black woman who eventually experiences tragedy because her daughter chooses to live her life as a white woman.

9 RECORDED SOUND SECTION

1. All these recordings are available in MBRS through the Recorded Sound Reference Center: Mamie Smith singing "Crazy Blues" (1920, Okeh 4169 or 169), the *Major Bowes' Amateur Hour* broadcast (LWO 7161 r22A) with Beverly Sills, Mary McLeod Bethune giving a talk broadcast by radio in 1939 (RWA 4895 B2–4896 A1), and the Jane Addams radio broadcast (RXA 5638 A5).

2. Michele Hilmes, *Radio Voices: American Broadcasting, 1922–1952* (Minneapolis: University of Minnesota Press, 1997), 278.

3. John Dunning, *Tune in Yesterday: The Ultimate Encyclopedia of Old-Time Radio, 1925–1976* (Englewood Cliffs, N.J.: Prentice-Hall, 1976), 549.

4. Raymond Stedman, *The Serials: Suspense and Drama by Installment*, 2nd ed. (Norman, Okla.: University of Oklahoma Press, 1977), 306–7.

5. Muriel G. Cantor and Suzanne Pingree, *The Soap Opera* (Beverly Hills, Calif.: Sage Publications, 1983), 44–45.

6. Madeleine Edmondson and David Rounds, *From Mary Noble to Mary Hartman* (New York: Stein and Day, 1976), 89.

7. Dunning, *Tune in Yesterday*, 55.

8. Ibid., 257–58.

9. Ibid., 474–76.

10. Message from Gene Frederickson, AFRTS Web site, <fredegw@dodmedia.osd.mil>, sent October 13, 1999.

11. Rainer E. Lotz and Ulrich Neuert, *The AFRS "Jubilee" Transcription Programs: An Exploratory Discography* (Frankfurt am Main: Ruecker, 1985), vii.

12. Hilmes, *Radio Voices*, 266.

10 MOVING IMAGE SECTION

1. *Moving Picture World*, June 22, 1907 (PN1993.M88), 252.

2. *Moving Picture World*, November 20, 1909 (PN1993.M88), 744.

3. Donald Bogle, *Blacks in American Films and Television: An Encyclopedia* (New York: Garland Publishers, 1988; PN1995.9.N4 B58 1988), 377.

4. Charles Musser, *Edison Motion Picture, 1890–1900: An Annotated Filmography* (Washington: Smithsonian Institution Press, 1997; PN1995.9.D6 M88 1997), 33–36.

5. Lizzie Francke, *Script Girls: Women Screenwriters in Hollywood* (London: British Film Institute, 1994; PN1995.9.W6 F675 1994), 6.

6. Cari Beauchamp, *Without Lying Down: Frances Marion and the Powerful Women of Early Hollywood* (New York: Scribner, 1997; PS3525.A6549 Z54 1997), 11.

11 AMERICAN FOLKLIFE CENTER

1. Undated, typed manuscript, with Sidney Robertson Cowell's handwritten notes, probably prepared for a newspaper columnist's article advertising a Cowell lecture. The WPA California Folk Music Project Collection, American Folklife Center.

2. For a detailed account of American Indian collections at the American Folklife Center (and in other divisions of the Library), see *Many Nations: A Library of Congress Resource Guide for the Study of Indian and Alaska Native Peoples of the United States* (Washington: Library of Congress, 1996).

3. Interview, Marianna Costa, Haledon, New Jersey, by David Taylor, August 20, 1994. Working in Paterson Folklife Project, American Folklife Center.

4. Interview, Marianna Costa, Haledon, New Jersey, by David Taylor, August 10, 1994. Working in Paterson Folklife Project, American Folklife Center.

12 AREA STUDIES COLLECTIONS

1. Malka Lee Rappaport, *Durkh kindershe oygn* (Through the eyes of childhood) (Buenos Aires: Farlag Yidbukh, 1955; PJ5129.R25 D8 Hebr), 160. Malka Lee Rappaport, "Through the Eyes of Childhood," *Found Treasures: Stories by Yiddish Women Writers*, edited by Frieda Forman, Ethel Raicus, Sarah Silberstein Swartz, and Margie Wolfe (Toronto: Second Story Press, 1994; PJ5191.E8F68 1994 GenColl), 172. These are Rappaport's thoughts as a new immigrant arriving in New York City in 1921.

2. Patrick Frazier, ed., *Many Nations: A Library of Congress Resource Guide for the Study of Indian and Alaska Native Peoples of the United States* (Washington: Library of Congress, 1996; Z1209.2.U5 L53 1996 GenColl) and Debra Newman Ham, ed., *The African-American Mosaic: A Library of Congress Resource Guide for the Study of Black History and Culture* (Washington: Library of Congress, 1993; Z1361.N39 L47 1993, Z663.A74 1993 GenColl).

3. Fabiola Cabeza de Baca Gilbert, *We Fed Them Cactus* (1954; Albuquerque: University of New Mexico Press, 1994; F392.L62 G55 1994 GenColl); "Yoshie Mary Tashima: Evacuation to Santa Anita Assembly Center," New York Times Oral History Program (Glen Rock, N.J.: Microfilming Corporation of America, 1977; Microfilm 49517 [E] MicRR); Monique Ugbaja, *In the Secret Place: The Ordeal of an African First Wife in America* (Manassas, Va.: REF Publishing, 1996; HQ836.R63 U43 1996 GenColl).

4. Jacob Rader Marcus, *The American Jewish Woman, 1654–1980* (New York: Ktav; Cincinnati: American Jewish Archives, 1981; HQ1172.M37 GenColl, MRRAlc, Hebr Ref), 113.

5. Isaac Metzker, ed., *A Bintel Brief: Sixty Years of Letters from the Lower East Side to the Jewish Daily Forward* (New York: Behrman House, 1982; 2 vols.,Garden City, N.Y.: Doubleday, 1971; F128.9.J5 B46 1982 GenColl), 69–70.

6. Also watch for Vicki L. Ruiz and Virginia Sanchez-Korrol, *Latinas in the United States: A Historical Encyclopedia* (Bloomington: Indiana University Press, forthcoming).

Alfred T. Palmer. Women workers installing fixtures and assemblies to the tail fuselage of a B-17F bomber at the Douglas Aircraft Company in Long Beach, California. Color slide, October 1942. Office of War Information Collection. Prints and Photographs Division. LC-USW361-128.

Tidy and familiar in appearance, these women were engaged in work that challenged traditional ideas of women's capabilities. Joined by millions more across the country—wiring and riveting wing sections on the night shift at a Boeing plant in Wichita, Kansas, carefully building bombs at Joliet Arsenal in Illinois, or ferry piloting combat planes to airfields—while their sisters in the military repaired engines in Florida or controlled air traffic at the busiest air base in San Diego, such women played a major role in ensuring American productivity and winning the war. Yet, once the war was won, the United States government urged them to return to their homes. Fortunately, many young women chose to take advantage of greater educational opportunities, preparing at schools like Park College, Pomona College, and the School of Nursing of the Hospital of the University of Pennsylvania to continue to make a difference as teachers, nurses, journalists, and scientists. Their "war stories" will make significant contributions to the National Veterans History Collection being collected today by the Library of Congress (see <www.loc.gov/folklife/vets>).

Index

Page numbers in **boldface** type indicate illustrations.
—Susan Fels, *Indexer*

Quaker Photo Service. "Miss America Getting a Permanent Wave." Photograph. Philadelphia, 1926. Specific Subjects File. Prints and Photographs Division. LC-USZ62-26742.

Norma Smallwood, Miss America 1926, smiles bravely through an electric permanent wave, as she ventures toward the outer limits of what a woman will endure for beauty. The fashion for bobbed hair in the 1920s greatly increased the popularity of the torturous twelve-hour procedure invented in Germany around 1905. Requiring the direct application of heat, the result was sometimes a frizzy disaster.

C

Frances Benjamin Johnston. Group of young women reading in library of normal school, Washington, D.C. Photograph, 1899. Frances Benjamin Johnston Collection. Prints and Photographs Division. LC-USZ62-100288.

Late in the spring term of 1899, Frances Benjamin Johnston photographed these young women pursuing an education with the intention of becoming educators themselves. Johnston had been commissioned to make a photographic survey of Washington, D.C., schools to show the public what was meant by the new, "progressive" education. Her photographs were displayed at the Paris Exposition of 1900 and were also used to illustrate a series of publications titled The New Education Illustrated. (See the Frances Benjamin Johnston Collection, pages 193–94.)

M

N

Lucretia Garfield with thirteen of her sixteen grandchildren at Lawnfield. Photograph by Edmond & Son, 1906. Harry A. Garfield Papers (container 195). Manuscript Division. LC-MS-21949-6.

Lucretia Garfield's tenure as first lady was short and tragic. She assumed her duties as mistress of the White House in March 1881, but all official activities came to a halt in May when she was stricken with malaria and taken to Elberon, New Jersey, to recuperate. While there, her husband of nearly twenty-three years was shot on July 2 by disappointed office-seeker Charles Guiteau. James A. Garfield lingered for eighty days, with his wife at his bedside, before succumbing on September 19. With the income from a congressional grant, her husband's congressional pension, and a generous fund raised by the American public, Lucretia was able to support herself and her five living children. She devoted her remaining thirty-six years to preserving her husband's memory, engaging in civic and political affairs, and serving as the beloved matriarch of a large and growing family, which visited her often at the family farm. (See the Garfield family papers, page 148.)

Q

R

S

Harriet Tubman. Photograph in Miller Scrapbook (Geneva, New York. 1910–11; JK1881.N357, sec. 16:9, NAWSA), p. 47. Photographer unknown. Rare Book and Special Collections Division.

Harriet Ross Tubman (ca. 1821–1913), one of the most daring "conductors" on the Underground Railroad, led more than three hundred slaves, including her parents, north to freedom during the decade preceding the Civil War. During the war she served the Union as a scout, spy, and nurse, for which she received official commendation but no pay. Settling in Auburn, New York, Tubman raised funds to assist freedmen and eventually opened her home as a refuge for elderly blacks. Active in promoting women's rights, Tubman attended many of the suffrage events organized by Elizabeth and Anne Miller in nearby Geneva. This rare photograph, pasted in the scrapbook among items dated 1911, was most likely taken at Tubman's home in Auburn about two years before her death. (See pages 112–13 for the Miller scrapbooks.)

Y

Z

ISBN 0-8444-1048-9
90000>
9 780844 410487

THE SENTIMENTS of an AMERICAN WOMAN.

ON the commencement of actual war, the Women of America manifeſted a firm reſolution to contribute as much as could depend on them, to the deliverance of their country. Animated by the pureſt patriotiſm, they are ſenſible of ſorrow at this day, in not offering more than barren wiſhes for the ſucceſs of ſo glorious a Revolution. They aſpire to render themſelves more really uſeful; and this ſentiment is univerſal from the north to the ſouth of the Thirteen United States. Our ambition is kindled by the ſame of thoſe heroines of antiquity, who have rendered their ſex illuſtrious, and have proved to the univerſe, that, if the weakneſs of our Conſtitution, if opinion and manners did not forbid us to march to glory by the ſame paths as the Men, we ſhould at leaſt equal, and ſometimes ſurpaſs them in our love for the public good. I glory in all that which my ſex has done great and commendable. I call to mind with enthuſiaſm and with admiration, all thoſe acts of courage, of conſtancy and patriotiſm, which hiſtory has tranſmitted to us: The people favoured by Heaven, preſerved from deſtruction by the virtues, the zeal and the reſolution of Deborah, of Judith, of Eſther! The fortitude of the mother of the Macchabees, in giving up her ſons to die before her eyes: Rome ſaved from the fury of a victorious enemy by the efforts of Volumnia, and other Roman Ladies: So many famous ſieges where the Women have been ſeen forgeting the weakneſs of their ſex, building new walls, digging trenches with their feeble hands; furniſhing arms to their defenders, they themſelves darting the miſſile weapons on the enemy, reſigning the ornaments of their apparel, and their fortune, to fill the public treaſury, and to haſten the deliverance of their country; burying themſelves under its ruins; throwing themſelves into the flames rather than ſubmit to the diſgrace of humiliation before a proud enemy.

Born for liberty, diſdaining to bear the irons of a tyrannic Government, we aſſociate ourſelves to the grandeur of thoſe Sovereigns, cheriſhed and revered, who have held with ſo much ſplendour the ſcepter of the greateſt States, The Batildas, the Elizabeths, the Maries, the Catharines, who have extended the empire of liberty, and contented to reign by ſweetneſs and juſtice, have broken the chains of ſlavery, forged by tyrants in the times of ignorance and barbarity. The Spaniſh Women, do they not make, at this moment, the moſt patriotic ſacrifices, to encreaſe the means of victory in the hands of their Sovereign. He is a friend to the French Nation. They are our allies. We call to mind, doubly intereſted, that it was a French Maid who kindled up amongſt her fellow-citizens, the flame of patriotiſm buried under long misfortunes: It was the Maid of Orleans who drove from the kingdom of France the anceſtors of thoſe ſame Britiſh, whoſe odious yoke we have juſt ſhaken off; and whom it is neceſſary that we drive from this Continent.

But I muſt limit myſelf to the recollection of this ſmall number of atchievements. Who knows if perſons diſpoſed to cenſure, and ſometimes too ſeverely with regard to us, may not diſapprove our appearing acquainted even with the actions of which our ſex boaſts? We are at leaſt certain, that he cannot be a good citizen who will not applaud our efforts for the relief of the armies which defend our lives, our poſſeſſions, our liberty? The ſituation of our ſoldiery has been repreſented to me; the evils inſeparable from war, and the firm and generous ſpirit which has enabled them to ſupport theſe. But it has been ſaid, that they may apprehend, that, in the courſe of a long war, the view of their diſtreſſes may be loſt, and their ſervices be forgotten. Forgotten! never; I can anſwer in the name of all my ſex. Brave Americans, your diſintereſtedneſs, your courage, and your conſtancy will always be dear to America, as long as ſhe ſhall preſerve her virtue.

We know that at a diſtance from the theatre of war, if we enjoy any tranquility, it is the fruit of your watchings, your labours, your dangers. If I live happy in the midſt of my family; if my huſband cultivates his field, and reaps his harveſt in peace; if, ſurrounded with my children, I myſelf nouriſh the youngeſt, and preſs it to my boſom, without being affraid of ſeeing myſelf ſeparated from it, by a ferocious enemy; if the houſe in which we dwell; if our barns, our orchards are ſafe at the preſent time from the hands of thoſe incendiaries, it is to you that we owe it. And ſhall we heſitate to evidence to you our gratitude? Shall we heſitate to wear a cloathing more ſimple; hair dreſſed leſs elegant, while at the price of this ſmall privation, we ſhall deſerve your benedictions. Who, amongſt us, will not renounce with the higheſt pleaſure, thoſe vain ornaments, when ſhe ſhall conſider that the valiant defenders of America will be able to draw ſome advantage from the money which ſhe may have laid out in theſe; that they will be better defended from the rigours of the ſeaſons, that after their painful toils, they will receive ſome extraordinary and unexpected relief; that theſe preſents will perhaps be valued by them at a greater price, when they will have it in their power to ſay: *This is the offering of the Ladies*. The time is arrived to diſplay the ſame ſentiments which animated us at the beginning of the Revolution, when we renounced the uſe of teas, however agreeable to our taſte, rather than receive them from our perſecutors; when we made it appear to them that we placed former neceſſaries in the rank of ſuperfluities, when our liberty was intereſted; when our republican and laborious hands ſpun the flax, prepared the linen intended for the uſe of our ſoldiers; when exiles and fugitives we ſupported with courage all the evils which are the concomitants of war. Let us not loſe a moment; let us be engaged to offer the homage of our gratitude at the altar of military valour, and you, our brave deliverers, while mercenary ſlaves combat to cauſe you to ſhare with them, the irons with which they are loaded, receive with a free hand our offering, the pureſt which can be preſented to your virtue,

BY AN AMERICAN WOMAN.